Techniques and Applications for Advanced Information Privacy and Security:
Emerging Organizational, Ethical, and Human Issues

Hamid R. Nemati
The University of North Carolina at Greensboro, USA

 **INFORMATION SCIENCE REFERENCE**

Hershey · New York

Director of Editorial Content:	Kristin Klinger
Senior Managing Editor:	Jamie Snavely
Managing Editor:	Jeff Ash
Assistant Managing Editor:	Carole Coulson
Typesetter:	Jeff Ash
Cover Design:	Lisa Tosheff
Printed at:	Yurchak Printing Inc.

Published in the United States of America by
Information Science Reference (an imprint of IGI Global)
701 E. Chocolate Avenue, Suite 200
Hershey PA 17033
Tel: 717-533-8845
Fax: 717-533-8661
E-mail: cust@igi-global.com
Web site: http://www.igi-global.com/reference

and in the United Kingdom by
Information Science Reference (an imprint of IGI Global)
3 Henrietta Street
Covent Garden
London WC2E 8LU
Tel: 44 20 7240 0856
Fax: 44 20 7379 0609
Web site: http://www.eurospanbookstore.com

Library of Congress Cataloging-in-Publication Data

Techniques and applications for advanced information privacy and security : emerging organizational, ethical, and human issues / Hamid R. Nemati, editor.
    p. cm.

Includes bibliographical references and index.
Summary: "This book provides a thorough understanding of issues and concerns in information technology security"--Provided by publisher.

ISBN 978-1-60566-210-7 (hardcover) -- ISBN 978-1-60566-211-4 (ebook) 1. Electronic commerce--Security measures. 2. Information technology--Security measures. 3. Computer security. 4. Data protection. I. Nemati, Hamid R., 1958-

HF5548.37.T43 2009
 658.4'78--dc22

                        2008051169

British Cataloguing in Publication Data
A Cataloguing in Publication record for this book is available from the British Library.

All work contributed to this book is new, previously-unpublished material. The views expressed in this book are those of the authors, but not necessarily of the publisher.

Advances in Information Security and Privacy (AISP) Series

Editor-in-Chief: Hamid Nemati, The University of North Carolina, USA

ISBN: Pending

Techniques and Applications for Advanced Information Privacy and Security:
Emerging Organizational, Ethical, and Human Issues
Edited By: Hamid Nemati, University of North Carolina at Greensboro, USA

> Information Science Reference
> Copyright 2009
> Pages: 389
> H/C (ISBN: 978-1-60566-210-7)
> Our Price: $195.00

Techniques and Applications for Advanced Information Privacy and Security: Emerging Organizational, Ethical, and Human Issues provides a thorough understanding of issues and concerns in information technology security. An advanced reference source covering topics such as security management, privacy preservation, and authentication, this book outlines the field and provides a basic understanding of the most salient issues in privacy concerns for researchers and practitioners.

Cyber Security and Global Information Assurance:
Threat Analysis and Response Solutions
Edited By: Kenneth J. Knapp, U.S. Air Force Academy, USA

> H/C (ISBN: 978-1-60566-326-5)
> Information Science Reference
> Copyright 2009
> Pages: 381
> Our Price: $195.00

Cyber Security and Global Information Assurance: Threat Analysis and Response Solutions provides a valuable resource for academicians and practitioners by addressing the most pressing issues facing cyber-security from both a national and global perspective. This reference source takes a holistic approach to cyber security and information assurance by treating both the technical as well as managerial sides of the field.

As information technology and the Internet become more and more ubiquitous and pervasive in our daily lives, there is an essential need for a more thorough understanding of information security and privacy issues and concerns. The *Advances in Information Security and Privacy (AISP) Book Series* will create and foster a forum where research in the theory and practice of information security and privacy is advanced. It seeks to publish high quality books dealing with a wide range of issues, ranging from technical, legal, regulatory, organizational, managerial, cultural, ethical and human aspects of information security and privacy. It will do so through a balanced mix of theoretical and empirical research contributions. AISP aims to provide researchers from all disciplines with comprehensive publications that best address the current state of security and privacy within technology and worldwide organizations. Because of the growing importance of this field, the series will serve to launch new developments with international importance and practical implication.

To the love of my life, my inspiration Mary and my precious Danny

Table of Contents

Section I
Information Security and Privacy:
Threats and Solutions

Vishal Vatsa, Indian Institute of Technology, India
Shamik Sural, Indian Institute of Technology, India
A. K. Majumdar, Indian Institute of Technology, India

Mohammad M. Masud, University of Texas at Dallas, USA
Latifur Khan, University of Texas at Dallas, USA
Bhavani Thuraisingham, University of Texas at Dallas, USA

Hamid Jahankhani, University of East London, UK
Shantha Fernando, University of Moratuwa, Sri Lanka
Mathews Z. Nkhoma, University of East London, UK

Kirk P. Arnett, Mississippi State University, USA
Mark B. Schmidt, St. Cloud State University, USA
Allen C. Johnston, University of Alabama, Birmingham, USA
Jongki Kim, Pusan National University, Korea
HJ Hwang, Catholic University of Daegu, Korea

Detailed Table of Contents

Section I
Information Security and Privacy:
Threats and Solutions

Chapter I

Traditional security mechanisms are often found to be inadequate for protection against attacks by unauthorized users or intruders posing as authorized users. This has drawn interest of the research community towards intrusion detection techniques. The authors model the conflicting motives between an intruder and an intrusion detection system as a multi-stage game between two players, each trying to maximize its payoff. They consider the specific application of credit card fraud detection and propose a two-tiered architecture having a rule-based component in the first tier and a Game-theoretic component in the second tier. Classical Game theory is considered useful in many situations because it permits the formulation of strategies that are optimal regardless of what the adversary does, negating the need for prediction of his behavior. However, they use it in a predictive application in the sense that we consider intruders as rational adversaries who would try to behave optimally, and the expected optimal behavior can be determined through Game theory.

Chapter II

This work applies data mining techniques to detect email worms. E-mail messages contain a number of different features such as the total number of words in message body/subject, presence/absence of binary attachments, type of attachments, and so on. The goal is to obtain an efficient classification model based on these features. The solution consists of several steps. First, the number of features is reduced using two different approaches: feature-selection and dimension-reduction. This step is necessary to reduce noise and redundancy from the data. The feature-selection technique is called Two-phase Selection (TPS), which is a novel combination of decision tree and greedy selection algorithm. The dimension-reduction is performed by Principal Component Analysis. Second, the reduced data is used to train a classifier. Different classification techniques have been used, such as Support Vector Machine (SVM), Naïve Bayes and their combination. Finally, the trained classifiers are tested on a dataset containing both known and unknown types of worms. These results have been compared with published results. It is found that the proposed TPS selection along with SVM classification achieves the best accuracy in detecting both known and unknown types of worms.

Chapter III

Hamid Jahankhani, University of East London, UK
Shantha Fernando, University of Moratuwa, Sri Lanka
Mathews Z. Nkhoma, University of East London, UK

In today's business environment it is difficult to obtain senior management approval for the expenditure of valuable resources to "guarantee" that a potentially disastrous event will not occur that could affect the ultimate survivability of the organization. The total information network flexibility achieved depends to a great extent on how network security is implemented. However, this implementation depends on the network designers at the initial stage and the network administrators in the long term. Initial security level design can be later changed, improved or compromised by the network administrators who look after day-to-day network and system functions. Their competencies and the motivation contribute in achieving the desired security objectives that are aligned with the business goals. Incompetent network administrator may pave the way to attacks that could take place either at once where an obvious vulnerability may exist or in several phases where it requires information gathering or scanning in order to enter into the target system. De-motivated network administrator may ignore the possible threats or find strategies to make his/ her presence vital for the existence of the network services. The latter may be an example of a competent network administrator who is not rewarded due to the lapses of the senior management, in which case backdoors or logic bombs may be deployed so that the administrator may take vengeance in case the career is terminated or someone else is given undue recognition. Two studies on real cases given in this paper highlights the influence of such network administrators. To preserve the confidentiality, the names of personnel or organizations are not revealed.

Chapter IV

Kirk P. Arnett, Mississippi State University, USA
Mark B. Schmidt, St. Cloud State University, USA
Allen C. Johnston, University of Alabama, Birmingham, USA
Jongki Kim, Pusan National University, Korea
HJ Hwang, Catholic University of Daegu, Korea

Respondents from eight Korean and United States higher education institutions were surveyed as to their knowledge and experience with various forms of computer malware. The surveys provide insight into knowledge of rootkits that have become coffee lounge discussion following the once secretive Sony rootkit news break in late 2005 and then the rash of accusations and acknowledgements of other rootkits that followed. The surveys provide an empirical assessment of perceptions between students in the two countries with regard to various forms of malware. The two groups are similar in many respects but they exhibit significant differences in self-reported perceptions of rootkit familiarity. U.S. respondents report higher levels of familiarity for all assessed malware types, including the fictional "Trilobyte" virus. A timeline-based comparison between virus and rootkit knowledge reveals that relatively little is known about rootkits today. This highlights dangers related to existing knowledge levels but presents hope for solutions and an accelerated rootkit awareness curve to improve worldwide malware protection.

Section II
Privacy Preservation and Techniques

Chapter V

Privacy-Preserving Data Mining (PPDM) refers to data mining techniques developed to protect sensitive data while allowing useful information to be discovered from the data. In this chapter the authors review PPDM and present a broad survey of related issues, techniques, measures, applications, and regulation guidelines. They observe that the rapid pace of change in information technologies available to sustain PPDM has created a gap between theory and practice. This chapter posits that without a clear understanding of the practice, this gap will be widening, which, ultimately will be detrimental to the field. They conclude by proposing a comprehensive research agenda intended to bridge the gap relevant to practice and as a reference basis for the future related legislation activities.

Chapter VI

While the sharing of data is known to be beneficial in data mining applications and widely acknowledged as advantageous in business, this information sharing can become controversial and thwarted by privacy regulations and other privacy concerns. Data clustering for instance could be more accurate if more information is available, hence the data sharing. Any solution needs to balance the clustering requirements and the privacy issues. Rather than simply hindering data owners from sharing information for data analysis, a solution could be designed to meet privacy requirements and guarantee valid data clustering results. To achieve this dual goal, this chapter introduces a method for privacy-preserving clustering, called Dimensionality Reduction-Based Transformation (DRBT). This method relies on the intuition behind random projection to protect the underlying attribute values subjected to cluster analysis. It is shown analytically and empirically that transforming a dataset using DRBT, a data owner can achieve privacy preservation and get accurate clustering with little overhead of communication cost. Such a method presents the following advantages: it is independent of distance-based clustering algorithms; it has a sound mathematical foundation; and it does not require CPU-intensive operations.

Chapter VII

  Song Han, Curtin University of Technology, Australia
  Vidyasagar Potdar, Curtin University of Technology, Australia
  Elizabeth Chang, Curtin University of Technology, Australia
  Tharam Dillon, Curtin University of Technology, Australia

This chapter introduces a new transaction protocol using mobile agents in electronic commerce. The authors first propose a new model for transactions in electronic commerce – mutual authenticated transactions using mobile agents. They then design a new protocol by this model. Furthermore, the authors analyse the new protocol in terms of authentication, construction and privacy. The aim of the protocol is to guarantee that the customer is committed to the server, and the server is committed to the customer. At the same time, the privacy of the customer is protected.

Chapter VIII

  Amr Ali Eldin, Accenture, The Netherlands

Despite the expected benefits behind context-awareness and the need for developing more and more context-aware applications, the authors enunciate that privacy represents a major challenge for the success and widespread adoption of these services. This is due to the collection of huge amount of users' contextual information, which would highly threaten their privacy concerns. Controlling users' information collection represents a logical way to let users get more acquainted with these context-aware services. Additionally, this control requires users to be able to make consent decisions which face a high degree of uncertainty due to the nature of this environment and the lack of experience from the user side with information collectors' privacy policies. Therefore, intelligent techniques are required in order to deal with this uncertainty. In this chapter, they propose a consent decision-making mechanism, ShEM, which allows users to exert automatic and manual control over their private information. An enhanced fuzzy logic approach was developed for the automatic decision making process. The proposed mechanism has been prototyped and integrated in a UMTS location-based services testbed on a university campus. Users have experienced the services in real time. A survey of users' responses on the privacy functionality has been carried out and analyzed as well. Users' response on the privacy functionality was positive. Additionally, results obtained showed that a combination of both manual and automatic privacy control modes in one approach is more likely to be accepted than only a complete automatic or a complete manual privacy control.

Many of the current issues with Information Privacy have been the result of inadequate consideration for privacy during the planning, design and implementation of Information Systems and communication networks. The area of Quantum Computation is still in its infancy, and a truly functional quantum computer has not been implemented. However, it is anticipated that within the next decade it may be feasible. This presents a unique opportunity to give due consideration to Information Privacy in the realm of future quantum computational devices and environments while they are still in their infancy. This chapter provides an overview of the key Information Privacy issues that the author feel may arise with the evolution and realization of quantum computation. Additionally they propose an integrated approach of technical, legal and social elements to address these issues.

Section III
Authentication Techniques

The design of an authentication system based on keystroke dynamics is made difficult by the fact that the typing behaviour of a person is subject to strong fluctuations. An asymmetrical method able to handle this difficulty by using a long text on enrolment and a short one at login is analysed in this paper. The results of an empirical study based on an extensive field test are presented. The study demonstrates that the advantages of the analysed method remain even if a predefined input text is used. The results also show that the method's quality highly depends on the amount of text typed on enrolment as well as on login, which makes the system scalable to different security levels. They also confirm the importance of using stable characteristics that are due e.g. to the user's right- or left-handedness. The method's learning velocity is shown to be high, which enables enrolment to be kept short. Moreover, the study demonstrates that admitting multiple login attempts significantly ameliorates the recognition performance without sacrificing security.

Chapter XI

Till now, the best defense against phishing is the use of two-factor authentication systems. Yet this protection is short-lived and comparatively weak. The absence of a fool-proof solution against Man-in-the-Middle, or Active Phishing, attacks have resulted in an avalanche of security practitioners painting bleak scenarios where Active Phishing attacks cripple the growth of Web-based transactional systems. Even with vigilant users and prudent applications, no solutions seem to have addressed the attacks comprehensively. In this chapter, the authors propose the new Two-factor Interlock Authentication Protocol (TIAP), adapted from the Interlock Protocol with two-factor authentication, which is able to defend successfully against Active Phishing attacks. They further scrutinize the TIAP by simulating a series of attacks against the protocol and demonstrate how each attack is defeated.

This chapter discusses a content-based authentication technique based on inter-coefficient relationship of Discrete Wavelet Transform (DWT). Watermark is generated from the first level DWT. An image digest (which is a binary string) is generated from the second level DWT. The watermark is embedded in the mid-frequency coefficients of first level DWT as directed by the image digest. Image authentication is done by computing the Completeness of Signature. The proposed scheme is capable of withstanding incidental image processing operations such as compression and identifies any malicious tampering done on the host image.

Section IV
Security and Privacy Management

This chapter presents a value exchange model of privacy and security for electronic customer relationship management within an electronic commerce environment. Enterprises and customers must carefully manage these new virtual relationships in order to ensure that they both derive value from them and minimize unintended consequences that result from the concomitant exchange of personal information that occurs in e-commerce. Based upon a customer's requirements of privacy and an enterprise requirement to establish markets and sell goods and services there is a value exchange relationship. The model is an integration of the customer sphere of privacy, sphere of security and privacy/security sphere of implementation.

Chapter XIV

Joseph A. Cazier, Appalachian State University, USA
E. Vance Wilson, Arizona State University, USA
B. Dawn Medlin, Appalachian State University, USA

In today's networked world, privacy risk is becoming a major concern for individuals using information technology. Every time someone visits a website or provides information online they have exposed themselves to possible harm. The information collected can be sold to third parties or kept by the site owners themselves for use in creating a profile of users' preferences and tastes. To gain insight into the role risk plays in the adoption process of technology, the authors studied the use of information systems in relation to a student registration and schedule management system at a major United States university. Further, they extended the Technology Acceptance Model (TAM) to include perceptual measures of privacy risk harm (RH) and privacy risk likelihood (RL) which apply to the extended model and predict students' intentions to use technology. Their finding indicated the growing importance of privacy risk in the use of information technology.

Chapter XV

Thomas P. Van Dyke, University of North Carolina, Greensboro, USA

Studies have shown that people claim that privacy matters to them but then they often do things while browsing that are risky in terms of privacy. The seeming inconsistency between professed privacy concerns and risky behavior on the internet may be more a consequence of ignorance rather than irrationality. It is possible that many people simply don't understand the technologies, risks, and regulations related to privacy and information gathering on the Web. In this study, they conducted an experiment to determine the answer to the following question: If people understood the risks and technology, would that knowledge alter their level of privacy concern and their preferences concerning e-commerce Web site personalization? Results indicate that increased awareness of information gathering technology resulted in significantly higher levels of privacy concern and significantly reduced preferences for web site personalization. Implications of the findings are discussed.

Section V
Web Security and Privacy Issues and Technologies

Chapter XVI

Stephen J.H. Yang, Central University, Taiwan
Blue C.W. Lan, Central University, Taiwan
James S.F. Hsieh, Ulead Systems Inc., Taiwan
Jen-Yao Chung, IBM T. J. Watson Research Center, USA

Web service technology enables seamlessly integration of different software to fulfill dynamic business demands in a platform-neutral fashion. However, the adoption of loosely coupled and distributed services will cause trustworthiness problems. In this chapter, the authors present an experience-based evaluation of service's trustworthiness based on trust experience (understanding) and trust requirements (policy). They utilize ontology to specify past experiences of services and trustworthy requirement of requester. Before invoking found services, the addressed method can help requester evaluate the trustworthiness of the services based on his trustworthy requirements and past experiences of the services. Furthermore, they also present an evaluation method for composite services by taking the structure of the composite services into account. The main contribution of the chapter is providing evaluation methods for Web services such that service requester can make better decision in selecting found services in terms of service's trustworthiness.

Chapter XVII

    Bhavani Thuraisingham, University of Texas at Dallas, USA
    Natasha Tsybulnik, University of Texas at Dallas, USA
    Ashraful Alam, University of Texas at Dallas, USA

The Semantic Web is essentially a collection of technologies to support machine understandable Web pages as well as Information Interoperability. There has been much progress made on the Semantic Web including standards for eXtensible Markup Language, Resource Description Framework and Onotlogies. However, administration policies and techniques for enforcing them have received little attention. These policies include policies for security, privacy, data quality, integrity, trust and timely information processing. This chapter discusses administration policies for the semantic web as well as techniques for enforcing them. In particular, the authors will discuss an approach for ensuring confidentiality, privacy and trust for the Semantic Web. They will also discuss the inference and privacy problems within the context of administration policies.

Chapter XVIII

    Almut Herzog, Linköpings Universitet, Sweden
    Nahid Shahmehri, Linköpings Universitet, Sweden
    Claudiu Duma, Linköpings Universitet, Sweden

The authors present a publicly available, OWL-based ontology of information security which models assets, threats, vulnerabilities and countermeasures and their relations. The ontology can be used as a general vocabulary, roadmap and extensible dictionary of the domain of information security. With its help, users can agree on a common language and definition of terms and relationships. In addition to browsing for information, the ontology is also useful for reasoning about relationships between its entities, that is, threats and countermeasures. The ontology helps answer questions like: Which countermeasures detect or prevent the violation of integrity of data? Which assets are protected by SSH? Which countermeasures thwart buffer overflow attacks? At the moment, the ontology comprises 88 threat classes, 79 asset classes, 133 countermeasure classes, and 34 relations between those classes. The authors provide means for extending the ontology, and provide examples of the extendibility with the countermeasure classes "memory protection" and "source code analysis". This chapter describes the content of the ontology as well as its usages, potential for extension, technical implementation and tools for working with it.

Section VI
Evaluating Information Security and Privacy:
Where are We Going from Here?

Taking a sequential qualitative-quantitative methodological approach, the authors propose and test a theoretical model that includes four variables through which top management can positively influence security effectiveness: user training, security culture, policy relevance, and policy enforcement. During the qualitative phase of the study, they generated the model based on textual responses to a series of questions given to a sample of 220 information security practitioners. During the quantitative phase, authors analyzed survey data collected from a sample of 740 information security practitioners. After data collection, they analyzed the survey responses using structural equation modeling and found evidence to support the hypothesized model. They also tested an alternative, higher-order factor version of the original model that demonstrated an improved overall fit and general applicability across the various demographics of the sampled data. They then linked the finding of this study to existing top management support literature, general deterrence theory research, and the theoretical notion of the dilemma of the supervisor.

The value of IS security evaluated by simulating interactions between an information system, its users and a population of attackers. Initial results suggest that the marginal value of additional security may be positive or negative as can the time rate of change of system value. This implies that IT security policy makers should be aware of the relative sensitivity of attackers and users to security before setting IT security policy.

Foreword

We are the first generation of humans where the capabilities of the technologies that support our information processing activities are truly revolutionary and far exceed those of our forefathers. Although this technological revolution has brought us closer and has made our lives easier and more productive, paradoxically, it has also made us more capable of harming one another and more vulnerable to be harmed by each other. Our vulnerabilities are the consequence of our capabilities. Mason (1986) argues that in this age of information, a new form of social contract is needed in order to deal with the potential threats to the information which defines us. Mason states "Our moral imperative is clear. We must ensure that information technology, and the information it handles, are used to enhance the dignity of mankind. To achieve these goals we must formulate a new social contract, one that insures everyone the right to fulfill his or her own human potential" (Mason, 1986, p 26). In light of the Aristotelian notion of the intellect, this new social contract has a profound implication in the way our society views information and the technologies that support them. For Information Technology (IT) to enhance the "human dignity", it should assist humans in exercising their intellects ethically. But is it possible to achieve this without assuring the trustworthiness of information and the integrity of the technologies we are using? Without security that guarantees the trustworthiness of information and the integrity our technologies, ethical uses of the information cannot be realized. This implies that securing information and its ethical uses are inherently intertwined and should be viewed synergistically. Therefore, we define *Information Privacy and Security* as an all encompassing term that refers to all activities needed to secure private information and systems that support it in order to facilitate its ethical use.

Until recently, information security was exclusively discussed in terms of mitigating risks associated with data and the organizational and technical infrastructure that supported it. With the emergence of the new paradigm in information technology, the role of *information security and ethics* has evolved. As Information Technology and the Internet become more and more ubiquitous and pervasive in our daily lives, a more thorough understanding of issues and concerns over the *information privacy and security* is becoming one of the hottest trends in the whirlwind of research and practice of information technology. This is chiefly due to the recognition that whilst advances in information technology have made it possible for generation, collection, storage, processing and transmission of data at a staggering rate from various sources by government, organizations and other groups for a variety of purposes, concerns over security of what is collected and the potential harm from personal privacy violations resulting from their unethical uses have also skyrocketed. Therefore, understanding of pertinent issues in *information security and ethics* vis-à-vis technical, theoretical, managerial and regulatory aspects of generation, collection, storage, processing, transmission and ultimately use of information are becoming increasingly important to researchers and industry practitioners alike. *Information privacy and security* has been viewed as one of the foremost areas of concern and interest by academic researchers and industry practitioners from diverse fields such as engineering, computer science, information systems, and management. Recent studies of major areas of interest for IT researchers and professionals point to information security and privacy as one of the most pertinent.

We have entered an exciting period of unparallel interest and growth in research and practice of all aspects of information security and ethics. *Information privacy and security* is the top IT priority facing organizations. According to the 18th Annual Top Technology Initiatives survey produced by the American Institute of Certified Public Accountants (AICPA, 2007) information security tops the list of ten most important IT priorities (http://infotech.aicpa.org/Resources/). According to the survey results, for the fifth consecutive year, *Information Security* is identified as the technology initiative expected to have the greatest impact in the upcoming year for organizations and is thus ranked as the top IT priority for organizations. Additionally, six out of the top ten technology initiatives discussed in this report are issues related to information security ethics, as are the top four. The interest in all aspects of information security and ethics is also manifested by the recent plethora of books, journal articles, special issues, and conferences in this area. This has resulted in a number of significant advances in technologies, methodologies, theories and practices of information security and ethics. These advances, in turn, have fundamentally altered the landscape of research in a wide variety of disciplines, ranging from information systems, computer science and engineering to social and behavioral sciences and the law. This confirms what information security and ethics professionals and researchers have known for a long time that information security and ethics is not just a *"technology"* issue any more. It impacts and permeates almost all aspects of business and the economy.

In this book, we will introduce the topic of information security and privacy and discuss fundamental concepts and theories from a technical, organizational and ethical point of view. We will broadly discuss tools and technologies used in achieving the goals of information security and privacy. We will consider the managerial, organizational and societal implications of information security and privacy and conclude by discussing a number of future developments and activities in information security and privacy on the horizon that we think will have an impact on this field. Our aim in developing this book is not to present an exhaustive literature review of the research in information security and privacy, nor is it intended to be a comprehensive introduction to the field. Our main goal here is to describe the broad outlines of the field and provide a basic understanding of the most salient issues for researchers and practitioners. This book is presented in six sections. In each section, we aim to provide a broad discussion of an important issue in information privacy and security.

Hamid R. Nemati
The Universtiy of North Carolina at Greensboro, USA

Preface

SECTION I: INFORMATION SECURITY AND PRIVACY: THREATS AND SOLUTIONS

The primary mission of information security is to ensure that information systems and their contents remain impervious to unauthorized access and modification, thereby guaranteeing the confidentiality, integrity and availability of information. Although Information Security can be defined in a number of ways, the most salient is set forth by the government of the United States. The National Institute of Standards and Technology (NIST) defines Information Security based on the 44 United States Code Section 3542(b)(2), which states "Information Security is protecting information and information systems from unauthorized access, use, disclosure, disruption, modification, or destruction in order to provide *integrity*, *confidentiality*, and *availability*" (NIST, 2003, p3). The Federal Information Security Management Act (FISMA, P.L. 107-296, Title X, 44 U.S.C. 3532) defines Information Security as "protecting information and information systems from unauthorized access, use, disclosure, disruption, modification, or destruction" and goes on to further define Information Security activities as those "carried out in order to identify and address the vulnerabilities of computer system, or computer network" (17 U.S.C. 1201(e), 1202(d)).

The overall goal of information security should be to enable an organization to meet all of its mission critical business objectives by implementing systems, policies and procedures to mitigate IT-related risks to the organization, its partners and customers (NIST, 2004). Information systems face attacks on a daily basis from threats both inside and outside the organization. Insider threats include, but are not limited to poorly trained employees, disgruntled employees, and ignorant employees. Outsider threats include hackers, crackers, phreakers, former employees and forces of nature (Whitman, 2004). Insider threats can be overcome with a combination of stringent formal policies and informal security education awareness and training (SETA) programs. Outsider threats, on the other hand, imply a non-stop cat-and-mouse game between the hackers and the IS security personnel on who outwits the other. More often than not it is the hackers who have the upper hand, as they have nothing to lose, while the organizations have no option but to come up with real-time solutions for each attack from the potential threats or stand to lose the very proprietary information which helps them gain a competitive advantage.

Any information security initiative aims to minimize risk by reducing or eliminating threats to vulnerable organizational information assets. The National Institute of Standards and Technology (NIST, 2003, p. 7) defines *risk* as "…a combination of: (i) the likelihood that a particular vulnerability in an agency information system will be either intentionally or unintentionally exploited by a particular threat resulting in a loss of confidentiality, integrity, or availability, and (ii) the potential impact or magnitude of harm that a loss of confidentiality, integrity, or availability will have on agency operations (including mission, functions, and public confidence in the agency), an agency's assets, or individuals (including privacy) should there be a threat exploitation of information system vulnerabilities," Risks are often characterized qualitatively as high, medium, or low (NIST, 2003, p 8). The same publication defines *threat* as "...any circumstance or event with the potential to intentionally or unintentionally exploit a specific vulnerability in an information system resulting in a loss of confidentiality, integrity, or availability," and *vulnerability* as "...a flaw or weakness in the design or implementation of an information system (including security procedures and security controls associated with the system) that could be intentionally or unintentionally exploited to adversely affect an agency's operations (including missions, functions, and public confidence in the agency), an agency's assets, or individuals (including privacy) through a loss of confidentiality, integrity, or availability" (NIST, 2003, 9). NetIQ (2004) discusses five different types of vulnerabilities that have direct impact on the governance of information security practices. They are: exposed user accounts or defaults, dangerous user behavior, configuration flaws, missing patches and dangerous or unnecessary service. An effective management of these vulnerabilities is critical for three basic reasons. First, an effective vulnerability management helps reducing the severity and growth of incidence. Second, it helps in regulatory compliance. And third and the most important reason can be summed as simply saying, it is a "good business practice" to be proactive in managing the vulnerabilities rather than be reactive by trying to control the damage from an incidence.

That sets the stage for *Section I* which highlights four different types of threats including credit card frauds, e-mail worms, rootkits, and threats from network administrators, and analyzes their impacts on the organization.

The first chapter in *Section I* focuses on the important issue of online credit card fraud and explores ways to protect against it. *"A Rule-Based and Gametheoretic Approach to On-Line Credit Card Fraud Detection"* is authored by Vishal Vatsa, Shamik Sural, and Arun K. Majumdar. The authors observe that as the use of credit cards increases, so does the possibility of fraud committed by thieves trying to steal credit card information. In this chapter, the authors present a novel approach to dealing with this problem. The model presented in this chapter is based on the assumption that the conflicting motives between an intruder, who is trying to commit fraud, and an intrusion detection system, that is trying to prevent it, can be viewed as a multistage game between two players, each trying to maximize its own payoff. Although the basic ideas of *game theory* have been applied successfully in many settings, their applications in information security and privacy have been very limited. In applying the game theory, the authors consider the specific application of credit card fraud detection systems and propose a two-tiered architecture having a rule-based component in the first tier and a game-theoretic component in the second tier. The ideas of game-theocratic are used to develop a predictive application in which the intruders are viewed as rational adversaries who would try to behave optimally, and therefore their expected optimal behavior can be determined through game theory.

The focus of the second chapter in this section, *"Email Worm Detection Using Data Mining"* authored by Mohammad M. Masud, Latifur Khan, and Bhavani Thuraisingham, is application of data mining techniques to detect e-mail worms. The authors explore three different data mining approaches to automatically detect e-mail worms. First, the authors apply either Naïve Bayes (NB) or Support Vector Machine (SVM) on the unreduced dataset, without any feature reduction, and train a classifier. In the second approach, the authors reduce dimensionality using Principal Component Analysis (PCA) and apply NB or SVM on the reduced data and train a classifier. The third approach is to apply a feature-selection technique is called Two-phase Selection (TPS), which is a novel combination of decision tree and greedy selection algorithm. Finally, the trained classifiers are tested on a dataset containing both known and unknown types of worms. The authors' experiments indicate that the best performance is achieved by TPS, and that the best classifier is SVM. Thus the authors strongly recommend applying SVM with our two-phase selection process for detecting novel email worms in a feature-based paradigm.

The third chapter in *Section I* is titled: *"Information Systems Security: Cases of Network Administrator Threats"* by professors Hamid Jahankhani, Shantha Fernando, and Mathews Nkhoma. The authors discuss the importance of network administrators in organizations achieving their desired network security objectives. The authors observe that while information systems network security depends on network designers at the early stages of implementation, in the long term, the network administrators who look after day-to-day network and system functions are the most important, since the initial security level designs can later be changed, improved, or compromised by the network administrators. To illustrate the authors provide two case studies where the influence of network administrators is highlighted.

The last chapter in this section: *"Rootkits and What we Know: Assessing U.S. and Korean Knowledge and Perceptions"* is authored by professors Kirk P. Arnett, Mark B. Schmidt, Allen C. Johnston, Jongki Kim, and HJ Hwang. The authors present the results of their survey conducted among students of eight Korean and U.S. higher educational institutions regarding their knowledge and experience of various forms of computer malware, in general and rootkits, in particular. A rootkit is a relatively new form of malware that allows its user to gain top level (root) privileges where the rootkit is installed. It is not a virus or a worm but it may deliver a virus or worm. Once installed, if a backdoor mechanism is made available to the attacker, the rootkit will allow the attacker to "own" the machine. The authors believe that rootkit threat levels are not well understood. The authors' goal is to assess the knowledge levels and perceptions of Korean and U.S. college students regarding rootkits and more traditional malware with an eye toward identifying possible problems or solutions that might surface. Results of the survey indicate that though the two groups are similar in many respects, they exhibit significant differences in self-reported perceptions of rootkit familiarity. U.S. respondents report a higher level of rootkit awareness compared to their Korean counterparts. Perhaps the greater issue here is that the awareness and knowledge of rootkits is limited in both countries. The authors believe that to solve this problem of limited awareness, proactive response must surface and the rootkit awareness curve accelerated to improve worldwide malware protection.

SECTION II: PRIVACY PRESERVATION AND TECHNIQUES

Information privacy is an elusive term to define. Although there are many attempts to articulate a definition for information privacy, the most salient one was first put forth by Westin (Westin, 1967) as a "right of an individual" to determine when, how, and to what extent information about him/her is communicated to others. Information security, on the other hand, has been more successfully defined. The United States' National Information Assurance Training and Education Center (NIATEC) defines information security as "*a system of administrative policies and procedures*" for identifying, controlling, and protecting information against unauthorized access to or modification, whether in storage, processing, or transit (NIATEC, 2006). These definitions have profound implications for the way information security and privacy is viewed as a field of study. These definitions imply that an individual has the right and must be able to exercise a substantial degree of control over the data about him/her and its use. However, the exercise of this control is contingent upon the security of systems that collect, store, process, and transmit that information. Hence, the relationship between information security and information privacy can be viewed as synergistic and mutually symbiotic in that, without information security, privacy protection cannot be guaranteed and, without a concerted concern over the protection of privacy, most information security promises can be construed as vain.

Advances in technology are causing new privacy concerns. According a survey by U.S. Department of Commerce, an increasing number of Americans are going online and engaging in several online activities, including online purchases and conducting banking online. The growth in Internet usage and e-commerce has offered businesses and governmental agencies the opportunity to collect and analyze information in ways never previously imagined. "Enormous amounts of consumer data have long been available through offline sources such as credit card transactions, phone orders, warranty cards, applications and a host of other traditional methods. What the digital revolution has done is increase the efficiency and effectiveness with which such information can be collected and put to use" (Adkinson, Eisenach, & Lenard, 2002). The significance of privacy has not been lost to the information security and ethics research and practitioners' communities as was revealed in Nemati and Barko (Nemati et al., 2001) of the major industry predictions that are expected to be key issues in the future (Nemati et al., 2001). Chiefly among them are concerns over the security of what is collected and the privacy violations of what is discovered ((Margulis, 1977), (Mason, 1986), (Culnan, 1993), (Smith, 1993), and (Milberg, S. J., Smith, & Kallman, 1995)). About 80 percent of survey respondents expect data mining and consumer privacy to be significant issues (Nemati et al., 2001).

Technologies such as data warehousing have allowed business organizations to collect massive amounts of data which could then be passed through data mining tools and techniques that intelligently and automatically sift through that data to discover meaningful and previously hidden information. If this new information is not used properly, it can create privacy concerns. People feel violated when their privacy is invaded. Privacy invasions lead directly to lost sales. The solution is to make privacy a corporate priority throughout all levels of the organization. The bottom line is that privacy preservation must be viewed as a business issue, not a compliance issue.

This important issue of privacy is the focus of *Section II* where different techniques such as privacy-preserving data mining, privacy-preserving clustering, privacy-preserving transactions protocol using mobile agents, and autonomous user privacy control are highlighted and the possibilities of using quantum computing to solve information privacy issues are explored.

The first chapter in *Section II* is titled, *"Privacy-Preserving Data Mining and the Need for Confluence of Research and Practice"* and is coauthored by professors Lixin Fu, Hamid Nemati, and Fereidoon Sadri. In this chapter, privacy-preserving data mining (PPDM) is defined as data mining techniques developed to protect the privacy of sensitive data while allowing useful information to be discovered from the data. In this chapter, the authors observe that the practice of privacy-preserving data mining, as mandated by the regulatory agencies, currently cannot keep up with the pace of advances in technologies supporting data mining. This incongruence in the research and the practice of privacy-preserving data mining makes it imperative that a comprehensive research agenda be charted relevant to practice and as a reference basis for future related legislation activities.

The second research chapter in this section is titled *"A Dimensionality Reduction-Based Transformation to Support Business Collaboration"* and is authored by Stanley R. M. Oliveira and Osmar R. Zaïane. In this chapter, the authors argue that while the benefits of data sharing for the purpose of data mining are immense, so are the concerns over the privacy violations resulting from such data sharing. Rather than simply preventing data sharing to enhance privacy, the authors present a solution designed to meet privacy requirements while guaranteeing valid data clustering results. The chapter introduces an innovative method called dimensionality reduction-based transformation (DRBT) that preserves privacy in a shared data environment.

The use of mobile agents in e-commerce to achieve privacy is the crux of the third chapter in *Section II*. The third chapter is titled, *"Privacy-Preserving Transactions Protocol Using Mobile Agents with Mutual Authentication"*, and is coauthored by Song Han, Vidyasagar Potdar, Elizabeth Chang, and Tharam Dillon. This chapter introduces a new transaction protocol using mobile agents in electronic commerce. This protocol is developed based on the assumption that a privacy-preserving e-commerce transaction requires that both the customer and the provider to become committed in protecting the privacy of the customer. This approach is based on mutually-authenticated transactions achieved by using mobile agents.

The focus of the fourth chapter in this section, *"Dynamic Control Mechanisms for User Privacy Enhancement"* authored by Amr Ali Eldin, is to allow end users to exert automatic and manual control over their private information. The authors propose a consent decision-making mechanism, the Sharing Evaluation Model (ShEM), for this purpose. The authors developed an enhanced fuzzy logic approach for the automatic decision-making process. The proposed mechanism has been prototyped and integrated in a UMTS location-based services testbed platform called Mobile Information and Entertainment Services (MIES) on a university campus. The service was implemented and used by two groups of users in real time. A survey of users' responses on the privacy functionality has been carried out and analyzed as well. Users' response on the privacy functionality was positive. Additionally, results obtained showed that a combination of both manual and automatic privacy control modes in one approach is more likely to be accepted than only a complete automatic or a complete manual privacy control.

The fifth chapter in *Section II* deals with the intriguing new idea of quantum computation and discusses its implications for information security, privacy research, and practice. *"A Projection of the Future Effects of Quantum Computation on Information Privacy"* by Geoff Skinner and Elizabeth Chang presents quantum computation as a digital/computing environment that utilizes quantum mechanical principles and technologies in its operation to process data. In traditional computers, data is represented as a series of binary bits, and computational processes are achieved by manipulation of these bits. However in quantum computers, the processing engine is a quantum computational environment, and data is represented as a series of *"qubits,"* where data can be either 0 or 1 or it can simultaneously hold two or more functional values. This has profound implications on how data is processed, including encryption and authentication. The authors point out that although the area of quantum computation is still in its infancy, and a truly functional quantum computer has not been implemented, it is anticipated that within the next decade it may be feasible. The authors provide an overview of the key issues in information privacy that will be impacted with the expected evolution and realization of quantum computation and provide guidelines for researchers in information security and privacy seeking to exploit the opportunities provided by it.

SECTION III: AUTHENTICATION TECHNIQUES

Authentication is the process of attempting to verify the digital identity of the sender of a communication by obtaining his / her identification credentials such as name and password and validating those credentials against some authority (OWASP, 2008). If the credentials are valid, the user is considered an authenticated identity. Authentication tools provide the ability to ensure that a message came from who it claims to have come from. All authentication schemes are based on the possession of some secret information known only to the user and possibly (but not necessarily) to the authentication system itself. Communications with other parties use this secret in a way that allows the recipient to verify that the user possesses the secret, but that does not divulge the secret itself. This means that the secret itself cannot be shared, since to do so would allow the recipient to impersonate the user on subsequent interactions with other parties. One of the major differences between authentication systems lies in how to prove you know the secret without telling it (Wells, 1996).

Authentication is defined as a *"Security measure designed to establish the validity of a transmission, message, or originator, or a means of verifying an individual's authorization to receive specific categories of information"* (CNSS, 2003. p 5). In order for a system to achieve security, it should require that all users identify themselves before they can perform any other system actions. Once the identification is achieved, authorization should be the next step. Authorization is process of granting permission to a subject to access a particular object. Authentication is the process of establishing the validity of the user attempting to gain access, and is thus a basic component of access control, in which unauthorized access to the resources, programs, processes, systems are controlled. Access control can be achieved by using a combination of methods for authenticating the user. The primary methods of user authentication are: access passwords, access tokens, something the user owns which can be based on a combination of software or hardware that allows authorized access to that system (e.g., smart cards and smart card readers), the use of biometrics (something the user is, such as a fingerprint, palm print or voice print), access location (such as a particular workstation), user profiling (such as expected or acceptable behavior), and data authentication, to verify that the integrity of data has not been compromised (CNSS, 2003).

Authentication is important as it forms the basis for *authorization* (determining whether a privilege will be granted to a particular user or process), *privacy* (keeping information from becoming known to non-participants), and *non-repudiation* (not being able to deny having done something that was authorized to be done based on the authentication) (Wells, 1996).

The vital topic of authentication receives well-deserved attention in *Section III* with chapters that focus on the design of authentication systems, use of the two-factor interlock authentication protocol to defeat phishing attacks, and use of watermarking to increase the authentication capabilities of existing mechanisms.

The focus of the first research chapter in *Section III* is on the design of authentication systems. This chapter, titled *"On the Design of an Authentication System Based on Keystroke Dynamics Using a Pre-defined Input Text"* is authored by Dieter Bartmann, Idir Bakdi, and Michael Achatz. The authors realize the difficulty in the design of authentication systems based on keystrokes dynamics, which are highly influenced by fluctuation of the individual typing behavior. This paper presents an asymmetrical method to overcome this difficulty. The paper presents the empirical results of an extensive field test study.

The second chapter in this section deals with a very timely issue of Internet phishing and how to defeat it. *"Defeating Active Phishing Attacks for Web-Based Transactions"* is authored by Xin Luo and Teik Guan Tan. Internet phishing is a term first used in 1996 by hackers who were trying to steal account information from AOL account holders. These hackers would collect personal and account information fraudulently by pretending to represent legitimate entities. In this chapter, the authors observe that up to now the best defense against Internet phishing has been the use of two-factor authentication systems and argue that this solution, while effective, is not fool-proof and provides no defense against *man-in-the-middle*, or active phishing. The authors provide evidence that active phishing attacks have crippled the growth of Web-based transactional systems and observe that even with vigilant users and prudent applications, no solutions seem to have addressed the attacks comprehensively. The authors propose a new *two-factor interlock authentication protocol* (TIAP), adapted from the interlock protocol with two-factor authentication, which is able to defend successfully against active phishing attacks. Through the use of simulating a series of attacks against this protocol, the authors assess the robustness of the TIAP protocol and demonstrate how each attack can be defeated.

The last chapter in *Section III* provides a very interesting watermarking approach to increase authentication mechanisms. *"A Content-Based Watermarking Scheme for Image Authentication Using Discrete Wavelet Transform Inter-Coefficient Relations"* is authored by Latha Parameswaran, and K. Anbumani. The authors observe that the proliferation of multimedia on the Internet has led to the need for developing authentication mechanisms and proposes a new blind watermarking scheme based on the contents of the image in the discrete wavelet transform domain for image authentication. Watermarking is a method in which an image or a digital pattern is embedded or sometimes hidden in an electronic document in order to enhance its authenticity. The approach presented in this chapter is based on a *"discrete wavelet transformation"* method in which the relationship between neighboring wavelet coefficients in each band of the second level decomposition is considered to construct the content-based watermark. The watermark is embedded in the first level mid frequency band, of the discrete wavelet transformed image. The received image is authenticated by extracting the watermark and determining the level of authenticity. This scheme is capable of tolerating content-preserving modifications and detecting content-changing modifications. Experimental results prove the efficiency of the scheme.

SECTION IV: SECURITY AND PRIVACY MANAGEMENT

Privacy is a set of expectations, with or without a legal basis, existing within certain relationships (for example: consumer / service provider) regarding the collection, control, use, transfer, storage and disclosure of information. Privacy management is quickly becoming a core business concern across most industries. Privacy management is no longer about just staying within the letter of the latest law or regulation. Privacy policies and procedures that cover all of the organization's online and offline operations must put in place. Regulatory complexity will grow as privacy concerns surface in scattered pieces of legislation. Companies need to respond quickly and comprehensively. They must recognize that privacy is a core business issue.

Privacy concerns are real and have profound and undeniable implications on people's attitude and behavior (Sullivan, 2002). The importance of preserving customers' privacy becomes evident when we study the following information: In its 1998 report, the World Trade Organization projected that the worldwide Electronic Commerce would reach a staggering $220 billion. A year later, Wharton Forum on E-commerce revised that WTO projection down to $133 billion. What accounted for this unkept promise of phenomenal growth? Census Bureau, in its February 2004 report stated that "Consumer privacy apprehensions continue to plague the Web and hinder its growth." In a report by Forrester Research it is stated that privacy fears will hold back roughly $15 billion in e-commerce revenue. In May 2005, Jupiter Research reported that privacy and security concerns could cost online sellers almost $25 billion by 2006. Whether justifiable or not, consumers have concerns about their privacy and these concerns have been reflected in their behavior. The chief privacy officer of Royal Bank of Canada said "Our research shows that 80% of our customers would walk away if we mishandled their personal information."

Privacy considerations will become more important to customers interacting electronically with businesses. As a result, privacy will become an import business driver. People (Customers) feel 'violated' when their privacy is invaded. They respond to it differently, despite the intensity of their feelings. Given this divergent and varied reaction to privacy violation, a lot of companies still do not appreciate the depth of consumer feelings and the need to revamp their information practices, as well as their infrastructure for dealing with privacy. Privacy is no longer about just staying within the letter of the latest law or regulation. As sweeping changes in attitudes of people their privacy will fuel an intense political debate and put once-routine business and corporate practices under the microscope. Two components of this revolution will concern business the most, rising consumer fears and a growing patchwork of regulations. Both are already underway. Regulatory complexity will grow as privacy concerns surface in scattered pieces of legislation. Companies need to respond quickly and comprehensively. They must recognize that privacy should be a core business issue. Privacy policies and procedures that cover all operations must be enacted. Privacy Preserving Identity Management should be viewed as a business issue, not a compliance issue.

Privacy implies many things to the organization. It means risk management, compliance, gaining a competitive advantage over competitors and forming a trust-building vehicle with customers. Managing privacy involves more than simply creating and posting a privacy policy. If an organization posts a policy and then does not verify that the policy is being followed in actual practice, the privacy policy can become more of a liability than an asset. Responsibly managing privacy involves a comprehensive process of assessing an organization's data use needs, putting in place appropriate privacy practices, posting a privacy policy that reflects those practices and establishing processes that allow management to verify compliance with the stated policy.

The chapters in *Section IV* are dedicated to ethical issues and privacy management and discuss the role of privacy in the age of eCRM, the role of privacy risk in its acceptance and the effect of increased knowledge on privacy concerns and e-commerce personalization preferences.

The first research chapter in *Section IV* looks at privacy and security issues in Electronic Customer Relationship Management (e-CRM). This chapter is titled, *"Privacy and Security in the Age of Electronic Customer Relationship Management"* and is coauthored by Nicholas Romano, Jr. and Jerry Fjermestad. This chapter presents a value exchange model of privacy and security for electronic customer relationship management. The value exchange model requires that customer preferences for privacy and security and the enterprise requirement to sell goods and services be balanced. The model is an integration of the customer sphere of privacy, the sphere of security, and the privacy/security sphere of implementation.

The second research chapter in this section presents an empirical study of the impact of privacy risk in the acceptance of information technology. The chapter is titled, *"The Impact of Privacy Risk Harm (RH) and Risk Likelihood (RL) on IT Acceptance"*, and is authored by Joseph A. Cazier, E. Vance Wilson, and B. Dawn Medlin. The authors speculate that risk and concerns over privacy violations impact the adoption of technology. Technology acceptance model (TAM) is extended to include perceptual measures of privacy risk harm and privacy risk likelihood. The result of their study confirms the notion that privacy risks play an important role in the use of information technology.

The final research chapter in *Section IV* presents a provocative idea that ignorance about privacy risks can be bliss. The chapter is titled *"Ignorance is Bliss: The Effect of Increased Knowledge on Privacy Concerns and Internet Shopping Site Personalization Preferences"* and is authored by Thomas P. Van Dyke. The author observes that while people claim that privacy matters to them, they often do things while browsing that are risky in terms of privacy and posit that this seeming inconsistency between professed privacy concerns and risky behavior on the Internet may be more a consequence of ignorance rather than irrationality. An experiment to determine if people understood the privacy violation risks of technology, would that knowledge alter their level of privacy concern and their preferences concerning e-commerce Web site personalization. Results indicate that increased awareness of information gathering technology resulted in significantly higher levels of privacy concern and significantly reduced preferences for Web site personalization.

SECTION V: WEB SECURITY AND PRIVACY ISSUES AND TECHNOLOGIES

The W3C defines a Web service as "a software system designed to support interoperable machine-to-machine interaction over a network. It has an interface described in a machine-processable format (specifically WSDL). Other systems interact with the Web service in a manner prescribed by its description using SOAP-messages, typically conveyed using HTTP with an XML serialization in conjunction with other Web-related standards." (W3C, 2004)

A Web service is simply an application that exposes a function that is accessible using standard Internet technologies and that adheres to Web services standards. Web services promote platform independence as they can be developed for and deployed onto any platform using any programming language. Web services use the Web Services Description Language (WSDL) to specify a service contract. A consumer of a Web service uses a service registry called Universal Description, Discovery and Integration (UDDI) to dynamically discover and locate the description for a Web service. Web service is one of the Web

2.0 technologies that organizations are embracing to drive up their bottom lines. In a McKinsey global survey conducted in January 2007, more than 80% of the respondents indicated that they were either currently using or planning to use Web services in the near future (McKinsey, 2007).

The W3C defines Semantic Web as a methodology that provides a common framework that allows data to be shared and reused across application, enterprise, and community boundaries. (W3C, 2004). The Semantic Web is a web of data. The Semantic Web is about two things. It is about common formats for integration and combination of data drawn from diverse sources, where on the original Web mainly concentrated on the interchange of documents. It is also about language for recording how the data relates to real world objects. That allows a person, or a machine, to start off in one database, and then move through an unending set of databases which are connected not by wires but by being about the same thing. The Semantic Web will bring structure to the meaningful content of Web pages, creating an environment where software agents roaming from page to page can readily carry out sophisticated tasks for users. The Semantic Web is not a separate Web but an extension of the current one, in which information is given well-defined meaning, better enabling computers and people to work in cooperation (Berners-Lee, 2007).

Together Web services and Semantic Web have the potential to transform the way computer-to-computer and people-to-computer communications take place. This forms the perfect backdrop for *Section V* which articulates the trustworthiness of Web services, privacy and trust management for the semantic web, and an ontology of information security.

The focus of the first chapter in this section is on the security of Web services. This chapter is titled, *"Trustworthy Web Services: An Experience-Based Model for Trustworthiness Evaluation"* and is coauthored by Stephen J. H. Yang, Blue C. W. Lan, James S. F. Hsieh, and Jen-Yao Chung. Web Services technology is defined as a set of software tools designed to support the interoperability of services over a network. This paradigm requires that the service provider and the service requester each follow a set of protocols. In this chapter, authors observe that although Web services technology has made seamless integration of different software possible, the trustworthiness of the component software remains problematic. This is due to the fact that to achieve a secure transaction in a Web services environment, the service requester needs to make an informed decision regarding the trustworthiness of the service provider. They present an experience-based method to evaluate the trustworthiness of the service provider. This approach is based on the understanding of trust experience and trust requirements of the service provider and the service requester. The use of ontology to specify past experience of services and the trustworthy requirements of the requester is presented.

The second chapter in *Section V* is titled, *"Administering the Semantic Web: Confidentiality, Privacy and Trust Management"* and is coauthored by Bhavani Thuraisingham, Natasha Tsybulnik, and Ashraful Alam. In this chapter, the authors introduce the Semantic Web as a collection of technologies to support information interoperability. They point out that in order to achieve secure, confidential, and private information interoperability, a set of administration policies needs to be defined. Administration policies of the Semantic Web have been described, and techniques for enforcing these policies are outlined. Specifically, the authors discuss an approach for ensuring confidentiality, privacy, and trust for the Semantic Web.

In the third chapter in this section *"An Ontology of Information Security"*, authors Almut Herzog, Nahid Shahmehri, and Claudiu Duma present a publicly available, OWL-based ontology of information security which models assets, threats, vulnerabilities and countermeasures and their relations. The authors' goal is to present an ontology that provides a general overview over the domain of information security, contains detailed domain vocabulary and is thus capable of answering queries about specific, technical security problems and solutions, and supports machine reasoning. The authors designed their ontology according to established ontology design principles and best practices to ensure that it is collaboratively developed and acceptable to the security and ontology community. All the core concepts are subclassed or instantiated to provide the domain vocabulary of information security. Relations connect concepts. Axioms, implemented as OWL restrictions, model constraints on relations and are used to express, for example, which countermeasure protects which asset and which security goal. Inference and the query language SPARQL allow additional views on the ontology. They can show countermeasures that protect the confidentiality of data, countermeasures that detect integrity violations, threats that can compromise the availability of a host etc. Inference also assists in finding countermeasures for a given threat. The authors propose that their work can be used as online learning material for human users, as a framework for comparing security products, security attacks or security vulnerabilities, as a publicly available knowledge base for rule-based reasoning with semantic web applications and as a starting point and framework for further extensions and refinements.

SECTION VI: EVALUATING INFORMATION SECURITY AND PRIVACY: WHERE ARE WE GOING FROM HERE?

The requirement to measure information security performance is driven by regulatory, financial, and organizational reasons. A number of existing laws, rules, and regulations cite information performance measurement, in general, and information security performance measurement in particular, as a requirement. These laws include the Clinger-Cohen Act, the Government Performance and Results Act (GPRA), the Government Paperwork Elimination Act (GPEA), and the Federal Information Security Management Act (FISMA) (NIST, 2008).

The key components of effective information security are strong upper-level management support, existence of information security policies and procedures backed by the authority necessary to enforce compliance, quantifiable performance measures that are designed to capture and provide meaningful performance data, and results-oriented performance measures analysis (NIST, 2008).

Evaluating information security is critical since it has the potential to shed light on the state of security within the organization, the level of threats facing the organization, the readiness of the organization to deal with incidents, the adequateness of the organization's disaster recovery and business continuity plans, and the effectiveness of protection of information assets of the organization.

The goal of *Section VI* is to bring the key issue of information security evaluation to the limelight by discussing the effectiveness of information security using a theoretical model and investigates a simulation model of information systems security.

The focus of the first research chapter in *Section VI* is in measuring the effectiveness of information security activities. The chapter is titled *"Information Security Effectiveness: Conceptualization and Validation of a Theory"* and is authored by Kenneth J. Knapp, Thomas E. Marshall, R. Kelly Rainer, Jr., and F. Nelson Ford. The chapter presents a sequential qualitative-quantitative methodological approach to propose and test a theoretical model of information security effectiveness. The proposed model includes four variables through which top management can positively influence security effectiveness: user training, security culture, policy relevance, and policy enforcement. The chapter links the finding of the study to existing top management support literature, general deterrence theory research, and the theoretical notion of the dilemma of the supervisor.

The second chapter in this section *"A Simulation Model of IS Security"* is authored by Norman Pendegraft and Mark Rounds. The purpose of this research chapter is to develop a model sufficiently robust to provide management insight into the merits of alternative responses. In this chapter, the authors offer a simulation model for simulating interactions between an information system (IS), its users, and a population of attackers. The model incorporates plausible interactions between the rate of attacks, the value of the IS, user sensitivity to security, user specific response curve to security and the level of security. These interactions are incorporated into a reservoir / flow model using the IThink simulation software. The model depends on four fundamental constructs: VALUE, USAGE, ATTACKS, and SECURITY. The authors perceive VALUE construct as a reservoir, USAGE and ATTACKS as flows, and SECURITY as a control parameter representing the management decision. Results suggest that the marginal value of additional security may be positive or negative as can the time rate of change of system value. This implies that IT security policy makers should be aware of where they are in the state space before setting IT security policy.

CONCLUSION AND FINAL THOUGHTS

Until recently, information security and privacy were exclusively discussed in terms of mitigating risks associated with data and the organizational and technical infrastructure that supported it. With the emergence of the new paradigm in information technology, the role of information security and privacy has evolved. As information technology and the Internet become more and more ubiquitous and pervasive in our daily lives, a more thorough understanding of issues and concerns over the information security and privacy is becoming one of the hottest trends in the whirlwind of research and practice of information technology. This is chiefly due to the recognition that whilst advances in information technology have made it possible for generation, collection, storage, processing and transmission of data at a staggering rate from various sources by government, organizations and other groups for a variety of purposes, concerns over security of what is collected and the potential harm from personal privacy violations resulting from their unethical uses have also skyrocketed. Therefore, understanding of pertinent issues in information security and privacy vis-à-vis technical, theoretical, managerial and regulatory aspects of generation, collection, storage, processing, transmission and ultimately use of information are becoming increasingly important to researchers and industry practitioners alike. Information security and privacy has been viewed as one of the foremost areas of concern and interest by academic researchers and industry practitioners from diverse fields such as engineering, computer science, information systems, and management. Recent studies of major areas of interest for IT researchers and professionals point to information security and privacy as one of the most pertinent.

REFERENCES

Adkinson, W., Eisenach, J., & Lenard, T. (2002). Privacy Online: A Report on the Information Practices and Policies of Commercial Web Sites. Retrieved August, 2006, from http://www.pff.org/publications/privacyonlinefinalael.pdf

American Institute of Certified Public Accountants (AICPA) information security tops the list of ten most important IT priorities, 2007. Accessed from: http://infotech.aicpa.org/Resources.

Barker, William and Lee, Anabelle, Information Security, Volume II: Appendices to Guide for Mapping Types of Information and Information Systems to Security Categories, National Institute of Standards and Technology, , NIST Special Publication 800- 60 Version II, 2004. Accessed from: http://csrc.nist.gov/publications/nistpubs/800-60/SP800-60V2-final.pdf

Barker, William, Guide for Mapping Types of Information and Information Systems to Security Categories, National Institute of Standards and Technology, NIST Special Publication 800- 60 Version 1.0, 2004, Accessed from: http://csrc.nist.gov/publications/nistpubs/800-60/SP800-60V1-final.pdf

Berners-Lee, Tim, The Semantic Web, 2007. Accessed from Scientific American at www.sciam.com.

Chew, L., Swanson, M., Stine, K., Bartol, N., Brown, A., and Robinson, W., Performance Measurement Guide for Information Security, National Institute of Standards and Technology, NIST Special Publication 800-55 Revision 1. 2008. Accessed from: http://csrc.nist.gov/publications/nistpubs/800-55-Rev1/SP800-55-rev1.pdf

Committee on National Security Systems (CNSS), National Security Agency, "National Information Assurance (IA) Glossary," CNSS Instruction No. 4009, May 2003, Accessed from: http://www.cnss.gov/Assets/pdf/cnssi_4009.pdf

Culnan, M. J. (1993). How did they get my name?" An exploratory investigation of consumer attitudes toward secondary information use. *MIS Quart., 17*(3), 341-363.

Grance, T., Stevens, M., and Myers M., Guide to Selecting Information Technology Security Products, National Institute of Standards and Technology, NIST Special Publication 800-36. 2003. Accessed from: http://csrc.nist.gov/publications/nistpubs/800-36/NIST-SP800-36.pdf

Margulis, S. T. (1977). Conceptions of privacy: current status and next steps. *J. of Social Issues, 33*, 5-10.

Mason, R., "Four ethical issues of the information age" *MIS Quarterly, 10*(1), 1986.

McKinsey, 2007. How Businesses are using Web 2.0: A McKinsey Global Survey. Accessed from http://www.mckinseyquarterly.com/

Milberg, S. J., S. J., B., Smith, H. J., & Kallman, E. A. (1995). Values, personal information privacy, and regulatory approaches. *Comm. of the ACM, 38*, 65-74.

National Information Assurance Training and Education Center (NIATEC), 2006. Accessed from http://niatec.info/index.aspx?page=215&glossid=2265.

Nemati, H., Barko, R., & Christopher, D. (2001). Issues in Organizational Data Mining: A Survey of Current Practices. *Journal of Data Warehousing, 6*(1), 25-36.

NetIQ, Controlling your Controls: Security Solutions for Sarbanes-Oxley, Accessed at: http://download.netiq.com/Library/White_Papers/NetIQ_SarbanesWP.pdf , 2004.

OWASP, Testing for Authentication. Accessed from http://www.owasp.org/index.php/Testing_for_authentication.

Smith, H. J. (1993). Privacy policies and practices: Inside the organizational maze. *Comm. of the ACM, 36*, 105-122.

Sullivan, B. (2002). Privacy groups debate DoubleClick settlement. Retrieved August, 2006, from http://www.cnn.com/2002/TECH/internet/05/24/doubleclick.settlement.idg/index.html

Wells, David (1996). Accessed from http://www.objs.com/survey/authent.htm

Westin, A. (1967). *Privacy and Freedom*. New York: Atheneum.

Whitman, M. & Mattord, H. (2004). *Principles of Information Security*. Course Technology.

World Wide Web Consortium (W3C), 2004. Accessed from http://www.w3.org/TR/ws-gloss/

Section I
Information Security and Privacy:
Threats and Solutions

Chapter I
A Rule-Based and Game-Theoretic Approach to On-Line Credit Card Fraud Detection

Vishal Vatsa
Indian Institute of Technology, India

Shamik Sural
Indian Institute of Technology, India

A. K. Majumdar
Indian Institute of Technology, India

ABSTRACT

Traditional security mechanisms are often found to be inadequate for protection against attacks by authorized users or intruders posing as authorized users. This has drawn interest of the research community towards intrusion detection techniques. The authors model the conflicting motives between an intruder and an intrusion detection system as a multi-stage game between two players, each trying to maximize its payoff. They consider the specific application of credit card fraud detection and propose a two-tiered architecture having a rule-based component in the first tier and a Game-theoretic component in the second tier. Classical Game theory is considered useful in many situations because it permits the formulation of strategies that are optimal regardless of what the adversary does, negating the need for prediction of his behavior. However, the authors use it in a predictive application in the sense that we consider intruders as rational adversaries who would try to behave optimally, and the expected optimal behavior can be determined through Game theory.

INTRODUCTION

The popularity of E-commerce applications like online shopping has been growing rapidly over the last several years. According to a recently conducted ACNielsen study, one-tenth of the world's population has now started shopping online (Global Consumer Attitude, 2006). Germany and Great Britain have the largest number of online shoppers and credit card is the most popular mode of payment (59%). As the number of credit card users is rising worldwide, opportunity for thieves to steal credit card details and subsequently commit fraud are also increasing. Credit card frauds can be broadly categorized into the following three types.

a) Physical card gets lost or stolen and is used by fraudster.
b) Card number is stolen and used in indirect shopping.
c) Credit card skimming where the data from a card magnetic strip is electronically copied onto another card.

The first type can lead to a huge financial loss as long as the card holder does not realize the loss of the card immediately. Once the card holder realizes the loss of the card, the institution issuing the card can cancel it. In the second and the third type of fraud, the card holder normally can realize the fraudulent transaction on his card after a long period of time. The only way to detect these two types of fraud is to analyze the transaction patterns of the card holder and find out unusual transactions.

Over the last several years, researchers have developed methods to prevent unauthorized access to database applications. All these techniques aim to detect malicious transactions, specifically in databases, but an open problem in this field is to protect the database from well-formed but damaging transactions while limiting the generation of too many false alarms. This assumes significance

especially in the domain of E-commerce where a service provider like a credit card company needs to minimize its losses due to fraudulent transactions but, at the same time, does not wish the cardholder to feel hassled too often. If it could confirm all transactions on a credit card with the genuine cardholder, then automated fraud detection would not have been necessary. But this is neither practical nor feasible. Further, there exists a finite possibility of the attacker being able to learn the defense mechanisms in place when involved in repeated attacks on the system. It is imperative that the detection system, in contrast, should be able to learn the strategies of an attacker and adopt a suitable counter-strategy.

Consider intrusion in an E-purchase situation: the fraudster, if in possession of somebody else's credit card details, can attempt a fraudulent transaction over the Internet posing as the genuine cardholder. The fraudster can obtain the credit card details of an unsuspecting cardholder through a number of ways such as shoulder surfing, dumpster diving, packet intercepting and database stealing (Li and Zhang, 2004). We also add the possibility that unscrupulous employees at merchant establishments, restaurants, gas stations, etc, can note down credit card details and possibly pass them on to an organized group of fraudsters. A fraudster aims at deriving the maximum benefit from such a pool of cards either in the short run (by making high value purchases, even risking detection) or in the long run (by making a number of small-value purchases to avoid obvious detection). The fraud detection system at the credit card company, oblivious of the type of customer it is interacting with, aims at minimizing its loss due to fraudulent transactions through early detection. This can be modeled as two players in a max-min situation, typical of a Game-theoretic problem.

The field of Game theory has been explored for problems ranging from auctions to chess and its application to the domain of information warfare seems promising. Hamilton et al. (2002a) bring out the possible role of Game theory in information warfare. They highlight that one can utilize well-developed Game-theoretic techniques to predict future attacks and possible courses of action to defend against them. They also identify the differences and challenges in this domain as compared to traditional games like chess. This includes the availability of only a few limited examples, multiple simultaneous moves and no time constraints (Hamilton et al., 2002b).

In the domain of database intrusion detection, an attacker can make multiple moves and does not play under time limitations, unlike the scenario in case of traditional games. Also, in contrast to traditional games, the possible set of moves is often ill defined. However, we feel that it may be advantageous to consider applicability of Game theory for specific situations. For example, in case of credit card fraud, theoretically the fraudster is not constrained by any time limit but in practical situations, he can believe that the malicious transactions will get detected and hence, tries to carry out successive fraudulent transactions as quickly as possible. Our work, thus, focuses on the problem of fraud detection in the domain of credit card transaction so as to be able to handle the application-specific rules and problems.

The rest of the paper is organized as follows. We first describe the existing work related to credit card fraud detection and then we propose a Game-theoretic model. Thereafter, we describe the two-tiered architecture of the proposed credit card fraud detection system followed by discussion on the results obtained from our simulation and experimental studies. Finally, we conclude the paper.

BACKGROUND AND RELATED WORK

Credit card fraud is a growing problem in the credit card industry. In the USA, the online retail sales were reported to be $ 144 billion in 2004, which was a 26% increase over 2003 (Complete

Website, 2005). It is also estimated that 87% of purchases made over the Internet are paid by credit card (Merchant Account, 2005). The Association of Payment and Clearing Services (APACS) report showed that in the UK, the cost of credit card fraud reached £ 504.8 ($ 966.74) million in 2004, which was an increase of 20% as compared to 2003 (Clearly Business 2005). According to the report, Card-not-present (CNP), such as Internet transactions, was the most frequent type of fraud, increasing by a quarter since 2003 to £ 150.8 ($ 288.8) million. CNP fraud in the UK has grown from £ 2.5 ($ 4.8) million in 1994 to £ 116.4 ($ 223) million in 2003. The sharp rise was attributed to increasing number of transactions made over phone, fax and the Internet. Another survey of over 160 companies revealed that online fraud (committed over Web or phone shopping) is 12 times higher than offline fraud (committed by using a stolen physical card) (Online Fraud, 2005). The growing number of credit card users worldwide provides more opportunities for "thieves" to steal credit card details and subsequently commit fraud.

Though there are a variety of ways in which credit card fraud can be perpetrated, we classify them into two broad categories. This brings out the difference in the way frauds are carried out and also in the detection techniques used against them.

(a) **Physical card.** The cardholder either loses the card or his card is stolen and is then used by somebody else. In this case a substantial financial loss would occur only if the cardholder does not realize the loss of his card. Intuitively, the fraudster would attempt large volume or large value purchases in the shortest possible time. This is not too difficult to detect by a fraud detection system in place.

(b) **Virtual card.** The second type of fraud can take place if the cardholder does not realize that someone else is in possession of his card details. This would also encompass the fraud that takes place due to counterfeit cards. These kinds of frauds may or may not get noticed, depending on the strength of the Fraud Detection System (FDS) in place. Further, the genuine cardholder in this case, may be able to detect the fraudulent transactions on his card only when he receives the card statement at the end of the month.

A variety of secure payment systems have been proposed to thwart credit card fraud such as Address Verification Service (AVS), Card Verification Value, Secure Electronic Transactions (SET) protocol and Secure Sockets Layer (SSL) (Peters, 2002). Notwithstanding the problems that may be peculiar to a particular payment system, it may be noted that in general, these methodologies are ineffective once the fraudster is in possession of the credit card details because they are sufficient for him to carry out any Web-based transaction.

Credit card fraud detection has drawn a lot of interest from the research community and a number of techniques, with special emphasis on data mining and neural networks, have been proposed to counter fraud in this field. Ghosh and Reilly (1994) carried out a feasibility study to determine the effectiveness of neural networks for credit card fraud detection. The authors conclude that it is possible to achieve a reduction of 20% to 40% in the total fraud losses. Aleskerov et al. (1997) present CARDWATCH, a database mining system based on a neural network learning module. Chan et al. (1999) divide a large data set of transactions into smaller subsets and then apply the mining techniques in parallel in a distributed data mining approach. The resultant base models are then combined to generate a meta-classifier. More recently, Syeda et al. (2002) proposed the use of parallel granular neural networks (PGNNs) for fast credit card fraud detection. The PGNN aims at speeding up the data mining and knowledge discovery process.

The above-mentioned techniques, in general, attempt to either train a neural network with training data and then classify fraudulent/legitimate transactions or detect anomalies from a large amount of data using data mining techniques. Even the commercially available systems such as MaxMind (Maxmind, 2005) and Fraud Detection Suite (Fraud Detection Suite, 2005) use a set of rules or filters to flag a fraudulent transaction. These approaches would largely be static in nature and fail in a scenario in which an attacker learns the methodology or strategy of his opponent (in this case, the FDS) over a period of time in order to outdo it. Once aware of the strategy, the attacker can act to maximize his payoff. Conversely, the goal of the detection system is to be able to learn the moves of the attacker dynamically so as to minimize its own loss.

The application of Game theory in the above-mentioned situation seems interesting and hence, we present a Game-theoretic approach for credit card fraud detection and propose architecture of a Fraud Detection System. The FDS improvises on the existing fraud detection systems by using Game-theoretic techniques for fraud detection in addition to the existing ones and *learns* at each step of the game. Liu and Li (2002) have presented a Game-theoretic attack prediction model for attacks on IDS-protected systems. The authors have considered choosing a threshold by the detection system depending on the profile of the customer and the availability weight provided by the system. It is clear that if the threshold is low, it may result in the genuine transactions being rejected causing a negative payoff to the cardholder, which is considered as zero by the authors. Further, in a real-world scenario, the genuine cardholder cannot be expected to choose his action according to Nash Equilibrium and any deviations can only be suspected. As the detection system increases the availability weight, to avoid denial of service to the customer, there is no pure strategy equilibrium and the thief can act to maximize his payoff. Our model is not limited by these assumptions. We use Game-theoretic techniques in addition to a number of static rules and include the possibility of 'learning' in a multi-stage game.

GAME-THEORETIC MODEL

One can visualize the transaction process between a potential client and a secure credit card processing system as two opponents pitted against each other. The system has no information about the type of client, who could be the genuine cardholder or a fraudster. The fraudster, in turn, is unaware of the exact rules of the system. The fraudster intends to maximize his payoff and launches attacks against the system in the form of fraudulent transactions. The detection system, on the other hand, intends to minimize its loss by detecting the fraudulent transactions at an early stage. At the same time, a benign transaction not being serviced by the system will result in a denial of service to the genuine cardholder. The fraudster, upon failure in his initial attempts, will try to learn from the experience such that he can evade detection. In contrast, the detection system would also attempt to learn the behavior of the fraudster. The presence of *two parties with conflicting goals* provided us with the initial impetus to use Game theory as a tool for credit card fraud detection.

Existing Models

In order to develop a Game-theoretic model for credit card fraud detection, we first attempted to model the problem in the form of some well-known games like the "Bridges Problem" (Game Theory, 2005), the "D-Day Game" (Andrew, 2002) and the "Inspection Game" (Ferguson and Melolidakis, 1998). We also considered the game proposed by Kodialam and Laxman (2003). They detect network intrusions via sampling with a Game-theoretic approach. The problem requires detecting an intruding packet in a communication network while not exceeding a given total sampling budget. The problem is modeled as a two-person zero-sum game in a Game-theoretic framework.

We observed subtle differences these traditional games have when compared to the situation we intended to work upon. For example, in the Bridges Problem, it may be safe to assume that the fraudster is likely to have a pre-conceived notion about the system trying to judge transactions based on their amount or broadly, on the amount range. However, this is based on the fact that the thief is aware of the risk/uncertainty associated with a "bridge" while we should consider the risks to be implicit in the credit card situation. Assumptions like, a smuggler learns of each inspection in the inspection game as it is made, or that the inspector may announce his mixed strategy would be too weak in case of credit card fraud detection. The D-day Game has a solution in mixed strategies but the payoff matrix in the incomplete information game pertaining to credit card fraud detection cannot be defined. Further, a fraudster has no notion of the number of ranges. Assuming an arbitrary payoff matrix and then, predicting actions based on a mixed strategy will be too limiting. Besides the four games mentioned above, we also considered a few other traditional games. However, none of them could be considered to be a valid model.

Fraud Model

It is clear that the credit card situation is different in many respects from the Game-theoretic situations discussed above. Noteworthy among them is the unavailability of complete knowledge to both the opponents, especially the fraudster. The FDS has the ability to have more knowledge than the fraudster in this situation since it can "see" the range of transaction amount used by a potential fraudster. The fraudster, however, does not know the move made by the FDS. In a repeated game environment, the fraudster can, however, try to learn the steps that need to be taken to arrive at the Nash Equilibrium, in order to cope with the incomplete knowledge that he has. We address these issues in our model and propose a different game as described below.

As stated earlier, it is safe to assume that a thief is likely to attempt a fraudulent transaction with the belief that his transaction may be monitored on the basis of transaction amount. For example, a very high value transaction is likely to raise an alarm. Hence, the aim of the thief is to avoid suspicion/detection by the FDS and to maximize his payoff, either in the long run or in a short time (for fear of the fraud being detected before long). On the other hand, the aim of the FDS is to minimize its loss by detecting the fraud at an early stage. In our model, the loss can be minimized if the system is able to correctly predict the next move of the potential thief in terms of a transaction value range. If the range is predicted correctly, it is assumed that a thief carried out the transaction, and the genuine cardholder is contacted for confirmation. In such a scenario, if the genuine cardholder confirms that the transaction was not carried out by him, we say that the thief has been *'caught'*. The dilemma for the thief, on the other side, is to be able to choose a transaction range that has not been predicted by the FDS.

One interesting point to note here is that we do not consider a transaction as being carried out by a thief unless the transaction amount matches with that predicted by the Game-theoretic component of the FDS using a validated fraud model. The advantage of this approach is that we can handle situations where fraudulent and benign transactions are interspersed, thus avoiding Denial of Service to the genuine cardholder. This notion makes our work unique in comparison with the other Game-theoretic approaches to Information Warfare. In fact, knowing that we are playing against an adversary and continuing the game is self-contradictory. The FDS should have called up the customer and verified in the first place. Thus, one of the challenges of this problem is for the FDS even to determine whether a game is at all on or not.

The game, in case of three transaction ranges, can be modeled as shown in Figure 1. The thief, oblivious of the ranges or the strategies used by the FDS, needs to choose the ith range from the possible 'n' (here n = 3) ranges. The FDS, in contrast, is unaware of the thief's choice and hence, all the possible choices form the information set for the FDS. A correct prediction of the ith range by the FDS results in the thief being caught.

Formally, we define our Fraud Model as a 6-tuple: $\{FDS, TS_{thief}, AS_{thief}, AS_{FDS}, SS_{thief}, SS_{FDS}\}$ where

(a) FDS is the Fraud Detection System.

(b) TS_{thief} is the type space for the thief. For example, the thief could be a first-time thief or a learned thief. He could also be a risk-loving or a risk-averse thief.

(c) AS_{thief} and AS_{FDS} are the action space for the thief and FDS, respectively. For simplicity, we define two actions possible for both players, namely, to choose either a *Low (L)* range or a *High (H)* range transaction.

(d) SS_{thief} and SS_{FDS} are the strategy space for the thief and the FDS, respectively. The thief can define his own strategy while we initialize the strategy space for the FDS to {LLL, HHH, LHL, HLH}. Essentially, these strategies are utilized by the Game-theoretic component to predict the next move of the thief. The strategies are based and can further build upon the FDS's belief

Figure 1. Modeling the game

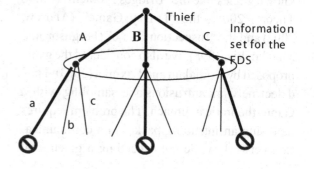

6

like a risk-averse thief may opt for only low value transactions or he is likely to repeat his successful move.

The heuristic strategies, as mentioned above, used to initialize the strategy space of the FDS cater for the type space of the thief. The fraud model is built on the belief that the FDS may be interacting with a 'first-time thief' or a 'learned thief'. Further, the former encompasses both sub-types of a 'risk-averse' or a 'risk-loving' thief. For example, it is natural for a fraudster to attempt low value transactions in order to evade detection and especially so, for a risk-averse thief. Intuitively, a successful transaction in a low range would encourage him to attempt subsequent transactions in the same range, thus, generating the strategy 'LLL'. Our model does not limit the number of subsequent transactions in the same range and this can be user-defined, necessitating a compromise between false-negatives and false-positives, though we feel that a strategy like 'LL' based on only two moves would be inappropriate since it could be more due to chance, resulting in higher number of false-positives. The strategy 'HHH' is explicable in a similar fashion and would be attempted by a risk-loving thief in order to gain the maximum in the shortest possible time. However, these action strategies will enable the thief to carry out a limited number of moves and he may attempt to alternate between the transaction amount ranges as his next move. This will strengthen the belief of the FDS, in terms of interacting with a learned thief, and has been catered for by the other two strategies, namely, LHL and HLH.

It may be noted that though we have chosen two ranges for the purpose of our study the system is not restricted by the number of ranges specified. However, choosing a large number of ranges will not only make prediction difficult for the system (as the search space gets deeper) but also provide more opportunity for the fraudster to get away with fraudulent transactions.

A pertinent question at this stage would be – "What is the validity of the fraud model?" To the best of our knowledge, there is no existing reference in scientific and technical literature on credit card fraud model. It is also hard to get ample data from credit card companies due to the sensitive nature of the problem. In order to study this aspect, we carried out an experiment in our institute comprising of senior undergraduate students, graduate students and faculties in which participants were required to fool a credit card fraud detection system developed by us. During this experiment, the participants demonstrated behavior similar to that described above. While students and professors may not behave exactly like professional credit card thieves, we could validate our model using data as close to real life as possible. Details of the experiment and corresponding results are given in our sub-section 'Experimental results'.

The other related issue is to determine the effect of genuine transactions interspersed with the fraudulent transactions in the proposed system. It should be clear that the genuine cardholder does not violate most of the static rules though this does not always guarantee a genuine transaction. We utilize this fact to filter out seemingly genuine transactions, while not neglecting the possibility of false negatives, and use the remaining transactions (on a particular card) to strengthen the belief of the FDS about the opponent being a fraudster or a genuine cardholder at each step of the game.

PROPOSED FRAUD DETECTION SYSTEM

The proposed fraud detection system has a two-tiered architecture, consisting of a *'Rule-based component'* and a *'Game-theoretic component'*. We extend some of the useful features available in commercial fraud detection systems while we improve upon it by including a layer working on

Game-theoretic strategies. In our architecture, the first line of defense is a rule-based system while the second uses Game-theoretic techniques. The Tier I of the fraud detection system uses a number of static rules, some of which are generic, while the rest are customer-specific. These rules are used to initially classify a transaction as seemingly genuine or suspect. The Tier II of the system uses dynamic strategies to predict the next action of the opponent (the fraudster in this case) and map its belief about the fraudster with respect to the fraud model. If the subsequent actions do not match with the fraud model, the belief that an adversary is active goes down. This represents a situation in which an infrequent unusual transaction was made by the genuine cardholder. The architecture of the system is shown in Figure 2.

Rule-Based Component

We felt the necessity of the first layer in our FDS structure not only for inclusion of useful features from existing systems but also to avoid handling of millions of transactions with the Game theory rules, most of which are carried out due to rou-tine use of credit cards. In an application such as credit card fraud detection, it is quite difficult to conclusively declare that a given transaction is fraudulent. One may initially only suspect a transaction to be fraudulent. Consider the most basic check used in many commercial systems and by various credit card companies, namely, "billing and shipping address mismatch". However, such a mismatch could be either due to a fraudster aiming to get items delivered at an address of his convenience or the actual cardholder gifting an item to a friend.

In view of this, the first tier of our proposed architecture uses generic as well as customer-specific rules to calculate an overall *suspicion score* for each submitted transaction. The main idea is that, given a transaction and a specific user, what confidence measure can be assigned for the transaction to be from the genuine cardholder. We have implemented a number of techniques, as mentioned below, to enrich the functionality of the first tier. This tier presently has one generic rule, namely, that of "Shipping address being different from billing address" and three customer-specific rules. The following techniques have been used

Figure 2. Architecture of the proposed fraud detection system

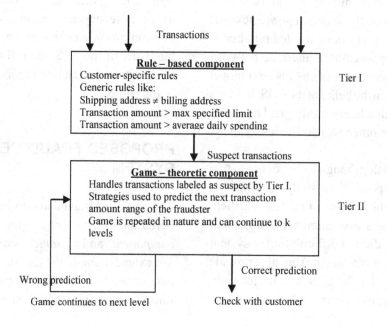

to extract the customer-specific rules and label a transaction as possibly suspect attributable to its deviation from the usual customer profile.

(i)   Outlier Detection
(ii) Break Point Analysis
(iii) Weighted Average Analysis

Intuitively, the first tier can filter out *seemingly* genuine transactions as is being done by existing credit card fraud detection systems. The architecture has been kept flexible in our implementation and other promising measures can be included at a later stage.

Address Mismatch

One of the basic rules that any purchase transaction, especially Web transaction, is subjected to, is to verify if the shipping address is the same as the billing address of the cardholder. Although we cannot declare a transaction to be fraudulent with certainty whenever this rule is violated, any transaction that satisfies this rule can be classified as genuine with a very high probability (except for the cases where the fraudster's aim is only to harass the cardholder). The transactions that violate this check are labeled as suspect with weight w_a, which can be user-defined.

Outlier Detection

Since a customer is likely to follow a particular pattern or carry out similar kind of transactions, these can be visualized as part of a group or a *cluster*. Similarly, since the fraudster is likely to deviate from the customer's profile, his transactions can be detected as exceptions to the cluster, a process also known as *outlier detection*. DBSCAN (Density Based Spatial Clustering of Applications with Noise) is a recently proposed density based clustering algorithm (Ester et al., 1996; Han and Kamber, 2001) in which for each point in a cluster, the neighborhood of a given

radius has to contain at least a minimum number of points, that is, the density in the neighborhood has to exceed a certain threshold.

Formally, let $T = \{t_1, t_2, \ldots, t_n\}$ be the set of existing transactions for the customer R_i. Then the transaction t_{n+1} is classified as an outlier if it does not belong to the existing set of clusters C. Consequently, the transaction is labeled as suspect with weight w_b. We have used transaction amount as an attribute for our implementation, but the algorithm can easily be extended to include other attributes as well.

Break Point Analysis

Break point analysis is used for behavioral fraud detection. The term "break point" signifies an observation or time when anomalous behavior is detected (Bolton and Hand, 2001). It identifies changes in spending behavior based on the transaction information in a single card. This is of significance to us since the Tier I of our system should be able to handle customer-specific rules and hence, we need to tackle individual cards. The advantage of using break point analysis in addition to outlier detection is that recent transactions on a credit card are compared with previous spending behavior to detect features such as rapid spending and an increase in the level of spending, features that would not necessarily be captured by the outlier detection technique.

For the credit card application, break point analysis operates at the card level, comparing sequences of transactions to detect a change in behavior for a particular card. A transaction that is found to deviate from the usual spending pattern of the cardholder is labeled as suspect with weight w_c.

Weighted Average Analysis

Weighted average is a technique of calculating an average that takes into account the proportional relevance of each component rather than treating each component equally. We use weighted average for the analysis of the purchase pattern of a particular cardholder. The purchase pattern here relates to the '*type of product*' that the customer purchases. This is useful in establishing a customer's profile based on the products that he usually purchases. Cardholders often use their credit cards for purchasing particular classes of products and even cardholders with multiple cards often use a particular card for certain types of products. For example, a cardholder may use one of his credit cards only for high-end purchases like jewelry, electronic items, etc and another for groceries or gasoline.

Any deviation from the usual profile of the cardholder is reported as anomalous. Suitable weights can also be assigned to a particular product. For example, unusual occurrences of sale-able products like jewelry can be assigned higher weight as compared to that of grocery. A transaction that deviates from the usual profile of the customer is labeled as suspect with weight w_d.

The first tier of the proposed architecture uses the above-mentioned techniques for computing the overall suspicion weight w_s $(= w_a + w_b + w_c + w_d)$ of any submitted transaction. The same is compared with a user-defined threshold weight w_t. If $w_s > w_t$, the transaction is submitted to the Game-theoretic component for further treatment. Else, the transaction is classified as genuine.

Game-Theoretic Component

The second tier of the proposed architecture is the Game-theoretic component. We consider the game between the fraudster and the FDS to be a multi-stage repeated game. This is essential because, firstly, the fraudster is likely to try again even if he fails with one card and secondly, no effective learning can take place in a one-time game.

It is also worthwhile to mention that the game being played between the FDS and the fraudster is one of incomplete information since the fraud-

ster would be completely unaware of the modus operandi of the detection system. However, the fraudster is likely to have some notions or beliefs about the strategy of the FDS, as stated earlier. Further, since we assume that the situation is one of repeated games, the fraudster can use his past experience to build upon his belief about the FDS strategy. For example, if the fraudster is successful in carrying out low value transactions since the FDS is detecting only high value transactions, then the fraudster learns that his best strategy in this case is to carry out only low value transactions. Therefore, such type of '*learning*' will help him to realize and then play according to a Nash Equilibrium strategy – a strategy such that he cannot play anything better given the current strategy of the FDS. The FDS, as the other player, needs to choose its own best strategy to counter this. One may realize that the advantage of the proposed approach is that this component is not one-time rule-based but will anticipate the next move of the opponent and anticipating the next move correctly is a definite advantage to either player.

The flow of events in the FDS has been depicted in Figure 3. The transaction for a particular card number is checked at Tier I. If it clears the checks at Tier I, it is logged as a genuine transaction, failing which it is passed to the Game-theoretic component and the card is marked as 'suspect'. This signifies the beginning of a game between the potential thief and the FDS. Tier II predicts the next move of the thief based on the fraud model and in the event of the prediction being correct, the card is declared as compromised and the thief is "Caught". In the event of the prediction being incorrect, the game continues to the next round. As the game progresses to subsequent rounds, the FDS strengthens its belief about the type of opponent it is playing against and his strategy in force so as to use the best counter-strategy. If at any point of time, the FDS realizes that the thief has possibly learnt its own strategy, it can dynamically switch to a different strategy. On the

Figure 3. Flow of events

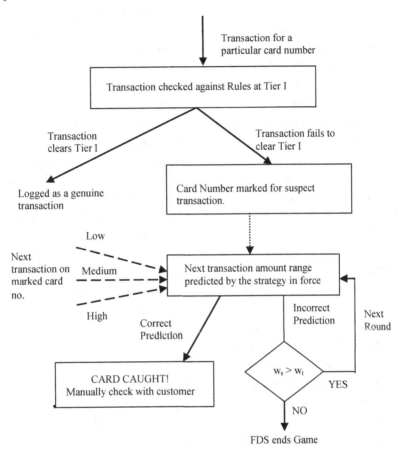

other hand, with the progression of the game, if the FDS realizes that the successive transactions or the behavior of the (unknown) customer does not conform to the fraud model, then the FDS strengthens its belief about the interacting client to be the genuine cardholder.

For example, consider that the FDS initially believes that the potential fraudster may carry out only low value transactions in order to evade detection or that he may carry out only high value transactions so as to maximize his payoff with a small number of transactions. This maps to our fraud model and hence, the FDS plays with the counter-strategies of LLL and HHH. The counter-strategy LLL used by the FDS considers the possibility of the fraudster repeatedly opting for the Low value (L) transactions in order to evade the FDS. Similarly, the strategy HHH caters for

the thief repeatedly opting for the high value transactions in order to extract the maximum benefit in a short time for the fear of being detected early. However, it is also possible that the fraudster has a notion of this strategy possibly due to his past interaction with the FDS, and hence he plays with the strategy LHL or HLH. Intuitively, as the belief of the FDS exceeds a threshold that the fraudster has learnt its strategy, the FDS switches its strategy to counter these strategies of the fraudster. It may be noted that the FDS will be able to handle the genuine transactions interspersed with the fraudulent ones due to the rules defined at Tier I.

We visualize this repeated game between the FDS and the fraudster as a finite one for several reasons. Firstly, the game is limited by the credit limit on the card. Secondly, the number of rounds of the game can be limited by the maximum loss that the card issuing authority can sustain. Thirdly, the fraudulent transactions may be identified by the genuine cardholder in his monthly statement and hence, any game in progress will be identified. Finally, the FDS can end the game if its belief that it is playing against a fraudster goes below the threshold due to a large number of consecutive transactions clearing Tier I rules. It may be noted that though we have considered transaction amount as an attribute for prediction, any other feature such as 'duration between transactions' can also be similarly considered.

SIMULATION AND EXPERIMENTAL RESULTS

Any fraud detection system should be tested to demonstrate its usefulness. However, unavailability of a large volume of real data is a bottleneck for testing a credit card fraud detection system. To overcome this problem, we have developed a simulator to generate genuine as well as fraudulent transactions. The simulator has been developed using T-SQL with the help of stored procedures and triggers on a Microsoft SQL Server database. The simulator can easily be modified to model patterns other than those that have already been covered in this work. We also carried out an on-campus experiment, with student and faculty volunteers, to validate the fraud model and the simulation results with data as close to real-life as possible. The volunteers for the experiments were able to update their belief over successive plays of the game and some of them were eventually able to learn the strategy of the FDS.

Simulation Results

Our fraud model considers a repeated game between the fraudster and the fraud detection system. The simulator has been designed to handle various scenarios that would be experienced in such a game. The typical issues that need to be handled are (i) In a multi-stage game, both the opponents can play with (a set of) strategies to maximize their payoff. (ii) An actual credit card database contains fraudulent transactions interspersed with genuine transactions. (iii) The genuine transactions would largely be similar for a given customer profile. For example, the transactions of an individual in the middle-income group usually comprises of medium range or low range amounts.

The simulator has been developed to handle these combinations, which are quite relevant to the credit card domain. It can generate transactions for different strategies of either of the opponents. While simulating genuine and fraudulent transactions, their inter-mixing can follow user-specified distributions. Further, the simulator can also handle different customer profiles for the generation of the genuine transactions.

During simulation, the first tier of the detection system filters out the seemingly genuine transactions and only the suspected transactions are subjected to the Game-theoretic component. Standard metrics have been used to study the different test cases. True negatives (TN) are the genuine transactions labeled as genuine, true positives (TP) are the fraudulent transactions caught by the system (also called hits), false negatives (FN) are the fraudulent transactions labeled as genuine (also called misses) and false positives (FP) are the genuine transactions labeled as fraudulent (also called false alarms).

The thief's transactions are modeled as a Markov process, comprising of two states - Low (L) and High (H). The thief can either stay in the same state (carry out a transaction in the same range) or transit to the other state (carry out a transaction in a different range) with a certain probability. The values of these probabilities can be varied to get different behaviors of the thief. For example, a pure strategy of LLL would mean that the thief starts in the Low state and always transits to the same state. We have considered the case where the thief is more probable to initiate the game with a low value transaction and hence, the initial probabilities for the Low state and the High state were fixed as 0.6 and 0.4, respectively. The Markov model for the thief is depicted in Figure 4. It may be noted that though this model considers only two states, it can easily be changed to cater for any other complex process.

The different strategies of the FDS were used against the fraudulent transaction separately in order to carry out a comparative study. An average of over 1000 transactions was taken to study the effect on true positives and false negatives with different strategies in place. It may be noted that the thief can play against the FDS with either a pure strategy or a mixed strategy. The greater the number of rounds that he is able to play without getting caught more is his payoff. A comparison of the different strategies of the thief against the FDS

with respect to his payoff (in terms of the number of successful rounds) was also carried out.

The fraudulent transactions for the thief were generated for two different sets of parameter values for the Markov process discussed above. The results for Set A = {p_1 = 0.8, p_2 = 0.2, p_3 = 0.8 and p_4 = 0.2} against different FDS strategies have been shown in Figures 5 to 7. The results for Set B = {p_1 = 0.5, p_2 = 0.5, p_3 = 0.5 and p_4 = 0.5} against different FDS strategies have been shown in Figures 8 to 10. Set A models the situation where a thief is likely to attempt a transaction in the same range as his last successful transaction. In contrast, Set B considers, firstly, the situation where the thief is likely to pick up any range with equal probability (excluding the initial state, which is determined by the initial probability) and secondly, the situation where the

Figure 4. Markov Model representation of thief strategy

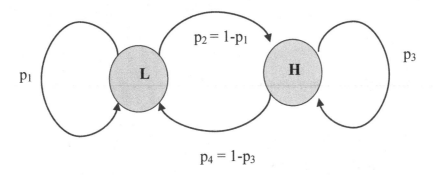

Figure 5. Percentage of TP with thief strategy of Set A

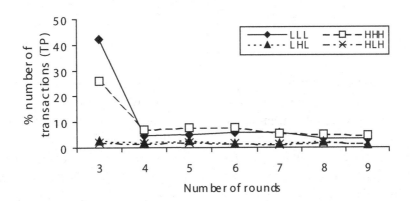

Figure 6. Cumulative % of TP with thief strategy of Set A

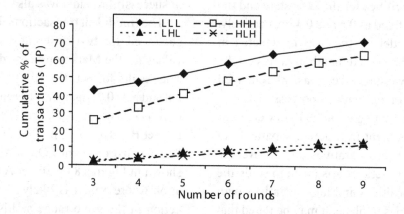

Figure 7. Number of false negatives with thief strategy of Set A

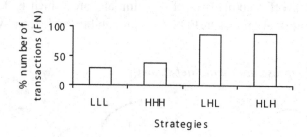

Figure 8. Percentage of TP with thief strategy of Set B

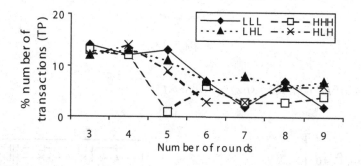

thief believes or may have learnt that he may get caught if he repeats transactions in the same range and hence, opts for alternating the transaction amount ranges. Figure 5 shows that the strategies LLL and HHH were successful in correctly predicting relatively large number of fraudulent transactions in the initial rounds of the game. It

is further clear from Figure 6, which plots the cumulative % of TP (percentage of TP get added up over each round), that the strategies LLL and HHH perform better as compared to LHL and HLH for thief's transactions according to strategy of Set A. The marginal difference between LLL and HHH is due to the initial probability being

Figure 9. Cumulative % of TP with thief strategy of Set B

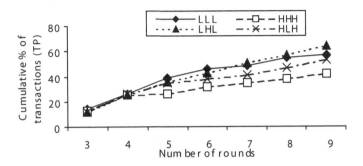

Figure 10. Number of false negatives with thief strategy of Set B

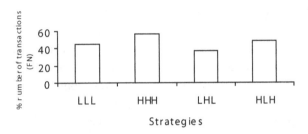

higher in the Low state than the High state. Intuitively, we fixed the initial probability of being in the Low state higher as a thief is more likely to carry out a low value transaction first for the fear of being detected or just trying out the card. A comparison of Figures 7 and 10 shows that the number of false negatives when the thief adopted strategy of Set A was less when FDS chose the strategies LLL or HHH while they were less when FDS chose strategy LHL against thief strategy of Set B. Similarly, Figure 9 depicts that the strategy LHL performs relatively better against thief's strategy according to that of Set B. This was in contrast to strategy LLL and HHH performing better against thief's strategy of Set A as seen in Figures 6 and 7.

The successive number of rounds that the thief can play with different strategies against the strategies implemented in the FDS, as was determined from the simulator, has been shown in Figure 11. It would be clear that given the strategy of the FDS, there exists the possibility of the thief being caught early resulting in a low payoff. However, there also exists a Nash Equilibrium strategy for the thief, which is the last strategy as shown in the figure, with which he can maximize his payoff. This strategy, in effect, avoids all the FDS strategies, namely, LLL, HHH, LHL and HLH.

Experimental Results

In spite of running large-scale simulations, one cannot be sure that the proposed model represents the behavior of a real-life credit card thief. At the same time, actual credit card data is not easily accessible. We have used a novel experiment in order to get data as close to real-life as possible. A 'Fool the FDS' contest, involving about 40 students and faculty members of our institute, was conducted to validate the proposed Fraud Model. Each volunteer was given a valid card number to

Figure 11. Payoff of thief playing different strategies over 30 transactions

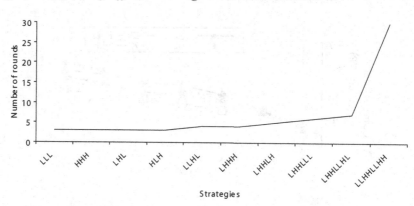

carry out transactions and in the event of getting caught, was given the next card number online (up to a maximum of 20 cards). The challenge for the volunteers was to be able to figure out the strategy being used by the FDS and then to carry out 10 successive transactions on a particular card number without getting caught. The purpose of the contest was to:

(a) Validate the Fraud Model.
(b) See whether learning can actually take place even with incomplete information
(c) See the possibility of learning with complex models and NOT to show that the particular FDS strategy is a good strategy. This is important as it proves that mapping credit card situations to complex games is not correct since the adversary may not be able to learn it and of course, the strategies cannot be disclosed a priori.

We introduced the concept of a dynamic strategy for the FDS in this contest. This was done with the purpose of achieving the final functionality of the FDS, i.e., the FDS starts with an initial belief about the fraudster and as its belief that the fraudster has possibly learnt its strategy crosses a threshold, it dynamically switches its strategy. The volunteers were assumed to be of the type 'first-time thief' when they were issued

with the first card and hence, assumed to be at the first level. The FDS used a relatively simple strategy for this level of players. As the belief of the FDS changed during the course of play, a player from first level was re-assigned to the second level where the strategy used by the FDS was relatively more complex. The FDS strategy space was initialized to Tit-for-Tat strategy (Tit for Tat, 2005), i.e., strategy space {LL, HH} for volunteers at the first level while the volunteers at the second level played against the strategy space {LLL, HHH, LHL, HLH}, as mentioned in the Fraud Model. The volunteers could graduate from first to second level after k successful stages where $k < 10$. Volunteers are said to have 'Learnt' the dynamic strategy if $k = 10$ successful transactions are made on a particular card. The percentage of volunteers who were able to learn the first strategy (Level I) and thereafter, the second strategy of the FDS (Level II), have been depicted in Figure 12.

It can be observed from the figure that learning does take place although it is slow in case of complex strategies. It was also observed that a large majority of the volunteers chose low value transactions to evade detection and tried to repeat their successful transaction, which was detected by the strategies defined in the Game-theoretic component.

Figure 12. FDS strategy learnt by volunteers (%)

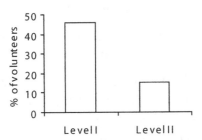

The contest also validated the notion that in the repeated game environment, the fraudster stands a chance to learn his Nash Equilibrium Strategy (NES) even under incomplete information in order to maximize his payoff. It did take place for 15% of the volunteers. Given the strategies of the FDS, the fraudster may initially succeed in carrying out only a few transactions but eventually, as he learns his NES, he can carry out any number of successful transactions. This has been depicted in Figure 13 for a window of 10 transactions and the strategy space of the FDS as specified in our Fraud Model. It may be noted that the result was similar to that obtained from the simulation studies.

The experimental result suggests that the thief is able to learn the NES, which is LLHHLLHH or HHLLHHLL, in this case. A very important observation, in this game, is that the thief could learn the strategy of the FDS. A learning scheme

Figure 13. Payoff of thief with different strategies

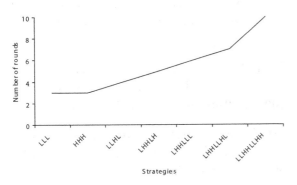

can be embedded in the present architecture so as to allow the FDS also to strengthen its belief about the extent to which the thief has learnt its NE strategy and this will enable the FDS to select alternative strategies dynamically, once its belief about thief's knowledge exceeds a certain threshold. Such a scenario essentially changes the scheme into a two-player competitive learning game for the players.

CONCLUSION

Though most of the fraud detection systems employ rule-based schemes, they suffer from the limitation that in a repeated game environment, a fraudster can eventually learn the defense mechanism adopted by the FDS. We have discussed the applicability of Game theory in such a scenario and suggested a novel approach for credit card fraud detection. A two-tiered architecture, which combines a rule-based component and a Game-theoretic component, has been proposed. The system uses a number of static techniques and improvises through the inclusion of a dynamic Game-theoretic component. The Game-theoretic model is based on a two-player repeated incomplete information game between a thief and the FDS. In this scenario, we have shown that it is indeed possible that the strategies can be learnt and hence, fraud detection systems should be designed with dynamically changing rules.

Though we have largely concentrated on a specific application, we feel that Game theory can be effectively used to counter intrusion in other database applications, such as online banking transactions or fraud in the telecommunications industry. With minor application-specific differences, such situations can be handled as an information warfare game between the attacker and the detection system. We intend to extend this work by augmenting the proposed architecture, especially the Game-theoretic component, equipped with other Game-theoretic strategies. The possibility of enhancing the capability of the Game-theoretic component by inclusion of learning features in the FDS is also being considered. This would enable the FDS to strengthen its belief about the extent to which the fraudster has learnt, thereby enabling it to switch to a counter-strategy.

REFERENCES

Aleskerov, E., Freisleben, B., & Rao, B. (1997). CARDWATCH: A neural network based database mining system for credit card fraud detection. *Proceedings of the Computational Intelligence for Financial Engineering Conference*, (pp. 220-226).

Andrew, K. (2002). *Formal theory for political science – Lecture Notes*.

Bolton, R. J., & Hand, D. J. (2001). Unsupervised profiling methods for fraud detection. *Proceedings of the Conference on Credit Scoring and Credit Control*, Edinburgh, UK.

Chan, P. K., Fan, W., Prodromidis, A. L., & Stolfo, S. J. (1999). Distributed Data Mining in Credit Card Fraud Detection. *IEEE Intelligent Systems*, (pp. 67-74).

Clearly Business (2005). *Clearly Business – Card Fraud*. Website: http://www.clearlybusiness.com/cb/articles/

Complete Website (2005). *Complete Website and E-commerce Solutions*. Website: http://www.haveninternet.com/welcome.htm

Ester, M., Kriegel, H-P., Sander, J., & Xu, X. (1996). A density-based algorithm for discovering clusters in large spatial databases with noise. *Proceedings of the Second International Conference on Knowledge Discovery and Data Mining*.

Ferguson, T. S., & Melolidakis, C. (1998). On the inspection game. *Naval Research Logistics 45*, 327-334.

Fraud Detection Suite (2005). *Fraud Detection Suite- White Paper*. Website: http://www.authorizenet.com/files/fdswhitpaper.pdf

Game Theory (2005). *Game Theory*. Website: http://plato.stanford.edu/entries/game-theory/

Ghosh, S., & Reilly, D. L. (1994). Credit card fraud detection with a neural network. *Proceedings of the 27th Annual Hawaii International Conference on System Sciences*, (pp. 621-630).

Global Consumer Attitude (2006). Global Consumer Attitude Towards Online Shopping. Website: http://www2.acnielsen.com/reports/documents/2005_cc_onlineshopping.pdf

Hamilton, S.N., Miller, W.L., Ott, A., & Saydjari, O.S. (2002). The role of game theory in information warfare. *Proceedings of the Fourth Information Survivability Workshop*.

Hamilton, S. N., Miller, W. L., Ott, A., & Saydjari, O. S. (2002). Challenges in applying game theory to the domain of information warfare. *Proceedings of the Fourth Information Survivability Workshop*.

Han, J., & Kamber, M. (2001). *Data Mining: Concepts and Techniques*. Morgan Kaufman.

Kodialam, M., & Lakshman, T.V. (2003). Detecting network intrusions via sampling: A game-theoretic approach. *Proceedings of the IEEE INFOCOM*, (pp. 1880-1889).

Li, Y., & Zhang, X. (2004). A security-enhanced one-time payment scheme for credit card. *Proceedings of the 14th International Workshop on Research Issues in Data Engineering*, (pp. 40-47).

Liu, P., & Li, L. (2002). A game-theoretic approach for attack prediction. Technical Report, PSU-S2-2002-01, Pennsylvania State University.

MAXMIND (2005). *MAXMIND – Geolocation and Credit Card Fraud Detection*. Website: http://www.maxmind.com/

Merchant Account (2005). *Merchant Account Credit Card Processing.* Website: http://www. aaa-merchant-account.com/

Online Fraud (2005). *Online Fraud is 12 Times Higher than Offline Fraud.* Website: http://selli-tontheweb.com/ezine/news0434.shtml

Peters, M.E. (2002). Emerging eCommerce credit and debit card protocols. *Proceedings of the 3rd International Symposium on Electronic Commerce,* (pp. 39-46).

Syeda, M., Zhang, Y. Q., & Pan, Y. (2002). Parallel granular neural networks for fast credit card fraud detection. *Proceedings of IEEE International Conference on Fuzzy Systems,* (pp. 572-577).

Tit For Tat (2005). *TIT FOR TAT.* Website: http://www.abc.net.au/science/slab/tittat/story.htm

Chapter II
Email Worm Detection Using Data Mining

Mohammad M. Masud
University of Texas at Dallas, USA

Latifur Khan
University of Texas at Dallas, USA

Bhavani Thuraisingham
University of Texas at Dallas, USA

ABSTRACT

This chapter applies data mining techniques to detect email worms. Email messages contain a number of different features such as the total number of words in message body/subject, presence/absence of binary attachments, type of attachments, and so on. The goal is to obtain an efficient classification model based on these features. The solution consists of several steps. First, the number of features is reduced using two different approaches: feature-selection and dimension-reduction. This step is necessary to reduce noise and redundancy from the data. The feature-selection technique is called Two-phase Selection (TPS), which is a novel combination of decision tree and greedy selection algorithm. The dimension-reduction is performed by Principal Component Analysis. Second, the reduced data is used to train a classifier. Different classification techniques have been used, such as Support Vector Machine (SVM), Naïve Bayes and their combination. Finally, the trained classifiers are tested on a dataset containing both known and unknown types of worms. These results have been compared with published results. It is found that the proposed TPS selection along with SVM classification achieves the best accuracy in detecting both known and unknown types of worms.

INTRODUCTION

Email worm spreads through infected email messages. The worm may be carried by attachment, or the email may contain links to an infected website. When the user opens the attachment, or clicks the link, the host gets infected immediately. The worm exploits the vulnerable email software in the host machine to send infected emails to addresses stored in address book. Thus, new machines get infected. Worms bring damage to computer and people in various ways. They may clog the network traffic, cause damage to the system and make the system unstable or even unusable.

The traditional way of worm detection is signature based. A signature is a unique pattern in the worm body that can identify it as a particular type of worm. Thus, a worm can be detected from its signature. But the problem with this approach is that it involves significant amount of human intervention and may take long time (from days to weeks) to discover the signature. Thus, this approach is not useful against "zero-day" attacks of computer worm. Besides, signature matching is not effective against polymorphism.

Thus, there is a growing need for a fast and effective detection mechanism that requires no manual intervention. Our work is directed towards automatic and efficient detection of email worms. We apply a feature-based approach for this purpose. A number of features of email messages have been identified in (Martin, Sewani, Nelson, Chen & Joseph, 2005a), and discussed in "Feature reduction & Classification" section. The total number of features is large, some of which may be redundant or noisy. So we apply two different feature-reduction techniques: a *dimension-reduction* technique called Principal Component Analysis (PCA), and our novel *feature-selection* technique called Two-phase Selection (TPS) that applies decision tree and greedy elimination. These features are used to train a classifier to obtain a classification model. We use three different classifiers for this task: Support Vector Machine (SVM), Naïve Bayes (NB), and a combination of SVM and NB, mentioned henceforth as the *Series* classifier. The Series approach was first proposed by Martin, Sewani, Nelson, Chen & Joseph (2005b).

We use the data set of (Martin et al., 2005a) for evaluation purpose. The original data distribution was unbalanced, so we balance it by rearranging. We divide the data set into two disjoint subsets: the *known worms set* or K-Set and the *novel worms set* or N-Set. The K-Set contains some clean emails and emails infected by five different types of worms. The K-Set contains emails infected by a sixth type worm, but no clean email. We run a three-fold cross validation on the K-Set. At each iteration of the cross validation, we test the accuracy of the trained classifiers on the N-Set. Thus, we obtain two different measures of accuracy, namely, the accuracy of the three-fold cross validation on K-Set, and the average accuracy of novel worm detection on N-Set.

Our contributions to this research work are as follows: First, we apply two special feature-reduction techniques to remove redundancy and noise from data. One technique is PCA, and the other is our novel TPS algorithm. PCA is commonly used to extract patterns from high dimensional data, especially when the data is noisy. Besides, it is a simple and nonparametric method. TPS applies decision tree C4.5 (Quinlan, 1993) for initial selection, and thereafter it applies greedy elimination technique (see section "Two-phase Feature Selection (TPS)"). Second, we create a balanced dataset as explained above. Finally, we compare the individual performances among NB, SVM, and Series and show empirically that the Series approach proposed by Martin et al. (2005b) performs worse than either NB or SVM.

The rest of this paper is organized as follows: section "Related Work" describes related work in automatic email worm detection; section "Feature Reduction and Classification Techniques" describes the feature-selection, dimension-reduction and classification techniques; section "Data Set" describes the distribution of the data set; section "Experimental setup" describes the experimental setup such as hardware, software and system parameters; section "Results" discusses the results; and section "Conclusions" concludes with future guidelines for research.

RELATED WORK

There are different approaches to automate the detection of worms. These approaches are mainly of two types: *behavioral* and *content-based*. Behavioral approaches analyze the behavior of messages like source-destination addresses, attachment types, message frequency etc. Content-based approaches look into the content of the message, and try to detect signature automatically. There are also combined methods that take advantage of both techniques.

An example of behavioral detection is social network analysis (Golbeck & Hendler, 2004; Newman, Forrest & Balthrop, 2002). It detects worm infected emails by creating graphs of network, where users are represented as nodes, and communications between users are represented as edges. A social network is a group of nodes among which there exists edges. Emails that propagate beyond the group boundary are considered to be infected. But the drawback of this system is that worms can easily bypass social networks by intelligently choosing recipient lists, by looking at recent emails in the user's outbox.

Another example of behavioral approach is the application of Email Mining Toolkit (EMT) (Stolfo, 2006). The EMT computes *behavior profiles* of user email accounts by analyzing email logs. They use some modeling techniques to achieve high detection rates with very low false positive rates. Statistical analysis of outgoing emails is another behavioral approach (Symantec, 2005; Schultz, Eskin & Zadok, 2001). Statistics collected from frequency of communication between clients and their mail server, byte sequences

in the attachment etc. are used to predict anomalies in emails and thus worms are detected.

An example of content based approach is the EarlyBird System (Singh, Estan, Varghese & Savage, 2003). In this system, statistics on highly repetitive packet contents are gathered. These statistics are analyzed to detect possible infection of host or server machines. This method generates content signature of worm without any human intervention. Results reported by this system indicated very low false positive rate of detection. Other examples are the Autograph (Kim & Karp, 2004), and the Polygraph (Newsome, Karp & Song, 2005), developed at Carnegie Mellon University.

There are other approaches to detect early spreading of worms, such as employing "honeypot". A honeypot (Honeypot, 2006) is a closely monitored decoy computer that attracts attacks for early detection and in-depth adversary analysis. The honeypots are designed to not send out email in normal situations. If a honeypot begins to send out emails after running the attachment of an email, it is determined that this email is an email worm.

Another approach by (Sidiroglou, Ioannidis, Keromytis & Stolfo, 2005) employs behavior-based anomaly detection, which is different from signature-based or statistical approaches. Their approach is to open all suspicious attachments inside an instrumented virtual machine looking for dangerous actions, such as writing to the Windows registry, and flag suspicious messages.

Our work is related to Martin et al., (2005a). They report an experiment with email data, where they apply a statistical approach to find an optimum subset of a large set of features to facilitate the classification of outgoing emails, and eventually, detect novel email worms. However, our approach is different from Martin et al.'s approach in that we apply PCA, and TPS to reduce noise and redundancy from data.

FEATURE REDUCTION AND CLASSIFICATION TECHNIQUES

First, we briefly describe the features that are used in email worm detection. These features are extracted from a repository of outgoing emails collected over a period of two years (Martin et al., 2005a). These features are categorized into two different groups: i) per-email feature and ii) per-window feature. Per-email features are features of a single email, while per-window features are features of a collection of emails sent/received within a window of time. Second, we describe our dimension-reduction and feature-selection techniques. Finally, we describe the classification techniques.

Feature Description

For a detailed description of the features please refer to (Martin et al., 2005a). Each of these features are either continuous valued or binary. Value of a binary feature is either 0 or 1, depending on the presence or absence of this feature in a data point. There are a total of 94 features. Here we describe some of them.

Per Email Features

HTML in body: Whether there is HTML in the email body. This feature is used because a bug in the HTML parser of the email client is a vulnerability that may be exploited by worm writers. It is a binary feature.

Embedded image: Whether there is any embedded image. This is used because a buggy image processor of the email client is also vulnerable to attacks.

Hyperlinks: Whether there are hyperlinks in the email body. Clicking an infected link causes the host to be infected. It is also a binary feature.

Binary Attachment: Whether there are any binary attachments. Worms are mainly propagated by binary attachments. This is also a binary feature.

Multipurpose Internet Mail Extensions (MIME) type of attachments: There are different MIME types, for example: "application/msword", "application/pdf", "image/gif", "text/plain" etc. Each of these types is used as a binary feature (total 27).

UNIX "magic number" of file attachments: Sometimes a different MIME type is assigned by the worm writers to evade detection. Magic numbers can accurately detect the MIME type. Each of these types is used as a binary feature (total 43).

Number of attachments: It is a continuous feature.

Number of words/characters in subject/body: These features are continuous. Most worms choose random text, whereas a user may have certain writing characteristics. Thus, these features are sometimes useful to detect infected emails.

Per Window Features

Number of emails sent in window: An infected host is supposed to send emails at a faster rate. This is a continuous feature.

Number of unique email recipients, senders: These are also important criteria to distinguish between normal and infected host. This is a continuous feature too.

Average number of words/characters per subject, body; average word length: These features are also useful in distinguishing between normal and viral activity.

Variance in number of words/characters per subject, body; variance in word length: These are also useful properties of email worms.

Ratio of emails to attachments: usually, normal emails do not contain attachments, whereas most infected emails do contain them.

Dimension Reduction

The high dimensionality of data always appears to be a major problem for classification tasks because i) it increases the running time of the classification algorithms, ii) increases chance of overfitting, and iii) large number of instances are required for learning tasks. We apply PCA in to obtain a reduced dimensional data in an attempt to eliminate these problems.

PCA finds a reduced set of attributes by projecting the original dimension into a lower dimension. PCA is also capable of discovering hidden patterns in data, thereby increasing classification accuracy. As high dimensional data contains redundancies and noises, it is much harder for the learning algorithms to find a hypothesis consistent with the training instances. The learned hypothesis is likely to be too complex and susceptible to overfitting. PCA reduces the dimension, without losing much information, and thus allows the learning algorithms to find a simpler hypothesis that is consistent with the training examples, and thereby reduces the chance of overfitting. But it should be noted that PCA projects data into a lower dimension in the direction of maximum dispersion. Maximum dispersion of data does not necessarily imply maximum separation of between–class data and/or maximum concentration of within – class data. If this is the case, then PCA reduction may result in poor performance.

Two-Phase Feature Selection (TPS)

Feature selection is different from dimension reduction because it selects a subset of the feature set, rather than projecting combination of features onto lower dimension. We apply a two-phase feature selection (TPS) process. In phase I, we build a decision tree from the training data. We select the features found at the internal nodes of the tree. In phase II, we apply a greedy selection algorithm. We combine these two selection processes because of the following reasons. The decision tree selection is fast, but the selected features may not be a good choice for the novel dataset. That is, the selected features may not perform well on the novel data, since the novel data may have a different set of important features.

We observe this fact when we apply decision tree on the Mydoom.M and and VBS.BubbleBoy dataset. That is why we apply another phase of selection, the greedy selection, on top of decision tree selection. Our goal is to determine if there is a more general feature set that covers all important features. In our experiments, we are able to find such a feature set using greedy selection. There are two reasons why we do not apply only greedy selection: first, it is very slow compared to decision tree selection. Because, at each iteration, we have to modify the data to keep only the selected features and run the classifiers to compute the accuracy. Second, the greedy elimination process may lead to a set of features that are inferior to the decision tree-selected set of features. That is why we keep the decision tree-selected features as the minimal features set.

Phase I

We apply decision tree as a feature selection tool in phase I. The main reason behind applying decision tree is that it selects the best attributes according to information gain. Information gain is a very effective metric in selecting features. Information gain can be defined as a measure of the effectiveness of an attribute (i.e., feature) in classifying the training data (Mitchell, 1997). If we split the training data on this attribute values, then information gain gives the measurement of the expected reduction in entropy after the split. The more an attribute can reduce entropy in the training data, the better the attribute in classifying the data. Information Gain of a binary attribute A on a collection of examples S is given by (1):

$$Gain(S, A) \equiv Entropy(S) - \sum_{V \in Values(A)} \frac{|S_v|}{|S|} Entropy(S_v)$$

$$(1)$$

Where Values(A) is the set of all possible values for attribute A, and S_v is the subset of S for which attribute A has value v. In our case, each binary attribute has only two possible values (0, 1). Entropy of subset S is computed using the following equation:

$$Entropy(S) = -\frac{p(s)}{n(s)+p(s)}\log_2(\frac{p(s)}{n(s)+p(s)}) - \frac{n(s)}{n(s)+p(s)}\log_2(\frac{n(s)}{n(s)+p(s)})$$

(2)

Where $p(S)$ is the number of positive examples in S and $n(S)$ is the total number of negative examples in S. Computation of information gain of a continuous attribute is a little tricky, because it has infinite number of possible values. One approach followed by Quinlan (Quinlan, 1993) is to find an optimal threshold, and split the data into two halves. The optimal threshold is found by searching a threshold value with highest information gain within the range of values of this attribute in the dataset.

We use J48 for building decision tree, which is an implementation of C4.5. Decision tree algorithms choose the best attribute based on information gain criterion at each level of recursion. Thus, the final tree actually consists of the most important attributes that can distinguish between the positive and negative instances. The tree is further pruned to reduce chances of overfitting. Thus, we are able to identify the features that are necessary and the features that are redundant, and use only the necessary features. Surprisingly enough, in our experiments we find that on average, only 4.5 features are selected by the decision tree algorithm, and the total number of nodes in tree is only 11. It indicates that only a few features are important. We have six different datasets for six different worm types. Each dataset is again divided into two subsets: the *known worms set* or K-Set, and the *novel worm set* or N-Set. We apply three-fold cross validation on the K-Set.

Phase II

In the second phase, we apply a greedy algorithm to select the best subset of features. We use the feature subset selected in phase I as the *minimal subset* (MS). At the beginning of the algorithm, we select all the features from the original set, and call it as the *potential feature set* (PFS). At each iteration of the algorithm, we compute the average novel detection accuracy of six dataset, using PFS as the feature set. Then we pick up a feature at random from the PFS, which is not in MS, and eliminate it from the PFS if the elimination does not reduce the accuracy of novel detection of any classifier (NB, SVM, Series). If the accuracy drops after elimination, then we do not eliminate the feature, and we add it to MS. In this way, we reduce PFS and continue until no further elimination is possible. Now the PFS contains the most effective subset of features. Although this process is time consuming, we finally come up with a subset of features that can outperform the original set.

Algorithm 1 sketches the two-phase feature selection process. At line 2, the decision tree is built using original feature set FS, and unreduced dataset D_{FS}. At line 3, the set of features selected by the decision tree is stored in the minimal subset, MS. Then the potential subset, PFS is initialized to the original set FS. Line 5 computes the average novel detection accuracy of three classifiers. The functions NB-Acc(PFS, D_{PFS}), SVM-Acc(PFS, D_{PFS}) and Series-Acc(PFS, D_{PFS}) return the average novel detection accuracy of NB, SVM and Series, respectively, using PFS as the feature set.

In the while loop, we randomly choose a feature X, such that $X \in PFS$ but $X \notin MS$, and delete it from PFS. The accuracy of the new PFS is calculated. If, after deletion, the accuracy increases or remains the same, then X is redundant. So we remove this feature permanently. Otherwise, if the accuracy drops after deletion, then this feature is essential, so we add it to the minimal set, MS (lines 13-14). In this way, we either delete a redundant feature or add it to the minimal selection. It is repeated until we have nothing more to select (i.e., MS equals PFS). We return the PFS as the best feature set.

Algorithm 1.

Algorithm 1 Two-phase feature selection

1: Two-Phase-Selection (*FS*, D_{FS}) returns *FeatureSet*
// *FS* : original set of features
// D_{FS} : original dataset with *FS* as the feature set
2: *T* ← Build-Decision-Tree (*FS*, D_{FS})
3: *MS* ← Feature-Set (*T*)   //minimal subset of features
4: *PFS* ← *FS*   //potential subset of features
//compute novel detection accuracy of *FS*
5: p_{avg} ← (NB-Acc(*PFS*, D_{PFS}) + SVM-Acc(*PFS*, D_{PFS})
          + Series-Acc(*PFS*, D_{PFS})) /3
6: **while** *PFS*<>*MS* **do**
7:     *X* ← a randomly chosen feature from *PFS* that is not in *MS*
8:     *PFS* ← *PFS* − *X*
       //compute novel detection accuracy of *PFS*
9:     C_{avg} ← (NB-Acc(*PFS*, D_{PFS}) + SVM-Acc(*PFS*, D_{PFS})
          + Series-Acc(*PFS*, D_{PFS})) /3
10:    **if** $C_{avg} \geq p_{avg}$
11:        p_{avg} ← C_{avg}
12:    **else**
13:        *PFS* ← *PFS* ∪ {*X*}
14:        *MS* ← *MS* ∪ {*X*}
15:    **end if**
16: **end while**
17:**return** *PFS*

Classification Techniques

We apply the NB (John & Langley, 1995), SVM (Boser, Guyon & Vapnik, 1992), and C4.5 decision tree (Quinlan, 1993) classifiers in our experiments. We also apply our implementation of the Series classifier (Martin et al., 2005b) to compare its performance with other classifiers. We briefly describe the Series approach here for the purpose of self-containment.

The Series or "two-layer approach" (as is called in Martin et al., 2005b) works as follows: in the first layer, SVM is applied as a novelty detector. The parameters of SVM are chosen such that it produces almost zero false positive. This means, if SVM classifies an email as infected, then with probability (almost) 100%, it is an infected email. If, otherwise, SVM classifies an email as clean, then it is sent to the second layer for further verification. This is because, with the above parameter settings, while SVM reduces false positive rate, it also increases the false negative rate. So, any email classified as negative must be further verified. In the second layer, NB classifier is applied to confirm whether the suspected emails are really infected. If NB classifies it as infected, then it is marked as infected, otherwise, it is marked as clean. Fig. 1 illustrates the Series approach.

DATA SET

We have collected the worm data set used in the experiment by Martin et al. (Martin et al., 2005a). They have accumulated several hundreds of clean and worm emails over a period of two years. All these emails are outgoing emails. Several features are extracted from these emails as explained in subsection "Feature Description".

There are six types of worms contained in the data set: VBS.BubbleBoy, W32.Mydoom.M, W32. Sobig.F, W32.Netsky.D, W32.Mydoom.U, and W32.Bagle.F. But the classification task is binary: {clean, infected}. The original data set contains six training and six test sets. Each training set is made up of 400 clean emails and 1000 infected emails, consisting of 200 samples from each of the five different worms. The sixth virus is then included in the test set, which contains 1200 clean emails and 200 infected messages. Table 1 clarifies this distribution. For ease of representation, we abbreviate the worm names as follows:

B: VBS.BubbleBoy
F: W32.Bagle.F
M: W32.Mydoom.M
N: W32.Netsky.D
S: W32.Sobig.F
U: W32.Mydoom.U

NB, SVM and the Series classifiers are applied on the original data, the PCA-reduced data, and the TPS-selected data. The decision tree is applied on the original data only.

We can easily notice that the original data set is unbalanced, because the ratio of clean emails to infected emails is 2:5 in the training set, whereas it is 5:1 in the test set. So, the results obtained from this dataset may not be reliable. We make it balanced by redistributing the examples. In our distribution, each balanced set contains two subsets. The *Known-worms set* or K-Set contains 1600 clean email messages, which are the combination of all the clean messages in the original data set (400 from training set, 1200 from test set). The K-Set also contains 1000 infected messages, which consists of five types of worms marked as the "known worms". The N-Set contains 200 infected messages of a sixth type of worm, marked as the "novel worm". Then we apply cross validation on K-Set. The cross validation is done as follows: we randomly divide the set of 2600 (1600 clean + 1000 viral) messages into three equal sized subsets, such that the ratio of clean messages to viral messages remains the same in all subsets. We take two subsets as training set and the remaining set as the test set. This is done three times by rotating the testing and training sets. We take the average accuracy of these three runs. This accuracy is shown under the column *accuracy* in following tables. Besides testing the accuracy of the test set, we also test the detection accuracy of each of the three learned classifier on the N-Set, and take the average. This accuracy is

Figure 1. Series combination of SVM and NB classifiers for email worm detection

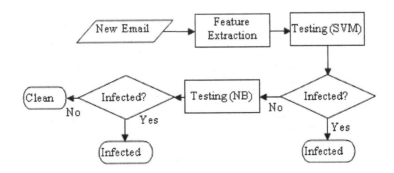

Table 1. Data distribution from the original data set

Set	Training set		Test set	
	Total clean emails	Total infected emails	Total clean emails	Total infected emails
B	400	1000 (= 200x5), 200 from each different types except B	1000	200 (only B)
M	400	1000 (= 200x5), 200 from each different types except M	1000	200 (only M)
S	400	1000 (= 200x5), 200 from each different types except S	1000	200 (only S)
N	400	1000 (= 200x5), 200 from each different types except N	1000	200 (only N)
U	400	1000 (= 200x5), 200 from each different types except U	1000	200 (only U)
F	400	1000 (= 200x5), 200 from each different types except F	1000	200 (only F)

also averaged over all runs and shown as *novel detection accuracy*. Table 2 displays the data distribution of our dataset.

EXPERIMENTAL SETUP

We run all our experiments on Windows XP machine with Java version 1.5 installed. For running SVM, we use libsvm (Libsvm, 2006) package. The type of classifier is C-Support Vector Classification (C-SVC) with the radial basis function. Parameter setting are "gamma" = 0.2 and "C"=1. We use our own C++ implementation of NB. We implement PCA with MATLAB. We vary the target dimension from 5 to 94 with step 5 increments. We use the WEKA (WEKA, 2006) implementation of decision tree, with pruning applied.

Table 2. Data distribution from the redistributed data set

Set	Cross validation set		Novel Worm set	
	Total clean emails	Total infected emails	Total clean emails	Total infected emails
B	1600	1000 (= 200x5), 200 from each different types except B	0	200 (only B)
M	1600	1000 (= 200x5), 200 from each different types except M	0	200 (only M)
S	1600	1000 (= 200x5), 200 from each different types except S	0	200 (only S)
N	1600	1000 (= 200x5), 200 from each different types except N	0	200 (only N)
U	1600	1000 (= 200x5), 200 from each different types except U	0	200 (only U)
F	1600	1000 (= 200x5), 200 from each different types except F	0	200 (only F)

RESULTS

We discuss the results in three separate subsections. In subsection "Results from Unreduced Data", we discuss the results found from unreduced data, i.e., data before any reduction or selection is applied. In subsection "Results from PCA-reduced Data", we discuss the results found from PCA-reduced data, and in subsection "Results obtained from Two-phase Selection", we discuss the results obtained using TPS-reduced data.

Results from Unreduced Data

Table 3 reports the accuracy of the cross validation accuracy and false positive for each set. The cross validation accuracy is shown under the column *Acc* and the false positive rate is shown under the column *FP*. The set names at the row headings are the abbreviated names as explained in "Data Set" section. From the results reported in Table 3, we see that SVM observes the best accuracy among all classifiers, although the difference with other classifiers is small.

Table 4 reports the accuracy of detecting novel worms. We see that SVM is very consistent over all sets but NB, Series, and decision tree performs significantly worse in Mydoom.M dataset.

Results from PCA-Reduced Data

The following chart (Fig. 2) shows the results of applying PCA on the original data. The X axis denotes dimension of the reduced dimensional data, which has been varied from 5 to 90, with step 5 increments. The last point on the X axis is the unreduced or original dimension. Fig. 2 shows the cross validation accuracy for different dimensions. The data from the chart should be read as follows: a point (x, y) on a given line, say the line for SVM, indicates the cross validation accuracy y of SVM, averaged over all six data sets, where each data set has been reduced to x dimension using PCA.

Fig. 2 indicates that at lower dimensions, cross validation accuracy is lower, for each of the three classifiers. But SVM achieves its near maximum accuracy at dimension 30. NB and Series reaches within 2% of maximum accuracy at dimension 30 and onwards. All classifiers attain their maximum at the highest dimension 94, which is actually the unreduced data. So, from this observation, we may conclude that PCA is not effective on this data set, in terms of cross validation accuracy. The reason behind this poorer performance on the reduced dimensional data is possibly the one that we have mentioned earlier in subsection "Dimension Reduction". The reduction by PCA

Table 3. Comparison of accuracy (%) and false positive (%) of different classifiers on the worm data set

	NB		SVM		Series		decision tree	
Set	Acc	FP	Acc	FP	Acc	FP	Acc	FP
M	99.3	0.6	99.5	0.6	99.4	0.5	99.3	0.6
S	99.1	0.6	99.5	0.6	99.2	0.5	99.4	0.6
N	99.2	0.5	99.5	0.6	99.2	0.4	99.2	1.1
U	99.1	0.6	99.5	0.6	99.2	0.5	99.2	0.8
F	99.2	0.6	99.5	0.7	99.3	0.4	99.4	0.4
B	99.2	0.6	99.3	0.8	99.2	0.6	99.6	0.4
Avg	**99.19**	**0.58**	**99.47**	**0.64**	**99.24**	**0.49**	**99.35**	**0.65**

Table 4. Comparison of novel detection accuracy (%) of different classifiers on the worm data set

Set name	NB	SVM	Series	decision tree
M	17.4	92.4	16.6	32.0
S	97.0	95.0	95.0	97.5
N	97.0	97.0	97.0	99.0
U	97.0	97.2	97.0	97.0
F	97.0	97.0	97.0	99.5
B	96.0	96.0	96.0	0.5
Avg	**83.58**	**95.77**	**83.11**	**70.92**

is not producing a lower dimensional data where dissimilar class instances are maximally dispersed and similar class instances are maximally concentrated. So, the classification accuracy is lower at lower dimensions.

We now present the results, at dimension 25, similar to the results presented in the previous subsection. Table 5 compares the novel detection accuracy and cross validation accuracy of different classifiers. The choice of this particular dimension is that, at this dimension all the classifiers seem to be the most balanced in all aspects: cross validation accuracy, false positive and false negative rate and novel detection accuracy. We conclude that this dimension is the optimal dimension for projection by PCA. From Table 5, it is evident that accuracies of all three classifiers on PCA-reduced data are lower than that of the unreduced data. It

is possible that some information, which is useful for classification, might have been lost during projection onto a lower dimension.

We see in Table 5 that both the accuracy and novel detection accuracy of NB has dropped significantly from the original dataset. The novel detection accuracy of NB on Mydoom.M dataset has become 0%, compared to 17% in the original set. The novel detection accuracy of SVM on the same dataset has dropped to 30%, compared to 92.4% in the original dataset. So, we can conclude that PCA-reduction does not help in novel detection.

Results from Two-Phase Selection

Our TPS selects the following features (without any ordering)

Figure 2. Average cross validation accuracy of the three classifiers on lower dimensional data, reduced by PCA

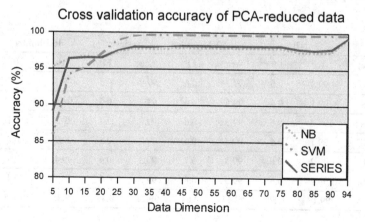

Table 5. Comparison of cross validation accuracy (Acc) and novel detection accuracy (NAcc) among different classifiers on the PCA reduced worm data set at dimension 25.

Set	NB		SVM		Series	
	Acc (%)	NAcc(%)	Acc (%)	NAcc(%)	Acc (%)	NAcc(%)
M	99.08	0.0	99.46	30.02	99.15	24.7
S	97.31	97.01	99.19	97.01	97.77	97.01
N	96.61	97.51	98.62	97.01	96.73	97.01
U	96.92	97.51	98.46	97.34	97.15	97.34
F	96.92	97.51	98.93	97.01	97.07	97.01
B	96.96	97.68	98.88	97.51	97.08	97.51
Avg	**97.3**	**81.2**	**98.92**	**85.98**	**97.49**	**85.1**

i. Attachment type *binary*
ii. MIME (magic) type of attachment *application/msdownload*
iii. MIME (magic) type of attachment *application/x-ms-dos-executable*
iv. Frequency of email sent in window
v. Mean words in body
vi. Mean characters in subject
vii. Number of attachments
viii. Number of From Address in Window
ix. Ratio of emails with attachment
x. Variance of attachment size
xi. Variance of words in body
xii. Number of HTML in email
xiii. Number of links in email
xiv. Number of To Address in Window
xv. Variance of characters in subject

The first three features actually reflects important characteristic of an infected email. Usually, infected emails have binary attachment, which is a dos/windows executable. Mean/variance of *words in body* and *characters in subject* are also considered as important symptoms, because usually infected emails contain random subject or body, thus having irregular size of body or subject. *Number of attachment* and *ratio of attachments*, and *links in email* are usually higher for infected emails. *Frequency of emails sent in window*, and *number of To address in window* are higher for an infected host, since a compromised host sends infected emails to many addresses and more frequently. Thus, most of the features selected by our algorithm are really practical and useful.

Table 6 reports the cross validation accuracy (%), and false positive rate (%) of the three classifiers on the TPS-reduced dataset. We see that both the accuracy and false positive rates are almost the same as the unreduced dataset. The accuracy of Mydoom.M dataset (shown at row **M**) is 99.3% for NB, 99.5% for SVM and 99.4% for Series. Table 7 reports the novel detection accuracy (%) of the three classifiers on the TPS-reduced dataset. We find that the average novel detection accuracy on TPS-reduced dataset is higher than the unreduced dataset. The main reason behind this improvement is due to a higher accuracy on the Mydoom.M set by NB and Series. The accuracy of NB on this dataset is 37.1% (row **M**), compared to 17.4% in the unreduced dataset (please refer to Table 4, row M). Also, the accuracy of Series on the same is 36.0%, compared to 16.6% on the unreduced dataset (as show in Table 4, row M). However, accuracy of SVM remains almost the same; 91.7%, compared to 92.4% in the unreduced dataset. In Table 8, we summarize the averages from all the tables from Table 3 – Table 7.

Table 6. Cross validation accuracy (%) and false positive (%) of three different classifiers on the TPS-reduced dataset

Set name	NB		SVM		Series	
	Acc	FP	Acc	FP	Acc	FP
M	99.3	0.6	99.5	0.6	99.4	0.5
S	99.1	0.7	99.5	0.6	99.2	0.5
N	99.1	0.6	99.5	0.6	99.2	0.4
U	99.1	0.7	99.5	0.6	99.2	0.5
F	99.2	0.6	99.5	0.6	99.3	0.4
B	99.2	0.6	99.3	0.8	99.2	0.6
Avg	99.16	0.58	99.49	0.6	99.25	0.49

The first three rows (after the header row) report the cross validation accuracy of all four classifiers that we have used in our experiments. Each row reports the average accuracy on a particular dataset. The first row reports the average accuracy for unreduced dataset; the second row reports the same for PCA-reduced dataset and the third row for TPS-reduced dataset. We see that the average accuracies are almost the same for TPS-reduced and unreduced set. For example, average accuracy of NB (shown under column NB) is the same for both, which is 99.2%; and accuracy of SVM (shown under column SVM) is also the same, 99.5%. The average accuracies of these classifiers on PCA-reduced dataset are

1-2% lower. There is no entry under the decision tree column for PCA-reduced and TPS-reduced dataset because we only test the decision tree on the unreduced dataset.

The middle three rows report the average false positive values and the last three rows report the average novel detection accuracies. We see that the average novel detection accuracy on the TPS-reduced dataset is the highest among all. The average novel detection accuracy of NB on this dataset is 86.7%, compared to 83.6% on the unreduced dataset, which is a 3.1% improvement on average. Also, Series has the novel detection accuracy of 86.3% on TPS-reduced dataset, compared to that of the unreduced dataset, which is 83.1%. Again, it is a 3.2% improvement on average. However, average accuracy of SVM remains almost the same (only 0.1% difference) on these two datasets. Thus, on average, we have an improvement in novel detection accuracy across different classifiers on the TPS-reduced dataset. While TPS-reduced dataset is the best among the three, the best classifier among the four is SVM. It has the highest average accuracy and novel detection accuracy on all datasets, and also very low average false positive rates.

In summary, we have two important findings from our experiments. First, SVM has the best performance among all four different classifiers:

Table 7. Comparison of novel detection accuracy (%) of different classifiers on the TPS-reduced dataset

Set name	NB	SVM	Series
M	37.1	91.7	36.0
S	97.0	95.0	95.0
N	97.0	97.0	97.0
U	97.0	97.2	97.0
F	97.0	97.0	97.0
B	96.0	96.0	96.0
Avg	86.87	95.66	86.34

Table 8. Summary of results (averages) obtained from different feature-based approaches

	Dataset	NB	SVM	Series	decision tree
Cross validation Accuracy	Unreduced	99.2	99.5	99.2	99.4
	PCA-reduced	97.3	98.9	97.5	--
	TPS-selected	99.2	99.5	99.3	--
False Positive	Unreduced	0.6	0.6	0.5	0.7
	PCA-reduced	0.9	1.5	0.6	--
	TPS- selected	0.6	0.6	0.5	--
Novel detection Accuracy	Unreduced	83.6	95.8	83.1	70.9
	PCA-reduced	81.2	86.0	81.0	--
	TPS- selected	86.7	95.7	86.3	--

NB, SVM, Series and decision tree. Second, feature selection using our TPS algorithm achieves the best accuracy, especially in detecting novel worms. Combining these two findings, we conclude that SVM, with TPS-reduction should work as the best novel worm detection tool on a feature-based dataset.

In future, we would like to continue our research in detecting worms by combining feature-based approach with content-based approach to make it more robust and efficient. Besides, we are also willing to focus on the statistical property of the contents of the messages for possible contamination of worms.

CONCLUSION

In this work, we explore three different data mining approaches to automatically detect worms email worms. The first approach is to apply either NB or SVM on the unreduced dataset, without any feature reduction, and train a classifier. The second approach is to reduce data dimension using PCA and apply NB or SVM on the reduced data and train a classifier. The third approach is to apply a two-phase selection to select the best features using decision tree and greedy algorithm. Results obtained from our experiments indicate that the best performance is achieved by TPS. We report the feature set that achieves this performance. We also find that the best classifier is SVM, achieving the highest average accuracy among all classifiers across different datasets. Thus, we strongly recommend applying SVM with our two-phase selection process for detecting novel email worms in a feature-based paradigm.

REFERENCES

Boser, B. E., Guyon, I. M., & Vapnik, V. N. (1992). *A training algorithm for optimal margin classifiers*. In D. Haussler, (Ed.), *5th Annual ACM Workshop on COLT*, (pp. 144-152). Pittsburgh, PA. ACM Press.

Golbeck, J., & Hendler, J. (2004). *Reputation network analysis for email filtering*. In CEAS.

Honeypot (2006). http://www.honeypots.net/

http://www.sarc.com/avcenter/venc/data/w32. beagle. bg@mm.html

John, G. H., & Langley, P. (1995). *Estimating Continuous Distributions in Bayesian Classifiers. In the Proceedings of the Eleventh Conference on Uncertainty in Artificial Intelligence* (pp. 338-345)., San Mateo: Morgan KaufMann Publishers.

Kim, H.-A., & Karp, B. (2004). Autograph: Toward Automated, Distributed Worm Signature Detection. *In the Proceedings of the 13th Usenix Security Symposium (Security 2004)*, San Diego, CA, August, 2004.

Libsvm. (2006). *A library for Support Vector Machine.* http://www.csie.ntu.edu.tw/~cjlin/libsvm/

Martin, S., Sewani, A., Nelson, B., Chen, K., & Joseph, A.D. (2005a). Analyzing Behavioral Features for Email Classification. *In the Proceedings of the IEEE Second Conference on Email and Anti-Spam (CEAS 2005)*, July 21 & 22, Stanford University.

Martin, S., Sewani, A., Nelson, B., Chen, K., & Joseph, A. D. (2005b). *A Two-Layer Approach for Novel Email Worm Detection.* Submitted to USENIX Steps on Reducing Unwanted Traffic on the Internet (SRUTI).

Mitchell, T. (1997). *Machine Learning.* McGraw Hill.

Newman, M. E. J., Forrest, S., & Balthrop, J. (2002). Email networks and the spread of computer viruses. *Physical Review, E 66*, 035101.

Newsome, J., Karp, B., & Song, D. (2005). Polygraph: Automatically Generating Signatures for Polymorphic Worms. *In Proceedings of the IEEE Symposium on Security and Privacy,* May 2005.

Quinlan, J. R. (1993). *C4.5: Programs for Machine Learning.* Morgan Kaufmann Publishers.

Schultz, M., Eskin, E., & Zadok, E. (2001). MEF: Malicious email filter, a UNIX mail filter that detects malicious windows executables. *In USENIX Annual Technical Conference - FREENIX* Track, June 2001.

Sidiroglou, S., Ioannidis, J., Keromytis, A. D., & Stolfo, S. J. (2005). An Email Worm Vaccine Architecture. *Proceedings of the First International Conference on Information Security Practice and Experience (ISPEC 2005)*, Singapore, April 11-14, pp. 97-108.

Singh, S., Estan, C., Varghese, G., & Savage, S. (2003) *The EarlyBird System for Real-time Detection of Unknown Worms.* Technical report - cs2003-0761, UCSD.

Stolfo, S. J., Hershkop, S., Hu, C. W., Li, W. Nimeskern, O., & Wang, K. (2006) *Behavior-based Modeling and its Application to Email Analysis.* ACM Transactions on Internet Technology (TOIT), Feb 2006.

Symantec Co. (2005). *W32.Beagle.BG.* Online.

WEKA (2006): *Data Mining Software in Java.* Online, http://www.cs.waikato.ac.nz/~ml/weka/

Chapter III
Information Systems Security:
Cases of Network Administrator Threats

Hamid Jahankhani
University of East London, UK

Shantha Fernando
University of Moratuwa, Sri Lanka

Mathews Z. Nkhoma
University of East London, UK

ABSTRACT

In today's business environment it is difficult to obtain senior management approval for the expenditure of valuable resources to "guarantee" that a potentially disastrous event will not occur that could affect the ultimate survivability of the organization. The total information network flexibility achieved depends to a great extent on how network security is implemented. However, this implementation depends on the network designers at the initial stage and the network administrators in the long term. Initial security level designed can be later changed, improved or compromised by the network administrators who look after day-to-day network and system functions. Their competencies and the motivation contribute in achieving the desired security objectives that are aligned with the business goals. Incompetent network administrator may pave the way to attacks that could take place either at once where an obvious vulnerability may exist or in several phases where it requires information gathering or scanning in order to enter into the target system. De-motivated network administrator may ignore the possible threats or find strategies to make his/ her presence vital for the existence of the network services. The latter may be an example of a competent network administrator who is not rewarded due to the lapses of the senior management, in which case backdoors or logic bombs may be deployed so that the administrator may take vengeance in case the career is terminated or someone else is given undue recognition. Two studies on real cases given in this paper highlights the influence of such network administrators. To preserve the confidentiality, the names of personnel or organizations are not revealed.

INTRODUCTION

Security threats to business-technology systems keep growing and despite this increase, fewer businesses rank security as a high priority, fewer plan to boost security spending, and a growing number say money isn't the biggest barrier to better security.

What do we want from secure computer systems? The advent of information technology has changed the face of doing business. Today, people through the information revolution can look at any part of business – whether an investment decision, an office building or an individual product – and examine all the individual costs to a single activity or good. Because of the convenience that IT provides, businesses had begun embracing it at an astonishing rate. The public and private sectors increasingly depend on information and telecommunications systems capabilities and services. In the face of rapid technological change, public and private organizations are undergoing significant changes in the way they conduct their business activities, including the use of wide area networking via public networks. These changes include mandates to reduce expenses, increase revenue, and, at the same time to compete in a global marketplace, (Potter, 2004).

Computers have found their way into all areas of business, industry, education, and government. Increasingly far-reaching information networks linking computers and databases provide important benefits, including greater staff productivity and a sharper competitive edge. The more that we expand the reach of our information networks, the more important network security becomes. The computer is the symbol of the modern, automated business. Its growing popularity plus the powerful business software, has resulted in an explosion of stand-alone data processing systems in many different departments of organizations throughout the world.

Further advancing the technology, information networks are now solving many work and productivity problems. Networks promote information exchange by interconnecting distributed departmental computers and associated terminals, printers, and other devices with centralized computers so that all units function as part of a single, unified communications system. Ideally, the result will be one, cohesive network in which authorized personnel can speedily and efficiently access computers and other system resources from any terminal or other device, whether they are in the same room, building, city, or even country. But whether this total information network flexibility is achieved depends to a great extent on how network security is implemented.

In today's business environment it is difficult to obtain senior management approval for the expenditure of valuable resources to "guarantee" that a potentially disastrous event will not occur that could affect the ultimate survivability of the organization.

The need for a reliable security network was also heightened by the issue of cyber-crime, which involves hacking into computers, creating and spreading computer viruses, perpetrating online fraud schemes, and stealing trade secrets and other intellectual property.

Advanced level of network security provides maximum network flexibility as well as an additional layer of protection against unauthorized computer access. Moreover, this advanced security level also makes possible an audit trail of network usage. Another benefit is that a user authorization can be quickly and efficiently rescinded from the network. In general, this advanced security level can help reduce, if not eliminate, the need for costly additional security hardware such as data encryption devices.

According to the technical report on Information Security Breaches Survey 2004, by Pricewaterhouse Coopers UK and Department of Trade and Industry UK (PWC/DTI, 2004b), analysing potential risk and the allocation of resources for computer network security and business continuity require strategic, long-term planning. Most companies tend to be reactive and respond with quick infrastructure solutions. A strategic approach to computer network security leads to a more efficient plan and a less expensive risk-management strategy. Aligning computer network security to corporate goals provides management with a framework for steering resources, whether it is toward infrastructure, improved controls, training, or insurance, based on a carefully thought-out process that analyses the level of risk the company is willing to absorb. Executive summary of Information Security Breaches Survey 2004, by Pricewaterhouse Coopers UK and Department of Trade and Industry UK (PWC/DTI, 2004a) states that this analysis leads to a better computer network risk management. As a consequence, the company achieves higher levels of efficiency and cost-effectiveness essential to its profitable growth.

NETWORK SECURITY AS A BUSINESS ISSUE

Many organizations run on information, and a well-planned network circulates this information life-blood to all parts of an organization as efficiently as possible. Inappropriate network security provisions, however, can reduce network flexibility and still not close the door against unauthorized access and information loss. The ability of a network to blend an advanced level of security with maximum operating flexibility, therefore, must be considered carefully in any network plans.

An effective information security program incorporates a combination of technological and human controls in order to avoid the loss of information, deter accidental or intentional unauthorised activities, prevent unauthorised data access, detect a loss or impending loss, recover after a loss has occurred, and correct system vulnerabilities to prevent the same loss from happening again (Jahankhani and Nkhoma, 2005).

Correspondence among businesses, internal or external, is conducted through data transmissions. Data transmissions pass in networks of interconnected portals where parties could get in touch with one another. Networks need to be protected from both outsiders such as hackers and crackers, and insiders such as employees and other individuals with access to the network.

Unprotected information and computer networks can seriously damage a business's future, (McClure, 2003). This happens because of the loss of classified or customer critical information, exposure of trade secrets, unacceptable business interruption, or lawsuits stemming from security breaches. As information and computer network security involves more than technology, companies are now spending more money and man-hours than necessary on cutting-edge technology. Inaccurate analysis of the company's needs can result in greater risk of information loss and higher frequency of security breaches.

Making computer and communication systems more secure is both a technological challenge and a managerial problem. The technology exists to incorporate adequate security safeguards within these systems, but the managerial demand for secure systems is virtually nonexistent outside of the defence and financial industries. That so many of our commercial systems provide marginal security at best is a reflection of the lack of managerial awareness and understanding of the need to protect the information stored in, and transmitted between, computers.

CSI/FBI Computer Crime and Security Survey 2004 (CSI/FBI, 2004) presents potential grim scenarios for companies if they do not emphasize the importance of network security. Unprotected information and computer networks mean loss of data that are deemed crucial and confidential for the company's own development; loss of confidential third-party data; and business interruption or slowdowns that significantly impact the business as well as other parties. Kolodzinski (2002) further stresses that any of these scenarios could result in loss of competitive advantage, lawsuit exposure, and unacceptable downtime (i.e. business interruption).

In collaboration with Information Week, Ernest and Young (2005) conducted another survey of 1320 high-level information technology managers. Threats against corporate data still continue to rise. More companies are storing increasing amounts of corporate data on information systems. Senior management expressed concern over the threat, but has done very little to counter the threat. Very few companies have established a dedicated information security staff. Most companies do not have a formal security policy. Many companies face problems in procuring skilled information security personnel. Senior managers fail to see information security as "value-added" contribution to "bottom line." It is true to say in 2004 the treat still is continuing to rise, because of the ever increase of inferences between IT and IS technology.

Senior managers are becoming more and more aware of the need to address security and information technology investments within the context of the corporation's business goals. As Schwartau (2005) has observed, Security is no longer just about security. Today, security is about resource and information management and it turns out that good security is a by-product of a well-run organization.

Information systems (IS) executives are most concerned with ensuring that their technology goals are consistent with those of the overall business, believing that an effective organization and usage of the company's data is a critical IS activity. In the annual CSC (2006) survey, it is found that executives consider networking technologies as key to future competitive positioning, and are looking to outsourcing in increasing numbers to help improve customer service. Aligning IS and corporate goals is the primary challenge for IS executives. In the survey, respondents focus on improving user productivity and collaboration through information networks. For example, the

IT infrastructure improvement initiative currently under way in most respondents' companies is "enhancing or developing information networks," and the three most critical technologies being used in companies' infrastructure initiatives are wide area networks, local area networks and client/server systems. In addition, IS executives consider networks a key competitive tool. When asked to name the five most critical emerging technologies their companies will have to adopt by the year 2000 to remain competitive, respondents chose the Internet/World Wide Web, electronic commerce, groupware, broadband networks and network security tools (CSC, 2006).

Williamson (1997) suggests an approach to setting priorities for IT projects and some criteria for IT investment decisions that are potentially applicable to information security investment decisions. This approach consists developing a formal, quantitative way to assess the business value of proposed projects; engaging customers in a dialogue about the available resources and business needs throughout the year, not just at budget time; interviewing customers about their wants and needs; communicating frequently with customers about the Information Security (IS) department's achievements, current projects and short-term plans.

Williamson (1997) also considers the importance of remembering the human element; take egos and the need for validation into account; working with committees structured to minimize the influence of any one individual or department; visiting with the business units; communicate clearly how priorities are set so that people can anticipate project funding decisions; and developing a business case for every project, assessing its risks, its business value, and the cost of building or buying it. Additionally, the said author' approach calls for the demonstration of interest in the constraints under which business customers operate, and staying on top of changes in the regulatory and competitive environment in which the business operates. Here, it is emphasized that decision-makers must be prepared to show how a proposed project fits with business goals.

According to Kolodzinski (2002), the primary goal then is to develop a scalable corporate security structure that is responsive to short- and long-term needs as well as shifts in technology. A basic tenet of such business driven computer network security planning is that senior management and its risk management function lead the charge on linking business strategies to computer network security and identifying where information is at risk. By knowing future needs, security planners can anticipate requirements for information protection with a view to making them able to expand or contract according to strategic actions that the company takes in pursuit of its targets and goals. Similarly, the planning process will be responsive to shifts in technology and needs should be known in advance and systems put in place that would allow for technology upgrades or additions.

THE FOCUS OF INVESTMENT ON NETWORK SECURITY

In all organisations the directors are faced with the problem of achieving organisational goals using limited resources available to them. Investing in network security should always seek to move the organisation nearer to securing the entire network. The directors should also keep in mind that investing in network security is an on going process as the threats are always being upgraded time and again. This is so due to the fact that the hacking tools are readily available on the market and minimal training is required. Investment decisions are essentially a search projects which are worth more than they cost to exploit and which thus create value.

Information security, right now, is a confused and paradoxical business. For example:

- You've increased spending significantly, and you're told this is a good thing, and yet it has had zero effect in mitigating security breaches.
- You're constantly warned about "digital Pearl Harbors" and yet the vast majority of incidents you report are relatively small, don't last long and don't cost much.
- You're told that aligning security and business strategies is a top priority, and yet those who have fared best in avoiding breaches, downtime and security-related damages are the least likely to be aligned with the business. But in another sense, you seem to be contributing to the confusion.
- Respondents who suffered the most damages from security incidents were two times more likely than the average respondent to plan on decreasing security spending next year.
- Those with the most damages were nearly half as likely to list staff training as one of their top three priorities.
- A quarter of you neither measured nor reviewed the effectiveness of your information security policies and procedures in the past year.

In short, as much as the emerging information security discipline has grown since its baptism—on Sept. 18, 2001 (one week after the terrorist attacks and the day the Nimda worm hit)—it hasn't much improved with age.

Network resources allow worldwide access to information, no matter where it resides, or where the users are located. Unfortunately, the physical and logical controls used by an organisation to secure its information offer no protection when that information is being electronically transmitted.

As Frankwood (2000) observed, a successful financial decision is one that creates value, that is, it is worth more than it costs to implement. The investment decision is perhaps the most important of all decision an organisation makes. In any organisation there are strategic, technical and political issues as well as financial aspects to tackle with, so it involves more than simply number-crunching or relative financial costs and benefits. Many costs and benefits in network security investment are difficult if not impossible to quantify. Moreover, the numbers are often secondary, what determines whether an investment is accepted or not depends on the strategic direction the organisation wants to pursue. Moreover, the approval of investment may hinge on the nature of the decision process within the organisation, i.e. investment approval in reality is often a question of internal politics. To obtain an approval of investment in network security management, managers must demonstrate that an investment is necessary to maintain security by replacing old or obsolete technology. Many organisations classify investments into various categories in which different amounts of information are required as inputs to the evaluation process.

HACKING AND CRACKING

Hacking is defined as an electronic break-in into a company for the purpose of harvesting a wealth of information or may be with some non-malicious intention. Hackers are those people who do not have any bad intention but want to learn everything about a computer system, while crackers are the ones who are breaking into computer systems illegally. The early hackers had a love of technology and a compelling need to know how it all worked, and their goal was to push programs beyond what they were designed to do. The word hacker did not have the negative connotation as it has today.

Present day hackers can be classified into different categories based on their knowledge and involvement in the field. There are some with in born talent who really want to learn more of the computer systems and they also create software

that helps to improve the overall technological infrastructure. Those who belong to this category with out any malicious intention are the highly respected computer pundits in the contemporary world. The second category hackers are not knowledgeable like the previous ones but they have experience with several operating systems and know how to exploit the vulnerabilities associated with them. Most of the security consultants fall into this category. Third and the last category often called crackers are those with least knowledge and use the codes and methods developed by other people to do their cracking.

It is not necessary that a cracker is knowledgeable in cracking any more. Figure 1 (Allen, et. al, 2000) illustrates that which was the expert's territory in the past has now become open to the average person due to the new innovations of tools, making the information systems more vulnerable. With the introduction of new Internet based applications, and new network vulnerability testing and intruder tools, it has become more difficult to keep organizational information assets secure.

The attacks take place in several phases such as information gathering or reconnaissance, scanning and finally entering into the target system. Information gathering involves methods of obtaining information or to open security holes. It is just like the way in which the orthodox type of robbery is carried out. The robber will find out the whole information about the place that wants to rob before making attempt. Just like this the computer attacker will try to find out information about the target. Social Engineering is one such method used by an attacker to get information.

PUTTING THEM ALL TOGETHER: CASES ON SECURITY BREACHES THROUGH NETWORK ADMINISTRATORS

It was discussed that the total information network flexibility achieved depends to a great extent on

Figure 1. Attack sophistication vs. intruder technical knowledge (Allen et al., 2000)

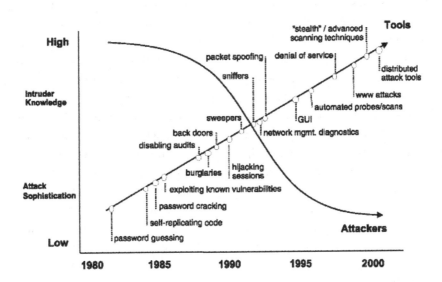

how network security is implemented. However, this implementation depends on the network designers at the initial stage and the network administrators in the long term. Initial security level designed can be later changed, improved or compromised by the network administrators who look after day-to-day network and system functions. Their competencies and the motivation contribute in achieving the desired security objectives that are aligned with the business goals. Competencies can depend on the training and experience, whereas the motivation can be greatly affected, either positively or negatively, by the behaviour, attitude and preferences of the senior management.

Incompetent network administrator may pave the way to attacks that could take place either at once where an obvious vulnerability may exist, or in several phases where it requires information gathering or scanning in order to enter into the target system.

De-motivated network administrator may ignore the possible threats or find strategies to make his or her presence vital for the existence of the network services. The latter case may be an example of a competent network administrator who is not rewarded due to the lapses of the

senior management, in which case backdoors or logic bombs may be deployed so that the administrator may take vengeance in case the career is terminated or someone else is given undue recognition.

In any of the above cases, ultimately it is the future of the business that is affected. Two studies on real cases given below were used to carry out the analysis. These two real cases emphasise the influence of such network administrators. To preserve the confidentiality, the names of personnel or organizations are not revealed.

Description of Cases

The Case 1: Vengeance of the Network Administrator

An Internet Service Provider had all the necessary firewalls with hardened operating systems and high-cost commercial application servers. Server capacities were sufficient enough for few more years of operations and required intensive marketing to bring them to an acceptable utilisation level. Hence the infrastructure was very much under utilized at the time of analysis. The company had not reached the break-even point in its initial three years time and hence was running at losses, which lead to the lower salary scales and dissatisfaction of the staff including the system administrator. It was the business analysis that over-predicted the Internet subscriptions and corporate connections, leading to the overspending on the capital for infrastructure. While the competent network administrator had taken every effort to keep the systems up to date and even gone to the extent of developing some administrative utilities to help him mange the network and systems efficiently, management was of the view that he is also partly responsible for the loss. However, the network administrator's view was that the marketing the service was not within the scope of his work and he was taking effort to make the services reliable. The situation led to tensions and instead of the network administrator being rewarded, the company was looking for a new network administrator who could generate revenue, which is due to lack of understanding of the network administrator's primary role. Senior management did not realise that he had the technical capability to have the full control of the entire system by creating backdoors and also some firewall rules that enabled him to use some utilities residing in the systems inside the network. Knowing the capabilities of the network administrator, he was offered an attractive job in a foreign country, and he officially handed over the tasks to the new network administrator and happily left the company. It was only after a few months time that the company discovered that many individuals free of charge utilize their Internet Service. Systems did not have any billing records for few user accounts that were heavily used, and the new network administrator was not vigilant enough to identify such user logins using audit trails. Many corporate and individual clients did not get the required bandwidth. Most of such free login entries were not in the audit trails, probably deleted, and hardly any trace was visible, unless a tool was used to analyse the audit trails. It was only the congestion of their international bandwidth, which was perceived as poor perfor-

mance of the systems that led to hiring experts to evaluate the network infrastructure, systems and applications. During this process it was revealed that the former unhappy network administrator had created several backdoors using the utilities he deployed or developed before, and that allowed him to create free Internet accounts for his friends through remote access and he also had the privilege to work with the audit trails. However, many of these utilities and firewall rules were set up while he was in the company with the consent of the senior management since they appeared to be for a business purpose than a backdoor for future use of the network administrator. However, the company did not take any legal actions against the former network administrator for several reasons, and some of the arguments could have turned out to be advantages for the network administrator than it was for the company under the prevailing employment regulations. It was also the opinion of some new senior managers that the former senior management did not act favourably to reward the competent staff. This case was described a vengeance of a network administrator.

The Case 2: Imprudence of the Network Administrator

A research institute had its services offered to the research community through the Internet. An on-line library of research publications, research fund applications and dissemination notices, projects coordination, etc., were among the services offered. The networking infrastructure was protected by firewalls but no auditing had been carried out on the configuration of the firewalls. Installation of Linux based web application servers followed proper guidelines so that even if some attack takes place the server would be secured. However, some staff in the institute wanted FTP access to upload the updates. At a subsequent stage the network administrator reluctantly enabled the staff to use FTP within the internal network assuming that the firewall will take care of external attempts. The internal staff had to phone the network administrator to enable FTP at a given time and then soon after that the FTP port would be closed. This was a weekly practice which no body thought would compromise their web application server.

All of a sudden the web application server stopped responding over the network, and the network administrator rebooted the server thinking that the server had got stuck. The server simply refused to boot. The expertise investigation was sought.

It was found that the entire root file system together with the web applications and data have been wiped off. Fortunately, some logs were backed up to a different partition from time to time. The logs revealed that the intruder has been monitoring the opening of FTP port, using a sniffing agent planted in a workstation through an e-mail sent to an internal user. Since the firewall allowed originating connections from within the network on higher TCP and UDP ports, the intruder was aware of the times at which the FTP was enabled. The cracker was able to plant an agent in the web application server using FTP (probably again sent as an e-mail attachment to an internal user) which sent some account details and vulnerabilities of the system. One day the cracker managed to use SSH which was a secure protocol allowed through the firewall to connect to the server and wipe out everything except the other partition that was not touched. Probably the mistake was that the cracker did not delete the other partition before hand or it was not found out that the logs were backed up there. Within few hours the services were restored since there were periodic backups, and preventive measures were taken to avoid a similar attack. Forensics process revealed the attacker's IP address and user privileges that were used. However, since it was originating from a DHCP allocated IP address from an ISP, the exact user was not identified.

Supporting secure document uploading through a web interface instead of FTP would have prevented this attack.

IMPLICATIONS OF CASES AND CONCLUSION

We illustrated that in today's business environment it is difficult to obtain senior management approval for the expenditure of valuable resources to "guarantee" that a potentially disastrous event will not occur that could affect the ultimate survivability of the organization. If the senior management of the first case was enlightened on this, the competent network administrator would not have left the organization and the harm would not have taken place.

We also highlighted the need for a reliable security network in the context of cyber-crime, which involves hacking into computers, creating and spreading computer viruses, perpetrating online fraud schemes, and stealing trade secrets and other intellectual property. This is the implication of the second case. This proves that the unprotected information and computer networks can seriously damage a business's future.

The first case proves what Schwartau (2005) has observed, i.e., Security is no longer just about security, and today, security is about resource and information management and it turns out that good security is a by-product of a well-run organization.

As it was expressed by CSC (2006), aligning IS and corporate goals is the primary challenge for IS executives. This also involves the proper identification of roles. In the survey, respondents focus on improving user productivity and collaboration through information networks. The frustration of both the network administrator and the senior management would have been avoided if this understanding were there.

In fact it was the forensics analyser was to able to figure out what went wrong and present them as stories in the above case studies. Such a forensics process is the process of gathering and analysing data in a manner as free from distortion or bias as possible to reconstruct data or what has happened in the past on a system (Farmer & Venema, 1999), or the court-proof preservation, identification, extraction, documentation and interpretation of computer data, which is often more of an art than a science (Piller & Wolfgarten, 2004).

However, there were several issues with the forensics analysis. Many IT systems are huge and complex, changes rapidly over a short period of time, and hence even the experts have knowledge only on a subset of system functions and utilities, out of the thousands available. Therefore it is practically impossible to ensure that everything in an information system is 100% secure or trustworthy. A criminal may be an expert of a particular set of utilities, sometimes may be even self-developed, of which forensics experts may not be the masters. Hence other forms of analysis, sometimes going into the physical and raw levels are necessities. This lack of complete knowledge has an effect on the forensics analysis process. However, much of the computer forensics work is based on the existing information and data in storage media. Heterogeneous systems with heterogeneous storage and backup techniques make it possible to gather data from different sources, yet, making it difficult to analyse them systematically. This was the case with the second case study above. Ultimately, analysis process will depend on the systems and utilities available. It was only the log files that were in the untouched partition could give some meaningful information. Many other workstations in the network were found to have virus infected and hence could not rely on them.

Forensics analysis is difficult when simultaneous, different, independent parties attack a computer system. It could be same type of attack by multiple parties or multiple attacks by multiple parties, leaving many ambiguities in the tracing process. In the second case again, though it was suspected that it was the same cracker who may used compromised workstations to attack the web application server, there was a direct SSH connection as well. Finding a correlation was difficult, though few things could be logically argued.

Another issue is the change of evidence that makes the analysis harder. This change may be due to the following reasons:

1. covering behaviour of the offender, purposely deleting the evidence
2. victims may delete evidence to avoid embarrassment
3. use of computer after the crime, innocently altering or deleting evidence
4. system administrators may delete suspicious accounts to prevent further damage to the system but deleting valuable evidence
5. old backup media to be used in comparative analysis may have been exposed to dust, humidity, electro-magnetic fields, floods, heat, etc. or decayed, causing the reference data non-recoverable
6. actions of the forensics analyser, sometimes by accident, but sometimes for a purpose, making it harder for a secondary forensics analyser.

Not that all information systems support forensics analysis. It is essential that the systems be made forensics aware. This has to be well thought of at the system installation process and all the subsequent upgrades and application deployments. For example, some utilities and application software does not keep audit trails in a meaningful, informative, concise but sufficient manner. Further, such audit trails should be secured by the system so that any attacker would not be able to change them, or at least any attempt for such an illegal change is recorded elsewhere so that the attacker would not be able to leave the system without a trace. One such example is the use of TCP wrappers to offer UNIX network services such as shells (ssh, telnet), file transfers (sftp, ftp), etc.

Conducting a systematic search for evidence, packaging the evidence in logical containers, drawing out relationships between such packages, and building up a chain of events or incidents is the task of the expert. All these processes will be conceptually similar but technically different in different systems. Even if it is the same line, the process may differ from version to version. For example, different UNIX implementations, different distributions of the same implementation such as Linux, or MS-Windows with different service packs applied, may require different ways of using tools in investigation (Farmer & Venema, 1999).

Every computer user or system administrator may not be able to carry out a forensics process. However, awareness building on the subject helps gathering information once an incident takes place. Making systems forensics aware, at the time of installation and right throughout the ongoing upgrades, is important for a proper forensics analysis, in case of an attack. In any forensics operation, though there is no black-&-white instructions, recommended guidelines help carrying out a proper operation.

REFERENCES

Allen, J., Alberts, C., Behrens, S., et al. (2000). Improving the Security of Networked Systems, *CrossTalk: The Journal of Defense Software Engineering*, October 2000.

CSC (2006). *Aligning technology and corporate goals is top concern again in annual CSC survey—networks seen as key competitive tool; Outsourcing gaining support, Computer Sciences Corporation.* Available at: http://www.csc.com/newsandevents/news/1298.shtml. Retrieved: 05/03/2006.

CSI/FBI (2004). *CSI/FBI Computer Crime and Security Survey 2004*, Computer Security Institute and Federal Bureau of Investigation (CSI/FBI). Available at: http://i.cmpnet.com/gocsi/db_area/pdfs/fbi/FBI2004.pdf

E&Y (2005). *5th Annual Information Security Survey*, Ernest and Young.

Farmer, D., & Venema, W. (1999). *Murder on the Internet Express, Computer Forensic Analysis Seminar*. IBM T.J. Watson Research Centre, Yorktown Heights, NY, USA.

Frankwood (2000). *Introduction to Accounting*. UK: Prentice Hall.

Jahankhani, H., & Nkhoma, M. Z. (2005). Information Systems Risk Assessment. *International Conference on information and Communication Technology in Management, Challenges and Prospects*, 23-25 May 2005, Malaysia.

Kolodzinski, O. (2002). Aligning Information Security Imperatives with Business Needs, *The CPA Journal*, 27(7), 20.

McClure, S., Scambray, J., & Kurtz, G. (2003). Hacking Exposed, *Network Security Secrets & Solutions*, 4th edition. McGraw-Hill Ryerson.

Piller, K., & Wolfgarten, S. (2004). Honeypot Forensics – No stone unturned or logs, what logs? *Risk Advisory Services*. Berlin: Ernst & Young.

Potter, G. (2001). *Business in a Virtual World: Exploiting Information for Competitive Advantage*. Houndmills, England: Macmillan.

PWC/DTI (2004a). *Information Security Breaches Survey 2004: Executive Summary*, Pricewaterhouse Coopers UK, Department of Trade and Industry UK, April 2004. Available at: http://www.pwc.com/images/gx/eng/about/svcs/grms/2004Exec_Summ.pdf.

PWC/DTI (2004b). *Information Security Breaches Survey 2004: Technical Report*, Pricewaterhouse Coopers UK, Department of Trade and Industry UK, April 2004. Available at: http://www.pwc.com/images/gx/eng/about/svcs/grms/2004Technical_Report.pdf

Schwartau, W. (2005). Securing the Enterprise. Technology alone won't make you safe. Tackle it as a management problem. *Network World*, January 27, 42.

Williamson, M. (1997). *Weighing the NO's and CON's CIO*, April 15, 49.

Chapter IV
Rootkits and What We Know:
Assessing U.S. and Korean Knowledge and Perceptions

Kirk P. Arnett
Mississippi State University, USA

Mark B. Schmidt
St. Cloud State University, USA

Allen C. Johnston
University of Alabama, Birmingham, USA

Jongki Kim
Pusan National University, Korea

HJ Hwang
Catholic University of Daegu, Korea

ABSTRACT

Respondents from eight Korean and United States higher education institutions were surveyed as to their knowledge and experience with various forms of computer malware. The surveys provide insight into knowledge of rootkits that have become coffee lounge discussion following the once secretive Sony rootkit news break in late 2005 and then the rash of accusations and acknowledgements of other rootkits that followed. The surveys provide an empirical assessment of perceptions between students in the two countries with regard to various forms of malware. The two groups are similar in many respects but they exhibit significant differences in self-reported perceptions of rootkit familiarity. U.S. respondents report higher levels of familiarity for all assessed malware types, including the fictional "Trilobyte" virus. A timeline-based comparison between virus and rootkit knowledge reveals that relatively little is known about rootkits today. This highlights dangers related to existing knowledge levels but presents hope for solutions and an accelerated rootkit awareness curve to improve worldwide malware protection.

INTRODUCTION

Korea and the U.S., along with the rest of the Internet enabled world, continually battle a growing number of computer attacks. The source of these attacks may be domestic or foreign. The attacks may be from government or terrorist sponsored organizations for intelligence gathering or they may be from criminal groups or individuals intent on financial gains. The attacks may be against personal, business, education, or governmental computer assets. Regardless of the source or target, each country must prepare for current attacks as well as attacks that will surely occur in the future. For maximum effect, the preparation must be to protect personal, business, and governmental assets, and the preparation must span the globe.

Countries around the globe need skilled persons to battle against attacks, and these countries certainly have attackers who are on the opposite side of the battle field. Each country houses hackers who create malware and each country trains computer hackers for offensive as well as defensive cyber attacks. Despite its lack of sophisticated digital infrastructure, North Korea has attacked both South Korean and U.S. governmental computer installations. The capabilities of graduates from Kim il Sung's North Korean hacker training academy, where students undergo five years of specialty courses for hacking careers, are said to be comparable to the best U.S. CIA trained hackers (Digital, 2005).

During this decade, U.S. Soldiers have been indicted for breaking into South Korean computer systems (Stars, 2001). We don't know whether or not this was government sponsored, but we do know that attacks are not only one-to-many or many-to-one events. Rather, cyber attacks are characterized as events in which many sources are involved in attacking many targets. South Korea's Ministry of National Defense said a five percent budget increase was allocated mainly for projects such as "the buildup of the core capability needed for coping with advanced scientific and information warfare." The report also revealed that South Korea's military has 177 computer training facilities and had trained more than 200,000 "information technicians" (Kramarento, 2003). Training efforts such as these are a necessary strategy for any country that is a part of today's malware infested landscape.

A relatively new form of malware is a rootkit. Although well known in the Unix arena, rootkits are now rapidly expanding in Windows environments. Even the newest software developments may not be immune to rootkits as Polish security researcher Joanna Rutkowska demonstrated blue pill – a proof of concept rootkit to circumvent pre-release Microsoft Vista security. A rootkit is a piece of software that allows its user to gain top level (root) privileges where the rootkit is installed. A rootkit is not a virus or a worm but it may deliver a virus or worm. Once installed, if a backdoor mechanism is made available to the attacker, the rootkit will allow the attacker to "own" the machine. Co-author of the now famous rootkit.com website, Jamie Butler, says that it is this stealth nature of a rootkit that is the real danger as a "rootkit is software used to hide other software from the user and security tools, to evade detection" (Williamson, 2007). The result is, because they are unknown, rootkit infections may last longer and therefore do more damage for longer periods than could a single worm or virus.

Our belief is that rootkit threat levels are not understood and our purpose is to describe the findings from a cross-cultural study. The research goal is to assess the knowledge levels and perceptions of Korean and U.S. college students regarding rootkits and more traditional malware with an eye toward identifying possible problems or solutions that might surface. The organization is to first examine selected relevant literature regarding Korea and the U.S. in today's digital world. Rootkits are then examined as to their current status and potential threat level. The study methodology is briefly described and the data comparisons are presented and discussed. Finally, the limitations that should be considered in interpreting the results are suggested and courses of action for these and other countries are recommended.

RELEVANT LITERATURE

F-Secure reports the Winevar e-mail worm was found in-the-wild in Korea at the end of November 2002 (Hulme, 2002). Apparently it was intentionally released by the virus writer during South Korea's Anti-Virus Researcher's Asian conference. The Korean born W32/Buchon@ mm mass mailer also delivers a keylogger. The Slammer virus that affected Windows machines running SQL Server was especially destructive in Korea, resulting in a massive DoS attack. At its time, the Code Red Worm, which was originally designed to attack White House computers (Lemos, 2001), infected at least 225,000 computers elsewhere and shut down Internet services in Korea for several hours in 2001. Korea and the U.S. have well known security firms to combat malware, they each have virus writers who release viruses in the wild, and they engage in training attackers and defenders for cyber warfare.

Korea is deemed to be more risk averse than the U.S. An evaluation of software risks by (Peterson and Kim, 2003) found there were few differences between the U.S. and Japan, yet a number of differences were found between the U.S. and Korea. Specifically, a lack of experienced IS development personnel was perceived to be a greater risk factor in Korea than in the U.S. This difference adds some weight to Hofstede's five cultural differences studies among more than 50 countries (ITIM, 2006). Although Hofstede's findings have been questioned, they are based on a large and broad-based data source on country cultural differences. Hofstede measured Korea's dimension of uncertainty avoidance index (or UAI) as its highest dimension at 85; whereas,

the U.S. UAI is relatively quite low at 46. This substantial difference indicates that individuals in South Korea would be more likely to be subject to and to accept tight rules and controls than would U.S. people who, according to the index, would have fewer rules and controls and would have a greater level of tolerance for variety. These two studies indicate that differences might be expected in terms of student perceptions of the extent of and potential for malware damage.

As this research examines perceptions and understanding from participants in two countries, cultural values that might affect participant learning and perceptions are relevant. Koreans have high educational achievements; so a natural query is to determine the factors that lead to these high achievements. Kim and Park (2006) outline limitations of prior studies that emphasize biological bases and educational structural features to explain high educational achievements among Koreans noting that, despite prior assumptions with regard to Korean education limitations, anomalies exist as Korean students "outperform their Western counterparts in reading, mathematics, and sciences" (p.287).

Their explanation employs an indigenous psychological approach. With this approach they find that Koreans 1) view education as a part of self cultivation which is a way to achieve personal, social, and occupational success, 2) believe ability is acquired through persistent effort and discipline, and 3) consider that parental influence, which occurs for life, is essential for success. Along with other findings, a cultural difference is that there is no self-serving bias – Koreans believe that success is due to effort and failure is due to lack of effort and ability (Kim and Park, 2006). Based on these findings, it is expected that knowledge or understanding of the rootkit phenomenon might be stronger for Koreans because of their efforts to learn about rootkit malware and to increase their depth of knowledge about malware in general. This would be aligned with learning and acquiring knowledge.

Calhoun, Teng, and Cheoan (2002) note that cultural values are often designed into technologies, but they are not always accepted in the receiving society because of cultural differences. Specifically EIS and GDSS provide examples of this rejection. Their findings from survey data regarding perceptions of technology use in decision making behavior indicates that some behaviors change while others do not. Yet, it is well known the Koreans are world leaders in egames, which is an indication of higher skills and knowledge of at least some computer skills in decision-type games. This expertise and familiarity should lead to more exposure to and/or better understanding of computer malware.

Today's always on connections and wireless capabilities have increased vulnerabilities for computer and Internet users. An empirical study for a model of hacking identified a positive correlation between broadband capacity and cyber attacks (Bento and Bento, 2004). This positive correlation is prevalent in high broadband use countries such as the U.S. and Korea. However, in terms of wireless technologies, South Korea has taken a lead. Also, a study of cellular technologies by Shim (2005) found that South Korea was a test bed for hi-tech cellular technologies. Korean mobile carriers had planned to roll-out the world's first handset-based satellite digital multimedia broadcasting (DMB) services via cellular phones. Shim also suggests that a young generation of cellular phone users in Japan and Korea associate the use of modern cellular phones with their social status (Shim, 2005).

Korea and the U.S. share common ground with regard to Internet usage. For instance, according to (Internet World, 2005) there is a 67.0% penetration of Internet users in South Korea and a 68.1% penetration in the U.S. Both countries have roughly the same extent of, but rapidly expanding, broadband usage so they both have large numbers of "always-on" Internet connections that can be compromised. Indeed, computer viruses are strong in Korea as "the country boasts the world's highest per-capita Internet penetration with about 12 million of the total 15.5 million households hooked up to the always-on Internet" (Korean, 2005).

The similarities and differences between the two countries and others should be explored in today's malware threat environment. Such studies have been made in the past for computer viruses, but none have been published to examine more modern threats such as rootkits in these countries. Previously cited studies indicate that the knowledge of the rootkit threat might be expected to be greater in Korea than in the U.S. because of users who would be more "high tech" and technology/Internet savvy (Calhoun et al. 2002; Shim, 2005; Korean, 2005) and who place high importance on learning (Kim and Park 2006). Rootkits have gained increased attention following the late 2005 revelation that Sony had installed rootkit software to monitor usage of their CDs. As such, it is reasonable to question what college students, who will be the business leaders of tomorrow, know about rootkits. This assessment should not be isolated to one, or even a few countries, as today's malware is frequently worldwide, gives zero day warnings, and spreads in minutes.

ROOTKITS: STATUS AND POTENTIAL

A 2006 eWeek.com article entitled "When's a Rootkit Not a Rootkit? In Search of Definitions," describes a vendor-neutral movement to find an unambiguous way to describe rootkits (Naraine, 2006). Rootkits were once almost exclusively associated with Unix-based hosts. Now they are gaining the attention of Windows users across the globe. Sony's use of rootkits on CDs has no doubt greatly added to this attention. But, even before Sony's debacle, rootkits were growing in the Windows world as Roberts (2005) warned in "Microsoft on Rootkits: Be afraid, be very afraid!" Further, Roberts' article is far from a lonely voice, as Seltzer (2005) predicts that this trend to focus on Windows based machines will continue in the foreseeable future.

A Rootkit is software that is designed to hide files, processes, or registry data, most often in an attempt to mask intrusion and to surreptitiously gain administrative rights to a computer system. When used in this malicious manner, rootkits can provide the mechanism by which various forms of malware, including viruses, spyware, and Trojans, attempt to hide themselves. Rootkits are not worms or viruses, but they can be delivered by worms and viruses. Moreover, rootkits can be extremely difficult to detect and remove. As described by Dillard (2005) rootkits target the extensible nature of operating systems, applying the same principles for value added application development as found in legitimate software.

In May of 2007, Johanna Rutkowska announced with a colleague her plans to open a new firm, *Invisible Things Lab*, obviously tailored from the rootkit moniker, and also to present previously unreleased code, techniques, and ideas at a Black Hat Briefings conference later in the year (Naraine, 2007). Also Symantec announced a merger with storage software vendor Veritas which, according to analysts, will enhance Symantec's rootkit detection capabilities because of Veritas' strength in deep raw disk scans, which are said to be one of the ways to uncover rootkits which traditional malware prevention techniques are missing. Yet rootkits are here. They are often hidden, and the authors who hide them are currently ahead of the defenders. This malware is exceedingly dangerous and will likely plague users for some time to come.

As rootkits become more prevalent, they are becoming a part of today's blended malware. Within the modern computer security paradigm, rootkits represent an under-reported, under-estimated threat to computer security. Their newness, stealth nature, and potential to lead to complete system compromise make them extremely danger-

ous. We need to learn more about rootkits, and this knowledge needs to quickly saturate a critical mass of users. An appropriate starting point is to gauge what college students know and believe about rootkits today.

METHODOLOGY AND MEASUREMENTS

To measure knowledge and perceptions we conducted student surveys which resulted in the accumulation of 199 surveys from five higher education institutions in Korea and 210 surveys from three institutions in the US. More than 80% of respondents from each group are full time college students, and as would be expected, the large majority of respondents from both countries are between 18 and 29 years of age. The survey instrument was first used in 1993 in *Computers and Security* (Jones et al. 1993) to gauge user knowledge of computer viruses and then in 2005 *Communications of the ACM* (Schmidt and Arnett 2005) to report user knowledge of spyware.

The U.S. survey respondents are predominantly male (57%), with more than five years of computer experience (74.3%). For Korea, the respondents are almost evenly divided in gender and 88.1% of them have more than 5 years of computer experience. Not only are both groups well experienced with computers, most individuals own one or more computers (U.S. 93.8%, Korea 91.6%). Table 1 presents details of selected respondent demographics.

The number of individuals who have heard of rootkits, and at least have an awareness of them, should be a measure of baseline knowledge. Responses indicate that only 16.2% of U.S. students and 10.4 % of Korean students have even *heard* of rootkits. Further, large percentages of the respondents have known of rootkits for less than one year (U.S. 82.1%, Korea 93.9%). These figures are alarming when compared to these individuals' knowledge of computer viruses where

Table 1. Selected profile of respondents

	Response category	U.S. respondents	Korean respondents
Age	18 to 29	82.6%	95.5%
	30 to 39	8.0%	4.5%
	40 to 49	8.5%	0%
	50 to 59	1.0%	0%
	60 and over	0%	0%
Gender	Female	42.4%	50.7%
	Male	57.6%	49.3%
Computer experience	< 1 year	2.5%	.5%
	1 to 2 years	2.5%	0%
	2 to 5 years	20.6%	11.3%
	5 to 10 years	45.2%	51.2%
	> 10 years	29.1%	36.9%
Occupation	Full time student	81.5%	96.0%
	Part time student		
	IT professional	7.3%	2.0%
	Other		
		6.8%	2.0%
		4.4%	0%
How many personal computers (or laptops) do you own?	0	6.2%	8.4%
	1	47.1%	60.1%
	2	31.4%	24.6%
	3	7.1%	5.9%
	4 or more	8.1%	1.0%

in contrast, 77.2% of U.S. respondents and 69.5% of Korean respondents have known of viruses for five or more years. One surprise shown in Table 2 below is the difference between the percentages of respondents who know about spyware. Only (9.3%) of Korean users have known about spyware for more than three years while 28.% of U.S. respondents indicate that they have known about spyware for more than three years.. These findings indicate the newness of rootkits within the Microsoft Windows user domain.

The survey included five-point Likert scale responses (1 = Strongly Disagree, 3 = Neutral, 5 = Strongly Agree) for the research items to facilitate self-reported measures of perceptions among both U.S. and Korean survey respondents. These perceptions can be examined to determine differences between the two countries. As Figure 1 illustrates, regardless of country of origin, students report more knowledge of viruses (3.04) and spyware (3.15) than of rootkits (1.30). Also, students of

both countries share similar perceptions of the knowledge possessed by their peers; believing them to know more about spyware and viruses than they do about rootkits (see Figure 2).

A comparison of responses provided by U.S. and Korean students suggests that there are significant differences in how the two student groups

Figure 1. Relative familiarity of malware types

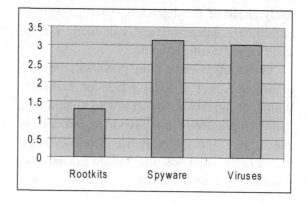

Figure 2. Perceptions of peers' familiarity of malware types

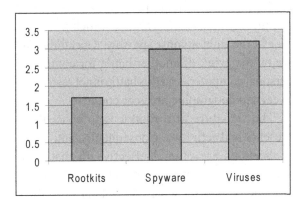

report their familiarity of rootkits, spyware, and viruses in general. For example, U.S. students report higher levels of familiarity with all three forms of malware than their Korean counterparts. As depicted in Table 2, this differential in perceptions is consistent for all forms of malware, and is significant for all variables ($p < 0.01$). Appendix 1 presents the ANOVA calculations. Included in the analysis is a fictitious threat, "Trilobyte," which was introduced to the study simply as a means for ascertaining the quality of the survey responses. U.S. students report higher levels of familiarity than Korean students with the "Trilobyte" virus, although neither group reports more than low to moderate familiarity. Interestingly, both groups believe their familiarity of the "Trilobyte" virus to be greater than that of rootkits. Also included in Table 2, perceptions of familiarity with the very real "Melissa" virus were different among the

student groups, with U.S. students again reporting a higher level of familiarity.

Interpretation

U.S. respondents report a higher level of rootkit awareness. While both groups report low perceptions of familiarity of how rootkits work, U.S. respondents report relatively higher levels. The reports of low familiarity may be indicative of limited exposure to the threat because of its newness and the stealth characteristics. It is expected that this level of familiarity will increase over the next few years as rootkits become more prevalent.

Similar to rootkit familiarity, U.S. respondents report relatively higher levels of spyware familiarity than their Korean counterparts. However, for spyware, the difference in reported levels of familiarity is much greater, with U.S. respondents reporting themselves as familiar and Korean respondents reporting themselves as unfamiliar. Factors that might contribute to this difference are increased interest in personal information theft by both hackers and owners of the information, particularly in the U.S. In effect the U.S. college student represents the low hanging, but valuable fruit of personal information.

The difference in familiarity between U.S. and Korean respondents is greatest for the general threat of computer viruses. This is somewhat surprising given the maturity of the threat because it seems that all college students should have had

Table 2. Comparison of U.S. and Korean responses

Survey Question	U.S. Mean	Korea Mean
I am familiar with how rootkits work	1.44	1.15
I am familiar with spyware	4.13	2.10
I am familiar with computer viruses	4.21	1.78
I am familiar with the "Trilobyte" virus	1.95	1.40
I am familiar with the "Melissa" virus	2.79	1.70

substantial exposure and mitigation information. This could be the result of widespread penetration of vulnerable Windows client machines in the U.S.

With regard to the trilobite virus, which is imaginary, U.S. respondents report relatively higher levels of familiarity than the Korean students. Because the virus in question is nonexistent, it might be that Korean students want to be more certain, and thereby precise, in their answers because of educational cultural differences. Here, we speculate that U.S. students feel less constrained to be exact and thereby more willing to guess, even if the guess is mistaken. This is consistent with previous findings that Koreans are more risk averse and have very high levels of uncertainty avoidance relative to the U.S.

For the widely successful Melissa virus, it is somewhat discouraging that neither group of students report even moderately high levels of familiarity. As with the other forms of malware, U.S. students report a higher degree of familiarity. Perhaps this is due to the origin of the virus.

ISSUES, CONCLUSIONS AND LIMITATIONS

This section presents the issues that arise in view of the findings of study. The conclusions and limitations are highlighted as well.

Issues

The limited awareness and knowledge of rootkits in both countries is especially alarming considering the recent "call to arms" against spyware and other forms of malicious malware. The *Communications of the ACM* recently devoted a special edition to the emergence and proliferation of the threat of spyware (Stafford, 2005). However, within these articles no mention was made as to the presence of rootkit technology or new forms of blended threat. To solve this

problem of limited awareness, proactive response must surface. What must occur next is a global intelligence and preparedness ramp-up by the IT community consistent with that which is occurring in the fight against spyware. Certainly, we are on the brink of another battle for control of personal computers and this battle is not restricted to certain geographic areas or countries.

The signature of a rootkit is to conceal its presence and activities. Consequently, anti-virus applications are often ineffective in that they cannot detect what they cannot see. Additionally, the manner in which rootkits are installed on systems further complicates their detection by traditional anti-malware software. Rootkits are often installed through tactics such as social engineering or through exploits of operating system vulnerabilities. Traditional symptoms of malware infestation, such as replication activities, are simply absent from rootkit manifestations. Conventional malware detection mechanisms such as anti-virus and anti-spyware software are now firmly established in the security practices of IT management; however, they must be revisited as to their ability to address rootkit exploits.

Conclusions

With the emergence of these blended threats, computer security managers must take actions above and beyond traditional anti-malware techniques and employ methods consistent with the requirements of advanced rootkit detection and removal. These actions must be taken everywhere. If one country's set of computers remain unprotected, their vulnerabilities will surely be compromised and used in the ever growing army of botnets against others. Partial protection among countries parallels locking the back door of your home and leaving the front door unlocked – the vulnerability still exists although it may not be as widespread.

Computer security measures such as network firewalls, email scanning, anti-malware utilities, intrusion detection applications, and intrusion prevention applications are synonymous with a holistic approach to IT security and should be regarded as a necessary first line of defense against rootkit infestation. Additionally, patches must be made available in a timely fashion. Attackers have the upper hand in exploiting vulnerabilities and their activities will likely dictate when patches should be developed and released to users. This is evidenced by the occasional Microsoft vulnerabilities where public pressure, and quick-fix patches created by other vendors, force Microsoft to issue patches before the scheduled "Patch Tuesday" release date. To successfully encourage the international user community to patch as needed, there must first be basic awareness and knowledge concerning the vulnerability. The user community should have basic awareness and knowledge of rootkits because of their damage potential and increasing movement into Windows computing environments.

Beyond the ramp-up of the IT community education efforts must be initiated, but these efforts must be widespread and tailored to the audience in order to combat the problem. Education will be needed for diverse groups such as lawmakers, consumers, home users, and IT professionals; and members of these groups will sometime overlap. Lawmakers are not traditional recipients of these education efforts but they should be included because of the international reach of malware and because of the scarcity of legal treaties that are intended to be global. Security vendors will need cooperative efforts, which are now only being seen in small numbers by current acquisitions and mergers, to strengthen their security offerings. Rootkits are not detected by traditional signature-based detection methods that are common now, and combined efforts that extend the time-tested detection methods may be used to improve software-driven combative efforts where client consumers and IT professionals each receive benefits. Corporate policy makers must be vigilant in their protection efforts. First they must gain awareness of the capabilities and characteristics of the anti-rootkit solutions. When appropriate solutions or preventative tasks are promulgated by policy, they must be enforced and penalties must occur when these codified solutions and tasks are violated.

Limitations

We believe this study presents a fair assessment of what college students in the two countries perceive concerning rootkits. The convenience samples were chosen by the authors, based on geographic proximity, and it could be argued that the findings are not generalizable to Korea and the U.S. as a whole. Also, the survey respondents are relatively young and most of them are full time college students who are not a part of the workplace where rootkits will surely cause business losses. However, these students are certainly experienced with computers and they indicate that they have access to one or more owned personal computers. It is further expected that they have a high level of skill in Internet surfing and digital downloads based on profiles of college students in other contexts. So, although this study is not without limitations, its currency and cross-country orientation should be valuable to those involved in training and/or education in the private or public sector. Furthermore, the results may serve as a baseline for researchers and security firms who examine awareness levels.

REFERENCES

Bento, A., & Bento, R. (2004) Empirical Test of Hacking Framework: An Exploratory Study. *Communications of the AIS, 14*, 678-690.

Calhoun, K. J., Teng, J. T. C., & Cheon, M. J. (2002). Impact of National Culture on Information Technology Usage Behavior: An Exploratory Study of Decision Making in Korea and the USA.

Behavior and Information Technology, (21.4), July/August 2002, 293-302.

Digital Chosunilbo. (2005). *N. Korea's Hackers Rival CIA*, Expert Warns. Retrieved from http://english.chosun.com/w21data/html/news/200506/200506020014.html

Dillard, K. (2005). What is a rootkit? from *SearchWindowsSecurity.com*

Hulme, G. V. (2002). *Rude Worm Insults.* then Wreaks Havoc. http://www.itnews.com.au/news-story.aspx?CIaNID=10532

Internet World Stats (2005). http://www.internet-worldstats.com/stats.htm

ITIM International (2006). http://www.geert-hofstede.com/

Jones, M. C., Arnett, K. P., Tang, J. T. E., & Chen, N. S. (1993). Perceptions of computer viruses a cross-cultural assessment. *Computers and Security, 12,* 191-197.

Kim, U., & Park, Y. S. (2006). Indigenous psychological analysis of academic achievement in Korea: The influence of self efficacy, parents, and culture.

International Journal of Psychology, 41(4) 287-292.

Korean Times (2005) Technology. It's English. *The Korean Times.*http://times.hankooki.com/lpage/tech/200512/kt2005120216444111780.htm

Kramarenko, D. (2003, January 25) Hackers or Cyber-soldiers? *Computer Crime Research Center.* http://www.crime-research.org/interviews/hacker0904/

Lemos, R. (2001) Web Worm Targets White House. *CNet News.com*

Naraine, R. (2006, January 18) eWeek.com When's a Rootkit Not a Rootkit? http://www.eweek.com/article2/0,1759,1913083,00.asp

Naraine, R. (2007, May 15) Rutkowska Announces Invisible Things Lab Startup.*ZDNet,* http://blogs.zdnet.com/security/?p=199.

Peterson, D. K., & Kim, C. (2003). Perceptions on IS Risks and Failure Types: A Comparison of Designers from the United States, Japan and Korea. *Journal of Global Information Management,* 11(3), 19-20, Jul-Sep.

Roberts, P. F. (2005). *Microsoft on 'Rootkits': Be Afraid, Be very Afraid.*

Schmidt, M. B., & Arnett, K. P. (2005). Spyware: A Little Knowledge is a Wonderful Thing. *Communications of the ACM,* 48(8), 67-70.

Seltzer, L. (2005). Rootkits: The Ultimate Stealth Attack. *PC Magazine, 24,* 76.

Shim, J. P. (2005) Korea's Lead in Mobile Cellular and DMB Phone Services., *Communications of the Association for Information Systems,15.*

Stafford, T. F. (2005). Spyware. *Communications of the ACM, 48*(8), 34-35.

Stars and Stripes (2001, July 27), S. Korea Indicts U.S. Service Member for Allegedly Hacking more than 50 Web Sites. http://ww2.pstripes.osd.mil/01/jul01/ed072701g.html

Williamson, M. (2007). A Conversation with Jamie Butler. *ACM Queue,* February 2007. 16-23.

APPENDIX

ANOVA results. Respondents provided answers on Likert scale with 1 "Strongly Disagree," 3 "Neutral," and 5 "Strongly Agree."

	N	Mean		Sum of Squares	df	Mean Square	F	Sig.
I am familiar with how rootkits work								
USA	209	1.44	Between Groups	9.13	1	9.1285	14.4552	0.000
Korea	199	1.15	Within Groups	256.39	406	0.6315		
Total	408	1.30	Total	265.52	407			
The "average" person at my institution is familiar with rootkits								
USA	210	1.94	Between Groups	25.61	1	25.6101	36.3942	0.000
Korea	199	1.44	Within Groups	286.40	407	0.7037		
Total	409	1.70	Total	312.01	408			
I am familiar with spyware								
USA	210	4.13	Between Groups	418.45	1	418.4463	357.6413	0.000
Korea	196	2.10	Within Groups	472.69	404	1.1700		
Total	406	3.15	Total	891.13	405			
The "average" person at my institution is familiar with spyware								
USA	210	3.85	Between Groups	331.75	1	331.7464	369.2223	0.000
Korea	195	2.04	Within Groups	362.10	403	0.8985		
Total	405	2.98	Total	693.84	404			
I am familiar with computer viruses								
USA	210	4.21	Between Groups	602.97	1	602.9662	841.5044	0.000
Korea	196	1.78	Within Groups	289.48	404	0.7165		
Total	406	3.04	Total	892.45	405			
The "average" person at my institution is familiar with computer viruses								
USA	210	4.12	Between Groups	381.74	1	381.7385	460.6763	0.000

continued on following page

APPENDIX. CONTINUED

Korea	196	2.18	Within Groups	334.77	404	0.8286		
Total	406	3.18	Total	716.51	405			

I am familiar with the "Trilobyte" virus

USA	208	1.95	Between Groups	30.56	1	30.5612	34.1501	0.000
Korea	191	1.40	Within Groups	355.28	397	0.8949		
Total	399	1.69	Total	385.84	398			

The "average" person at my institution is familiar with the "Trilobyte" virus

USA	209	2.31	Between Groups	50.96	1	50.9615	62.1123	0.000
Korea	191	1.59	Within Groups	326.55	398	0.8205		
Total	400	1.97	Total	377.51	399			

I am familiar with the "Melissa" virus

USA	210	2.79	Between Groups	116.46	1	116.4585	112.5560	0.000
Korea	189	1.70	Within Groups	410.76	397	1.0347		
Total	399	2.27	Total	527.22	398			

The "average" person at my institution is familiar with the "Melissa" virus

USA	210	3.78	Between Groups	54.35	1	54.3472	33.8593	0.000
Korea	189	3.04	Within Groups	637.22	397	1.6051		
Total	399	3.43	Total	691.57	398			

Section II
Privacy Preservation and Techniques

Chapter V
Privacy–Preserving Data Mining and the Need for Confluence of Research and Practice

Lixin Fu
University of North Carolina, Greensboro, USA

Hamid Nemati
University of North Carolina, Greensboro, USA

Fereidoon Sadri
University of North Carolina, Greensboro, USA

ABSTRACT

Privacy-Preserving Data Mining (PPDM) refers to data mining techniques developed to protect sensitive data while allowing useful information to be discovered from the data. In this chapter the review PPDM and present a broad survey of related issues, techniques, measures, applications, and regulation guidelines. The authors observe that the rapid pace of change in information technologies available to sustain PPDM has created a gap between theory and practice. They posit that without a clear understanding of the practice, this gap will be widening, which, ultimately will be detrimental to the field. They conclude by proposing a comprehensive research agenda intended to bridge the gap relevant to practice and as a reference basis for the future related legislation activities.

1. INTRODUCTION

Technological advances, decreased costs of hardware and software, and the world-wide-web revolution have allowed for vast amounts of data to be generated, collected, stored, processed, analyzed, distributed and used at an ever-increasing rate by organizations and governmental agencies. According a survey by U.S. Department of Commerce, an increasing number of Americans are going online and engaging in several online activities, including online purchases and conducting banking online. The growth in Internet usage and e-commerce has offered businesses and governmental agencies the opportunity to collect and analyze information in ways never previously imagined. "Enormous amounts of consumer data have long been available through offline sources such as credit card transactions, phone orders, warranty cards, applications and a host of other traditional methods. What the digital revolution has done is increase the efficiency and effectiveness with which such information can be collected and put to use" (Adkinson, Eisenach, & Lenard, 2002).

Simultaneously, there is a growing awareness that by leveraging their data resources to develop and deploy data mining technologies to enhance their decision-making capabilities, organizations can gain and sustain a competitive advantage (Eckerson & Watson, 2001). If correctly deployed, Data Mining (DM) offers organizations an indispensable decision-enhancing process that optimizes resource allocation and exploits new opportunities by transforming data into valuable knowledge (Nemati, Barko, & Christopher, 2001). Correctly deploying data mining has the potential of significantly increasing a company's profits and reducing its costs by helping to identify areas of potential business, or areas that the company needs to focus its attention on, or areas that should be discontinued because of poor sales or returns over a period of time. For example, data mining can identify customer buying patterns and preferences which would allow for a better management of inventory and new merchandising opportunities. However, when data contains personally identifiable attributes, if data mining is used in the wrong context, it can be very harmful to individuals. Data mining may "pose a threat to privacy" in the sense that sensitive personal data may be exposed directly or discovered patterns can reveal confidential personal attributes about individuals, classify individuals into categories, revealing in

that way confidential personal information with certain probability. Moreover, such patterns may lead to generation of stereotypes, raising very sensitive and controversial issues, especially if they involve attributes such as race, gender or religion. An example is the debate about studies of intelligence across different races." (Estivill-Castro, Brankovic, & Dowe, 1999). As another example, individual patient medical records are stored in electronic databases by government and private medical providers (Hodge, Gostin, & Jacobson, 1999). The proliferation of medical databases within the healthcare information infrastructure presents significant benefits for medical providers and patients, including enhanced patient autonomy, improved clinical treatment, advances in health research and public health surveillance (Hodge et al., 1999). However, use and mining of this type of data presents a significant risk of privacy. Therefore not only protecting the confidentiality of personally identifiable health data is critical, but also insufficient protections of what could be mined from it can subject the individuals to possible embarrassment, social stigma, and discrimination (Hodge et al., 1999).

The significance of data security and privacy has not been lost to the data mining research community as was revealed in Nemati and Barko (Nemati et al., 2001) of the major industry predictions that are expected to be key issues in the future (Nemati et al., 2001). Chiefly among them are concerns over the security of what is collected and the privacy violations of what is discovered ((Margulis, 1977), (Mason, 1986), (Culnan, 1993), (Smith, 1993), (Milberg, S. J., Smith, & Kallman, 1995), and (Smith, Milberg, & Burke, 1996)). About 80 percent of survey respondents expect data mining and consumer privacy to be significant issues (Nemati et al., 2001).

Recently, research in privacy as well as that of data mining has garnered considerable interest among academic and practitioners' communities from diverse perspectives – for example, technical, behavioral, sociological, governmental, and organizational perspectives. Although, there is an extensive pool of literature that addresses many aspects of both privacy and data mining, it is often unclear as to how this literature relates and integrates to define an integrated privacy preserving data mining research discipline. Part of the problem is that there is no clear framework that defines the privacy preserving data mining paradigm for research. As a result, privacy preserving data mining research seems to be fluid and often fragmented. Hence, it is difficult to articulate what defines and bounds PPDM research and to identify what research streams exist within it. For academics, these issues can become problematic when seeking to define the contribution of intellectual activities in this discipline. Given the importance of this area of research, the need for its viability as an increasingly distinct discipline, a laudable move toward a tighter and conceptually better developed research has recently become more evident. This trend has clearly been beneficial to the development of PPDM as an independent and viable field. Therefore to succeed, in conducting research in PPDM, it is important to aim for the greatest degree of practical validity possible while maintaining a rigorous theoretical framework. However, the rapid pace of change in information technologies available to sustain PPDM has created a gap between theory and practice. Without a clear understanding of the practice, this gap will be widening which, ultimately will be detrimental to the field. It is therefore imperative to foster a coexistence of theoretical and methodological rigor with managerial, organizational and governmental relevance that ultimately enhances the practice and the theory of this field of research.

In this paper, we will begin by discussing the importance of data and data mining. Then we concentrate on the issue of privacy. A survey of PPDM research and evaluation of PPDM techniques are presented next. After that, we discuss governmental regulation issues related to privacy. Lastly, we propose some open issues and give promising research areas in PPDM.

Data Data Everywhere Data

Several studies ((Brancheau, Janz, & Wetherbe, 1996); (Niederman, Brancheau, & Wetherbe, 1991)) show that data has been ranked as one of the top priorities for IT executives as an organizational resource. Similar research ((Rockart & DeLong, 1988); (Watson, Rainer Jr, & Koh, 1991)) has also revealed that data is an important part of a decision support system since it forms the basis of the information that is delivered to decision makers. The formidable challenge facing organizations involves the collection, management, and presentation of its data to enable management to make well-informed and timely decisions. With the emergence of web technologies, the collection and storage of data, both internal and external to an organization, has increased dramatically. Data experts estimate that in 2002 the world generated 5 exabytes[1] of data. This amount of data is more than all the words ever spoken by human beings. The rate of growth is just as staggering – the amount of data produced in 2002 was up 68% from just two years earlier. The size of the typical business database has grown a hundred-fold during the past five years as a result of internet commerce, ever-expanding computer systems and mandated recordkeeping by government regulations. To better grasp how much data this is, consider the following: if one byte of data is the equivalent of this dot (•), the amount of data produced globally in 2002 would equal the diameter of 4,000 suns. Moreover, that amount probably doubles every two years (Hardy, 2004). In spite of this enormous growth in enterprise databases, research from IBM reveals that organizations use less than 1 percent of their data for analysis (Brown, 2002). This is the fundamental irony of the information age we live in: Organizations possess enormous amounts of business data, yet have so little real business information, and to magnify the problem further, a leading business intelligence firm recently surveyed executives at 450 companies and discovered that 90 percent of these organizations rely on instinct rather than hard facts for most of their decisions because they lack the necessary information when they need it (Brown, 2002). Moreover, in cases where sufficient business information is available, organizations are only able to utilize less than 7 percent of it (Economist, 2001).

Data what is in it?

This proclamation about data volume growth is no longer surprising, but continues to amaze even the experts. For businesses, more data isn't always better. Organizations must assess what data they need to collect and how to best leverage it. Collecting, storing and managing business data and associated databases can be costly, and expending scarce resources to acquire and manage extraneous data fuels inefficiency and hinders optimal performance. The generation and management of business data also loses much of its potential organizational value unless important conclusions can be extracted from it quickly enough to influence decision making while the business opportunity is still present. Managers must rapidly and thoroughly understand the factors driving their business in order to sustain a competitive advantage. Organizational speed and agility supported by fact-based decision making are critical to ensure an organization remains at least one step ahead of its competitors.

The events of September 11, 2001, have accelerated the governmental agencies need for and use of personally identifiable information. These needs and uses are being justified in the name of protecting and promoting national, public, or individual security. For example organizations and local, state, or federal agencies need to identify individuals faster and to make assessments and judgments about people more accurately and more reliably, in real or near-real time. They also need to authenticate the identities of individuals, check backgrounds and histories and to verify their credentials and authorizations. In order to

do this in a timely fashion, they need to access and sift through massive amounts of personal data quickly from many sources, both public & private, and across numerous jurisdictions, intercept communications and monitor electronic activities. Government agencies and organizations also need to share data and intelligence across different jurisdictions and domains. Data sharing, in particular, magnifies privacy violation risks and underlines the need for reliable Privacy-Preserving Data Mining techniques.

The manner in which companies interact with their customers has changed tremendously over the past few years. Customers no longer guarantee their loyal patronage, and this has resulted in organizations attempting to better understand them, predict their future needs, and decrease response times in fulfilling their demands. Customer retention is now widely viewed by organizations as a significant marketing strategy in creating a competitive advantage, and rightly so. Research suggests that as little as a 5% increase in retention can mean as much as a 95% boost in profit, and repeat customers generate over twice as much gross income as new customers (Winer, 2001). In addition, many business executives today have replaced their cost reduction strategies with a customer retention strategy—it costs approximately five to ten times more to acquire new customers than to retain established customers (Pan & Lee, 2003). It has been shown that protecting customers' personal information has a direct relationship with their retention. A study by (Liu, Marchewka, & Yu, 2004) concluded that privacy has a strong influence on whether a consumer trusts an e-vendor. Their results also indicate that trust subsequently influences behavioral intentions to purchase, visit the site again, or recommend the site to others.

Privacy Definitions and Issues

Privacy is defined as "the state of being free from unsanctioned intrusion" (Dictionary.com,

2006). Westin (Westin, 1967) defined the right to privacy as "the right of the individuals... to determine for themselves when, how, and to what extent information about them is communicated to others." The Forth Amendment to the US Constitution's Bill of Rights states that "The right of the people to be secure in their persons, houses, papers, and effects, against unreasonable searches and seizures, shall not be violated." This belief carries back through history in such expressions from England, at least circa 1603, "Every man's house is his castle." The Supreme Court has since ruled that "We have recognized that the principal object of the Fourth Amendment is the protection of privacy rather than property, and have increasingly discarded fictional and procedural barriers rested on property concepts." Thus, because the Amendment "protects people, not places," the requirement of actual physical trespass is dispensed with and electronic surveillance was made subject to the Amendment's requirements (Findlaw.com, 2006).

Generally the definitions of privacy in regards to business are quite clear. On the Internet, however, privacy raises greater concerns as consumers realize how much information can be collected without their knowledge. Companies are facing an increasingly competitive business environment which forces them to collect vast amounts of customer data in order to customize their offerings. Eventually, as consumers become aware of these technologies new privacy concerns will arise, and these concerns will gain a higher level of importance. The security of personal data and subsequent misuse or wrongful use without prior permission of an individual raise privacy concerns and often end up in questioning the intent behind collecting private information in the first place (Dhillon & Moores, 2001). Privacy information holds the key to power over the individual. When privacy information is held by organizations that have collected the information without the knowledge or permission of the individual the rights of the individual are at risk. By 1997, consumer privacy had become a prominent issue in the United States (Dyson, 1998).

Cost of Privacy and Why Privacy Matters

In practice, information privacy deals with an individual's ability to control and release personal information. The individual is in control of the release process: to whom information is released, how much is released and for what purpose the information is to be used.

"If a person considers the type and amount of information known about them to be inappropriate, then their perceived privacy is at risk"(Roddick & Wahlstrom, 2001). Consumers are likely to lose confidence in the online marketplace because of these privacy concerns. Business must understand consumers' concern about these issues and aim to build consumer trust. It is important to note that knowledge about data collection can have a negative influence on a customer's trust and confidence level online.

Privacy concerns are real and have profound and undeniable implications on people's attitude and behavior (Sullivan, 2002). The importance of preserving customers' privacy becomes evident when we study the following information: In its 1998 report, the World Trade Organization projected that the worldwide Electronic Commerce would reach a staggering $220 billion. A year later, Wharton Forum on E-commerce revised that WTO projection down to $133 billion. What accounts for this unkept promise of phenomenal growth? Census Bureau, in its February 2004 report states that "Consumer privacy apprehensions continue to plague the Web and hinder its growth." In a report by Forrester Research it is stated that privacy fears will hold back roughly $15 billion in e-commerce revenue. In May 2005, Jupiter Research reported that privacy and security concerns could cost online sellers almost $25 billion by 2006. Whether justifiable or not, consumers have concerns about their privacy and these concerns have been reflected in their behavior. The chief privacy officer of Royal Bank of Canada said "Our research shows that 80% of our customers would walk away if we mishandled their personal information."

2. A SURVEY OF PRIVACY-PRESERVING DATA MINING

What is Data Mining?

Data mining refers to discovering knowledge from large data sets typically stored in databases (Han & Kamber, 2001). It is also known as knowledge discovery in databases (KDD). Data mining is the process of discovering and interpreting previously unknown patterns in databases. It is a powerful technology that converts data into information and potentially actionable knowledge. However, obtaining new knowledge in an organizational vacuum does not facilitate optimal decision making in a business setting. The unique organizational challenge of understanding and leveraging DM to engineer actionable knowledge requires assimilating insights from a variety of organizational and technical fields and developing a comprehensive framework that supports an organization's quest for a sustainable competitive advantage. These multidisciplinary fields include data mining, business strategy, organizational learning and behavior, organizational culture, organizational politics, business ethics and privacy, knowledge management, information sciences and decision support systems. These fundamental elements of DM can be summarized into three main groups: Artificial Intelligence (AI), Information Technology (IT), and Organizational Theory (OT). Our research and industry experience suggest that successfully leveraging DM requires integrating insights from all three categories in an organizational setting typically characterized by complexity and uncertainty. This

is the essence and uniqueness of DM. Obtaining maximum value from DM involves a cross-department team effort that includes statisticians/data miners, software engineers, business analysts, line-of-business managers, subject matter experts, and upper management support. Today, there are extensive vertical data mining applications providing analysis in the domains of banking and credit, bioinformatics, CRM, e-CRM, healthcare, human resources, e-commerce, insurance, investment, manufacturing, marketing, retail, entertainment, and telecommunications.

What is PPDM?

PPDM allows one to derive useful statistical information from large data sets (this includes predication models, association rules, classification, etc.) but, at the same time, protects sensitive information. One of the main techniques of PPDM is to develop algorithms to modify the original data in certain way so that even after the mining process, the private data and private knowledge are still private. In this section we provide a summary of PPDM techniques. Our presentation is neither detailed nor comprehensive. Interested readers can consult the references for more in-depth discussions.

In the area of statistical databases, extensive research has been conducted to provide statistics information, such as sum, count, average, min, max, and percentiles, without releasing sensitive information of individuals (Adam & Wortman, 1989). The work is broadly in two categories: query restriction (restricting the size of the query result, controlling the overlap among successive queries, keeping audit trail, clustering into mutually exclusive populations etc.) and data perturbation.

Privacy-preserving data mining approaches, in general, use a combination of data suppression and data perturbation to protect sensitive data while making it possible to obtain statistical information. Data suppression refers to removing parts of data. For example, identifying fields, such as social security numbers, are normally removed from the data. Data perturbation refers to changing data values from the original. It should be done in a way that the statistical information that is mined is still valid. There have been many approaches to data perturbation, including

- **Generalization:** A specific data value can be replaced by a less specific range of values. For example, we can decide to categorize age into ten-year intervals 0-9, 10-19, 20-29, etc., and replace each age by its corresponding range. Another example is to replace a street address by a less specific city, county, state, or region. Generalization is one of the most widely used techniques for anonymizing data.

- **Adding *noise* to data values:** This approach can be used for numeric data. It has been shown (R. Agrawal & Srikant, 2000) that valid statistical distributions can be derived from data that is altered by adding a random value from a known distribution. Based on the reconstructed distributions, they built a decision-tree classifier whose accuracy is comparable to the one using the original data. The work in (D. Agrawal & Aggarwal, 2001) uses an Expectation Maximization (EM) algorithm for distribution to improve over the Bayesian-based method. Papers (Evfimievski, Srikant, Agrawal, & Gehrke, 2002) and (Rizvi & Haritsa, 2002) address the perturbation for binary and categorical data.

- **Swapping values between tuples** (Denning, 1982): In this approach data values are preserved but association between data values are altered. Hence, it becomes difficult if not impossible to determine which sensitive data value belongs to which individual. Statistical information mined from the anonymized data set still remains valid.

- **Sampling data:** (Liew, Choi, & Liew, 1985) **or sampling query results:** (Denning, 1980)

- **Retaining some data, and replacing others probabilistically:** An example of this technique is discussed in (Evfimievski et al., 2002) for association rule mining. Each sales transaction containing a list of items is randomized by retaining a subset of items at random, and possibly adding more items that are not in the original transaction randomly.

A survey paper written by Verykios et al. gave a classification hierarchy for existing works related to PPDM (Verykios, Bertino et al., 2004). Their categorization of works done in PPDM is based on the following five dimensions: data distribution, data modification, data mining techniques, data or rule hiding, and selective modification of data for privacy preservation.

Secure Multiparty Computation (SMC)

Another promising direction for Privacy-Preserving Data Mining is to develop algorithms for distributed data mining that also preserve privacy. In this approach, which has been called *Secure Multiparty Computation* (SMC), data is distributed over many sources. Examples include banking and health systems. Multiple sources collaborate to mine the collective data. The data at each source is private to that source and should be protected from other sources. Many of the algorithms are based on cryptographic techniques (Pinkas, 2002). Examples of SMC techniques include association rule mining for horizontally distributed data (Kantarcioglu & Clifton, 2004), and for vertically distributed data (J. Vaidya & Clifton, 2005), classification (Lindell & Pinkas, 2002), and clustering on horizontally and vertically distributed data (Clifton, Kantarcioglu, Vaidya, Lin, & Zhu, 2002). A survey of these techniques can be found in (Jaideep Vaidya & Clifton, 2004).

Examples

The following simple example demonstrates data suppression, generalization, and noise addition techniques. Original data is shown in the following table:

SSN	NAME	AGE	SALARY
123456789	Kay	31	40
234234234	Joe	45	55
444444444	Albert	26	35
...	...	...	...

Randomized data is shown below. Identifying fields (SSN and NAME) are suppressed, age is generalized, and random values in the [-50, +50] range are added to salary. If the size of data is adequately large, statistical inferences (such as average salary, average salary per age group) computed from randomized data will be close approximations of real statistics.

AGE	SALARY
0-40	52
40-45	14
20-30	87
...	...

The next example, taken from (Jaideep Vaidya & Clifton, 2004), shows the value of distributed data mining. Here we have vertically distributed data, one from health care, and the other from a cell phone company. Combined data indicates the possibility that Li/Ion phone batteries may lead to brain tumors in diabetics. Each data set is private and can not be disclosed to the other party. SMC techniques make it possible to mine distributed data securely.

RPJ	Brain tumor	Diabetic
CAC	No tumor	Nondiabetic
...	...	...
PTR	No tumor	Diabetic

Medical Records

RPJ	5210	Li/Ion
CAC	None	None
...	...	...
PTR	3650	NiCd

Cell Phone Data

3. EVALUATING PPDM TECHNIQUES

How can we evaluate a PPDM technique? There are many aspects that should be considered:

- **Application domain:** Some PPDM techniques are specific to certain applications. For example, there are techniques specifically designed for mining association rules for horizontally distributed data. Some techniques, such as data perturbation, are more general. These techniques are used to alter (*randomize, anonymize, sanitize*) source data. The randomized data set is then made available (published) to interested parties for data mining.
- **Speed:** Different techniques achieve different degrees of efficiency. In general, SMC techniques are slower compared to single-source PPDM techniques.
- **Nature of data:** Different techniques are used for numeric data and non-numeric data. Further, data distribution (single source, horizontal distribution, vertical distribution) call for different techniques.

In addition to the aspects listed above, there are two very important factors in evaluating any PPDM technique:

1. The degree of privacy achieved by the PPDM technique
2. The degree of usefulness of the technique (*i.e.*, the accuracy of the rules and patterns that can be mined)

Despite significant research, there are still many open problems with respect to these factors. For example, policy makers such as governments and international associations have specified a series of policies and regulations with respect to privacy. On the other hand, PPDM researchers have also attempted to define numerous measures to quantify the degree of privacy. No single measure, among the many proposed, is widely accepted at this time. More importantly, there is a gap between privacy measures from the scientific community, and privacy policies from social and legal communities. It is not even clear whether it is possible to relate these attempts to define and quantify privacy to each other. In the following we will try to present some of the measures from the scientific community, and provide, to the extent possible, the intuition behind the different definitions. Governmental privacy regulations will be discussed in Section 4.

There is a subtle balance between the degree of privacy offered and the utility achieved by a given PPDM approach. Utility refers to the extent to which useful information can be extracted from anonymized data set. Obviously, suppressing all data provides the maximum privacy, but nothing can be mined. On the other end of the spectrum, the original data provides the maximum opportunity for mining useful information but provides no privacy. Researchers have been struggling with the issues of privacy and utility and many metrics have been proposed to quantify the degrees of privacy and utility offered by a given approach. The issue is more complicated

than it appears because we would like to protect the privacy against adversaries that may have their own additional information (usually called background information), and adversaries that may collude to break down the privacy offered by a given approach. In the following we examine some of the privacy and utility metrics.

Privacy Measures

*   **Perfect privacy:** Intuitively, sensitive information is defined as a set of queries, and a perfect privacy policy only allows queries and access that does not compromise sensitive data in any way. Although attractive from a privacy preservation point of view, this approach has been shown to be excessively restrictive (hence, of very low utility) (Miklau & Suciu, 2004). More practical measures are needed for PPDM.
*   **K-anonymity:** Proposed by Sweeney (Sweeney, 2002), this measure states that the anonymized data should have at least k tuples with given values for non-sensitive attributes. For example, an anonymized health records table with attributes age-range, gender, state, diagnosis, satisfies k-anonymity for k=20 if, for each (age-range, gender, state) value, the anonymized table contains at least 20 tuples with those values. Hence, an adversary that knows (age, gender, address) of an individual, can only narrow down the search for the medical diagnosis of that individual to 20 (or more) tuples in the anonymized data set. Obviously, large k-values would be more desirable for privacy preservation.
*   **L-diversity:** K-anonymity alone is not adequate for formalizing privacy protection. In our health information system above, given the additional background information (age, gender, address) of an adversary, it may happen that the 20 tuples in the anonymized dataset all have the same diagnosis. In which

case the sensitive information of the individual has been compromised. Even when the number of diagnosis is not 1, but a small number (say, 3), the adversary has gained some information about the individual. The ℓ-diversity measure was proposed recently to remedy this shortcoming (Machanavajjhala, Gehrke, Kifer, & Venkitasubramaniam, 2006). Intuitively, ℓ-diversity states that among the tuples that have the same values for non-sensitive attributes, there should be at least 1 different values for the sensitive attribute. For example, in our health information example, k-anonymity plus ℓ-diversity for k=20 and l=10 states that given (age, gender, address), the anonymized dataset contains at least 20 tuples with those values, and these tuples have at least 10 different diagnoses. So, the adversary who has additional background knowledge can only narrow down the sensitive information to 10 or more possible values.

• The metric of privacy in secure multiparty computation techniques is based on the notion of *computational indistinguishability*. Two distributions are said to be computationally indistinguishable if no polynomial-time program can distinguish between them. Intuitively, this means obtaining the original data from the (perturbed or encrypted) information revealed by a source is very difficult. A truly secure SMC protocol enforces computational indistinguishability.

Utility Measures

Utility measures try to quantify the degree to which an anonymized data set can be used to obtain valid statistical information. Obviously, maximum privacy can be obtained if no data is revealed at all. But lack of data does not allow any statistical inference either. So, we need to be able to assess the utility of an anonymized data set. Many utility measures are proposed for this purpose. These measures try to quantify the degree of *information loss* suffered as a result of the anonymization process. Below, we will mention some of the utility measures proposed without going into technical details.

Simple utility measures for generalization-based techniques include *generalization height* (Samarati, 2001), *average size of anonymized groups* (Machanavajjhala et al., 2006), and *discernibility factor* (Bayardo & Agrawal, 2005). More sophisticated measures have been proposed that also take data distribution into account. Examples include *classification metric* (Iyengar, 2002) and *information-gain-privacy-loss ratio* (Wang, Fung, & Yu, 2005). More recently, an information-theoretic utility measure was proposed (Kifer & Gehrke, 2006), and its relationship to other well-known concepts such as entropy measure, divergence, and log-linear models was shown.

The bottom line is to design *efficient* algorithms for anonymization and data mining of anonymized data sets, with *high degrees* of *privacy preservation* and *utility*. Choice of these measures can have a significant impact on the efficiency of the algorithms.

The Need to Protect the Outcome of Data Mining

In the movie "Minority Report" would-be criminals are identified before they commit any crime, and are put away by the police. Whether technology would advance to a degree that such horror predications become a reality is debatable, but we already witness scenarios where advances in technology, coupled with data mining techniques, can come close to making certain critical predictions. For example, researchers are actively relating genetic information to likelihood of contracting certain diseases. Such advanced techniques are double-edged swords. An individual may be denied employment, or may face very high medical insurance premiums due to his/her genetic information. On the other hand, genetics can play an important role in the ability to cure diseases, for example, by determining the best treatment for a certain condition based on genetic makeup. Further, the prediction ability makes it possible for increased monitoring and pre-emptive treatment measures for high-risk individuals.

So, in addition to protecting individual data, another important issue in privacy-preserving data mining is the need to selectively protect the results of data mining. The issue has a legal dimension: Legislation is needed to regulate use of prediction methods for the purposes of employment, health care insurance premiums, and similar domains where there is a need for protection against discrimination. There are also technological issues. For example, techniques have been developed to allow corporations to share data through anonymization or other PPDM techniques, but to hide sensitive corporate information that can provide competitive advantage (Atallah et al., 1999). Simply put, the data should be anonymized in a way not to reveal any rules and patterns that are considered sensitive to the business that owns the data, while permitting collective mining for other useful knowledge. How can we transform database D into D', the released database, so that all the rules except for the sensitive rules, R_h, can still be mined? (Atallah et al., 1999) gives a formal proof that the optimal sanitization is NP-hard for the hiding of sensitive large itemsets in discovering association rules. A later work on association rule hiding is reported in (Verykios et al., 2004).

4. GOVERNMENTAL AND REGULATORY ACTIVITIES CONCERNING PRIVACY

Data mining and accompanying technologies have advanced at a rapid rate and have outpaced legislation designed to protect consumers. Governmental regulatory agencies and other policy makers need to be vigilant by developing laws and regulations that protect the privacy rights of the individual while accommodating the needs of businesses and government. In addition to the existing regulations already being enforced, it appears by the plethora of recent regulatory activities that the policy makers have released that they need to be more proactive. The Center for Democracy and Technology in its 2004 review of the 108th US congress found that at least twelve bills related to privacy and the Internet were debated in the US congress (Anonymous, 2004).

The most widely accepted principles on which many privacy laws in the United States, Canada, European Union and other parts of the world are based are the Fair Information Practice Principles (FIPP). The Principles were first formulated by the U. S. Department of Health, Education and Welfare in 1973 for collecting and use of information on consumers. FIPP are quoted here from the Organization for Economic Cooperation and Development's Guidelines on the Protection of Privacy and Transborder Flows of Personal Data (Text here is reproduced from the report available at http://www1.oecd.org/publications/e-book/9302011E.PDF).

Openness

There should be a general policy of openness about developments, practices and policies with respect to personal data. Means should be readily available for establishing the existence and nature of personal data, and the main purposes of their use, as well as the identity and usual residence of the data controller.

Collection Limitation

There should be limits to the collection of personal data and any such data should be obtain by lawful and fair means and, where appropriate, with the knowledge or consent of the data subject.

Purpose Specification

The purpose for which personal data are collected should be specified not later than at the time of data collection and the subsequent use limited to the fulfillment of those purposes or such others as are not incompatible with those purposes and as are specified on each occasion of change of purpose.

Use Limitation

Personal data should not be disclosed, made available or otherwise used for purposes other than those specified as described above, except with the consent of the data subject or by the authority of law.

Data Quality

Personal data should be relevant to the purposes for which they are to be used, and, to the extent necessary for those purposes, should be accurate, complete, relevant and kept up-to-date.

Individual Participation

An individual should have the right: a) to obtain from a data controller, or otherwise, confirmation of whether or not the data controller has data relating to him; b) to have communicated to him, data relating to him within a reasonable time; at a charge, if any, that is not excessive; in a reasonable manner; and in a form that is readily intelligible to him; c) to be given reasons if a request is denied and to be able to challenge such denial; and d) to challenge data relating to him and, if the challenge is successful, to have the data erased, rectified, completed or amended.

Security Safeguards

Personal data should be protected by reasonable security safeguards against such risks as loss or unauthorized access, destruction, use, modification or disclosure of data.

Accountability

A data controller should be accountable for complying with measures which give effect to the principles stated above.

The Federal Trade Commission (FTC) is the primary federal agency responsible for the enforcement of various laws governing the privacy of an individual's information on the Internet. The Federal Trade Commission Act (FTCA), 15 U.S.C. § 45(a), gives the FTC investigative and enforcement authority over businesses and organizations engaged in interstate commerce. While waiting on the enactment of new legislation, the FTC utilizes existing laws to protect consumers from unfair and deceptive trade practices. The FTC has allowed most businesses to self-regulate. However, the government has regulated some industries such as healthcare and financial services. They also require web sites to follow specific rules when obtaining information from children.

The FTC would like to see self-regulation of industries. However, if businesses don't effectively comply, the FTC is prepared to step in and apply existing laws to protect consumers. In March 2000, the Federal Trade Commission conducted a survey showing that most websites collect a vast amount of personal information from and about consumers. The survey found that 97% of sites collect email address or other personal information. However, only 20% implement the fair information practice principle: notice, choice, access, security. Unfortunately, these numbers are even higher when considering only the most popular websites. The FTC Chairman, Robert Pitofsky, on July 21, 1998 stated that "new laws may be needed to eliminate concerns raised by the online collection of personal information. …While some industry players may form and join self-regulatory programs, many may not. …This would result in a lack of uniform privacy protections that the

Commission believes are necessary for electronic commerce to flourish. The Commission believes that unless industry can demonstrate that it has developed and implemented broad-based and effective self-regulatory programs by the end of 1998, additional governmental authority in this area would be appropriate and necessary."

One of the most far reaching laws with privacy implication impacting data mining research and practitioner communities is Health Insurance Portability and Accountability Act of 1996. Health information is subject to HIPPA. The original legislation went into effect in 2001 and the final modifications took effect in April, 2003. A core aspect of HIPAA is to appropriately secure electronic medical records. The act applies to health information created or maintained by health care providers who engage in certain electronic transactions, health plans, and health care clearinghouses. The Office for Civil Rights (OCR) is responsible for implementing and enforcing the HIPPA privacy regulation. The act sets standards to protect privacy in regards to individuals' medical information. The act provides individuals access to their medical records, giving them more control over how their protected health information is used and disclosed, and providing a clear avenue of recourse if their medical privacy is compromised (Anonymous, 2006). Improper use or disclosure of protected health information has the potential for both criminal and civil sanctions. For example, fines up to $25,000 for multiple violations of a single privacy standard in a calendar year and the penalties for intentional or willful violations of the privacy rule are much more severe with fines up to $250,000 and/or imprisonment up to 10 years for knowing misuse of personal health data. There are more immediate risks of private lawsuits relying on the HIPAA standard of care. Data Miners must take care not to violate this regulation or they will face penalties, which may include fines and/or imprisonment.

Special care must be taken when dealing with information obtained from Children. The

Children's Online Privacy Act of 1998 (COPPA) 15 U.S.C. §§ 6501 et. seq., governs the online collection of personal information of children under the age of thirteen. The regulation requires that websites get parental consent before collecting personal data from children. Websites are also required to post a privacy statement detailing what information will be collected, how it will use that information, if it will make the information available to third parties and a contact at the site. When utilizing data mining, one should be aware of how the data to be used for mining was obtained. The user can be held responsible for utilizing data that was illegally obtained. This is not limited to solely to children and pertains to all data.

Financial information is routinely mined to improve customer service, marketing and to increase an organization's bottom line. It is essential that this data be adequately protected from fraudulent use. The illegal and fraudulent use of financial information is widespread, causing harm to individuals and opening the organization and individual(s) responsible for the lapse in security to liability for the damage and hardship caused by inadequately protecting personal financial data. Financial information is subject to Gramm-Leach-Bliley Act, 15 U.S.C. §§ 6801 et seq. The act requires financial institutions to protect data collected from routine transactions (i.e. names, addresses and phone numbers; bank and credit card account numbers; income and credit histories; and Social Security numbers). Financial institutions must develop a written information security plan that describes their program to protect customer information. All programs must be appropriate to the financial institution's size and complexity, the nature and scope of its activities, and the sensitivity of the customer information at issue (Pitofsky, 2006). Privacy and security experts suggest that three areas of operation present special challenges and risks to information security and privacy: employee training and management; information systems, including network and software design, and information processing, storage, transmission and retrieval; and security and privacy management, including the prevention, detection and response to attacks, intrusions or other system failures. The Rule requires financial institutions to pay special attention to these areas (Pitofsky, 2006).

These regulations were prescribed to protect the privacy of personal information collected from and about individuals on the Internet, to provide greater individual control over the collection and use of that information and other purposes. However, data mining presents a new set of challenges to the regulatory agencies when considering that self-regulatory programs may not work or workability of them are at best very questionable. For example, in a space of six months, during 1989, TRUSTe, a nonprofit privacy initiative had three of their licensees – RealNetworks, Microsoft and Deja News investigated for privacy violations (Lemos, 1999a). Organizations such as TRUSTe provide website owners with seals once they meet certain criteria relating to consumer privacy. Sites qualify for the seals by agreeing to post their privacy policies online, and allowing the seal providers to audit their operations to ensure they're adhering to the policy. When violations are discovered, TRUSTe and other privacy services "come in after the fact and say what the company did was bad, but they don't do anything to solve the problems," said Richard Smith, an independent Internet consultant who has uncovered several of the worst incidences of online privacy infringement (Lemos, 1999b).

The Patriot Act

The events of September 11, 2001 have led to new legislation designed to help law enforcement agencies combat terrorism. The Patriot Act (Uniting and Strengthening America by Providing Appropriate Tools Required to Intercept and Obstruct Terrorism Act, H. R. 3162, October 24, 2001) covers a broad range of topics including: wiretapping and intelligence surveillance, criminal justice, student privacy, financial privacy and immigration. The legislation increased law enforcement's powers while lowered the burden of proof needed for searches and surveillance. Due to the Patriot Act, the government has been given easier access to individuals' records and their eventual uses. These records could be personal such as medical, educational, mental health as well as financial. To gain access to such private data, the FBI needs to do is to certify that the records may be relevant to an investigation. The FBI will undoubtedly be collecting and integrating and mining more databases in the future.

5. SOME OPEN ISSUES: A PROMISING RESEARCH AGENDA

In this new age of information glut and terrorism concerns researchers from various disciplines have been concerned about privacy issues vis-à-vis, PPDM. There is every reason to believe that researchers would have continued to be interested in information privacy as information technology applications and use continue to increase. Because of the fast pace of advances in technologies and methodologies that support the goal of discovering knowledge from vast amounts of data, there is a substantial gap between what is theoretically possible and what is legally, ethically, or organizationally permissible.

Can the consumer really trust that his or her privacy is being protected as data mining techniques become powerful and integrated? Is the government really doing enough to assure that such self regulations are adequate? Can the regulatory agencies do more? The government is enacting regulations and is trying monitoring the situation but it is unclear when, if ever, the legislation will be able to keep pace with the technology. There are many important issues in PPDM that require further investigation, such as:

1. Scientists have been proposing many different measures for privacy and utility. On the other hand, policy makers have been producing large bodies of rules and regulations for privacy in many different application domains. These are two significantly different means of specifying and quantifying privacy, and it is very difficult, if not impossible, to reconcile these different approaches to the definition and measurement of privacy. We need to be able to evaluate PPDM techniques regarding their compliance with privacy laws and regulations. Also, the legislation should take advantage of PPDM research results. On one hand, given the existing laws and practices, PPDM research needs to find new algorithms or methods to implement the regulations. On the other hand, the legislation body should include PPDM research scientists as members to ensure that the regulations are based on solid, deep research foundation.

2. There has been significant progress in the scientific community in the establishment of metrics for privacy and utility. Often a proposed metric becomes popular and becomes a de facto standard, until new research exposes the weakness of the approach, and comes up with newer measures to fix the deficiency. For example, k-anonymity was proposed in late 90's as a measure of privacy, and gained significant popularity due to its simplicity and discovery of efficient algorithms to enforce k-anonymity. Yet, recently, it was shown that k-anonymity alone may not be an adequate measure for privacy. It was shown that simple attacks can effectively breach privacy of k-anonymized data (Machanavajjhala et al., 2006). An additional measure, ℓ-diversity was proposed to remedy this problem. But the question remains: Are these measures adequate for protecting privacy? The answer is "maybe, but we can not be sure." The improvement

is undoubtedly more powerful. That much is certain. As another example, simple anonymization became popular for PPDM approaches for association rule mining. Yet, it was shown recently (Lakshmanan, Ng, & Ramesh, 2005) that the degree of privacy achieved by simple anonymization is highly dependant on the data itself. Authors propose certain tests to determine whether anonymization provide adequate privacy for the given data set. Again, the question remains: Given a specific PPDM technique, how can we be assured that it is safe? The bottom line is, we are making steady progress into more secure PPDM techniques, but the ultimate decision to accept a PPDM approach remains a difficult decision to be made by policy makers.

3. We need to define different measures, utilities, matrices, that are not just "scientific" but are also based on organizational and managerial, governmental, considerations. Does the PPDM research community need to become more proactive or more reactive to the laws and regulations. Should they become more active in shaping the debate on what is the legal definition of privacy or should they just stay in their labs and develop ever more sophisticated algorithms?

4. A recent cover story article in Businessweek points out that "...the tool that probably has the most potential to thwart terrorism is data mining. Think of it as a form of surveillance that casts its eye on computer networks" (Businessweek, 2001). This enormous potential that data mining techniques show in fighting terrorism provides a great opportunity and challenges for data miners. The government is actively investing in data mining technologies, providing research grants and leading the effort to increase the ability of technological tools to be used for law enforcement and surveillance. Data miners need to assist investigators with

the current technology and develop new or improve current data mining tools. The government utilizes very powerful surveillance tools based on data mining and there maybe legitimate concerns regarding accuracy of data, and concerns over privacy violations of what these tools produce. It is imperative that those who utilize data mining and other technologies be aware of the potential abuses and limitations of these technologies. As the data mining becomes more widely used by governmental agencies in the hunt for suspected terrorists, data miners will and should be playing a more prominent role in not only developing the appropriate data mining algorithms and methodologies, but also in shaping the debate over the use of these methods and how to protect the privacy of people.

6. CONCLUSION

We are living in an age of data explosion. Unless we can mine useful knowledge nuggets from large amounts of data, these data sets at best remain "hidden treasures." However, the sophisticated data mining technologies may put the important issue of privacy protection in serious concern. Government has already passed regulations and laws that are aimed to protect the privacy of the citizens' sensitive data. We pointed out that even defining privacy strictly and universally itself is still an open issue. We have conducted a comprehensive survey of PPDM technologies, and privacy and utility measures. In particular, we discussed the main PPDM approaches such as data perturbation and SMC, and gave an evaluation of these techniques. We have recognized the gap between the research community and regulating government bodies, and tried to charter a research agenda of important and promising fields to close the gap.

REFERENCES

Adam, N. R., & Wortman, J. C. (1989). Security-control Methods for Statistical Databases. *ACM Computing Surveys, 21*(4), 515-556.

Adkinson, W., Eisenach, J., & Lenard, T. (2002). *Privacy Online: A Report on the Information Practices and Policies of Commercial Web Sites.* Retrieved August, 2006, from http://www.pff.org/publications/privacyonlinefinalael.pdf

Agrawal, D., & Aggarwal, C. C. (2001, May 2001). *On the design and quantification of privacy preserving data mining algorithms.* Paper presented at the Proceedings of the twentieth ACM SIGMOD-SIGACT-SIGART symposium on Principles of database systems, Santa Barbara, California, United States.

Agrawal, R., & Srikant, R. (2000). Privacy-preserving data mining. In *ACM SIGMOD Record, Proceedings of the 2000 ACM SIGMOD international conference on Management of data SIGMOD '00* (Vol. 29, pp. 439-450): ACM Press.

Anonymous. (2004). *Privacy Legislation Affecting the Internet: 108th Congress.* Retrieved August, 2006, from http://www.cdt.org/legislation/108th/privacy/

Anonymous. (2006). Retrieved August, 2006, from http://www.hhs.gov/ocr/index.html

Atallah, M., Elmagarmid, A., Ibrahim, M., Bertino, E., & Verykios, V. (1999). *Disclosure Limitation of Sensitive Rules.* Paper presented at the Proceedings of the 1999 Workshop on Knowledge and Data Engineering Exchange.

Bayardo, R. J., & Agrawal, R. (2005). *Data privacy through optimal k-anonymization.* Paper presented at the ICDE.

Brancheau, J. C., Janz, B. D., & Wetherbe, J. C. (1996). Key issues in information systems management: 1994-95 SIM Delphi Results. *MIS Quart., 20*(2), 225-242.

Brown, E. (2002, April 1). Analyze This. *Forbes, 169*, 96-98.

Businessweek. (2001), Privacy in an Age of Terror. *Businessweek*.

Clifton, C., Kantarcioglu, M., Vaidya, J., Lin, X., & Zhu, M. (2002). Tools for privacy preserving distributed data mining. *ACM SIGKDD Explorations Newsletter, 4*(2), 28-34.

Culnan, M. J. (1993). How did they my name?" An exploratory investigation of consumer attitudes toward secondary information use. *MIS Quart., 17*(3), 341-363.

Denning, D. (1980). Secure statistical databases with random sample queries. *ACM Transactions on Database Systems (TODS), 5*(3), 291-315.

Denning, D. (1982). *Cryptography and Data Security*: Addison-Wesley.

Dhillon, G., & Moores, T. (2001). Internet privacy: Interpreting key issues. *Information Resources Management Journal, 14*(4).

Dictionary.com. (2006). Retrieved July 2006, 2006, from http://dictionary.reference.com/browse/privacy

Dyson, E. (1998). Release 2.0 : A Design for Living in the Digital Age. *Bantam Doubleday Dell Pub*.

Eckerson, W., & Watson, H. (2001). Harnessing Customer Information for Strategic Advantage: Technical Challenges and Business Solutions, Industry Study 2000, Executive Summary. In *The Data Warehousing Institute*.

Economist. (2001, February 17). The slow progress of fast wires, *358*.

Estivill-Castro, V., Brankovic, L., & Dowe, D. L. (1999). *Privacy in Data Mining*. Retrieved August, 2006, from http://www.acs.org.au/nsw/articles/1999082.htm

Evfimievski, A., Srikant, R., Agrawal, R., & Gehrke, J. (2002). Privacy preserving mining of association rules. In *Proceedings of the eighth ACM SIGKDD international conference on Knowledge discovery and data mining, July 2002, Edmonton, Alberta, Canada* (pp. 217-228).

Findlaw.com. (2006). *Findlaw Homepage*. Retrieved July, 2006, from http://public.findlaw.com/

Han, J., & Kamber, M. (2001). *Data Mining: Concepts and Techniques*: Morgan Kaufmann Publishers.

Hardy, Q. (2004, May 10). Data of Reckoning. *Forbes, 173*, 151-154.

Hodge, J. G., Gostin, L. O., & Jacobson, P. (1999). Legal Issues Concerning Electronic Health Information: Privacy, Quality, and Liability, JAMA. *The Journal of the American Medical Association, 282*(15), 1466-1471.

Iyengar, V. S. (2002). *Transforming data to satisfy privacy constraints*. Paper presented at the KDD.

Kantarcioglu, M., & Clifton, C. (2004). Privacy-Preserving Distributed Mining of Association Rules on Horizontally Partitioned Data. *IEEE Trans. Knowledge Data Eng., 16*(9), 1026-1037.

Kifer, D., & Gehrke, J. (2006). *Injecting utility into anonymized datasets*. Paper presented at the Proceedings of the 2006 ACM SIGMOD international conference on Management of data, Chicago, IL, USA.

Lakshmanan, L. V. S., Ng, R. T., & Ramesh, G. (2005). *To do or not to do: the dilemma of disclosing anonymized data*. Paper presented at the Proceedings of the 2005 ACM SIGMOD international conference on Management of data, Baltimore, Maryland.

Lemos, R. (1999a). *Can you trust TRUSTe?* Retrieved Oct 14, 2002, from http://zdnet.com.com/2100-11-516377.html?legacy=zdnn

Lemos, R. (1999b). *RealNetworks rewrites privacy policy ZDNet News*. Retrieved 1999, October 31, from http://zdnet.com.com/2100-11-516330.html?legacy=zdnn

Liew, C. K., Choi, U. J., & Liew, C. J. (1985). A data distortion by probability distribution. *ACM Transactions on Database Systems (TODS), 10*(3), 395-411.

Lindell, Y., & Pinkas, B. (2002). Privacy Preserving Data Mining. *J. Cryptology, 15*(3), 177-206.

Liu, J. T., Marchewka, J. L., & Yu, C. S. (2004). Beyond concern: a privacy-trust-behavioral intention model of electronic commerce. *Information & Management*(42), 127-142.

Machanavajjhala, A., Gehrke, J., Kifer, D., & Venkitasubramaniam, M. (2006). *l-Diversity: Privacy Beyond k -Anonymity*. Paper presented at the 22nd International Conference on Data Engineering (ICDE'06).

Margulis, S. T. (1977). Conceptions of privacy: current status and next steps. *J. of Social Issues*(33), 5-10.

Mason, R. O. (1986). Four ethical issues of the information age. *MIS Quart., 10*(1), 4-12.

Miklau, G., & Suciu, D. (2004). A Formal Analysis of Information Disclosure in Data Exchange. In *SIGMOD 2004* (pp. 575-586).

Milberg, S. J., S. J., B., Smith, H. J., & Kallman, E. A. (1995). Values, personal information privacy, and regulatory approaches. *Comm. of the ACM, 38*, 65-74.

Nemati, H., Barko, R., & Christopher, D. (2001). Issues in Organizational Data Mining: A Survey of Current Practices. *Journal of Data Warehousing, 6*(1), 25-36.

Niederman, F., Brancheau, J. C., & Wetherbe, J. C. (1991). Information systems management issues for the 1990's. *MIS Quart., 15*, 474-500.

Pan, S. L., & Lee, J.-N. (2003). Using E-CRM for a Unified View of the Customer. *Communications of the ACM, 46*(4), 95-99.

Pinkas, B. (2002). Crytographic techniques for privacy-preserving data mining. *SIGKDD Exploreations, 4*(2), 12-19.

Pitofsky, R. (2006). *Privacy Online: Fair Information Practices in the Electronic Marketplace, a Report to Congress*. Retrieved August, 2006, from http://www.ftc.gov/reports/privacy2000/privacy2000.pdfFTC

Rizvi, S. J., & Haritsa, J. R. (2002). *Maintaing data privacy in association rule mining*. Paper presented at the Proceedings of the 28th International Conference on Very Large Databases.

Rockart, J. F., & DeLong, D. W. (1988). *Executive Support Systems: The Emergence of Top Management Computer Use*. Paper presented at the Dow Jones-Irwin, Homewood, IL.

Roddick, J., & Wahlstrom, K. (2001). On the Impact of Knowledge Discovery and Data Mining. *Australian Computer Society, Inc.*

Samarati, P. (2001). Protecting respondents' identities in microdata release. *IEEE Transactions on Knowledge and Data Engineering*, 1010-1027.

Smith, H. J. (1993). Privacy policies and practices: Inside the organizational maze. *Comm. of the ACM, 36*, 105-122.

Smith, H. J., Milberg, S. J., & Burke, S. J. (1996). Information privacy: Measuring individuals' concerns about organizational practices. *MIS Quart.*, 167-196.

Sullivan, B. (2002). *Privacy groups debate DoubleClick settlement*. Retrieved August, 2006, from http://www.cnn.com/2002/TECH/internet/05/24/doubleclick.settlement.idg/index.html

Sweeney, L. (2002). k-Anonymity: a model for protecting privacy. *International Journal on*

Uncertainty, Fuziness and Knowledge-based Systems, 10(5), 557-570.

Vaidya, J., & Clifton, C. (2004). Privacy-Preserving Data Mining: Why, How, and When. *IEEE Security and Privacy, 2*(6), 19-27.

Vaidya, J., & Clifton, C. (2005). Secure Set Intersection Cardinality with Application to Association Rule Mining. *J. Computer Security.*

Verykios, V. S., Bertino, E., Fovino, I. N., Provenza, L. P., Saygin, Y., & Theodoridis, Y. (2004). State-of-the-art in privacy preserving data mining. In *SIGMOD Record* (Vol. 33, pp. 50-57).

Verykios, V. S., Elmagarmid, A. K., Bertino, E., Saygin, Y., & Dasseni, E. (2004). Association Rule Hiding. *IEEE Transactions on Knowledge and Data Engineering, 16*(4), 434-447.

Wang, K., Fung, B. C. M., & Yu, P. S. (2005). *Template-based privacy preservation in classification problems.* Paper presented at the ICDM.

Watson, H. J., Rainer Jr, R. K., & Koh, C. E. (1991). Executive information systems: a framework for development and a survey of current practices. *MIS Quart.*, 13-30.

Westin, A. (1967). Privacy and Freedom. *New York: Atheneum.*

Winer, R. S. (2001). A framework for Customer Relationship Management. *California Management Review, 43*(4), 89-106.

ENDNOTE

[1] An Exabyte is 2^{16} bytes, or, approximately, 1,150,000,000,000,000,000 bytes.

Chapter VI
A Dimensionality Reduction–Based Transformation to Support Business Collaboration

Stanley R. M. Oliveira
Embrapa Informática Agropecuária, Brasil

Osmar R. Zaïane
University of Alberta, Canada

ABSTRACT

While the sharing of data is known to be beneficial in data mining applications and widely acknowledged as advantageous in business, this information sharing can become controversial and thwarted by privacy regulations and other privacy concerns. Data clustering for instance could be more accurate if more information is available, hence the data sharing. Any solution needs to balance the clustering requirements and the privacy issues. Rather than simply hindering data owners from sharing information for data analysis, a solution could be designed to meet privacy requirements and guarantee valid data clustering results. To achieve this dual goal, this chapter introduces a method for privacy-preserving clustering, called Dimensionality Reduction-Based Transformation (DRBT). This method relies on the intuition behind random projection to protect the underlying attribute values subjected to cluster analysis. It is shown analytically and empirically that transforming a dataset using DRBT, a data owner can achieve privacy preservation and get accurate clustering with little overhead of communication cost. Such a method presents the following advantages: it is independent of distance-based clustering algorithms; it has a sound mathematical foundation; and it does not require CPU-intensive operations.

INTRODUCTION

Data clustering is of capital importance in business and it fosters business collaboration as sharing data for clustering improves the prospects of identifying optimal customer targets, market more effectively and understand customer behaviour. Data Clustering maximizes return on investment supporting business collaboration (Lo, 2002; Berry & Linoff, 1997). Often combining different data sources provides better clustering analysis opportunities. Limiting the clustering on only some attributes of the data confines the correctness of the grouping, while benefiting from additional attributes could yield more accurate and actionable clusters. For example, it does not suffice to cluster customers based on their purchasing history, but combining purchasing history, vital statistics and other demographic and financial information for clustering purposes can lead to better and more accurate customer behaviour analysis. More often than not, needed data sources are distributed, partitioned and owned by different parties insinuating a requirement for sharing data, often sensitive, between parties. Despite its benefits to support both modern business and social goals, clustering can also, in the absence of adequate safeguards, jeopardize individuals' privacy. The fundamental question addressed in this chapter is: how can data owners protect personal data shared for cluster analysis and meet their needs to support decision making or to promote social benefits? To address this problem, data owners must not only meet privacy requirements but also guarantee valid clustering results.

Attaining good clustering may require data sharing between parties and data sharing may jeopardize privacy, a dilemma facing many modern data mining applications. Achieving privacy preservation, when sharing data for clustering, poses challenges for novel uses of data mining technology. Each application poses a new set of challenges. Let us consider two real-life examples in which the sharing of data poses different constraints:

- Two organizations, an Internet marketing company and an on-line retail company, have datasets with different attributes for a common set of individuals. These organizations decide to share their data for clustering to find the optimal customer targets so as to maximize return on investments. How can these organizations learn about their clusters using each other's data without learning anything about the attribute values of each other?

- Suppose that a hospital shares some data for research purposes (e.g., to group patients who have a similar disease). The hospital's security administrator may suppress some identifiers (e.g., name, address, phone number, etc) from patient records to meet privacy requirements. However, the released data may not be fully protected. A patient record may contain other information that can be linked with other datasets to re-identify individuals or entities (Samarati, 2001; Sweeney, 2002). How can we identify groups of patients with a similar pathology or characteristics without revealing the values of the attributes associated with them?

The above scenarios describe two different problems of privacy-preserving clustering (PPC). We refer to the former as PPC over centralized data and the latter as PPC over vertically partitioned data. To address these scenarios, we introduce a new PPC method called Dimensionality Reduction-Based Transformation (DRBT). This method allows data owners to find a trade-off between privacy, accuracy, and communication cost. Communication cost is the cost (typically in size) of the data exchanged between parties in order to achieve secure clustering.

Dimensionality reduction techniques have been studied in the context of pattern recognition (Fukunaga, 1990), information retrieval (Bingham & Mannila, 2001; Faloutsos & Lin, 1995; Jagadish, 1991), and data mining (Fern &

Brodley, 2003; Faloutsos & Lin, 1995). To the best of our knowledge, dimensionality reduction has not been used in the context of data privacy in any detail, except in (Oliveira & Zaïane, 2004b). Although there exists a number of methods for reducing the dimensionality of data, such as feature extraction methods (Kaski, 1999), multi-dimensional scaling (Young, 1987) and principal component analysis (PCA) (Fukunaga, 1990), this chapter focuses on random projection, a powerful method for dimensionality reduction. The accuracy obtained after the dimensionality has been reduced, using random projection, is almost as good as the original accuracy (Kaski, 1999; Achlioptas, 2001; Bingham & Mannila, 2001). More formally, when a vector in d-dimensional space is projected onto a random k dimensional subspace, the distances between any pair of points are not distorted by more than a factor of $(1 \pm \varepsilon)$, for any $0 < \varepsilon < 1$, with probability $O(1/n^2)$, where n is the number of objects under analysis (Johnson & Lindenstrauss, 1984).

The motivation for exploring random projection is based on the following aspects. First, it is a general data reduction technique. In contrast to the other methods, such as PCA, random projection does not use any defined interestingness criterion to optimize the projection. Second, random projection has shown to have promising theoretical properties for high dimensional data clustering (Fern & Brodley, 2003; Bingham & Mannila, 2001). Third, despite its computational simplicity, random projection does not introduce a significant distortion in the data. Finally, the dimensions found by random projection are not a subset of the original dimensions but rather a transformation, which is relevant for privacy preservation.

In this work, random projection is used to mask the underlying attribute values subjected to clustering, protecting them from being revealed. In tandem with the benefit of privacy preservation, the method DRBT benefits from the fact that random projection preserves the distances

(or similarities) between data objects quite nicely, which is desirable in cluster analysis. We show analytically and experimentally that using DRBT, a data owner can meet privacy requirements without losing the benefit of clustering. The major features of our method DRBT are: a) it is independent of distance-based clustering algorithms; b) it has a sound mathematical foundation; and c) it does not require CPU intensive operations.

This chapter is organized as follows. In the next section, we provide the basic concepts that are necessary to understand the issues addressed in this chapter. We then describe the research problem employed in our study. Subsequently, we introduce our method DRBT to address PPC over centralized data and over vertically partitioned data. A taxonomy of PPC solutions is then introduced. Subsequently, the experimental results are presented followed by our conclusions.

BACKGROUND

In this section, we briefly review the basics of clustering, notably the concepts of data matrix and dissimilarity matrix. Subsequently, we review the basics of dimensionality reduction. In particular, we focus on the background of random projection.

Data Matrix

Objects (e.g., individuals, observations, events) are usually represented as points (vectors) in a multi-dimensional space. Each dimension represents a distinct attribute describing the object. Thus, objects are represented as an $m \times n$ matrix D, where there are m rows, one for each object, and n columns, one for each attribute. This matrix may contain binary, categorical, or numerical attributes. It is referred to as a data matrix, represented as follows:

$$D = \begin{bmatrix} a_{11} & \cdots & a_{1k} & \cdots & a_{1n} \\ a_{21} & \cdots & a_{2k} & \cdots & a_{2n} \\ \vdots & & \vdots & \ddots & \vdots \\ a_{m1} & \cdots & a_{mk} & \cdots & a_{mn} \end{bmatrix} \quad (1)$$

The attributes in a data matrix are sometimes transformed before being used. The main reason is that different attributes may be measured on different scales (e.g., centimeters and kilograms). When the range of values differs widely from attribute to attribute, attributes with large range can influence the results of the cluster analysis. For this reason, it is common to standardize the data so that all attributes are on the same scale. There are many methods for data normalization (Han & Kamber, 2001). We review only two of them in this section: *min-max normalization* and *z-score normalization*.

Min-max normalization performs a linear transformation on the original data. Each attribute is normalized by scaling its values so that they fall within a small specific range, such as 0.0 and 1.0. Min-max normalization maps a value v of an attribute A to v' as follows:

$$v' = \frac{v - min_A}{max_A - min_A} \times (new\_max_A - new\_min_A) + new\_min_A$$

$$(2)$$

where min_A and max_A represent the minimum and maximum values of an attribute A, respectively, while new_min_A and new_max_A are the new range in which the normalized data will fall. When the actual minimum and maximum of an attribute are unknown, or when there are outliers that dominate the min-max normalization, z-score normalization (also called zero-mean normalization) should be used. In z-score normalization, the values for an attribute A are normalized based on the mean and the standard deviation of A. A value v is mapped to v' as follows:

$$v' = \frac{v - \overline{A}}{\sigma_A} \quad (3)$$

where $\overline{A}$ and σ_A are the mean and the standard deviation of the attribute A, respectively.

Dissimilarity Matrix

A dissimilarity matrix stores a collection of proximities that are available for all pairs of objects. This matrix is often represented by an $m \times m$ table such as:

$$DM = \begin{bmatrix} 0 & & & & \\ d(2,1) & 0 & & & \\ d(3,1) & d(3,2) & 0 & & \\ \cdots & \cdots & \cdots & & \\ d(m,1) & d(m,2) & \cdots & \cdots & 0 \end{bmatrix} \quad (4)$$

We can see the dissimilarity matrix DM corresponding to the data matrix D in *(1)*, where each element $d(i, j)$ represents the difference or dissimilarity between objects i and j. In general, $d(i,j)$ is a non-negative number that is close to zero when the objects i and j are very similar to each other, and becomes larger the more they differ. Several distance measures could be used to calculate the dissimilarity matrix of a set of points in d-dimensional space (Han & Kamber, 2001). The Euclidean distance is the most popular distance measure. If $i = (x_{i1}, x_{i2}, ..., x_{in})$ and $j = (x_{j1}, x_{j2}, ..., x_{jn})$ are n-dimensional data objects, the Euclidean distance between i and j is given by:

$$d(i,j) = \sqrt{\sum_{k=1}^{n} |x_{ik} - x_{jk}|^2} \quad (5)$$

The Euclidean distance satisfies the following constraints:

- $d(i, j) \geq 0$: distance is a non-negative number.
- $d(i, i) = 0$: the distance of an object to itself.
- $d(i, j) = d(j, i)$: distance is a symmetric function.

- $d(i, j) \leq d(i, k) + d(k, j)$: distance satisfies the triangular inequality.

Dimensionality Reduction

In many applications of data mining, the high dimensionality of the data restricts the choice of data processing methods. Examples of such applications include market basket data, text classification, and clustering. In these cases, the dimensionality is large due to either a wealth of alternative products, a large vocabulary, or an expressive number of attributes to be analyzed in Euclidean space, respectively.

When data vectors are defined in a high-dimensional space, it is computationally intractable to use data analysis or pattern recognition algorithms which repeatedly compute similarities or distances in the original data space. It is therefore necessary to reduce the dimensionality before, for instance, clustering the data (Kaski, 1999; Fern & Brodley, 2003).

The goal of the methods designed for dimensionality reduction is to map d-dimensional objects into k-dimensional objects, where $k \ll d$ (Kruskal & Wish, 1978). These methods map each object to a point in a k-dimensional space minimizing the stress function:

$$stress^2 = \frac{\sum_{i,j}\left(\hat{d}_{ij} - d_{ij}\right)^2}{\sum_{i,j}d_{ij}^2} \qquad (6)$$

where d_{ij} is the dissimilarity measure between objects i and j in a d-dimensional space, and $\hat{d}_{ij}$ is the dissimilarity measure between objects i and j in a k-dimensional space. The function *stress* gives the relative error that the distances in k-d space suffer from, on the average.

There are numerous methods for reducing the dimensionality of data, ranging from different feature extraction methods to multidimensional scaling. The feature extraction methods are often performed according to the nature of the data, and therefore they are not generally applicable in all data mining tasks (Kaski, 1999). The multidimensional scaling (MDS) methods, on the other hand, have been used in several diverse fields (e.g, social sciences, psychology, market research, and physics) to analyze subjective evaluations of pairwise similarities of entities (Young, 1987).

Another alternative for dimensionality reduction is to project the data onto a lower-dimensional orthogonal subspace that captures as much of the variation of the data as possible. The best and most widely way to do so is Principal Component Analysis (Fukunaga, 1990). Principal component analysis (PCA) involves a mathematical procedure that transforms a number of (possibly) correlated variables into a smaller number of uncorrelated variables called principal components. The first principal component accounts for as much of the variability in the data as possible, and each succeeding component accounts for as much of the remaining variability as possible. Unfortunately, PCA is quite expensive to compute for high-dimensional datasets.

Although the above methods have been widely used in data analysis and compression, these methods are computationally costly and if the dimensionality of the original data points is very high it is infeasible to apply these methods to dimensionality reduction.

Random projection has recently emerged as a powerful method for dimensionality reduction.

The accuracy obtained after the dimensionality has been reduced, using random projection, is almost as good as the original accuracy (Kaski, 1999; Achlioptas, 2001; Bingham & Mannila, 2001). The key idea of random projection arises from the Johnson-Lindenstrauss lemma (Johnson & Lindenstrauss, 1984): "if points in a vector space are projected onto a randomly selected subspace of suitably high dimension, then the distances between the points are approximately preserved."

Lemma 1 *(Johnson & Lindenstrauss, 1984).*
Given $\varepsilon > 0$ and an integer n, let k be a positive integer such that $k \geq k_0 = O(\varepsilon^{-2}log\ n)$. For every set P of n points in $\mathfrak{R}^d$ there exists f: $\mathfrak{R}^d \rightarrow \mathfrak{R}^k$ such that for all u, v $\boxtimes$ P $(1-\varepsilon)\|u-v\|^2 \leq \|f(u)-f(v)\|^2 \leq (1+\varepsilon)\|u-v\|^2$.

The classic result of Johnson and Lindenstrauss (Johnson & Lindenstrauss, 1984) asserts that any set of *n* points in *d*-dimensional Euclidean space can be embedded into *k*-dimensional space, where *k* is logarithmic in *n* and independent of *d*.

In this work, we focus on random projection for privacy-preserving clustering. Our motivation for exploring random projection is based on the following aspects. First, it is a general data reduction technique. In contrast to the other methods, such as PCA, random projection does not use any defined interestingness criterion to optimize the projection. Second, random projection has shown to have promising theoretical properties for high dimensional data clustering (Fern & Brodley, 2003; Bingham & Mannila, 2001). Third, despite its computational simplicity, random projection does not introduce a significant distortion in the data. Finally, the dimensions found by random projection are not a subset of the original dimensions but rather a transformation, which is relevant for privacy preservation. We provide the background of random projection in the next section.

Random Projection

A random projection from *d* dimensions to *k* dimensions is a linear transformation represented by a *d×k* matrix *R*, which is generated by first setting each entry of the matrix to a value drawn from an i.i.d. $\sim N(0,1)$ distribution (i.e., zero mean and unit variance) and then normalizing the columns to unit length. Given a *d*-dimensional dataset represented as an $n \times d$ matrix *D*, the mapping $D \times R$ results in a reduced-dimension dataset *D'*, i.e.,

$$D'_{n \times k} = D_{n \times d} R_{d \times k} \tag{7}$$

Random projection is computationally very simple. Given the random matrix *R* and projecting the $n \times d$ matrix *D* into *k* dimensions is of the order $O(ndk)$, and if the matrix *D* is sparse with about *c* nonzero entries per column, the complexity is of the order $O(cnk)$ (Papadimitriou, Tamaki, Raghavan, & Vempala, 1998).

After applying random projection to a dataset, the distance between two *d*-dimensional vectors *i* and *j* is approximated by the scaled Euclidean distance of these vectors in the reduced space as follows:

$$\sqrt{\frac{d}{k}}\|R_i - R_j\| \tag{8}$$

where *d* is the original and *k* the reduced dimensionality of the dataset. The scaling term $\sqrt{d/k}$ takes into account the decrease in the dimensionality of the data.

To satisfy Lemma 1, the random matrix *R* must hold the follow constraints:

- The columns of the random matrix *R* are composed of orthonormal vectors, i.e, they have unit length and are orthogonal.
- The elements r_{ij} of *R* have zero mean and unit variance.

Clearly, the choice of the random matrix *R* is one of the key points of interest. The elements r_{ij} of *R* are often Gaussian distributed, but this need not to be the case. Achlioptas (Achlioptas, 2001) showed that the Gaussian distribution can be replaced by a much simpler distribution, as follows:

$$r_{ij} = \sqrt{3} \times \begin{cases} +1 & with \quad probability \quad 1/6 \\ 0 & with \quad probability \quad 2/3 \\ -1 & with \quad probability \quad 1/6 \end{cases} \tag{9}$$

In fact, practically all zero mean, unit variance distributions of r_{ij} would give a mapping that still satisfies the Johnson-Lindenstrauss lemma. Achlioptas' result means further computational savings in database applications since the computations can be performed using integer arithmetic.

PROBLEM DEFINITION

The goal of privacy-preserving clustering is to protect the underlying attribute values of objects subjected to clustering analysis. In doing so, the privacy of individuals would be protected.

The problem of privacy preservation in clustering can be stated as follows: Let D be a relational database and C a set of clusters generated from D. The goal is to transform D into D' so that the following restrictions hold:

- A transformation T when applied to D must preserve the privacy of individual records, so that the released database D' conceals the values of confidential attributes, such as salary, disease diagnosis, credit rating, and others.
- The similarity between objects in D' must be the same as that one in D, or just slightly altered by the transformation process. Although the transformed database D' looks very different from D, the clusters in D and D' should be as close as possible since the distances between objects are preserved or marginally changed.

We will approach the problem of PPC by first dividing it into two sub-problems: PPC over centralized data and PPC over vertically partitioned data. In the centralized data approach, different entities are described with the same schema in a unique centralized data repository, while in a vertical partition, the attributes of the same entities are split across the partitions. We do not address the case of horizontally partitioned data.

PPC over Centralized Data

In this scenario, two parties, **A** and **B**, are involved, party **A** owning a dataset D and party **B** wanting to mine it for clustering. In this context, the data are assumed to be a matrix $D_{m \times n}$, where each of the m rows represents an object, and each object contains values for each of the n attributes.

We assume that the matrix $D_{m \times n}$ contains numerical attributes only, and the attribute values associated with an object are private and must be protected. After transformation, the attribute values of an object in D would look very different from the original. Therefore, miners would rely on the transformed data to build valid results, i.e., clusters.

Before sharing the dataset D with party **B**, party **A** must transform D to preserve the privacy of individual data records. However, the transformation applied to D must not jeopardize the similarity between objects. Our second real-life motivating example, in the Introduction of this chapter, is a particular case of PPC over centralized data.

PPC over Vertically Partitioned Data

Consider a scenario wherein k parties, such that $k \geq 2$, have different attributes for a common set of objects, as mentioned in the first real-life example, in Section *Introduction*. Here, the goal is to do a join over the k parties and cluster the common objects. The data matrix for this case is given as follows:

$$
\begin{array}{cccc}
Party_1 & Party_2 & \cdots & Party_k
\end{array}
$$
$$
\begin{bmatrix}
a_{11} & \cdots & a_{1i} & a_{1i+1} & \cdots & a_{1j} & a_{1p+1} & \cdots & a_{1n} \\
& \vdots & & & \vdots & & \cdots & \vdots & \\
a_{m1} & \cdots & a_{mi} & a_{mi+1} & \cdots & a_{mj} & a_{mp+1} & \cdots & a_{mn}
\end{bmatrix}
$$

$$(10)$$

Note that, after doing a join over the k parties, the problem of PPC over vertically partitioned data becomes a problem of PPC over centralized data.

For simplicity, we do not consider communication cost here since this issue is addressed later.

In our model for PPC over vertically partitioned data, one of the parties is the central one which is in charge of merging the data and finding the clusters in the merged data. After finding the clusters, the central party would share the clustering results with the other parties. The challenge here is how to move the data from each party to a central party concealing the values of the attributes of each party. However, before moving the data to a central party, each party must transform its data to protect the privacy of the attribute values. We assume that the existence of an object (ID) should be revealed for the purpose of the join operation, but the values of the associated attributes are private.

The Communication Protocol

To address the problem of PPC over vertically partitioned data, we need to design a communication protocol. This protocol is used between two parties: the first party is the central one and the other represents any of the $k - 1$ parties, assuming that we have k parties. We refer to the central party as *party(c)* and any of the other parties as *party(k)*. There are two threads on the *party(k)* side, one for selecting the attributes to be shared, as can be seen in Table 1, and the other for selecting the objects before the sharing data, as can be seen in Table 2.

THE DIMENSIONALITY REDUCTION-BASED TRANSFORMATION

In this section, we show that the triple-goal of achieving privacy preservation and valid clustering results at a reduced communication cost in PPC can be accomplished by dimensionality reduction. By reducing the dimensionality of a dataset to a sufficiently small value, one can find a trade-off between privacy, accuracy, and communication cost. In particular, random project can fulfill this triple-goal. We refer to this solution as the Dimensionality Reduction-Based Transformation (DRBT).

General Assumptions

The solution to the problem of PPC based on random projection draws the following assumptions:

- The data matrix D subjected to clustering contains only numerical attributes that must be transformed to protect individuals' data values before the data sharing for clustering occurs.
- In PPC over centralized data, the existence of an object (ID) should be replaced by a fictitious identifier. In PPC over vertically partitioned data, the IDs of the objects are used for the join purposes between the parties involved in the solution, and the existence of an object at a site is not considered private.

Table 1. Thread of selecting the attributes on the party(k) side

Steps to select the attributes for clustering on the *party(k)* side:
1. Negotiate the attributes for clustering before the sharing of data.
2. Wait for the list of attributes available in *party(c)*.
3. Upon receiving the list of attributes from *party(c)*:   Select the attributes of the objects to be shared.

Table 2. Thread of selecting the objects on the party(k) side

Steps to select the list of objects on the *party(k)* side:

1. Negotiate the list of *m* objects before the sharing of data.
2. Wait for the list of *m* object IDs.
3. Upon receiving the list of *m* object IDs from *party(c)*:
  a) Select the *m* objects to be shared;
  b) Transform the attribute values of the *m* objects;
  c) Send the transformed *m* objects to *party(c)*.

- The transformation (random projection) applied to the original data might slightly modify the distance between data points. Such a transformation justifies the trade-off between privacy, accuracy, and communication cost.

One interesting characteristic of the solution based on random projection is that, once the dimensionality of a database is reduced, the attribute names in the released database are irrelevant. In other words, the released database preserves, in general, the similarity between the objects, but the underlying data values are completely different from the original ones. We refer to the released database as a *disguised database*, which is shared for clustering.

PPC over Centralized Data

To address PPC over centralized data, the DRBT performs three major steps before sharing the data for clustering:

- *Step 1 - Suppressing identifiers*: Attributes that are not subjected to clustering (e.g., address, phone number, etc.) are suppressed.
- *Step 2 - Reducing the dimension of the original dataset*: After pre-processing the data according to *Step 1*, an original dataset *D* is then transformed into the disguised dataset *D'* using random projection.
- *Step 3 - Computing the stress function*: This function is used to determine whether the accuracy of the transformed dataset is marginally modified, which guarantees the usefulness of the data for clustering. A data owner can compute the stress function using Equation (6).

To illustrate how this solution works, let us consider the sample relational database in Table 3.

This sample contains real data from the Cardiac Arrhythmia Database available at the UCI Repository of Machine Learning Databases (Blake & Merz, 1998). The attributes for this example are: *age*, *weight*, *h rate* (number of heart beats per minute), *int def* (number of intrinsic deflections), *QRS* (average of QRS duration in msec.), and *PR int* (average duration between onset of P and Q waves in msec.).

We are going to reduce the dimension of this dataset from 6 to 3, one at a time, and compute the error (stress function). To reduce the dimension of this dataset, we apply Equation (7). In set corresponds to the matrix *D*. We compute a random matrix R_1 by setting each entry of the

Table 3. A cardiac arrhythmia database

ID	age	weight	H_rate	Int_def	QRS	PR_int
123	75	80	63	32	91	193
342	56	64	53	24	81	174
254	40	52	70	24	77	129
446	28	58	76	40	83	251
286	44	90	68	44	109	128

Table 4. The relative error that the distances in 6-3 space suffer from, on the average

Transformations	k=6	k=5	k=4	K=3
RP_1	0.0000	0.0223	0.0490	0.2425
RP_2	0.0000	0.0281	0.0375	0.1120

matrix to a value drawn from an independent and identically distributed (i.i.d.) $N(0,1)$ distribution and then normalizing the columns to unit length. We also compute a random matrix R_2 where each element r_{ij} is computed using Equation (9). We transform D into D' using both R_1 and R_2. The random transformation RP_1 refers to the random projection using R_1, and RP_2 refers to the random projection using R_2.

The relative error that the distances in 6-3 space suffer from, on the average, is computed using Equation (6). Table 4 shows the values of the error using RP_1 and RP_2. In this Table, k represents the number of dimensions in the disguised database D'.

In this case, we have reduced the dimension of D from 6 to 3, i.e, the transformed dataset has only 50% of the dimensions in the original dataset. Note that the error is relatively small for both RP_1 and RP_2, especially for RP_2. However, this error is minimized when the random projection is applied to high dimensional datasets, as can be seen in Figure 2, in Section *Measuring the effectiveness of the DRBT Over Centralized Data.*

After applying random projection to a dataset, the attribute values of the transformed dataset are completely disguised to preserve the privacy of individuals. Table 5 shows the attribute values of the transformed database with 3 dimensions, using both RP_1 and RP_2. In this table, we have the attributes labeled *Att1, Att2,* and *Att3* since we do not know the labels for the disguised dataset. Using random projection, one cannot select the attributes to be reduced beforehand. The attributes are reduced randomly. More formally, $\forall i$ if $Attr_i \in D'$, then $Attr_i \notin D$.

As can be seen in Table 5, the attribute values are entirely different from those in Table 3.

PPC over Vertically Partitioned Data

The solution for PPC over vertically partitioned data is a generalization of the solution for PPC over centralized data. In particular, if we have k parties involved in this case, each party must apply the random projection over its dataset and then send the reduced data matrix to a central party. Note that any of the k parties can be the central one. When k parties ($k \geq 2$) share some data for PPC over vertically partitioned data, these parties must satisfy the following constraints:

Table 5. Disguised dataset D_ using RP1 and RP2

ID	D' using RP_1			D' using RP_2		
	Att1	Att2	Att3	Att1	Att2	Att3
123	-50.40	17.33	12.31	-55.50	-95.26	-107.96
342	-37.08	6.27	12.22	-51.00	-84.29	-83.13
254	-55.86	20.69	-0.66	-65.50	-70.43	-66.97
446	-37.61	-31.66	-17.58	-85.50	-140.87	-72.74
286	-62.72	37.64	18.16	-88.50	-50.22	-102.76

- *Agreement*: The k parties must follow the communication protocol described in Section *The communication protocol*.
- *Mutual exclusivity*: We assume that the attribute split across the k parties are mutually exclusive. More formally, if $A(D1)$, $A(D2)...,A(Dk)$ are a set of attributes of the k parties, $\forall i \neq j\ A(Di) \cap A(Dj) = \phi$. The only exception is that IDs are shared for the join purpose.

The solution based on random projection for PPC over vertically partitioned data is performed as follows:

- *Step 1 - Individual transformation*: If k parties, $k \geq 2$, share their data in a collaborative project for clustering, each party k_i must transform its data according to the steps in Section *PPC Over Centralized Data*.
- *Step 2 - Data exchanging or sharing*: Once the data are disguised by using random projection, the k parties are able to exchange the data among themselves. However, one party could be the central one to aggregate and cluster the data.
- *Step 3 - Sharing clustering results*: After the data have been aggregated and mined in a central party k_j, the results could be shared with the other parties.

How Secure is the DRBT?

In the previous sections, we showed that transforming a database using random projection is a promising solution for PPC over centralized data and consequently for PPC over vertically partitioned data since the similarities between objects are marginally changed. Now we show that random projection also has promising theoretical properties for privacy preservation. In particular, we demonstrate that a random projection from d dimensions to k, where $k \ll d$, is a non-invertible transformation.

Lemma 2 *A random projection from d dimensions to k dimensions, where k ≪ d, is a noninvertible linear transformation.*

Proof: A classic result from Linear Algebra asserts that there is no invertible linear transformation between Euclidean spaces of different dimensions (Auer, 1991). Thus, if there is an invertible linear transformations from $\Re^m$ to $\Re^n$, then the constraint $m = n$ must hold. A random projection is a linear transformation from $\Re^d$ to $\Re^k$, where $k \ll d$. Hence, a random projection from d dimensions to k dimensions is a non-invertible linear transformation.

Even when sufficient care is taken, a solution that adheres to DRBT can be still vulnerable to disclosure. For instance, if an adversary knows the positions of $d + 1$ points (where d is the number of dimensions), and the distances between these points, then one can make some estimates of the coordinates of all points. However, it is important to note that the violation of the solution that adheres to DRBT becomes progressively harder as the number of attributes (dimensions) in a database increases since an adversary would need to know $d + 1$ points to disclose the original data. On the other hand, when the number of dimensions grows, the accuracy regarding the distances between points is improved.

The Accuracy of the DRBT

When using random projection, a perfect reproduction of the Euclidean distances may not be the best possible result. The clusters in the transformed datasets should be equal to those in the original database. However, this is not always the case, and we have some potential problems after dimensionality reduction: a) a noise data point ends up clustered; b) a point from a cluster becomes a noise point; and c) a point from a cluster migrates to a different cluster. In this research, we focus primarily on partitioning methods. In particular, we use K-means (Macqueen, 1967), one of the most used clustering algorithms. Since K-means is sensitive to noise points and clusters all the points in a dataset, we have to deal with the third problem mentioned above (a point from a cluster migrates to a different cluster).

Our evaluation approach focuses on the overall quality of generated clusters after dimensionality reduction. We compare how closely each cluster in the transformed data matches its corresponding cluster in the original dataset. To do so, we first identify the matching of clusters by computing the matrix of frequencies showed in Table 6. We refer to such a matrix as the clustering membership matrix (CMM), where the rows represent the clusters in the original dataset, the columns represent the clusters in the transformed dataset, and $freq_{i,j}$ is the number of points in cluster c_i that falls in cluster c'_j in the transformed dataset.

After computing the frequencies $freq_{i,j}$, we scan the clustering membership matrix calculating precision, recall, and F-measure for each cluster c'_j with respect to c_i in the original dataset (Larsen & Aone, 1999). These formulas are given by the following equations:

$$Pr\,ecision(P) = \frac{freq_{i,j}}{\left|c'_i\right|} \qquad (11)$$

$$Re\,call(R) = \frac{freq_{i,j}}{\left|c_i\right|} \qquad (12)$$

$$F - measure(F) = \frac{2 \times P \times R}{(P + R)} \qquad (13)$$

Table 6. The number of points in cluster c_i that falls in cluster c'_j in the transformed dataset

	c'_1	c'_2	...	c'_k
c_1	$freq_{1,1}$	$freq_{1,2}$	...	$freq_{1,k}$
c_2	$freq_{2,1}$	$freq_{2,2}$	...	$freq_{2,k}$
...	...	...	...	...
c_k	$freq_{k,1}$	$freq_{k,2}$	...	$freq_{k,k}$

where $|X|$ is the number of points in the cluster X.

For each cluster c_i, we first find a cluster c'_j that has the highest F-measure among all the c'_l, $1 \leq l \leq k$. Let $F(c_i)$ be the highest F-measure for cluster c_i, we denote the overall F-measure (OF) as the weighted average of $F(c_i)$, $1 \leq i \leq k$, as follows:

$$OF = \frac{\sum_{i=1}^{k}\left|c_i\right| \times F(c_i)}{\sum_{i=1}^{k}\left|c_i\right|} \qquad (14)$$

In the section *Experimental Results*, we present our performance evaluation results for clustering based on Equation (14).

The Complexity of the DRBT

One of the major benefits of a solution that adheres to the DRBT is the communication cost to send a disguised dataset from one party to a central one. In general, a disguised data matrix is of size $m \times k$, where m is the number of objects and k is the number of attributes (dimensions).

The complexity of DRBT is of the order $O(m \times k)$, however $k \ll m$.

To quantify the communication cost of one solution, we consider the number of bits or words required to transmit a dataset from one party to a central or third party. Using DRBT, the bit communication cost to transmit a dataset from one party to another is $O(mlk)$, where l represents the size (in bits) of one element of the $m \times k$ disguised data matrix.

A TAXONOMY OF PPC SOLUTIONS

Some effort has been made to address the problem of PPC. In this section, we present a taxonomy of the existing solutions. We categorize these solutions into two major groups: *PPC over centralized data* and *PPC over distributed data*. In the former approach, different objects are described with the same schema in a unique centralized data repository, while in the latter approach, either the attributes or the records of objects are split across many partitions.

Solutions for PPC Over Centralized Data

Methods for PPC over centralized data are categorized into two groups: *Attribute Masking* and *Pairwise Object Similarity*.

Attribute value masking: This data transformation makes the original attribute values difficult to perceive or understand and preserves all the information for clustering analysis. Our data transformation that falls into this category is called Rotation-Based Transformation (RBT) (Oliveira & Zaïane, 2004a). The idea behind this technique is that the attributes of a database are split into pairwise attributes selected randomly. One attribute can be selected and rotated more than once, and the angle θ between an attribute pair is also selected randomly. RBT can be seen as a technique bording obfuscation. Obfuscation techniques aim at making information highly illegible without actually changing its inner meaning (Collberg, Thomborson & Low, 1997). In other words, using RBT the original data are masked so that the transformed data capture all the information for clustering analysis while protecting the underlying data values. One interesting application of RBT is privacy preservation of health data (Armstrong, Rushton & Zimmerman, 1999).

Pairwise object similarity: This technique is a data matrix representation in which a data owner shares the distance between data objects instead of the location of the data points. This technique relies on the idea of the similarity between objects, i.e., a data owner shares some data for clustering analysis by simply computing the dissimilarity matrix (matrix of distances) between the objects and then sharing such a matrix with a third party (Oliveira & Zaïane, 2004b). This solution is simple to implement and addresses PPC over centralized

data. One of the most important advantages of this solution is that it can be applied to either categorical, binary, numerical attributes, or even a combination of these attributes. On the other hand, this solution can sometimes be restrictive since it requires a high communication cost.

Solutions for PPC Over Distributed Data

Regarding PPC over distributed data, we classify the existing solutions in two groups: *PPC over vertically partitioned data* and *PPC over horizontally partitioned data*.

Vertically partitioned data: In a vertical partition approach, the attributes of the same objects are split across the partitions. The idea behind this solution is that two or more parties want to conduct a computation based on their private inputs. The issue here is how to conduct such a computation so that no party knows anything except its own input and the results. This problem is referred to as the secure multi-party computation problem (Goldreich, Micali & Wigderson, 1987; Pinkas, 2002). The existing solution that falls in this category was introduced in (Vaidya & Clifton, 2003). Specifically, a method for k-means was proposed when different sites contain different attributes for a common set of entities. In this solution, each site learns the global clusters, but learns nothing about the attributes at other sites. This work ensures reasonable privacy while limiting communication cost.

Horizontally partitioned data: In a horizontal partition approach, different objects are described with the same schema in all partitions. A solution for PPC over horizontally partitioned data was proposed in (Meregu & Ghosh, 2003). This solution is based on generative models. In this approach, rather than sharing parts of the original data or perturbed data, the parameters of suitable generative models are built at each local site. Then such parameters are transmitted to a central location. The best representative of all data is a certain "mean" model. It was empirically shown that such a model can be approximated by generating artificial samples from the underlying distributions using Markov Chain Monte Carlo techniques. This approach achieves high quality distributed clustering with acceptable privacy loss and low communication cost.

Attribute reduction: This is the approach presented in this chapter: the attributes of a database are reduced to a smaller number. The small number of attributes is not a subset of the original attributes since the transformation disguises the original attribute values by projecting them onto a random space. Our data transformation that lies in this category is called Dimensionality Reduction-Based Transformation (DRBT) (Oliveira & Zaïane, 2004b). This data transformation can be applied to both PPC over centralized data and PPC over vertically partitioned data. The idea behind this data transformation is that by reducing the dimensionality of a database to a sufficiently small value, one can find a trade-off between privacy and accuracy. Once the dimensionality of a database is reduced, the released database preserves (or slightly modifies) the distances between data points. In tandem with the benefit of preserving the similarity between points, this solution protects individuals' privacy since the underlying data values of the objects subjected

to clustering are completely different from the original ones.

As can be seen in Figure 1, the only solution to address both PPC over centralized data and PPC over distributed data is the DRBT.

EXPERIMENTAL RESULTS

In this section, we empirically validate our method DRBT. We start by describing the real datasets used in our experiments. We then describe the methodology used to validate our method. Subsequently, we study the effectiveness of our method to address PPC over centralized data and PPC over vertically partitioned data. We conclude this section discussing the main lessons learned from our experiments.

Datasets

We validated our method DRBT for privacy-preserving clustering using five real datasets. These datasets are described as follows:

1. **Accidents:** This dataset concerning traffic accidents was obtained from the National Institute of Statistics (NIS) for the region of Flanders in Belgium. The transactions are

Figure 1. A taxonomy of PPC solutions

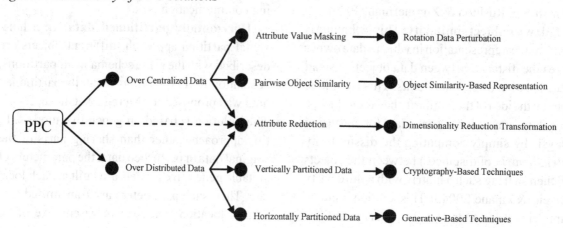

traffic accident forms filled out by police officers for each traffic accident that occurred involving injuries or deaths on a public road in Belgium. There are 340,183 traffic accident records included in the dataset. We used 18 columns of this dataset after removing missing values.

2. **Mushroom:** This dataset is available at the UCI Repository of Machine Learning Databases (Blake & Merz, 1998). Mushroom contains records drawn from The Audubon Society Field Guide to North American Mushrooms. There are 8,124 records and 23 numerical attributes.

3. **Chess:** The format for instances in this database is a sequence of 37 attribute values. Each instance is a board-descriptions of a chess endgame. The first 36 attributes describe the board. The last (37th) attribute is the classification: "win" or "nowin". Chess is available at the UCI Repository of Machine Learning Databases (Blake & Merz, 1998) and contains 3,196 records. There is no missing value in this dataset.

4. **Connect:** This database contains all legal 8-ply positions in the game of connect-4 in which neither player has won yet, and in which the next move is not forced. Connect is composed of 67,557 records and 43 attributes without missing values. This dataset is also available at the UCI Repository of Machine Learning Databases (Blake & Merz, 1998).

5. **Pumsb:** The Pumsb dataset contains census data for population and housing. This dataset is available at http://www.almaden. ibm.com/software/quest. There are 49,046 records and 74 attribute values without missing values.

Table 7 shows the summary of the datasets used in our experiments. The columns represent, respectively, the database name, the total number of records, and the number of attributes in each dataset.

Table 7. A summary of the datasets used in our experiments

Dataset	# Records	# Attributes
Accidents	340,183	18
Mushroom	8,124	23
Chess	3,196	37
Connect	67,557	43
Pumsb	49,046	74

Methodology

We performed two series of experiments to evaluate the effectiveness of DRBT when addressing PPC over centralized data and PPC over vertically partitioned data. Our evaluation approach focused on the overall quality of generated clusters after dimensionality reduction. One question that we wanted to answer was: *What is the quality of the clustering results mined from the transformed data when the data are both sparse and dense?*

Our performance evaluation was carried out through the following steps:

Step 1: we normalized the attribute values of the five real datasets used in our experiments. To do so, we used the z-score normalization given in Equation (3). The results presented in the next sections were obtained after normalization.

Step 2: we considered random projection based on two different approaches. First, the traditional way to compute random projection, by setting each entry of the random matrix R_1 to a value drawn from an i.i.d. $N(0,1)$ distribution and then normalizing the columns to unit length. Second, we used the random matrix R_2 where each element r_{ij} is computed using Equation (9). We refer to the former random projection as RP_1 and the latter as RP_2. We repeated each experiment (for random projection) 5 times. In the next section, we present results by showing only the average value.

Step 3: we computed the relative error that the distances in *d-k* space suffer from, on the average, by using the stress function given in Equation (6). The stress function was computed for each dataset.

Step 4: we selected K-means to find the clusters in our performance evaluation. Our selection was influenced by the following aspects: (a) K-means is one of the best known clustering algorithm and is scalable; (b) When using random projection, a perfect reproduction of the Euclidean distances may not be the best possible result. However, the rank order of the distances between the vectors is meaningful. Thus, when running K-means over the transformed data, one can find the clusters that would be mined from the original datasets with a reasonable accuracy.

Step 5: we compared how closely each cluster in the transformed dataset matches its corresponding cluster in the original dataset. We expressed the quality of the generated clusters by computing the F-measure given in Equation (14). Considering that K-means is not deterministic (due to its use of random seed selection), we repeated each experiment 10 times. We then computed the minimum, average, maximum, and standard deviation for each measured value of the F-measure. We present the results by showing only the average value.

We should point out that the steps described above were performed to evaluate the effectiveness of the DRBT when addressing PPC over centralized and vertically partitioned data.

Measuring the Effectiveness of the DRBT over Centralized Data

To measure the effectiveness of DRBT in PPC over centralized data, we started by computing the relative error that the distances in *d-k* space suffer from, on the average. To do so, we used the two random projection approaches (RP_1 and RP_2) mentioned in Step 3 of Section *Methodology*.

A word of notation: hereafter we denote the original dimension of a dataset as d_o and reduced dimension of the transformed dataset as d_r. This notation is to avoid confusion between the reduced dimension of a dataset (k) and the number of clusters used as input of the algorithm K-means.

An important feature of the DRBT is its versatility to trade privacy, accuracy, and communication cost. The privacy preservation is assured because random projection is a non-invertible transformation, as discussed in Section *How Secure is the DRBT?* We here study the trade-off between accuracy and communication cost. The accuracy is represented by the error that the distances in d_o-d_r space suffer from, while the communication cost is represented by the number of dimensions that we reduce in the datasets. We selected two datasets: Pumsb and Chess with 74 and 37 dimensions, respectively. We reduced the dimensions of these datasets and computed the error. Figure 2(a) shows the error produced by RP_1 and RP_2 on the dataset Pumsb and Figure 2(b) shows the error produced by RP_1 and RP_2 on the dataset Chess. These results represent the average value of five trials. The error produced by RP_1 and RP_2 on the other datasets are available at Appendix A.

We observed that, in general, RP_2 yielded the best results in terms of the error produced on the datasets (the lower the better). In the dataset Chess the difference between RP_2 and RP_1 was not significant. These results confirm the same findings in (Bingham & Mannila, 2001) and backup the theory of random projection (the choice of the random matrix) proposed in (Achlioptas, 2001). We noticed from the figures that the DRBT trades well accuracy (error) and communication cost (number of reduced dimensions) when the data are reduced up to 50% of the dimensions. In this case, the trade-off between the error and the communication cost is linear. However, reducing more than 50% of the dimensions, the communication cost is improved but the accuracy is compromised since the error produced on the datasets grows faster. Therefore, a data owner should consider carefully this trade-off before releasing some data for clustering.

After evaluating the error produced on the datasets, we used the algorithm K-means to find the clusters in the original and transformed datasets. We varied the number of clusters from 2 to 5 in the five datasets. Subsequently, we compared how closely each cluster in the transformed dataset matches its corresponding cluster in the original dataset by computing the F-measure given in Equation (14).

Table 8 shows the results of the F-measure for the Accidents dataset. We reduced the original 18 dimensions to 12. We repeated each experiment 10 times and computed the minimum, average, maximum, and standard deviation for each measured value of the F-measure. We simplify the results by showing only one dataset (Accidents). The values of the F-measure for the other datasets can be found in Appendix B. Note that we computed the values of the F-measure only for the random projection RP_2 since its results were slightly better than those yielded by RP_1.

We noticed that the values of the F-measure for the Chess and Connect datasets (see Appendix B) were relatively low when compared with the results of the F-measure for the other datasets. The main reason is that the data points in these datasets are densely distributed. Thus, applying a partitioning clustering algorithm (e.g., K-means) to datasets of this nature increases the number of misclassified data points. On the other hand, when the attribute values of the objects are sparsely distributed, the clustering results are much better. Consider, for example, the Iris dataset available at the UCI Repository of Machine Learning Databases. Iris is perhaps the best known database to be found in the pattern recognition literature. This dataset has two clusters well defined and the data are sparsely distributed. We reduced the original 5 dimensions to 3. Then we applied random projection RP_2 to the Iris dataset and computed the minimum, average, maximum, and standard deviation for each measured value of the F-measure. We repeated each experiment 10 times. Table 9 shows that the standard deviation for two clusters ($k = 2$) was zero and the average of the F-measure was one.

Figure 2. (a) The error produced on the dataset Pumsb (do = 74); (b) The error produced on the dataset Chess (do = 37)

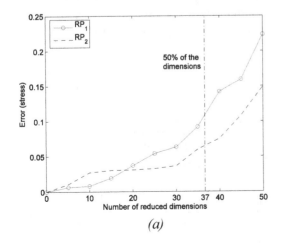
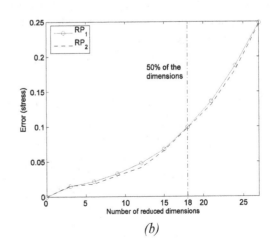

(a)   *(b)*

Table 8. Average of the F-measure (10 trials) for the Accidents dataset (do = 18, dr = 12)

Data Transformation	k=2				k=3			
	Min	Max	Avg	Std	Min	Max	Avg	Std
RP_2	0.931	0.952	0.941	0.014	0.903	0.921	0.912	0.009
Data Transformation	k=4				k=5			
	Min	Max	Avg	Std	Min	Max	Avg	Std
RP_2	0.870	0.891	0.881	0.010	0.878	0.898	0.885	0.006

Table 9. Average of the F-measure (10 trials) for the Iris dataset ($d_o = 5$, $d_r = 3$)

Data Transformation	k=2				k=3			
	Min	Max	Avg	Std	Min	Max	Avg	Std
RP_2	1.000	1.000	1.000	0.000	0.094	0.096	0.948	0.010
Data Transformation	k=4				k=5			
	Min	Max	Avg	Std	Min	Max	Avg	Std
RP_2	0.773	0.973	0.858	0.089	0.711	0.960	0.833	0.072

Measuring the Effectiveness of the DRBT over Vertically Partitioned Data

Now we move on to measure the effectiveness of DRBT to address PPC over vertically partitioned data. To do so, we split the Pumsb dataset (74 dimensions) from 1 up to 4 parties (partitions) and fixed the number of dimensions to be reduced (38 dimensions). Table 10 shows the number of parties, the number of attributes per party, and the number of attributes in the merged dataset which is subjected to clustering. Recall that in a vertically partitioned data approach, one of the parties will centralize the data before mining.

In this example, each partition with 37, 25, 24, 19, and 18 attributes was reduced to 19, 13, 12, 10, and 9 attributes, respectively. We applied the random projections RP_1 and RP_2 to each partition and then merged the partitions in one central repository. Subsequently, we computed the stress error on the merged dataset and compared the error with that one produced on the original dataset (without partitioning). Figure 3 shows the error produced on the Pumsb dataset in the vertically partitioned data approach. As we can see, the results yielded by RP_2 were again slightly better than those yielded by RP_1. Note that we reduced approximately 50% of the dimensions

Table 10. An example of partitioning for the Pumsb dataset

No. of parties	No. of attributes per party	No. of attributes in the merged dataset
1	1 partition with 74 attributes	38
2	2 partitions with 37 attributes	38
3	2 partitions with 25 and 1 with 24 attributes	38
4	2 partitions with 18 and 2 with 19 attributes	38

Figure 3. The error produced on the dataset Pumsb over vertically partitioned data

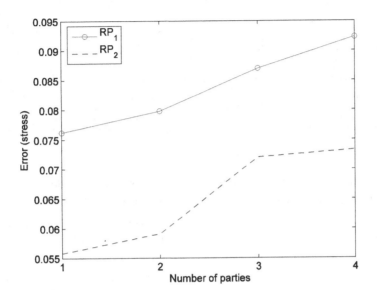

of the dataset Pumsb and the trade-off between accuracy and communication cost is still efficient for PPC over vertically partitioned data.

We also evaluated the quality of clusters generated by mining the merged dataset and comparing the clustering results with those mined from the original dataset. To do so, we computed the F-measure for the merged dataset in each scenario, i.e., from 1 up to 4 parties. We varied the number of clusters from 2 to 5. Table 11 shows values of the F-measure (average and standard deviation) for the Pumsb dataset over vertically partitioned data. These values represent the average of 10 trials considering the random projection RP_2.

We notice from Table 11 that the results of the F-measure slightly decrease when we increase the number of parties in the scenario of PPC over vertically partitioned data. Despite this fact, the DRBT is still effective to address PPC over vertically partitioned data in preserving the quality of the clustering results as measured by F-measure.

Discussion on the DRBT When Addressing PPC

The evaluation of the DRBT involves three important issues: security, communication cost, and quality of the clustering results. We previously discussed the issues of security based on Lemma 2, and the issues of communication cost and space requirements in Section *The Complexity of the DRBT*. In this Section, we have focused on the quality of the clustering results.

We have evaluated our proposed data transformation method (DRBT) to address PPC. We have learned some lessons from this evaluation, as follows:

- *The application domain of the DRBT:* we observed that the DRBT does not present acceptable clustering results in terms of accuracy when the data subjected to clustering are dense. Slightly changing the distances between data points by random projection results in misclassification, i.e., points will migrate from one cluster to another in

Table 11. Average of the F-measure (10 trials) for the Pumsb dataset over vertically partitioned data

No. of parties	k=2		k=3		k=4		k=5	
	Avg	Std	Avg	Std	Avg	Std	Avg	Std
1	0.909	0.140	0.965	0.081	0.891	0.028	0.838	0.041
2	0.904	0.117	0.931	0.101	0.894	0.059	0.840	0.047
3	0.874	0.168	0.887	0.095	0.873	0.081	0.801	0.073
4	0.802	0.155	0.812	0.117	0.866	0.088	0.831	0.078

the transformed dataset. This problem is somehow understandable since partitioning clustering methods are not effective to find clusters in dense data. The Connect dataset is one example which confirms this finding. On the other hand, our experiments demonstrated that the quality of the clustering results obtained from sparse data is promising.

- *The versatility of the DRBT*: using the DRBT, a data owner can tune the number of dimensions to be reduced in a dataset trading privacy, accuracy, and communication costs before sharing the dataset for clustering. Most importantly, the DRBT can be used to address PPC over centralized and vertically partitioned data.

- *The choice of the random matrix*: from the performance evaluation of the DRBT we noticed that the random projection RP_2 yielded the best results for the error produced on the datasets and the values of F-measure, in general. The random projection RP_2 is based on the random matrix proposed in Equation (9).

CONCLUSION

In this chapter, we introduced a new method to address Privacy-Preserving Clustering (PPC) over centralized data and over vertically partitioned data, called the Dimensionality Reduction-Based Transformation (DRBT) and showed analytically and experimentally that PPC is possible.

Our method was designed to support business collaboration considering privacy regulations, without losing the benefit of data analysis.

Random projection has recently emerged as a powerful method for dimensionality reduction. It preserves distances between data objects quite nicely, which is desirable in cluster analysis. Our privacy-preserving clustering method, DRBT, relies on the idea behind random projection to protect the underlying attribute values subjected to clustering.

We evaluated the DRBT taking into account three important issues: security, communication cost, and accuracy (quality of the clustering results). Our experiments revealed that using DRBT, a data owner can meet privacy requirements without losing the benefit of clustering since the similarity between data points is preserved or marginally changed. From the performance evaluation, we suggested guidance on which scenario a data owner can achieve the best quality of the clustering when using the DRBT. In addition, we suggested guidance on the choice of the random matrix to obtain the best results in terms of the error produced on the datasets and the values of F-measure.

The advantages of the DRBT are that the method is independent of distance-based clustering algorithms. We used k-means for our experiments but other clustering algorithms are also possible; DRBT has a sound mathematical foundation; the method does not require CPU-intensive operations; and it can be applied to address PPC over centralized data a well as PPC over vertically partitioned data.

REFERENCES

Achlioptas, D. (2001). Database-Friendly Random Projections. In Proc. of the 20th ACM Symposium on Principles of Database Systems (p. 274-281). Santa Barbara, CA, USA.

Armstrong, M. P.; Rushton, G.; Zimmerman, D. L. (1999). Geographically Masking Health Data to Preserve Confidentiality. *Statistics in Medicine, 18*, 497–525, 1999.

Auer, J. W. (1991). *Linear Algebra With Applications*. Prentice-Hall Canada Inc., Scarborough, Ontario, Canada.

Berry, M., & Linoff, G. (1997). *Data Mining Techniques - for Marketing, Sales, and Customer Support*. New York, USA: John Wiley and Sons.

Bingham, E., & Mannila, H. (2001). Random Projection in Dimensionality Reduction: Applications to Image and Text Data. *In Proc. of the 7th ACM SIGKDD International Conference on Knowledge Discovery and Data Mining* (pp. 245-250). San Francisco, CA, USA.

Blake, C., & Merz, C. (1998). *UCI Repository of Machine Learning Databases*, University of California, Irvine, Dept. of Information and Computer Sciences.

Collberg, C., Thomborson, C., & Low, D. (1997). *A Taxonomy of Obfuscating Transformations*. Technical report, TR–148, Department of Computer Science, University of Auckland, New Zealand, July.

Faloutsos, C., & Lin, K.-I. (1995). FastMap: A Fast Algorithm for Indexing, Data-Mining and Visualization of Traditional and Multimedia Datasets. *In Proc. of the 1995 ACM SIGMOD International Conference on Management of Data* (pp. 163-174). San Jose, CA, USA.

Fern, X. Z., & Brodley, C. E. (2003). Random Projection for High Dimensional Data Clustering: A Cluster Ensemble Approach. *In Proc. of the 20th International Conference on Machine Learning (ICML 2003)*. Washington DC, USA.

Fukunaga, K. (1990). Introduction to Statistical Pattern Recognition. 2nd. Edition. Academic Press.

Goldreich, O., Micali, S., & Wigderson, A. (1987). How to Play Any Mental Game - A Completeness Theorem for Protocols with Honest Majority. In *Proc. of the 19th Annual ACM Symposium on Theory of Computing*, (pp. 218–229), New York City, USA, May.

Han, J., & Kamber, M. (2006). *Data Mining: Concepts and Techniques*. Morgan Kaufmann Publishers, San Francisco, CA.

Jagadish, H. V. (1991). A Retrieval Technique For Similar Shapes. *In Proc. of the 1991 ACM SIGMOD International Conference on Management of Data* (pp. 208-217). Denver, Colorado, USA.

Johnson, W. B., & Lindenstrauss, J. (1984). Extensions of Lipshitz Mapping Into Hilbert Space. *In Proc. of the Conference in Modern Analysis and Probability* (pp. 189-206). Volume 26 of Contemporary Mathematics.

Kaski, S. (1999). Dimensionality Reduction by Random Mapping. *In Proc. of the International Joint Conference on Neural Networks* (pp. 413-418). Anchorage, Alaska.

Kruskal, J. B., & Wish, M. (1978). *Multidimensional Scaling*. Sage Publications, Beverly Hills, CA, USA.

Larsen, B., & Aone, C. (1999). Fast and Effective Text Mining Using Linear-Time Document Clustering. *In Proceedings of the 5th ACM SIGKDD International Conference on Knowledge Discovery and Data Mining* (pp. 16-22). San Diego, CA, USA.

Lo, V. S. Y. (2002). The True Lift Model - A Novel Data Mining Approach to Response Modeling in Database Marketing. *SIGKDD Explorations, 4*(2), 78-86.

Macqueen, J. (1967). Some Methods for Classification and Analysis of Multivariate Observations. *In Proc. of the 5th Berkeley Symposium on Mathematical Statistics and Probability* (pp. 281-297). Berkeley: University of California Press, Vol. 1.

Meregu, S., & Ghosh, J. (2003). Privacy-Preserving Distributed Clustering Using Generative Models. *In Proc. of the 3rd IEEE International Conference on Data Mining (ICDM'03)* (pp. 211-218). Melbourne, Florida, USA.

Oliveira, S. R. M., & Zaïane, O. R. (2004a). Achieving Privacy Preservation When Sharing Data For Clustering. In *Proc. of the Workshop on Secure Data Management in a Connected World (SDM'04) in conjunction with VLDB'2004*, (pp. 67–82), Toronto, Ontario, Canada, August.

Oliveira, S. R. M., & Zaïane, O. R. (2004b). Privacy-Preserving Clustering by Object Similarity-Based Representation and Dimensionality Reduction Transformation. *In Proc. of the Workshop on Privacy and Security Aspects of Data Mining (PSADM'04) in conjunction with the Fourth IEEE International Conference on Data Mining (ICDM'04)* (pp. 21-30). Brighton, UK.

Oliveira, S. R. M. (2005). *Data Transformation For Privacy-Preserving Data Mining.* PhD thesis, Department of Computing Science, University of Alberta, Edmonton, AB, Canada, June.

Papadimitriou, C. H., Tamaki, H., Raghavan, P., & Vempala, S. (1998). Latent Semantic Indexing: A Probabilistic Analysis. *In Proc. of the 17th ACM Symposium on Principles of Database Systems* (pp. 159-168). Seattle, WA, USA.

Pinkas, B. (2002). Cryptographic Techniques For Privacy-Preserving Data Mining. *SIGKDD Explorations, 4*(2), 12–19, December 2002.

Samarati, P. (2001). Protecting Respondents' Identities in Microdata Release. IEEE Transactions on Knowledge and Data Engineering, 13 (6), 1010-1027.

Sweeney, L. (2002). k-Anonymity: A Model for Protecting Privacy. *International Journal on Uncertainty, Fuzziness and Knowledge-Based Systems, 10*(5), 557-570.

Vaidya, J., & Clifton, C. (2003). Privacy-Preserving K-Means Clustering Over Vertically Partitioned Data. *In Proc. of the 9th ACM SIGKDD Intl. Conf. on Knowledge Discovery and Data Mining* (pp. 206-215). Washington, DC, USA.

Young, F. W. (1987). *Multidimensional Scaling.* Lawrence Erlbaum Associates, Hillsdale, New Jersey.

APPENDIX A: RESULTS OF THE STRESS FUNCTION APPLIED TO THE DATASETS

Table 12. The error produced on the Chess dataset ($d_o=37$)

Chess	dr = 37	dr = 34	dr = 31	dr = 28	dr = 25	dr = 22	dr = 16
PR₁	0.000	0.015	0.024	0.033	0.045	0.072	0.141
PR₂	0.000	0.014	0.019	0.032	0.041	0.067	0.131

Table 13. The error produced on the Mushroom dataset ($d_o=23$)

Mushroom	dr = 23	dr = 21	dr = 19	dr = 17	dr = 15	dr = 13	dr = 9
PR₁	0.000	0.020	0.031	0.035	0.048	0.078	0.155
PR₂	0.000	0.017	0.028	0.029	0.040	0.079	0.137

Table 14. The error produced on the Pumsb dataset ($d_o=74$)

Pumsb	dr = 74	dr = 69	dr = 64	dr = 59	dr = 49	dr = 39	dr = 29
PR₁	0.000	0.006	0.022	0.029	0.049	0.078	0.157
PR₂	0.000	0.007	0.030	0.030	0.032	0.060	0.108

Table 15. The error produced on the Connect dataset ($d_o=43$)

Connect	dr = 43	dr = 37	dr = 31	dr = 25	dr = 19	dr = 16	dr = 13
PR₁	0.000	0.016	0.037	0.063	0.141	0.159	0.219
PR₂	0.000	0.016	0.028	0.062	0.122	0.149	0.212

Table 16. The error produced on the Accidents dataset ($d_o=18$)

Accidents	dr = 18	dr = 16	dr = 14	dr = 12	dr = 10	dr = 8	dr = 6
PR₁	0.000	0.033	0.034	0.044	0.094	0.144	0.273
PR₂	0.000	0.018	0.023	0.036	0.057	0.108	0.209

APPENDIX B: RESULTS OF F-MEASURE FOR THE CLUSTERS MINED FROM TRANSFORMED DATASETS

Table 17. Average of the F-measure (10 trials) for the Chess dataset ($d_o = 37$, $d_r = 25$)

Data Transformation	k=2				k=3			
	Min	Max	Avg	Std	Min	Max	Avg	Std
RP$_2$	0.529	0.873	0.805	0.143	0.592	0.752	0.735	0.050
Data Transformation	k=4				k=5			
	Min	Max	Avg	Std	Min	Max	Avg	Std
RP$_2$	0.597	0.770	0.695	0.063	0.569	0.761	0.665	0.060

Table 18. Average of the F-measure (10 trials) for the Mushroom dataset ($d_o = 23$, $d_r = 15$)

Data Transformation	k=2				k=3			
	Min	Max	Avg	Std	Min	Max	Avg	Std
RP$_2$	0.972	0.975	0.974	0.001	0.689	0.960	0.781	0.105
Data Transformation	k=4				k=5			
	Min	Max	Avg	Std	Min	Max	Avg	Std
RP$_2$	0.727	0.864	0.811	0.058	0.747	0.884	0.824	0.051

Table 19. Average of the F-measure (10 trials) for the Pumsb dataset ($d_o = 74$, $d_r = 38$)

Data Transformation	k=2				k=3			
	Min	Max	Avg	Std	Min	Max	Avg	Std
RP$_2$	0.611	0.994	0.909	0.140	0.735	0.991	0.965	0.081
Data Transformation	k=4				k=5			
	Min	Max	Avg	Std	Min	Max	Avg	Std
RP$_2$	0.846	0.925	0.891	0.028	0.765	0.992	0.838	0.041

Table 20. Average of the F-measure (10 trials) for the Connect dataset ($d_o = 43$, $d_r = 28$)

Data Transformation	k=2				k=3			
	Min	Max	Avg	Std	Min	Max	Avg	Std
RP$_2$	0.596	0.863	0.734	0.066	0.486	0.863	0.623	0.103
Data Transformation	k=4				k=5			
	Min	Max	Avg	Std	Min	Max	Avg	Std
RP$_2$	0.618	0.819	0.687	0.069	0.572	0.763	0.669	0.069

Chapter VII
Privacy–Preserving Transactions Protocol using Mobile Agents with Mutual Authentication

Song Han
Curtin University of Technology, Australia

Vidyasagar Potdar
Curtin University of Technology, Australia

Elizabeth Chang
Curtin University of Technology, Australia

Tharam Dillon
Curtin University of Technology, Australia

ABSTRACT

This chapter introduces a new transaction protocol using mobile agents in electronic commerce. The authors first propose a new model for transactions in electronic commerce – mutual authenticated transactions using mobile agents. They then design a new protocol by this model. Furthermore, the authors analyse the new protocol in terms of authentication, construction and privacy. The aim of the protocol is to guarantee that the customer is committed to the server, and the server is committed to the customer. At the same time, the privacy of the customer is protected.

INTRODUCTION

Security and Privacy are the paramount concerns in Electronic Commerce (Eklund, 2006). Mobile agent systems are becoming involved in e-commerce (Claessens et al., 2003). However, security and privacy within mobile agents must be addressed before mobile agents can be used in a wide range of electronic commerce applications.

The security in the electronic transactions with mobile agents can be classified into two different aspects:

- *One is **the security of the hosts**, to which the mobile agents will travel.*
- *The other is **the security of the mobile agents**, by which some sensitive information may be transported to the hosts.*

The above first security is used to protect the hosts, since the mobile agents may be malicious. For example, the mobile agent may be in the disguise of a legal mobile agent. Therefore, the host will interact with the mobile agent on an electronic transaction. However, the mobile agent tries to obtain some sensitive information (e.g. the secret development plan, the financial report, etc.) about the host. This case will damage the benefit of the host. Therefore, it is very important to maintain the security of the host if some malicious mobile agents travel to the hosts.

The above second security is used to protect the mobile agents, since the hosts may be hostile. For example, when the mobile agents with some sensitive information arrive at the host, those sensitive information (e.g. the private key, bank account password, home address, etc.) are paramount important to the mobile agents' owner. Therefore, the host may try to attain the information through interacting with the mobile agents. As a result, the customer (the owner of the mobile agents) may be blackmailed by the host, since the host holds some sensitive information obtained from the underlying mobile agents. Therefore, it

is imperative to design some security mechanism to maintain the security of the mobile agents.

Hosts' security mechanisms include: (1) Authentication; (2) Verification; (3) Authorisation; and (4) Payment for services (Claessens et al. 2003). In this paper, we will utilise the method of authentication to preserve the security of the host. Authentication is one of the cryptographic techniques. The implication of authentication is to *assure that the entity (customer, host, mobile agents, etc.) requesting access or interaction is the entity that it claims to be.*

Mobile agents' security mechanism (Kotzanikolaou et al., 2000) include: (1) Authentication; (2) Encryption algorithms; and (3) Digital signatures. In this paper, we will utilise the digital signature technique. Digital signature is another cryptographic technique. A digital signature scheme is a method of signing a message stored in electronic form. As such, a signed message can be transmitted over a computer network. Also, signature can be verified using a publicly known verification algorithm. Therefore, anyone who knows the verification algorithm can verify a digital signature. The essence of digital signatures is to convince the recipient that a message (attached to its valid digital signature) is really sent from the signer.

In a virtual community, delegation of signing rights is an important issue since security and privacy are concerned. Consider the following scenario: An international logistics company, AuHouse's President is scheduled to sign a major contract with an Automobile Company in Europe on Feb 28. However, because of a management emergency the President is required to attend a meeting held in the General Building of AuHouse in Australia on the same day. This meeting is vital to the future of the AuHouse. However, the contract in Europe is also very important to the organisation. How then can the President be in two places at once and sign the contract, even though he cannot be physically in Europe? Undetachable signature protocol will help the President to solve this issue since the undetachable signature protocol can provide the delegation of signing power whilst preserving the privacy of the President.

Undetachable signatures are one of the digital signatures which could provide secure delegation of signing rights whilst preserving privacy. So far only a few undetachable signatures have been created (Kotzanikolaou et al., 2000; Coppersmith et al., 1993; Sander et al., 1998). Sander and Tschudin first proposed the undetachable signatures (Sander et al. 1998). The construction is based on the birational functions (Shamir, 1993). However, Stern et al proved that undetachable signatures based on birational functions are insecure and vulnerable to the attacks (Coppersmith et al., 1993). Another construction on RSA cryptosystem was proposed (Burmester et al., 2000). This undetachable signature scheme is secure since its security is based on the security of RSA signatures. However, it is known that RSA signatures usually need to be about 1024 bit-length or much more in order to maintain an optimal security level (Lauter, 2004). At the same time, mobile agents are working in an environment of mobile communications. Therefore, low bandwidth and efficient communications are much satisfactory for mobile agents, since the mobile agents often migrate from its owner to a server and from this server to other servers.

Two secure transaction protocols having short signatures have been proposed (Han et al. 2005a, 2005b). However, their schemes do not have the mutual authentication mechanism. Therefore, their protocol can not guarantee that the server is committed to the customer, and the customer is committed to the server.

In this article, we will design a mutual authenticated transaction protocol with mobile agents. We will provide the mutual authentication mechanism to assure that the mobile agent is really the one it claims to be sent by its owner, the customer. Simultaneously, we will provide a new undetachable signature to protect the privacy of the customer.

The organization of the rest of this article is as follows: We first provide the model of mutual authenticated electronic transactions with mobile agents, and the definition of undetachable signatures. Secondly, some mathematical preliminaries are presented, that will be used in the new protocol. Thirdly, a new transaction protocol with mutual authentication using mobile agents is proposed. Then, the analysis and proofs are provided, mainly including authentication analysis and construction analysis, as well as privacy analysis – a very important property for a practical virtual community. The conclusions appear in the last section.

MODEL OF MUTUAL AUTHENTICATED TRANSACTIONS WITH MA AND DEFINITION OF UNDETACHABLE SIGNATURES

In this section, we will provide a new model of the transactions using mobile agents (MA) with mutual authentication between the server and the mobile agents (de facto the customer) and the definition of undetachable signatures. Note that it is the first definition for undetachable signatures to the best of our knowledge. An undetachable signature scheme consists of four algorithms, namely Setup, Key, Sign and Verify.

Model of Mutual Authenticated Transactions with MA

There are at least four participants involving in the model. The participants are: a customer C (which plays the role of the identifier of the customer), a number of servers (i.e. electronic shops) $S_1, S_2, ..., S_n$ (which play the roles of all the servers, respectively), a key certificate authority KCA (which plays the role of the identifier of the key certificate authority) and a number of mobile agents MA_1, $MA_2, ..., MA_n$ (which play the roles of these mobile agents, respectively). Besides these participants, there are six procedures for the proposed model. These procedures deliver the specifications for the mutual authenticated electronic transactions protocol using mobile agents (MAs). The details of this model are as follows:

Setup Algorithm: It generates public key and private key for the customer,. and also some public parameters for the corresponding servers. In this algorithm, the customer will construct her purchase requirements $\mathrm{Re}q_C$ according to her purchase plan. The server will construct Bid_S, that defines the bid of the server for a selling activity.

Key Algorithm: In this algorithm, a key certificate authority will also be involved. The customer, a key certificate authority, and some servers will collaborate to assign some public and private parameters. A suitable public key encryption algorithm $E_{pub \otimes prv}$ will be known to the customer and those servers. The private keys and public keys will be certificated by the key certificate authority, respectively. In addition, there is an shared key between the key certificate authority. That will be used for the authentication before the mobile agent migrates to the underlying server.

Mobile Agents Preparing: It involves the interactions between the customer and its mobile agents. The customer will construct some mobile codes for each mobile agent $MA_j(1 \le j \le n)$. These mobile codes include: *TBI*, $\mathrm{Re}q_C$, and a pair of undetachable signature functions; where *TBI* is the temporary identifier of the customer. The undetachable signature function pair are used to generate the bid tuple on the purchase requirement. Therefore, these mobile agents will travel with the mobile codes to these servers.

Mutual Authentications: This algorithm is used to take authentications between the customer and the servers $S_1, S_2, ..., S_n$. This authentication is mu-

tual means that the customer and the underlying server authenticate in a symmetrical way. It will assure that: *the underlying server is committed to the customer; and the customer is committed to the server.*

Mobile Agent Execution: This algorithm will make the server attend the bidding for the purchase brought with the mobile agent. Each mobile agent will take the mobile codes to the server. And then, the server will design its bid and sign on the bid. In the end, the server arranges the mobile agent to travel back to the customer.

Transactions Verifying: The customer first checks whether the time-stamp is still valid. If it is valid, the customer will verify the signature on the bid. If it is legal, and also the bid is an optimal one, the customer will accept this bid.

Definition of Undetachable Signatures

Undetachable signature is in fact a kind of encrypted functions. Some private parameters will be embedded in the function. And the recipient of this function can execute the computation of the function with some inputs chosen by herself. We utilise the definition proposed by Han and Chang (2006).

Setup is a probabilistic polynomial time algorithm which takes as input a security parameter k and outputs a family of system parameters.

Key is a probabilistic polynomial time algorithm which is executed by a trusted centre and the signers. The input contains system parameters, as well as random parameters which are chosen by the trusted centre and the signers. The output includes a public key $pk \in \underline{K}$ and a corresponding secret key sk.

Sign is a probabilistic polynomial time algorithm, which takes as input a secret key sk and a message $m \in \underline{M}$ and outputs a signature $Sig_{sk} \in \underline{S}$. In general, there are many valid signatures for any pair $(m, pk) \in \underline{M} \times \underline{K}$.

Verify is a deterministic polynomial time algorithm. The input includes a message and its allayed signature $Sig_{sk} \in \underline{S}$, as well as system parameters. The output is 'Accept' or 'Otherwise'.

PRELIMINARIES

In this section, we will provide some mathematical knowledge that are used in the design and analysis in the proposed protocol. There are two multiplicative cyclic group G_1 and G_2 of prime order q. g_1 is a generator of G_1 and g_2 is a generator of G_2.

A bilinear map is a map $e : G_1 \times G_2 \rightarrow G_T$ with these three properties:

- **Bi-linearity:** for any $P \in G_1$, $Q \in G_2$ and x, $y \in Z$, $e(P^x, q^y) = e(P,Q)^{xy}$.

- **Non-degenerate:** if g_1 is a generator of G_1 and g_2 is a generator of G_2, then $e(g_1, g_2) = 1$.

- **Efficient Computability:** there is an efficient algorithm to compute $e(P,Q)$ for any P and Q.

We will use the general case $G_1 \neq G_2$ so that we can take advantage of certain families of elliptic curves to obtain short signatures. Specifically, elements of G_1 have a short representation whereas elements of G_2 might not.

We say that (G_1, G_2) are bilinear groups if there exists a group G_T, an isomorphism $\psi : G_2 \rightarrow G_1$, and a bilinear map $e : G_1 \times G_2 \rightarrow G_T$, and e, ψ, and the group action in G_1, G_2, and G_T can be computed efficiently. Generally, the isomorphism ψ is constructed by the trace map over elliptic curves.

Each customer selects two generators $g_1 \in G_1, g_2 \in G_2$, and e(. , .) as above. He will choose $x \in Z_p^*$ and compute $v = g_2^x \in G_2$. There are four cryptographic hash functions will be used: H_1, H_2, H_3 and H_4, where $H_1 : \{0,1\}^* \times \{0,1\}^* \mapsto Z_p$

$H_2 : Z_p \mapsto Z_p$, $H_3 : \{0,1\}^* \times Z_p^* \mapsto Z_p$ and $H_4 : \{0,1\}^* \times \{0,1\}^* \times Z_p \mapsto Z_p$.

TRANSACTIONS PROTOCOL WITH MUTUAL AUTHENTICATION

A new undetachable signature scheme will be proposed for the protocol of secure transactions. This new undetachable scheme belongs to the domain of short signatures (Boneh et al., 2004; Courtois, 2004; Lauter, 2004). As described in the previous section, short signatures have the characteristics of shorter bit-length of signatures, fast signature generation, as well as fast signature verification. These characteristics are imperative for mobile agents, which take part in the secure transactions between a customer and any server.

Setup Algorithm

Setup algorithm is mainly to set up the compulsory parameters assigned to each participant. We will use the mathematical settings of bilinear mapping groups introduced as above. Each customer will do the following steps:

1. Customer selects $g_1 \in G_1$, $g_2 \in G_2$ two generators.
2. Customer Selects bilinear mapping $e(\cdot, \cdot)$ as above.
3. Customer randomly selects $x \in Z_p^*$ and computes $v = g_2^x \in G_2$.
4. Customer selects two securely cryptographic hash functions H_1 and H_2: $H_1 : \{0,1\}^* \times \{0,1\}^* \mapsto Z_p, H_2 : Z_p \mapsto Z_p$

In addition, there another two secure cryptographic hash functions H_3 and H_4, such as SHA-1 (Stinson, 1995, p. 248, pp. 251-253); where $H_3 : \{0,1\}^* \times Z_p^* \mapsto Z_p$ and $H_4 : \{0,1\}^* \times \{0,1\}^* \times Z_p \mapsto Z_p$.

Therefore, the private key of the customer is x; the public key is $g_1, g_2, e(\cdot, \cdot), H_1, H_2, H_3$ and

H_4. All these public parameters are also known to the servers. Note that H_3 and H_4 will be used for the authentication between the underlying server and the mobile agent (de facto the customer) in subsection 4. D. Another point is all the public keys are certificated by the key certificate authority, in order to maintain the integration and non-repudiation.

Since we are constructing a transactions protocol, we should specify some corresponding information about the customer and the server. For example, who is the buyer? And who is the bidder (de facto seller). That is, what is the corresponding information of the customer and the server. Here, the server represents the host computer the mobile agents will visit in the transactions.

For permanent usability, we let C be a permanent identifier for the customer, and S be a permanent identifier of the server. For a specific purchase (i.e. e-transactions), we define *TSI* as the temporary bidder identifier. In fact, *TSI* is derived from S and the corresponding purchase/selling information (for example, valid period for this bid). We also define *TBI* as the temporary buyer identifier (this may represent the mobile agent). At the same time, t is a time-stamp generated by the underlying server. R is a random element generated by the key certificate authority. R_1 is a random element generated by the customer. These items will be used for the authentication before the mobile agent takes the transactions with the underlying server.

In addition, we denote the constraints of the customer by $\mathrm{Re}\,q_C$, and the bid of the server by Bid_S. The two items are defined as follows:

$\mathrm{Re}\,q_C$ defines the requirements of the customer for a specific purchase. It includes: (1) the description of a desired product; (2) an expiration date and time stamp; (3) the maximum price that is acceptable to the customer; (4) a deadline for the delivery of the product.

Bid_S defines the bid of the server for a selling activity. It includes: (1) the description of the

server's product; (2) the minimum price that will be acceptable to the server; (3) a deadline for the delivery of the product; (4) a deadline for paying money into the bank account of the server; (5) an expiration date and time stamp.

Key Algorithm

The *Key algorithm* is a probabilistic polynomial time algorithm. The key certificate authority, the customer and each server will collaborate to assign some keys. All the keys specified here have two fundamental functions: some of them are used to maintain the privacy of the underlying participants; the others are used to maintain the authentication between the customer and the underlying server.

1. The key certificate authority determines a practical public key encryption algorithm $E_{pub \otimes prv}$ for the customer and the underlying server. Note that, the customer and the underlying server cannot agree on $E_{pub \otimes prv}$ by themselves, since they need mutual authentication in the underlying transactions protocol.

2. The key certificate authority generates a random secret element $k \in Z_p^*$ for the underlying server. Therefore, the key certificate authority and the underlying server will share this element. This key will be used for the authentication before the mobile agent migrates to the server.

3. The key certificate authority sends a pair of public key pub_C and private key prv_C to the customer securely.

4. The key certificate authority sends a pair of public key pub_S and private key prv_S to the underlying server securely.

All these public keys and private keys will be involved when the customer initiates the e-Transaction with the server. The public key encryption algorithm can maintain the private communications between the customer and the server.

Mobile Agents Preparing

This algorithm is used to equip the mobile agent with executable codes. The customer constructs the executable codes by using his private key. However, the private key will be presented as a blinded version, since the mobile agent will migrate with the executable does to the underlying server. This will not leak any useful information about the private key. The customer equips the Mobile Agent with executable codes. The executable codes are in fact an undetachable signature function pair:

$$y(\ ) = (\ ) - x_1 \pmod q \text{ and}$$

$$y_{signed}(\ ) = x_2 \times g^{H_2((\ )-x_1)}.$$

where $x_1 = H_1(TBI, \mathrm{Re}\,q_C)$ is bounded by q; $x_2 = g_1^{\overline{x}} \in G_1$, where the exponentiation is computed modular q. x_2 can be seen as a variant version of the short signature:

$$x_1 = H_1(TBI, \mathrm{Re}\,q_C)(\mathrm{mod}\ q)$$

$$x_2 = g_1^{\frac{x}{x}} \in G_1$$

Where C is a message, $\mathrm{Re}\,q_C$ is a random element. Therefore, x_1 and x_2 could be treated as the signature (Han and Chang, 2006): $\sigma = h(m,r)^{\frac{1}{x}}$ on the message m; where $h(m,r) = g_1^{x_1}$. The security is based on an assumption of q-SDH (Han and Chang, 2006).

Equipped with the executable codes, the mobile agent will migrate from the customer to the server. This agent will carry *TBI* and $\mathrm{Re}\,q_C$ as part of its data. Also, the mobile agent can sign any purchase (restricted by the purchase requirement) on behalf of the customer. Therefore, this algorithm realises the delegation of signing rights from the customer to the mobile agent.

Before the mobile agent migrates to the underlying server, the customer and the server need to authenticate with each other. Note that, this process is actually executed between the mobile agent and the server. Here, the mobile agent, in fact, represents its owner, i.e. the customer. However, for the simplicity of the deployment, we arrange the customer and the server to take the process of authentication. The process will assure that: (1) the customer is the purchaser (de facto the buyer); (2) the underlying server is truly the bidder (de facto the seller).

Mutual Authentication

If the mutual authentication is successful, this algorithm can verify that: (a) *the underlying server is committed to the customer for the coming transaction;* (b) *the customer is committed to the server for the coming transaction.* The customer, the underlying server, and the key certificate authority will attend this algorithm. The followings are the details:

1. In order to win the indent (transaction order), the server promulgates her selling information and sends an authentication request to the customer. This request includes *TSI* and *t*.

2. The customer sends *TSI* along with *t* and his permanent identifier *C* to the key certificate authority through a secure channel.

3. After the key certificate authority receives the information, it first checks whether the permanent identifier *C* is legal and *t* is valid. If one them is not valid, the process stops here; Otherwise, the key certificate authority computes $AU_C = H_3(t, k)$ and $K_t = H_3(R, k)$. Then, the key certificate authority sends the tuple $\{AU_C, R, K_t\}$ to the customer through a secure channel.

4. Once the customer receives the tuple from the key certificate authority, he computes $AU_S = H_4(R, t, K_t)$ and stores it in his database. Then, the customer sends the tuple $\{AU_C, R, t\}$ to the underlying server.

5. Once the server gets the tuple, she first checks whether t is valid. If t is valid, the process stops here; otherwise, the server calculates $AU_C^* = H_3(t, k)$ and compares it with the received AU_C. If they are not equal, the transaction is terminated here; otherwise, the customer is authenticated. The server then computes $K_t^* = H_3(R, k)$ and $AU_S^* = H_4(R, t, K_t^*)$, and sends both of them to the customer.

6. After receiving AU_S^* and K_t^*, the customer compares AU_S^* with the one AU_S stored in this database. If the following two equations hold:

$$K_t^* = K_t$$
$$AU_S^* = AU_S.$$

Then, the server is authenticated successfully. After the mutual authentication is completed successfully, the customer will arrange the mobile agent to take the transaction with the underlying server.

Mobile Agent Execution

After the mobile agent arrives at the server, the agent will give all its data and the executable code to the server. The server will execute the executable code provided by mobile agent, i.e. $y()$ and $y_{signed}()$. The details are as follows:

1. The server computes $y_1 = H_1(TBI, TSI, Bid_S)$ with a bid.
2. The server computes
   $$r = y(x) = y_1 - x_1 \pmod{q}.$$
   If $r \equiv 0 \bmod q$, the server will stop.
3. The server computes:
   $$y_2 = y_{signed}(y_1)$$
   $$= x_2 \times g^{H_2(y_1 - x_1)}$$
   $$= g_1^{\frac{x_1}{x}} \times (g_1^x)^{H_2(y_1 - x_1)}$$
   $$= g_1^{\left(\frac{x_1}{x} + xH_2(y_1 - x_1)\right)(\bmod q)} \in G_1$$

where $g = g_1^x \in G_1$.

4. The server outputs the x-coordinate x_3 of y_2, where x_3 is an element in Z_q.
5. The server hands the mobile agent a tuple
   $$TBI, TSI, Bid_S, y_1, m, x_3;$$
   This tuple will represent part of the transaction.
6. The mobile agent with the tuple migrates to its owner, i.e. the customer.

Remark: *In the above algorithm, we let TBI and TSI involve the computation of the transaction. This will help to protect the permanent identity of the customer as well as the underlying server. This principle is reasonable, since the temporary identifier is privately linked to the permanent identifier.*

Transaction Verifying

This algorithm is used to verify the fulfilled transaction is an optimal one. If it is, the customer will accept the transaction. The details are as follows: When the mobile agent returns from the server, the customer will check the returned data provided by the mobile agent. The customer will need to follow these steps:

1. The customer will check the undetachable signature (r, x_3) for this transaction by utilizing the following formula.
2. The customer will find whether there is a point in G_1: $g_3 = (x_3, y_3)$ (where t is an element in Z_p)
   Such that the following equation holds in G_1:

   $$e(g_3, v^{H_2(r)}) = e(g_1, g_2)^{(x_1 + x^2 H_2(r))H_2(r)}$$

If there is no such point, then the customer will not accept this transaction. Otherwise, she will accept this transaction.

That is to say: If the above equality holds, that certifies the transaction is valid. And then the customer will accept the transaction. Otherwise, the customer will arrange the current mobile agent or another mobile agent to migrate to another server to seek a desirable bid and accomplish the transaction.

ANALYSIS OF THE TRANSACTIONS PROTOCOL

This section we will analyze the proposed protocol of transactions with mobile agents and provide authentication analysis, security proof and privacy analysis. We first provide the authentication analysis - mutual authentication analysis. We will show that how the customer is committed to the server, and how the server is committed to the customer. Construction analysis tells how the protocol works, what the principal of the protocol is, how the mobile agents help the transactions. Security proof shows how to extract the signature scheme from transactions. Subsequently, we will analysis how the privacy is preserved for both the customer and the server.

Authentication Analysis

In this subsection, we will analyze the authentication mechanism. As previously described, we know that the temporary identifier TSI is derived from the permanent identifier S, and the temporary identifier TBI derived from the permanent identifier C. Therefore, TSI is linked to S, and TBI is linked to C.

1. Mutual authentication fulfils the mutual commitment between the buyer and the seller, i.e. the customer and the underlying server. If the seller is committed to the buyer, and the buyer is not committed to the seller, then it will be probable that the buyer would not accept or confirm the transactions. This

will result in the buyer presenting no responsibility for the underlying purchase. On the other hand, only the temporary identifiers of the customer and the server are involved in the mobile agent preparing algorithm and the mobile agent execution algorithm. It is known that the temporary identifier has specific and short-term valid period. Therefore, it is necessary to accomplish the mutual authentication.

2. The mechanism of authentication is as follow: on the one hand, the underlying server is authenticated through: (1) the customer checks whether $K_t^* = K_t$; and (2) the customer checks whether $AU_S^* = AU_S$. In fact, $K_t^* = K_t$ reflects the underlying server has a shared private element with the key certificate authority. $AU_S^* = AU_S$ implies that the server constructs AU_S^* using the elements from the customer. On the other hand, the customer is authenticated through: (1) the server checks whether the timestamp t is valid; and (2) the server checks whether $AU_C^* = AU_C$. In fact, That t is valid implies that the customer really receives t and replies correctly. $AU_C^* = AU_C$ implies that the customer attains the element AU_C from the key certificate authority, since only the server and the key certificate authority can compute the value of AU_C^* and AU_C.

3. The proposed transaction protocol indicates that the authentication process can not be forged by the server as well as the customer. Consequently, anyone else (excluding the customer, server, and the key certificate authority) cannot forge the authentication. The security of the mutual authentication is based on the property of cryptographic hash functions (Stinson, 1995).

Construction Analysis

We will deploy the proposed transactions protocol from the construction point of view. This will help us to further understand the transaction protocol.

Note that a key certificate authority is involved in the following three algorithms: setup algorithm, key algorithm, and authentication algorithm. Therefore, the function of the key certificate authority can be deployed according to the three aspects:

a. The key certificate authority certifies the public keys (signing algorithm) for the customer in the setup algorithm.

b. The key certificate authority determines the public key algorithm for the customer and the underlying server in the key algorithm. This assures the private communications between the customer and the server.

c. The key certificate authority helps to accomplish the mutual authentication between the customer and the server. This is realised through: (1) a shared private key between the key certificate authority and the underlying server; (2) computing $AU_C = H_3(t,k)$ and $K_t = H_3(R,k)$; as well as (3) confirming the legality of the permanent identifier of the customer. All these three are presented in the authentication algorithm.

Next, we deploy the proposed transaction protocol from the delegation-of-signing-right point of view.

In the transaction protocol, the mobile agent is awarded a pair of functions ($y(\ )$ *and* $y_{signed}(\ )$) and migrates with them to the server. This pair of functions maintains the un-leakage of the signing algorithm (actually the signing private key) of the customer. The input x of the server is linked to the server's bid. At the same time, the mobile agent is also given the certified requirements of the customer (a, b), satisfying $y(\ ) = (\ ) - x_1 \pmod{q}$, and $y_{signed}(\ ) = x_2 \times g^{H_2(\ (\ ) - x_1)} y$ in G_1. The parameters of function $y(\ )$ are such that the output of this function includes the customer's constraints. The server modifies these by including the bid, Bid_S in the input y_1, in such a way as to satisfy:

- The message m links the constraints of the customer to the bid of the server.
- Get an undetachable signature (r, x_3) for the transaction, where $r = (y_1 - x_1) \pmod{q}$ and x_3 is the x-coordinate of the point *beta*. This serves as a certificate which is authenticated by the customer as follows

$$e\left(g_3, v^{H_2(r)}\right) = e\left(g_1, g_2\right)^{(x_1 + x^2 H_2(r))H_2(r)}.$$

The certified constraints of the customer $Re\, q_C$, and the bid of the server, Bid_S restrict the scope of *the context* of *the transaction*, i.e. the certificate (r, x_3) to 'optimal bid' transactions with the appropriate time-limits (or more generally, to whatever requirements the customer and the server stipulate).

Note that even if a server ignores the customer's constraints $Re\, q_C$ and executes the mobile agent associated with the executable code $y(\ )$ and $y_{signed}(\ )$ in order to produce an undetachable signature of the customer for a bogus bid, the signature will be invalid. If a server is not willing to bid for a purchase, then the mobile agent will travel to another server to obtain an optimal bid for the transaction.

Privacy Analysis

Privacy is the most concern in respect to financial issues of the participants in the transactions (Eklund, 2006). Therefore, besides the security analysis, it is also necessary to analyze the privacy of the proposed protocol. We will analyze the privacy of the transactions protocol from the following four aspects:

1. Privacy of the signing key of the customer: This privacy is maintained by the mobile agent's executable code, i.e. the pair of functions $y(\ )$ *and* $y_{signed}(\ )$ since the signing key is implied and embedded in the content of $y_{signed}(\ )$.

2. Privacy of the identity of the customer: This privacy is maintained through the encrypted communication. In fact, when the customer sends the mobile agent to some servers to seek 'optimal purchase', she will encrypt the whole or part of the tuple $(y(\ ), y_{signed}(\ ), TBI, \mathrm{Re}\, q_C)$ (if necessary for the whole content), by utilizing her private key prv_C of the underlying public key encryption.

3. Privacy of the context of the Transaction initiated between the customer and a server: This privacy is maintained through the mutual encrypted communications between the customer and the server, who will utilize the public key encryption algorithm established in the Setup algorithm of the e-Transaction protocol.

4. Privacy of the identity of the underlying server: This privacy is maintained through the fact: when the server hands the tuple $TBI, TSI, Bid_S, y_1, r, x_3$ to the mobile agent to migrate to the customer, the server will encrypt the part of the tuple in which is related to its identity information, by utilizing her private key prv_S of the underlying public key encryption.

CONCLUSION

In this article, we have defined a model of mutual authenticated transactions with mobile agents. And then, a new electronic transaction protocol is presented according to the proposed model. We have provided the corresponding analysis and proofs for the proposed transaction protocol. In detail, there are authentication analysis, construction analysis, and privacy proof. For authentication analysis, we deploy it from the mechanism of mutual authentication, as well as the unforgeable authentication elements. The construction analysis helps to better understand the

principles of the proposed protocol. For privacy analysis, it is told that the privacy is maintained through the involvement of the public key algorithm, an undetachable signature function, and the temporary identifiers.

REFERENCES

Boneh, D., & Boyen, X. (2004). Short signatures without random oracles. *Proceedings of Eurocrypt 2004, LNCS 3027*, 56-73.

Claessens, J., Preneel, B., & Vandewalle. J. (2003). How can mobile agents do secure electronic transactions on untrusted hosts? *ACM Trans. Internet Tech, 3*(1), 28-48.

Coppersmith, D., Stern, J., & Vaudenay, S. (1993). Attacks on the birational permutation signature schemes. *CRYPTO 1993, LNCS 773*, 435-443.

Courtois, N. (2004) *Short signatures, provable security, generic attacks and computational security of multivariate polynomial schemes such as HFE, Quartz and Sflash*. Eprint 2004/143.

Digital Signature Algorithm (DSA), (ECDSA; as specified in ANSI X9.62), RSA (as specified in ANSI X9.31), and Elliptic Curve DSA FIPS 186-2.

Edjlali, G., Acharya, A., & Chaudhary, V. (1998). *History-based access control for mobile code. ACM CCS 1998*, (pp. 38-48).

Eklund, E. (2006). *Controlling and securing personal privacy and anonymity in the information society.* http://www.niksula.cs.hut.fi/~eklund/Opinnot/netsec.html

Han, S., Chang, E., & Dillon, T., (2005a). Secure e-transactions using mobile agents with agent broker. *Proceedings of the Second IEEE Conference on Service Systems and Service Management, 2*, 849-855, Jun.13-15, Chongqing University, China.

Han, S., Chang, E., & Dillon, T. (2005b). Secure transactions using mobile agents with TTP. *Proceedings of the Second IEEE Conference on Service Systems and Service Management, 2,* 856-862, Jun. 13-15, Chongqing University.

Han, S., & Chang, E. (2006). *New efficient undetachable sigantures.* Technical Report, IS-CBS2006.

Kolaczek, G. (2003). *Specification and verification of constraints in role based access control for enterprise security system.* WETICE 2003, (pp. 190-195).

Kotzanikolaou, P., Burmester, M., & Chrissikopoulos, V. (2000). Secure transactions with mobile agents in hostile environments. *ACISP 2000, LNCS 1841,* 289-297.

Lauter, K. (2004). The advantages of elliptic curve cryptography for wireless security. *IEEE Wireless Communications Magazine.*

Rivest, R.L., Shamir, A., & Adleman, L.M. (1978). A method for obtaining digital signatures and public-key cryptosystems. *Commun. ACM 21*(2), 120-126.

Sander, T., & Tschudin, C.F. (1998). Protecting mobile agents against malicious hosts. *Mobile Agents and Security 1998, LNCS 1419,* 44-60.

Shamir, A. (1984). Efficient signature schemes based on birational permutations. *Advances in Cryptology - CRYPTO 93, LNCS 773,* 1-12.

Stinson, D. R. (1995) Cryptography: practice and theory. CRC Press, Boca Raton.

Patarin, J., Courtois, N., & Goubin, L. (2001). QUARTZ, 128-bit long digital signatures. *CT-RSA 2001,* (pp. 282-297).

Chapter VIII
Dynamic Control Mechanisms for User Privacy Enhancement

Amr Ali Eldin
Accenture, The Netherlands

ABSTRACT

Despite the expected benefits behind context-awareness and the need for developing more and more context-aware applications, we enunciate that privacy represents a major challenge for the success and widespread adoption of these services. This is due to the collection of huge amount of users' contextual information, which would highly threaten their privacy concerns. Controlling users' information collection represents a logical way to let users get more acquainted with these context-aware services. Additionally, this control requires users to be able to make consent decisions which face a high degree of uncertainty due to the nature of this environment and the lack of experience from the user side with information collectors' privacy policies. Therefore, intelligent techniques are required in order to deal with this uncertainty. In this chapter, the auhtors propose a consent decision-making mechanism, ShEM, which allows users to exert automatic and manual control over their private information. An enhanced fuzzy logic approach was developed for the automatic decision making process. The proposed mechanism has been prototyped and integrated in a UMTS location-based services testbed on a university campus. Users have experienced the services in real time. A survey of users' responses on the privacy functionality has been carried out and analyzed as well. Users' response on the privacy functionality was positive. Additionally, results obtained showed that a combination of both manual and automatic privacy control modes in one approach is more likely to be accepted than only a complete automatic or a complete manual privacy control.

INTRODUCTION

Advances in mobile network access technology with increasingly higher bandwidth capacity, intelligent mobile devices, and smart miniaturized sensors, have opened up a whole range of new possibilities. Ubiquitous computing brings new challenges to information and computer science; one of those challenges is to deal with privacy threats, how to present sensitive information about individuals such as location, preferences and activities. In addition, the possibility that users' profiles may be shared among different parties without the user's consent may also pose a serious threat to user privacy. For example, mobile health applications make it possible to monitor patients who might become ill due to a disease: for instance to prevent epileptic seizures or hypoglycaemic conditions in case of diabetics, especially during times when their treatment is being set-up or adjusted. Small medical sensors combined with higher bandwidth and more reliable mobile network technologies make it possible for such patients to be monitored and even treated anytime and anywhere. This allows patients to live more 'normal' lives, and it helps improve their quality of life and well-being. However, it also has a serious impact on a patient's privacy, a factor that should be given serious consideration.

There is a trade off between a user's privacy requirements and the reasons he or she may have to allow information to be made available. Complete privacy is impossible in a society where a user has to interact with other members of the society such as colleagues, friends, or family members. Each flow of user information will reveal some private information about the user at least to the information receiver. Since this flow of information is needed, and maybe self-initiated by the user, a user needs to make sure that the other party (the destination) is going to adhere to his or her privacy requirements.

Privacy policies and legal contracts can be used to help users and service providers reach an agreement on the type of privacy users will have. However, these contracts do not provide enough flexibility for users with respect to choosing the type of privacy they need. They also do not guarantee that a user's privacy will not be violated but what they do is that they give the user the right to sue an organization if the privacy contract was broken. Although a lot of efforts on privacy protection has been exerted in the literature (Ackerman, Darrell, & Weitzner, 2001; Camenisch & Herreweghen, 2002; Casal, 2001), not many efforts has realized the option that privacy could be negotiable. A user Ben might be willing to share his information with information collectors in order to get some cheaper service or a better offer. What makes it complex is that users' privacy concerns could be influenced not only by mostly known factors such as culture, age, etc., but also by their context or situation when the information is requested. This influence of context becomes noticeable in environments where users context is expected to change.

Context may be defined as any information that can be used to characterize the situation of an entity, where an entity can be a person, place, physical or computational object that is considered relevant to the interaction between an entity and an application. Contextual information matches any relevant object in the user's environment or user description: examples would be Ben's location, time, mobile device capabilities, network bandwidth, etc. Contextual information can come from different network locations, protocol layers and device entities. Context-aware applications are applications that collect users' context and give content that is adapted to it.

Informed consent is one of the requirements of privacy set up by the European directives (European Directive, 2002). Accordingly, a user should be asked to give his/her informed consent before any context collection. From a usability point of view, it would be difficult to let each user enter his/her response each time context is collected. Increasingly, the type of collected data would highly influence his/her privacy concerns. The problem becomes more complex when more than one party gets involved in collecting users information, for example third parties. Third parties of a certain information collector represent unknown parties to the user. Despite that the first information collector might list in its privacy policy that users information is being given to those third parties in one way or another, it is not possible yet in the literature (Hauser & Kabatnik, 2001) to provide a means for the user to know which party collects which information. Thus uncertainty takes over when a user Ben gets pushed information or services from unknown collectors whether to give them access or not. Although he did not give explicit consent to unrelated third parties in his privacy preferences, he did not mention he would block them either.

Privacy strictness varies from one user to another. It is not possible to generalize it or to have a common agreement on which data elements should be given away and which should not since privacy is mainly a personal matter. In this sense, Ben should be able to define how he thinks his personal information should be dealt with. Which information practices are acceptable and which ones he does not approve in what is known as privacy preferences description. Although this might look simple, defining effective preferences that match each user and that is efficient in describing their privacy needs is still immature (Ali Eldin & Wagenaar, 2004). When a lot of application domains get involved in exchanging Ben's information with different types of information demands and different types of services, the process of managing these preferences gets higher in complexity as well.

In context-aware services such as mobile location-based services, mobile healthcare services, etc., users' collected context would be expected to change from time to time, due to the change in the surrounding circumstances and environmental influences. We assume that a user's privacy preference would not only be context dependent but also context driven. Current privacy preferences architectures such as P3P (Cranor, Langheinrich, Marchiori, Presler-Marshall, & Reagle, 2004) do not support this feature of context-aware systems. Additionally, the user is burdened with taking care of updating his/her privacy preferences that adds more complexity to him/her in keeping privacy. We assume that a flexible privacy approach should be a user centric one because users are the only ones capable of setting up their own privacy concerns and also due to the changing demands of their privacy. However, we also assume that not all users know exactly what they need. Increasingly, most users will prefer more a user-friendly way, which reduces their interactions as much as possible and at the same time, satisfies their personal information privacy requirements.

In this chapter, we develop a consent decision-making mechanism that fulfils the dynamic consent requirement by adopting dynamic user profiles with privacy preferences descriptions and intelligent decision-making. The chapter has been structured as follows. Section 2 discusses the proposed consent decision-making approach. In section 3, we present the proposed privacy preferences model together with the proposed architecture. Section 4 deals with the experimental details and findings that were collected by prototypes we constructed. Section 5 concludes the chapter.

TOWARDS AUTOMATIC CONSENT DECISION-MAKING

In this section, we present the consent decision mechanism needed in order to autonomously estimate users consent decisions.

Consent Decision Dependences

It seems clear that there are a number of factors upon which a user takes a decision whether to share his/her information with others. These factors differ from one user to another in their roles and impact on users' decisions. It is not the intention of this research to find out a full survey of factors that are affecting users consent decisions but to develop a way of modeling the impact of these factors and to effectively and flexibly implement this way of modeling. In this section, we focus on the most observable factors from plain reasoning (see Figure 1).

Trustworthiness of Information Collector

Trust analysis and measurement have been of major interest in the literature (Gambetta 1988, Currall & Judge 1995, Glaeser et al. 2000). However, still users cognition of trust is not efficiently mapped onto physical measurements. For example: how to measure trust or how to define trust is still object of extensive study. Trustworthiness of the information collector plays a major role in users' willingness to give up or to continue the service. For example, a user might choose to continue yahoo e-mail although yahoo might send some information to third parties just because s/he trusts that e-mail service.

Increasingly, trustworthiness of an information collector can imply a number of factors such as quality of service to the users, users' need of the service, and users' expectations of the information collector regarding their information collection. Besides, the user's former experience with an information collector will also impact the user's trust in that collector.

Personal Information Confidentiality

Personal information confidentiality largely determines whether users will give their consent, or not, to an information collector. Information confidentiality is driven by a number of factors. Information value to a user can affect its confidentiality and hence its confidence. Increasingly, the culture itself may have different effects on personal information confidentiality. For example, a user salary, in the Netherlands, represents one of the most confidential information to him/her while in Sweden, salaries are published online and the public will realize how much a user earns, based on the type of work, s/he is doing. On the other hand, medical healthcare information varies in their confidentiality according to how much serious

Figure 1. Consent decision influencing factors

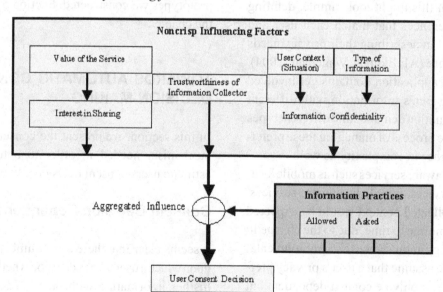

it is but not the culture. In addition, information confidentiality can vary according to user context. To conclude, confidentiality thus depends on the type of collected information as well as context in which information is collected.

Users Interest in Information Sharing

The higher the user interest in information sharing or in other words, the higher the user willingness to share information is, the lower the possibility not to allow the sharing for any reason. For instance, a user interest or need for a service might be high enough that s/he gave up some of his/her private information. Some freeware programs install a lot of ad ware on a user's computer and most users allow that just because of their interest in those freeware programs. An example is Kazaa free media desktop, which installs in addition to itself other ad ware programs that could violate a person's privacy.

Information Practices

The above-mentioned factors represent a group of factors that cannot be crisply quantified. In this subsection, another type of influence on users consent decisions is considered. This type corresponds to the evaluation of users' preferences against information collectors' privacy policies. This comparison or evaluation reflects how much the information collector way of dealing with a user's information matches with the user approved way of dealing with his/her information. In contrast to previously mentioned factors, this factor could be crisply measured, for instance by the density of matching hits obtained.

Each user would define how s/he thinks his/her personal information should be dealt with. Preferences can lead to perfect representation of users' privacy requirements if well defined. It is not easy to define preferences that match each user and that is efficient in describing their privacy needs. Increasingly, as information systems get

more complex, and a lot of information collectors do exist with different types of information demands and different types of services, the process of managing these preferences gets higher in complexity as well. P3P (Cranor et al., 2004) and APPEL (Cranor, Langheinrich, & Marchiori, 2002) are considerable efforts in representing users preferences and matching them with information collector privacy policies. Based on this evaluation procedure, a user agent can summarize the situation to the user and give hem/her responsibility to decide whether to continue and the type of consent to give.

THE SHARING EVALUATOR MODEL (*SHEM*)

In this section, we present the architecture based on which a final consent decision could be made regarding the transfer of information to an information collector "*SP*". The architecture is known as ShEM as acronym of *Sharing Evaluator Model*. The architecture functionalities are based on privacy requirements presented in (Ali Eldin & Wagenaar, 2003). In this section, we briefly discuss the component details of the sharing evaluator model (*ShEM*): compare_pref, consent decider and consent evaluator (see Figure 2).

A Users Privacy Preferences Model

We assume that the basic control element of any privacy support architecture consists of users' predefined preferences that govern the process of their data collection. Users' preferences play an important role in the consent decisions. These preferences will be checked each time a decision is required regarding the user's permission to collect his/her information. Users would be able to control these preferences and change them during run time. In this subsection, we present the proposed privacy preferences model as shown in Figure 4.

*Figure 2. The Sharing evaluator model (**ShEM**) architecture*

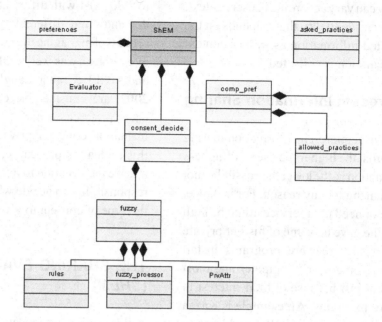

Privacy Attributes

We assume that there exists a correlation between privacy and a number of attributes. In this research, we only consider three privacy attributes: confidentiality of the information, trustworthiness of information collector and users interest in sharing. Privacy attributes are attributes that evaluate users' willingness to share their information with information collectors. They are used by the consent decider component in order to develop autonomously an estimated permission decision by the use of fuzzy logic.

The following preferences are associated with each of them:

- Value: this is the value of each attribute.
- Mode: mode represents how these values are updated. There are three modes of updating:
  - Self: where the user chooses to self update his/her preferences.
  - Group: where the user chooses to update his/her preferences based on other users experiences or voting.

  - System: where the *ShEM* updates users' preferences autonomously based on default preferences.

Valuating Privacy Attributes

Users are assumed to have the full capabilities to assign values for these attributes. This could be sufficient enough in case of context information *confidentiality* and *interest in sharing* since both attributes highly depend on the user perception and could vary from one user to another. In addition to being personally dependent, *interest in sharing* could be influenced by other users' experiences as well which we denote by *"group assigned values"*. On the other hand, trustworthiness of the information collector represents a different type of attribute, which could be highly affected by the users' own experience, other users' experiences or by trusted third parties' experiences. Therefore, we enunciate three modes of valuating privacy attributes: self assigned values ($UsrValue_k$), group assigned values ($GrpValue_k$) and system assigned values ($SysAttrb_k$). The total value of the attribute could be assumed as a linear combination of the three values such that:

Figure 3. Preferences model

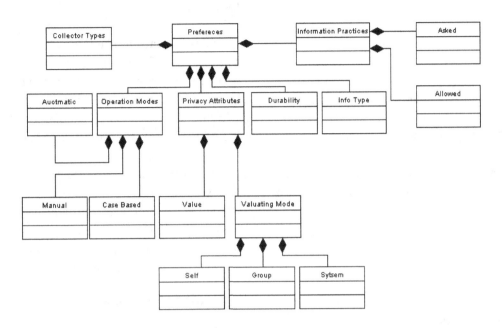

$$Pr\,vValue_k = \qquad\qquad (4)$$
$$Wr \times UsrValue_k + Wg \times GrpValue_k + Ws \times SysAttrb_k$$

Wr, Wg and Ws represent weighting factors of the different contributing values.

Users can specify in the preferences how the attributes could be valuated: self, group or system based assignment. This is controlled via the constants Wr, Wg, and Ws (see Table 1 for an example). In addition, there could be two possibilities for valuating privacy attributes. The first is to specify on a certain scale, for example scale (1-10), the final value of a variable. The other approach

is to set the membership function parameters by allowing custom membership functions. In this work, the former approach is adopted.

Self Assigned Values

In this case, a user k self valuates the attribute with a value $UsrValue_k = U_k$

Group Assigned Attributes

In this case, other users experience is used in valuating the attribute,

Table 1. A valuating privacy attributes example

	Self Assigned	Group Assigned	System Assigned
Confidentiality ($Wr=1$, $Wg=0$ and $Ws=0$)	✓	✗	✗
Interest in Sharing (Wr, $Wg=1$ and $Ws=0$)	✓	✓	✗
Trustworthiness of collector ($Wr=0$, $Wg=0$ and $Ws=1$)	✗	✗	✓

$$GrpValue_k = \sum_{i=1}^{n} w_i \times U_i$$

Where

w : a weighting factor
n : number of users in the group

System Assigned Value

The ShEM system itself automatically assigns a value based on predefined history with third parties:

$$SysAttrb_k = \sum_{j=1}^{m} y_j \times Utp_j$$

where

m: number of system values
Utp: attribute value assigned by a third party *tp*

Information Practices

Information practices, as a part of users' privacy preferences model, control the way the information collector should deal with users' information after being received. The information collector publishes its information practices, which we call asked information practices, online so that it is available for evaluation by information owners. A user defines his/her own allowed practices. However, both the information collectors and the information owners should use the same semantics in describing these practices. The platform of privacy preferences (P3P) (Cranor et al., 2004) represents a well-known standard, based on XML, that covers this issue. P3P has defined a number of data practices that together constitute a P3P privacy policy. Data practices describe the ways users' data would be dealt with. Examples of such practices are purpose: explaining the purpose of data collection, recipient: explaining who collects the data and retention: the durability of storing data.

In this context, we define two groups of information practices:

Asked information practices:
These are the information practices of the collector or the requester of the information that describe how the information collector is going to deal with users' information. Usually, it's stored in the information collector privacy policy.

Allowed information practices:
Allowed information practices specify how users would like their information to be dealt with. It is stored in the user profile and compared to the information collector privacy policy each time a request is received for information collection.

Privacy Control Modes

Users are able to switch among a combination of three control modes regarding evaluating access to their private information. The ShEM then takes those modes into consideration in the consent evaluation part:

Manual mode: In this mode, the user is capable of manually controlling his/her information submission to information collectors. S/he decides completely whether to give information to an information collector or not. The ShEM directly gets a response from the user without passing through the evaluation process. Users' interactions are also stored in their profile so that the system learns from the users' preferences and makes use of it later in future requests.

Automatic mode: In this mode, the user is only capable of controlling his/her data through valuating the privacy attributes that govern the autonomous decision making process. S/he defines also allowed information practices. Evaluation of information collector requests is then performed autonomously by the *ShEM* and based on the results; the system recommends a decision without the need for users' interaction. However, there might be a case where *ShEM* cannot sharply define a decision. In this case, the system would switch to the manual mode and get user response manually.

Other Preferences

Information types: These allow evaluation to take place as per a group of information items. Users can categorize information items into groups or categories according to its confidentiality or content for example professional, personal and public. In this case, evaluation would take place per group rather than per the whole information items.

Collector groups: These allow evaluation to take place as per a group of information collectors, which have a common value, or interest for the user. Default groups of information collectors, such as trusted or non-trusted information collectors. This preference can help in bypassing the evaluation process and enforcing default evaluation by the running system.

Durability: Since we deal with dynamic environments, a need for dynamic preferences does exist as well. The durability preference refers to the time needed before an update is asked by the system for the user to update his/her preferences.

Comp_Pref Component: In this step, users' preferences on how their collected information should be used are compared to service providers' privacy policies. In this work, we adopt the platform of privacy preferences (P3P) specifications in modeling both information types. In (Cranor et al., 2002), a P3P preference exchange language (APPEL) was proposed as the language for expressing users' preferences. APPEL is a machine-readable specification of user's preferences that can be programmatically compared against a privacy policy. A P3P privacy policy is a step towards automating and simplifying user assessments of an information collector through the use of user agents and APPEL. When a service provider issues a request for user data, Comp_Pref

component would request for the privacy policy of the service provider on behalf of the user. Then Comp_Pref would automatically compare the privacy policy of the service provider with users privacy preferences expressed as a set of APPEL rules. Depending on rules evaluation, three types of consent would be issued: *request*, *limited* and *block*. *Request* results in all asked user data to be transmitted. When *limited*, only identity information is being blocked while a *block* consent blocks all information from being transmitted.

Automatic Consent Decision-Making Architecture (Consent Decider)

It is obvious that when users want to have control capabilities over their private information and, at the same time, want to achieve this control with as less as possible manual effort, uncertainty takes over. In addition, in a context-aware environment where a user is surrounded by a number of context sensors, it would be impossible for the user or the device to recognize all the information collectors and to manually take the right decisions. After all, users' decisions with minimizing their interactions should be carefully considered by the system by deriving (actually predicting) the next decisions based on previous decisions and actions. It is also extremely difficult to crisply quantify all influences mentioned above; for example how much confidential an information object is, or how much trustworthy an information collector is. Therefore, it is clear that dealing with such environment should be done in a way that allows effective dealing with uncertainty.

The use of fuzzy logic helps in supporting reasoning under uncertainty (Dubois & Prade, 1995). Since fuzzy inference systems are linguistically interpretable, it provides a useful way of combining collected data with expert knowledge . Therefore, we assume that the notation of fuzzy sets could help in better understanding of these factors and better classification and evaluation of their rules on the users final consent decisions.

In this chapter we adopt the fuzzy approach developed in (Ali Eldin, van den Berg, & Wagenaar, 2004) to develop consent decisions with regard to information collection. Their approach is based on the assumption that the existence of a correlation between privacy and a number of factors. These factors will be referred to as *privacy attributes*. In their work, they consider three factors as: Confidentiality of the information (*C*), trustworthiness of information collector (*T*) and users' interest in sharing (*I*). This assumption is expected not to influence the effectiveness of the proposed approach and in the future more factors could be added. Users are assumed to have the full capabilities to assign values for these factors. This could be realistic in case of context information confidentiality and interest in sharing. Both factors highly depend on the user perception and could vary from one user to another. However, trustworthiness of the information collector represents a different type of factors, which could be highly affected by other users' experiences or by the information collector reputation (Daskapan, Vree, & Ali Eldin, 2003).

The concept of fuzzy logic was first introduced by Zadeh (1973). Fuzzy logic employs fuzzy sets to deal with imprecise and incomplete phenomena (Bojadziev & Bojadziev, 1997). A fuzzy set is defined by a so-called membership function. A fuzzy set is a set without a crisp boundary, which qualifies it to represent human brain concepts and cognitive process (Konar, 2000). The Consent Decider component (see Figure 4) implements a mapping $X \rightarrow S$ where, for every context element, an *L*-dimensional input vector $x = (x_1, x_2, \ldots, x_L)$ of privacy attribute values is mapped into a calculated consent value *S*. The Consent Decider uses a Mamdani type (Mamdani, 1976) of fuzzy system architecture, so its kernel consists of a Mamdani reasoning engine together with a fuzzy rule base. Each privacy attribute variable x_i is given a set of appropriate linguistic values A_{ij} defined by membership functions $\mu_j(x_i)$. Similarly, the consent variable *S* is given a set of linguistic

values B_k defined by membership functions $\mu_k(s)$. Using these notations, rule *q* (*q=1, 2... Q*) of the rule base can be written as:

If x_1 is A_{1q} and x_2 is A_{2q} and ... x_L is A_{Lq}, then $S = B_q$.

A set of fuzzy rules is required: (a) to aggregate the output membership function values for each input vector $x = (x_1, x_2, \ldots, x_L)$, (b) to calculate the output membership function values and (c) to calculate the final crisp consent value (after a so-called 'de-fuzzification' step). The type and parameters of the membership functions A_{ij} and B_k can be defined empirically based on domain experience. Generally speaking, it is difficult to define the impact of the input variables on the final decision of user consent, because assessing these variables impact may differ from one user to another. In addition, there are situations where multiple of possibilities can exist with equal probability of occurrence. Additionally, fuzzy systems usually have static and predefined rule engines, which are an issue that makes it difficult to design personalized fuzzy systems. Therefore, in order to meet different users' demands and to provide a certain level of personalization, we suggest that each fuzzy rule be assigned a weighting value, which can be set by the users themselves. Hence, all possible rules are stored in a fuzzy rule repository or a rule space *RS* (see also Figure 4).

Figure 4. Consent decider: fuzzy system architecture

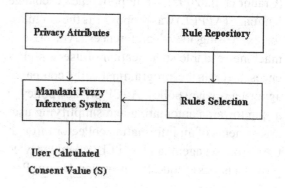

Users can assign a value called degree of support ($D_q \in [0,1]$) to each qth rule to rank or prioritize its validity against others in situations where a number of possibilities exist. So rules with "*0*" degree of support will not be "fired".

Consent Evaluator

The calculated consent value (*FnCalcCs*) from the consent decider component will vary from 0 to 1. The consent variable in the fuzzy process is considered as a fuzzy set of three value categories {Low, Medium, High}. Then the consent decider output *FnCalcCs* will be checked in which region of output values it is, based on threshold values δ_L and δ_H. A calculated value *Medium* means that the consent decider component could not define sharply the impact of the set of privacy attributes. In this case, we rely on the user on giving a definitive consent value for the system to continue its decision. At the same time, Comp_Pref generates an output, which is defined into three categories according to threshold values Ω_L and Ω_H (see Figure 5). Both outputs represent input to the consent evaluator.

The consent evaluator rules can be summarized as follows:

- The evaluator checks first whether automatic control mode is set.
- If the automatic control mode is set to false, then the consent decision will be made by manual interference of the user.
- If the automatic control mode is set to true, then the consent decision process will go through the comp_pref, and consent decider components.
- The evaluator rules in aggregating both values from comp_pref and consent decider component are represented as follows:

```
If (FnCalcCs = comp_pref) then
consent = comp_pref
If (FnCalcCs = comp_pref +) then
consent = comp_pref
If FnCalcCs = comp_pref ++) then
consent = comp_pref +
else
set manual control mode to
"true".
End if
```

Figure 5. Evaluator rules

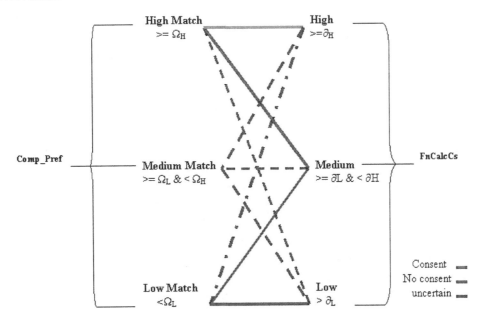

Where comp_pref + means one stage higher, and comp_pref ++ means two stages higher than comp_pref value. For example, if comp_pref = "Low", then comp_pref + = "Medium" and comp_pref ++ = "High".

EXPERIMENTAL WORK

In this section, we discuss the design, implementation and operational results of two prototypes of the ShEM model architecture. The objective of this experimental work is to verify the feasibility and usefulness of the suggested architecture by implementing and testing it with technology and real users. It also helps in understanding different dimensions of the investigated problem in domain specific applications and to refine the proposed solution. In this experimental work, we implemented *ShEM* with a location-based service scenario called "Finding people". Actually, two

prototypes have been implemented of the ShEM model: one that depends mainly on automatic control by using fuzzy technology, and the other that adopts a fully manual control via short messages. The two prototypes differ basically in privacy evaluation and also in the test groups, which will be described later (see Figure 6).

Design Features and Functionalities

The aim was to have a privacy aware finding people service designed in such away that it enables users to specify their allowed information practices and privacy attributes in order to evaluate consent decisions on any incoming request for users' data. Finding people service was developed to be one of the services offered by a UMTS test bed platform called MIES (Kar, 2004), an acronym for Mobile Information and Entertainment Services. MIES offers GIS location-based services and tourist information to

Figure 6. Experimental work layout

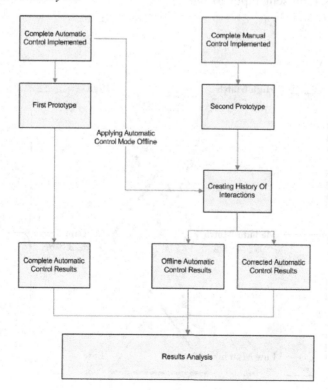

university campus visitors. It also enables users to locate and to contact each other. We have designed *ShEM* for this service to allow users to search for other users of MIES and to locate them, taking into consideration privacy issues.

MIES services were delivered to users through an UMTS network, provided by a mobile service provider with a UMTS license. For the MIES project this role was fulfilled on the campus by T-Mobile. With its higher bandwidth than GPRS (and also GSM on which it is based), the UMTS network is a 3G broadband packet-based transmission network for text, digitized voice, video and multimedia at data rates up to 2 Megabits/second theoretically. Content providers make available their content for MIES users via secure connections to their intranets via the Internet. Users are equipped with an HP/Compaq iPAQ PDA UMTS cell phone and a GPS receiver, either a separate one connected to the iPAQ via Bluetooth, or a slot-loading GPS receiver clicking into the iPAQ (Kar, 2004).

On the iPAQ, Tom-Tom Navigator is installed. For the sake of simplicity, maps were all stored locally on the iPAQ. Besides, there is the MIES position updater (MPU), a program specifically developed by the MIES project, that sends the current GPS location of the iPAQ to a web server application, and receives a (latitude, longitude) position from it in return. If the web server application returns a position to the MPU, it opens the Tom-Tom Navigator map-view and shows the (latitude, longitude) location on the screen.

Context Information Clusters

Users profile has been defined into three clusters of information:

Personal information: this includes any information that is personal in nature such as name, date of birth, telephone numbers, address etc.

Professional Information: This includes information that is professional in nature such as job title, organization, work address, visiting address, e-mail address, research interests, research fields, etc.

Location information: this includes information about users' device IP addresses and users' GPS location. Location is assumed to represent context since knowing location in the campus can reveal a users activity or context for example, being in the library, office or in a restaurant.

Getting Users Data Input and Privacy Preferences

Users were asked to fill in two online web forms, the first one with their personal and professional data, while the second one asks about their privacy preferences. Users' identity information such as IP address was simultaneously collected as well. The GPS location was captured from a

Figure 7. Finding people menus

GPS satellite by a GPS receiver connected to the iPAQ and the corresponding latitude and longitude coordinates were stored in the database with a 5 seconds refresh rate.

Valuating Privacy Attributes

Privacy attributes represent factors that influence users' willingness to share their information with other users in the MIES. Users were responsible to fill in their privacy attributes through a web-based form with values from 1 to 10. The three privacy attributes: *I, C* and *T* refer to "*users interest in sharing*", "*confidentiality of the information*" and "*trustworthiness of information collector*" respectively. Each user has three records of privacy attributes, one per each group of information. Each record contains values of the privacy attributes. Context clusters of information and privacy attributes have been developed and implemented by a MySQL relational database, and on an Apache server.

The main functionality of 'Finding people' is to facilitate subscribed users of the service to have access to each other's stored information. Users have to specify search criteria based on which requested data are retrieved back to them. The search criteria consist of the following: name, language and field of research.

Embedded Consent Decision-Making

The Mathwork Matlab[1] Mamdani fuzzy inference system was used in implementing the consent decider fuzzy system. All variables were considered to have three fuzzy membership functions: low, medium and high. The Gaussian function was used in implementing the fuzzy membership functions for all variables. According to common sense reasoning, it could be assumed that confidentiality of an information object and trust in an information collector are correlated and that their effect could be seen on the users willingness to sharing via the attribute: user interest in sharing

by decreasing it or increasing it. Therefore, the following rules were used in generating the FIS rule space:

Per each context element and an information collector, a rule q could be formulated as:

If $(\|T_q\| > \|C_q\|)$ Then $\|S_q\| = \|I_q\|$-- ➜ (Less strictness)

If $(\|T_q\| = \|C_q\|)$ Then $\|S_q\| = \|I_q\|$ ➜ (Highly depends on the user)

If $(\|T_q\| < \|C_q\|)$ Then $\|S_q\| = \|I_q\|$++ ➜ (more strictness),

Where

'I' strictness decreases from Low (L) towards High (H), passing by Medium (M).

'I++' means current 'I' value or the next lower ones in strictness.

'I—' means current 'I' values or the previous higher ones in strictness.

- Note: if $(\|I_k\| = M)$ then $\|I_k\|$++ $= L$ & $\|I_k\|$-- $= H)$, $q = 1,..,Q$.

Inspired by P3P (Cranor et al., 2004), we define the output consent set into three elements {Block Limit, Request} and represent the membership functions by the Gaussian membership function, such that:

- Block: rejects the sending of user information
- Limit: rejects sending all the information that helps identifying the user such as address, name, location, ID, etc.
- Request: allows sending all user information.

The *ShEM* functional components were compiled into a stand-alone win32 application and integrated into the other components of the system (see Figure 8).

Automatic Privacy Evaluation

Before a search request is actually carried out, privacy consent evaluation takes place in order to determine what type of data could be retrieved. In the first prototype of SHEM, a complete automatic privacy evaluation was carried out. For the sake of simplicity, there was only one information practice considered, "Purpose of search", representing purpose of collection. Purpose of search is provided by the 'requesting user' and describes what type of action the requesting user would take up at receiving the user data searched for. On the other hand, each user is asked to determine the purposes they allow. Three categories of purpose collection were distinguished:

Personal Knowledge. It represents the default purpose of collection, meaning that the information collector collects the information for his/her own personal knowledge interest.

Formal Appointments. Users are allowed to collect knowledge about the other user for the purpose of personal interest and to ask for professional appointments.

Informal Appointments. Similar as to the previous one, but now users are also allowed to ask for informal appointments such as coffee breaks, dinners etc.

When a user requests to access specific information of a certain user, his/her request passes through the consent evaluator (*CnsEval) procedures* which in turns decide whether to give access to the requesting user or not. Each specific block of information has a record in the database with all related privacy attributes and consent values. Before the *CnsEval procedures* are called, the attributes values are retrieved, and the *consent decider* component is activated. For the sake of simplicity, the consent decider fuzzy rules were implemented with (*DoS) =1*. The *CnsEval procedure* is called with both requesting and searched users purposes calculating consent values and then returning a Boolean value "true or false" corresponding to the user final consent[2].

Two consent evaluator procedures were implemented CnsEvalPers and CnsEvalProf (see APPENDIX 1). All personal and professional information delivered to the requesting user is

Figure 8. Generating CalcCs from privacy attributes

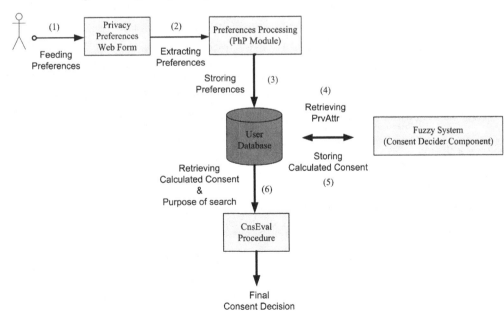

presented simultaneously on the same page. In this prototype, location information was not included in the consent evaluation due to time constraints related to the MIES project availability; however, its evaluation in theory would have been done similar to other information types except that the MPU application would be called each time to define the location (using a Tom-Tom Navigator map). If the output of CnsEvalPers is true then the following personal information will be shown: Name, Address, City, Country, Email address and Organization. If the output is false then only Name will be shown in the final form (see Figure 9). To retrieve the CalcCS for professional information, the Boolean function CnsEvalProf with the parameters CalcCS, PurposeOfSearch and purpose allowed would check if professional information could be retrieved. If CnsEvalProf output is *true* then professional fields will be shown: Profession and Research area; if CnsEvalProf output is *false* then no fields at all will be shown (see Figure 10).

Manual Privacy Evaluation

In the second prototype, a manual evaluation of privacy was implemented. Users were able to fully control which user has access to which information. With short messages (SMS based) a user has to send an access request for a certain type of information; the requested user has to respond manually with the type of consent s/he gives. Users were asked to freely experiment with the service for a week. Their responses were stored in the history database.

We assumed that fully manual control of user information collection by others could be effectively achieved through messages. For example, as a user's location will change, a user's willingness to allow others to see his/her location will change. However, this option of letting users have manually full control capabilities of their information access by others is somehow cumbersome for the users themselves. We expect that manual control

Figure 10. Example of restriction on personal information, no restriction on professional information

Figure 9. Example of consent to all information

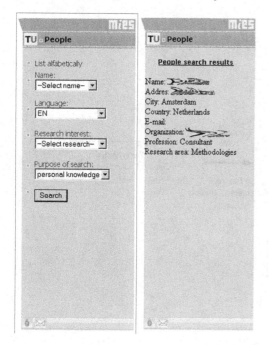

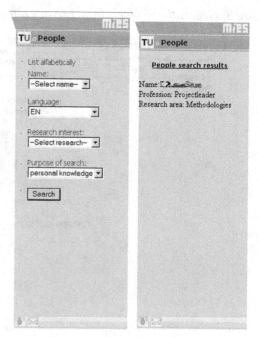

is not acceptable for usability reasons in this context-aware environment and so we do need a way of having this control function performed automatically as well. However, a flexible approach to solve this issue is a challenging one. The objective of this manual prototype was to study the feasibility and effect of manual control on enhancing the automatically calculated consent. Manual control is regarded as a separate mode of operation, which users specify in their preferences. Figure 11 shows how this manual control was implemented. Firstly a user would navigate to the Find people form. In this form, s/he would choose search criteria. Then, s/he would specify the type of requested information. *ShEM* would respond with list of users matching the specified search criteria. The further user (information owner) would receive a short message with user name and type of information s/he is asking. The further user would then have to give consent

manually to the requested type of information s/he would allow.

RESULTS ANALYSIS

As mentioned above, in the first prototype a complete real time automatic control was implemented while in the second prototype a complete manual control was implemented. In the second prototype, each manual response was associated with an offline calculated automatic consent value. The correction formula (3) was applied and a new consent value was created per each response. In both prototypes, users were asked to evaluate their satisfaction with the privacy functionality through a questionnaire. In the questionnaire, they were asked about what type of privacy control they preferred. Unexpectedly, the average agreement among users was to be able to manually

Figure 11. Manual control

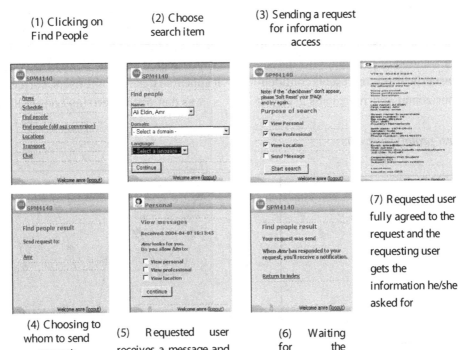

(1) Clicking on Find People

(2) Choose search item

(3) Sending a request for information access

(4) Choosing to whom to send request

(5) Requested user receives a message and is asked to give consent for information to show

(6) Waiting for the requested user response

(7) Requested user fully agreed to the request and the requesting user gets the information he/she asked for

control their information collection by others, although they were not against automatic control by SHEM as such. It could be inferred that most users wanted to have both manual and automatic control capabilities of their information collection. Accordingly, we enunciate that there should be a way of balancing this issue. A fully automatic control of users' information is not feasible in daily life interactions, since it is impossible to perfectly model each user's behavior. On the other hand, a fully manual control challenges user friendliness and the overall performance of the application.

Automatic Control Prototype

There were 12 registered users to the MIES service in the first prototype, most of them foreign visitors to the university campus attending for a conference. They used the MIES services for three consecutive days. Initial results, obtained in the automatic control experiment, showed that most users have had different preferences regarding their privacy attributes, and that the three groups of information differed in confidentiality from low, in case of professional information, up to high in case of location or personal information (see Figure 12a: vertical axis represents confidentiality while horizontal axis represents users). It

was also noticed that only four users had different calculated consent values per each group of information and that calculated consent was the highest in case of professional information for all users, while location was recorded to be of lower consent value than personal information in case of user 12 only (see Figure 12b). Most users had equal calculated consent values for both personal and location information.

Manual Control Prototype

For the second prototype a group of 22 students was asked to test the service for a week. Pairs of 2 students got again an iPAQ, a phone and a GPS receiver. During the manual control experiment, a history of user interactions was recorded. Each time a consent decision is made by a user, a corresponding consent is calculated automatically and associated with that manually defined consent. The fuzzy system (consent decider component), tested in the first prototype, was called offline to calculate a consent S_t given users privacy attributes. Then, these calculated values were corrected using based on users' experiences and per each request there was three consent values; manual consent $\bar{S}_t$, corrected consent $\hat{S}_t$ and fuzzy consent (S_t). It appeared that for some users, corrected consent $\hat{S}_t$ was damped to zero (no consent) because us-

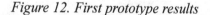

Figure 12. First prototype results

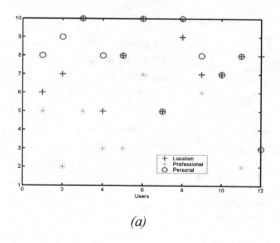

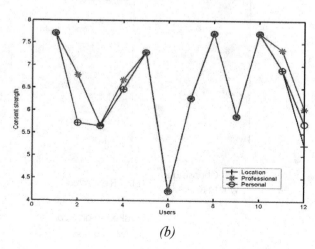

(a)   (b)

ers did not accept these requests ($\bar{S}_t = 0$). The majority had fuzzy calculated permissions (S_f) that were very close to the manual ones. Further, users estimated consent values differed depending on who was requesting for their information, which implies the effect of trustworthiness on consent decisions.

Figure 13 *show the influence of correction on customizing users' consent decisions according to their own experiences:* horizontal axis refers to the requests and vertical axis refers to calculated consent values per requester.

Evaluation Tests

The participants were asked if they agreed or disagreed with the statements as listed in the questionnaire (see appendix 2). Score could range from "1 highly agree" to "7 highly disagree". From these scores an average score for each participant for each statement was derived in addition to an overall average of users' responses. Users were asked about the overall performance of the system in terms of their satisfaction of privacy protection, type of preferred control modes and whether they need to add more preferences to the predefined preferences.

Having experimented with the first prototype, the group of 12 conference visitors to the campus was asked if they agreed or disagreed with the following statements:

- I could easily define my privacy settings.
- People could contact me though I did not ask for that.
- By SHEM I am able to self control my privacy.
- My privacy is guaranteed with SHEM.

The overall mean of the four statements per respondent is seen to be "4" which means that most of the respondents were neutral whether privacy performance of SHEM was acceptable.

Next, answers were given to more specific questions regarding the privacy preferences of the users:

- SHEM should always and automatically handle users request for my info. The mean is 3.8 so most respondents *almost agreed* to the statement.
- SHEM should always ask me before letting others contact me. The mean is 2.5; most respondents *agreed* to this statement.

Figure 13. Final estimated permissions per location information

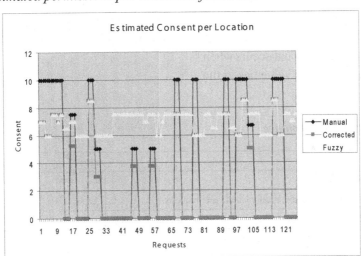

- I need to add new privacy preferences to SHEM. The mean is 4.0; 50% of the respondents (do not) agree to this statement (*neutral*).

For the second test round, a brainstorm was held on what problems one encountered, what was missing and what could be improved. The respondents of the second test round were equally positive/negative about the privacy performance of the service. They agreed less on the statement that SHEM always should ask the user before letting others contact the user (see Table 2).

DISCUSSION AND CONCLUSION

Before ambient systems become widely available, a number of challenges need to be addressed. End users control of their private contextual information should be effectively achieved. In addition, this control by end users should be optimized in such a way that it allows them to combine both manual and automatic control features. In this chapter, we developed and tested the *ShEM* model. A UMTS location-based service was implemented and used by two groups of real users.

Results obtained showed that users are not willing to rely on a fully automatic control of their contextual data sharing. They need to have more manual control capabilities as well. Additionally, from the technical point of view, using the consent decider component still yields calculated results that are uncertain in some cases. That occurs when the finally estimated permission value lies in the

medium region (neither low nor high). Hence, we enunciate that any privacy control architecture should take into consideration the possibility that users are asked explicitly to give consent.

Based on questionnaire evaluation, it appeared that the overall privacy performance of the fully automatic control prototype was not satisfactory due to users need to have more control capabilities. In the second fully manual prototype, the overall privacy performance was again not evaluated as satisfactory, and users reported the need for more automatic handling of requests by SHEM on behalf of them. Therefore, we could conclude that better privacy control would be achieved via an approach that can combine both manual and automatic control capabilities and to flexibly allow users to switch between the two modes. However, this switching between modes - if done manually - would not ensure high flexibility and usability, unless it is also automated. In other words, it should be able to allow this switching autonomously and/or manually if necessary. In order to allow this dynamic mode of operation, intelligent learning mechanisms are required such as case based reasoning techniques where the system learns from previous cases on which decisions to make in the future. This issue is to be taken into consideration in the design of the preferences part. In addition, and in order to deal with the uncertainty problems, more sophisticated fuzzy or probabilistic approaches might be taken into consideration. This is currently subject of further research by our group.

Table 2. Overall privacy performance

Experiment		First	Second
Privacy performance		4,0	3,8
Privacy preferences	Automatically handle user requests	3,8	4,5
	Always ask me before letting others contact me	2,5	4,2
	I need to add new preferences	4,0	4,3

ACKNOWLEDGMENT

This work was performed during the author employment by Delft University of Technology. He would like to submit this work to the soul of Professor René Wagenaar who had supported this work in every possible way.

REFERENCES

Ackerman, M., Darrell, T., & Weitzner, D. J. (2001). Privacy in context. *HCI, 16*(2), 167-179.

Ali Eldin, A., van den Berg, J., & Wagenaar, R. (2004). *A Fuzzy reasoning scheme for context sharing decision making.* Paper presented at the the 6th International Conference on Electronic Commerce, Delft, The Netherlands.

Ali Eldin, A., & Wagenaar, R. (2003). *Towards a Component based Privacy Protector Architecture.* Paper presented at the 15. CAiSE 2003 Short Papers, Klagenfurt, Austria.

Ali Eldin, A., & Wagenaar, R. (2004). *Towards a users driven privacy control.* Paper presented at the the IEEE conference on Systems, Man, and Cybernetics (SMC 2004), The Hague.

Bojadziev, G., & Bojadziev, M. (1997). *Fuzzy Logic for Business, Finance, and Management*: World Scientific.

Camenisch, J., & Herreweghen, E. V. (2002). *Design and Implementation of Idemix Anonymous Credential System*: IBM Zurich Research Laboratory.

Casal, C. R. (2001). *Privacy Protection For Location Based Mobile Services in Europe.* Paper presented at the the 5th World Multi-Conference on Systems, Cybernetics, and Informatics (SCI2001), Orlando, Florida USA.

Cranor, L., Langheinrich, M., & Marchiori, M. (2002). *A P3P Preference Exchange Language 1.0 (APPEL1.0) W3C Working Draft.*

Cranor, L., Langheinrich, M., Marchiori, M., Presler-Marshall, M., & Reagle, J. (2004). *The Platform for Privacy Preferences 1.1 (P3P1.1) Specification W3C Working Draft.*

Daskapan, S., Vree, W. G., & Ali Eldin, A. (2003). *Trust metrics for survivable security systems.* Paper presented at the The IEEE International Conference on Systems, Man & Cybernetics,, Washington.

Dubois, D., & Prade, H. (1995). What does fuzzy logic bring to AI? *ACM Computing Surveys (CSUR),, 27*(3).

EuropeanDirective. (2002). Directive 2002/58/EC of the European Parliament and of the Council of 12 July 2002, electronic communications sector (Directive on privacy and electronic communications). *Official Journal of the European Communities, L*, 201-237.

Hauser, C., & Kabatnik, M. (2001). *Towards Privacy Support in a Global Location Service.* Paper presented at the the IFIP Workshop on IP and ATM Traffic Management (WATM/EUNICE 2001), Paris.

Kar, E. A. M. v. d. (2004). *Designing mobile information services; An Approach for Organisations in a Value Network.* Unpublished Doctoral dissertation, Delft University of Technology, Delft, The Netherlands.

Konar, A. (2000). *Artificial Intelligence and Soft Computing: Behavioral and Cognitive Modeling of the Human Brain.* New York: CRC Press.

Mamdani, E. H. (1976). Advances in the Linguistic Synthesis of Fuzzy Controllers. *Journal of Man-Machine Studies, 8*, 669-678.

Nilsson, M., Lindskog, H., & Fischer-Hübner, S. (2001). *Privacy Enhancements in the Mobile Internet.* Paper presented at the the IFIP WG 9.6/11.7 working conference on Security and Control of IT in Society, Bratislava.

Zadeh, L. A. (1973). Outline of a new approach to the analysis of complex systems and decision processes. *IEEE Trans. on Systems, Man and Cybernetics, 3*(1), 28-44.

ENDNOTES

[1] http://www.mathworks.com/products/matlab/

[2] when the CalcCs is in uncertainty area, we took an average of "5" between high and low CalcCs values.

APPENDIX A.

```
Function CnsEvalPers(CalcCs, PurposeOfSearch, PurposeAllowed)
CnsEvalPers = False
IF PurposeOfSearch > PurposeAllowed then
CnsEvalPers = False
ElseIf PurposeOfSearch <= PurposeAllowed And CalcCs => 5 then
CnsEvalPers = True
ElseIF PurposeOfSearch <= PurposeAllowed And CalcCs < 5 then
CnsEvalPers = False
Else
CnsEvalPers = False
End If
End Function


Function CnsEvalProf(CalcCs, PurposeOfSearch, PurposeAllowed)
CnsEvalProf = False
IF PurposeOfSearch > PurposeAllowed then
CnsEvalProf = False
ElseIf PurposeOfSearch <= PurposeAllowed And CalcCs => 5 then
CnsEvalProf = True
ElseIF PurposeOfSearch <= PurposeAllowed And CalcCs < 5 then
CnsEvalProf = False
Else
CnsEvalProf = False
End If
End Function
```

APPENDIX B. QUESTIONNAIRE

Statements	Highly agree	Agree	Almost agree	Neutral	Almost disagree	Disagree	Highly disagree
	1	2	3	4	5	6	7
I could easily define my privacy settings							
People could contact me, though I didn't ask for that							
SHEM should always and automatically handle users requests for my w WHAinfo							
SHEM should always ask me before letting others contact me							
I need to add new privacy preferences to SHEM							
By SHEM, I am able to self control my privacy							
My privacy is guaranteed with SHEM							

Chapter IX
A Projection of the Future Effects of Quantum Computation on Information Privacy

Geoff Skinner
Curtin University of Technology, Australia

Elizabeth Chang
Curtin University of Technology, Australia

ABSTRACT

Many of the current issues with Information Privacy have been the result of inadequate consideration for privacy during the planning, design and implementation of Information Systems and communication networks. The area of Quantum Computation is still in its infancy, and a truly functional quantum computer has not been implemented. However, it is anticipated that within the next decade it may be feasible. This presents a unique opportunity to give due consideration to Information Privacy in the realm of future quantum computational devices and environments while they are still in their infancy. This chapter provides an overview of the key Information Privacy issues that the authors feel may arise with the evolution and realization of quantum computation. Additionally they propose an integrated approach of technical, legal and social elements to address these issues.

INTRODUCTION

Recent research into the field of Quantum Computation has produced many interesting issues and alternative approaches to information and communication security. As with classical computer system evolution the new field of quantum computation is already at risk of following a similar path of overlooking information privacy concerns. Clarke (1999) defines information privacy as being a combination of communications privacy and data privacy. He formally defines it as '… the interest an individual has in controlling, or at least significantly influencing, the handling of data about themselves' (Clarke, 1999). An individual's concern about their information privacy is a significant issue regardless of the technology used to .implement the information systems the entities are interacting with. It is widely regarded that many of the current information systems privacy inadequacies derive from the fact that privacy was never a serious consideration during the development life cycle of the systems (Skinner and Chang, 2005). This is in addition to the fact that the idea of privacy is itself very subjective in nature, unique to each individual and influenced by a broad range of factors from context to culture (He, 2006; Wishart, 2005). From a financial perspective the ability to place monetary values on individual privacy is very difficult and therefore hard to integrate such factors into system design specifications and costing (Faja, 2005).

Modern privacy solutions are often derived from the application, both in combination and isolation, of the four main models of privacy protection (EPIC, 2003). The models are Comprehensive Laws, Sectoral Laws, Self Regulation, and Technologies of Privacy. Of interest to our own work is the impact of quantum computation on privacy enhancing technologies (PETs). The reason being is that many of the technology of privacy solutions rely on varying levels of computationally secure methods, such as encryption, to provide security and privacy of personal data (Skinner and Chang, 2006a). With the advent of quantum computation and the possible realization in the near future of a quantum computer, many previous computationally secure methodologies will become redundant as they are tested in quantum networks and environments. For example the application of Shor's Algorithm (Shor, 1994) to find prime factors of a large number in polynomial

time jeopardizes many cryptographic algorithms, such as RSA and PGP, many of which are used in privacy protection mechanisms.

While the advent of quantum computation does raise serious concerns to the effectiveness of many current privacy protection mechanisms, it is not all negative. Quantum computation also offers many advantages, which through its proper use, combined with other features of quantum mechanics and specific classical computational elements can be used to provide better privacy protection. Some areas currently under research and generating a lot of interest include quantum cryptography (Bennett, 1984), Quantum based Private Information Retrieval (PIR) (Wehner, 2004), Quantum anonymous transmissions Christandl, 2005), and quantum privacy amplification (Deutsch, 1996). The focus of this paper is to provide a foundational perspective of our work investigating Information Privacy issues in the realm of quantum computation. We propose that solutions to address the increased privacy threats posed by quantum computation are similar to a degree of those required for current information privacy issues. That is, not only does Information Privacy conformance need to be integrated from system inception, but an effective privacy solution must be a symbiotic molding of technical, legal, and social elements.

The rest of the paper follows a common structure outline as follows. The next section provides relevant background material on Information Privacy for data at rest and in transit. Additional supplementary quantum computation areas are also discussed. The next section provides a number of quantum, terms defined for the context of our work, in addition to applicability to information privacy. Our research summary of a number of Quantum Computational technologies and their impact on Information Privacy is included in the section that follows, entitled 'Information Privacy in the Quantum Era'. The section 'What Can Be Done?' provides our proposals on what can be done to insure information privacy protection in

Quantum Computational capable environments. A brief conclusion and future work is provided in the final section before the references.

BACKGROUND AND RELATED WORK

Quantum Computation reaches its full potential when the operational environment is what is termed a quantum network. A quantum network consists of quantum computing devices representing the nodes connected with quantum communication lines (Giedke, 2006). As the topology of a network is abstracted from the technology of nodes and communication lines a number of security and privacy issues faced with classical networking environments are also applicable to quantum networks. While it is acknowledged that researchers still have a long way to go in understanding the potential and limitations of quantum computation, one group has a stated goal of building a "quantum Internet" (Robinson, 2000). So with the potential realization of quantum networks and a quantum Internet individuals are still faced with Information Privacy issues and questions about the privacy implications of the new technology. Our research aims to address these issues and find potential privacy benefits of quantum computation.

Quantum computation and the operational environment of quantum networks may inherent many of the same privacy issues that are faced by classical information systems and communication technologies (IBM, 2003). However, it is the possibility that many unseen problems may be part of the new technology and therefore need investigation in respect to the quantum operational context. Our focus is on Information Privacy rather than Information Security, and specifically Privacy Enhancing Technologies (Goldberg, 2002). The uniqueness of privacy in terms of its subjective nature and openness to individual interpretation and representation has allowed it

to evolve with advances in technology, society, culture and values (Davison, 2003). In the field of IS research privacy solutions are not always based on technological approaches. The use and enforcement of legal regulations, laws (sectoral and comprehensive), and even self regulation attempts will still be applicable to information privacy in quantum networks. However, protection against intentional malicious attacks is still heavily reliant on technological solutions. Therefore, when approaching information privacy issues in the age of quantum computation, our objective is to focus on the technological components.

According to the Common Criteria (CC, 2003) privacy requirements for identity and privacy protection are concerned with Anonymity, Pseudonymity, Unlinkability and Unobservability. These set of requirements also provide a baseline level of protection requirements for privacy enhancing technologies (PETs). A major set of tools that facilitate these requirements is that of encryption. Encryption in general is used to protect information stored on a computer or transmitted over communication networks. By preventing access to data it also helps protect privacy. A number of PETs make extensive use of encryption in some form to help protect privacy. These include the Identity Protector (Blarkom, 2003), Privacy Shield (Skinner, 2006b), and Privacy Protector (Gritzalis, 2004). The form of encryption used is normally based on some form of Public Key Infrastructure (PKI), RSA, and other computationally hard (from a classical sense) algorithms. However, it has been shown that through the application of Shor's (Shor, 1994) work on factorization using quantum principles, many of the previous computationally secure encryption schemes can be compromised. Therefore any levels of privacy protection offered by PET's using encryption tools as part of their infrastructure will be in jeopardy. Another not so obvious threat to privacy with the advent of quantum computation is Grover's algorithm (Grover, 1997). Basically this application of quantum principles dramatically decreases the amount of time it takes to search for a specific marked item in an unsorted database. Applied to many such data sources, in combination with advanced data mining and profiling algorithms, access and generation of personal profiles would be even more accessible.

With any new information technology with potential risks for privacy also come the potential for privacy benefits. The field of quantum computation is no exception. Perhaps the biggest advantage of the new technology is the fact it is so new. Being in its infancy allows system designers to hopefully learn from previous mistakes, in particular the design oversights of classical systems when considering information privacy. Privacy by design is a key concept that should be applied to all new information systems, whether they are classical or quantum in nature. Even hybrid combinations of both technologies can offer better privacy protection to the users of the systems. For example, while quantum computers are still some time away from general use, quantum cryptography over both classical and quantum communication networks has been achieved and commercial products are now available (Giedke, 2003; Robinson, 2000). So while quantum cryptography may still provide no protection against "man-in-the-middle" attacks they do offer unsurpassed levels of encryption protection through their creative application. For example, the classical Vernam code (Protechnix, 2001), which is unbreakable, has always suffered from key distribution problems. Through the application of quantum mechanical principles this issue is solved. The details are not provided here but may be found in (Bennett, 1984). What is important is the fact that information privacy benefited from such an application. Our work serves two purposes then. Firstly to highlight potential threats to information privacy and any advantages that may be gained from the quantum era we may soon be immersed in when applied to information privacy protection. Secondly,

we propose some ideas to address the threats to privacy in the Quantum Era. We show that many of these solutions will require a unique molding of technical, legal and social elements to ensure information privacy is preserved.

QUANTUM CONCEPTS AS THEY RELATE TO INFORMATION PRIVACY

Quantum computation is a relatively new field of research open to many new ideas, concepts, and proposals. In the absence of widely accepted formal definitions it is beneficial for new works to provide definitions for the terminology to be used throughout the work. This section elaborates on a number of concepts and technologies discussed in the previous sections in the context of information privacy. It should be noted that the definitions provided are the authors own interpretations for use throughout our work.

Quantum Computation: We use the term quantum computation to encompass any digital/computing environment that utilizes quantum mechanical principles and technologies in its operation. For example, it may involve the use of a quantum computer to solve a particular problem, such as attempting to break RSA encryption technologies. In general quantum computation offers a number of benefits and risks to information privacy. From a benefits perspective information privacy can be maintained or even improved through the application of quantum encryption to ensure data security of sensitive personal information both at rest and in transit. However, information privacy may be at risk in traditional information systems where quantum computation can be applied in malicious ways. This includes attacking classical encryption methods, shown to be significantly weakened when subjected to quantum computational attacks as well as the ability to search large data stores in significantly reduced amounts of time. The ability for an entity to be profiled or have vast amounts of personal information collected about them is possible with quantum computation.

Quantum Computers: We use the term quantum computers to represent the actual devices that are capable of executing quantum computational processes. That is, quantum mechanical technologies provide the functionality of the computing device permitting significantly faster processing speeds over traditional or classical computer systems. Quantum computers are capable of manipulating atoms and photos rather than electronic signals found in traditional or classical computers. Again quantum computers can provide both a number of benefits and risks to information privacy. Advantages include quantum computers being able to implement quantum encryption to protect the data residing on and being transmitted out of the computer. Information privacy disadvantages include the ability to use the quantum computer as a tool for maliciously 'attacking' encrypted data that is not intended to be accessed by the attacking entity.

Quantum Networks: We use this term to describe digital networks that are capable of supporting quantum mechanical operations. This includes the transmission of data in quantum states, therefore fiber optic channels and other supporting network infrastructure are required to facilitate the generation of the photons and the transmission of the particles between locations. Quantum networks support the use of quantum cryptography which provides information privacy protection in quantum computational environments. Potential information privacy drawbacks include the need to re-transmit signals if they have found to be corrupted by intentional or unintentional interference.

The fundamental difference in digital computational capabilities between classical computing environments compared with those in quantum computing environments is the methods of data representation and manipulation. That is, atoms and photos replace electric signals for binary data representations of the bits 1 and 0.

INFORMATION PRIVACY IN THE QUANTUM ERA

With space limitations of a short paper the best approach to represent our work in progress is consideration of the key elements under investigation. This translates to consideration of key Quantum computational technologies that have either been realized or are still theoretical in nature. Discussion of each quantum technology is from an Information Privacy perspective in regards to potential threats to or and benefits for privacy. The topics included here are not a complete list but rather areas of particular relevance to Information Privacy issues that should be considered in a quantum network, whether realized or theoretical.

Quantum Computers and Shor's Algorithm: The central premise to quantum computing is the derivation and use of algorithms based on quantum mechanical properties in order to process information faster (Giedke, 2003). The algorithm that would represent the pinnacle of such research is one that provides an exponential speed increase. That is, solving a problem by quantum means in polynomial time, where it would normally take exponential time with classical computers. To date, the most useful proposed algorithm is the one developed by Shor (Shor, 1994). Simply stated it would allow a quantum computer to find the prime factors of a large number in polynomial time. What would take a computational infeasible amount of time on a classical computer could be achieved in seconds on a quantum machine. The obvious threat here is that many modern encryption algorithms are based in this principle. That is, it would take an extraordinary if not impossible amount of time to find the prime factors of a very large number (RSA, PKI methods, etc). So infrastructures using these encryption algorithms for encrypting data at rest and transmitted over communication networks would be at risk. As a direct consequence any personal data included would be exposed and an individual's privacy compromised.

Quantum Computers and Grover's Algorithm: Like Shor's proposal Grover (Grover, 1997) has put forward an algorithm that takes advantage of quantum mechanical properties for processing speed increases. In this case it reduces the number of queries needed to search for a marked item in an unsorted database of N entries from N, classically, to about the square root of N, by quantum computation. Threats to information privacy may not be immediately evident until we consider applications such as data mining, profiling, and sharing of data from different organizations and data sources, such as data intelligence gathering. Many previous searches may have been seen as unfeasible, ineffective, or to costly use of resources as the time and number of queries needed to extract useful information was far too large. However, quantum computation and the use of Grover's algorithm have the potential to bring many of these searches into the realm of feasibility. As not all profiling and data mining is done with an individual's best interest in mind it represents a threat to information privacy and personal data protection. Many schemes that relied on anonymity or even pseudo-anonymity through obfuscation or hiding among large data sets may also be at risk for similar reasons.

Quantum Cryptography: Quantum cryptography relies on the laws of physics rather than various mathematical techniques to encrypt data. Classical cryptography, besides implementation of the Vernam cipher which has proved difficult and therefore impractical with classical implementation methods, can not guarantee absolute security of information. Therefore where that information is personal data it can not guarantee absolute privacy either. Quantum cryptography provides complete security of communication allowing two parties to exchange an enciphering key over a private channel. With secure key exchanges one time pads (Vernam) ciphers can be used to ensure both secure communication and privacy of any personal data communicated. It should be noted however that currently quantum cryptographic techniques are still susceptible to "man-in-the-middle attack" known as brigade attack. This issue is the focus of many research groups and there are positive signs for issue resolution.

Private Information Retrieval (PIR): PIR enables a user to retrieve an entry from a database, while hiding the index of the requested entry (Wehner, 2004). Through the use of quantum computation it has been shown that the communication complexity of PIR can be significantly reduced. A quantum PIR is characterized by a quantum server and communication over a quantum channel. The whole premise of PIR forms an important component of privacy protecting systems. Quantum computation makes its use for feasible for the technology to widely available.

Anonymous Transmissions: Protocols used to hide the sender and recipient of message are known as anonymous transmission protocols. They provide another privacy protection tool in that they are able to hide the identities of entities involved in data exchanges. Many classical protocols of this nature are under threat with the advent of quantum computation for similar reasons most classical encryption methods are at threat. However, in (Wehner, 2004; Christandl, 2005) a new quantum protocol has been proposed that provides anonymous transmission with perfect repudiation. Such a protocol ensures the future privacy of an entity's identity in a quantum computation environment.

Quantum Privacy Amplification: Privacy amplification is a sort of cryptographic version of error correction, which addresses some of the problems with the brigand attacks used on quantum cryptography. The idea is to start with long similar initial keys that the communicating parties assume an eavesdropper has some knowledge about. From these long keys the communicating parties make shorter shared random keys which are identical and unknown to an eavesdropper. It has been shown that quantum cryptography allows privacy amplification to be carried out directly, making it more efficient.

WHAT CAN BE DONE?

Research to date strongly indicates that no single model of privacy protection is sufficient to provide a complete information privacy solution (EPIC, 2003). Therefore, we propose that a solution to this issue is to develop systems and operating environments that integrate a symbiotic molding of all four models of privacy protection. In addition, privacy by design and information system Hippocratic principles (Skinner, 2005; Skinner and Chang, 2006b) should be adhered to throughout the systems life cycle. To compliment the for-mentioned factors and provide robust information privacy protection architectures, the operating contexts (Skinner and Chang, 2006c; Ackerman, 2004) as well as social and cultural environmental conditions need to be accounted for within the framework during development and deployment.

While technology achievements advance at a rapid rate, so to do the threats to privacy and an entities identity. Many PET's that have been proposed only deal with immediate threats to information privacy and do not look far beyond the current computational capabilities of systems and information processing environments. Not only are the computational abilities of systems increasing but also their level of ubiquity. Pervasive computing environments are becoming more common, and when coupled with increased computational capabilities dramatically increase the risks to information privacy. So in the event that quantum computation becomes feasible it will further place at risk entity privacy. Even early deployment of quantum computation capable systems, where perhaps only a central server may be quantum enabled, pose a serious threat to privacy. These central servers can be assigned dedicated tasks such as data profiling and mining, which if used maliciously, suddenly become privacy invasive technologies.

Any privacy solution must take into consideration all current and foreseeable future factors that pose a threat to information privacy. Therefore, we propose a solution entitled T.L.C. (Technical, Legal, and Contextual) Privacy Protection, referred to as TLC-PP. It is an approach that combines all four models of privacy protection (EPIC, 2003), as well as consideration for the influence of social and cultural ideas and perceptions. It supports the implementation and methods of enforcement for both comprehensive and sectoral laws, self regulation and certification schemes, and the impact the operating context has on all of these components (Skinner and Chang, 2007). The TLC-PP objective is to address the issue of information privacy that is at risk from the increasing computational capacities of current and future computing environments. In particular, we are concerned with the possibility that in the near future quantum computational systems may be realized and soon become integral components of many computing environments. The diagram in Figure 1 provides a visual representation of the three TLC cornerstones of privacy protection and their respective components.

Technological advances should be applied in equal measure to ensure privacy protection. With increased collection and processing of information it is imperative that industries and researchers contributing to technological advances also develop complimentary methods of privacy protection. For example, as discussed in Section 3, with the advent of Quantum Computation there is the risk of compromising many of the widely used encryption technologies that help provide privacy protection. In order to offset this problem then it is possible to leverage the new technology to also provide better encryption methods such as the use of quantum cryptography. Additionally whether ever possible the use of anonymous and pseudo-anonymous identities should be used. This approach to identity and privacy protection can be abstracted from the technological implementation details. Therefore, no matter the computational capabilities of the computing environment, PET's should be in place that provides anonymous and

Figure 1. The TLC model for Information privacy protection in quantum computational environments

Addressing Information Privacy in Quantum Computational Environments

Integration of Quantum Technology for PET's
Use of Anonymous and Psuedo-Anonymous Identities
Use of Anonymous Transmission

Technical

Consistency of Laws and Regulations
Methods of enforcement and recrimination procedures
Consideration of long term technological advances
Burden and costs upon the organizations and system owners not on the users

Legal

TLC - PP
Technical, Legal, and Contextual Privacy Protection

Contextual

User awareness and comprehension
Customizable privacy preferences
Consideration of situational and cultural influence on privacy
Minimize data collection by changing the general perception of the need to collect vast amounts of data.

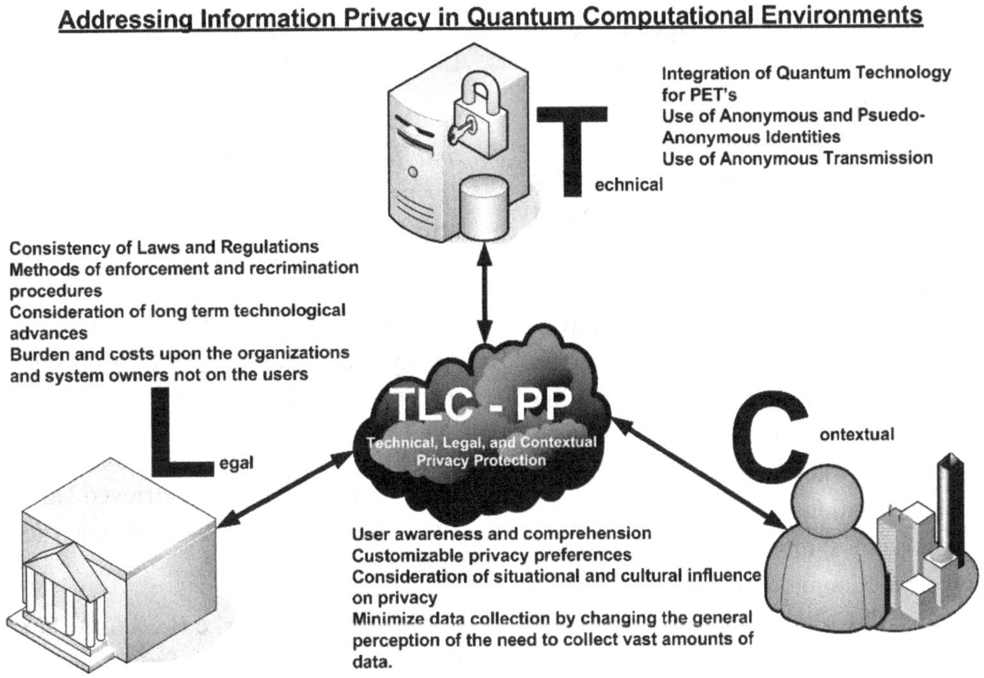

pseudo-anonymous services. This also includes the use of anonymous transmission for network communications of private data, which coupled with quantum enhanced PIR (private information retrieval) can help ensure strong privacy protection.

Legal approaches to privacy protection have the advantage of being even further abstracted from technological advances. However, the need in the future will be to ensure consistency of privacy laws and regulations across all of globe. Equally important will be the ability to enforce the laws and regulations that are put in place. The burden and costs involved to pursue information privacy breaches should not be placed upon the user. Rather the onus should be on the system owners to ensure they correctly adhere to the privacy laws and regulations governing their operation. Currently the EU seems to be focusing on comprehensive privacy legislation rather than the sectoral approach seen in other countries and regions. Australia has made a number of promising steps towards improving their information

privacy laws; however there still seems to be a lack of consumer awareness and organizational uptake. While this may be seen as a negative for current information privacy advocates at least one positive can be to be drawn from such a state. That is, it provides opportunities to incorporate measures that take into consideration future threats to information privacy such as the power of quantum computational environments.

Contextual conditions also play an important part in information privacy protection. Foremost of these initiatives should be the increasing social awareness of data collection and usage, and the need to protect their own privacy. Not all users or even cultures are the same when dealing with privacy. Certain societies and different contexts affect an entities need for and perception of privacy. Therefore, future systems need to not allow users to customize their privacy preferences based on different contexts, social and situational conditions (Skinner and Chang, 2006c). Entities and system users should also be able to clearly understand and comprehend the privacy and data usage policies of the system they are using.

CONCLUSION AND FUTURE WORK

With any new technology there is a much to learn often through trial an error. Privacy advocates are fortunate however in that many of the information privacy mistakes and issues that have been made with classical computing systems are ones that can be avoided or at least addressed with Quantum based systems. Privacy laws and regulations and self regulation are applicable to any information systems, regardless of the implementation technology. Our work is focused on the challenges faced to Information Privacy with the advent of quantum based technologies. We have discussed a number of key technologies and areas of quantum computational research in this paper. We have proposed a symbiotic molding of various privacy protection models into an approach we have termed TLC-PP (Technical, Legal, and Contextual Privacy Protection).

TLC-PP incorporates many components and elements that affect information privacy. The TLC-PP approach caters for advances in computational processing capabilities of future systems, in particular the possible realization of quantum processing environments. Our ongoing work encompass many other quantum computational developments as they impact upon information privacy, whether is in a negative or positive way. An important objective of the research is to highlight the need for Information Privacy awareness from an early development stage for quantum computational systems and protocols. This can be further achieved by the integration of privacy by design principles.

REFERENCES

Ackerman, M., Darrell, T., & Weitzner, D.J. (2001). Privacy In Context. *Human-Computer Interaction, 16*(2), 167-176.

Bennett, C. H., & Brassard, G. (1984). BB84. *Proceedings of IEEE International Conference on Computers, Systems, and Signal Processing.* Los Alamitos, CA: IEEE Press (pp. 175-184).

Clarke, R. (1999). *Introduction to Dataveillance and Information Privacy, and Definitions of Terms.* Retrieved November 20, 2006, from, http://www.anu.edu.au/people/Roger.Clarke/Intro.html

Christandl, M., & Wehner, S. (2005). Quantum Anonymous Transmissions. *Proceedings of 11th ASIACRYPT, LNCS 3788,* 217-235.

Common Criteria Project (2006, November 16). *The Common Criteria.* Retrieved November 16, 2006, from, http://www.commoncriteriaportal.org/

Davison, R. M., Clarke R., Smith, J., Langford, D., & Kuo, B. (2003). Information Privacy in a Globally Networked Society: Implications for IS Research. *Communications of the Association for Information Systems, 12,* 341-365.

Deutsch, D., Ekert, A., Jozsa, R., Macchiavello, C., Popescu, S., & Sanpera, A. (1996). Quantum privacy amplification and the security of quantum cryptography over noisy channels. *Physics Review Letters, 77*(13), 2818-2821.

EPIC (2003). *Privacy and Human Rights 2003. Electronic Privacy Information Centre.* Retrieved October 9, 2006, from http://www.epic.org

Faja, S. (2005). Privacy in E-Commerce: Understanding User Trade-Offs. *Issues in Information Systems, 6*(2).

Giedke, G. (2006, March 14). *What is Quantum Information Processing.* MagiQ, retrieved March 14, 2006, from http://www.magiqtech.com/index.php

Goldberg I. (2002). Privacy-enhancing technologies for the Internet II: Five years later. *Proceedings of the Workshop on Privacy Enhancing Technologies, LNCS 2009,* 1-12.

Gritzalis, D. A. (2004). Embedding privacy in IT applications development. *Information Management and Computer Security, 12*(1), 8-26.

Grover, L. (1997). Quantum Mechanics helps in searching for a needle in a haystack. *Physics Review Letter, 79*(22), 325-328.

He, Y., & Dawn N., & Jutla, N. D. (2006). Contextual e-Negotiation for the Handling of Private Data in e-Commerce on a Semantic Web. HICSS. *Proceedings of the 39th Annual Hawaii International Conference on System Sciences (HICSS'06),* 62-66.

IBM Research (2003, September). *Views of Privacy: Business Drivers, Strategy, and Directions.* IBM Research Division. Retrieved November 16, 2006, from, www.zurich.ibm.com/pdf/privacy/IBM_RC_on_Views_of_Privacy.pdf

Protechnix (2006, October 9). Cryptology and Data Secrecy: The Vernam Cipher. Retrieved 9 October, 2006, from, http://www.pro-technix.com/information/crypto/pages/vernam_base.html

Robinson, S. (2000, March 7). Gauging the Limits of Quantum Computing. *The New York Times On The Web,* Retrieved November 22, 2006, from, http://www.nytimes.com/library/national/science/030700sci-quantum-computing.html.

Skinner, G., & E. Chang E. (2005). PP-SDLC: The Privacy Protecting Systems Development Life Cycle. *IPSI-2005,* Carcassonne, FRANCE.

Skinner G., Han, S., & Chang, E. (2006a). The Computational View of Information Privacy for Privacy Enhancing Technologies. *The First International Conference on Legal, Security and Privacy Issues in IT (LSPI),* Germany.

Skinner, G., & Chang, E. (2006b). A Conceptual Framework for Information Privacy and Security in Collaborative Environments. *International Journal of Computer Science and Network Security, 6*(2)B, 45-51.

Skinner, G., & Chang, E. (2006c). Fair Privacy Principles and Preferences (F3P) – Evaluating Context Based Privacy Preferences. *The 10th WSEAS International Conference on Computers, ICCOMP-06,* Vouliagmeni, Athens, Greece.

Skinner, G., & Chang, E. (2007). An Environmentally Adaptive Conceptual Framework for Addressing Information Privacy Issues in Digital Ecosystems. Presented at DEST2007, Cairns, Australia.

Shor, P. W. (1994). Polynomial-Time Algorithms for Prime Factorization and Discrete Logarithms on a Quantum Computer. *Proceedings of the 35th Annual Symposium on Foundations of Computer Science,* USA.

van Blarkom G. W., Borking, J. J., & Olk, J. G. E. (2003). Handbook of Privacy and Privacy-Enhancing Technologies. *Privacy Incorporated Software Agent (PISA) Consortium,* The Hague, Amsterdam.

Wehner, S. (2004). *Quantum Computation and Privacy.* Unpublished masters thesis, University of Amsterdam, Amsterdam.

Wishart R., Henricksen K., & Indulska J. (2005). An access control scheme for ubiquitous computing environments based on context-dependent privacy preferences. *10th Australasian Conference on Information Security and Privacy,* Brisbane Australia.

Section III
Authentication Techniques

Chapter X
On the Design of an Authentication System Based on Keystroke Dynamics Using a Predefined Input Text

Dieter Bartmann
Universität Regensburg, Germany

Idir Bakdi
Universität Regensburg, Germany

Michael Achatz
Universität Regensburg, Germany

ABSTRACT

The design of an authentication system based on keystroke dynamics is made difficult by the fact that the typing behaviour of a person is subject to strong fluctuations. An asymmetrical method able to handle this difficulty by using a long text on enrolment and a short one at login is analysed in this paper. The results of an empirical study based on an extensive field test are presented. The study demonstrates that the advantages of the analysed method remain even if a predefined input text is used. The results also show that the method's quality highly depends on the amount of text typed on enrolment as well as on login, which makes the system scalable to different security levels. They also confirm the importance of using stable characteristics that are due, that is, to the user's right- or left-handedness. The method's learning velocity is shown to be high, which enables enrolment to be kept short. Moreover, the study demonstrates that admitting multiple login attempts significantly ameliorates the recognition performance without sacrificing security.

1. INTRODUCTION

At the end of the 19th century, analyzing the typing behaviour of telegraphers, the discovery was made that each human being has his own pattern when transmitting dots and lines (Bryan & Harter, 1897). Transfer of this observation to typing behaviour on a computer keyboard for the purpose of identifying persons started with (Spillane, 1975). A patent was first time assigned to Garcia (1986) in 1986. Recently, many publications on the subject of authentication based on keystroke dynamics have appeared (Clarke et al., 2003; Cho et al., 2001; Dowland et al., 2002; Furnell & Dowland, 2000; Monrose et al., 2001; Obaidat & Sadoun, 1997). This demonstrates an increasing interest in this biometrical method. The greatest advantage of this kind of biometrics is that no additional hardware is required for its use on a conventional PC or notebook. A standard keyboard takes over the task of a recording sensor. This saves time and costs otherwise needed for purchasing, installing and maintaining additional hardware.

Nevertheless, a breakthrough of keystroke dynamics based biometrics to a broad usage in practice did not yet occur, in spite of intensive research and development efforts. The reasons for this lay in the nature of the typing behaviour itself. An evident problem is the fact that the manner in which a person types is not constant. Typing severely changes depending on the time of day, the individual mood of the user and on external circumstances (e.g. simultaneous telephoning, a change in keyboards etc.). Because of this, the method for successful user authentication using keystroke dynamics has to be, on the one hand, very tolerant towards typing fluctuations of the authorized user, and on the other hand, to reject impostors with a high probability. This apparent antagonism is very difficult to resolve, the most probable way to handle it being the use of a very long text. This, however, would result in an application impracticable in most use cases.

This problem can be eased by methods that take into account the asymmetry between the data captured at enrolment time and that registered at authentication time. The individual traits of keystroke dynamics, e.g. the duration of a stroke or the transition times from one key to the next, can be captured by a statistical model. On enrolment, a long text is typed in. Out of the data collected during enrolment, the method estimates the different parameters of the statistical model. On login, the user only needs to type a short sentence. Asymmetrical methods based on statistical models have the advantage that an arbitrary text may be used. An example for such a method from early literature on keystroke biometrics is the patent script by Young and Hammon (Young & Hammon, 1989).

A more recent example is the method of Bartmann (2000). This method uses stable statistical characteristics in addition to pure keystroke dynamics (Bartmann & Bartmann, 1997). The former characteristics are hardly subject to the daily condition and mood of a user, and are not influenced by external circumstances. These characteristics include the right- or left-handedness of the user or the way he learned to type. Both characteristics influence the way he uses the shift keys. Usually, a shift key is pressed by the "weak" hand and the capital letter by the "strong" one. This fact can be interpreted as right- or left-handedness. If a person is mostly using one shift key, he has probably learned typing by himself, while the interchanging use of both shift keys shows that the user is typing according to the ten finger typing system. Equally, the (rare) use of the numerical pad carries valuable information.

Another stable characteristic of typing behaviour is the precision of the keystroke. Its precision is high, if the second key is pressed only after the first key has been released. Often, however, the second key is pressed too early. Sometimes, this can be observed on the screen when a word beginning with a capital letter is typed. In case the shift key is released too late, the following letter will be capital, as well. According to research (Bartmann & Breu, 2004), keystroke precision is very individual and very much influenced by finger flexibility, but hardly subject to the daily condition of a user. It is the expression of a ground-in typing behaviour. Besides the use of such stable characteristics the method analyzed in this work does not do the verification on login through a direct comparison of samples. Instead, every single character or group of characters is put through a test of hypothesis. Moreover, a customized, individual weighting of the different features is calculated by a multilayer perceptron neural network consisting of three layers (with 13 neurons in the input layer, 6 neurons in the hidden layer and 1 output neuron). A standard backpropagation algorithm was used for the training of the neural network (Bartmann, 2000).

This paper presents the results of some extensive tests that were conducted using the method developed by Bartmann (2000) in order to measure the influence of different design parameters (e.g. the length of enrolment text and of login text, the number of samples used for the enrolment, etc.) on the recognition quality.

2. RESEARCH QUESTIONS

In order to use the described method solely on login, it is not necessary to allow the use of free text input. A predefined text is sufficient for this purpose. Thus, the authentication system described above is used along with predefined input text, while the statistical model remains the same. On enrolment, the user is prompted to type a fixed sentence several times. This variant of the method is called the predefined input text variant in this paper as opposed to the arbitrary input text variant. In the predefined text variant, the system is specifically trained on the typing behaviour characteristics appearing within a chosen login sentence. The question is how the method

behaves when confined to such a predefined text. In what extent do the results depend on the length of the enrolment and the login texts? Are there favourable values for these parameters? Are the results independent of the input text or is it possible to influence them by choosing an appropriate login sentence? How many typing samples should be used for the training of the artificial neural network? Behind these questions lies the goal of optimizing the authentication system by customizing the various parameters.

More precisely, the following issues are analyzed:

Concerning the length of the predefined login sentence:

- Is the quality of the method dependent on the length of the input text?
- If it is, how far can the input text be reduced without a conceivable loss of quality?

Concerning the use of shift keys:

- Is it important to include capital letters in the input text? In most of the widely spread languages except German this is rarely the case. If the feature "use of shift keys" plays an important role, the choice of the input text should be especially adjusted.

Concerning the length of the enrolment text:

- How many typing samples should the user provide the system with?

Concerning the training of the neural network:

- How many known impostor samples have to be used?
- How many different known impostors have to provide these samples?

Concerning authentication:

- How many login attempts should be allowed?

3. EXPERIMENTAL SETUP

The research questions posed above have to be answered empirically. The limits of empirical experiments while testing biometrical methods have, however, to be kept in mind. The greatest challenge lies in the gathering of a sufficiently high amount of typing samples from a large group of different users. According to Peacock et al. (2004) most of the previous works on keystroke dynamics based authentication have used less than 25 test persons each for their evaluations. Gunetti & Picardi (2005) state that they have examined the so far largest group of test persons. However, from the 205 persons contemplated by Gunetti & Picardi (2005) only 40 have provided enough typing samples for the calculation of a typing behaviour profile. The typing data of the remaining 165 test persons has been used solely for generating impostor samples.

The results of the present paper are based on several field tests we have conducted. Most data has been collected under realistic conditions, as approx. 20 employees of our institute have been using typing biometrics for daily authentication at their workstations. A special authentication module embedded into the Microsoft® Windows OS has been developed for this purpose. Additional data has been collected by a web front-end using a browser plug-in for recording typing samples.

The users had always to type the same sentence: "Hello User: It never rains in Southern California.", which is 50 characters long, counting spaces. The length of this sentence has been proven to provide a high level of security in previous tests (Bartmann & Breu, 2004) and is, at the same time, short enough to be considered user-friendly. In section 5 we examine, amongst other issues, the impact of shortening the text length below 50

characters. To input this sentence the user has to press the shift key six times, which renders possible the analysis of the importance of the "choice of keys" characteristic.

A total of 87 users have provided the typing samples. Among them were persons of both genders, of different ages and varying education levels. The test persons were familiar with the use of a keyboard, but unequally trained with it. There were test persons typing by the ten finger system as well as individuals that were having only limited access to a computer over the last years. The results of this paper are based on 21053 different typing samples altogether, which corresponds to an average of about 242 typing samples per person. The 87 test persons can be roughly divided into two groups. The first group counts 59 users that have provided 20-30 typing samples each. The members of the second group, on the other hand, have supplied distinctly more typing samples, namely up to 2058. Some users, mostly members of the first group, have delivered their typing samples in the course of a single session, while the typing samples of the other users, mainly members of the second group, have been gathered over a period of 17 months.

In the following section we illustrate the method used to evaluate the influence of the different factors on the recognition quality based on this data set.

4. METHODOLOGY OF ANALYSIS

4.1. The Equal Error Rate

The identification quality of biometrical methods is usually described by two error rates: the *false acceptance rate* (FAR) and the *false rejection rate* (FRR). The false acceptance rate describes the probability of admitting the wrong user, whereas the false rejection rate (FRR) stands for the probability of an authorised person's false rejection (Mansfield & Wayman, 2002, p.5). The FAR is a measure for system security, the FRR for its user-friendliness.

As most biometrical systems, the method developed by Bartmann (2000) employs a threshold that regulates the strictness of the verification process. When a login attempt occurs, the system calculates a matching score between the observed typing behaviour and the user's typing profile. This value is compared with the threshold. If the calculated matching score is higher than the threshold the authentication is considered successful, otherwise it is rejected. As Fig. 1 shows, the FRR increases with a higher threshold while the FAR decreases and vice versa. Hence, the threshold offers an opportunity to make a trade-off between user-friendliness (i.e. lower FRR) and security (i.e. lower FAR).

In order to evaluate a biometrical method independently of the threshold, the so called *equal error rate* (EER) is often used. The EER is defined as the intercept point of the FAR and FRR curves (see Fig. 1). It is a common measure for the quality of a biometrical method. Kotani & Horii (2005) describe its use in the context of keystroke dynamics based authentication.

4.2. Estimating the EER

On enrolment, the user types a predefined input text several times. From these typing samples,

the system calculates his typing profile. First, we will consider how an EER can be estimated for a single profile. The FRR curve is defined by the matching scores the user achieves during several logins. To estimate the corresponding FAR curve, the matching scores resulting from a number of attacks are used. Finally, the EER is taken as the ordinate of the interception point of both curves. The so estimated EER is referring to exactly one profile. As this does not supply a measure representative of a method's quality, the average EER of many profiles by many users has to be used instead.

4.3. Estimating the Average EER

The *average equal error rate* is estimated by simulation using a large number of typing samples from different users. The easiest way of determining an EER for a given user U is the so-called *holdout method*. This method first divides the data of the user U into a learning set L_U and a test set T_U. This step is repeated using the impostor samples, i.e. the samples coming from the other users. This way, an impostor learning set L_A and an impostor testing set T_A are defined. Next, a new typing profile is calculated from the learning sets L_U and L_A. The samples of the learning set L_A are needed to train the neural network. Then, some login attempts are simulated using the test sets T_U

Figure 1. Connection between the tolerance threshold, FAR, FRR and EER

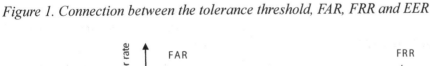

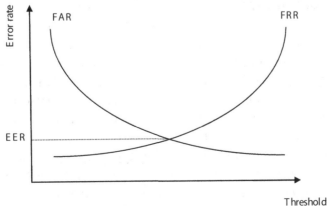

and T_A. The resulting matching scores are finally used to estimate the EER as described above.

Unfortunately, the holdout method has three decisive disadvantages. Firstly, the data of the test set T_U cannot be dispensed with, as the number of samples is already small for most users. Secondly, an "unfortunate" division into learning and test sets can lead to the wrong results. If the holdout method was repeatedly used to estimate the EER choosing each time a different division of the samples into learning and test sets, the results of the individual estimations would vary too much. Thus, no significant results could be derived. Finally, the resulting EER is dependent on whether the learning set L_A contains typing samples of impostors that also provided samples for the test set T_A. This is because the system can reject a given impostor the better, the more exactly it knows his typing behavior.

The first two problems are met in this paper with the help of so called *re-sampling methods*. These are methods that, starting from a given set of samples, randomly generate "new" sets of samples. They are used to derive significant results, even when the available data set is relatively small (Gutierrez-Osuna, 2005). The re-sampling methods used in the present paper are the methods of random subsampling and bootstrapping described below. A more detailed presentation of these methods is given by Hastie et al. (2001). First, however, the solution of the third problem is illustrated in the following subsection.

4.3. Known vs. Unknown Impostors

As described above, impostor samples are needed for two purposes when estimating an EER for a given user U. The impostor learning set L_A contains samples that are used during profile creation, while the impostor test set T_A is needed to estimate the FAR curve. Thus, in order to compute the EER for a given user U, all the other users are divided into two disjoint groups. The first group represents the so-called *known impostors*. The samples

of these users constitute the impostor learning set L_A. Members of the second group are called *unknown impostors*. Their samples constitute the test set T_A used to estimate the FAR curve. This way, a rather conservative EER estimation is made, as only impostors that the system has never observed before are assumed when estimating the FAR curve.

In the literature, the performance of authentication methods based on keystroke dynamics is often measured using only data of known impostors. In this lies the risk of estimating the error rates too optimistically. Gunetti & Picardi (2005) mention several papers on the subject of keystroke dynamics based authentication that do not distinguish between known and unknown impostors.

4.4. Random Subsampling

For every system configuration to be analysed (e.g. for a certain length of the input text), n test runs per user are made. In every test run that is made for a given user U, all the other users are regarded as impostors. A single subsampling run consists of the following steps:

1. A learning set L_U of a predefined size is chosen at random without replacement from the available samples of user U.
2. A test set T_U of a predefined size is chosen at random without replacement from the remaining samples of user U.
3. The impostors are divided into known and unknown ones.
4. A learning set L_A of a predefined size is chosen at random with replacement from the samples of the known impostors.
5. A test set T_A of a predefined size is chosen at random with replacement from the samples of the unknown impostors.
6. Using the learning sets L_U and L_A, a new typing profile for user U is produced.
7. A matching score between every sample in T_U and the new profile is calculated, thus obtaining a FRR curve.

8. A matching score between every sample in T_A and the new profile is calculated, thus obtaining a FAR curve.

9. Finally, the intersection point of the two curves is used to estimate the EER.

If samples of m users are used this method produces a total of $n \cdot m$ EER values. In order to not only calculate an average value, but to be also able to make a statement about the significance of the results using confidence intervals, the bootstrap method described below is employed.

4.5. Bootstrapping

Bolle et al. (1999) suggest the use of bootstrapping when evaluating biometrical systems in order to obtain confidence intervals. A similar approach has been adapted in this paper. In every bootstrap run a new set of $n \cdot m$ EER values is taken at random with replacement out of the $n \cdot m$ EER values calculated in the different subsampling runs. The values of this set are averaged, so that each bootstrap run results in one average EER. A certain number of bootstrap cycles brings forth an estimate of the distribution of the average EER and therefore of the confidence interval for a given significance level α. In the results presented in the following section, α was set to 5%, which means that the probability of the actual EER value lying within the specified confidence intervals is at least 95%.

These methods, however carefully chosen, do not ensure the EER being always constant. The absolute value of the EER also depends on the design of the experiment, which is in turn dictated by the research question in case. If, for instance, the research goes into analyzing the dependency of the method's quality on the number of typing samples entered on enrolment, the group of test persons is restricted to those who provided a large enough amount of typing samples. This changes the underlying set of data and thus the absolute value of the estimated average EER.

5. RESULT[1]

5.1. Concerning the Input Text

Significant Scalability with Text Length

The influence of a change in the length of the input text upon the recognition rate was analysed for the predefined text variant. The starting point was a sentence containing 50 characters as described above. Its length was gradually decreased to 40, 30, 26, 21 and finally to 15 characters by leaving corresponding segments out of account. As shown by the curves of Fig. 2, the recognition quality improves when the length of the input text grows. The confidence intervals further show that the improvement is significant. One can clearly observe a critical length of the input text, below which the quality of recognition greatly decreases (see the steep decline of the curves when the text length is below 25 characters). This observation goes in parallel with the suggestion of Sheng et al. (2005) stating that the input text should have at least a length of about 30 characters. The result also confirms the expected advantageous feature of behavioural biometrics. By changing the length of the input text the method can be tailored to different security needs, a possibility that image processing biometrics do not offer.

Significant Influence of the Characteristic "Use of Shift Keys"

The next research question goes into the role of an explicit modelling of users' behaviour at the choice of shift keys. Comparing the curves in Fig. 2 one can see that this characteristic leads to a significant improvement of the results. This improvement lies at 1% minimum at all recorded text lengths. The fact that the degree of improvement is unequal at different text lengths is mainly due to two reasons. On the one hand, the improvement is the higher, the more shift events occur in the text sample at hand. On the other hand,

Figure 2. Impact of text length and the characteristic "use of shift keys" upon the average equal error rate

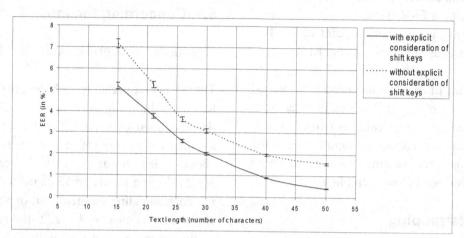

this characteristic becomes less important with increasing text length if the total number of shift events is assumed to be constant, because in this case the relative importance of other characteristics increases.

All the following results have been calculated using uncut typing samples (i.e. including all of the 50 characters) and explicitly modelling the choice of shift keys.

5.2 Concerning Enrolment

Learning Effort

The effort on enrolment is decisive for the user-friendliness of a biometrical system. In the case of an authentication system based on keystroke dynamics, this effort can be measured by the number of typing samples the user has to provide on enrolment. Hence, this paper examines the impact of the number of learning typing samples upon the recognition rate. The results of this experiment are shown in Fig. 3.

As shown in this chart, the recognition rate is ameliorating along with an increase in the number of learning samples. This improvement becomes very faint starting from about 20 samples and no more significant starting from 30 typing

samples (see the confidence intervals in Fig. 3). The fact that the quality stabilises rather quickly demonstrates the method's high velocity of learning. The method can determine a representative profile out of just 9 typing samples. As with the text length, the number of learning samples should not fall below a certain value. If only 5 samples are used on enrolment instead of 20, the average EER approximately doubles.

The experiments described below have been conducted using profiles calculated from 30 learning samples each.

Effort of Collecting Known Impostor Samples

A further issue coming up on enrolment concerns the number of imposter typing samples employed to train the neural network. To determine the impact of this parameter, the number of known impostor samples was varied, while the number of users providing these samples (i.e. the number of known impostors) remained constant. The results of this experiment are illustrated in Fig.4.

Fig. 4 shows that the quality of the method is improving with an increasing number of known impostor samples. With 50 impostor samples the results are already good, with over 100 impostor

Figure 3. Impact of the number of user samples used for profile creation upon the average equal error rate

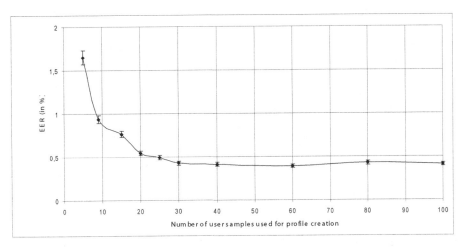

samples the improvement stops. This provides further evidence for the high learning velocity of the analysed method.

Number of Known Impostors

Finally, it is important to know whether to prefer many different known impostors providing a few samples each for the training of the neural network, or the other way around. To clarify this matter, the total number of impostor samples has been set to a constant 100 while the number of known impostors providing these samples was varied.

The results in Fig. 5 show the importance of using impostor samples from different users. Nevertheless, starting from 20 known impostors, a further increase in their number does not lead to a significant improvement.

Figure 4. Influence of the number of known impostor samples used for profile creation upon the average equal error rate

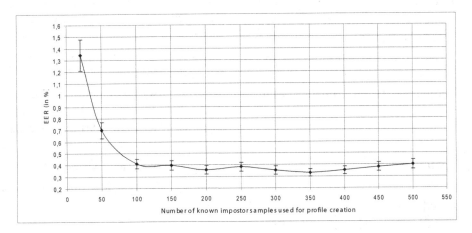

Figure 5. Influence of the number of known impostors upon the average equal error rate

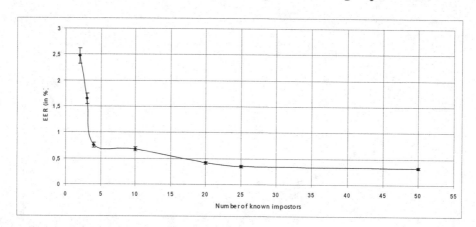

5.3 Concerning the Authentication Procedure

Strong Scalability with the Number of Admitted Login Attempts

If a user is not recognised after the first login attempt it does not necessarily mean that he does not get access to the system anymore. The method could allow him to retry and ultimately reject him only after a certain number of unsuccessful attempts. The influence of the number of admitted login attempts upon the recognition quality is depicted in Fig. 6.

As demonstrated by Fig. 6, the average EER strongly ameliorates when the number of admitted login attempts increases. The highest impact can be observed when allowing up to two logins instead of a single one. This improves the average EER by 0,2%. The improvement is explainable through the fact that although the FAR deteriorates with an increased number of admitted login attempts, the FRR ameliorates in a stronger manner.

6. CONCLUSION

The tests conducted above are extensive compared to other studies of biometrical methods and the methodology of analysis has a solid theoretical basis. Thus, the results achieved can be considered reliable. The analysis in details offers the following conclusions:

The restriction to the predefined input text maintains the basic qualities of scalability and quality improvement through stable characteristics. A possible risk could have been a loss of importance of the "use of shift keys" feature. Not only does this not occur, but this characteristic proves to be very essential. With its help the average EER is reduced by up to 50%. The improvement is relatively stable regardless of the length of the input text.

The learning velocity of the method is demonstrated by a strong "elbow effect" in Fig. 3. The EER curve steeply decreases with an increasing number of learning samples and it is quickly saturated. The bend in the curve being so evident, the issue of minimum effort on enrolment can be resolved rather easily. This is an important matter, as the user wants to type as little as possible. After the user has entered just ten samples the method works rather well and it reaches its full capacity after a few additional logins. The high learning velocity also makes it easy to adapt to changes in the user's typing behaviour that may occur e.g. when he does not type for a long time or because of an illness.

Figure 6. Influence of the number of admitted login attempts upon the average equal error rate

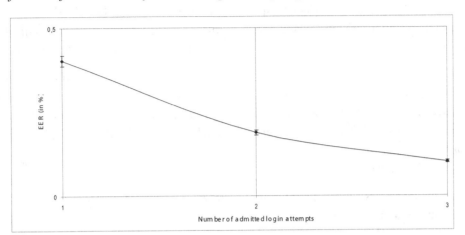

For the method to be accepted by the users, it is very important that they succeed when trying to login in, even if they have to make several attempts. Concerning this aspect, the method shows the expected characteristic of behavioural biometrics. If a user is erroneously rejected, every following login provides the system with additional information which makes it accept the user in the end. This renders the risk of an authorised user being definitely rejected very small, without sacrificing the system's security.

A number of further questions remain to be solved, e.g. on how stable the method is towards different keyboards. Also, a secure system does not only depend on the recognition quality. Another important aspect is, for instance, its protection against replay attacks. It would be interesting to analyse in how far the use of an input text which varies slightly on each login could help to avert such an attack. Reliable answers to these questions would greatly contribute to moving biometrical authentication methods based on keystroke dynamics towards practical applications.

REFERENCES

Bartmann, D., & Bartmann, D. (1997). *Method for Verifying the Identity of a User of a Data Processing Unit with a Keyboard Designed to Produce Alphanumeric Characters*. European patent number: EP 0 917 678 B1.

Bartmann, D., & Breu, C. (2004). Eignung des biometrischen Merkmals Tippverhalten zur Benutzerauthentisierung. In D. Bartmann, (Eds.), *Überbetriebliche Integration von Anwendungssystemen* (pp. 321-343). FORWIN-Tagung, Aachen.

Bartmann, D. jun (2000). *Benutzerauthentisierung durch Analyse des Tippverhaltens mit Hilfe einer Kombination aus statistischen und neuronalen Verfahren*. Dissertation, Technical University of Munich.

Bolle, R. M., Ratha, N. K., & Pankanti, S. (1999). Evaluating Authentication Systems Using Bootstrap Confidence Intervals. *Proceedings of the 1999 IEEE Workshop on Automatic Identification Advanced Technologies (WAIAT-99)*, Morristown NJ, USA.

Bryan, W. L., & Harter, N. (1897). Studies in the Physiology and Psychology of the Telegraphic Language. *Psychological Review, 4*(1), 27-53.

Cho, S., Han, C., Han, D., & Kim, H. (2001). Web based keystroke dynamics identity verification using neural networks. *Journal of Organisational Computing & Electronic Commerce, 10*(4), 295-307.

Clarke, N., Furnell, S., Reynolds, P., & Lines, B. (2003). Using Keystroke Analysis is a Mechanism for Subscriber Authentication on Mobile Handsets. *SEC*, (pp. 97-108).

Dowland, P. S., & Furnell, M. S., & Steven M., & Papadaki, M. (2002). Keystroke Analysis as a Method of Advanced User Authentication and Response. *Proceedings of IFIP/SEC - 17ᵗʰ International Conference on Information Security*, Cairo, Egypt, (pp. 215-226).

Furnell S. M., & Dowland P. S. (2000). Enhancing Operating System Authentication Techniques. *In Proceedings of the Second International Network Conference*, Plymouth, England (pp. 253-261).

Garcia, J. D. (1986). *Personal identification apparatus*. United States patent number: 4 621 334.

Gunetti, D., & Picardi, C. (2005). Keystroke Analysis of Free Text. *ACM Transactions on Information and System Security, 3*(5), 312-347.

Gutierrez-Osuna, R. (2005). *Introduction to Pattern Analysis, Cross-validation*. http://research. cs.tamu.edu/prism/lectures/pr/pr_l13.pdf, last visited on 2006-11-13.

Hastie, T., Tibshirani, R., & Friedman, J. (2001). *The Elements of Statistical Learning; Data Mining, Inference*. New York: Spring-Verlag.

Kotani, K., & Horii, K. (2005). Evaluation on a keystroke authentication system by keying force incorporated with temporal characteristics of keystroke dynamics. *Behaviour & Information Technology, 4*(24), 289-302.

Mansfield, A. J., & Wayman, J. L. (2002). *Best Practices in Testing and Reporting Performance of Biometric Devices - Version 2.01*. http://www. npl.co.uk/scientific_software/publications/bio-metrics/bestprac_v2_1.pdf, last visited on 2006-11-14.

Monrose, F., Reiter, M. K., & Wetzel, S. (2001). Password hardening based on keystroke dynamics. *International Journal of Information Security, 1*(2). New York: Springer-Verlag,

Obaidat, M. S., & Sadoun, B. (1997). Verification of Computer User Using Keystroke Dynamics. *IEEE Transactions on Systems, Man, and Cybernetics - Part B, 27*(2), 261-269.

Peacock, A., Ke, X., & Wilkerson, M. (2004). Typing Patterns: A Key to User Identification. *IEEE Security and Privacy, 5*(2), 40-47.

Sheng, Y., Phoha, V. V., & Rovnyak, S.M. (2005). A Parallel Decision Tree-Based Method for User Authentication Based on Keystroke Patterns. *IEEE Transactions on Systems, Man, and Cybernetics - Part B, 35*(4), 826-833.

Spillane, R. J. (1975). Keyboard apparatus for personal identification. *IBM Technical Disclosure Bulletin, 17*(11), 3346.

Young, J. R., & Hammon, R. W. (1989). *Method and apparatus for verifying an individual's identity*. United States patent number: 4 805 222.

ENDNOTE

[1]   Since the first release of this paper the result has significantly improved. All charts reflect the technical state at the end of 2007. Recent developments show further improvements.

Chapter XI
Defeating Active Phishing Attacks for Web–Based Transactions

Xin Luo
Virginia State University, USA

Teik Guan Tan
Data Security Systems Solutions Pte Ltd, Singapore

ABSTRACT

Till now, the best defense against phishing is the use of two-factor authentication systems. Yet this protection is short-lived and comparatively weak. The absence of a fool-proof solution against Man-in-the-Middle, or Active Phishing, attacks have resulted in an avalanche of security practitioners painting bleak scenarios where Active Phishing attacks cripple the growth of web-based transactional systems. Even with vigilant users and prudent applications, no solutions seem to have addressed the attacks comprehensively. In this chapter, the authors propose the new Two-factor Interlock Authentication Protocol (TIAP), adapted from the Interlock Protocol with two-factor authentication, which is able to defend successfully against Active Phishing attacks. They further scrutinize the TIAP by simulating a series of attacks against the protocol and demonstrate how each attack is defeated.

INTRODUCTION

The current wave of phishing attacks against Internet Banking and Transaction web sites is only the tip of the hacking iceberg in the field of information systems security. Yet, these relatively unsophisticated attacks have already catastrophically resulted in significant monetary loss and a major source of embarrassment to the financial institutions. This predicament has drawn increasing attention from both security researchers and practitioners. Early research has shed light on such tactical anti-phishing methods as having Internet service providers (ISPs) involved to close phishing websites and launching retaliatory services to proactively block phishing traffic. However, these approaches are time-consuming and expensive, and are even useless in countries that lack relevant anti-phishing regulations (Geer, 2005). While organizations are scrambling to deploy costly two-factor authentication solutions (i.e. having a one-time password in addition to a normal password) to cope with the problem, such remedies may just be short-lived as the hackers can easily deploy the more sophisticated active phishing attacks to thwart the security and the additional effort could cause consumers to avoid Internet banking (Geer, 2005).

Defined as attacks that use both social engineering and technical subterfuge to steal consumers' personal identity data and financial account credentials (Goth, 2005), phishing incidents have gradually eroded consumer confidence in online banking (Geer, 2005) and further imposed immeasurable losses for corporations in terms of time and resources. In addition to public education, authentication such as one-time password technology may be successful at preventing offline or Static Phishing attacks (Bellovin, 2004). While researchers have previously addressed the technological concerns of Static Phishing and proposed relevant solutions such as phishing webpage detection based on visual similarity (Liu et al., 2005), mail filtering method (Inomata et al., 2005) and XUL and JavaScript-based browser extensions (Kirda and Kruegel, 2005), the field of Active Phishing is still unexplored as the possibility of Active Phishing or on-line Man-in-the-Middle attacks has been troubling security practitioners and consultants (Schneier, 2005) for a while already. In general, Active Phishing can be defined as the use of a reverse proxy in the middle to dynamically access the actual site while phishing the user, thus giving the impression that the user is communicating with the correct site, while the hacker in the middle has actual control

of the session and may modify the contents to achieve illegitimate gains.

Along with Herzberg's argument that SSL/TLS is limited and weak for site impersonation and scam sites (Herzberg, 2004), we believe that the difficulty in preventing Active Phishing attacks for web-based transactions is due to the fact that the HTTP-over-SSL protocol is easily reverse-proxied. In fact, all SSL-VPN solutions exploit this reverse-proxy capability somewhat to support a seamless VPN tunnel between the browser through the SSL-VPN gateway to the backend application server. Hence, the SSL-VPN gateway is in fact functioning as a "good" man-in-the-middle to provide the VPN encryption functionality.

The problem is further acerbated by the inherent fact that the Client executable content (i.e. the HTML/Javascript in the browser) is actually downloaded from the Server. This means that the server with which the browser is communicating with has full control over whatever content is executed on the browser. Should the browser be communicating with a phishing server, there is no way that the actual server is able to bypass this problem.

The painted scenario is bleak. A security-conscious bank with a security-conscious user base does not guarantee that the Internet banking sessions between them are secure. Already, a case of active phishing has been reported (Kirk, 2005), and it is only a matter of time before the exploitation of the vulnerability becomes widespread.

THEORETICAL BACKGROUND

The Interlock Protocol by Rivest and Shamir (1984) is an elegant solution designed to defeat hackers who attempt to eavesdrop on the communication. In Figure 1, Alice and Bob is using the Diffie-Hellman exponential key exchange protocol (Diffie and Hellman, 1976) to establish a shared secret key which can be used subsequently to encrypt the session. The Diffie-Hellman exponential key exchange works by first having a large public value n, used as the modulus, a public random value g and a secret random value a generated by Alice. Alice computes g^a mod n and sends over the result, along with g and n. a remains secret in Alice's possession. Bob, would generate a secret random value b, compute g^b mod n, and return the result of the modulo exponent to Alice. Both Alice and Bob are able to compute g^{ab} mod n[1], thus arriving at a shared secret key k which no one else is able to cryptographically derive. Using the shared secret key k, Alice would be able to encrypt any secret information, denoted as $E_k(..)$, and send it securely to Bob, with certainty that only Bob is able to decrypt it, and vice versa. However, the communication is easily susceptible to man-in-the-middle attacks.

With Mallory in Figure 2, he will perform a key exchange with both Alice and Bob, posing as the opposite party to obtain a shared secret key k with Alice, and a different shared secret key k' with Bob. Whatever information that Alice encrypts using k can be decrypted by Mallory and re-encrypted using k' to be forwarded to Bob, thus achieving the Man-in-the-Middle attack.

In this scenario, the secret information encrypted by the session key is accessible by Mallory, and subject to illegal modifications. The Interlock protocol breaks the Man-in-the-middle attack by destroying Mallory's ability to decrypt using one key, and re-encrypt using a different key in real time. After Mallory has successfully negotiated the secret keys, the trick in the Interlock protocol is that it requires that the information encrypted by the session key be divided into two halves[2], and each half is sent after receiving a half from the other party (See Figure 3).

This method defeats Mallory's attempt at the Man-in-the-Middle attack as on the onset of the communication, since Mallory only has received half of the secret info and thus is unable to determine what information, denoted by $E_k(??)$, to send to the other party. He is at best able to receive 1 proper message from either Alice or Bob, but is unable to continue the conversation between Alice and Bob.

Positive as it may seem, the Interlock protocol is not entirely suitable for preventing Man-in-the-Middle authentication attacks. Bellovin and Merritt (1992) proposed that by doing a slightly more sophisticated attack, Mallory is able to

Figure 1. Exponential key exchange

Alice (user)		Bob (server)
g^a mod n	$\rightarrow$	
	$\leftarrow$	g^b mod n
k = g^{ba} mod n		k = g^{ab} mod n
E_k (secret info$_a$)	$\rightarrow$	
	$\leftarrow$	E_k (secret info$_b$)

Figure 2. Man-in-the-middle attack on exponential key exchange

Alice		Mallory		Bob
g^a mod n	$\rightarrow$			
	$\leftarrow$	g^m mod n		
		g^m mod n	$\rightarrow$	
			$\leftarrow$	g^b mod n
k = g^{ma} mod n		k = g^{am} mod n k' = g^{bm} mod n		k' = g^{mb} mod n
E_k (secret info$_a$)	$\rightarrow$	$E_{k'}$ (secret info$_a$)	$\rightarrow$	
	$\leftarrow$	E_k (secret info$_b$)	$\leftarrow$	$E_{k'}$ (secret info$_b$)

Figure 3. Interlock protocol to defeat man-in-the-middle attack

Alice		Mallory		Bob
$g^a \bmod n$	→			
	←	$g^m \bmod n$		
		$g^m \bmod n$	→	
			←	$g^b \bmod n$
$k = g^{ma} \bmod n$		$K = g^{am} \bmod n$ $K' = g^{bm} \bmod n$		$K' = g^{mb} \bmod n$
$E_k(\text{secret info}_{a1})$	→	$E_{k'}(??)$	→	
	←	$E_k(??)$	←	$E_{k'}(\text{secret info}_{b1})$
$E_k(\text{secret info}_{a2})$	→	got secret info$_a$!! $E_{k'}(??)$	→	
				REJECT

steal Alice's authentication credentials and open a session with Bob (and even potentially stealing Bob's authentication credentials)

Additionally, the other acknowledged solution is the Encrypted Key Exchange. The Encrypted Key Exchange (EKE) by Bellovin and Merritt (1994) was designed initially to address the frequent use of poorly chosen passwords used by users during authentication. By using these passwords to encrypt a randomly generated public key pair, the EKE achieves the ability to prevent the poorly chosen passwords from being easily guessable. The solution also has the advantage of preventing the Man-in-the-Middle attack illustrated in Figure 4.

However, the downside in the EKE protocol is its inability to fully support two-factor one-time password authentication. This is because EKE

Figure 4. Interlock protocol is unable to defeat man-in-the-middle attack for authentication

Alice		Mallory		Bob
$g^a \bmod n$	→			
	←	$g^m \bmod n$		
		$g^m \bmod n$	→	
			←	$g^b \bmod n$
$k = g^{ma} \bmod n$		$k = g^{am} \bmod n$ $k' = g^{bm} \bmod n$		$K' = g^{mb} \bmod n$
$E_k(\text{auth info}_{a1})$	→			
	←	$E_k(??)$		
$E_k(\text{auth info}_{a2})$	→	got auth info$_a$!!		
	←	Disconnect Alice		
		$E_{k'}(\text{auth info}_{a1})$	→	
			←	$E_{k'}(\text{auth info}_{b1})$
		$E_{k'}(\text{auth info}_{a2})$	→	
			←	$E_{k'}(\text{auth info}_{b2})$

requires that the password be used to encrypt the randomly generated key. The server is expected to have the same password to decrypt the generated key which may not be possible since most one-time password implementations (e.g. S/Key (Haller et al., 2005), RSA SecurID, VASCO Digipass) at the server-end only verify, and do not or cannot produce the expected one-time password.

FURTHER OBSERVATIONS

Both the Interlock protocol and Encrypted Key Exchange protocol have shown some potential in preventing Man-in-the-Middle attacks. However, by simply applying the protocols to web-based transactions is not viable as both solutions rely heavily on both the client and server performing a stipulated set of operations as per required in the protocol. In the case of web-based transactions, there is no way this can be ensured since the executable content on User's browser is determined by the hacker. Mallory could easily present a set of similar looking HTML content on the browser and Alice would be fooled to think that the actual cryptographic protocol was taking place, when in fact, the authentication information entered by Alice was presented directly to Mallory.

In Figure 5a, Alice is phished for the authentication information and the Interlock / EKE protocol implemented by Bob cannot prevent Mallory from carrying out a Man-in-the-Middle attack.

To complete the last piece of the puzzle, we postulate the scenario that even if Alice and Bob authenticated each other correctly during the login process, Alice is still vulnerable to the Man-in-the-Middle attack as Mallory can easily hijack the web session after the authentication has taken place.

This is because the HTTPS session encryption between the browser and the web server is not correlated to the authentication exchange between the communicating parties. The authentication information entered by Alice played no part in deciding the session encryption key used for that session. In fact, the session encryption negotiation would have already taken place before Alice entered the authentication information. To achieve the attack, Mallory has to simply compromise the HTTPS session encryption by operating as a pass-through proxy, and hijack the session after the authentication has successfully taken place.

The challenge therefore is to find a web-based authentication implementation that:

○ prevents Alice from falling prey to Mallory's fake login webpage
○ cannot be successfully operated by Mallory using a reverse-proxy / pass-through implementation
○ is able to support two-factor authentication
○ is still convenient to Alice for web-based usage.

Figure 5a. Phishing attack for authentication

Alice		Mallory		Bob
	←	fake login webpage		
enter auth info	→			
		Perform protocol exchange with Bob using auth info provided by Alice	↔	Interlock / EKE protocol
				Ok
			←	secret info$_b$
	←	secret info$_b$		

Figure 5b. Session hijack after successful authentication

Alice		Mallory		Bob
Perform protocol exchange with Bob	↔	pass-through proxy	↔	Interlock / EKE protocol
				Ok
			←	secret info$_b$
	←	secret info$_b$		

PROPOSED SOLUTION: TWO-FACTOR INTERLOCK AUTHENTICATION

Our proposed solution exploits the cryptographic foundation of the Interlock protocol, with the advantages of two-factor authentication, and certain practical aspects of web-browser usage to arrive at a realistic solution in defeating active phishing. The EKE is not suitable for two-factor one-time password authentication as it relies on the knowledge of the password in order to derive the encryption key. This is not possible in the server-end for many one-time password systems.

We will firstly illustrate the proposed Two-factor Interlock Authentication protocol (TIAP) before describing the solution. The idea is to split the two-factor authentication information into two portions, the static password and the one-time password (OTP), of which the one-time password (OTP) is first presented, before the static password (Pwd). By doing so, we will be able to defend against Bellovin and Merritt's attack on the Interlock protocol (Bellovin and Merritt, 1992). The proposed protocol is as follows:

In Figure 6,
- Steps 1 to 3 is unchanged from the standard Diffie-Hellman exponential key exchange protocol, and simply describe a means for both Alice and Bob to obtain a session encryption key. Besides using the Diffie-Hellman Exponential Key Exchange protocols, the use of other public key based protocols,

such as RSA is also possible. The important requirement in the key exchange is that the session key must not be solely determined by only one party but by the combination of two parties.
- Step 4 to Step 7 is the Interlock Protocol where the one-time password is submitted Alice to Bob, while the user info is sent from Bob to Alice. In Step 4, the one-time password (OTP) information is encrypted and only the 1st half of this information is sent to Bob. Alice will also indicate specific user information (such as the user name, salutation, last login time, and last failed attempt) that Bob has to present to Alice. The reason why the one-time password is sent first, rather that the static password, is to prevent a replay attack by Mallory.
- In Step 5, Bob will encrypt the session-chosen user-specific information, and send the 1st half of the user information back to Alice.
- In Step 6, Alice will send the 2nd half of the OTP information to Bob.
- In Step 7, Bob will first verify that the OTP information is correct, before sending the 2nd half of the user information to Alice. Now as a follow on from Step 7 to Step 9, an additional round trip of information from Alice to Bob has to take place. This is essential to break Bellovin and Merritt's attacks on the Interlock Protocol for Authentication (Bellovin and Merritt, 1992).

Figure 6. Two-factor interlock authentication protocol (TIAP)

Step	Alice (user)		Bob (server)	Remarks
1	g^a mod n	$\rightarrow$		This is essentially a Diffie-Hellman exponential key exchange.
2		$\leftarrow$	g^b mod n	
3	$k = g^{ba}$ mod n		$k = g^{ab}$ mod n	
4	E_k (OTP info$_{a1}$)	$\rightarrow$		Doing the first Interlock protocol will defeat the Man-in-the-Middle attack as shown by Rivest and Shamir (1984). Since we are exchanging only the OTP (one-time-password) here, the danger of a replay attack is removed.
5		$\leftarrow$	E_k (user info$_{b1}$)	
6	E_k (OTP info$_{a2}$)	$\rightarrow$		
7		$\leftarrow$	Check OTP info$_a$ E_k (user info$_{b2}$)	By enforcing a round-trip exchange of information both from Alice to Bob and from Alice to Bob, Bellovin and Merritt's attack (1992) on the Interlock protocol will not succeed.
8	Check user info$_b$ E_k (Pwd info$_a$)	$\rightarrow$		
9		$\leftarrow$	Check Pwd info$_a$ Ok	
10	E_k (secret info$_a$)	$\rightarrow$		
11		$\leftarrow$	E_k (secret info$_b$)	

- In Step 8, Alice will be prompted with the user information from Bob and asked to verify that the user information is correct before encrypting and sending the static password information to Bob.
- In Step 9, Bob will verify the static password information, and proceed with the session if verified correct.
- Now that the authentication protocol has established a common session key between Alice and Bob, sensitive information (e.g. transaction data) to be transferred between Alice and Bob should be encrypted using this session key.

We propose that the implementation of the Two-factor Interlock Authentication Protocol on Alice's side will be by means of a Java applet (or ActiveX) plug-in embedded within the browser. It is important to use compiled plug-ins, rather than script-based content (e.g. Javascript), as current reverse-proxy implementations are unable to lift content displayed by the compiled plug-ins. The Java applet plug-in will be responsible for:

- negotiating the session key (Step 1 to 3)
- prompting the entry of the one-time password, and encrypting it (Step 4)
- transmitting the 1st half of the encrypted one-time password to Bob (Step 4)
- transmitting the 2nd half of the encrypted one-time password to Bob (Step 6)
- decrypting the user information, and displaying it ito Alice for verification (Step 8)
- prompting the entry of the static password and encrypting it (Step 8). This step could be enhanced with the use of EKE to strengthen the transmission security of the static password, but this is not related to defending against phishing attacks.
- transmitting the encrypted static password to Bob (Step 8)
- functioning as a cryptographic API to encrypt / decrypt sensitive information to be exchanged between Alice and Bob.

As for the server-side implementation, the authentication service operated by Bob has to be able to handle the TIAP exchange, and importantly be able to authenticate the one-time password and static password separately.

PROTOCOL ANALYSIS

We will analyze the proposed Two-factor Interlock Authentication protocol (TIAP) by simulating the possible hacking attacks to be carried out by Mallory in the various steps. The places of attack are:

- Eavesdrop the entire conversation
- Collect Alice's OTP information before masquerading as Alice to Bob
- Collect Bob's user information before masquerading as Bob to Alice
- Send fake HTML content to Alice to prevent Alice from using the protocol
- Perform a session-hijack on the session after authentication has taken place

Hacking Attempt 1: Eavesdrop the Entire Conversation

We first assume that Mallory has been successful at compromising the session key (steps 1 to 3).

In attempting to simply eavesdrop on the authentication flow, the hacking attempt by Mallory is thwarted by the Interlock protocol between Alice and Bob in Step 4b.

Hacking Attempt 2: Masquerade as Alice

In the 2nd attempt, Mallory becomes smarter and attempts to collect Alice's OTP information before opening a connection to Bob in step 4b.

By deferring the communication with Bob, Mallory is able to first collect Alice's OTP information and open a valid channel with Bob. However, this hacking attempt is again thwarted by the Interlock protocol as Mallory is unable to present the user information to Alice in Step 8a.

Figure 7. Hacking Attack 1: Eavesdropping

Step	Alice		Mallory		Bob
1	$g^a \bmod n$	→			
2a		←	$g^m \bmod n$		
2b			$g^m \bmod n$	→	
2c				←	$g^b \bmod n$
3	$k = g^{ma} \bmod n$		$k = g^{am} \bmod n$ $k' = g^{bm} \bmod n$		$k' = g^{mb} \bmod n$
4a	$E_k(OTP\ info_{a1})$	→			
4b			$E_{k'}(??)$	→	
5a				←	$E_{k'}(user\ info_{b1})$
5b		←	$E_k(??)$		
6a	$E_k(OTP\ info_{a2})$	→	got OTP info$_a$!!		
6b			$E_{k'}(??)$	→	Incorrect OTP !! no part 2 of user info sent

Hacking Attempt 3: Masquerade as Bob

Now that Mallory has captured a specific set of Alice's user information, he will attempt to masquerade as Bob to obtain Alice's static password information before opening the connection to Bob. This attack is carried out by first performing the attack in Figure 8. When Alice re-attempts to connect to Bob, Mallory will attempt to masquerade as Bob.

This attack would succeed if not for the requirement in Step 4 of the Two-factor Interlock protocol which requires that Alice indicates user-specific information (such as the user name, salutation, last login time, and last failed attempt) that Bob has to return. In Alice's re-attempt to connect to Bob, the user information specified by Alice in Step 4a should be different from the first attempt, ensuring that Mallory is unable to present the correct user information back to Alice. Since there are so many different possibilities of user information to choose from, it would be very difficult for Mallory to phish Alice for all the possibilities without Alice being suspicious. Naturally, this protocol requires for Alice to be vigilant in checking for the user information.

Hacking Attempt 4: Fake Client Content

Mallory would have realized by now that the protocol is not possible to break. Instead, he deploys fake HTML content in Alice's browser in an attempt to circumvent the Interlock protocol.

This hacking attempt is thwarted by the use of Java Applet plug-ins to carry out the protocol as well as to display the user information returned by Bob. Since current reverse-proxy technology is unable to capture whatever is displayed by an Applet in Step 7b, Mallory is unable to dynamically present the user information back to Alice and hence is prevented from succeeding in the hacking attempt. Not to forget that it is possible for Mallory to perform an offline reverse-engineer on the Applet to allow the user information to be extractable in real time, it is important for Bob to deploy the use of different applets, each varying

Figure 8. Hacking Attack 2: Masquerade as Alice

Step	Alice		Mallory		Bob
1	$g^a \bmod n$	$\rightarrow$			
2a		$\leftarrow$	$g^m \bmod n$		
2b			$g^m \bmod n$	$\rightarrow$	
2c				$\leftarrow$	$g^b \bmod n$
3	$k = g^{ma} \bmod n$		$k = g^{am} \bmod n$ $k' = g^{bm} \bmod n$		$k' = g^{mb} \bmod n$
4a	$E_k (OTP\ info_{a1})$	$\rightarrow$			
4b		$\leftarrow$	$E_k (??)$		
6a	$E_k (OTP\ info_{a2})$	$\rightarrow$	got OTP $info_a$!!		
6b			$E_{k'} (OTP\ info_{a1})$	$\rightarrow$	
6c				$\leftarrow$	$E_{k'} (user\ info_{b1})$
6d			$E_{k'}(OTP\ info_{a2})$	$\rightarrow$	
7a			Got user info !!	$\leftarrow$	$E_{k'} (user\ info_{b2})$
8a	no user info, no Pwd info sent	$\leftarrow$	$E_k (??)$		

Figure 9. Hacking Attack 3: Masquerade as Bob

Step	Alice		Mallory		Bob
Perform Hacking attempt 2 to get Alice's user information.					
1	g^a mod n	$\rightarrow$			
2a		$\leftarrow$	g^m mod n		
2b			g^m mod n	$\rightarrow$	
2c				$\leftarrow$	g^b mod n
3	$k = g^{ma}$ mod n		$k = g^{am}$ mod n $\\$ $k' = g^{bm}$ mod n		$k' = g^{mb}$ mod n
4a	E_k (OTP info$_{a1}$)	$\rightarrow$			
4b		$\leftarrow$	E_k (user info$_{b1}$)		
6a	E_k (OTP info$_{a2}$)	$\rightarrow$	got OTP info$_a$!!		
7a		$\leftarrow$	E_k (user info$_{b2}$)		
8a	Incorrect user info, no Pwd info sent				

in the Diffie-Hellman public keys as well as the way the two halves of the data is split and joined, for different authentication sessions.

Hacking Attempt 5: Session Hijack after Authentication

In the final hacking attempt, Mallory will allow the entire authentication flow to pass through before taking over the session.

This attack would have been easily carried out if not for the shared session key between Alice and Bob. While Mallory retains control of the underlying HTTPS session, he is unable to access/modify information exchanged between Alice and Bob which is encrypted using the shared session key, thus effectively shutting Mallory out from the communication.

FUTURE RESEARCH

We have proposed and described the Two-factor Interlock Authentication Protocol which is an adaptation of the Interlock protocol with two-factor authentication and deployment recommendations to suit the protocol for defeating active phishing in web-based transactions. We have also comprehensively carried out hacking scenarios to attempt to break the protocol which seem to be able to withstand the attacks. We believe that the proposed approach can be used as a part of the enterprise-wide anti-phishing strategy.

At face value, the protocol is not entirely foolproof as the weakest point in the protocol still relies on the vigilance of the end-user to check for user information returned by the server in order to detect possible malicious activity. This paper also did not cover how Trojan horses or viruses on the users' machine may affect the solution as we believe that this problem should be addressed through the use of anti-virus software installed on the machine. Hence, in deploying this protocol, it is also important to incorporate a security-awareness program to constantly remind users on the proper usage of the website. Future research would be to deploy a reference implementation, most likely with an SSL VPN, to understand other practical aspects (such as performance tuning, streamlining the protocol) of the TIAP solution before possibly claiming victory against the phishing attacks.

Figure 10. Hacking Attack 4: Fake client content

Step	Alice		Mallory		Bob
		←	fake web site		
1		→			
1a			$g^m \bmod n$	→	
2a				←	$g^b \bmod n$
3			$k' = g^{bm} \bmod n$		$k' = g^{mb} \bmod n$
4a	Alice enters OTP	→			
6a		→	got OTP $info_a$!!		
6b			$E_{k'}(OTP\ info_{a1})$	→	
6c				←	$E_{k'}(user\ info_{b1})$
6d			$E_{k'}(OTP\ info_{a2})$	→	
7a			Got user info !!	←	$E_{k'}(user\ info_{b2})$
7b			Reverse proxy unable to extract user information from Applet		
8a	no user info, no Pwd info sent	←	??		

Figure 11. Hacking Attack 5: Session hijack after authentication

Step	Alice		Mallory		Bob
1	$g^a \bmod n$	→	$g^a \bmod n$	→	
2		←	$g^b \bmod n$	←	$g^b \bmod n$
3	$k = g^{ba} \bmod n$				$k = g^{ab} \bmod n$
4	$E_k(OTP\ info_{a1})$	→	$E_k(OTP\ info_{a1})$	→	
5		←	$E_k(user\ info_{b1})$	←	$E_k(user\ info_{b1})$
6	$E_k(OTP\ info_{a2})$	→	$E_k(OTP\ info_{a2})$	→	
7		←	$E_k(user\ info_{b2})$	←	$E_k(user\ info_{b2})$
8	$E_k(Pwd\ info)$	→	$E_k(Pwd\ info)$	→	
9		←	Ok	←	Ok
	session is hijacked				
10a	$Info_a$	→	Got $Info_a$ $Info_m$	→	
10b			Got $Info_b$ $Info_m$	←	$Info_b$
		←			
10c	$E_k(Info_a)$	→	??		
10d			??	←	$E_k(Info_b)$

REFERENCES

Bellovin, S., & Merritt, M. (1992). *Encrypted key exchange: password-based protocols secure against dictionary attacks.* Paper presented at the IEEE Symposium on Security and Privacy, Oakland, California.

Bellovin, S., & Merritt, M. (1994). An attack on the Interlock Protocol when used for authentication. *IEEE Transactions on Information Theory, 40*(1), 273-275.

Bellovin, S. M. (2004). Spamming, phishing, authentication, and privacy. *Communications of the ACM, 47*(12), 144.

Diffie, W., & Hellman, M. E. (1976). New directions in cryptography. *IEEE Transactions on Information Theory, IT-22,* 644-654.

Geer, D. (2005). Security technologies go phishing. *IEEE Computer, 38*(6), 18 - 21.

Goth, G. (2005). Phishing attacks rising, but dollar losses down. *IEEE Security and Privacy, 3*(1), 8.

Haller, N., Metz, C., Nesser, P., & Straw, M. (2005). A one-time password system. Retrieved May 5, 2006, from http://www.faqs.org/rfcs/rfc2289.html

Herzberg, A. (2004). *Web spoofing and phishing attacks and their prevention.* Paper presented at the The Fifth Mexican International Conference in Computer Science, Colima, Mexico.

Inomata, A., Rahman, M., Okamoto, T., & Okamoto, E. (2005). *A novel mail filtering method against phishing.* Paper presented at the IEEE Pacific Rim Conference on Communications, Computers and signal Processing, Victoria, B.C., Canada.

Kirda, E., & Kruegel, C. (2005). *Protecting users against phishing attacks with antiPhish.* Paper presented at the 29th Annual International on Computer Software and Applications Conference, Edinburgh, Scotland.

Kirk, J. (2005). Yahoo users get phished. Retrieved May 6, 2006, from http://www.pcworld.com/news/article/0,aid,122707,00.asp

Liu, W., Huang, G., Liu, X., Deng, X., & Zhang, M. (2005). *Phishing web page detection.* Paper presented at the Eighth International Conference on Document Analysis and Recognition, Daejeon, Korea.

Rivest, R., & Shamir, A. (1984). How to expose an eavesdropper. *Communications of the ACM, 27*(4), 393 - 394.

Schneier, B. (2005). The failure of two-factor authentication. Retrieved May 6, 2006, from http://www.schneier.com/blob/archives/2005/03/the_failure_of.html

ENDNOTES

[1] Alice would use $(g^b \bmod n)^a \bmod n = g^{ab} \bmod n$, while Bob would use $(g^a \bmod n)^b \bmod n = g^{ab} \bmod n$

[2] How the halves are derived depends on the encryption algorithm. In the case of a block cipher such as 3DES, the 2 halves will correspond to the first 4 bytes and last 4 bytes of each 8 byte encrypted block.

Chapter XII

A Content–Based Watermarking Scheme for Image Authentication Using Discrete Wavelet Transform Inter–Coefficient Relations

Latha Parameswaran
Amrita University, India

K. Anbumani
Karunya University, India

ABSTRACT

This chapter discusses a content-based authentication technique based on inter-coefficient relationship of Discrete Wavelet Transform (DWT). Watermark is generated from the first level DWT. An image digest (which is a binary string) is generated from the second level DWT. The watermark is embedded in the mid-frequency coefficients of first level DWT as directed by the image digest. Image authentication is done by computing the Completeness of Signature. The proposed scheme is capable of withstanding incidental image processing operations such as compression and identifies any malicious tampering done on the host image.

INTRODUCTION

With the proliferation of the Internet, distribution of digital multimedia has grown enormously in the recent years. Multimedia normally refers to data such as text, images, sound, video, graphics etc. With the availability of simple and economic tools, multimedia contents can be easily pirated or altered either incidentally or intentionally. The low cost of reproduction, storage and distribution, also paves way for large-scale commercial infringement (Eskicioglu et.al 2003). Digital watermarking is one of the significant technologies available for multimedia security.

A *digital watermark* is a piece of information that is hidden in a multimedia content, in such a way that it is imperceptible to a human observer, but easily detected by a computer. The principal advantage is that the watermark is inseparable from the content (Cox et.al 2002). Digital watermarking is the process of hiding the watermark imperceptibly in the content. This technique was initially used in paper and currency as a measure of authenticity.

Digital Watermarking involves two major phases:

(i)   Watermark embedding, and
(ii)   Watermark extraction.

Digital watermarks can be a pseudo random sequence or a logo of a company or an image or content-based ie. features derived from the image itself. Watermark embedding is done in the watermark carriers such as Discrete Cosine Transform (DCT) or Discrete Wavelet Transform (DWT), etc of the original data resulting in watermarked data. The watermarked data may be compressed to reduce its size, corrupted by noise during its transmission through a noisy channel. It may be subjected to other normal image processing operations such as filtering, histogram modification etc. Also malicious intruders may tamper the data. Watermark extraction is on the received image. Metrics like correlation are used to verify the integrity of the received image.

Digital watermarking is a multidisciplinary field that combines media and signal processing with cryptography, communication theory, coding theory, signal compression and the theory of human perception (Dittaman 2001).

As watermarks are inseparable from its host data, they are suitable for several applications (Cox et. al 2002, Cox et.al 1999):

*   Broadcast and publication monitoring
*   Owner identification
*   Copyright protection or proof of ownership
*   Transaction tracking
*   Content authentication
*   Copy control

Content authentication is one of the applications of watermarking. The objective is to provide a method to authenticate the image and ensure the integrity of the image.

Authentication is quite independent of encryption. In encryption-based systems, the intent is to ensure the secrecy of a given data and to provide assurance that the received data has not been tampered or altered. In some cases, modifications on image may be unintentional and may not affect the content. In other cases, modifications may be intentional and may inadvertently affect the interpretation of the host image. For example, an inadvertent change in an X-ray image might result in misdiagnosis; similarly, malicious tampering of photographic evidence in a trial can result in wrong conviction or acquittal (Cox et. al, 2002, and Cox et.al, 1999).

In the context of content authentication, normal image processing operations like compression, filtering and noise are considered as legitimate, content-preserving modifications.

Other modifications on the image such as:

*   Geometric transformations like rotation, scaling, translation etc,
*   Cropping, and
*   Addition or removal of objects from the host image are considered as illegitimate, malicious, content-changing and tampering.

Three basic methods are available in the literature for image content authentication:

- *Robust authentication* systems tolerate legitimate modifications.
- *Exact authentication or fragile watermarking* systems consider the received image as unauthentic even if altered slightly.
- *Selective authentication or semi-fragile watermarking* tolerates legitimate modifications such as compression but detects illegitimate modifications. These systems also identify the tampered regions.

Types of watermarks used in content authentication techniques are:

(i) *Host image independent watermarks* such as an image or logo of a company, or a pseudo-random sequence.
(ii) *Host image dependent* i.e. *content-based watermarks* consisting of features derived from the image.

Motivation for Content-Based Watermarking

For authentication of images it is desirable if the watermark to be embedded is content-dependent i.e. derived from the host image itself, instead of image independent watermark like a pseudo-random sequence. If a pseudo-random sequence is adopted as the watermark, the seed for each image has to be securely communicated to the legitimate recipient. On the contrary, if the watermark is content-based there is no need for such secure communication of additional data which has to be different for different images transmitted.

Many authentication methods based on watermarking have the ability to identify the maliciously tampered regions if any in the received image. This capability is referred as localization. Most localization methods rely on blockwise authentication, in which the image is divided into a number of disjoint regions, each of which is authenticated separately (Roberto et.al 2003) and (Yang and Cot, 2006). All authentication watermarking techniques are required to have these characteristics (Memon et al., 2000 and Wu, 2002):

- Authenticate the content and not the representation of the image.
- Embed the watermark in the image.
- Extract watermark by withstanding content-preserving modifications.
- Identify exact regions of content-changing modifications.
- Design computationally efficient algorithms to implement in terms of software and hardware.

Watermarking systems have a number of characteristics and their relative importance depends on the applications (Cox et. al, 2002, and Cox et.al, 1999). Interpretation of the characteristics varies with applications. Important properties of the watermark are discussed below.

Fidelity: Fidelity refers to the perceptual similarity between the unwatermarked and watermarked images. The watermark should neither be noticeable to the viewer nor degrade the visual quality of the content.

Robustness: The ability of the watermark extractor to extract the watermark from the received image even after common signal processing operations such as compression is termed as robustness.

Fragility: In some applications, the exact opposite of robustness is required. Watermarks that do not survive even slightest modification on the watermarked image are said to be fragile. This property is essential in certain applications that authenticate sensitive multimedia data such as currency notes or X-ray images.

False positive rate: In certain applications, it is essential to distinguish unwatermarked and watermarked data. The false positive rate of a watermark detection system is the probability that it will identify an unwatermarked data as containing a watermark. The significance of such an error depends on the application.

Modification and multiple watermarks: Certain applications require watermark alterations after embedding. Just as in the case of digital video discs, a disc may be watermarked to allow only a single copy. Once this copy has been made, it is then necessary to modify the watermark on the original disc to prevent further copying. Allowing multiple watermarks to co-exist is required to track content from manufacturing to distribution and to eventual sales, since each point in the distribution chain can insert their own unique watermark.

Data payload: Data payload of a watermark is the number of bits a watermark encodes within a host image and varies with application.

Computational cost: In commercial use, the computational costs of embedding and detecting watermarks are significant and depend on the application. In broadcast monitoring, watermark embedding and detection demand very high speed as they run in real-time; whereas in copyright protection, speed of the watermark detectors is not that important.

Performance of watermarking systems is evaluated considering the visual quality of the watermarked image and quality of the extracted watermark. The widely used metrics for evaluating the quality of the watermarked image is given in Table 1 (Cox et.al, 2002), (Kutter and Petitcolas 1999), and (Ismail et.al 2001). Host image is represented as I of size n x n and the watermarked image is represented as I^* of the same size.

EXISTING RESEARCH WORK

Watermarking techniques based on the relationship between neighboring coefficients in a transform domain or pixel values in the spatial domain are available in the literature (Wu, 2002), (Da-Chun Wu, 2003), (Lu and Lia 2003) and, (Tang and Chen, 2004).

Table 1. Commonly used performance metrics

Difference distortion metrics	
Mean Square Error (MSE)	$\left(\dfrac{1}{n^2}\right)\sum\left(I-I^*\right)^2$
Peak Signal to Noise Ratio (PSNR)	$10\log_{10}\left(\dfrac{\max\left(I^2\right)}{MSE}\right)$
Image Fidelity (IF)	$1-\dfrac{\sum\left(I-I^*\right)^2}{\sum I^2}$
Correlation-based metrics	
Normalized Cross Correlation (NCC)	$\dfrac{\sum I*I^*}{\sum I^2}$
Pearson Correlation Coefficient (PCC)	$\dfrac{\left(\sum I*I^*\right)-\sum I\sum I^*}{\sqrt{\sigma^2(I)\,\sigma^2(I^*)}}$

In (Wu 2002) a watermarking technique based on coefficient relationship in DCT is proposed. In his scheme, the host image is segmented into blocks and DCT is applied to each block. DCT coefficients are scaled and quantized. Based on the relationship between the original and quantized DCT coefficients a binary string is generated. This binary string is encrypted and a watermark is computed. The computed watermark is stored in the image header and not embedded in the image.

In (Da-Chun Wu, 2003) a watermarking scheme based on the relationship between neighbouring pixel values in spatial domain is discussed. This scheme embeds a secret message into a gray scale image. The host image is segmented into blocks of two consecutive pixels. Image blocks are classified based on the difference between pixel values. This difference is replaced by the message to be embedded. This scheme is not robust against normal signal processing operations.

Another image authentication scheme based on the relationship between interscale coefficients in DWT is discussed in (Lu and Lia 2003). In this scheme, a watermark string is generated based on the difference between the DWT coefficients at the first level and the second level. This watermark is encrypted using the RSA encryption algorithm and then stored for authentication. This technique does not embed the watermark in the host image. Authentication is carried out by computing the Completeness of Signature (CoS).

Tang and Chen (Tang and Chen 2004) have proposed a watermarking scheme using relationship between DWT coefficients. In their scheme the watermark is generated based on the difference between the neighbouring coefficients considering all the subbands. A quantization based method is used to embed the watermark in the mid-frequency bands. Their non-blind scheme is capable of withstanding incidental distortions and identifies malicious tampering.

PROPOSED CONTENT-BASED WATERMARKING USING INTER-COEFFICIENT RELATIONS

In the schemes (Wu, 2002) and (Da-Chun Wu, 2003), the watermark is not embedded in the host image. In Da-Chun Wu, 2003), a chosen watermark is embedded in the host and in (Tang and Chen 2004) a quantization approach is used to embed the watermark. In the scheme proposed in this chapter the watermark is generated based on the relationship between the neighbouring coefficients in second level DWT and embedding is done in the first level DWT. The quality of the watermarked image is much better than (Tang and Chen 2004) and also the proposed scheme is blind while Tang and Chen (Tang and Chen 2004) scheme is non-blind.

This proposed watermarking technique has for major phases:

(i)   Image digest computation,
(ii)   Watermark generation,
(iii)   Watermark embedding, and
(iv)   Watermark extraction and authentication.

Image Digest Computation

In this proposed technique, DWT is applied on the host image. Let $DWT_S^\theta (p,q)$ denote the wavelet coefficient at location *(p, q)*, where *s* denotes the wavelet decomposition level and θ denotes the subband i.e. approximation band, horizontal band, vertical band and diagonal band. For example $DWT_2^2 (p,q)$ refers to the wavelet coefficient at *(p, q)* at the second level decomposition in the vertical subband. The coefficients in second level are scanned horizontally and continuously in alternate direction as shown in Fig. 1.

Image digest is generated based on these second level coefficients. Each pair of neighboring coefficients $DWT_2^\theta (p,q)$ and $DWT_2^\theta (p,q+1)$ in each subband is compared. If $DWT_2^\theta (p,q) > DWT_2^\theta (p,q+1)$, the image digest bit is stored

Figure 1. Scanning of coefficients for image digest computation

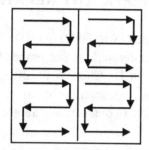

as 1; otherwise it is stored as 0. For each pair of coefficients a 4-bit image digest is generated from all the four subbands. This results in a binary string that denotes the relationship between all the coefficients in all the four subbands in the second level decomposition. Detailed steps of image digest computation are given below.

1. Perform DWT on the host image I and extract the approximation band coefficients.
2. Perform DWT on the approximation band to generate second level subbands.
3. Compare the neighboring coefficients $DWT_2^\theta(p,q)$ and $DWT_2^\theta(p,q+1)$ in the second level decomposition in all the four subbands and compute image digest bit D_i.
   If $DWT_2^\theta(p,q) > DWT_2^\theta(p,q+1)$ then $D_i = 1$; else $D_i = 0$.
4. Repeat this comparison for all the coefficients in all the four subbands. The resultant is the image digest (binary string) D.

Watermark Embedding

The content-based watermark in this scheme is the maximum of the two corresponding DWT coefficients in the mid-frequency bands, (horizontal and vertical) added to a scaled difference between them. Watermark embedding is done by modifying the mid-frequency coefficients of first level DWT directed by the image digest. Steps of watermark embedding are given below.

1. Perform DWT on the host image I.
2. Compute the difference between the corresponding coefficients in the mid-frequency subband in first level decomposition.

$$d = \left| DWT_1^1(p,q) - DWT_1^2(p,q) \right|$$

3. Compute the watermark to be embedded.

$$w = \max \left\{ DWT_1^1(p,q), DWT_1^2(p,q) \right\} + \lfloor d \rfloor * \alpha$$

4. Based on the image digest, replace the coefficients in the horizontal (LH) and vertical (HL) bands.

$$DWT_1^1(p,q) = \begin{cases} +w & \text{if } D_i = 1 \\ -w & \text{if } D_i = 0 \end{cases}$$

$$DWT_1^2(p,q) = \begin{cases} -w & \text{if } Di = 0 \\ +w & \text{if } Di = 1 \end{cases}$$

5. Repeat updating all the coefficients with the watermark in the mid-frequency bands, based on the bits of image digest D.
6. Perform inverse DWT and construct watermarked image I^*.

Watermark Extraction and Authentication

Watermark extraction is done on the received image. The embedded image digest is extracted from the mid-frequency DWT coefficients and an image digest is computed from the received image applying the same watermark generation procedure. The computed and extracted image digests are compared by calculating the Completeness of Signature (CoS) (Lu and Lia, 2003):

$$CoS = \frac{(N^+ - N^-)}{N_d}$$

where N^+ denotes the number of pairs that match, N^- denotes the number of pairs that do not match and N_d denotes the number of pairs considered for watermark computation. Detailed steps for watermark extraction are given below.

1. Perform watermark generation on the received image I' and obtain the computed watermark D'.
2. Perform DWT on the received image I'.
3. Extract the mid-frequency coefficients from LH (horizontal) band DWT_1^2.
4. Extract the image digest bit D_i^* if $DWT_1^2(p,q) > 0$ then $D_i^* = 1$; else $D_i^* = 0$.
5. Repeat extracting the image digest from all the locations in the horizontal band. This gives the extracted image digest D^*.
6. Compute Completeness of Signature (CoS) using D^* and D'.
7. If the value of CoS is high and nearly one, the received image is deemed authentic.
8. If CoS is low, the received image is unauthentic.

Thus the proposed scheme performs authentication on the received image and ably detects malicious tamper.

EXPERIMENTAL RESULTS

The proposed technique has been evaluated on a set of three different categories of 512 x 512 gray scale images: (i) standard images, (ii) natural images, and (iii) images created using imaging tools. Performance of these proposed scheme is evaluated along the dimensions:

(i) Quality of the watermarked image,
(ii) Extraction efficacy,
(iii) Robustness against incidental image processing operations,
(iv) Detection of tampering, and

Choice of Parameters

For choosing a suitable value for the embedding strength α, statistics of the mid-frequency DWT coefficient values are obtained, specifically its standard deviation σ_x. Similarly the standard deviation σ_w is obtained for the watermark. Value of the embedding factor α is determined such that the watermark values are suitably scaled to have the same range of variation as that of the mid-frequency DWT coefficients.

$$\alpha = \frac{\sigma_x}{\sigma_w}.$$

Experimentation for this technique, gave the values $\sigma_x = 0.5709$ and $\sigma_w = 1.1012$. Hence α has been calculated as

$$\alpha = \frac{0.5709}{1.1012} = 0.5.$$

Threshold for the Completeness of Signature (CoS) T has also been experimentally determined as 0.8. Lower thresholds resulted in false negatives.

Quality of the Watermarked Image

The images after watermarking using this proposed watermarking technique based on inter-coefficient relations are shown in Fig. 2. The performance metrics PSNR, Pearson Correlation Coefficient (PCC), Normalized Cross Correlation (NCC), and Image Fidelity (IF) are calculated between the host image and the watermarked image.

It is observed that there is no perceptually apparent difference in the images due to watermarking. Performance metrics values for the test images given in Table 2 also demonstrate this. PSNR values range from 51.96 to 78.28, with an average of 60.13 over all the test images, which is quite high.

The other metrics, PCC, NCC, and IF are also high. This demonstrates that the visual quality of the image has not reduced due to watermark embedding.

Figure 2. Images after watermarking using inter-coefficient relations

continued on following page

Figure 2. continued

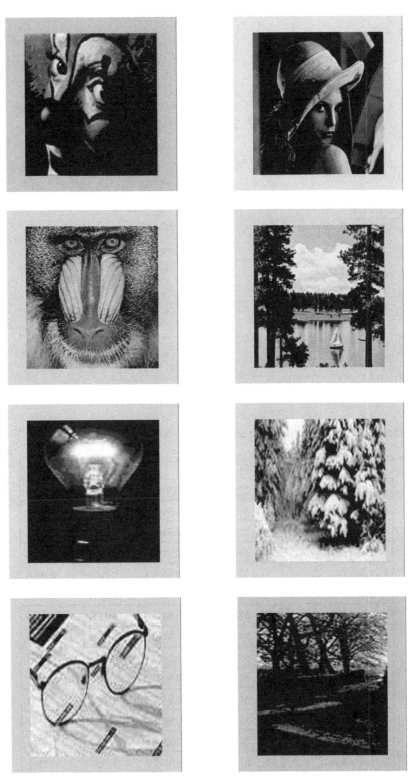

continued on following page

Figure 2. continued

Table 2. Quality metrics after watermarking using inter-coefficient relations

Image	PSNR	IF	NCC	PCC
Bridge	53.8666	0.9495	0.9396	0.9588
Boy	59.0879	0.9498	0.9399	0.9597
Building	52.4300	0.9493	0.9395	0.9581
Cameraman	54.1818	0.9496	0.9397	0.9591
Clown	77.3726	0.9500	0.9400	0.9600
Couple	63.1946	0.9500	0.9400	0.9599
Jet Plane	57.7332	0.9499	0.9399	0.9594
Lena	54.8574	0.9492	0.9393	0.9589
Living Room	55.9750	0.9497	0.9398	0.9589
Mandrill	54.5345	0.9496	0.9397	0.9581
Peppers	57.3255	0.9498	0.9398	0.9595
Sail Boat	53.7448	0.9496	0.9397	0.9591
Bulb	78.2800	0.9300	0.9960	0.9710
Snow Tree	67.7522	0.9100	0.9150	0.9561
Specs	68.4941	0.9450	0.9710	0.9860

continued on following page

Table 2. continued

Trees	66.0251	0.9370	0.9910	0.9559
KeyClock	55.5314	0.9498	0.9499	0.9489
SunBark	51.9680	0.9495	0.9496	0.9481
Decor	61.9157	0.9500	0.9500	0.9499
Lamp	56.9793	0.9499	0.9500	0.9494
Average	60.1308	0.9454	0.9472	0.9598
Minimum	51.9680	0.9100	0.9150	0.9481
Maximum	78.2800	0.9500	0.9960	0.9860

Extraction Efficacy

The efficacy of the proposed scheme for correctly extracting the watermark is determined by the Completeness of Signature (CoS) between the extracted and embedded image digest from the received image.

Observation of Table 3 shows that the CoS is high ranging from 0.8103 to 0.8933 giving an average of 0.8518. High values of CoS indicate that the scheme efficiently extracts the watermark. Since all CoS values are higher than the threshold 0.8 (chosen experimentally), it is evident that no tampering has been done on the watermarked images.

Robustness against Incidental Image Processing

Robustness of the proposed scheme against normal signal processing operations such as compression, noise and filtering has been experimentally evaluated on all the test images.

In this proposed watermarking technique the watermarked image is subjected to three sets of distortions: compression, noise, and filter. Watermarked image has been compressed using JPEG compression with different quality factors. Additive white Gaussian noise (AWGN) and uniform noise has been added to the watermarked image. Also filtering such as low pass, sharpening,

Table 3. Results after watermark extraction without attacks

Image	Completeness of Signature (CoS) after extraction without attacks
Bridge	0.8933
Boy	0.8361
Building	0.8804
Cameraman	0.8340
Clown	0.8358
Couple	0.8229
Jet Plane	0.8829
Lena	0.8746
Living Room	0.8421
Mandrill	0.8103
Peppers	0.8488
Sail Boat	0.8620
Bulb	0.8526
Snow Tree	0.8605
Specs	0.8505
Trees	0.8492
KeyClock	0.8540
SunBark	0.8427
Decor	0.8347
Lamp	0.8350
Average	0.8518
Minimum	0.8103
Maximum	0.8933

histogram equalization, and contrast stretching has been applied on the watermarked image. Completeness of Signature (CoS) is computed between the embedded and extracted image digest. Results of the test image Lena after these incidental image processing operations are tabulated in Table 4. The CoS values range from 0.8518 to 0.8732. Since all CoS values are higher than the threshold 0.8, it is evident that there is no tampering and the image is authentic.

Similar good performance of robustness of the proposed scheme has been obtained for other test images also. For example, Fig. 3 shows the robustness of the various test images against:

- JPEG compression medium quality (Quality factor = 5)
- AWGN with noise 5%
- Low pass filter with standard deviation 10.

Detection of Tampering

To demonstrate the ability of the proposed scheme to detect tampering, the watermarked Lena image has been intentionally tampered by introducing small patches as shown in Fig. 4. The image digest extracted after the tampering is compared with the embedded image digest using CoS. These values are given in Table 5. Low values of CoS (much less than the adopted threshold 0.8) indicate that the image is unauthentic and prompts us to suspect that the received image is tampered.

Similar tampering has been carried out on other test images. In all the cases, this proposed technique correctly identified malicious tampering and declared the image as unauthentic.

Table 4. Results after incidental distortions on Lena

Attacks	Parameters	Completeness of Signature (CoS) after attacks
JPEG Compression		
Maximum	Quality Factor = 10	0.8732
High	Quality Factor = 8	0.8712
Medium	Quality Factor = 5	0.8616
Low	Quality Factor = 3	0.8538
Noise		
AWGN	Noise = 5%	0.8636
Uniform	Noise = 5%	0.8714
Filter		
Low pass	Standard Deviation = 10	0.8678
Sharpening	-	0.8714
Histogram Equalization	-	0.8518
Gamma Correction	Gamma value = 3	0.8525
Contrast Stretching	Brightness = 15 Contrast = 15	0.8623
Average		0.8637
Maximum		0.8732
Minimum		0.8518

Figure 3. Robustness of inter-coefficient relations technique after incidental image processing

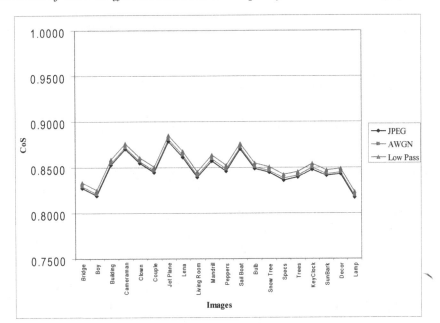

Figure 4. Tampered Lena for the inter-coefficient relations based technique

Table 5. Results after intentional tamper on Lena

Locations of Tamper	Completeness of Signature (CoS) after intentional tamper
Top	0.5582
Hat	0.6901
Shoulder	0.5786
Hair	0.5923

CONCLUSION

A content-based watermarking scheme for image authentication using inter-coefficient relations in DWT has been discussed in this chapter. This proposed technique withstands incidental image processing operations like compression and noise and declares the image as authentic; further it has the capability of correctly sensing malicious alterations on the received image declaring the image as unauthentic. Exhaustive experimentation has shown the efficiency of this technique in establishing authenticity and properly identifying malicious tampering. This scheme can find applications in authenticating documents such as identity cards, driving licenses, and so forth, stored as digital images.

REFERENCES

Ahmet, M. E., Town, J., & Delp, E. J. (2003, April). Security of digital entertainment content from creation to consumption. *Signal Processing: Image Communication, Special Issue on Image security, 18*(4), 237-262.

Avcybasb, I., Memon, N., & Sankurb, B. (2001, February). Steganalysis based on image quality metrics. *Proceedings of International Conference on Security and Watermarking of Multimedia contents.*

Caldelli, R., Bartiloni, F., & Cappellini, V. (2003). Standard metadata embedding in a digital image.

Proceedings of 14th International Workshop on Database and Expert Systems Applications.

Cox, I. J., Miller, M. L., & Bloom, J. A. (2002). *Digital Watermarking.* Morgan Kaufmann Publishers.

Dittmann, J. (2001, December). Using cryptographic and watermarking algorithms. *IEEE Multimedia and Security,* (pp. 54-65).

Kutter, M., & Petitcolas, F. A. P. (1999, January). A fair benchmark for image watermarking systems. *Proceedings of SPIE: Security and Watermarking of Multimedia Contents, 3637,* 226-239. San Jose, USA.

Kutter, M., & Petitcolas, F. A. P. (1999, January). A fair benchmark for image watermarking systems. *Proceedings of SPIE: Security and Watermarking of Multimedia Contents, 3637,* 226-239. San Jose, USA.

Lu, C-S., & Lia, M Y. A. (2003, June). Structural digital signature for image authentication: An incidental distortion resistant scheme. *IEEE Transactions on Multimedia, 5*(2), 161-173.

Memon, N., Vora, P., Yeo, B-L., & Yeung, M. (2000, February). Distortion bounded authentication techniques. *Proceedings of International Conference on Watermarking and Multimedia Contents.*

Miller, M. L., Cox, I. J., Linnartz, J-P. M. G., & Kalker, T. (1999). A review of watermarking principles and practices. *Digital Signal Process-*

ing in Multimedia Systems, pp. 461-485). Marcell Dekker Inc.

Tang, Y-L., & Chen, C-T. (2004). Image authentication using relation measures of wavelet coefficients. *Proceedings of IEEE International Conference on e-Technology, e-Commerce and e-Service.*

Wu, C. W. (2002, September). On the design of content-based multimedia authentication systems. *IEEE Transactions on Multimedia, 4*(3), 385-393.

Wu, D-C., & Tsai, W-H. (2003). A Steganographic method for images by pixel differencing. *Pattern Recognition Letters* (pp. 1613-1626). Elsevier.

Yang, H., & Kot, A. C. (2006, December). Binary image authentication with tampering localization by embedding cryptographic signature and block identifier. *IEEE Signal Processing Letters, 13*(12), 741-744.

Section IV
Security and Privacy Management

Chapter XIII
Privacy and Security in the Age of Electronic Customer Relationship Management

Nicholas C. Romano, Jr.
Oklahoma State University, USA

Jerry Fjermestad
New Jersey Institute of Technology, USA

ABSTRACT

New technologies have fostered a shift from a transaction-based economy through an Electronic Data Interchange (EDI) informational-exchange economy to relationship-based Electronic Commerce (EC) one (Keen 1999.) We have moved from "first order" transactional value exchanges through "second-order" informational value exchanges to "third-order" relational value exchanges (Widmeyer 2004.) Three important types of EC relationships have been identified: between enterprises and customers (B2C); between enterprises (B2B); and between customers (C2C) (Kalakota 1996.). Additional relationships between Governments (G2G), enterprises (G2B) and customers (G2C) have become more important as EC and e-government have matured and legislation, regulation and oversight have increased (Friel 2004; Reddick 2004); however these are not the focus of this paper. Relational value exchanges have become central to success and competitive advantage in B2C EC and it here that we focus on privacy and security in the age of virtual relationships.

INTRODUCTION

Both enterprises and customers must carefully manage these new virtual relationships to ensure that they derive value from them and to minimize the possible unintended negative consequences that result from the concomitant exchange of personal information that occurs when goods are services are purchased through EC. The need to manage these relationships has resulted in the development of Electronic Customer Relationship Management (eCRM) systems and processes (Romano and Fjermestad 2001-2002). eCRM is used for different reasons by enterprises and customers. It is important to understand how and why both of the players participate in "*relational value exchanges*" that accompany the economic transaction and informational value exchanges of EC.

Enterprises use eCRM to establish and maintain *intimate virtual relationships* with their *economically valuable* customers to derive additional value beyond that which results from economic value exchanges to improve return-on-investment from customer relationships.

Customers obtain goods, services and information (economic value) through EC for purposes such as convenience, increased selection and reduced costs. EC requires customers to reveal personal information to organizations in order for transactions to be completed. The exchange of information between customers and organizations leads to the possibility of privacy violations perpetrated against the customer and the responsibility for organizations to provide privacy policies and security measures that will engender customer trust.

In this paper we present a series of models "*sphere of privacy model,*" "*sphere of security model,*" "*privacy/security sphere of implementation model,*" and then integrate them into the "*relational value exchange model*" to explain privacy and security in the context of eCRM from the perspective of both customers and enterprises to provide guidance for future research and practice in this important area. It is important for both customers and firms to understand each others' vested interests in terms of privacy and security and to establish and maintain policies and measures that ensure both are satisfactorily implemented to minimize damage in terms of unintended consequences associated with security breaches that violate privacy and lead to relationship breakdowns.

The reminder of this paper is structured as follows: First, we explain why privacy and security are critically important issues for companies and customers that engage in EC and the consequences that can result from failure to recognize their importance or poor implementation of measures to ensure both for the organization and its customers. Second, we define privacy and security and their interrelationship in the context of CRM. Third, we present our relational value exchange model for privacy and security in eCRM; next, we discuss

Customer Relationship Management Privacy and Security: Who Cares?

"The data contained within a CRM application is often a company's most critical asset, yet because of the pivotal role this information plays in day-to-day business activities, it is also often the most vulnerable to security breaches and disruptions." (Seitz 2006)

Before we explain and define privacy and security in detail and our models and the relational value exchange model we will describe the costs associated with failure to understand these concepts and failure to effectively ensure that both are protected in terms that firms and customers can understand: dollars and lost customers.

Economic Cost of Customer Security Breaches

The economic cost of security breaches, that is the release or loss of customers personal information, has been studied in a number of surveys over the past decade and while some studies show declines in the total and average losses over time the costs are still staggering for many firms and new threats and vulnerabilities have arisen in the recent past and these lower costs are most likely offset by increased expenditures to implement security measures and training.

The Computer Security Institute (CSI) and the Federal Bureau of Investigation (FBI) have conducted eleven annual surveys of computer crime and security since 1995. Some of the results of the last seven are presented (Power 2002; Richardson 2003; Gordon, et al. 2004; Gordon, et al. 2005; Gordon, et al. 2006). The Ponemon Institute also conducted two surveys on the costs and effects of data security breaches (Ponemon 2005a; Ponemon 2005b) and we will also present a portion of their results as well.

The CSI/FBI surveys have tracked the costs (losses) associated with security breaches for thirteen years; we focus on summary data from the last seven years to illustrate trends and changes in the economic costs of security breaches for organizations that responded with loss data. Table 1 reveals some interesting aspects about security breach costs over the past seven years. Several types of costs have been reported across all the years of the survey, these include: theft of proprietary information, sabotage of data or networks, system penetration, insider abuse of network access, financial fraud, denial of service, viruses, unauthorized insider access, telecom fraud, and laptop theft.

Other types of losses were reported in early years of the period but not in later periods or were reported in only the last three or even only the final survey in 2006; indicating that some threats have been better managed and new ones have arisen or been identified and quantified. Specifically, losses from telecom eavesdropping were reported to be on average from a high of $1.2M in 2002 to a low on $15K in 2003; however there were no reported losses in 2004, 2005 or 2006. Active wiretapping is another loss that was reported as an average of $5M in 2000 and 4325K in 2003, but not reported in any of the other years. Theft of proprietary information was reported as the highest loss for the four years from 200 to 2003; then viruses took over the top spot in 2004 and remained the highest loss IN 2005 and 2006. The results also show that between 2002 and 2003 that there is a

62% reduction in the reported losses and between 2003 and 2004 there is a 90% reduction in the losses. Thus, the enterprises are responding to the need for privacy and security. In 2004 three new loss types were reported: website defacement, misuse of a public web application, and abuse of wireless networks. All three of these losses were also reported in 2005 and 2006. Six new losses were reported in 2006: Bots (zombies) within the organization; Phishing in which your organization was fraudulently represented as sender; instant messaging misuse; password sniffing; DNS server exploitation; and a general category of other.

The time-series results reveal the dynamic nature of the security environment and the threats and costs over time as companies identify them and take actions t try to minimize or eliminate losses. Figure 1 reveals that losses from security breaches appear to be going down over time, which is a positive finding; however they do not tell the whole story because the same surveys from which the data in table 1 are taken also found that budgets in terms of operating expenses and capitol investment for security and training and also rose at the same time.

Figure 2 shows the reported average expenditure per employee for operations, capitol investment and awareness training from 2004 to 2006 for four different sized companies based on reported revenues. It is important to keep in mind that these are *average* expenditures *per employee* and so for any given company the total outlay would be calculated by multiplying the number of employees in the organization by their actual expenditures, which could be higher or lower than the average.

This time series of expenditures for security reveals interesting trends as well. One is that there appear to be economies of scale for security measures, that is organizations with higher revenue seem to have smaller expenditures per employee (Gordon et al., 2006), but that may not translate into smaller overall expenditures. A second similar trend is that lower revenue firms seem

Table 1. Average loss per year per loss type

	2000	2001	2002	2003	2004	2005	2006
Theft of proprietary info.	$ 3,032,818	$ 4,447,900	$ 6,571,000	$ 2,699,842	$ 42,602	$ 48,408	$ 19,278
Sabotage of data or networks	$ 969,577	$ 199,350	$ 541,000	$ 214,521	$ 3,238	$ 533	$ 831
Telecom eavesdropping	$ 66,080	$ 55,375	$ 1,205,000	$ 15,200			
System penetration by outsider	$ 244,965	$ 453,967	$ 226,000	$ 56,212	$ 3,351	$ 1,317	$ 2,422
Insider abuse of Net access	$ 307,524	$ 357,160	$ 536,000	$ 135,255	$ 39,409	$ 10,730	$ 5,910
Financial fraud	$ 1,646,941	$ 4,420,738	$ 4,632,000	$ 328,594	$ 28,515	$ 4,014	$ 8,169
Denial of service	$ 108,717	$ 122,389	$ 297,000	$ 1,427,028	$ 96,892	$ 11,441	$ 9,335
Virus	$ 180,092	$ 243,835	$ 283,000	$ 199,871	$ 204,661	$ 66,961	$ 50,132
Unauthorized insider access	$ 1,124,725	$ 275,636	$ 300,000	$ 31,254	$ 15,904	$ 48,878	$ 33,920
Telecom fraud	$ 212,000	$ 502,278	$ 22,000	$ 50,107	$ 14,861	$ 379	$ 4,033
Active wiretapping	$ 5,000,000	$ -	$ -	$ 352,500			
Laptop theft	$ 58,794	$ 61,881	$ 89,000	$ 47,107	$ 25,035	$ 6,428	$ 21,223
Web site defacement					$ 3,562	$ 180	$ 519
Misuse of public web application					$ 10,212	$ 3,486	$ 861
Abuse of wireless network					$ 37,767	$ 852	$ 1,498
Bots (zombies) within the organization							$ 2,951
Phishing in which your organization was fraudulently represented as sender							$ 2,069
instant messaging misuse							$ 931
password sniffing							$ 515
DNS server exploitation							$ 288
Other							$ 2,827
Totals	$12,886,153	$10,688,458	$14,702,000	$5,557,491	$438,809	$203,661	$167712

(Data from (Power 2002; Richardson 2003; Gordon, et al. 2004; Gordon, et al. 2005; Gordon, et al. 2006)

to have had increases in security expenditures while higher revenue firms have seen decreases. Regardless of these trends the reduction in losses due to security breaches and attacks have been accompanied by increased investment in security software, hardware and training; therefore it is logical to conclude that either through losses or through increased defense expenditures security continues to have a large economic impact on firms. Finally it also reveals that in 2006 firms began to spend funds for security awareness training that were not reported in the previous years of the CSI/FBI surveys.

Figure 1. Total reported losses per year across 7 CSI/FBI surveys

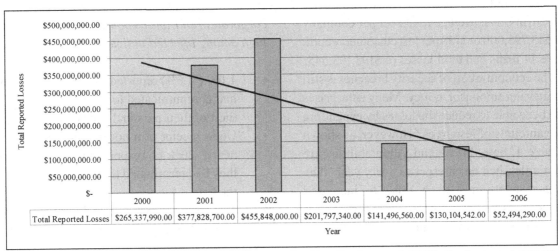

	2000	2001	2002	2003	2004	2005	2006
Total Reported Losses	$265,337,990.00	$377,828,700.00	$455,848,000.00	$201,797,340.00	$141,496,560.00	$130,104,542.00	$52,494,290.00

(Data from (Power 2002; Richardson 2003; Gordon, et al. 2004; Gordon, et al. 2005; Gordon, et al. 2006))

Figure 2. Reported average expenditure per employee

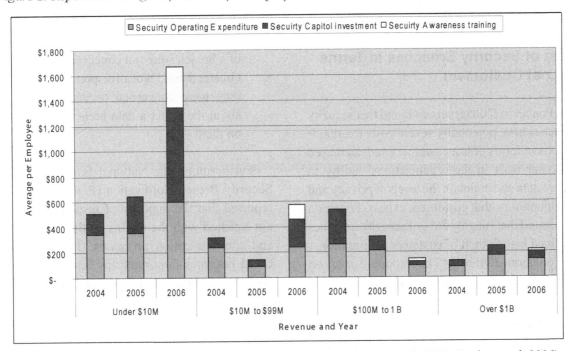

(Data from (Power 2002; Richardson 2003; Gordon, et al. 2004; Gordon, et al. 2005; Gordon, et al. 2006)

In November 2005 The Ponemon Institute (Ponemon 2005a) surveyed the costs incurred by 14 firms in 11 different industries that experienced security breaches. The size of the breaches in terms of customer records ranged from 900,000 to 1,500 for a total of 1,395,340 records and an average of 99,667 per breach.

Table 2 summarizes total average cost (including direct, indirect, and opportunity costs) for all 14 firms. The average total cost per company was $13,795,000 or $138 per lost customer record. These 14 firms had total losses of $193,103,545.

The economic cost of security breaches is still a staggering amount of money. Many enterprises have been able to reduce the losses by expending large amounts of resources. However, as shown in Table 1, new threats and vulnerabilities are being unleashed on enterprises every year. The lower costs are most likely offset by increased expenditures to implement new security measures and training. These economic costs are only part of the story; because there are also costs associated with lost customers and opportunity costs associated with potential customers going elsewhere due the security breach publicity. The next section discusses losses in these less tangible, but critically important areas.

Cost of Security Breaches in Terms of Lost Customers

The Ponemon (2005a) survey found that security breaches have potentially severe costs to organizations in terms of lost customers and decreased customer trust in the organizations' ability to secure data and maintain the levels of privacy and confidentiality that customers expect. Ponemon also found that roughly 86% of security breaches involved loss or theft of customer information.

Ponemon (2005b) in "The National Survey on Data Security Breach Notification" polled 9,154 adult-aged respondents in all major US regions and found that "*Damage to corporate reputation, corporate brand, and customer retention was very high among affected individuals*":

- 1,109 (11.6%) reported that an organization had communicated to them a loss or theft of their personal information.
- Upon receipt of a notification of a breach nearly 20% of respondents reported that they had terminated their relationship with the firm.
- 40% of those that received notification reported they might terminate the relationship due to the breach.
- 58% reported that they believed that the breach had lowered their confidence and trust in the organization that reported it.
- 92% of respondents blamed the company that notified them for the breach.
- Only 14% of respondents that were notified of a breach were not concerned.
- Greater than 85% of all respondents reported they were concerned or very concerned about the effect a data breach would have on them.

Furthermore, the National Survey on Data Security Breach Notification (Ponemon 2005b) reported that the majority of respondents were not satisfied with the quality of the notification and communication processes. This is where CRM becomes important and how enterprises communicate security breaches to their custom-

Table 2. Costs of security breaches for 14 firms in 2005

	Direct Costs	Indirect Costs	Lost Customer costs	Total Costs
Total Cost for all companies	$49,840,593	$123,262,952	(factored into indirect costs)	$193,103,545
Average Cost Per Company	$4,990,000	$1,347,000	$7,458,000	$13,795,000
Average Cost Per Lost Record	$50	$14	$75	$138

(Data from (Ponemon 2005a))

ers has an impact. The survey highlighted the following communication experiences:

- Companies that reported breaches to consumers were more than four times (417%) as likely to experience customer churn if they **failed** to communicate to the victim in a clear, consistent and timely fashion.
- Companies that sent e-mails or form letters to communicate a breach of consumer data were more than three times (326%) as likely to experience customer churn than companies that used telephone or personalized letters (or a combination of both).
- Over 82% of respondents believed that it is always necessary for an organization to report a breach even if the lost or stolen data was encrypted, or there was no criminal intent. The type of information involved in the breach was also not a factor.
- About 59% of respondents do not have confidence in U.S. state or federal regulations to protect the public from data security breaches by organizations.

The high cost of security breaches comes from efforts to prevent them and the cost of the aftermath of a breach. Customers appear to be more likely to terminate their relationship with an enterprise after a security breach. In addition, the timeliness and manner in which a breach notification is delivered is important. It appears that telephone calls immediately after (or at least before a public discloser) followed up with a personal letter is best to maintain trust and manage the relationship with the customer. Customers are concerned about protecting their privacy and identity and they expect companies to be vigilant in securing any data they share. In the next two sections we discuss and define both privacy and security within the context of EC and eCRM.

PRIVACY DEFINED

The concept of privacy dates back into antiquity: for example Aristotle (384–327 BCE) made explicit distinctions between a public sphere and political life 'πολιχ' (*polis*, city) and one's private sphere or family life 'οικοχ' (*oikos, home*) *that refers to a separate private domain* (Roy 1999; Rykwert 2001; DeCew 2002).

DeCew (2002) explains that privacy does not have a single shared definition:

"The term 'privacy' is used frequently in ordinary language as well as in philosophical, political and legal discussions, yet there is no single definition or analysis or meaning of the term. The concept of privacy has broad historical roots in sociological and anthropological discussions about how extensively it is valued and preserved in various cultures. Moreover, the concept has historical origins in well known philosophical discussions, most notably Aristotle's distinction between the public sphere of political activity and the private sphere associated with family and domestic life. Yet historical use of the term is not uniform, and there remains confusion over the meaning, value and scope of the concept of privacy."

DeCew (2002) further explains that there are several specific types or meanings of privacy that include control of information, Human dignity (individual dignity and integrity, personal autonomy and independence), degrees of intimacy, social relationships, and unwanted access by others. Each of these conceptualizations of privacy is important and meaningful; however within the scope of this paper, and information systems (IS) research and practice in general and EC specifically we adopt the concept of '*informational privacy*' (DeCew 2002). Privacy is an important issue for EC because new technologies have enabled personal information to be communicated in ways that were not possible in earlier time periods. Next we discuss the historical background of informational privacy and define privacy within the scope of this article.

Informational Privacy

Warren and Brandeis (*later Supreme Court Justice Brandeis*) (Warren and Brandeis) in their well known essay "*The Right to Privacy*" cited "*political, social, and economic changes*" and recognized "*the right to be let alone*" to argue that extent law at the time did afford for protection of individual privacy. In 1890 technologies such as newspapers, photography and others had led to privacy invasions through dissemination of details of peoples' private lives (Warren and Brandeis 1890). They argued that the right to privacy is based on the general principle of "*the right to one's personality*" and the more specific principle of "*inviolate personality*" (Warren and Brandeis 1890).

They asserted that the privacy principle was a part of the common law and the protection of a "*man's house as his castle;*" however they also argued that new technologies had changed how private information was disseminated and thus required recognition of a separate and explicit protection of individual privacy (Warren and Brandeis 1890). Their essay laid the foundation for what would become the idea of privacy as a person's control over information about themselves.

Two theories of privacy have stood the test of time and also have figured prominently in major privacy reviews in the 1970s, 1980's and 1990s (Margulis 2003): Westin's (1967) four states and four functions of privacy and Altman's five properties of privacy. We focus here on Westin's theory.

Westin (1967) defined four states of privacy; that is how privacy is achieved (Margulis 2003):

1. **Solitude:** an individual separated from the group and freed from the observation of other persons.
2. **Intimacy:** an individual as part of a small unit.
3. **Anonymity:** an individual in public but still seeks and finds freedom from identification and surveillance.
4. **Reserve:** based on a desire to limit disclosures to others; it requires others to recognize and respect that desire.

and four functions (purposes) privacy; that is why one seeks privacy (Margulis 2003):

1. **Personal autonomy:** desire to avoid being manipulated, dominated, or exposed by others or control over when information is made public
2. **Emotional release:** release from the tensions of social life such as role demands, emotional states, minor deviances, and the management of losses and of bodily functions. Privacy, whether alone or with supportive others, provides the "time out" from social demands, hence opportunities for emotional release.
3. **Self-evaluation:** integrating experience into meaningful patterns and exerting individuality on events. It includes processing information, supporting the planning process (e.g., the timing of disclosures), integrating experiences, and allowing moral and religious contemplation.
4. **Limited and protected communication:** Limited communication sets interpersonal boundaries; protected communication provides for sharing personal information with trusted others.

Westin's (1967) definition is the one that we adopt for this paper and we think is the one that should be adopted by IS researchers and practitioners as well as EC customers:

"Privacy is the claim of individuals, groups or institutions to determine for themselves when, how, and to what extent information about them is communicated to others."

Westin (1967) also pointed out that privacy is not an absolute but that:

"Each individual is continually engaged in a personal adjustment process in which he balances the desire for privacy with the desire for disclosure and communication...."

With this definition in mind we again turn to recent surveys of consumers and businesses to gain an understanding of how security breaches that violate privacy are perceived and handled. Ackerman et al. (1999) surveyed consumers to learn how comfortable they were with providing different types on personal information with businesses; while Ponemon (2005b) gathered data on actual breaches. Table 3 illustrates that data from the Ackerman, et al. (1999) survey of consumer concerns and the Ponemon (2005b) survey of actual data breaches reveals that there may be a mismatch in terms of what information consumers would prefer not to have revealed and what has actually been lost or stolen. Ponemon (2005b) surprisingly found that some of the more sensitive information that consumers are most reticent to reveal and that could result in the most damage are the ones that are most often released.

Only 1% of consumers surveyed were comfortable always or usually providing information their Social security numbers (Ackerman, et al. 1999), yet 38% of all breaches reported in another survey involved SSNs (Ponemon 2005b). Similar types of mismatches can be seen for several other data types in Table 3. These results illustrate that companies may not secure the types of personal information that consumers are most concerned about well enough (SSNs, credit Card Numbers and Home Telephone) and may place to much emphasis on the security of information that

Table 3. Comparison of actual data types released and consumer concern

Data Type	Data released	Consumer Comfort Level
Name	54%	54%
SSN	38%	1%
Credit Card Number	37%	3%
Home Telephone	36%	11%
Mailing address	23%	44%
E-mail Addresses	10%	76%

Data from (Ackerman et al., 1999) and (Ponemon, 2005b)

consumers are more willing to share (i.e. email addresses and mailing addresses.) This leads us to question whether firms take into consideration the privacy expectations of consumers when they decide how to protect different types of data. We think that firms should take consumer expectations and willingness to reveal information into account when establishing security measures to protect different types of information as this would focus resources in such a way as to engender trust from the consumer and also to minimize potential losses due to breaches.

Figure 3 presents our model of the Personal "Sphere of privacy" based on Ackerman's findings that illustrates how firms might establish levels of security that are consonant with both consumer willingness (comfort) to reveal information and also with the potential amount of damage that could occur from a breach of specific types of customer information.

We argue that firms should be most vigilant in securing information that consumers would most like to protect and should establish levels or zones of security of different strengths. Later in the paper we will tie this model to security strategies and technology implications.

Based on Ackerman et al. (1999) and Ponemon's (2005b) data (see Table 3) it is clear the consumers want their SSNs, credit card numbers and telephone numbers kept private. In other words

Figure 3. Model of the customer "sphere of privacy"

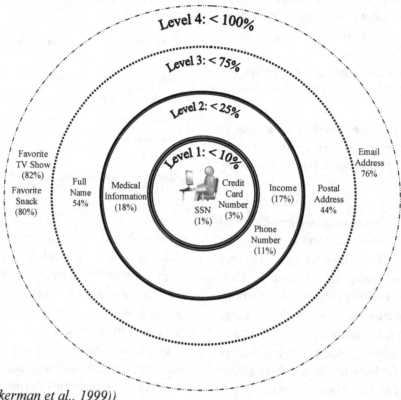

(Data from (Ackerman et al., 1999))

consumers place maximum value on these data items in contrast to their mailing address and their email address. Enterprises need to be sure and recognize what information is critical so as to protect it and ensure business continuity (Gordon and Loeb, 2002).

This leads us to the next section on security. Security is the technology and policies that an enterprise and consumer have to keep their valuable information secure.

SECURITY

Security breaches affect most enterprises and government agencies. A recent survey reports that 84% of all enterprises will be affected by a security breach, which is a 17% increase over the last three years (2004-2006) (Ferguson 2006). Those enterprises and government agencies in the survey reported that when a security breach happened 54 percent lost productivity, 20 percent reported lost revenue and 25 percent claimed to have suffered some sort of public backlash with either damage to their reputation or loss of customer trust. http://www.eweek.com/category2/0,1874,1728963,00.aspThirty-eight percent of these organizations reported that the breach was internal. Furthermore, according to the survey many of them did not take the issue seriously enough. Only one percent of those surveyed thought IT security spending was too high, while 38 percent said it was much too low (Ferguson 2006). The results suggest that even though organizations are investing in security technologies, they still aren't achieving the results they seek.

Security Defined

The term security can be used in reference to crime and accidents of all kinds. Security is a vast topic including security of countries against terrorist attack, security of computers against hackers, home security against burglars and other intruders, financial security against economic collapse and many other related situations.

Following are four definitions that provide a narrower focus:

1. **Security:** A very general term covering everything.
2. **Computer security:** the discipline that helps free us from worrying about our computers."(Landwehr 2001) Computer security is the effort to create a secure computing platform, designed so that agents (users or programs) can only perform actions that have been allowed. This involves specifying and implementing a security policy. The actions in question can be reduced to operations of access, modification and deletion. Computer security can be seen as a subfield of security engineering, which looks at broader security issues in addition to computer security.
3. **Information security:** is the protection of information systems against unauthorized access to or modification of information whether in storage, processing, or transit, and against denial of service to authorized users, including those measures necessary to detect, document, and counter such threats. (**NSTISSC** 1999) IS Security has previously concentrated on confidentiality of information stored electronically. The rapid growth in the volume of such information and the uptake of E-commerce within organizations have heightened the need for increased security to protect the privacy of this information and prevent fraudulent activities (Spinellis, et al. 1999)
4. **Data security:** the most important part of security- securing the data from unauthorized use.

From the point of view of eCRM the above definitions do not help us much. In the section on privacy information such as SSN and credit card numbers were more critical to consumers than an email address. Thus, we need to look at the security components.

Security Components

A recent meta-analysis of critical themes in electronic commerce research by Wareham et al.(Wareham, et al. 2005) identified security as an underserved area in IS Research. They suggest and support Gordon and Loeb's (2002) assertion that information is an asset of value to an organization and consequently needs to be suitably protected in order to ensure business continuity, minimize business damage, maximize ROIs, and business opportunities (BSI 1999). The purpose of information security could be characterized as the preservation of confidentiality, integrity and availability for information asset to keep business value (BSI 1999; Sheth, et al. 2000; Gordon and Loeb 2002) Then, in general, IS security is the effective implementation of policies to ensure the confidentiality, availability, and integrity of information and assets to protect from theft, tampering, manipulation, or corruption. (Smith and Jamieson 2006) This also follows from the ISO 1799 Information Security Standard (ISO/IEC 2005).

The ISO 17799 standard is an internationally recognized information security management guidance standard (ISO/IEC 2005), ISO 17799 is high level, broad in scope, and conceptual in nature. This approach allows it to be applied across multiple types of enterprises and applications. It has also made the standard controversial among those who believe standards should be more precise. In spite of this controversy, ISO

17799 is the only "standard" devoted to Information Security Management in a field generally governed by "Guidelines" and "Best Practices." (ISO/IEC 2005)

ISO 17799 defines information as an asset that may exist in many forms and has value to an organization. Thus, the goal of information security is to suitably protect this asset in order to ensure business continuity, minimize business damage, and maximize return on investments. The objective of the standard is to safe guard:

- **Confidentiality:** Ensuring that information is accessible only to those authorized to have access.
- **Integrity:** Safeguarding the accuracy and completeness of information and processing methods.
- **Availability:** Ensuring that authorized users have access to information and associated assets when required.

Thus, our basic definition of security in the e-commerce environment is the necessary hardware, software, network controls, data encryption, policies and procedures in place for an enterprise to ensure that a consumer's information is confidential, has integrity and is available for use, e-commerce use.

Enterprise and Consumer Views of Security

Enterprises ands the consumers will view the security components some what differently.

Table 4 shows the enterprise and the consumer view. For confidentiality, both the enterprise and consumer expect the security features to prevent unauthorized access to the data. For integrity the enterprise must use the data supplied by the consumer only for business purposes and must not sell or release the personal data to other enterprises without authorization from the consumer. It us the consumers obligation to assure that the data is correct. For availability it is the enterprises responsibility to assure that the data is available for the consumer and for e-commerce. From the consumers point of view the data need to be available for modification (i.e. change of address, change of preferences).

IS Security has previously concentrated on confidentiality of information stored electronically. The rapid growth in the volume of such information and the uptake of E-commerce within organizations have heightened the need for increased security to protect the privacy of this information and prevent fraudulent activities (Spinellis, et al. 1999)

Computer security is the effort to create a secure computing platform, designed so that agents (users or programs) can only perform actions that have been allowed. This involves specifying and implementing a security policy. The actions in question can be reduced to operations of access, modification and deletion. Computer security can be seen as a subfield of security engineering, which looks at broader security issues in addition to computer security.

Table 4. Security components

Security Components	Enterprise/Organization	Consumers
Confidentiality	Prevent unauthorized access Secure all personal information	Prevent unauthorized access How my data is being protected
Integrity	Data used for only business purposes Data not sold without authorization	Data is correct
Availability	Data available for customer Data available for e-commerce	Data available for modification

Security Threats and Vulnerabilities

Table 5 highlights the major threats and vulnerabilities of enterprise networks and consumer use. Threats are any type of unwanted or unauthorized intrusions, attach , or exploit on to the system (Volonino and Robinson 2004). Vulnerabilities are two fold: from the consumer point of view - human error- using poor passwords, participating in chat rooms; from the enterprise side- is the complexity of the software which results in misconfigurations, programming errors, or other flaws. The major internet security breaches are shown in Table 5 (Volonino and Robinson 2004).

In a recent trade press article (August 29, 2006), AT&T revealed (Preimesberger 2006) that an undisclosed number of unauthorized persons had illegally hacked into one of its computer systems and accessed the personal data, including credit card information, of about 19,000 customers who had purchased DSL equipment through the company's online store. The unauthorized electronic access took place over the weekend of Aug. 26-27, 2006 and was discovered within hours, according to a company spokesperson. The electronic store was shut down immediately and remained offline as we write this paper. The cost of this security breach has not been disclosed, however, the company is also working with law enforcement to investigate the incident and pursue the perpetrators. The 19,000 customers are being notified by e-mail, phone calls and letters. Furthermore, AT&T intends to pay for credit monitoring services for customers whose accounts have been impacted. Clearly breaches are still occurring, even to the largest companies that we would expect would have adequate security in place.

Security: No more than Managing Risk

Gordon and Loeb (2002) suggest that the optimal amount to spend on information security is an increasing function of the level of vulnerability of the information. However, the optimal amount to spend on information security does not always increase with the level of vulnerability of such information. They further suggest that managers should budget for security on information that is in a midrange of vulnerability to security breaches. Furthermore, managers may want to consider partitioning information sets into low, middle, and high levels of security breach vulnerability. Some information may be difficult to protect at a high security level and thus is best defended at a more moderate level. Their findings suggest that the optimal amount to spend on information security never exceeds 37% of the expected loss resulting from a security breach.

Smith and Spafford (2004) also suggest that security is managing risk. In addition, they suggest that the major security challenges are:

Table 5. Security threats and vulnerabilities

Internal Threats		External Threats	
Organizations	**Consumers**	**Organizations**	**Consumers**
• Illness of personnel • Temporary staff • Loss of key personnel • Loss of network service • Disgruntled employees • Disgruntled consultants • Labor dispute • Malware • Software bugs	• User misuse • Malware • Software bugs • Poor passwords • Chat room participation	• Severe storms • Utility outage • Natural disasters • Theft of hardware • Software compromise • Hackers • Adversaries	• Severe storms • Utility outage • Natural disasters • Unauthorized access • Unauthorized sale • Theft of computer • Hackers • Denial of service

1. Stop epidemic-style attacks
2. Build trustworthy large-scale systems
3. Make quantitative information systems risk management as good as quantitative financial risk management
4. Give end users security they can understand and privacy they can control

Kuper (2005) suggests that the sole reason that information technology exists is to leverage the critical asset of data. Thus, security is data and network integrity, the protection of and access to the data. Also, (Kuper 2005) from 2000 to 2005 enterprises have spent $15 billion on perimeter level security (antivirus, firewalls, and approximately $1.5 billion on encryption software, one of the more obvious technologies for protecting the data. This supports Gordon and Loeb (2002) assertion that the amount spent does not always match the required level of vulnerability.

Kuper (2005) suggests several new approaches to data security:

1. **Data and network integrity:** Protecting access to data
2. **Inclusion/exclusion security:** Trusted, known users are handled differently than unknown users (nodes)
3. **Embedded security:** More security into all aspects of IT components (hardware, software, or service)
4. **Improved approaches:** Dynamic XML and web service architectures.

In this regard, enterprises need to work at the data level (using encryption) to secure the most critical data. The second element is that of trust, trusted consumers should be treated differently than unknown consumers. This is one of the objectives of CRM. Next, embedded security for the enterprise at the hardware/software and server level can help to minimize security breaches. Last, new dynamic approaches can be used.

Table 6 illustrates how privacy and security are interrelated in terms of the levels of data, security strategy and technologies required to achieve appropriate vigilance. Our model of the sphere of privacy suggests that some information is not as critical to secure (i.e. email address) while other information, consumer's SSN, is critical to secure. Kuper (2005) suggests that initially enterprises focused security at the perimeter, but as they learned from persistent attacks they moved from the edge down deeper, layer by layer, to secure the very data itself through encryption. We rename this as the Enterprise "Sphere of Security" model (See Figure 4.) Different technologies are required at the different levels and the most crucial level data requires encryption to ensure that it is not released (Volonino and Robinson, 2004). At the perimeter (level 4) firewalls and malware prevention software may offer enough protection for data that is no as sensitive.

Enterprise Privacy/Security Sphere of Implementation

There is an adage that you cannot ensure privacy if you don't first have security. Thus enterprises

Table 6. Complementarity of privacy, security and technology

Sphere of Privacy (Ackerman , 1999)	Sphere of Security (derived from Kuper, 2005)	Technology (Volonino & Robinson, 2004)
Level 4: Email	Perimeter	Hardware/Software
Level 3: Full name	Network	Network Security
Level 2: Phone #	Application	Process & Procedures
Level 1: SSN	Data	Encryption

Figure 4. Model of the enterprise "sphere of security"

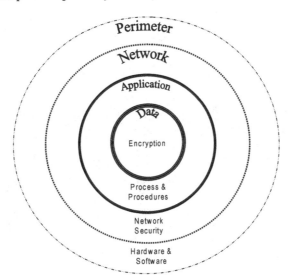

and consumers need to be prepared for an increasingly hostile public network. Both must provide the right (and updateable) hardware control, data and software controls, and encryption controls to ensure optimal security. Both must also consider the risks, costs and possible consequences of releasing private information.

A complete solution to either the security or the privacy problem requires the following three steps which become our privacy/security sphere of implementation model:

Policy: The first step is to develop a security or privacy policy. The policy precisely defines the requirements that are to be implemented within the hardware and software of the computing system and those that are external to the computing system, including physical, personnel, and procedural controls. The policy lays down broad goals without specifying how to achieve them.

Mechanism: The security or privacy policy is made more concrete with the mechanism necessary to implement the requirements of the policy. It is important that the mechanism perform the intended functions.

Assurance: The last step deals with the assurance issue. It provides guidelines for ensuring that the mechanism meets the policy requirements with a high degree of assurance. Assurance is directly related to the effort required to subvert the mechanism. Low-assurance mechanisms are easy to implement, but also relatively easy to subvert; on the other hand, high-assurance mechanisms are notoriously difficult to implement.

CONDITIONAL RELATIONAL "VALUE EXCHANGE" MODEL

Figure 5 illustrates customer data flow and some privacy and security issues related to eCRM. The figure shows that each customer has their own personal identity as well as personal and confidential information they may choose to share or unknowingly (unwittingly) share with online businesses with which they interact or with others that obtain the information through some other mechanism than a known direct transfer. The figure illustrates both intentional and unintentional information transfer from customers to other entities. Three representative customers interact with one or more of three online businesses, as well as other players. Several different scenarios that can affect privacy and security are depicted in the figure.

Figure 5. Customer dataflow and privacy and security issues

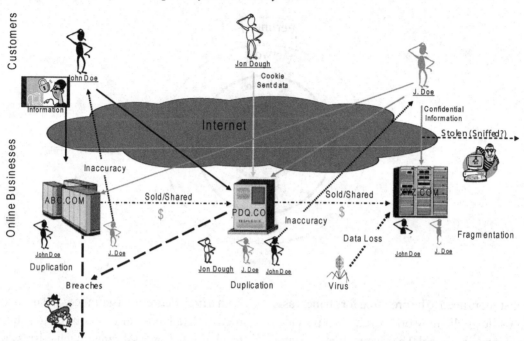

Scenarios for Customer John Doe. Mr. Doe interacts with online businesses ABC.COM and PDQ.COM and reveals 'some' personally identifiable information to both; but not necessarily the same information. Once this data is revealed ABC.COM and PDQ.COM have a responsibility to keep it secure and accurate; however both may fail in these responsibilities. If they share or sell the information to other companies there will then be duplicate copies of the information in multiple systems, each of which has different levels of security and protection and the risk that John Doe's information may be used for purposes other than he intended increases. Additionally, duplicate copies may not be updated if Mr. Doe changes his address, email or phone number and thus inaccuracies due to redundant data that is not synchronized can and do multiply. Another possible security and privacy issue is that data from other customers with similar names to John Doe may be inaccurately associated with him; or he may be inaccurately associated with their data. This can result in unwanted offers being sent, invalid information being released or even

inaccurate information that changes the customers status and affects their credit score, ability to purchase or reputation. The complex data exchange environment and the increase in the number and types of attacks and threats makes it very hard for customers to be confident that their data will be secured and their privacy not violated.

Figures 6 and 7 present our conditional relational "value exchange" model. The basic value exchange model (Figure 6) integrates our customer sphere of privacy with our sphere of security model and the enterprise privacy/security sphere of implementation. If an enterprise is to succeed in the EC environment, it must provide the necessary security to attract and retain customers. Surveys have shown that (Ackerman, et al., 1999; Ponemon, 2005a) customers will churn if they feel that there privacy has been or may be violated.

The value exchange model works through the EC system. The customer interested in obtaining information, evaluating a product or service, or even buying a product or service connects with the EC system and then provides the information that is required from their sphere of privacy.

Figure 6. Conditional relational "value exchange" model

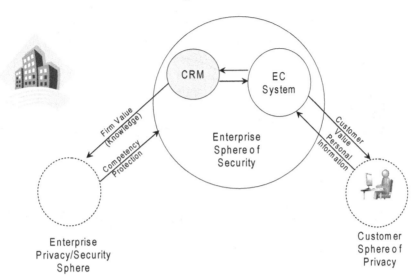

Simultaneous with the customer's inquiry or purchase (the customer's value exchange) the eCRM system is updated. This in turn becomes the enterprise's value exchange. Then based upon detailed internal and external analysis the enterprise's privacy/security policies, assurances and mechanisms should be modified.

Clearly this is a value exchange model. Prabhaker (2000) suggests that business can add value to their EC offerings by leveraging Internet technology (the sphere of security) in coordination with proactive measures (Privacy/Security Sphere of implementation) to preserve consumer privacy (the customer sphere of privacy). This is further supported by Schoder and Madeja (2004) who suggest that eCRM built upon knowledge about their customers and their ability to serve their customers based on that knowledge has proven to be a key success factor in EC. They also suggest that the most effective way to collect customer data online is through an interactive, feature-rich environment that matches the customers' expectations of an enterprise. In other words, there should be a match between the enterprise's sphere of security and the customer's sphere of privacy.

Figure 7 is the extended value exchange model. This model adds in the interrelationships between the customers, the enterprise, the government, standards organizations, industry and society and watchdogs agencies (i.e. the Better Business Bureau BBB). This is a very complex open model. Fletcher (2003) suggests consumer backlash to perceived invasions of privacy is causing government agencies, standards organizations, industry and other watchdogs to be more proactive in developing guidelines and policies. Most major EC companies have a detailed privacy statement on their home page. For example, Amazon.com has 11 major items from "What personal information about customers does Amazon.com gather?" to "Examples of information collected. Their objective is to assure that the information that they collects from customers helps them personalize and continually improve the customer's shopping experience at Amazon.com (http:\\www.amazon.com Accessed 8/31/2006).

IMPLICATIONS FOR ENTERPRISES AND CUSTOMERS

Enterprises continue to collect more and more personal information from online transactions and are using this data to improve sales and service

Figure 7. Extended model with Watchdogs, Government, Society, and Standards organizations

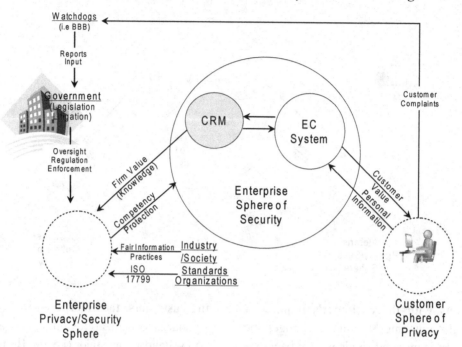

effectiveness (Fletcher, 2003; Romano and Fjermestad, 2003) this is eCRM in the e-commerce environment. This has become one of the most significant issues confronting enterprises in the electronic age. The issues are securing privacy and security of consumer data while using advanced information systems technology (i.e. eCRM, business intelligence, data warehousing, and data mining) to sell more goods and services to the consumer.

Consumers on the other hand want to get benefits (i.e. reduced time and reduced costs) from e-commerce, however, they are not willing to sacrifice data items such as SSN and credit card number to achieve these benefits. Consumers require the enterprises safeguard their data.

CONCLUSION AND DIRECTIONS FOR FUTURE RESEARCH

The objective of this paper was to develop an integrated value exchange model for enterprises

and consumers in an e-commerce environment. Enterprises want to attract and retain economically valuuable customers (Romano and Fjermestad, 2001-2002). Typically this is through eCRM. However, the prime ingredient is customer data. Thus, an enterprise must employ the right levels of privacy, security, and policy spheres to enable the continued collection and use of consumer data. Gordon and Lobe (2002) suggest that information is an asset of value to an organization and consequently needs to be suitably protected in order to ensure business continuity, minimize business damage, maximize ROIs, and business opportunities. Information security is then characterized as the preservation of confidentiality, integrity and availability of this information asset to maintain business value (BSI 1999; Sheth, et al. 2000; Gordon and Loeb 2002.) IS security is the effective implementation of policies to ensure the confidentiality, availability, and integrity of information and assets to protect it from theft, tampering, manipulation, or corruption (Smith and Jamieson 2006).

Enterprises can lose customers if they do not respond quickly enough and through the right communication channel after a security breach. Research suggests that this is best handled with personal telephone calls and follow-up personal letters (Ponemon 2005b). The use of spam e-mail will not be effective and can in fact make customers more upset due to feeling disrespected on top of their personal information being lost.

Our contributions are four-fold. First is our model of the customer sphere of privacy adapted from Ackerman, et al.'s (1999) survey findings. This model presents the idea of levels of privacy for a consumer in terms of how willing they are to reveal personal information of different types. The highest level, level 1, corresponds to any personal information that consumers are almost never comfortable revealing, such as their Social Security Number or Credit card numbers. Consumers will not revel such information unless they fully trust the recipient. The lowest level, level 4, corresponds to personal information that many consumers are very comfortable revealing, such as their email address. These levels also correspond with the potential seriousness of consequences from the consumers' information getting into the wrong hands. Release of an SSN or Credit card number can result in identity theft or monetary losses; while release of an email address may only result in additional spam email. Both are negative consequences; but clearly the former is much more serious than the latter.

The second contribution is our enterprise sphere of security derived from Kuper's (2005) levels of security. This model represents the level of security required to support customer privacy ranging from the deepest internal data level to the externally focused perimeter level. Accompanying this model is the technology required to support it. At the perimeter level hardware and software (i.e. routers and firewalls) provide a modest level of protection; while at the data level more secure technologies such as encryption or perturbation are required to more vigilantly ensure protection

of consumer privacy. The third contribution is the enterprise privacy/security sphere of implementation. These are the policies, mechanisms, and assurances to support privacy and security. Many enterprises provide such a policy statement on their website.

Our fourth contribution is the integrated value exchange model and the extended model. This model is built upon the interrelationships among the three spheres. The model proposes that both the enterprise and customer exchange information when they transact via EC. The customer exchanges personal information in order to obtain customer value (reduced time and cost, as well as the goods, services or information purchased). The enterprise gains customers and via aggregation and data mining competitive advantage from the knowledge about their customers. In order to keep their customers the enterprise must provide competent protection for the customers' information. The extended model shows that there is substantial input from industry, standards organizations, the government and other watchdog organizations.

In many case the major asset of an enterprise is its customers and data about them. There is a delicate balance (as the value exchange model illustrates) that must be maintained. The customers are only a mouse click away from an enterprise's competitors. Customers also have responsibilities to be careful and vigilant when that they must give up personal information in order to receive the benefits of EC. They must provide accurate and reliable information and also verify that a firm is trustworthy and employing adequate levels of security before revealing personal information. They should also think carefully about what information is required for a given transaction and not provide additional information that is not necessary. This can assist customers to make more informed queries and purchases and at the same time helps the enterprise market to them and to other customers more effectively through new mechanisms such a recommender systems, cross selling and preference discounts.

In the Age of ECRM Enterprises and Customers have vast new opportunities to exchange value more quickly and effectively than ever before; however along with these come new vulnerabilities and responsibilities to secure and protect privacy. Enterprises that fail to protect the privacy of their customers may find that many leave for the competition that will do so. ECRM is about establishing and maintaining intimate relationships with customers to generate additional value and long term loyalty; enterprises cannot do this if they do not provide the security required to protect their customers' privacy at the level of vigilance they expect. It may be necessary to provide personalized levels of security for the very best customers if they demand it. Just as investors can choose the level of risk they are willing to take for a potential return on investment, consumers will also choose which firms to do business with via EC based on the level of perceived risk they associate with them. Future research and practice in Information Assurance (Security and Privacy) will have to take the consumer's perspective more into account than at present.

REFERENCES

Ackerman, M. S., L. F. Cranor, & Reagle, J. (1999). *Beyond Concern: Understanding Net Users' Attitudes About Online Privacy, AT&T Labs. 2006*, online at: http://citeseer.ist.psu.edu/cranor-99beyond.html (accessed 8-31-2006).

BSI. (1999). *Information Security Management – Part 1, Code of Practice for Information Security Management*, BS 7799-1, BSI Group, London, UK.

DeCew, J. (2002). *Privacy. The Stanford Encyclopedia of Philosophy.* E. N. Zalta online at: http://plato.stanford.edu/archives/sum2002/entries/privacy/ (accessed 8-31-2006).

Ferguson, S. (2006). Study: Security Breaches Afflict Most Enterprises, Governments.

eWeek, July 7, 2006. http://www.eweek.com/article2/0,1895,1986066,00.asp (accessed 8-31-2006).

Fletcher, K. (2003). Consumer power and privacy: the changing nature of CRM. *International Journal of Advertising, 22*, 249-272.

Friel, A. L. (2004). Privacy Patchwork. *Marketing Management, 13*(6), 48-51.

Gordon, A. A., & Loeb, M. P. (2002). The economics of information security investment. *ACM Transactions on Information and System Security, 5*(4), 438-457.

Gordon, L. A., Loeb, M. P, Lucyshyn, W., & Richardson, R. (2004). Ninth Annual CSI/FBI Computer Crime And Security Survey, Computer Security Institute.

ISO/IEC, Ed. (2005). ISO/IEC 17799:2005 Information technology - Security techniques - Code of practice for information security management, International Organization for Standardization.

Kalakota, R. & Whinston, A. B. (1996). Frontiers of Electronic Commerce, 1st edition, Addison Wesley Publishing Co., New York, NY, USA

Keen, P. G. W. (1999). Competing in chapter 2 of internet business: Navigating in a new world. Eburon Publishers, Delft, The Netherlands.

Kuper, P. (2005). The state of security. *IEEE Security and Privacy 3*(5), 51-53.

Landwehr, C. E. (2001). Computer security. *International Journal of Information Security, 1*(1), 3-13.

Margulis, S. T. (2003). On the Status and Contribution of Westin's and Altman's Theories of Privacy. *Journal of Social Issues, 59*(2), 411-429.

NSTISSC (1999). *National Information Systems security (INFOSEC) Glossary, National security Telecommunications and Information Systems security Committee (NSTISSC): 4.*

Ponemon, L. (2005a). *Lost Customer Information: What Does a Data Breach Cost Companies?* Ponemon Institue, Tucson, Arizona, USA. (online at: http://www.securitymanagement. com/library/Ponemon_DataStudy0106.pdf) (accessed 8-31-2006)

Ponemon, L. (2005b). *The National Survey on Data Security Breach Notification*, Ponemon Institute, Tucson, Arizona, USA. (online at: http://www.whitecase.com/files/Publication/ bdf5cd75-ecd2-41f2-a54d-a087ea9c0029/Presentation/PublicationAttachment/2f92d91b-a565-4a07-bf68-aa21118006bb/Security_Breach_ Survey%5B1%5D.pdf) (accessed 8-31-2006)

Power, R. (2002). CSI/FBI computer crime and security survey. *Computer Security Issues & Trends VIH,* (1), 1-22.

Preimesberger, C. (2006). Hackers Hit AT&T System, Get Credit Card Info. *eWeek,* August 29, 2006, http://www.eweek.com/article2/0,1895,2010001,00.asp?kc=EWNAVEMN L083006EOA (accessed 8-31-2006).

Reddick, C. G. (2004). A two-stage model of e-government growth: Theories and empirical evidence for U.S. cities. *Government Information Quarterly, 21*(1), 51-64.

Richardson, R. (2003). Eighth Annual CSI/FBI Computer Crime And Security Survey, Computer Security Institute: Online at. http://www. reddshell.com/docs/csi_fbi_2003.pdf#search=% 22Eighth%20Annual%20CSI%2FFBI%20COM PUTER%20CRIME%20AND%20SECURITY %20SURVEY%22 (accessed 8-31-2006)

Romano, N. C., Jr., & Fjermestad, J. (2001-2002). Customer Relationship Management Research: An Assessment of Research. *International Journal of Electronic Commerce, 6*(3 Winter)), 61-114.

Romano, N.C., Jr. & Fjermestad, J. (2003). Electronic Commerce Customer Relationship Management: A Research Agenda. *Information Technology and Management, 4,* 233-258.

Roy, J. (1999). Polis and oikos in classical Athens. *Greece & Rome 46*(1), 1-18.

Rykwert, J. (2001). Privacy in Antiquity. *Social Research, 68*(1), 29-40.

Schoder, D. & Madeja, N. (2004). Is customer relationship management a success factor in electronic commerce? *Journal of Electronic Commerce Research, 5*(1), 38-53.

Seitz, K. (2006). Taking Steps To Ensure CRM Data Security. *Customer Inter@ction Solutions 24*(11), 62-64,66.

Sheth, J. N., Sisodia, R. S., & Sharma, S. (2000). The antecedents and consequences of customer-centric marketing. *Journal of the Academy of Marketing Science, 28*(1 Winter), 55-66.

Smith, S. & R. Jamieson (2006). Determining Key Factors In E-Government Information System Security. *Information Systems Management, 23*(2), 23-33.

Smith, S. W., & Spafford, E.H. (2004). Grand challenges in information security: process and output. *IEEE Security and Privacy, 2*(1), 69-71.

Spinellis, D., Kokolakis, D., & Gritzalis, S. (1999). Security requirements, risks and recommendations for small enterprise and home-office environments. *Information Management & Computer security, 7*(3), 121-128.

Volonino, L., & Robinson, S.R. (2004). *Principles and Practice of Information Security.* Upper Saddle River, NJ, USA, Pearson Prentice Hall.

Wareham, J., Zheng, J.G., & Straub, D. (2005). Critical themes in electronic commerce research: a meta-analysis. *Journal of Information Technology, 20*(1), 1-19.

Warren, S., & Brandeis, L. (1890). The Right to Privacy. *Harvard Law Review, 4*(5 December), 193-220.

Westin, A. (1967). *Privacy and Freedom.* New York, NY, USA, Atheneum.

Widmeyer, G. R. (2004). The Trichotomy Of Processes: A Philosophical Basis For Information Systems. *The Australian Journal of Information Systems, 11*(1), 3-11.

Chapter XIV
The Impact of Privacy Risk Harm (RH) and Risk Likelihood (RL) on IT Acceptance:
An Examination of a Student Information System

Joseph A. Cazier
Appalachian State University, USA

E. Vance Wilson
Arizona State University, USA

B. Dawn Medlin
Appalachian State University, USA

ABSTRACT

In today's networked world, privacy risk is becoming a major concern for individuals using information technology. Every time someone visits a website or provides information online they have exposed themselves to possible harm. The information collected can be sold to third parties or kept by the site owners themselves for use in creating a profile of users' preferences and tastes. To gain insight into the role risk plays in the adoption process of technology, the authors studied the use of information systems in relation to a student registration and schedule management system at a major United States university. Further, they extended the Technology Acceptance Model (TAM) to include perceptual measures of privacy risk harm (RH) and privacy risk likelihood (RL) which apply to the extended model and predict students' intentions to use technology. Their finding indicated the growing importance of privacy risk in the use of information technology.

INTRODUCTION

The past few decades have seen the proliferation of information technology (IT) into virtually every aspect of the personal and professional lives of Americans. As a nation, we regularly employ information technologies to file taxes, conduct banking and financial transactions, order pizzas, and even search for a mate. The general trend has been to consider IT in terms of the benefits that can accrue to individuals or organizations. However, information technology is "morally neutral" in that it can be employed for either positive or negative uses (Conca, Medlin, & Dave, 2005, p. 167). As an example, e-mail can be a highly useful form of communication in routine work situations or for sharing information among friends or family. However, email can also be used for the dissemination of malicious computer code and viruses such as the case with the Email-Worm.Win32.NetSky.q in 2008 that spread using the Internet as an attachment to infected messages. It is also able to propagate via P2P networks and accessible http and ftp directories (VirusList.com, 2008).

Privacy concerns are among some of the largest fears that Americans have identified when using information technologies (Garfinkel, Gopal and Goes, 2002), and privacy practices appear as a key determinant of trust for websites (Bart, Shankar, Sultan and Urban, 2005). In response to negative occurrences, many Americans have discontinued activities formerly done online - for example, a recent IBM study finds 18% of participants have stopped paying bills online and that most Americans believe they are more likely to be a victim of a cyber attack than a physical crime (IBM, 2006).

Where in the past security was mainly the responsibility of the consumer, most of the privacy risks today are controlled by others, such as third party vendors or e-commerce organizations. As individuals lose control of their information and incidents occur such as identity theft, anxiety and stress will likely increase, making it even more important to study privacy risk today than in the past (Schneier, 2005). Certainly, as more individuals have given up control of their information, opportunities for abuse have escalated. Consumers must balance the cost of supplying information with the benefits received from providing it (Ng-Kruelle, Swatman, Rebne, Hampe, 2002). This balancing act is often a difficult one, as consumers begin to rely on more online services.

In the future, privacy risk will likely be even more important as mobile commerce introduces new security and privacy risks above and beyond those of simple online e-commerce activities (Gosh and Swaminatha, 2001). This transition requires that privacy become an even more important issue to understand as we currently prepare to adopt this new type commerce and the technologies that it incorporates.

We propose that it is becoming increasingly important to evaluate individuals' risk perceptions in understanding the adoption and use of IT. This paper presents an exploratory study of the role of users' perceived privacy risk (PPR) as measured by its components risk harm (RH) and risk likelihood (RL) in forming behavioral intentions toward continued use of IT. In the following sections we briefly review the IT acceptance literature and then define the elements of risk relating to privacy of individuals and organizations.

THEORETICAL DEVELOPMENT

We frame this paper as an extension of the Technology Acceptance Model (TAM) (Davis, Bagozzi, & Warshaw 1989). TAM is a derivation of the theory of reasoned action (TRA) (Ajzen & Fishbein, 1980) that is customized for prediction of IT adoption and use. TRA and TAM represent a rational decision-making approach to the prediction of behaviors in which individual beliefs are mediated by attitude and behavioral intentions leading to subsequent use or non-use of technologies. For example, TAM posits that

IT use will be predicted judiciously by perceived usefulness (PU) and perceived ease of use (PEOU), as mediated by behavioral intention (BI)[1]. Thus, all factors in TAM except IT use are typically measured as the individual's perceptions of his or her beliefs and intentions. The ease of administering and measuring TAM through questionnaires and interviews has no doubt contributed to the popularity of this model among researchers.

In practice, TAM has proven to be both powerful and parsimonious. In a review of 101 TAM studies conducted across a wide range of IT types and usage contexts, Lee, Kozar, and Larsen (2003) report overwhelming support for the central relationships in TAM. Among the studies which assessed each specific relationship, 88% find PU influences BI, 71% find PEOU influences BI, 84% find PEOU influences PU, and 87% find BI influences IT use. In addition, Lee et al. describe 25 external factors that have been studied as contributors to TAM, ranging from measures of voluntariness of use to users' prior experiences with the technology. However, none of the external factors they describe in their study address privacy risks of computer use[2].

Featherman and Pavlou (2003) in their research draw upon the theory of perceived risk, which conveys the importance of expanding TAM by looking at the negative utility factors such as perceived risk. Their more balanced approach increases the likelihood of a broader range of factors, and thus their results can produce more in-depth findings. The vast majority of prior TAM literature focuses on positive utility measures, leaving untapped a wide domain of negative utility factors that can be used to explore a more realistic and complete picture of technology acceptance. Privacy risk in our study is a negative utility concern, thus making it an important contribution to the literature.

Using Featherman and Pavlou's introduction of the concept of privacy risk to perceived risk theory, we were able to draw on this concept for our paper. They define privacy risk as the "potential loss of control over personal information."

Our definition also includes the components of risk harm and risk likelihood.

Privacy Concerns

Advances in information technology have lead to the ability and practice of collecting vast amounts of information about individuals by commercial and government organizations. Subsequently, consumers are growing increasingly concerned about information privacy (Henderson and Snyder, 1999). Earp and Baumer (2003) found that consumers were more reluctant to share sensitive personal information with websites with which they were less familiar than websites that were more well-known. This suggests that consumers have the ability to discriminate the sharing of information based on characteristics of the website or sponsoring organization.

In addition, Awad and Krishnan (2006) found that companies often face a privacy paradox, where privacy-sensitive minorities are unwilling to participate in online profiling, even with additional privacy features and benefits. This further suggests that privacy is a paramount concern for an increasing number of individuals. The advances in data mining, personalization and profiling will be of little benefit if consumers refuse to participate in the technology or if there is a wave of consumer backlash at the use and perceived abuse of these technologies. An understanding of the consumer's perception of risk and risk tolerance is an important part of addressing these issues for the future.

Liu et al. (2005) found that a company's visible privacy practice, as illustrated by their notice, access, choice and security, had a strong impact on a consumer's willingness to trust that organization and thus their intent to transact with them. Both privacy and trust are very important topics when studying or practicing online activities. Based on the above evidence, many consumers are concerned about online privacy to the point where it may have a significant impact on their online behavior. In the next section we explore possible risks that are behind some of the privacy concerns of consumers.

Risk Factors

Westin (2005) asserted that the general public is fairly sophisticated in its use and understanding of privacy issues and is not controlled by mono-mindset single issue ideas about privacy. For both consumers and companies there are many trade-offs, cost-benefits, risks and rewards to consider. New technologies and data gathering techniques potentially have a lot to offer, but these risks are great and also need to be considered. Raab and Bennett (1998) noted that individuals are often not fully aware of how data is being used and processed or of the lack of transparency in the data disclosure process, which may breed rumors and fear based on horror stories and worst case scenarios. Additionally, they argue that unless we obtain more information and a better understanding of privacy risks, our ability to implement good policies will be impaired.

A number of researchers have studied monetary risks in online computing associated with e-commerce. Hoffman, Novak & Peralta (1999) find that when users perceived the online environment to be risky, they are less likely to purchase online. Labuschagne and Eloff write, "The major reason most people are still skeptical about electronic commerce is the perceived security risks associated with electronic transactions over the internet" (2000, pg 154). Heijden, Verhagen, and Creemers (2003) found that the trust antecedent "perceived risk" directly influences an individual's attitude toward making online purchases. In their study, the effect of risk on attitude is an order of magnitude greater than the effect of PEOU and PU. The risk used in their research is more general than the risk tested in our paper. Our research makes a significant contribution by focusing on privacy risk. In addition, we obtain a greater degree of granularity and insight by separating

risk into the components, risk likelihood and risk harm. By addressing risk in this way we acquire a more accurate picture of the components of risk and their relative importance. It also provides greater insight into what companies can do to address risk perceptions, e.g. focus on risk harm or risk likelihood and which of the components will provide a better return for customers.

In the present study we focus on privacy risk, which we define as the risks involved in the privacy of personal or organizational information. The specialized study of privacy risks in online computing is now becoming important because of the increasing presence of online activities that are intended to breach privacy of individuals and organizations, such as phishing and spyware. According to Drennan, Mort and Previte (2006), perception of risk is fundamental to the understanding of consumer concerns about privacy online and the relationship among the factors of privacy, risk and intentions. When people perceive risks they change their behaviors accordingly, often by performing a risk benefit calculation that assists them in deciding whether they should or should not disclose private information (Milne and Culnan, 2004).

One of the most evident types of privacy risk is that of identity theft, in which identification documents or identifying numbers are stolen. Victims of identity theft often spend years attempting to resolve the problems created by identity theft. Problems such as bounced checks, loan denials, credit card application rejections and debt collection harassment can all be results of identity theft.

As reported by the Identity Theft Resource Center in 2007, they documented 446 paper and electronic security breaches, potentially affecting more than 127 million records. This is a significant increase from 2005 where there were 158 incidents affecting more than 64.8 million people, and in 2006 which listed in excess of 315 publicized breaches affecting nearly 20 million individuals (http://www.idtheftcenter.org/artman2/publish/lib_survey/ITRC_2008).

In more recent years identity theft has been accompanied by additional privacy threats such as phishing and spyware. Phishing attacks can use both social engineering and technical subterfuge to steal consumers' personal identity data and account credentials (http://www.antiphishing.org). But just as disconcerting is the fact that some agencies and organizations have simply given away private information about its customers and clients through careless actions.

Listed below are a few of the current phishing and other activities which have affected consumers' information:

- In May 2008, the FBI warned consumers of reported spam email purportedly from the Internal Revenue Service (IRS) which is actually an attempt to steal consumer information. The email advises the recipient that direct deposit is the fastest and easiest way to receive their economic stimulus tax rebate. The message contains a hyperlink to a fraudulent from which requests the recipient's personally identifiable information, including bank account information. To convince consumers to reply, the email warns that a failure to complete the form in a timely manner will delay the issuance of the rebate check.
- Reported in the Los Angeles Times on February 16th, 2008, computer equipment containing the private financial data of every employee of the Los Angeles Department of Water and Power was stolen, prompting the utility to pay for a credit monitoring service for each of its 8,275 workers.
- In June 2008, the Associated Press reported that the University of Florida was sending letters to more than 11,000 current and former students to notify them that their Social Security numbers, names and addresses were accidentally posted online.
- An undisclosed number of management-level workers at AT&T have been notified

that their personal information was stored unencrypted on a stolen laptop from the car of an employee on May 15th, 2008.

Loss of privacy exposes individuals and organizations to monetary costs, such as unauthorized bank account withdrawals, and nonmonetary costs, such as public exposure of personal affairs. If the privacy risks of online computing are increasingly viewed as costly, then we anticipate this perception will obstruct continued use of online IT and will deny individuals and organizations many of the benefits that online IT currently delivers. This problem is compounded by evolving online technology, such as mobile commerce, which can be expected to introduce new privacy risks (Gosh and Swaminatha, 2001). The current increasing level of privacy risks and potential for new privacy risks in online computing suggest it is essential to begin research that explains and predicts how privacy risks will influence adoption and use of online IT.

Forrester Research estimated in 1999 that the tangible and intangible costs of computer security breaches in three hypothetical situations. Their analysis indicated that, if thieves were to illegally wire $1 million from an on-line bank, the cost impact to the bank would be $106 million. They also estimated that, in the hypothetical situation that cyber techniques are used to divert a week's worth of tires from an auto manufacturer; the auto manufacturer would sustain losses of $21 million. Finally, they estimated that if a law firm were to lose significant confidential information, the impact would be almost $35 million (D'Amico, A., 2000).

Despite the identification of online privacy as a major problem hampering the development of e-commerce, this topic has still received little attention from the IS community (Malhotra, Kim, and Agarwal, 2004). Risk beliefs, according to Malhotra, Kim and Agarwal (2004), were found to have a very significant and direct impact on behavioral intentions, similar to those presented in our model.

Research Model and Hypotheses

Risk is calculated as the probability of an event occurring multiplied by the loss or amount of harm that could be done if that loss is realized (Straub and Welke, 1998). Our conceptualization of privacy risk follows the suggestion of Kim and Leem (2005) that risk involves two elements: the probability of an event occurring, which we denote as perceived privacy risk likelihood; and a loss amount, which we denote as perceived privacy risk harm[3]. Risk likelihood is the perception of probability that a privacy breach will occur. Risk harm is the perception of the level of damage that would occur in event of a privacy breach.

Our research model augments TAM with risk likelihood and risk harm (see Figure 1). Based on predominating findings in the TAM literature, we anticipate PEOU will have a positive effect on both PU and BI toward IT use, and we anticipate PU will have a positive effect on BI. We do not assess IT use in the present study.

We propose that perception of privacy risk will influence decisions toward use of IT. We anticipate BI toward IT use will diminish where

privacy risk is perceived to be high and increase where it is perceived to be low. In the present study, we operationalize privacy risk through its two elemental components, risk harm (RH) and risk likelihood (RL). We hypothesize that both factors will negatively influence BI.

H1: Increasing RH will reduce BI toward IT use.

H2: Increasing RL will reduce BI toward IT use.

RESEARCH METHOD

The research methodology was conducted using an online survey instrument that assesses the perceptions and usage intentions of students toward their university's student registration and schedule management system. Students use the system for many interactions with their university, such as registering, adding and dropping classes, checking course grades, changing contact information, making advising appointments, and the monitoring of financial aid applications.

Figure 1. Privacy risk research model

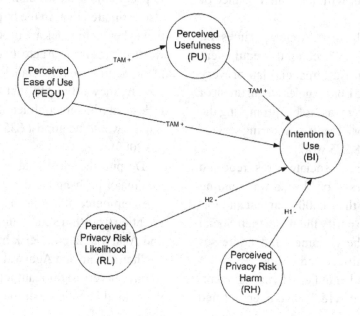

Survey Instrument

The online survey stored responses in a database and was designed to prevent missing data by redisplaying any question for which a response was missing. Participants responded to scale items using a seven-point Likert scale with endpoints labeled "Strongly Disagree" / "Very Little" (Value =1) and "Strongly Agree" / "Very Much" (Value = 7) as dictated by the form in which the item was stated.

Measurement Items

Items measuring TAM constructs were drawn from Davis (1989). Items measuring risk harm and risk likelihood were developed as part of the present study using techniques prescribed by Gable and Wolf (1993). Five items were created to represent the essential content of each construct. For risk likelihood, the items assess the perception that a privacy breach is likely. For risk harm, the items assess the perception of the degree of damage that would result from a privacy breach. These items were then subjected to scale validation.

Scale Validation

We applied factor analysis methods to prune scale items, as recommended by Gable and Wolf (1993), and to confirm convergent and discriminate validity of the resulting scales. All items loaded cleanly on a single factor representing the intended construct (see Table 1).

As a further confirmation of the reliability of the scales we also examined the Cronbach's Alpha and present the results in Column 1 of Table 1 It is recommended that the acceptable reliability for the Cronbach's Coefficient Alpha is .70 or greater (Peterson, 1994). All the alpha values for our scales exceed this criteria.

Subjects

Undergraduate business students at a major U.S. university participated in the research. A total of 331 participants completed the entire questionnaire.

RESULTS

Descriptive Statistics

As seen in Table 1, mean response to items measuring PU, PEOU, and BI tend toward agreement, ranging in value from 4.41-5.73. Responses to risk likelihood and risk harm items have low means, ranging from 2.75-2.95, indicating that respondents generally believe the risk to be low. Their assessment may relate to the institutional nature of the IT or to the types of registration and schedule management tasks this IT is used for. However, the standard deviation of responses to privacy questions is higher than responses to other questions, indicating that there is a relatively high degree of uncertainty in the assessment of privacy risk by respondents.

SEM Analysis

In order to test the research model, we conducted structural equation modeling (SEM) analysis using AMOS 4.0 software (Arbuckle & Wothke, 1999). Fit of the model with the data was examined using prominent fit indices. Fit of the model us excellent on all measures (see Table 2). The values of GFI, NFI, RFI, IFI, and CFI are well above the .90 level recommended by Kelloway (1998). The value of RMSEA is well below the .10 level recommended by Kelloway (1998).

Results of SEM analysis are shown in Figure 2. All paths in the model are significant, with direct and indirect relationships explaining 30 percent of the variance in BI. Covariance was tested

Table 1. Rotated factor matrix

Factor / Alpha	Items	Description	Mean	Std. Dev.	Factor Loadings*				
					1	2	3	4	5
PU	PU1	Using this software improves the quality of my work.	4.46	1.378	**.879**	.152	-.024	.128	.045
α = .93	PU2	Using this software enhances my effectiveness in my work.	4.47	1.335	**.910**	.132	-.010	.140	.013
	PU3	Using this software improves my work.	4.41	1.360	**.855**	.204	-.031	.180	.046
PEOU	PEOU1	Learning to use this software was easy for me.	5.44	1.557	.130	**.881**	-.075	.073	-.018
α = .92	PEOU2	This software is easy to use.	5.54	1.473	.136	**.947**	-.074	.086	-.061
	PEOU3	My interaction with this software is clear and understandable.	5.28	1.420	.208	**.771**	-.080	.169	.004
BI	BI1	I intend to continue using this software.	5.73	1.210	.182	.182	-.220	**.760**	-.119
α = .79	BI2	I intend to increase my use of this software	4.81	1.334	.225	.012	-.027	**.614**	.073
	BI3	I predict I would use this software.	5.47	1.296	.018	.148	-.180	**.780**	-.151
RL	RL1	How likely is it that the organization that manages this software would use your private personal information in a way that you would not approve of?	2.79	1.512	-.006	-.092	**.845**	-.102	-.006
α = .89	RL2	How likely is it that this organization would abuse some of your personal information?	2.75	1.475	-.015	-.108	**.929**	-.147	.010
	RL3	How likely is it that someone will break into this software and steal your personal information?	2.95	1.507	-.036	-.019	**.768**	-.122	-.057
RH	RH1	How much harm could be done to you if someone broke into this software? *reversed*	2.76	1.735	.014	-.049	-.051	-.046	**.674**
α = .80	RH2	How much harm could be done to you if the organization that manages this software abused your information? *reversed*	2.75	1.641	.073	.008	.014	-.080	**.994**

* Conducted using unconstrained maximum likelihood extraction and varimax rotation

between risk harm and risk likelihood, however, this relationship was not found to be significant was not included in the final model.

Model Interpretation

Hypothesis 1 states that increasing risk harm will reduce BI toward IT use. The hypothesis was supported (path coeff. = -.21, p < .0001).

The influence of risk harm on BI is in the same numeric range as the effect of PEOU.

Hypothesis 2 states that increasing risk likelihood will reduce BI toward IT use. This hypothesis also was supported (path coeff. = -.33, p < .0001). The influence of risk harm on BI is in the same numeric range as the effect of PU.

Although we did not hypothesize effects relating to TAM components in the research model,

Table 2. Fit statistics

Fit Measure	Abbreviation	Fit Statistics
Chi-square	χ^2	141.96
Degrees of freedom	df	72
Discrepancy/df	χ^2/df	1.972
Goodness of fit index	GFI	0.943
Normed fit index	NFI	0.953
Relative fit index	RFI	0.940
Incremental fit index	IFI	0.976
Comparative fit index	CFI	0.976
Root mean square error of approximation	RMSEA	0.054

all relationships predicted by TAM were found. PEOU contributes positively to PU (path coeff. = .29, p < .0001) and BI (path coeff. = .16, p = .002). PU contributes positively to BI (path coeff. = .34, p < .0001). In order to test whether risk harm and risk likelihood add to predictiveness of TAM, we tested the research model without these factors. This model explains significantly less than the full research model. We further tested whether risk harm or risk likelihood are mediated by TAM PEOU or PU belief factors by adding relationships between the two risk factors and PEOU and PU. None of these relationships was found to be significant.

DISCUSSION

We have argued previously that privacy risk is a key contributor to IT acceptance. In our extension of TAM, we find risk harm and risk likelihood as important as TAM's PEOU and PU factors in predicting BI. Because privacy risk factors have not previously been associated with IT acceptance (Lee et al., 2003) these findings make a valuable contribution to the IS literature.

The fact that these constructs have not been previously addressed in detail in the TAM literature is likely due to the changing nature of technology and the increasing privacy risks that are associ-

ated with online computing. Privacy risks were less common in the offline, stand-alone systems and organizational networks that characterized IT before the widespread adoption of the Internet. But along with numerous benefits, the Internet has provided a ready mechanism for privacy breaches relating to identity theft, phishing, and spyware. Our findings indicate that perceptions of privacy risk have emerged as important new predictors of IT acceptance in online computing environments, and this has implications both for research and practice.

Implications for Research

The primary implication of these findings for IS researchers is to question the assumption that current online computing is fundamentally similar to traditional computing, an assumption that underpins the application of TAM to predict individuals' acceptance and use of online IT. As pointed out by Lee et al. (2003), TAM is a mature theoretical model that has been tested across a wide range of IT. However, most of these tests used offline IT or were conducted before privacy risks became commonplace in online computing. Our finding that privacy risks directly influence BI without mediation by PEOU or PU presents a challenge to TAM. PEOU and PU are considered to be "fundamental determinants of user accep-

Figure 2. SEM analysis of research model

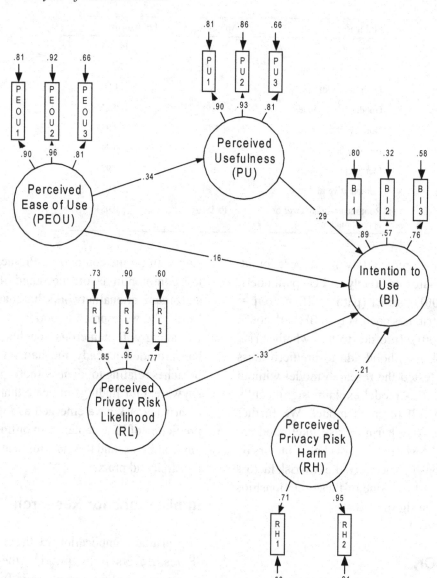

tance" of IT (Davis, 1989, p. 319). Yet effects of privacy risk factors in the present study are approximately as strong as the combined effects of PEOU and PU in predicting BI. Although TAM has been extended in many ways (Lee et al., 2003), we find no prior research has been directed toward privacy risks, including recent integrated approaches to IT acceptance, such as the unified theory of acceptance and use of technology (UTAUT) (Venkatesh, et al., 2003).

If online computing is to continue to deliver benefits to users, these users must decide to accept and use IT. Our findings suggest this decision is guided not only by the usefulness and ease of use that individuals perceive, but also by the privacy risk that is associated with IT use. This suggests future research should be directed toward finding ways to mitigate privacy risk. It is obvious that better security methods can help, but it also will be important to understand how to manage perception of risk, especially when perceptions are overblown in relation to the inherent harm and likelihood associated with online computing.

Future research is also needed that addresses the fact that a perceived level of risk cannot be taken as an unexplained prior condition. To address these conditions we can do experiments looking at what safeguards influence privacy risk on what factors and what organizations can do to overcome the risk perceptions in consumers (Raab and Bennett, 1998).

In addition, further research should be conducted to identify characteristics of online computing that may also play a role beyond PEOU and PU in predicting acceptance of online IT. Several recent studies have presented findings that improve on TAM in online computing environments. For example, both frequency of prior IT use (Kim & Malhotra, 2005) and regularity of prior IT use (Wilson, Mao, & Lankton, 2005) have been identified as strong contributors to BI and continued IT use in online computing. More research should be conducted to quantify differences between traditional computing and online computing.

Implications for Practice

As previously discussed, it will be important for researchers to identify new ways of mitigating privacy risk. However, one practical method for organizations to reduce perceptions of privacy risk is to build a feeling of trust among users to assure them that the likelihood of risk is controlled and that the organization will minimize any harm that may arise. According to Milne and Boza (1998, pg. 267) "Trust can be enhanced by building a reputation for fairness, by communicating information sharing policies up front and stressing the relational benefits, and by constantly informing the consumers of the organization's activities to serve them better." We propose it is important for organizations to ensure that they can safely and securely manage IT users' private information.

Promising fast counter measures and "no harm" guarantees in the event of a breach is just one example of accomplishing this goal.

Limitations

The present study addresses an online system that subjects perceive to be a relatively secure and safe. This is not surprising, given its university affiliation. In addition, while this system involves the exchange of information, there is not an online exchange of money. Thus, we anticipate our findings may *underestimate* the degree to which privacy risk plays a role in IT acceptance for those online IT activities that are perceived to have greater privacy risks, such as financial fraud or transactions involving bank accounts and credit cards. Future research should address computing in "riskier" domains.

Another limitation in the present study is that the use of IT is quasi-voluntary. Alternative means exist to accomplish all activities that this system supports; however, these typically require additional effort on the part of the student. Thus, results may be different in completely voluntary contexts, such as e-commerce sites where customers can choose among many different companies with which to do business. Potentially, privacy risk may be more important in voluntary contexts than in the present study; however, future research will be necessary to confirm this speculation.

CONCLUSION

Our rationale in conducting this research was to address the increase in privacy risk that we saw occurring in online computing, particularly as it affects individuals' perceptions and decisions toward use. We find that perceptions of privacy risk have become surprisingly important determinants of intention toward IT use, and this finding is troubling for the future of online computing. It is important for this reason to redouble efforts to reduce "frontier-style" online lawlessness. However, we propose it is equally important to find ways to avoid over-dramatizing privacy risk and to better match perceptions with reality regarding risk.

REFERENCES

Ajzen, I., & Fishbein, M. (1980). *Understanding attitudes and predicting social behavior.* Englewood Cliffs, NJ: Prentice-Hall.

Arbuckle, J., & Wothke, W. (1999). *AMOS 4.0 user's guide.* Chicago, IL: Smallwaters Corporation.

Awad, N. F., & Krishnan, M. S. (2006) The Personalization Privacy Paradox: An Empirical Evaluation of Information Transparency and the Willingness to be Profiled Online for Personalization. *Management Information Systems Quarterly*, March 2006, (30)1, 13-28.

Bart, Y., Shankar, V., Sultan, F., & Urban, G. L., (2005). Are the Drivers and Role of Online Trust the Same for All Web Sites and Consumers? A Large-Scale Exploratory Empirical Study. *Journal of Marketing*, 69, 133-152.

Bollen, K. A. (1989). *Structural equation modeling with latent variables.* New York: John Wiley & Sons Inc.

Conca, C., Medlin, D., & Dave, D. (2005). Technology-based security threats: taxonomy of sources, targets and a process model of alleviation. *International Journal Information Technology Management*, 4(2) 166-177.

D'Amico, A. (2000). What Does a Computer Security Breach Really Cost? Retrieved from http://www.avatier.com/files/docs/CostsOfBreaches-SANSInstitute.doc on June 9, 2008.

Davis, F. D. (1989). Perceived usefulness, perceived ease of use, and user acceptance of information technology. *MIS Quarterly, 13*(3), 319-329.

Davis, F. D., Bagozzi, R. P., & Warshaw, P. R. (1989). User acceptance of computer technology: A comparison of two theoretical models. *Management Science,* 35, 982-1002.

Drennan, J., Mort, G. S., & Previte, J. (2006). Privacy, Risk Perception, and Expert Online Behavior: an exploratory study of household end users. *Journal of Organizational and End User Computing:* (18)1, 1-22.

VirusList.com (2008) Email-Worm.Win32. NetSky.q. (2008). Retrieved from http://www.viruslist.com/en/viruses/encyclopedia?virusid=22760 on June 8, 2008.

Earp, J. B. & Baumer, D. (2003). Innovative Web Use to Learn about Consumer Behavior and Online Privacy. *Communications of the ACM,* (46)4, 81-83.

Featherman, M. S., & Pavlou, P. A. (2003). Predicting e-services adoption: a perceived risk facets perspective. *International Journal of Human-Computer Studies*, 59, 451-474.

Federal Trade Commission Identity Theft Clearing House, Retrieved on January 23, 2006 from http://www.consumer.gov/idtheft/http://www.consumer.gov/idtheft/.

Fishbein, M., & Ajzen, I. (1975). *Belief, attitude, intention, and behavior.* Reading, MA: Addison-Wesley.

Garfinkel, R., Gopal, R., & Goes, P., (2002). Privacy Protection of Binary Confidential Data Against Deterministic, Stochastic, and Insider Threat. *Management Science,* 48(6), 749 - 764.

Gable, R. K., & Wolf, M. B. (1993). *Instrument development in the affective domain* (second edition). Boston, MA: Kluwer Academic Publishing.

Gosh, A. K. & Swaminatha, T. M. (2001). Software Security and Privacy Risks in Mobile E-Commerce: Examining the risks in wireless computing that will likely influence the emerging m-commerce market. *Communication of the ACM*, (44)2, 51-57.

Heijden, H., Verhagen, T., & Creemers, M. (2003). Understanding online purchase intentions: contributions from technology and trust perspectives. *European Journal of Information Systems*, 12, 41-48.

Henderson, S. C. & Snyder, C. A. (1999). Personal Information Privacy: Implications for MIS Managers. *Information & Management*, (36), 213-220.

Hoffman, D.L., Novak, T.P., & Peralta, M. (2004). Building consumer trust online" Association for Computing Machinery. *Communications of the ACM*, (42)4, 80-86.

IBM Survey: Consumers Think Cybercrime Now Three Times More Likely Than Physical Crime: Changing Nature of Crime Leads to Significant Behavior-Changes. Retrieved on January 27, 2006 from http://www 03.ibm.com/press/us/en/press-release/19154.wss

ITRC 2008 Breach List. (2008). Retrieved from http://www.idtheftcenter.org/artman2/publish/lib_survey/ITRC_2008 on June 11, 2008.

Kelloway, E. K. (1998). *Using LISREL for structural equation modeling: A researcher's guide.* Thousand Oaks, CA: Sage Publications.

Kim, S. & Leem, C. S. (2005). Security of the internet-based instant messenger: Risk and safeguards. *Internet Research*, (15)1, 68-98.

Kim, S. S., & Malhotra, N. K. (2005a). A longitudinal model of continued IS use: An integrative view of four mechanisms underlying postadoption phenomena. *Management Science, 51*(5), 741-755.

Labuschagne, L. & Eloff, J. H. P. (2000). Electronic Commerce: the information-security challenge. *Information Management & Computer Security,* (8)3, 54-159.

Lee, Y., Kozar, K. A., & Larsen, K. R. T. (2003). The technology acceptance model: Past, present, and future. *Communications of AIS,* 12(50), 752-780.

Liu, C., Marchewka, J. T., Lu, J., & Yu, C. (2005). Beyond Concern - a Privacy -Trust - Behavioral Intention Model of Eclectronic Commerce. *Information & Management*, (42), 289-304.

Malhotra, N. K., Kim, S. S., & Agarwal, J., (2004). Internet users' Information Privacy concerns (IUIPC): The Construct, the Scale and a Casual Model. *Information Systems Research,* (15)4, 336-355.

Miller, R. (2006). Retrieved from http://news.netcraft.com/archives/security.htm on February 2, 2006.

Milne, G. R., & Boza, M.E. (1998). Trust and Concern in Consumers' Perceptions of Marketing Information Management Practices. *Marketing Science Institute Working Paper Report,* 98-117.

Milne, G. R., & Culnan, M. J. (2004). Strategies for reducing online privacy risks: Why consumers read (or don't read) online privacy notices. *Journal of Interactive Marketing*, (18)3, 15-29.

Peterson, Robert A. (1994). A meta analysis of Cronbach's coefficient alpha. *Journal of Consumer Research*, 21(2), 381-391.

Raab, C. D., & Bennett, C. J., (1998), The Distribution of Privacy Risks: Who Needs Protection? *The Information Society*, 14, 263-274.

Schneier, B., (2005). Risks of Third-Party Data. *Communication of the ACM*, 48(5),136.

Straub, D. W., & Welke, R. J. (1998). Coping with systems risk: Security planning models for management decision making. *MIS Quarterly*, (22)4, 441-469.

Venkatesh, V., & Davis, F.D. (2000). A theoretical extension of the technology acceptance model:

Four longitudinal field studies. *Management Science*, 46, 186-204

Venkatesh, V. (2000). Determinants of Perceived Ease of Use: Integrating Perceived Behavioral Control, Computer Anxiety and Enjoyment into the Technology Acceptance Model. *Information Systems Research* (11) 342-365.

Venkatesh, V., Morris, M. G., Davis, F. D., & Davis, G. B. (2003). User acceptance of information technology: Toward a unified view. *MIS Quarterly*, 27, 425-478.

Weston, A. F. (2005). American Attitudes on Health Care and Privacy. *I-Ways, Digest of Electronic commerce Policy and Regulation*, IOS Press, (28), 79-84.

Wilson, E. V., Mao, E., & Lankton, N. K. (2005). Predicting continuing acceptance of IT in conditions of sporadic use. In *Proceedings of the 2005 Americas Conference on Information Systems* (AMCIS), Omaha, NE.

ENDNOTES

[1] Although attitude was included in the initial development of TAM, most subsequent studies do not include an attitude measure (Lee et al., 2003)

[2] Computer anxiety measures certain aspects of risk, but these focus on apprehensions that the individual will be unsuccessful or inadequate in using the computer rather than concerns for privacy.

[3] For brevity we refer to these terms as risk likelihood (RL) and risk harm (RH) throughout the remainder of the paper.

Chapter XV
Ignorance is Bliss:
The Effect of Increased Knowledge on Privacy Concerns and Internet Shopping Site Personalization Preferences

Thomas P. Van Dyke
University of North Carolina, Greensboro, USA

ABSTRACT

Studies have shown that people claim that privacy matters to them but then they often do things while browsing that are risky in terms of privacy. The seeming inconsistency between professed privacy concerns and risky behavior on the internet may be more a consequence of ignorance rather than irrationality. It is possible that many people simply don't understand the technologies, risks, and regulations related to privacy and information gathering on the Web. In this study, the authors conducted an experiment to determine the answer to the following question: If people understood the risks and technology, would that knowledge alter their level of privacy concern and their preferences concerning e-commerce Web site personalization? Results indicate that increased awareness of information gathering technology resulted in significantly higher levels of privacy concern and significantly reduced preferences for Web site personalization. Implications of the findings are discussed.

INTRODUCTION

Individuals are willing to participate in diverse activities online – from emailing friends and looking up personal medical information to purchasing a wide variety of goods and services. While consumers benefit from their activities online, businesses also benefit from information gained while consumers browse. The internet environment allows business to collect and analyze more personal information with greater ease and efficiency than ever before. Firms can use several methods to collect information about visitors to their sites. These include overt methods such as registration forms, web surveys and order forms as well as covert methods including spyware, web bugs and cookies. The information gathered serves as an important input into marketing, advertising, customer service and product-related decisions by on line firms. The information gathered also allows firms to offer personalization (i.e. mass customization) to the web site. This has the potential to benefit both the customer, through added convenience and options, as well as the firm by encouraging increased sales.

However, the consequences of information gathering are not all positive. The ability of firms to gather so much information creates the risk of possible misuse and generates concerns over information privacy among users. These privacy concerns impede e-commerce. The Federal Trade Commission estimates that on-line retail sales were reduced by $18 billion due to privacy concerns in 2002. (Gellman, 2002).

Users claim that privacy is important to them (Westin, 2003). However, they are constantly taking actions that are risky in terms of privacy. Internet users are often required to make tradeoffs, taking actions that sacrifice privacy in return for convenience such as web-site personalization. These actions often appear to be in contradiction of their professed attitudes regarding their personal privacy.

For example, internet users have consistently indicated that they did not want firms to track their web surfing habits (Westin, 2003). However, people routinely accept cookies through their web-browsers by default. According to one study, users rejected fewer than 1% of cookies in over a billion page views (Websidestory, 2001).

There are several possible explanations for the seeming contradictions between user attitudes and actions. According to Kristol (2001) these include:

- Users know how cookies can collect information and track them but are unconcerned.
- Users don't know how cookies can be used to track them.

- Users have inadequate means to select which cookies to accept so they just give up and select them all.
- Users assume that the firms collecting the information will protect it and use it discreetly. (not true in all cases)
- Users assume (incorrectly) that that they are protected by governmental regulations that will prevent Web sites from misusing information about them.

Determining which of these explanations are true regarding users has important policy implications. Companies and interests groups that benefit from the information collected on the net back self-regulation and that is the current model used in the United States. Research by authors such as Westin (2003) can be used to support self-regulation on the grounds that people are free to make a choice. According to surveys, the majority of internet users fall into group that Westin refers to as privacy pragmatists. These people make informed cost-benefit decisions regarding internet privacy (Westin, 2003). However, such reasoning presupposes that respondents accurately assess their level of knowledge and understanding. It is possible that many who believe they are making informed, rational decisions are, in fact, making irrational decisions based on an unrecognized ignorance of the technologies, laws, and data flows related to on-line information gathering. If people do not understand the technology, regulations etc., then it is unrealistic to expect them to make an informed choice. Such findings could be used to argue for increased government regulation.

Unfortunately there is evidence that many people do not understand the technology, risks, or regulations related to information gathering on the Web. For example, research shows that "many individuals are unaware of the extent of the personal data stored by government and private corporations" (Roddick, 2001). In addition, the Pew Internet & American Life project found that 56% of Internet users could not identify a cookie and that *even those who claimed to have knowledge of cookies seem confused about the technology* (Fox, 2000). If people understood the type of information collected, the technology used to gather the information and the potential uses of the information, how would this alter their level of privacy concern and their desire for e-commerce web site personalization?

In this chapter, we examine the effect of increased knowledge on privacy concerns and desire for mass customization (internet shopping preferences). In the following sections, we first review the literature on privacy risks, web site personalization, also known as mass-customization and consumer attitudes towards privacy. Next we present a series of hypothesis based on previous research. Then we describe an experiment used to test the hypotheses. Data analysis results are presented. Finally we will discuss the results in the context of earlier research and attempt to explain the implications of our findings.

REVIEW OF THE LITURATURE

Privacy Concerns on the Internet

Since its inception in the mid 1990's, the growth of B2C e-commerce has been phenomenal. According to the department of commerce, on-line retail sales grew from $36.4 billion in 2000 to $54.9 billion in 2003 (http://www.census.gov/ mrts/ www/current.html). These sales figures could have been many billions of dollars higher except for the fact that many consumers simply refuse to make purchases online. One important factor restraining the growth in Internet sales is the increase in privacy concerns among Internet users (Hoffman et al., 1999) In a survey by AC Nielson, consumers rated the disclosure of personal information and comfort in using a credit card online as the biggest barriers to online purchasing (AC Nielsen, 2001). The Federal Trade Commission estimates that on-line retail sales

were reduced by up to $18 Billion due to concerns over privacy (Gellman, 2002). Considerable progress has been made in the development of technological mechanisms for secure payment. Unfortunately while these advances have indeed improved online security, they have done little to alleviate privacy concerns.

Privacy concerns are not merely psychological constructs. There is ample evidence that privacy concerns actually alter consumer behavior in a number of negative ways. According to a survey by AT Kearny, 52% of respondents reported abandoning an on-line purchase transaction due to privacy concerns (Ragnathan and Grandon, 2002). Total avoidance of online shopping, refusal to provide information and abandoning transactions are not the only responses to privacy concerns. Polls show that 30-40% (Hoffman et al. 1999) of web-users provide false information online. Reasons given include the desire to remain anonymous, avoidance of spam e-mail, and concern about how the website will use the information. A consequence of this on-line lying is that much of the information collected by websites is wrong. This both increases the cost and decreases the value of the data collected (Gellman, 2002).

Electronic commerce has increased people's concerns about privacy because the Internet environment allows business to collect and analyze more personal information with greater ease and efficiency than ever before. "Enormous amounts of consumer data have long been available through offline sources such as credit card transactions, phone orders, warranty cards, applications and a host of other traditional methods. What the digital revolution has done is increase the efficiency and effectiveness with which such information can be collected and put to use" (Adkinson, 2002). Studies have shown that the amount of data collected is truly vast. A March 2000 Federal Trade Commission survey found that 97% of sites collected some form of personal information. However, only 20% implement the fair information practice principles of notice, choice, access, and security (FTC, 2000).

Firms use several methods to collect information about visitors to their sites. These methods include registration forms, web surveys, order forms spyware and cookies. The information thus gathered serves as an important input into marketing, advertising, customer service and product-related decisions made by on-line retailers. However, the collection of this information creates the risk of possible misuse and generates concerns over information privacy. In a report to congress the FTC cited a survey showing that 92% of households with Internet access stated that they do not trust online companies to keep their personal information confidential (FTC, 2000).

Smith et al. (1996) suggest several dimensions of concern related to information privacy. *Collection* is a general concern that large amounts of personally identifiable data are being collected and stored. *Unauthorized Secondary Use (internal)* is the concern that information collected for one purpose could be used for another, unauthorized purpose by the same organization. *Unauthorized Secondary Use (external)* is the concern that information collected for one purpose could be used for another, unauthorized purpose after disclosure to an external organization. *Improper Access* is the concern that personal data are available to people not properly authorized to view the data. *Errors* names the concern that the protections against deliberate or accidental errors are not adequate. One concern that Smith et al. listed as tangential to the privacy issue, but which seems relevant in an e-commerce setting is *Combining Data*. This is the concern that several seemingly innocuous pieces of information in disparate databases may be combined to create personally identifying information that the user does not wish to disclose.

Even though all of these specific concerns have been identified, most consumers cannot articulate specific threats to privacy but rather speak of a vague feeling that there is too much information about them "out there". Unstructured interviews with Internet users show that many have a vague fear that unspecified people unknown to them will have access to personal information. Interviews also indicate that many web users have little understanding of technology. For example they don't really know what a cookie is or how it works. There is also evidence of confusion over privacy rights. Many consumers mistakenly believe that they are protected by "the privacy act" (Gellman, 2002) or that privacy statements are mandated by law.

Whether specific or vague, there is evidence that consumer's concerns about privacy risks associated with e-commerce are justified. In January 2000, the merger of the online advertising company DoubleClick and the database marketing firm Abacus Direct started a federal investigation when it was revealed that the company had compiled profiles of 100,000 online users, without their consent, and intended to sell the information (Kristol, 2001). More recently, the FTC reported 214,905 instances of identity theft in 2003. This represented 42% of all complaints up from 40% in 2002 (FTC 2004). Clearly, some threats to privacy and security related to internet shopping and on-line information gathering are real.

Web Site Personalization

E-commerce retailers are increasingly utilizing personalized features on web sites, also known as mass-customization, in order to build relationships with customers and increase the number of purchases made by each customer (Cranor, 2003). Web site personalization has been shown to be popular with customers and effective at increasing sales (Manber et al. , 2000; Personalization Consortium 2000; Personalization Consortium, 2001). However, e-commerce web site personalization adds new risks that can contribute to an increase in privacy concern.

Cranor (2003) suggests four dimensions that can be used to differentiate between types of personalization systems.

Explicit vs. Implicit Data Collection

In explicit data collection systems personalization is based on demographics, preferences, ratings or other information explicitly provided by the user. In implicit data collection systems, personalization is based on information inferred about a user from such things as purchase history, browsing habits, or query history.

Duration

Task or session focused personalization systems make recommendations based on actions taken by the user during the current session. Profile based personalization systems utilize profiles of users that are updated each time the user returns to the site. These systems often use cookies to recognize customers and retrieve their stored profiles. Logins may also be used to identify the customer and retrieve the corresponding profile.

User Involvement

Personalization may be either user initiated or system initiated. Some systems allow the users to customize their own web page while other sites attempt to customize for every customer whether they request customization or not.

Reliance on Prediction

Prediction based personalization systems use explicit or implicit ratings to build a profile that is then compared to others. If similar profiles are found, it predicts that they will have similar preferences and makes recommendations accordingly. Content-based personalization systems also provide customization or recommendations. However, they are based only on the actions of the user, not on profiles of others deemed similar (Herlocker, 2001).

Risks Related to Personalization

Personalization systems can create or exacerbate a number of risks to user privacy. Unsolicited marketing and the possibility of a firm selling information to a third party are generic concerns associated with internet use. However, these risks are heightened by the fact that personalization systems can collect and store detailed profiles containing considerable amounts of information that go beyond the type of single-purchase information collected by less sophisticated sites.

Another privacy risk associated with personalization systems is fear of prediction. Many people are uncomfortable with the concept that computers are able to make predictions about their habits and interests (Cranor, 2003). Interestingly some users fear that the predictions are too accurate and that the system can figure out information about the user that they would normally be unwilling to divulge. On the other hand, some fear that inaccurate predictions may cause the system to draw incorrect and possible damaging conclusions about the users (Zaslow, 2002).

Personalization systems also increase the risk of inadvertently revealing information to others who use the same computer. Persistent cookies stored on the machine can be used for authentification and provide access to the user's profile. Through this technology, others using the computer could have access to information such as purchasing records, health queries etc. Profiles often include passwords that then might be used to gain unauthorized access to a user's other accounts (Cranor, 2003).

In addition, highly detailed profile information could be accesses by third parties, hackers, or e-commerce company employees. It is also possible that profile information could be subpoenaed in court or used by the government in profiling of surveillance activities. The risks from online profiling led the Federal Trade Commission to recommend that Congress enact legislation to ensure consumer privacy online (FTC, 2000 Online Profiling).

Consumer Attitudes Towards Privacy

Alan Westin has been surveying consumers about privacy since 1967. In 1995, the Harris-Westin survey segmented the public on consumer privacy issues into three groups. *Privacy fundamentalists* who rejected consumer benefit claims for data uses and sought legal and regulatory protections. The *privacy unconcerned* group on the other hand were generally willing to supply their personal information to business and government and were largely unconcerned about privacy risks. Between these two extremes were the *privacy pragmatists*. According to Westin (2003) this group holds a balanced privacy position. They examine the benefits to them or society of the data collection and use. They wanted to know specific privacy risks and how organizations proposed to control those. Armed with this knowledge the privacy pragmatists would then decide whether to trust the organization or seek legal oversight.

Responses to some of the individual questions used to segment the population can be compared over time to show a trend toward increased public concern about privacy issues. Respondents concerned about threats to personal privacy jumped from 64% in 1978 to 84% in 1995 and had risen to 94% by 1999 (Louis Harris & Associates & Westin, 1999). Surveys in 2000 – 2002 recorded a dramatic shift in public attitudes (Westin 2003). By 2002, a majority of consumers (56%) felt that most businesses did *not* handle the personal information they collected in a confidential manner. This number was up from only 34% in 1999. Sixty-two percent responded that they did *not* believe that existing laws and organizational practices provided a reasonable level of privacy protection, up from 38% in 1999 (Westin, 2003).

Along with the changes in attitude, the segmentation of consumers has also moved in the direc-

tion of increased privacy concern. The privacy unconcerned group dropped from 22% in 1999 to only 8% in 2001. Privacy fundamentalists rose from 25% to 34%. Privacy pragmatists remained the majority at 58%. Policymakers have followed the change in opinion by passing hundreds privacy related laws at the state level and several at the national level. There is an ongoing debate as to the best method to protect privacy while at the same time facilitating electronic commerce. The ability of users to make informed decisions regarding internet privacy is at the center of that debate.

HYPOTHESES

It is clear that privacy risks exist. It is also apparent that some users do not fully understand the technology or specific risks associated with information gathering on the internet. This ignorance may explain why users claim that privacy is important but continue to perform activities that put their privacy at risk. In order to investigate if an increase in understanding would alter users' level of privacy concern or their preferences for web site personalization, we developed two sets of hypothesis.

Pre-Demonstration Hypotheses

Based on the results of previous research, we tested for between-group differences in privacy concern and preferences for web site personalization prior to the experimental treatment.

An Annenberg Public Policy Center survey by Turow and Nir (2000) found that teenagers are more likely to give away personal information than their parents. However, a study by Garbarino and Strahilevitz (2002) indicated that age did not have a significant effect on perceived risk of online shopping. We sought to clarify what effect, if any, that age had on privacy concern or preferences for web-site personalization.

H1a: *The level of privacy concern associated with Internet use is affected by age.*

H1b: *The proportion of users who prefer a website to remember them is affected by age.*

H1c: *The proportion of users who prefer that a website make recommendations based on previous visits is affected by age.*

Mayer (2002) found difference between internet users based on education level. As the education level of participants rose they were more likely to say that a promise of confidentiality would make a difference in their decisions, that there were risks associated with a lack of confidentiality, and that there was no guarantee associated with a promise of confidentiality. We developed three hypotheses to test for the effect of education.

H2a: *The level of privacy concern associated with Internet use is affected by education level*

H2b: *The proportion of users who prefer a website to remember them will be affected by education level.*

H2c: *The proportion of users who prefer that a website make recommendations based on previous visits is affected by education level.*

According to Fernandez and Miyazaki (2001), those who use the Internet frequently have a low perceived risk about the associated technologies. Those who purchase online infrequently will consequently have less knowledge of online technologies, and may be shocked by their capabilities. In 2001, Fernandez and Miyazaki found that "higher Internet experience...[is] related to lower levels of perceived risk toward online shopping, which in turn results in higher online purchase rates." They also state that "experience gained through simple usage of the Internet for non-purchase purposes such as information gathering and noncommercial communication will lead consumers to discover that privacy and security risks are often exaggerated." Three hypotheses were developed to test for the impact of internet usage levels.

H3a: *The level of privacy concern associated with Internet use is affected by the level of Internet usage.*

H3b: *The proportion of users who prefer a website to remember them will be affected by the level of Internet Usage.*

H3c: *The proportion of users who prefer that a website make recommendations based on previous visits is affected by the level of Internet Usage.*

Multiple studies have shown that trust is a significant antecedent of customer's willingness to transact with an on-line vendor (Gefen, 2000; Jarvenpaa et al., 2000). Jarvenpaa et al. posit that the mechanism by which trust affects one's willingness to transact is by reducing the perceived risk of doing business with the vendor. Perceived risk is a person's belief in the likelihood that they will be harmed as a consequence of taking a particular action. Gefen (2000) found that an increase in customer trust resulted in a decrease in the perceived risk associated with doing business with an on-line vendor. The two most widely cited risks associated with on-line shopping are privacy risk and security risk. Given the demonstrated relationship between trust and overall perceived risk, it is logical to assume that a similar relationship holds between trust and the level of privacy concern. If this relationship does not hold, we might need to re-evaluate the way that we operationalize the construct of privacy concern.

H4: *Those who are more trusting of people in general will tend to have lower levels of privacy concern.*

Post-Demonstration Hypotheses

The post-demonstration hypotheses are the focus of this paper. They are designed to investigate the impact of the experimental treatment, education concerning information gathering on the internet through a demonstration, on the dependent variables of Privacy Concern and two questions related to Internet shopping/personalization preferences. The hypotheses also focus investigation on the possibility of differential impact across various groups.

H5a: *The demonstration of privacy risks associated with internet cookies will increase the level of privacy concern.*

H5b: *The demonstration will have a greater impact on the privacy concerns of older voters.*

H5c: *The demonstration will have a greater impact on the privacy concerns of those with lower levels of education.*

H5d: *The demonstration will have a greater impact on the privacy concerns of those who demonstrate lower levels of internet usage.*

H6: *The demonstration of privacy risks will decrease the proportion of people preferring web cites remember them.*

H7: *The demonstration of privacy risks will decrease the proportion of people preferring to receive recommendations from web sites.*

METHODOLOGY

To test whether or not incongruities could be based upon lack of knowledge, we asked respondents a series of questions to measure their level of trust, on-line privacy concern and internet-shopping preferences. Basic demographics were also collected.

After a respondent answered questions as described above, we attempted to educate them. On one page of an internet web site, we displayed information about that respondent including their IP address, domain name, and computer information. See Figure 1. The following is the text that accompanied the information:

"The information below was collected from you in just a few short moments without your permission. This is only a simple example. Online companies have the capability to collect much more detailed data. Each time you visit a web site in fact, you are leaving a 'virtual footprint'. Your information may be actively collected and aggregated by third party companies that can then re-sell your profile."

After the respondents viewed the collected information, they were asked to re-answer the questions pertaining to online privacy concerns and preferences for mass customization. In order to ensure participant privacy, the capture of data was kept confidential. Information stored was limited only to responses and did not include any identifying information.

Measures

Several demographic questions were included so that respondents could be categorized by age, education, level of internet usage and general level of trust. The study utilized two dependent variables, Privacy Concern and Preferences for Web Site Personalization. The level of Privacy Concern was measured using a two-item, Likert-type scale. The scale demonstrated a reliability coefficient of .861. Two binary response (Yes/No) questions were used to capture the respondent's preferences toward e-commerce web site personalization.

1. Do you prefer for web sites you visit to remember you?

Figure 1.

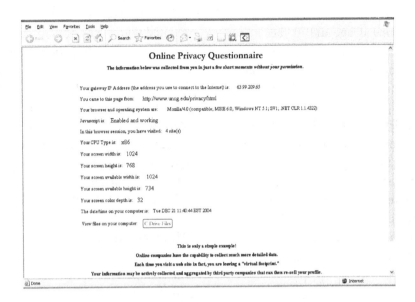

2. When you visit a site, do you prefer recommendations based upon your previous visits?

Data Collection

The investigation was conducted via an Internet survey. The survey instrument was initially reviewed by three experienced industry professionals to help ensure content validity. A web site containing the survey was developed. We utilized a convenience sample. The sample included employees from 5 different companies in the Southeast United States as well as undergraduate and graduate students from a Southeastern university. Of the 124 useful responses collected 70% were employees of various regional firms and only 30% were students.

Data Analysis

Several different analytical techniques were used to analyze the data. Simple T-tests were used to test between-group differences in Privacy Concern. Z-tests of proportion were used to test for differences

in the proportion of respondents answering the binary response format (yes/no) questions related to internet personalization preferences. ANOVA (SPSS General Linear Model) was used to test for differences between pre-test and post-test scores for Privacy Concern and for interaction effects. In order to test for differences in the proportions related to the binary response questions from before and after the treatment, McNemar's test for significance of changes in bivariate nominal scale data was used.

RESULTS

Demographics

In analyzing our sample, we found that most of the respondents were heavy Internet users. In fact, 54% claimed to spend 10 or more hours per week on the Internet and the majority, 83% had purchased more than one item online during the last year. Furthermore, respondents were also mainly college graduates with 72% having a Bachelors degree or above.

Age

In order to determine if age did in fact affect respondent's reactions to our questions, we broke our sample into two age groups – 18 to 30 and 30 and above. Results indicate no significant difference in the level of privacy concern between the two groups (Table 1.). Analysis of results utilizing the Z test of proportion indicate no significant difference between the age groups related to preferences for internet shopping site personalization (Table 2.). These results are consistent with the findings of Garbarino and Strahilevitz (2002) that indicated that age did not have a significant effect on perceived risk of online shopping

Education Level

Respondents were divided into two groups based on education level. One group included those with a Bachelor's degree or higher and the other group include those with less than a Bachelor's degree. Results indicate no difference in Privacy Concern between the two groups (Table 3). These findings are inconsistent with the findings of Mayer (2002) who found difference between internet users based on education level. Mayer reported that

as the education level of participants rose they were more likely to say that there were risks associated with a lack of confidentiality. Although there was no difference between the two groups in the proportion that preferred web sites remember them, there was a difference in the proportion that preferred recommendations from the web sites. 43.8 % of those with a Bachelor's degree or higher preferred recommendations based on previous visits compared to only 22.9% of those with less than a Bachelor's degree. This difference is significant at the .05 level (see Table 4).

Internet Usage

Our sample was split into two groups – those online more than 10 hours per week (heavy Internet user) and those online less than 10 hours per week. Results indicate a significant difference (p = .011) between the two groups in their level of privacy concern. Interestingly, the heavy internet users displayed higher levels of privacy concern than the less frequent users (see Table 5). There were no significant differences in preferences for personalization between the two groups (Table 6). The findings related to level of privacy concern may be inconsistent with the findings of Fernandez

Table 1. H1a: The effect of age on privacy concern

Age	N	Mean	Std. Dev	t	Sig. (2-tailed)
18-30	74	3.06	.653	1.042	.299
30+	50	3.19	.652		

Table 2. H1b&H1c: The effect of age on internet shopping personalization preferences

		18-30 (n=74)	>30 (n=50)	Z	Sig.
H1b: Prefer web sites to remember them	Yes	39.2%	40.0%	0.089	.92
	No	60.8%	60.0%		
H1c:Prefer recommendations based on previous visits	Yes	35.1%	42.0%	0.772	.44
	No	64.9%	58.0%		

Table 3. H2a: The effect of education level on privacy concern

Education Level	N	Mean	Std. Dev	t	Sig. (2-tailed)
Assoc. Degree or less	35	3.114	.718	-.014	.989
Bachelors or Higher	89	3.112	.664		

Table 4. H2b&H2c: The effect of education level on internet shopping preferences

		Assoc. or less (n=35)	Bachelor or higher (n=89)	Z	Sig.
H1b: Prefer web sites to remember them	Yes	37.1%	40.4%	0.337	.74
	No	62.9%	59.6%		
H1c:Prefer recommendations based on previous visits	Yes	22.9%	43.8%	2.38	.017*
	No	77.1%	56.2%		

Table 5. H3a The effect of internet usage levels on privacy concern

Internet Usage Level	N	Mean	Std. Dev	T	Sig. (2-tailed)
<10 hours/week	57	2.947	.698	2.56	.011*
>10 hours/week	67	3.253	.629		

Table 6. H2b&H2c: The effect of Internet usage levels on Internet shopping preferences

		<10 hrs. week (n=57)	>10 hrs. week (n=67)	Z	Sig.
H3b: Prefer web sites to remember them	yes	43.9%	35.8%	0.92	.36
	No	56.1%	64.2%		
H3c: Prefer recommendations based on previous visits	yes	35.1%	40.3%	0.59	.55
	No	64.9%	59.7%		

and Miyazaki (2001). According to Fernandez and Miyazaki (2001), those who use the Internet frequently have a low perceived risk about the associated technologies. The difference in findings may be accounted for by the slightly different dependent variables. Fernandez and Miyazaki (2001) used "perceived risk" as opposed to our construct of "privacy concern". Given that perceived risk is a more general construct that includes both privacy concerns and security concerns it may be possible for experienced uses to have a higher level of privacy concern while still perceiving a lower level of overall risk than less experienced users. While little has been done to address privacy risks, security technology, encryption, e-wallets etc. have made financial transactions on the net much more secure over the last few years. It is possible that experienced users' knowledge of security technology and the low risks related to online use of credit cards might account for the lower level of perceived risk. If experience is related to knowledge of the technologies and risks associated with e-commerce then these experienced users may be more aware of the privacy risks associated with persistent cookies, data miners, spyware and other information gathering technology. If true, this would be consistent with our findings. Likewise, the lower level of privacy concern reported by those who used the internet less supports the idea that ignorance is bliss. Those with the lowest level of use, and presumably a lower level of understanding, report the lowest level of privacy concern.

Level of Trust

H4: *Those who are more trusting will tend to have lower levels of Privacy Concern.*

To determine if trust affects the level of privacy concern, our sample was split into two groups – high and low trust consumers. Those who answered that they tend to trust people were placed within the high-trust category whereas those who did not tend to trust people were placed in the low-trust category. Results of a T-test indicate that low-trust individuals exhibited higher levels of privacy concern. Since privacy concern is related to a fear of potential harm from others, it is

consistent that those with low levels of trust would report higher levels of privacy concern. Given the similarity of the two constructs, this finding could be interpreted as evidence of convergent validity of the privacy concern scale.

Post Treatment Results

Hypothesis 5a is the represents the main focus of this study. The results of the paired samples t-test indicate a significant difference for all users between pre-test and post-test scores. Analysis shows that educating users about the technology of information gathering resulted in a significant ($p < .000$) increase in the level of Privacy Concern (see Table 8 and Figure 2).

ANOVA SPSS (General Linear Model for repeated measures) indicates a significant main effect of the treatment but no significant interaction effect between treatment and age (see Table 9).

Results indicated no interaction effect between the treatment and the user's education level (See Table 10)

An analysis of the results indicates a differential effect of the treatment based on the level of internet usage (see Table 11). The treatment had a significantly greater effect on those with lower levels of internet usage (see Figure 3).

The non-parametric test known as McNemar's test for significance of changes was used to evaluate the data for hypotheses H6 and H7. The test is

Table 7. Effect of general level of trust on level of privacy concern

General Level of Trust	N	Mean	Std. Dev	T	Sig. (2-tailed)
Low	25	3.340	.607	2.04	.048*
High	99	3.056	.684		

Table 8. H5a: The effect of TREATMENT on privacy concern

	N	Mean	Std. Dev	t	Sig. (2-tailed)
Pre-test	124	3.112	.677	-6.869	.000**
Post-test	124	3.419	.679		

Figure 2. The effect of the treatment on all users

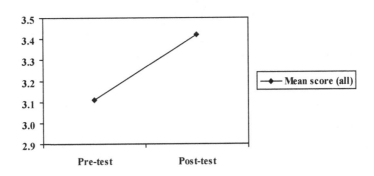

Effect of Treatment on Privacy Concern

Table 9. H5b: The interaction effects between age and TREATMENT on privacy concern

Age Group	N
18-30	74
>30	50

Source	F	Sig.
Within-Subjects Effects		
TREATMENT	44.302	0.000**
TREATMENT x Age_Group	.091	0.763
Between-Subjects Effects		
Age Group	0.433	0.785

Table 10. H5c: The interaction effects between TREATMENT and education level on privacy concern

Education Level	N
Less than Bachelor	35
Bachelor of Higher	89

Source	F	Sig.
Within-Subjects Effects		
TREATMENT	45.923	0.000**
TREATMENT x Education Level	1.740	0.190
Between-Subjects Effects		
Education Level	0.282	0.596

Table 11. H5d: The interaction effect of TREATMENT and Internet usage levels on privacy concern

Internet Usage Level	N
Less than10 hrs/week	57
>10 hrs/week	67

Source	F	Sig.
Within-Subjects Effects		
TREATMENT	55.433	0.000**
TREATMENT x Internet Usage Level	9.043	0.003**
Between-Subjects Effects		
Internet Usage Level	2.423	0.122

Figure 3. Effect of TREATMENT on privacy concern for different levels of Internet usage

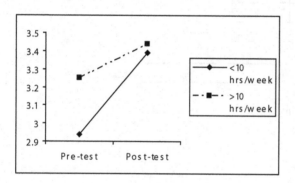

used to determine the significance of the proportion of respondents that change their preferences after the treatment.

H6: *The demonstration of privacy risks will decrease the proportion of people preferring web sites remember them.*

The contingency table above indicates that 25 people responded yes both before and after the treatment. 24 people responded YES before and changed to NO after treatment, 4 people answered no before and yes afterwards, and 71 people answered no both before and after the treatment (see Table 12). The results indicate that a statistically significant number of users

altered their preferences after being educated about information gathering technology online. The direction of change was consistent with the hypothesis. A significant proportion of those who initially preferred to be remembered by web sites chose NOT to be remembered after the demonstration.

H7: *The demonstration of privacy risks will decrease the proportion of people preferring to receive recommendations from web sites.*

The results shown in Table 13 indicate that a statistically significant number of users altered their preferences regarding receiving recommendations from web sites based on previous visits after being educated about information gathering technology online. The direction of change was consistent with hypothesis H7. A significant proportion of those who initially preferred to

Table 12. H6: Contingency table (Do you prefer web sites you visit to remember you?)

Before	After	
	Yes	No
Yes	25	24
No	4	71

*N = 124, Chi Square = 12.893, sig <0.000**

Table 13. H7: Contingency table (When you visit a site, do you prefer recommendations based upon your previous visits?)

Before	After	
	Yes	No
Yes	30	17
No	0	77

N = 124, Chi Square = 11.135, sig. <0.000**

receive recommendations from web sites chose NOT to receive those recommendations after the demonstration.

DISCUSSION AND CONCLUSION

Demographic Differences

Table 14 presents an overview of the pre-demonstration results. Several hypotheses were tested for between group differences prior to the demonstration. There was no difference in the level of privacy concern between groups based on age or education level. Although others have found significant differences, our failure to discover many differences in the level of privacy concern based on age or education level is consistent with the findings of Ackerman et al. (1999). The demographic variable that did result in a difference between groups was the level of internet usage, with heavy users (>10 hours/week) displaying a higher level of privacy concern.

Preferences toward e-commerce web site personalization were also relatively invariant across groups. The proportion of users that preferred for web sites to remember them was invariant across age, education, and internet usage levels. The only significant difference was for those who preferred that web sites make recommendations based on the results of previous visits between groups divided by educational level. Those with a Bachelor's degree or higher were more likely

Table 14. Overview of results – pre-demonstration hypotheses

	Hypothesis	Result
H1a:	The level of privacy concern associated with Internet use is affected by age.	Rejected
H1b:	The proportion of users who prefer a website to remember them is affected by age.	Rejected
H1c:	The proportion of users who prefer that a website make recommendations based on previous visits is affected by age.	Rejected
H2a:	The level of privacy concern associated with Internet use is affected by education level	Rejected
H2b:	The proportion of users who prefer a website to remember them will be affected by education level.	Rejected
H2c:	The proportion of users who prefer that a website make recommendations based on previous visits is affected by education level.	Accepted
H3a:	The level of privacy concern associated with Internet use is affected by the level of Internet usage.	Accepted
H3b:	The proportion of users who prefer a website to remember them will be affected by the level of Internet Usage.	Rejected
H3c:	The proportion of users who prefer that a website make recommendations based on previous visits is affected by the level of Internet Usage.	Rejected
H4:	Those who are more trusting of people in general will tend to have lower levels of privacy concern.	Accepted

to prefer the recommendations than those with less education.

The overall paucity of between-group differences based on age and education level simplify the interpretation of the results and improve the generalizability of the post-demonstration findings. It is not age or education level but how much the respondent uses the internet that has the greatest impact on the level of privacy concern.

Post-Demonstration Differences

The main focus of this research can be found in the pre-test, post-test results (see Table 15). Notice that the direct effect of the treatment was significant on all three dependent variables, (see hypotheses 5a, 6, and 7 in Table 15). An increased awareness of the types of information collected, information gathering technology, and the potential uses of that information significantly increased the level of privacy concerns of users. Such increased awareness also significantly reduced the proportion of users who prefer e-commerce web-site personalization. It significantly reduced both the proportion who wished for web sites to remember them and the proportion that preferred recommendations from the web sites based on previous visits.

When it comes to the level of privacy concern, it appears that ignorance is bliss. It is clear from these results that many users do not understand the amount or types of information that are collected about them on the internet. It also suggests that many have little understanding of the technologies, such as persistent cookies, that are used to collect personal information. It is this pre-existing lack of understanding that makes the effect of the treatment in this experiment so significant in its impact on the level of privacy concern and preferences for web site personalization. It is logical to assume (although not proven by this experiment) that those who are heavy internet users would have a better understanding of information gathering technology such as cookies than those who use the internet much less. Even before the treatment, the heavy internet users demonstrated higher levels of privacy concern than the light users. Those who used the web the least had the lowest levels of privacy concern (see Figure 3.). Although the treatment increased the level of privacy concern for both groups, the effect was significantly greater for the light users than for the heavy users. The two groups began with significantly different levels of privacy concern. However, after the treatment, both groups showed increased levels but the two groups were no longer significantly different from each other.

Table 15. Overview of results – post-demonstration hypotheses

	Hypothesis	Result
H5a:	The demonstration of privacy risks associated with internet cookies will increase the level of privacy concern.	Accepted
H5b:	The demonstration will have a greater impact on the privacy concerns of older voters.	Rejected
H5c:	The demonstration will have a greater impact on the privacy concerns of those with lower levels of education.	Rejected
H5d:	The demonstration will have a greater impact on the privacy concerns of those who demonstrate lower levels of internet usage.	**Accepted**
H6:	The demonstration of privacy risks will decrease the proportion of people preferring web cites remember them.	Accepted
H7:	The demonstration of privacy risks will decrease the proportion of people preferring to receive recommendations from web sites.	Accepted

Those with the least experience seemed to have been the most shocked by the information in the treatment and therefore they made a significantly greater change in their perceptions.

CONCLUSION

These findings have implication for consumers, e-commerce firms, and policy makers. On the consumer side, it is essential to protect one's own privacy. Our results indicate that consumers do not in fact fully understand online data collection and the related privacy issues. Therefore, consumers should begin by educating themselves about internet privacy risks and technology. Those consumers who are concerned about online privacy should be meticulous in reading privacy policies in order to establish what information is collected and how it will be employed. If a consumer is uncomfortable with the information that will be collected and/or how that information will be employed, they have the opportunity to visit another site or eschew the risky transaction. Consumers should also be aware of the technology available to help protect privacy. Browsers can be configured to block offending cookies. Sites such as bug-me-not.com can be used for anonymous registration. Encryption technology can also be used to help protect personal privacy. In addition, consumers must become aware that an inherent tradeoff exists between the convenience of mass customization and privacy risks online. Consumers must weigh the potential benefits versus the potential risks and make an informed choice regarding preferences for web site personalization.

These finding also have implications for e-commerce firms. Our findings showed increased levels of privacy concern as consumers were made aware of information gathering technology. Olivero and Lunt (2004) found that an increase in privacy risk awareness reduces the level of trust and increases the demand for control over information use thus complicating the relationship

between the retailer and consumer. Other studies have shown that trust is related to the willingness to transact business with an online firm (Jarvenpaa et al., 2000). Firms should not become complacent and assume that consumers trust them and choose to participate in surreptitious information exchange simply because consumers fail to block their cookies. Our findings indicate that it is ignorance, not acquiescence that causes people to allow cookies. If knowledge of internet information gathering increases, consumers are likely to lose confidence in the online marketplace. Businesses must understand consumers' concern about these issues and aim to build consumer trust. At a minimum, an online company should attempt to instill trust in consumers through contracts such as privacy policies and/or disclosure agreements that adhere to the FTC's fair information privacy guidelines of notice, choice, access and security (FTC, 2000).

Policy makers will also have to deal with the issue of on-line privacy in the coming years. According to the Center for Democracy & Technology (2004), there were at least twelve bills introduced in the 108th US congress related to privacy and the internet. We find the number of people that claim to be concerned about privacy is increasing (Turow, 2003), yet people continue to perform activities that are risky in terms of privacy. There is a debate as to the best method to protect privacy while at the same time facilitating electronic commerce. Some researchers and interest groups argue for self regulation on the grounds that consumers are free to make a choice with respect to participating in on-line information exchange (Turow, 2003). Their argument is bolstered by the findings of Westin (2002) who submits that the majority of internet consumers are "privacy pragmatists". His description of these users suggests that they make informed cost-benefit decisions regarding internet privacy risks. Our findings dispute this assertion. The results of this study suggest that a significant number of people do not understand the technology and risks associated with surreptitious information collection on the internet. If people do not understand the fast changing technology, regulations, and privacy laws that govern internet privacy, it is unrealistic to expect them to make an informed choice. Our findings support the need for further regulation and increased consumer education concerning surreptitious data collection on the internet.

REFERENCES

Ackerman, M., Cranor, L. F., & Reagle, J. (1999). *Beyond Concern: Understanding Net Users' Attitudes About Online Privacy.* AT&T Research Technical Report. Retrieved May 20, 2005, from http://www.research.att.com/library/trs/TRs/99/99.4/

ACNielson (2001). *ACNielsen Internet Confidence Index.* Retrieved December 10, 2005 from http://acnielsen.com/news/corp/001/20010627b.htm

Adkinson, W., Eisenach, J., & Lenard, T. (2002). *Privacy Online: A Report on the Information Practices and Policies of Commercial Web Sites.* Retrieved November 4, 2005 from http://www.pff.org/publications/privacyonlinefinalael.pdf

Center for Democracy & Privacy (2004). *Privacy Legislation Affecting the Internet: 108th Congress.* Retrieved December 12, 2005 from http://www.cdt.org/legislation/108th/privacy/

Fernandez, A., & Miyazaki, A. (2001). Consumer perceptions of privacy and security risks for online shopping. *The Journal of Consumer Affairs, 35*(1), 27-44.

Fox, S. (2000). *Trust and Privacy Online: Why Americans want to re-write the rules.* Pew Internet & American Life Project. Retrieved December 20, 2004 from http://www.pewinternet.org/reports/pdfs/PIP_Trust_Privacy_Report.pdf

FTC(2000). Federal Trade Commission. *Online Profiling: A Report to Congress.* June 2000, Retrieved May 23, 2005 from http://www.ftc.gov/os/2000/06/onlineprofilingreportjune2000.pdf

FTC (2000). *Privacy Online: Fair Information Practices in the Electronic Marketplace a Report to Congress.* Retrieved May 23, 2005 from http://www..gov/reports/privacy2000/privacy2000.pdf

FTC (2004). Federal Trade Commission. *National and State Trends in Fraud and Identity Theft.* Retrieved May 23, 2005 from http://www.consumer.gov/sentinel/pubs/Top10Fraud2003.pdf

Garbarino, E., & Strahilevitz, M. (2002). Gender differences in the perceived risk of buying online and the effects of receiving a site recommendation. *Journal of Business Research 57*(7), 768-775.

Gefen, D. (2000). E-Commerce: The Role of Familiarity and Trust. *Omega 28*(6), 735-737.

Gefen D. (2002). Customer Loyalty in E-Commerce. *Journal of the Association of Information Systems, 3*, 27-51.

Gellman, R. (2002). *Privacy, Consumers, and Costs: How the Lack of Privacy Costs Consumers and Why Business Studies of Privacy Costs are Biased and Incomplete.* Retrieved January 8, 2006 from http://www.epic.org/reports/dmf-privacy.html

Herlocker, J. L., & Konstan, J. A. (2001). Content-Independent Task-Focused Recommendation. *IEEE Internet Computing, 5*(6), 40-47.

Hoffman, D. L., Novak, T. P., & Peralta, M. (1999). Building consumer trust online. *Communications of the ACM, 42*(4), 80-85.

Jackson, L. A., von Eye, A., Barbatsis, G., Biocca, F., Zhao, Y., & Fitzgerald, H. (2003). Internet attitudes and Internet use: some surprising findings from the HomeNetToo Project. *International Journal of Human-Computer Studies, 59*, 355–382

Jarvenpaa, S. Tactinsky, N., & Vitale, M. (2000). Consumer Trust in an Internet Store. *Information Technology and Management, 1,* 45-71.

Kristol, D. M. (2001). HTTP Cookies: Standards, Privacy, and Politics. *ACM Transactions on Internet Technology, 1*(2) 151-198.

Manber, U., Patel, A., & Robinson, L. (2000). Experience with Personalization on Yahoo! *Communications of the ACM, 43*(8), 35-39.

Mayer, T. S. (2002). Privacy and Confidentiality Research and the U.S. Census Bureau Recommendations Based on a Review of the Literature. *Statistical Research Division U.S. Bureau of the Census.*

Olivero, N., & Lunt, P. (2003). Privacy versus willingness to disclose in E-commerce exchanges: the effect of risk awareness on the relative role of trust and control. *Journal of Economic Psychology, 25,* 243-262.

Personalization Consortium. (2000). *Survey Finds Few Consumers Unwilling to Provide Personal Information to Web Marketers in Exchange for Better Services.* Retrieved March15, 2005 from http://www.personalization.org/surveypress. html

Personalization Consortium. (2001). *New Survey Shows Consumers are More Likely to Purchase at Web Sites That Offer Personalization* Retrieved March 15, 2005 from http://www.personalization. org/pr050901.html

Ragnathan, C., & Grandon E. (2002). An Exploratory Examination of Factors Affecting Online Sales. *Journal of Computer Information Systems, 42*(3) 87-93.

Smith, H. J., Milberg, S. & Burke, S. (1996). Information Privacy: Measuring Individuals Concerns About Organizational Practices. *MIS Quarterly, 20*(6), 167-196.

Turner, E. C. (2003). Privacy on the web: an examination of user concerns, technology, and implications for Business organizations and individuals. *Information Systems Management, 20*(1), 8-18.

Turow, J., & Lilach N. (2000). *The Internet and the family 2000: The view from parents, the view from kids.* Annenberg Public Policy Center of the University of Pennsylvania.

Wahlstrom, K., & Roddick, J.F. (2001). On the Impact of Knowledge Discovery and Data Mining. In J. Weckert (Ed.), *Selected Papers from the Second Australian Institute of Computer Ethics Conference.* Australian Computer Society, Inc., Canberra, 22-27.

WebSideStory (2001). *Cookie rejection less than 1% on the Web.* Retrieved June 13, 2004 from http://www.wesidestory.com/cgi-bin/wss. cgi?corporate&news&press_2_124

Zaslow, J. (2002). *If TiVo Thinks You are Gay, Here's How to Set It Straight: What You Buy Affects Recommendations On Amazon.com, Too The Wallstreet Journal,* November 26, 2002. Retrieved July 6, 2004 from Http://online.wsj.com/article_ email/0,,SB1038261936872356908,00.thml

Section V
Web Security and Privacy Issues and Technologies

Chapter XVI
Trustworthy Web Services:
An Experience–Based Model for Trustworthiness Evaluation

Stephen J.H. Yang
National Central University, Taiwan

Blue C.W. Lan
National Central University, Taiwan

James S.F. Hsieh
Ulead Systems Inc., Taiwan

Jen-Yao Chung
IBM T. J. Watson Research Center, USA

ABSTRACT

Web service technology enables seamlessly integration of different software to fulfill dynamic business demands in a platform-neutral fashion. However, the adoption of loosely coupled and distributed services will cause trustworthiness problems. In this chapter, the authors present an experience-based evaluation of service's trustworthiness based on trust experience (understanding) and trust requirements (policy). The authors utilize ontology to specify past experiences of services and trustworthy requirement of requester. Before invoking found services, the addressed method can help requester evaluate the trustworthiness of the services based on his trustworthy requirements and past experiences of the services. Furthermore, they also present an evaluation method for composite services by taking the structure of the composite services into account. The main contribution of the paper is providing evaluation methods for Web services such that service requester can make better decision in selecting found services in terms of service's trustworthiness.

INTRODUCTION

The evolution of Internet and Web based technologies energize enterprises to conduct worldwide business transactions with greater ease than before. Various B2C and B2B applications have been developed to provide continuing business services for customers and partners. However, tightly coupled applications only enable enterprises a static business pattern, which cannot fulfill a great deal of diverse demands in today's fast-moving business environment. How to deliver adapted business services to customers and partners in a timely manner becomes a hot issue for e-business development now. Web service is an emerging solution that aims to support cross-functional integration beyond organizational boundaries. A number of de facto standards including SOAP (Mitra, 2003), WSDL (Chinnici, 2004), UDDI (Bellwood, 2003) and BPEL4WS (Andrew, 2003) are proposed for service communication, description, advertisement and orchestration respectively. By providing a uniform framework to solve the heterogeneity of programming languages and platforms, Web services can help e-business utilize virtual service components to build Web-based enterprises information systems that automate business processes in an inter-enterprise manner. Web services will not only make enterprises be more responsive, efficiency and productivity but also make it easier to conduct B2B e-commerce via standard interface. Gartner Group (Pezzini, 2003) predicts that there are more than 60% of businesses will adopt Web services by 2008. Furthermore, some enterprises have adopted Web services to conduct their businesses among their partners and customers now, for example, Galileo International (Galileo, 2006) and Triple A (Triple A, 2006).

However, delegating a computing task to dynamically found services have to undertake the risk of unknown service providers and unknown services qualities. The uncertainties in such a distributed, loosely organized, flexible and dynamic computing environment will cause a lot of trustworthiness problems including (1) Quality of Service (QoS): What are the service's availability, reliability, scalability, performance and integrity? From service requesters' perspective, they care about not only the functionality of a service but also its QoS issues. How can service requesters ensure that a found service will be available and will work reliably? Can a service deliver its functionality consistently under different loading? How does a service rollback its execution state if it fails in the middle? (2) Security of message based communications: How do service requesters and service providers keep confidentialities of transmitted data over secured or unsecured communication channels? They have to prevent classified information from internal and external eavesdropping. How can service requesters and service providers maintain data integrity? All interactions and data exchanging between the service requester and the service provider should comply with some kind of agreements. Any unauthorized modifications may lead to violations of agreements or misunderstanding of original intendment. (3) Management of trust relationships: Can service requesters trust service advertisements? What is the reputation of the corresponding service provider? How to measure the service's functional and non-functional performances is the key for evaluating the trustworthiness of the service advertisements and the service provider. It is also helpful for both service requesters and service providers to maintain trust relationships among them such that they can have higher confidence in choosing the service provider or service requester based on collected past experiences.

The trustworthiness concern can be classified into three levels, infrastructure, understanding and policy. Infrastructure is the first level focuses on keeping the trust of service's infrastructure. In other words, the essence of a trustworthy Web service is that the underlying system of the Web service is trusted (Grandison, 2000). For example, the underlying software and hardware of a Web service must be trustworthy to ensure the trustworthiness of the service. The network should guarantee that network transmission is reliable and secure. Recently, most of research efforts focused trustworthiness problems on fundamental security issues. W3C is presently developing XML Signature, XML Encryption and P3P projects. Moreover, many researchers also have proposed some related specifications to enhance the trustworthiness of Web services such as WS-Security (Anthony, 2004), WS-Policy (Bajaj, 2004), WS-Trust (IBM, 2002), Web Service Level Agreements (IBM Corporation, 2003) and WS-Quality (Mani, 2002). Understanding is the second layer. Huhns and Buell (2002) pointed out that we are more likely to trust something if we understand it. That means you will not trust what you do not understand. We need to confirm that services, which are performed by service providers or agents, are trusted when we invoke them. An active approach is to analyze the behaviors of services based on abstract behavior models of service providers and agents. A passive approach is to analyze experiences and estimate degree of trust based on requester's experiences of the service (Singh, 2002). Passive approaches such as rating service, reputation mechanism, referral network and social network are technologies for exchanging experiences and reputation based on a third party certification group (Grandison, 2000) or a peer-to-peer sharing mechanism (Yolum, 2002). The third layer, policy is used to describe requirements of trust, security, privacy and societal conventions to reach high-level trustworthy objectives (Huhns, 2002; Singh, 2002). In general, the policy provides many specific description-methods for requesters to define what states and situations we could accept. In other words, policy works like a rule set used to decide what behaviors and states could acquire authorizations.

In this paper, we present an experience-based evaluation of service's trustworthiness based on understanding and policy levels. We utilized ontology to specify past experiences of services

and trustworthy requirement of requester. Before invoking found services, the addressed method can help requester evaluate the trustworthiness of the services based on his trustworthy requirements and past experiences of the services. Furthermore, we also present an evaluation method for composite services by taking the structure of the composite services into account. The main contribution of the paper is providing evaluation methods for Web services such that service requester can make better decision in selecting found services in terms of service's trustworthiness.

The rest of this paper is organized as follows. An overview of related works is given, then follows the architecture of our experience-based trust management. The method of evaluating single service's trustworthiness and the evaluation method of composite service's trustworthiness are shown then. Finally, the concluding remarks and future works are presented.

RELATED WORKS

In order to improve the reliability of modern computer systems and promise to develop more trustworthy computing environments, both industrial vendors and academic institutes spend a lot of efforts on trust computing studies and form a number of open organizations such as TCG (TCG, 2005) and TRUST (TRUST, 2005) dedicated to providing various solutions with joint efforts. Trusted Computing Group (TCG) is a not-for-profit organization formed to develop, define and promote open standards for hardware-enabled trusted computing and security technologies across multiple platforms, peripherals and devices. From TCG's viewpoint, trust is the expectation that a device will behave in a particular manner for a specific purpose. A trusted platform should provide at least three basic features namely protected capabilities, integrity measurement and integrity reporting. Hence they design Trusted Platform Module (TPM) as the basis for enhancing the security of computing environment in disparate platforms including mobile devices, PC clients, servers and storage systems etc. TPM is the root of trust, which indicates it is the component that must be trusted without external oversight, and it provides numerous cryptographic capabilities such as encryption/decryption, digital signature and integrity measurement etc. With the combination of transitive trust and TPM, trust boundary can be extended from trusted execution kernel up to OS loader codes, OS codes and application codes by proving system's integrity to the remote party. Generally, TPM is implemented as a micro-controller to store keys, passwords and digital certificates such that it can be used in different computing platforms to assist in performing protected capabilities, integrity measurement and integrity reporting and IBM 4758 cryptographic coprocessor (Doorn, 2006) shows how to use TPM in an open way.

Team for research in ubiquitous secure technology (TRUST) is a new science and technology center established by U.S. National Science Foundation. TRUST brings a lot of top U.S. universities in security research together including Berkeley, Stanford, Carneige Mellon and San Jose State University etc. Due to a rapid increase in computer security attacks at all levels in the last decade, TRUST recognizes that computer trustworthiness is a pressing scientific, economic and social problem. They try to solve the problem from three directions: (1) Security science – includes software security, trusted platforms, applied cryptographic protocols and network security. (2) System science – includes complex inter-dependency modeling and analysis, secure network embedded systems, model-based integration of trusted components and secure information management software tools. (3) Social science – includes economics, public policy and societal challenges, digital forensics and privacy and human computer interfaces and security. Besides, TRUST will have an education and outreach component that focuses not only on integrating

research and inquiry-based education but also on transferring new and existing knowledge to undergraduate colleges, educational institutions serving under-represented populations and the K-12 community. For the long-term considerations, such activities can help lay the groundwork for training the scientists and engineers who will develop the next generation of trustworthy systems as well as help prepare the individuals who will ultimately become the users and consumers in the future.

There are also many different attempts on offering trustworthy solutions in the service level including QoS-aware service delivery, trustworthy service selections, reliable service compositions and validation-based access control etc. wsBus (Erradi, 2005) is an enhanced service registry as well as an intermediary that augments and manages the delivery of Web services by providing run-time support for reliable messaging, securing, monitoring and managing of Web services. It acts as a mediator between service requesters and service providers. All messages are intercepted by a messaging gateway and messages will be placed onto a queue for follow-up processing if they succeed in passing three reliability checks of message's expiration, duplication and ordering. In the mean time, wsBus will keep all messages in a persistent storage to provide fault tolerance and reliable message delivery such that messages can be re-sent when communication failures occur. Besides, wsBus also supports multiple transport protocols such as MSMQ, TCP, JMS and HTTP/R and thus it can offer reliable service delivery by taking advantage of underlying protocol's reliable communications capabilities. Wang (2004) proposed an integrated quality of service (QoS) management in service-oriented enterprise architectures. The integrated QoS management is to provide QoS support in a consistent and coordinated fashion across all layers of enterprise systems, ranging from enterprise policies, applications, middleware platforms and down to network layers. They classified QoS characteristics into four categories as well as developed an XML-based language for service requesters to express QoS requirements: Performance – response time, message throughput, payload size and end-to-end delay; Reliability – delivery guarantee, duplication elimination, message ordering, loss probabilities, error rate, retry threshold, message persistency and criticality; Timeliness – time-to-live, deadline, constant bit-rate, frame time and priority; Security – message signing and encryption. The integrated QoS management architecture consists of various component services to help service providers determine whether QoS requirements of required services from a client can be satisfied based on evaluations of current work loadings and resource allocations. In addition, the architecture supports run-time QoS monitoring and adaptations as well.

Tosic (2005) tried to assist service requesters in selecting appropriate Web services with comprehensive contractual descriptions. From technical contract perspective, they claimed that comprehensive descriptions of Web services require several different types of contracts and they classified all kinds of contractual descriptions into three broad categories: Functionality contracts – syntactic contract, behavioral contract, synchronization contract and compositional contract; Quality contracts – QoS contract and pricing contracts; Infrastructure contracts – communication contract, security contract and management contract. Based on the categories, they examined a number of existing Web service languages including WSDL (Chinnici, 2004), BPEL4WS (Andrew, 2003), WS-CDL (Kavantzas, 2004), WS-Policy (Bajaj, 2004), WSLA (Keller, 2003), WSOL (Tosic, 2003) and OWL-S (OWL-S Coalition, 2006) to check what types of contracts can be specified with them. However, none of the previous specifications can provide comprehensive description capabilities. On the other hand, Zhang (2004) presented another method to help service requesters select trustworthy Web services. They proposed a user-centered, mobile agent based,

fault injection equipped and assertion oriented approach to assist service requesters in selecting trustworthy Web services. Upon their UMFA approach, service requester can employ mobile agents with test data and predefined semantic assertions to determine whether targeted services can fulfill both functional and trustworthy requirements thoroughly.

In the case of Web services compositions, the QoS and trustworthiness problems are more complex than the problems in individual services due to various compositional patterns. Jaeger (2005) provided a mechanism to help service requesters determine the overall QoS of a Web services composition by aggregating the QoS of the individual services. Based on defined composition patterns including Sequence, Loop, XOR-XOR, AND-AND, AND-DISC, OR-OR and OR-DISC, they gave the corresponding aggregation rules for mean execution time, mean cost and mean fidelity. In order to get a closer estimation of the service composition, the aggregation method will take dependencies into account if dependencies between particular services exist. The effectiveness of such considerations is obvious when services of a particular dependency domain are integrated within different composition patterns of the whole composition.

EXPERIENCE BASED TRUSTWORTHINESS EVALUATION

In this Section, we present our experience based trustworthiness evaluation architecture based on CMU's RETSINA agent architecture (http://www.cs.cmu.edu/~softagents/) by incorporating three additional modules including *inquiry mosdel*, *evaluation module*, and *choice module* as shown in Figure 1.

The *inquiry module* queries past experience data of services in a task plan from reputation system or social network. It computes confidence of services based on requirement hypothesis,

Figure 1. Architecture of experience based trustworthiness evaluation

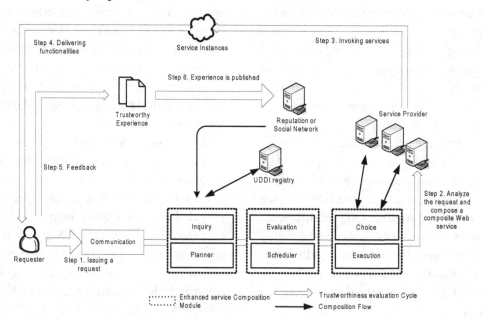

which will be explained in details in the next section. The *evaluation module* is an extension of the original scheduler module, which generates appropriate schedules (workflow or process) to coordinate service's executions. The *evaluation module* retrieves confidence of services from the *inquiry module* and then performs trustworthy evaluation with Petri nets based modeling and verification, which will be presented in details in next section. The *choice module* is an extension of the original execution module is designed to choose the most suitable task plan and schedule based on the evaluation results of *evaluation module*. Execution module will coordinate all services with the selected schedule. There are six steps in our experience based trust management: 1) A service requester issues a request with functional and trustworthy requirements. The trustworthy requirement contains policies in the forms of rule set to specify the requester's acceptable risk degree represented by two ontologies of general aspects and domain aspects. 2) The functional requirement will be analyzed to discover the requested services while the trustworthy requirement will be evaluated by the extended *evaluation module*. 3) Service

provider delivers offer service functionality with service instances according to invocations of the execution module and the results will be reported to the communication module. 4) The requester consumes the service instances. 5) The requester sends feedbacks of his experiences regarding the consumed service instances. 6) The experiences received in step 5 will be saved in the reputation and social network inside the trust management system so that the system can refer to the experiences when some other requesters issue a similar request of trust evaluation later.

INQUIRY MODULE FOR EXPERIENCE SPECIFICATION

We have utilized ontology to specify experience of trust. Ontology employs classes to describe concepts (Maximilien, 2004) so that we construct instances from classes and describe past experiences with facts. For example, we list the experiences from two aspects, general and domain specific samples for online bookstore services as shown in Table 1.

Table 1. Description of experience regarding bookstore services

General aspect		
Functional	1.	Does the service request have been fulfilled?
Non-Functional		
Network performance	1.	What is the response time of the service instance in this service?
	2.	What is the turnaround time of service instance in this service?
	3.	What is the packet miss rate of service instance in this service?
Security	1.	Does the service use RSA technology?
	2.	Does the service use DES technology?
Quality	1.	What is availability of this service?
	2.	What is usability of this service?
Domain aspect		
Selling		
Bookstore	1.	How long will it take to deliver a requested book in this service?
	2.	Does the book have been damaged during delivery in this service?
	3.	What is the list price of the requested book in this service?

The experiences regarding bookstore services can be modeled by several "trustworthy aspect ontologies" as shown in Figure 2. We define a class "Experience of Trust" to represent the abstract model of experiences. The "Experience of Trust" class consists of two abstract classes: "General aspect" and "Domain aspect" to express multi-dimensional aspects and concepts of the experiences. The general aspect describes the general functionality and non-functional properties with functional and non-functional classes and domain aspect considers different domain specific properties such as Selling, Booking and others. The experience instance will be shown in details in the next sub-section.

Table 2 is an experience instance of the "Experience of Trust" class based on the class diagram in Figure 2 and the description of experience in Table 1.

Trustworthy requirement is a kind of rule-based policy that we utilize to determine whether described experiences are acceptable to meet service requester's trustworthy requirement. The rules for trustworthy requirements are similar to

Figure 2. Trustworthy aspect ontology

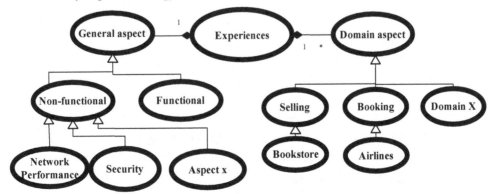

Table 2. Description of experience instance tr regarding bookstore service

Aspect	Property	Value
Functional	Reach	True
Non-Functional		
Network performance	Response time	510 ms
	Turnaround time	2100 ms
	Packet miss rate	1.5 %
Security	RSA technology	True
	DES technology	True
Bookstore	Book delivery time	2 Days 3 Hours
	Damage	False
	Price	$ 53.5

sentences appeared in propositional logic. What follows are two examples of trustworthy requirements rules. The trustworthy requirement rules are constructed by requester's requirements (see Box 1).

By adopting propositional logic based inference engine, we can issue two queries *TELL* and *ASK* to knowledge base *KB* with. *TELL* is used to query whether some experience instance *tr* meets requester's trustworthy requirements. *ASK* is used to determine whether a service can satisfy the request.

We utilize experiences to infer whether a trustworthy requirement is acceptable. For example, based on experience instance *tr* in Table 2, we can infer that requirement s_1 is non-acceptable but requirement s_2 is acceptable with knowledge base *KB*. Therefore the experience instance *tr* meet requester's trustworthy requirement.

EVALUATION MODULE FOF TRUSTWORTHINESS EVALUATION

Evaluating Single Service

We utilize sampling of binomial probability to calculate the confidence, which is used to determine whether a service conforms to the requester's trustworthy requirements based on a 95% confidence interval in terms of probability (Mitchell, 1997). The following terms are defined:

- *S* is defined as a set of service instances representing samples of total past service instances for one service, and is denoted by $S = \{s_1, s_2, ... s_n\}$.
- *Tr* is defined as a set of trust evaluation values of past experience instance, and is denoted by $Tr = \{tr_1, tr_2, ... tr_n\}$.
- *Rating* : $S \rightarrow Tr$ *Rating*(*s*): The Rating function maps the service instance *s* to past experience instance, *tr*. In other words, the

Box 1.

S_1 : *Accept* $\Leftarrow$ *Functional.Reach* $\wedge$ *Smaller*(*Network performance.Response time, 700ms*)$\wedge$
        Smaller(*Bookstore.Book delivery time, 2 Days*)$\wedge$ *Smaller*(*Bookstore.Price, $50*)

S_2 : *Accept* $\Leftarrow$ *Functional.Reach* $\wedge$ *Security.RSA technology* $\wedge$ $\neg$*Bookstore.Damage* $\wedge$
        Smaller(*Network performance.Packet miss rate, 2%*)

function associates past service instance with past experience instance, and the experiences are collected by past requesters. For example, the function $Rating(s) = tr$ represents a trust evaluation tr of instance s ($s \in S, tr \in Tr$).

- $Accpet : Tr \rightarrow \{0,1\}$ A requirement hypothesis can be denoted as *Accpet* function. The output of Accept function is 1 when past experience instance is accepted by requester, otherwise is 0. The *ASK* function is a query for the knowledge base *KB*.

$$Accpet\,(tr) \equiv \begin{cases} 1 & ASK\,(KB, tr) = Accept \\ 0 & otherwise \end{cases}$$

Based on the usage of Large-Sample of Hypothesis for a Binomial Proportion to evaluate the simple error and true error of a hypothesis addressed in (Mitchell, 1997, Mendenhall, 1999), the result of the hypothesis assesses the sample is a Boolean value (true or false). Thus we can see that the hypothesis assesses the sample as a Bernoulli trial and the distribution of Bernoulli trial is a binomial distribution. The binomial distribution approximates the normal distribution when the number of sample is enough. Simple error is correct rate in samples and true error is correct rate in population. We will get a confidence interval according to the simple error and the area of confidence interval represents a probability which true error fall in the interval. In the normal distribution, the true error is 95% probabilities falling within the range of $mean \pm 1.96 \times SD$ (Standard Deviation) in compliance with the experience rule. In other words, we can utilize the confidence interval to evaluate lowest true error of the evaluating hypotheses.

Let *Accpet* function be the hypothesis and then we can evaluate the possible true error of the hypothesis based on the past instances s according to the Evaluating Hypotheses theory (Mitchell, 1997). Whether the tr ($tr \in E$) is accepted by *Accpet* is a binomial distribution which approximates the normal distribution when the

number of samples is large enough. Thus we can utilize the normal distribution to calculate that the sample error closes with the true error. The true error is of 95% probabilities falling within a confidence interval, which will be approved as a trustworthy service in the general application.

We define the confidence symbol as the lowest bound of the true error. The trust of service conforms to the request's requirement when the confidence is higher.

$$\hat{p} = \frac{1}{n} \sum_{s \in S} Accpet(Rating(s)), SD = \sqrt{\frac{\hat{p} \times (1 - \hat{p})}{n}}$$

$$Confidence \equiv \max\{\hat{p} - z_{95\%} \times SD, 0\}$$

As the number of samples increases, the standard deviation decreases relatively and the confidence will be closer to the true error. For example, the past instances of the bookstore service are $S |S| = 256$. Requester proposes a Requirement Hypothesis *Accpet*. If the result of calculation is $\hat{p} = 0.6$, the confidence can be calculated from the following equation.

$$\hat{p} = \frac{1}{256} \sum_{s \in S} Accpet(Rating(s)) = 0.6, z_{95\%} = 1.96$$

$$Confidence = \hat{p} - z_{95\%} \times \sqrt{\frac{\hat{p} \times (1 - \hat{p})}{256}} \cong$$

$$0.6 - 0.060012 = 0.539987$$

The calculated confidence is 53.99%, which means the value is that the service has 53.99% probability to meet the trustworthy requirement based on 95% confidence interval. Hence we can assert that trust of the service have 53.99% probability of conforming to the requester's requirements.

Evaluating Composite Services

We define Trustworthy Web Service Evaluation Petri Net (TWSEPN) which is extended from Petri nets to model composite Web service. Furthermore we applied coverability graph of TWSEPN to simulate states of service execution (behavior analysis) (Narayanan, 2002). Based on the simulation, we can compute the variation of trustworthy confidence in a composite Web service.

Trustworthy Web Service Evaluation Petri Nets (TWSEPN)

Petri nets are characterized by its graphical modeling and mathematical computation power, which is very suitable for Web service modeling and simulation. In addition, Petri nets are more powerful than state machine to model concurrent and distributed systems and it can verify both structural and behavioral properties of the system. Petri nets can also be represented as mathematical models such as state equations so it is able to apply different mathematical techniques such as matrix operations to calculate system's behaviors. The details of TWSEPN is defined as follows:

$$TWSEPN = \left(P, T, F, M_{initial}, M_{finial}, Conf\right)$$

I. $P = \left\{p_1, p_2 \dots p_j\right\}$ is a finite set of places, each place represents a pre-condition and post-condition in a service.

II. $T = \left\{t_1, t_2 \dots t_k\right\}$ is a finite set of transitions, each transition represents a *sub-service* or *control-service* in a composite service. The transitions of sub-services are represented services, which organize the composite service, and the transitions of control-services are represented flow control in the TWSEPN.

III. $F \subseteq \left(P \times T\right) \cup \left(T \times P\right)$ is a set of arcs, each arc represent the control flow between *sub-services* in a service.

IV. $M_{initial} \in \{0,1\}^y$ represents the initial marking in the *TWSEPN*.

V. $M_{finial} \in \{0,1\}^y$ represents the final marking in the *TWSEPN*.

VI. *Conf:T $\rightarrow$ Confidence* is a mapping function which maps the *sub-services* to these confidences.

We use the *Requirement Hypothesis Accpet* to compute the *Confidence* of *sub-services*.

$$Conf\left(t\right) \equiv \begin{cases} Confidence \; _{of\,the\,t} & t \; _{is\,a} \; sub\text{-}service \\ 1 & t \; _{is\,a} \; control\text{-}service \end{cases}$$

In order to model different workflow patterns, we define several useful control constructs and their corresponding confidences, including sequence, split, split-join, if-then-else and iterate etc. as illustrated in Figure 3.

Trustworthy Evaluation with TWSEPN

According to the $M_{initial}$ and firing rules, we deduce all covered markings into a coverability graph to express the transformation of markings (states). The classical coverability graph algorithm proposed by (Murata, 1989). It has been optimized later by (Finkel, 1993) who has proposed an algorithm to construct the minimal coverability graph. We have used the algorithm to construct the coverability graph of the TWSEPN. Based on TWSEPN's definitions and control patterns, we parse a composite service, generate the corresponding model and derive its coverability graph easily as shown in Box 2 and Figure 4.

CHOICE MODULE FOR SELECTING TRUSTWORTHY COMPOSITE SERVICES

Every arc in a coverability graph represents a confidence value denoted by formula *Conf(t)* ($t \in T$). Hence, it is easy to find out the *minimum confidence* of a TWSEPN model by investigating all possible product values (firing sequences). Since a coverability graph is a directed graph, which might contain cycles, we need to consider the two different cases: the first one is that the coverability graph is a directed acyclic graph and the other is that the coverability graph contains cycles.

Figure 3. Control patterns in TWSEPN

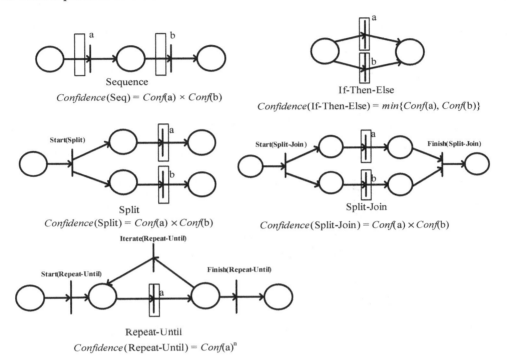

Box 2.

```
Program 1
...ignore

<process:CompositeProcess rdf:ID="CompositionService">
    <process:composedOf>
        <process:If-Then-Else>
            <process:ifCondition>...</process:ifCondition>
            <process:then>
                <process:AtomicProcess rdf:about="#ser1"/>
            </process:then>
            <process:else>
                <process:SplitJoin>
                    <process:AtomicProcess rdf:about="#ser2"/>
                    <process:Repeat-Until>
                        <process:untilCondition>...</process:untilCondition>
                        <process:untilProcess>...
                            <process:AtomicProcessrdf:about="#ser3"/>
                        </process:untilProcess>
                    </process:Repeat-Until>
                </process:SplitJoin>
            </process:else>
        </process:If-Then-Else>
    </process:composedOf>
</process:CompositeProcess>

...Ignore
```

Figure 4. The TWSEPN model of Program 1 and its coverability graph

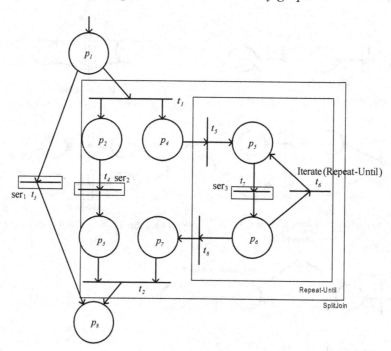

$$Conf\left(t_3\right) = a, \; Conf\left(t_4\right) = b, and \; Conf\left(t_7\right) = c$$

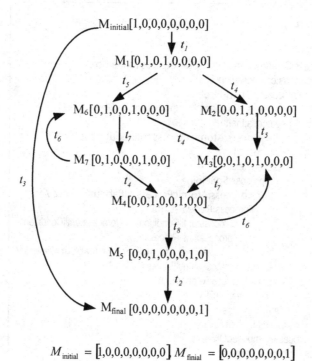

$$M_{initial} = \left[1,0,0,0,0,0,0,0\right] \; M_{finial} = \left[0,0,0,0,0,0,0,1\right]$$

Algorithm 1.

Algorithm 1

Step 1. $\forall M_x \in M, \quad CompositeConf(M_x) \leftarrow 1$

Step 2. I sort the Coverability Graph with topological order, and the result is saved in an ordinal list
$L = \{M_{initial} \dots M_{final}\}$.

Step 3. If the list L is not empty, then delete the head M_x of the list L and execute the following:

    Step 3.1. Each outgoing edge e which the mark is the transition t connects the M_x to the $M_y(M_y \in L)$.
    If $t \in T$, then do the following:
    $CompositeConf(M_y) \leftarrow \min\{CompositeConf(M_x) \times Conf(t), CompositeConf(M_y)\}$

    Step 3.2. Come to step 3.

Step 4. The value of $CompositeConf(M_{final})$ is the Composition Confidence (*minimal confidence product*).

Find Minimum Confidence

If the coverability graph is a directed acyclic graph (DAG), the graph is an Activity on Edge Network (AOE). In an AOE, every activity is attached to the arcs and AOE can be serialized by topological order. Every arc represents a state transformation and the confidence value of the transformation is attached to the arc. The algorithm of calculating minimum confidence of all possible product values is presented below.

In order to determine the minimum confidence of all possible product values in a cyclic graph, we present a method based on (Cormen, 1999) to determine the Strongly Connected Components (SCC) of the coverability graph in linear time (Tarjan's algorithm). Then we can compress the SCC into two vertexes and one arc to transform the directed cyclic graph into a DAG. The vertexes which construct the SCC, and the weights of edges which are in the SCC are denoted as

$$M^{SCC} = \{M_a, M_b \dots\}, \text{ and } T^{SCC} = \{t_\alpha, t_\beta \dots\}$$
$$(T^{SCC} \subseteq T).$$

Two of the compressed vertexes are denoted as $M_{ab\dots}$ and $M'_{ab\dots}$. A special symbol δ is defined to represent the infinite property. The lower bound of the confidence is

$$\left(\prod_{t \in T^{SCC} and\ t \in T} Conf(t)\right)^\delta \text{ in the compressed SCC.}$$

We substitute for the confidence values of arcs between $M_{ab\dots}$ and $M'_{ab\dots}$. Then we must ensure that the lower bound of the confidence is

$$\left(\prod_{t \in T^{SCC} and\ t \in T} Conf(t)\right)^\delta \text{ in the SCC.}$$

The lowest confidence loop is formed by the set $T' (T' \subseteq T^{SCC})$ in the SCC. The confidence of the loop is denoted as C and

$$c = \prod_{t \in T' and\ t \in T} Conf(t)^{\gamma_t}, \gamma_t \in \text{N. Let}$$

$$\gamma = \max_{t \in T' and\ t \in T} \{\delta_t\}.$$

A special symbol δ is defined to represent the infinite property and the symbol δ exists for each integer $n, \delta > n \times \gamma$. Thus the following formula can be derived:

$$c = \prod_{t \in T' and\ t \in T} Conf(t)^\gamma \geq \left(\prod_{t \in T' and\ t \in T} Conf(t)\right)^\gamma \geq \left(\prod_{t \in T^{SCC} and\ t \in T} Conf(t)\right)^\delta$$

There are two kinds of arcs in the original incoming ones. An arc e connects to $M (M \in M^{SCC})$ and the graph contains an arc e' which connects

M with M' ($M' \in M^{SCC}$). Otherwise, the arc e is connected to M'$_{a,b...}$. Finally, the minimum confidence of all possible product values can be determined by the following formula.

$$\min \left\{ CompositeConf(M_x) \times Conf(t), CompositeConf(M_y) \right\}$$

Choose Best Schedule of Service Execution

As the production of the confidence values includes an exponential variable δ, we have to decide which the minimum is. The evaluation of two composite confidences cc and cc' is shown as follows:

- If both cc and cc' do not include the variable δ, using scalar comparison to evaluate the situation.
- If both cc and cc' include the variable δ. The comparison of the confidences, which include the variable, δ is performed. If the confidences are equal, the comparison of

the confidences, which do not include the variable, δ is performed.

- If one of cc and cc' includes the variable, δ. The smaller of two confidences is the one, which includes variable, δ.
- The system decides a scalar and use scalar comparison to evaluate the situation.

The fore-mentioned method can be used to choose the best schedule. For example, according to Figure 4, the SCCs are detected as shown in Figure 5. Based on the addressed method, the coverability graph can be transformed into a DAG as shown in Figure 6. In accordance with algorithms 1, we can evaluate the *composition confidence* of a composite Web service. In the final step, we could decide whether this composite service conforms to the trustworthy requirements. In the scenario, the minimal composition confidence of this service is $min\{a, b \times c^\delta\}$. If some composite services can reach the same goal and the minimal composition confidence is greater than $min\{a, b \times c^\delta\}$, we will choose the greater one to ensure that the choice is the most trustworthy one.

Figure 5. Detected SCCs in coverability graph of Figure 4

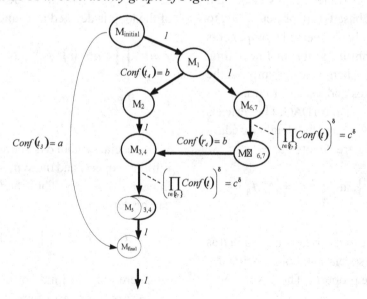

$$CompositonConfidence = min\left\{a, \ b \times c^\delta \right\}$$

Figure 6. Transformation of a coverability graph into a DAG

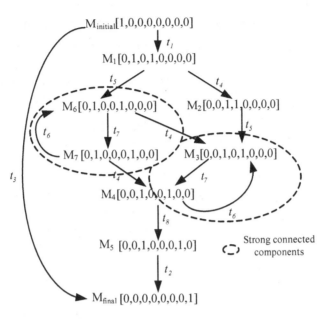

$$CompositonConfidence = min\{a, b \times c^\delta\}$$

CONCLUSION AND FUTURE RESEARCHES

In this paper, we have presented an experience based trustworthy evaluation model based on trust experience (understanding) and trust requirement (policy). In *inquiry model*, we utilize ontology to describe experiences and requirements to infer individual confidence degree of all sub-services. In *evaluation module*, we have presented TWSEPN to model a schedule (workflow or process) of a composite Web service and evaluate the whole confidence degree of the composite Web service with TWSEPN's coverability graph and individual confidence of sub-services. Finally, we developed a *choice module* to import various trust requirements in order to determine best plan of a composite Web service for service execution.

In the near future, we will introduce concepts of penalty and insurance to improve evaluation of trustworthy degree in Web services. If a service provider ever provided a failed service, his trustworthy degree will degrade due to the penalty. In addition, service providers need to address service insurance with a digital agreement and service requesters can file a damage claim based on the digital agreement if the offered service fails to meet the agreement.

ACKNOWLEDGMENT

This work is supported by National Science Council, Taiwan under grants NSC 94-2524-S-008-001.

REFERENCES

Andrew, T. et al. (2003). *Business Process Execution Language for Web Service Version 1.1*. June 1, 2006, from http://www.ibm.com/developerworks/library/ws-bpel

Anthony, N., Chris, K., Phillip H., & Ronald, M. (2004). *Web Services Security: SOAP Message*

Security 1.0 (WS-Security 2004). June 1, 2006, from http://docs.oasis-open.org/wss/2004/01/oasis-200401-wss- soap-message-security-1.0

Bajaj, S. et al. (2004). *Web Services Policy Framework (WS-Policy)*. June 1, 2006, from http://www-106.ibm.com/developerworks/library/specification/ws-polfram/

Bellwood, T. et al. (2003). *UDDI Version 3.0.1*. June 1, 2006, from http://uddi.org/pubs/uddi_v3.htm

Chinnici, R. et al. (2004). *Web Services Description Language (WSDL) Version 2.0 Part 1: Core Language,* June 1, 2006, from http://www.w3.org/TR/wsdl20/

Cormen, T. H., Leiserson, C. E., & Rivest, R. L. (1999). Introduction to Algorithms. *The MIT Press and McGraw-Hill,* (pp. 489-490).

Doorn, L. v. et al. (2006). *4758/Linux Project*. June 1, 2006, from http://www.research.ibm.com/secure_systems_department/projects/linux4758/index.html

Erradi, A., & Maheshwari, P. (2005). wsBus: QoS-aware Middleware for Reliable Web Services Interactions. *Proc. of IEEE EEE05*, (pp. 634-639).

Finkel, A. (1993). The Minimal Coverability Graph for Petri Nets. *Advances in Petri Nets 1993, Springer Verlag Lecture Notes in Computer Science, 674*, 210-243. Galileo International. (2006) June 1, 2006, from http://www.galileo.com/galileo/

Grandison, T., & Sloman, M. (2000). A Survey of Trust in Internet Applications. *IEEE Communications Surveys,* (pp. 2-16).

Huhns, M. N., & Buell, D. A. (2002). Trusted autonomy. *IEEE Internet Computing,* (pp. 92-95).

IBM Corporation (2003). *Web Services Level Agreements*. June 1, 2006, from http://www.research.ibm.com/wsla/WSLASpecV1-20030128.pdf

IBM, BEA Systems, Microsoft, Layer 7 Technologies, Oblix, VeriSign, Actional, Computer Associates, OpenNetwork Technologies, Ping Identity, Reactivity and RSA Security, (2004). *Web Services Trust Language*. June 1, 2006, from http://www-128.ibm.com/developerworks/webservices/library /specification/ws-trust/

Jaeger, M. C. et al. (2005). QoS Aggregation in Web Service Compositions. *Proc. of IEEE EEE05,* (pp. 181-185).

Kavantzas, N. et al. (2004). *Web Services Choreography Description Language Version 1.0*. June 1, 2006, from http://www.w3.org/TR/2004/WD-ws-cdl-10-20041217/

Keller, A., & Ludwig, H. (2003). The WSLA Framework: Specifying and Monitoring Service Level Agreements for Web Services. *Plenum Publishing, Journal of Network and Systems Management, 11*(1), 57-81.

Mani, A. and Nagarajan, A. (2002). *Understanding Quality of Service for Web Services*. June 1, 2006, from http://www-106.ibm.com/developerworks/webservices/library/ws-quality.html

Maximilien, E. M., & Singh, M. P. (2002). Conceptual Model of Web Service Reputation. *SIGMOD Record, 31*(4), 36–41.

Maximilien, E. M., & Singh, M. P. (2004). A Framework and Ontology for Dynamic Web Services Selection. *IEEE Internet Computing, 8*(5), 84–93.

Mendenhall, W., & Beaver, R. J. (1999). Introduction to Probability and Statistics. *Duxbury Press,* (pp. 442-446).

Mitchell, T. (1997). Machine Learning. *WCB McGraw-Hill,* (pp. 128-141).

Mitra, N. (2003). *SOAP Version 1.2 Part 0: Primer*. June 1, 2006, from http://www.w3.org/TR/2003/REC-soap12-part0-20030624/.

Murata, T. (1989). Petri Nets: Properties, Analysis and Applications. *Proceedings of the IEEE, 77*(4), 541-580.

Narayanan, S., & McIlraith, S. A. (2002). Simulation, Verification and Automated Composition of Web Services. *Proceedings ACM WWW 2002,* (pp. 77-88).

Pezzini, M. (2003). Composite Applications Head Toward the Mainstream. *Gartner Group*, ID Number AV-21-1772.

Shadbolt, N. (2002). A Matter of Trust. *IEEE Intelligent Systems,* (pp. 2-3).

Singh, M. P. (2002). Trustworthy Service Composition: Challenges and Research Questions. *Proceedings of the Autonomous Agents and Multi-Agent Systems Workshop on Deception, Fraud and Trust in Agent Societies,* (pp. 39-52).

The OWL Services Coalition. (2006). *OWL-S: Semantic Markup for Web Service Version 1.0.* June 1, 2006, from http://www.daml.org/services/owl-s/1.0/owl-s.html.

Tosic, V. et al. (2003). Management Applications of the Web Service Offerings Language (WSOL). *Springer-Verlag, Proc. of CAiSE03,* (pp. 468-484).

Tosic, V., & Pagurek, B. (2005). On Comprehensive Contractual Descriptions of Web Services. *Proc. of IEEE EEE05,* (pp. 444-449).

Triple A. (2006) June 1, 2006, from http://www.infoworld.com/articles/hn/xml/02/08/12/020812hntriplea.html?0814wewebservices

TRUST. (2005). *Team for Research in Ubiquitous Secure Technology (TRUST).* June 1, 2006, from http://trust.eecs.berkeley.edu/.

Trusted Computing Group. (2005). *Trusted Computing Group.* June 1, 2006, from https://www.trustedcomputinggroup.org/.

Wang, G. et al. (2004). Integrated Quality of Service (QoS) Management in Service-Oriented Enterprise Architectures. *Proc. of IEEE EDOC04,* (pp. 21-32).

Yolum, P., & Singh, M. P. (2002). An Agent-Based Approach for Trustworthy Service Location. *Proceedings of 1st International Workshop on Agents and Peer-to-Peer Computing (AP2PC),* (pp. 45-56).

Zhang, J. et al. (2004). An Approach to Help Select Trustworthy Web Services. *Proc. of IEEE CEC-East,* (pp. 84–91).

Chapter XVII
Administering the Semantic Web:
Confidentiality, Privacy and Trust Management

Bhavani Thuraisingham
University of Texas at Dallas, USA

Natasha Tsybulnik
University of Texas at Dallas, USA

Ashraful Alam
University of Texas at Dallas, USA

ABSTRACT

The Semantic Web is essentially a collection of technologies to support machine understandable Web pages as well as Information Interoperability. There has been much progress made on the Semantic Web including standards for eXtensible Markup Language, Resource Description Framework and Onotlogies. However, administration policies and techniques for enforcing them have received little attention. These policies include policies for security, privacy, data quality, integrity, trust and timely information processing. This chapter discusses administration policies for the Semantic Web as well as techniques for enforcing them. In particular, the authors will discuss an approach for ensuring confidentiality, privacy and trust for the Semantic Web. We will also discuss the inference and privacy problems within the context of administration policies.

INTRODUCTION

A semantic web can be thought of as a web that is highly intelligent and sophisticated so that one needs little or no human intervention to carry out tasks such as scheduling appointments, coordinating activities, searching for complex documents as well as integrating disparate databases and information systems (Lee, 2001). Recently there have been many developments on the semantic web (see for example, (Thuraisingham 2002). The World Wide Web consortium (W3C) is specifying standards for the semantic web. These standards include specifications for XML (eXtensible Markup Language), RDF (Resource Description Framework), and Ontologies.

While much progress has been made toward developing such an intelligent web, there is still a lot to be done in terms of security, privacy, data quality, integrity and trust management. It is critical that the semantic web be secure and trustworthy. That is, the components that constitute the semantic web have to be secure. The components include XML, RDF and Ontologies. In addition, we need secure information integration. We also need to examine trust issues for the semantic web. Essentially what we need is a set of administration policies as well as techniques for enforcing these policies for the semantic web.

This paper focuses on administration issues for the semantic web with emphasis on confidentiality, privacy and trust management. In the case of security policies, which we will also call confidentiality policies, we will discuss XML security, RDF security, and secure information integration. We also discuss privacy for the semantic web. Trust management issues include the extent to which we can trust the users and the web sites to enforce security and privacy policies.

The organization of this paper is as follows. Our definitions of confidentiality, privacy and trust as well as the current status on administering the semantic web will be discussed first. This will be followed by a discussion of our proposed framework for securing the semantic web which we call CPT (Confidentiality, Privacy and Trust). Next we will take each of the features Confidentiality, Privacy and Trust and discuss various aspects as they relate to the semantic web. An integrated architecture for CPT as well as inference and privacy control will also be discussed. Finally the paper is summarized and future directions are given.

TRUST, PRIVACY, AND CONFIDENTIALITY

In this section we will discuss issues on confidentiality, privacy and trust.

Definitions

Confidentiality, privacy, trust, integrity, and availability will be briefly defined with an examination of how these issues specifically relate to the trust management and inference problem. Confidentiality is preventing the release of unauthorized information. Privacy is a subset of confidentiality in that it is the prevention of unauthorized information from being released in regards to an individual. Integrity of data is the prevention of any modifications made by an unauthorized entity. Availability is the prevention of unauthorized omission of data. Trust is a measure of confidence in data correctness and legitimacy from a particular source.

Integrity, availability, and trust are all very closely related in the sense that data quality is of particular importance and all require individuals or entities processing and sending information to not alter the data in an unauthorized manner. If all of these issues, confidentiality, privacy, trust, integrity, and availability, are guaranteed, a system can be considered secure. Thus if the inference problem can be solved such that unauthorized information is not released, the rules of confidentiality, privacy, and trust will not be broken. A technique such as inference can either be used to aid or impair the cause of integrity, availability, and trust. If correctly used, inference can be used to infer trust management policies. Thus inference can be used for good or bad purposes. The intention is to prevent inferred unauthorized conclusions and to use inference to apply trust management.

Current Successes and Potential Failures

W3C is proposing encryption techniques for securing XML documents. Furthermore, logic, proof and trust belong to one of the layers of the semantic web. However, by trust in that context is meant whether the semantic web can trust the statements such as data and rules. In our definition, by trust we mean to what extent we can believe that the user and the web site will enforce the confidentiality and privacy policies as specified. Privacy has been discussed by the semantic web community. The main contribution of this community is developing the Platform for Privacy Preferences (P3P).

P3P requires the web developer of the server to create a privacy policy, validate it, and then place it in a specific location on the server as well as write a privacy policy in English. When the user enters the website, the browser will discover the privacy policy and if the privacy policy matches the user's browser security specifications, then the user can simply enter the site. If the policy does not match the user's specifications then the user will be informed of the site's intentions and the user can then choose to enter or leave.

While this is a great start, it is lacking in certain areas. One concern is the fact that the privacy policy must be placed in a specific location. If a website, for example a student website on a school's server, is to implement P3P and can not place it in a folder directly from the school's server, then the user's browser will not find the privacy policy.

Another problem with P3P is that it requires the data collector on the server side to follow exactly what is promised in the privacy policy. If the data collections services on the server side decide to abuse the policy and instead do other things not

stated in the agreement, then no real consequences occur. The server's privacy policy can simply choose to state that it will correct the problem upon discovery, but if the user never knows it until the data is shared publicly, correcting it to show the data is private will not simply solve the problem. Accountability should be addressed, where it is not the server's decision but rather lawmaker's decisions. When someone breaks a law or doesn't abide by contractual agreements, we do not turn to the accused and ask what punishment they deem necessary. Instead we look to the law and apply each law when applicable.

Another point of contention is trust and inference. Before beginning any discussions of privacy, a user and a server must evaluate how much the other party can be trusted. If neither party trusts each other how can either party expect the other to follow a privacy policy? Currently P3P only uses tags to define actions; it uses no web rules for inference or specific negotiations regarding confidentiality and privacy. With inference a user can decide if certain information should not be given because it would allow the distrusted server to infer information that the user would prefer to remain private or sensitive.

Motivation for a Framework

While P3P is a great initiative to approaching the privacy problem for users of the semantic web, it becomes obvious from the above discussion, that more work must be continued on this process. Furthermore, we need to integrate confidentiality and privacy within the context of trust management.

A new approach, to be discussed later, must be used to address these issues, such that the user can establish trust, preserve privacy and anonymity, and ensure confidentiality. Once the server and client have negotiated trust, the user can begin to decide what data can be submitted that will not violate his/her privacy. These security policies, one for each trust, privacy, and confidentiality, are described with web rules. Describing policies with web rules can allow an inference engine to determine what is in either the client or server's best interest and help advise each party accordingly. Also with web rules in place, a user and server can begin to negotiate confidentiality. Thus if a user does not agree with a server's privacy policies but would still like to use some services, a user may begin negotiating confidentiality with the server to determine if the user can still use some services but not all (depending on the final conclusion of the agreement). The goal of this new approach is to simulate real world negotiations, thus giving semantics to the current web and providing much needed security.

CPT FRAMEWORK

In this section we will discuss a framework for enforcing Confidentiality, Privacy and Trust (CPT) for the semantic web. We first discuss the basic framework where rules are enforced to ensure confidentiality, privacy and trust. In the advanced framework, we include inference controllers that will reason about the application and determine whether confidentiality, privacy and trust violations have occurred.

The Role of the Server

In the previous section, focus was placed on the client's needs; now we will discuss the server's needs in this process. The first obvious need is that the server must be able to evaluate the client in order to grant specific resources. Therefore the primary goal is to establish trust regarding the client's identity and based on this identity grant various permissions to specific data. Not only must the server be able to evaluate the client, but also be able to evaluate its own ability to grant permission with standards and metrics. The server also needs to be able to grant or deny a request appropriately without giving away classified information or instead of giving away classified information, the server may desire to give a cover story. Either of the scenarios, a cover story or protecting classified resources, must be completed within the guidelines of a stated privacy policy in order to guarantee a client's confidentiality. One other key aspect is that all of these events must occur in a timely manner such that security is not compromised.

CPT Process

Now that the client's and server's needs have been discussed, focus will be placed on the actual process of our system CPT. First a general overview of the process will be presented. After the reader has garnered a simple overview, this paper will continue to discuss two systems, Advanced CPT and Basic CPT, based on the general process previously discussed. The general process of CPT is to first establish a relationship of trust and then negotiate privacy and confidentiality policies. Figure 1 shows the general process.

Notice that both parties partake in establishing trust. The client must determine the degree to which it can trust the server in order to decide how much trust to place in the resources supplied by the server and also to negotiate privacy policies. The server must determine the degree to which it can trust the client in order to determine what privileges and resources it can allow the client to access as well as how to present the data. The server and client will base their decisions of trust on credentials of each other. Once trust is established, the client and server must come to an agreement of privacy policies to be applied to the data that the client provides the server. Privacy must follow trust because the degree to which the client trusts the server will affect the privacy degree. The privacy degree affects what data the client chooses to send. Once the client is comfortable with the privacy policies negotiated, the client will then begin requesting data. Based on the initial trust agreement, the server will determine what and when the client views these resources. The client will make decisions regarding confidentiality and what data can be given to the user based on its own confidential-

Figure 1. Basic framework for CPT

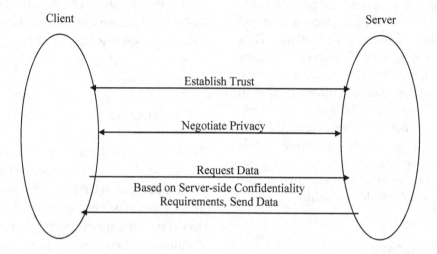

ity requirements and confidentiality degree. It is also important to note that the server and client must make these decisions and then configure the system to act upon these decisions. The Basic CPT system will not advise the client or server in any way regarding outcomes of any decisions. Figure 2 illustrates the communication between the different components.

Advanced CPT

The previous section discussed the Basic CPT system; the Advanced CPT system is an extension of the Basic system. The Advanced CPT system is outlined in Figure 3, which incorporates three new entities not found in the Basic system. These three new entities are the Trust Inference Engine (TIE), the Privacy Inference Engine (PIE), and the Confidentiality Inference Engine (CIE).

The first step of sending credentials and establishing trust is the same as the Basic system except that both parties consult with their own TIE. Once each party makes a decision, the client receives the privacy policies from the server and then uses these policies in configuration with PIE to agree, disagree, or negotiate. Once the client and server have come to an agreement about the client's privacy, the client will send a request for various resources. Based on the degree of trust

that the server has assigned to a particular client, the server will determine what resources it can give to the client. However, in this step the server will consult the CIE to determine what data is preferable to give to the client and what data, if given, could have disastrous consequences. Once the server has made a conclusion regarding data the client can receive, it can then begin transmitting data over the network.

Trust, Privacy, and Confidentiality Inference Engines

In regards to trust, the server must realize that if it chooses to assign a certain percentage of trust then this implies the client will have access to the specific privileged resources and can possibly infer other data from granted permissions. Thus, the primary responsibility of the trust inference engine is to determine what information can be inferred and is this behavior acceptable. Likewise, the client must realize the percentage of trust it assigns to the server will affect permissions of viewing the site as well as affecting how data given to the client will be processed. The inference engine in the client's scenario will guide the client regarding what can or will occur based on the trust assignment given to the server.

Figure 2. Communication between the components for basic CPT

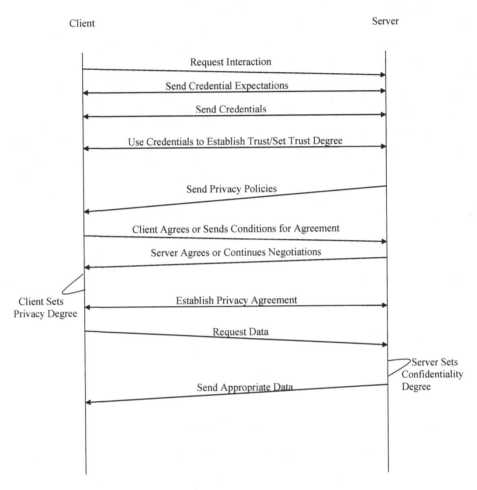

Once trust is established, the privacy inference engine will continue the inference process. It is important to note that the privacy inference engine only resides on the client side. The server will have its own privacy policies but these policies may not be acceptable to the client. It is impossible for the server to evaluate each client and determine how to implement an individual privacy policy without first consulting the client. Thus the privacy inference engine is unnecessary on the server's side.

The privacy inference engine must guide the client in negotiating privacy policies. In order to guide the client through negotiations, the inference engine must be able to determine how the server will use data the client gives it as well as who else will have access to the submitted data. Once this is determined, the inference engine

must evaluate the data given by the client to the server. If the inference engine determines that this data can be used to infer other data that the client would prefer to remain private, the inference engine must warn the client and then allow the client to choose the next appropriate measure of either sending or not sending the data.

Once the client and server have agreed on the privacy policies to be implemented, the client will naturally begin requesting data and the server will have to determine what data to send based on confidentiality requirements. It is important to note that the confidentiality inference engine is located only on the server side. The client has already negotiated its personal privacy issues and is ready to view the data thus leaving the server to decide what the next appropriate action is. The confidentiality inference engine must first determine what data will be currently available to the client, based on the current trust assignment. Once the inference engine has determined this, the inference engine must explore what policies or data can be potentially inferred if the data is given to the client. The primary objective of the confidentiality inference engine is to ponder how the client might be able to use the information given to it and then guide the server through the process of deciding a client's access to resources.

CONFIDENTIALITY FOR THE SEMANTIC WEB

This section will detail various aspects of confidentiality for the semantic web.

Layered Architecture

By confidentiality we mean secrecy which is what we also usually refer to as security, although in reality security may include integrity as well as trust. In this section by security issues we essentially mean confidentiality issues. In particular we provide an overview of security issues for the semantic web with special emphasis on XML security, RDF security and secure information integration. Note that according to the vision of Tim Berners Lee, logic, proof and trust are at the highest layers of the semantic web. That is, how can we trust the information that the web site gives us? Trusting the information that the web site gives us is essentially about trusting the quality of the information. We will not discuss that

Figure 3. Communication between components for advanced CPT

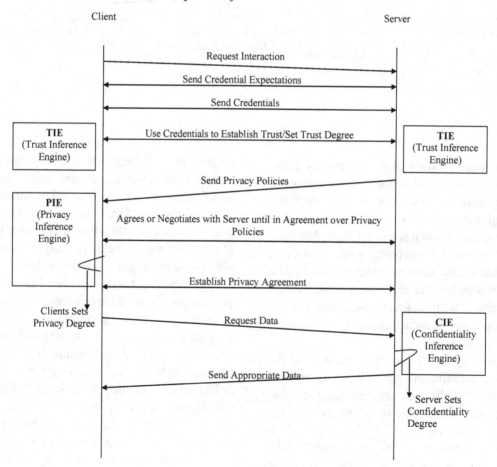

aspect of trust further in this paper. Instead, we will discuss trust from the viewpoint of trusting the web site or the user/ client.

Security cannot be considered in isolation. That is, there is no one layer that should focus on security. Security cuts across all layers and this is a challenge. That is, we need security for each of the layers and we must also ensure secure interoperability as illustrated in Figure 4. For example, consider the lowest layer. One needs secure TCP/IP, secure sockets, and secure HTTP. There are now security protocols for these various lower layer protocols. One needs end-to-end security. That is, one cannot just have secure TCP/IP built on untrusted communication layers. That is, we need network security. Next layer is XML and XML schemas. One needs secure XML. That is, access must be controlled to various portions of the document for reading, browsing and modifications. There is research on securing XML and XML schemas. The next step is securing RDF. Now with RDF not only do we need secure XML, we also need security for the interpretations and semantics. For example, under certain contexts, portions of the document may be Unclassified while under certain other contexts the document may be Classified. As an example, one could declassify an RDF document, once the war is over. Much work has been carried out on security constraint processing for relational databases. One needs to determine whether these

results could be applied for the semantic web (Thuraisingham, 1993).

Once XML and RDF have been secured, the next step is to examine security for ontologies. That is, ontologies may have security levels attached to them. Certain parts of the ontologies could be Secret while certain other parts may be Unclassified. The challenge is how does one use these ontologies for secure information integration? Researchers have done some work on the secure interoperability of databases. We need to revisit this research and then determine what else needs to be done so that the information on the web can be managed, integrated and exchanged securely.

We also need to examine the inference problem for the semantic web. Inference is the process of posing queries and deducing new information. It becomes a problem when the deduced information is something the user is unauthorized to know. With the semantic web, and especially with data mining tools, one can make all kinds of inferences. Recently there has been some research on controlling unauthorized inferences on the semantic web (Stoica, 2004)

Security should not be an afterthought. We have often heard that one needs to insert security into the system right from the beginning. Similarly security cannot be an afterthought for the semantic web technologies. Note also that XML, RDF and Ontologies may be used to specify the security policies also. Therefore, not only do we need to secure XML, RDF and Ontology documents, but these languages can also be used to specify policies (Thuraisingham, 2006). In the remaining subsections we will discuss security for the different layers of the semantic web.

XML Security

Various research efforts have been reported on XML security (Bertino, 2002). We briefly discuss some of the key points. XML documents have graph structures. The main challenge is whether to give access to entire XML documents or parts of the documents. Bertino et al have developed

Figure 4. Layers for the secure Semantic Web

Logic, Proof and Trust with respect
Security for Rules/Query
Security for RDF, Ontologies
Security for XML, XML Schemas
Security for the Protocols

authorization models for XML. They have focused on access control policies as well as on dissemination policies. They also considered push and pull architectures. They specified the policies in XML. The policy specification contains information about which users can access which portions of the documents. In (Bertino, 2002) algorithms for access control as well as computing views of the results are presented. In addition, architectures for securing XML documents are also discussed. In (Bertino, 2004) the authors go further and describe how XML documents may be published on the web. The idea is for owners to publish documents, subjects to request access to the documents and untrusted publishers to give the subjects the views of the documents they are authorized to see.

W3C (World Wide Web Consortium) is specifying standards for XML security. The XML security project (see XML Security) is focusing on providing the implementation of security standards for XML. The focus is on XML-Signature Syntax and Processing, XML-Encryption Syntax and Processing and XML Key Management. W3C also has a number of working groups including XML Signature working group (see XML Signature) and XML encryption working group (see XML Encryption). While the standards are focusing on what can be implemented in the near-term, the work reported in (Bertino, 2002) and (Bertino, 2004) sets the direction for access control and secure publishing of XML documents. Note also that the Bertino and others have also specified confidentiality and privacy policies in XML. In other words not only is there research on securing XML documents, but there is also research in specifying policies in XML (see also, Thuraisingham, 2005a).

RDF Security

RDF is the foundations of the semantic web. While XML is limited in providing machine understandable documents, RDF handles this limitation. As a result, RDF provides better support for interoperability as well as searching and cataloging. It also describes contents of documents as well as relationships between various entities in the document. While XML provides syntax and notations, RDF supplements this by providing semantic information in a standardized way.

The basic RDF model has three types: they are resources, properties and statements. Resource is anything described by RDF expressions. It could be a web page or a collection of pages. Property is a specific attribute used to describe a resource. RDF statements are resources together with a named property plus the value of the property. Statement components are subject, predicate and object. So for example, if we have a sentence of the form "John is the creator of xxx", then xxx is the subject or resource, Property or predicate is "Creator" and object or literal is "John". There are RDF diagrams very much like Entity-Relationship diagrams or object diagrams to represent statements.

There are various aspects specific to RDF syntax and for more details we refer to the various documents on RDF published by W3C. Also, it is very important that the intended interpretation be used for RDF sentences. This is accomplished by RDF schemas (Antoniou, 2004). More advanced concepts in RDF include the container model and statements about statements. The container model has three types of container objects and they are Bag, Sequence, and Alternative. A bag is an unordered list of resources or literals. It is used to mean that a property has multiple values but the order is not important. A sequence is a list of ordered resources. Here the order is important. Alternative is a list of resources that represent alternatives for the value of a property. Various tutorials in RDF describe the syntax of containers in more detail.

RDF also provides support for making statements about other statements. For example, with this facility one can make statements of the form "The statement A is false" where A is the statement "John is the creator of X". Again one can use object-like diagrams to represent containers and statements about statements. RDF also has a formal model associated with it. This formal model has a formal grammar. For further information on RDF we refer to the work of W3C reports (see RDF Primer). As in the case of any language or model, RDF will continue to evolve.

Now to make the semantic web secure, we need to ensure that RDF documents are secure. This would involve securing XML from a syntactic point of view. However with RDF we also need to ensure that security is preserved at the semantic level. The issues include the security implications of the concepts resource, properties and statements. That is, how is access control ensured? How can statements, properties and statements be protected? How can one provide access control at a finer grain of granularity? What are the security properties of the container model? How can bags, lists and alternatives be protected? Can we specify security policies in RDF? How can we resolve semantic inconsistencies for the policies? How can we express security constraints in RDF? What are the security implications of statements about statements? How can we protect RDF schemas? Some initial directions on RDF security are given in (Carminati, 2004). More details are given in (Thuraisingham, 2006).

Secure Information Interoperability

Information is everywhere on the web. Information is essentially data that makes sense. The database community has been working on database integration for several decades. They encountered many challenges including interoperability of heterogeneous data sources. They used schemas to integrate the various databases. Schemas are essentially data describing the data in the databases (see Sheth, 1990).

Now with the web, one needs to integrate the diverse and disparate data sources. The data may not be in databases. It could be in files both structured and unstructured. Data could be in the form of tables or in the form of text, images, audio and video. One needs to come up with technologies to integrate the diverse information sources on the web. Essentially one needs the

semantic web services to integrate the information on the web.

The challenge is how does one integrate the information securely? For example, in (Thuraisingham, 1994) the schema integration work of Sheth and Larson was extended for security policies. That is, different sites have security policies and these policies have to be integrated to provide a policy for the federated database system. One needs to examine these issues for the semantic web. Each node on the web may have its own policy. Is it feasible to have a common policy for a community on the web? Do we need a tight integration of the policies or do we focus on dynamic policy integration?

Ontologies are playing a major role in information integration on the web. How can ontologies play a role in secure information integration? How do we provide access control for ontologies? Do we have ontologies for specifying the security policies? How can we use some of the ideas discussed in (Bertino, 2004) to integrate information securely on the web? That is, what sort of encryption schemes do we need? How do we minimize the trust placed on information integrators on the web? We are investigating issues related to the above questions.

Secure Query and Rules Processing for the Semantic Web

The layer above the Secure RDF layer is the Secure Query and Rules processing layer. While RDF can be used to specify security policies (see for example, Carminati, 2004), the web rules language being developed by W3C is more powerful to specify complex policies. Furthermore, an inference engine is also being proposed to process the rules. One could integrate ideas from the database inference controller that we have developed (Thuraisingham, 1993) with web rules processing to develop an inference or privacy controller for the semantic web.

The query-processing module is responsible for accessing the heterogeneous data and information sources on the semantic web. W3C is examining ways to integrate techniques from web query processing with semantic web technologies to locate, query and integrate the heterogeneous data and information sources.

OUR APPROACH TO CONFIDENTIALITY MANAGEMENT

We utilize two popular semantic web technologies in our prototype called Intellidimension RDF Gateway and Infered (see Intellidimension, the RDF Gateway) and Jena (see JENA). RDF Gateway is a database and integrated web server, utilizing RDF, and built from the group up rather than on top of existing web servers or databases (RDF Primer). It functions as a data repository for RDF data and also as an interface to various data sources, external or internal, that can be queried. Jena is a Java application programming package to create, modify, store, query and perform other processing task on RDF/XML (eXtensible Markup Language) documents from Java programs. RDF documents can be created from the scratch or pre-formatted documents can be read into memory to explore various parts. The node-arc-node feature of RDF is closely resembled in how Jena accesses an RDF document. Through different class objects subjects, properties and objects can be iterated. It also has a built-in query engine designed on top of RDFQL (RDF Query Language) that allows querying documents using standard RDFQL query statements.

Using these technologies we specify the confidentiality policies. The confidentiality engine will then ensure that the policies are enforced correctly. If we assume the basic framework then the confidentiality engine will enforce the policies and will not examine security violations via inference. In the advanced approach, the confidentiality engine will include what we call an inference controller. We utilize a similar approach for ensuring privacy for the semantic web and will be discussed in a later section.

Inference/Confidentiality Controller for the Semantic Web

Inference is the process of forming conclusions from the response obtained to queries. If the conclusions are not authorized then the problem is called the inference problem. Inference controller is the system that ensures that confidentiality violations via inference do not occur. We have designed and developed inference controllers for a database system (Thuraisingham, 1993). In such a system users with different roles access and share a database consisting of data at different security levels. A powerful and dynamic approach to assigning privacy levels to data is one which utilizes security constraints. Security constraints provide an effective and versatile confidentiality policy. They can be used to assign security levels to the data depending on their content and the context in which the data is displayed. They can also be used to dynamically reclassify the data. An architecture for an inference controller for database systems is illustrated in Figure 5.

While much of our previous work focused on security control in relational databases, our recent work is focusing on extending this approach to the semantic web. Figure 6 illustrates an inference controller for the semantic web. The semantic web is augmented by an inference controller that examines the policies specified as ontologies and rules and utilizes the inference engine embedded in the web rules language, reasons about the applications and deduces the security violations via inference. In particular we focus on the design and implementation of an inference controller where the data is represented as RDF documents.

PRIVACY FOR THE SEMANTIC WEB

Privacy is about protecting information about individuals. Furthermore, an individual can specify say to a web service provider the information that

Figure 5. Confidentiality enhanced database management system

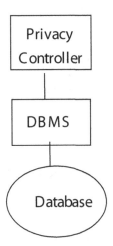

can be released about him or her. Privacy has been discussed a great deal in the past especially when it relates to protecting medical information about patients. Social scientists as well as technologists have been working on privacy issues. However, privacy has received enormous attention during the past year. This is mainly because of the advent of the web, the semantic web, counter-terrorism and national security. For example in order to extract information about various individuals and perhaps prevent and/or detect potential terrorist attacks data mining tools are being examined. We have heard much about national security vs.

privacy in the media. This is mainly due to the fact that people are now realizing that to handle terrorism, the government may need to collect data about individuals and mine the data to extract information. Data may be in relational databases or it may be text, video and images. This is causing a major concern with various civil liberties unions (Thuraisingham, 2003). We have utilized the same semantic web technologies that we used for our work on the inference controller to develop the privacy controller. (i.e., Intellidimension RDF Gateway and Infered and Jena)

From a technology policy of view our privacy controller is identical to the confidentiality controller we have designed and developed (Thuraisingham, 2005b). The privacy controller illustrated in Figure 7 is however implemented at the client side. Before the client gives out information to a web site it will check whether the web site can divulge aggregated information to the third party and subsequently result in privacy violations. For example, the web site may give out medical records without the identity so that the third party can study the patterns of flu or other infectious diseases. Furthermore, at some other time the web site may give out the names. However, if the web site gives out the link between the names and diseases then there could be privacy violations. The inference engine will make such deductions and determine whether the client should give out personal data to the web site.

Figure 6. Inference controller for the Semantic Web

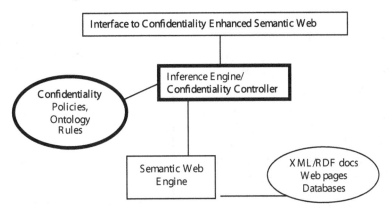

Figure 7. Privacy controller for the Semantic Web

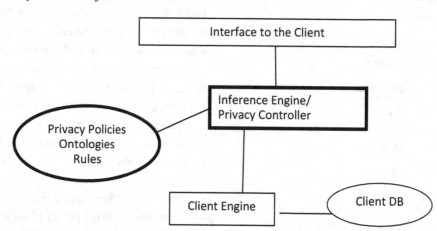

TRUST FOR THE SEMANTIC WEB

Researchers are working on protocols for trust management. Languages for specifying trust management constructs are also being developed. Also there is research on the foundations of trust management. For example, if A trusts B and B trusts C, then can A trust C? How do you share the data and information on the semantic web and still maintain autonomy. How do you propagate trust? For example, if A trusts B say 50% of the time and B trusts C 30% of the time, then what value do you assign for A trusting C? How do you incorporate trust into semantic interoperability? What are the quality of service primitives for trust and negotiation? That is, for certain situations one may need 100% trust while for certain other situations 50% trust may suffice (see also Yu, 2003).

Another topic that is being investigated is trust propagation and propagating privileges. For example, if you grant privileges to A, what privileges can A transfer to B? How can you compose privileges? Is there an algebra and calculus for the composition of privileges? Much research still needs to be done here. One of the layers of the semantic web is Logic, Proof and Trust. Essentially this layer deals with trust management and negotiation between different agents and examining the foundations and developing logics

for trust management. Some interesting work has been carried out by Finin et al. (see Denker, 2003, Finin, 2002, Kagal, 2003]).

For example if given data A and B can someone deduce classified data X (i.e. A + B → X). The inference engines will also use an inverse inference module to determine if classified information can be inferred if a user employs inverse resolution techniques. For example if given data A and the user wants to guarantee that data X remains classified, the user can determine that B, which combined with A implies X, must remain classified as well (i.e. A + ? → X; the question mark results with B). Once the expert system has received the results from the inference engines, it can conclude a recommendation and then pass this recommendation to the client or server who will have the option to either accept or reject the suggestion.

Figure 8. Trust probabilities

```
      Trust degree = 59%
          90 Policy1
          75 Policy2
          70 Policy3
          60 Policy4
          50 Policy5
          35 Policy6
          10 Policy7
           0 Policy8
```

Figure 9. Example policies

```
Policy1: if A then B else C
Policy2: not A or B
Policy3: A or C
Policy4: A or C or D or not E
Policy5: not (A or C)
```

In order to establish trust, privacy, and confidentiality, it is necessary to have an intelligent system that can evaluate the user's preferences. The system will be designed as an expert system to store trust, privacy, and confidentiality policies. These policies can be written using a web rules language with foundations of First Order Logic. Traditional theorem provers can then be applied to the rules to check for inconsistencies and alert the user (Antoniou, 2004). Once the user approves of all the policies, the system can take action and properly apply these policies during any transaction occurring on a site. Also the user can place percentages next to the policies in order to apply probabilistic scenarios. Figure 9 gives an example of a probabilistic scenario occurring with a trust policy.

In Figure 8, the user set the trust degree to 59%. Because the user trusts another person 59%, only policies 5-8 will be applied. Figure 9 shows some example policies. These example policies will be converted into a web rules language, such as the Semantics Web Rules Language (See SWRL) and enforced by the Trust engine. Figure 10 illustrates an integrated architecture for ensuring confidentiality, privacy and trust for the semantic web. The web server as well as the client have trust management modules. The web server has a confidentiality engine whereas client has a privacy engine. We are currently designing and developing such an Integrated CPT System with XML, RDF and Web Rules Technologies. Some details of the modules are illustrated in Figure 10.

In Figure 11, ontologies, CPT policies, and credentials are given to the expert system such that the expert system can advise the client or server who should receive access to what particular resource and how these resources should further be regulated. The expert system will send the policies to the WCOP (web rules, credentials, ontologies, and policies) parser to check for syntax errors and validate the inputs. The information contained within the dashed box is a part of the system that is only included in the Advanced

Figure 10. Integrated architecture for confidentiality, privacy and trust

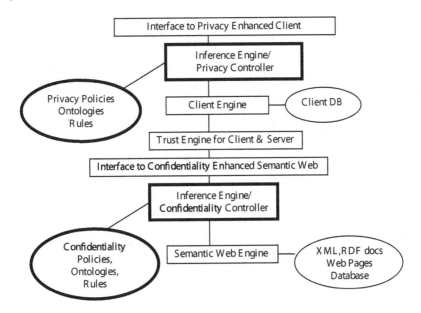

Figure 11. Modules of CPT controller

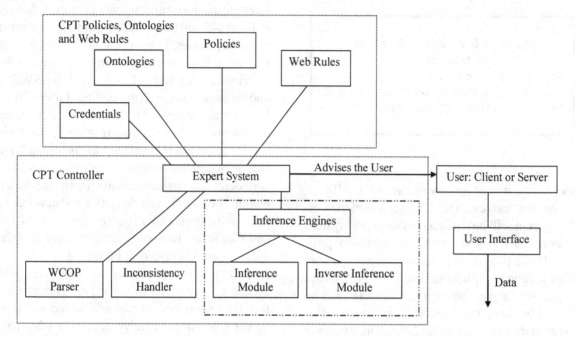

TP&C system. The inference engines (e.g., TIE, PIE, and CIE) will use an inference module to determine if classified information can be inferred based on the given

SUMMARY AND DIRECTIONS

This paper has provided an overview of administration issues for the semantic web. We first discussed a framework for enforcing confidentiality, privacy and trust for the semantic web. Then we discussed security issues for the semantic web. We argued that security must cut across all the layers.

Next we provided more details on XML security, RDF security, secure information integration and trust. If the semantic web is to be secure we need all of its components to be secure. We also described our approach to confidentiality and inference control. Next we discussed privacy for the semantic web. Finally, we discussed trust management as well as an integrated framework for CPT.

There are many directions for further work. We need to continue with the research on confidentiality, privacy as well as trust for the semantic web. Then we need to develop the integrated framework for CPT. Finally we need to formalize the notions of CPT and build a security model.

Standards play an important role in the development of the semantic web. W3C has been very effective in specifying standards for XML, RDF and the semantic web. We need to continue with the developments and try as much as possible to transfer the research to the standards effort as well as incorporate security into these efforts. We also need to transfer the research and standards to commercial products.

REFERENCES

Antoniou, G., & Harmelen, F. V. (2004). *A Semantic Web Primer*. MIT press.

Bertino, E., et al. (2002). *Access Control for XML Documents, Data and Knowledge Engineering, 43*(3).

Bertino, E. et al. (2004). Secure Third Party Publication of XML Documents. To appear in *IEEE Transactions on Knowledge and Data Engineering.*

Carminati, B., et al. (2004). Security for RDF. *Proceedings of the DEXA Conference Workshop on Web Semantics*, Zaragoza, Spain.

Berners Lee, T., et al. (2001, May). *The Semantic Web.* Scientific American.

Denker, G., et al. (2003). Security for DAML Web Services: Annotation and Matchmaking. *International Semantic Web Conference.*

Finin, T., & Joshi, A. (2002). Agents, Trust, and Information Access on the Semantic Web, *ACM SIGMOD.*

Kagal, L., Finin, T., & Joshi, A. (2003) A Policy Based Approach to Security for the Semantic Web. *International Semantic Web Conference.*

Intellidimension, the RDF Gateway. http://www. intellidimension.com/

JENA. http://jena.sourceforge.net/.

RDF Primer. http://www.w3.org/TR/rdf-primer/

Sheth, A., & Larson, J. (1990). Federated Database Systems. *ACM Computing Surveys, 22*(3).

Stoica, A., & Farkas, C. (2004). Ontology Guided XML Security Engine. *Journal of Intelligent Information Systems, 3*(23).

SWRL: Semantic Web Rules Language. (2004). http://www.w3.org/Submission/SWRL/

Thuraisingham, B., et al. (1993). Design and Implementation of a Database Inference Controller. *Data and Knowledge Engineering Journal, 11*(3).

Thuraisingham, B. (1994). Security Issues for Federated Database Systems, *Computers and Security, 13*(6).

Thuraisingham, B. (2002). *XML, Databases and the Semantic Web.* CRC Press, FL.

Thuraisingham, B. (2003). *Data Mining, National Security and Privacy.* ACM SIGKDD.

Thuraisingham, B. (2005a). *Standards for the Semantic Web, Computer Standards and Interface Journal.*

Thuraisingham, B. (2005b). Privacy Constraint Processing in a Privacy Enhanced Database System. *Data and Knowledge Engineering Journal.*

Thuraisingham, B. (2006). *Building Trustworthy Semantic Webs.* CRC Press, To appear.

World Wide Web Consortium(W3C): www.w3c.org

XML Security. http://xml.apache.org/security/

XML Signature. http://www.w3.org/Signature/

XML Encryption. http://www.w3.org/Encryption/2001/

Yu, T., & Winslett, M. (2003). A Unified Scheme for Resource Protection in Automated Trust Negotiation. *IEEE Symposium on Security and Privacy*, Oakland, CA.

Chapter XVIII
An Ontology of Information Security

Almut Herzog
Linköpings Universitet, Sweden

Nahid Shahmehri
Linköpings Universitet, Sweden

Claudiu Duma
Linköpings Universitet, Sweden

ABSTRACT

The authors present a publicly available, OWL-based ontology of information security which models assets, threats, vulnerabilities and countermeasures and their relations. The ontology can be used as a general vocabulary, roadmap and extensible dictionary of the domain of information security. With its help, users can agree on a common language and definition of terms and relationships. In addition to browsing for information, the ontology is also useful for reasoning about relationships between its entities, that is, threats and countermeasures. The ontology helps answer questions like: Which countermeasures detect or prevent the violation of integrity of data? Which assets are protected by SSH? Which countermeasures thwart buffer overflow attacks? At the moment, the ontology comprises 88 threat classes, 79 asset classes, 133 countermeasure classes and 34 relations between those classes. The authors provide means for extending the ontology, and provide examples of the extendibility with the countermeasure classes "memory protection" and "source code analysis". This chapter describes the content of the ontology as well as its usages, potential for extension, technical implementation and tools for working with it.

INTRODUCTION

Agreeing on the meaning of concepts and their relations is useful in all domains because the consequences of a misunderstanding can be time-consuming and costly. In the domain of information security many concepts are vaguely defined, even for security professionals. Is a password "a unique character string held by each user, a copy of which is stored within the system" (Oxford University Press, 2004) or "an example of an authentication mechanism based on what people know" (Bishop, 2003, p. 310)?

Such ambiguities could be mitigated by a common repository of domain knowledge for the security domain. In this article, we present such a repository by means of an ontology. An ontology "defines the basic terms and relations comprising the vocabulary of a topic area, as well as the rules for combining terms and relations to define extensions to the vocabulary" (Neches et al., 1991).

The need for an ontology of information security has also been clearly verbalised by Donner (2003):

"What the field needs is an ontology—a set of descriptions of the most important concepts and the relationship among them. ... Maybe we [the community of security professionals] can set the example by building our ontology in a machine-usable form in using XML and developing it collaboratively."

Previous work, such as Schumacher (2003); Kim et al. (2005); Jutla and Bodorik (2005); Squicciarini et al. (2006); Nejdl et al. (2005); Undercoffer et al. (2004); Tsoumas et al. (2005); Takahashi et al. (2005), has only partly addressed these needs, and, so far, an ontology of information security that provides general and specific concepts, is machine-usable, and can be developed collaboratively is still missing.

In this article we present an ontology that (1) provides a general overview over the domain of information security, (2) contains detailed domain vocabulary and is thus capable of answering queries about specific, technical security problems and solutions, and (3) supports machine reasoning.

As a step towards an ontology that is collaboratively developed and acceptable by the security and ontology community, we have designed our ontology according to established ontology design principles (Gruber, 1995) and best practices (obofoundry.org1) and make our ontology available online. Consequently, users can browse the ontology online. They can extend it either by downloading and modifying it or by importing the ontology from the web and extending it with new concepts.

Our security ontology builds upon the classic components of risk analysis (Whitman and Mattord, 2005, p. 110ff.): assets, threats, vulnerabilities and countermeasures. By modelling these four basic building blocks of information security and their relations, and refining each block with technical concepts, we arrive at an ontology that provides the "big picture" of the domain of information security as well as a classification and definition of specific domain vocabulary.

Our ontology provides natural language definitions for general terms such as 'asset', as well as domain-specific, technical terms, such as 'SSH'. By implementing high-level relations for specific, technical concepts, one can also find answers to questions such as "What and how does SSH protect?". Other examples of questions that our ontology helps answer are: Which threats threaten user authentication? Which countermeasures protect the confidentiality of data? Which vulnerabilities enable a buffer overflow attack? Which countermeasures protect against buffer overflow attacks? Which countermeasures use encryption?

Users may find our ontology useful (1) as a reference book or hyper-text learning material on information security, (2) as a template for classifying and comparing security products, security attacks or security vulnerabilities, (3) as a framework for plugging in new or existing detailed security taxonomies, and (4) as a knowledge base for reasoning with semantic web applications.

We have implemented our ontology in OWL (Web Ontology Language) (Bechhofer et al., 2004), a markup language based on RDF/XML (Resource Description Framework/Extensible Markup Language) (Powers, 2003), specifically devised for creating extensible ontologies for the semantic web. Thus, our ontology uses a commonly accepted notation for describing ontologies, and supports querying and acquisition of new knowledge through inference and rule-based reasoning using OWL reasoners and OWL query languages.

The remainder of the article is structured as follows. An overview of our ontology is given in the following section. Then we present refinements of the core concepts. After that we provide examples that demonstrate the power of inference and querying. We also describe useful tools for creating and working with ontologies. Towards the end we presents related work, critically discuss our ontology, address future work and conclude the article. An appendix explains the concepts of OWL, needed for understanding ontology details in earlier sections.

ONTOLOGY OVERVIEW

An ontology may be domain-oriented and address a very specific part of a domain; it may be task-oriented so that it achieves a specific task or it may be generic with a focus on high-level concepts (Stevens et al., 2000). An ontology may be used as an application-neutral knowledge base, as a basis for software development, as common information access for humans and applications and as support for information search (Stevens et al., 2000; Lambrix, 2004). An ontology can range in complexity from a controlled vocabulary that consists of a flat list of concepts to logic-based knowledge bases that contain concepts, instances, relations and axioms and provide reasoning services (Lambrix et al., 2007).

The ontology that we have created is a generic knowledge base with reasoning services, mainly intended as a source for common information access, containing key concepts, instances, relations and axioms from the domain of information security.

Our security ontology builds upon the classic components of risk analysis—assets, threats, vulnerabilities, countermeasures—and their relations to each other. These components are core concepts in our ontology and, together with their relations, provide an overview of the domain of information security. While the concepts are taken from literature, e.g. Whitman and Mattord (2005), relations between the concepts are only mentioned implicitly in the literature. It is our contribution to state them explicitly.

Figure 1 presents a simplified overview of our security ontology using an adapted notation of extended entity-relation (EER) diagrams (Chen, 1976). In the text, relations, core and non-core concepts are denoted in *italics*, at least upon their first occurrence, and appear with the same name in figure 1. Refinements are denoted with 'single quotes'.

An *asset* is connected to the concept *vulnerability* through its *has vulnerability*-relation. An asset is *threatened* by *threats* that also denote which *security goal* they threaten. An asset is *protected* by *countermeasures*; a countermeasure is also an asset. A *countermeasure protects* a *security goal* and an asset with a *defence strategy*. For example: The countermeasure 'backup' *protects* the integrity and availability (security goals) of the asset 'data' through recovery (defence strategy). Instances of the concept *defence strategy* are prevention, detection, recovery, correction, deterrence and deflection. Instances of the concept *security goal* are confidentiality, integrity, availability, authentication, accountability, anonymity, authenticity, authorisation, correctness, identification, non-repudiation, policy compliance, privacy, secrecy and trust. Security goals may be related. For example privacy *has the related goals* confidentiality, anonymity and secrecy.

In addition to its *protects*-relation, a countermeasure can make use of additional countermeasures. For example: The countermeasure 'SSL' *uses* 'symmetric encryption' and 'public-key encryption' (two countermeasure subconcepts). A countermeasure can also support other countermeasures. 'Key management' (a countermeasure) *supports*, for example, 'encryption' (a countermeasure).

A *threat* (e.g. 'eavesdropping') *threatens* a security goal (e.g. confidentiality) and an asset (e.g. 'network packet'). The countermeasure against a threat is found by matching assets and security goals of the *threatens*- and *protects*relation. For example: 'Eavesdropping' *threatens* the confidentiality of 'data in transit'; 'VPN' (virtual private network), 'SSH' (secure shell), 'SSL' (secure socket layer) etc. *protect* the confidentiality of 'data in transit'. A threat is *enabled by* one or more *vulnerabilities*.

The core ontology gives an overview of the general concepts and their relations in information security. However, to answer specific questions such as "What is SSH?" and "What and how does SSH protect?", the ontology must also be populated with specific concepts that refine the core concepts and implement the core relations. A few core refinements are shown in figure 1; they are further described and illustrated in the following section.

To answer questions such as "Which are the products that contain SSH?" or "For which operating systems is SSH available?" we also need to model concepts such as *product* and *operating system*. These concepts are not central to information security and should therefore be imported from external ontologies. In the ontology overview of Figure 1, we denote these concepts as non-core.

The non-core concepts that we have identified, and which are shown in figure 1, are useful for comparing security products and countermeasures. For example, the *product* concept denotes which countermeasure is contained in which product, e.g. 'access control' *is contained in* 'Microsoft Word'. The product concept could be further refined by an external taxonomy of software, hardware and system products; the *contained in*-relation, however, must be populated by the person that plugs in the product taxonomy. A product *consists of* one or more technological assets. For example, a 'database management system' *consists of* 'database files', 'executable program files' and 'configuration files'. Other non-core concepts can be added to the ontology depending on the queries that have to be supported by the ontology.

REFINEMENT OF THE CORE ONTOLOGY

The refinements or subconcepts for countermeasures, assets, threats and vulnerabilities consist of specific, technical domain vocabulary and are described in the following subsections. The vocabulary was collected from literature and from security taxonomies (cf. Related Work). The actual ontologies are accessible with browsable documentation and as OWL files from http://www.ida.liu.se/~iislab/projects/secont.

Our ontology is implemented in OWL, therefore, in this section, we use some OWL terminology to talk about the ontology. In OWL, concepts are implemented as classes, relations are implemented as properties and axioms are implemented with restrictions. An introduction to OWL is given in the appendix.

Countermeasures

In the asserted ontology, the first level of subconcepts of the countermeasure concept are 'access

Figure 1. Overview of the security ontology

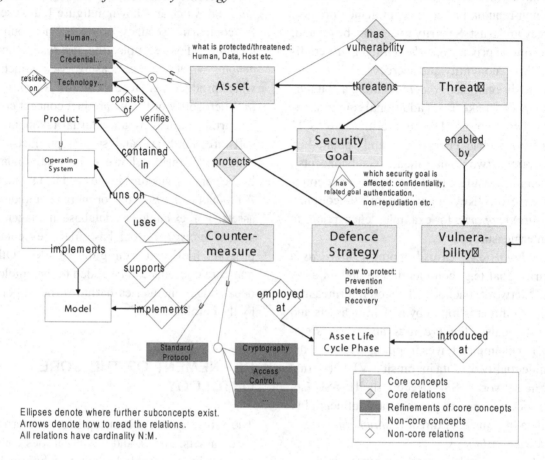

Ellipses denote where further subconcepts exist.
Arrows denote how to read the relations.
All relations have cardinality N:M.

control', 'cryptography' or 'encryption', 'secure network communication'. These and more sub-concepts are shown in Figure 2 where lines denote generalisation-specialisation-relations. Typically, countermeasures that are subconcepts of 'secure network communication' are also subconcepts of 'standard or protocol', e.g. 'SSL', 'IPSec' (Internet Protocol Security), 'DNSSEC' (Domain Name System Security Extensions). The concept 'technology mistakenly used as countermeasure' is a container for technologies that are not designed to be countermeasures but are commonly used as such. 'NAT' (network address translation) is such a technology. It was designed to remedy the shortcoming of the IPv4 address space but is sometimes used instead of a firewall to hide a network.

The *protects*-relation of Figure 1 denotes which assets and security goals the countermeasure protects through which defence strategy. Each countermeasure contains constraining axioms, in OWL called restriction, as to what it protects. An example is the countermeasure 'backup', whose OWL representation looks as shown in Box 1.

The OWL code expresses that backup is a countermeasure. A backup must protect at least (denoted by the someValuesFrom-restrictions) availability, integrity and data through recovery and not more (as denoted by the allValuesFrom-restrictions). More details and explanations of the OWL syntax are shown in the appendix.

If one wants to know all details about a countermeasure, one can browse to it in the OWL or html representation of the ontology and examine its definitions and restrictions. If a user wonders

Box 1.

```
Class (Backup partial
        Countermeasure
        restriction(protects allValuesFrom(intersectionOf(
        unionOf(_Availability _Integrity) _Data _Recovery)))
        restriction(protects someValuesFrom(_Availability))
        restriction(protects someValuesFrom(_Data))
        restriction(protects someValuesFrom(_Recovery))
        restriction(protects someValuesFrom(_Integrity)))
)
```

"What is SSH and what does it protect?", the ontology provides answers. SSH is textually described in the ontology as "a network protocol designed for logging into and executing commands on a networked computer, replacing the insecure ftp, telnet and rlogin protocol". Its class definition (Box 2) states that SSH is a countermeasure that belongs to the subconcepts of 'secure network communication' and 'standard'. It is a preventive measure, protects the confidentiality and integrity of data in transit and provides host authentication. The allValuesFrom-restriction on the *protects*-property contains the intersection of the expressions in the someValuesFrom-restrictions, meaning that

Box 2.

```
Class (SSH partial
    SecureNetworkCommunication
    Standard
    restriction(protects allValuesFrom(intersectionOf(
        _Prevention
        unionOf(
                intersectionOf(_Host _Authentication)
                intersectionOf( unionOf(_Confidentiality _Integrity) _DataInTransit)
        )
    )))
    restriction(protects someValuesFrom(_Prevention))
    restriction(protects someValuesFrom(
    intersectionOf(_Confidentiality _DataInTransit)))
    restriction(protects someValuesFrom(
    intersectionOf(_Integrity _DataInTransit)))
    restriction(protects someValuesFrom(
    intersectionOf(_Host _Authentication)))
    restriction(uses someValuesFrom(SymmetricEncryption))
    restriction(uses someValuesFrom(Public-KeyEncryption))
    )
```

Figure 2. Countermeasure classification

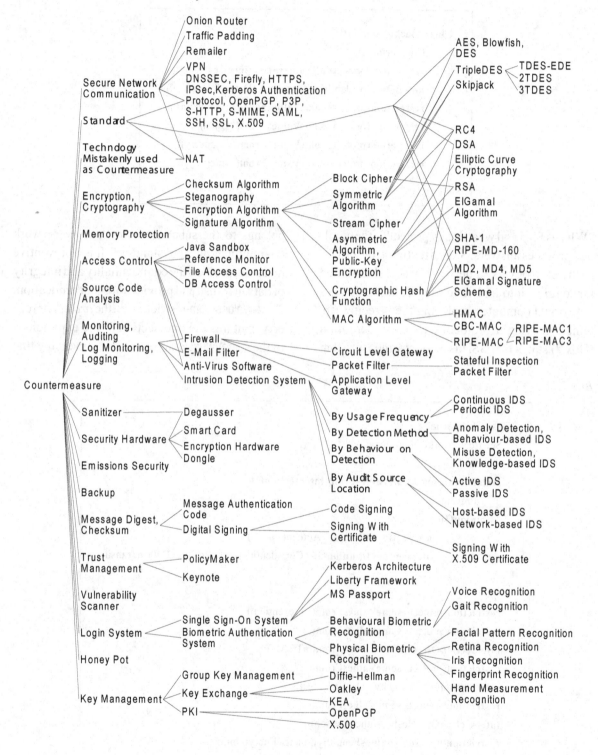

SSH does not protect more than what is stated as someValuesFrom-restrictions. SSH uses both symmetric and public-key encryption.

Restrictions like the ones described for backup and SSH are given for all 133 countermeasures, which makes up one major strength of our ontology, as these restrictions are used for inference as shown later.

Assets

Figure 3 shows the asset subconcepts in our ontology. The direct subconcepts are 'human', 'technology', 'credential' and also 'countermeasure'.

All countermeasures are assets—they deserve protection, they have a value.

A credential is an asset that is typically verified by 'login system' countermeasures. This is implemented by the *credentialVerifiedBy*-relation between credential and countermeasure. Credentials are grouped into biometric, physical and electronic tokens (Kim et al., 2005). The biometric tokens that are not fully shown in Figure 3 contain 'gait' and 'voice' (behavioural) as well as 'facial

pattern', 'fingerprint', 'hand measurement', 'iris' and 'retina' (physical biometric credential).

The asset 'technology' is further developed as 'data', 'hardware', 'process' and 'network'. 'Network' is further split up into e.g. 'ad-hoc network', 'wireless network', 'Intranet' etc. 'Hardware' is, among others, refined by 'host' that is further developed into 'bastion host', 'router', 'wireless access point', 'local host' and more. 'Data' is specialised by many file types, but also by 'data in transit' that is further refined as 'application layer packets' such as 'e-mail' or 'http traffic', as 'transport layer packets' and 'network layer packets' with the additional subconcepts of 'TCP', 'UDP' and 'IP packet'.

The asset 'human' is refined by 'sender' and 'receiver' which are used in certain network communication countermeasures to denote whether the privacy of sender or receiver is protected.

The interdependency of assets is described by the *resides on*-relation for technical assets. It expresses that e.g. the asset 'data' resides on a 'hard disk' which resides on a 'host' which resides on a 'network'. Thus, a countermeasure that protects

Figure 3. Some levels of assets. Ellipses show where further subconcepts exist.

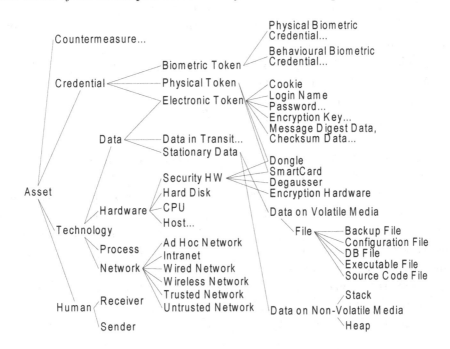

a network may also be useful in protecting data on a networked host.

Threats or Attacks

In this work, we use the words 'threat' and 'attack' interchangeably. Some publications, notably Whitman and Mattord (2005), use the word 'threat' for high-level threats such as 'act of human error or failure' or 'compromises to intellectual property' and the word 'attack' for more specific threats such as 'virus' or 'web site defacement'. The distinction is not clear as, for example, one threat is called a 'deliberate software attack' (Whitman and Mattord, 2005). At the moment, our ontology focuses more on specific attacks than on highlevel threats.

The attacks or threats as well as their hierarchical classification in the ontology have been taken from other books or articles, mentioned in the related work section. The sources are also documented in the ontology, either as comments or as annotations that point out the actual publication. The top level classification is *passive* and *active* attacks (Ince, 2001; Neumann, 1995) (see Figure 4). A passive attack is an attack that does not modify the attacked system but violates the confidentiality of the system. Typical passive attacks are eavesdropping, statistical attacks on databases, scavenging data from object residue, system mapping and side channel attacks. Typical active threats are unauthorised system modification, spoofing, denial of service attacks and more.

Sometimes a countermeasure can also be a threat. A vulnerability scanner in the hands of a system administrator is a countermeasure, in the hands of a malicious user it may prepare an active attack and is thus a threat. Our ontology allows such modelling. The vulnerability scanner appears both as a countermeasure and as a threat.

Each threat threatens a security goal and an asset, usually expressed together as in the example 'confidentiality (security goal) of data (asset)'.

Each threat concept is modelled with axioms that indicate what it threatens. For example, the threat posed by spyware is implemented as (Box 3), which reads: Spyware is malicious code. Minimally, it threatens the privacy of humans, the availability of the host—because it consumes resources—and the integrity of the host—because it was installed without the user's consent.

The threat of stack overflow shows how further properties for threats are used (Box 4). This reads: Stack overflow is a kind of buffer overflow. It threatens the integrity of the stack. If successful the threat may lead to the additional threats of malicious code or usurpation—using the *ifSuccessfulLeadsToThreat*-relation. Stack overflow is at least enabled by the use of a vulnerable programming language and missing input validation (*enabledByVulnerability*).

Similar axioms are provided for all 88 threats in the ontology and are used for finding countermeasures against threats as shown in the Inference section.

Vulnerabilities

The vulnerability concept is the least developed concept of the core ontology and its refinement is future work. At the moment we only model 13 vulnerabilities. A vulnerability participates in the *enablesThreat*-relation and the *existOnAsset*-

Box 3.

```
Class (Spyware partial
    MaliciousCode
    restriction(threatens someValuesFrom(
        intersectionOf (_Privacy _Human)))
    restriction(threatens someValuesFrom(
        intersectionOf (_Availability _Host)))
    restriction(threatens someValuesFrom(
        intersectionOf (_Integrity _Host)))
)
```

Box 4.

```
Class (StackOverflow partial
    BufferOverflow
    restriction(threatens someValuesFrom(
            intersectionOf(_Integrity _Stack)))
    restriction(threatens allValuesFrom(
            intersectionOf(_Integrity _Stack)))
    restriction(ifSuccessfulLeadsToThreat allValuesFrom(
            unionOf(MaliciousCode Usurpation)))
    restriction(enabledByVulnerability someValuesFrom(
            UseOfVulnerableProgrammingLanguage))
    restriction(enabledByVulnerability someValuesFrom(
            MissingInputValidation))
)
```

relation. For example: The vulnerability 'missing input validation' enables the threat 'malformed input', a superclass of, among other things, buffer overflows, and exists on the asset 'program source code file'.

Further Refinement of Two Countermeasure Concepts

To demonstrate how users can use our security ontology for comparing tools or products, we refined the countermeasure concepts 'memory protection' and 'source code analysis' with additional subconcepts representing tools used in the respective areas. For the implementation of these two subontologies, we imported our general security ontology into new OWL files and then implemented the new concepts. Thus the two in-depth ontologies are updated automatically with the latest general security ontology when they are opened. It also means that the new ontologies are very small in size because only the additional classes and restrictions reside in the new OWL files. All the basic structure comes from the general security ontology.

The source for the facts in the two ontologies are two studies (Wilander, 2005; Wilander and Kamkar, 2003) that contain an overview of tools that are useful for providing memory protection (28 concepts) and C source code analysis (25 concepts) respectively. The resulting two subontologies are basically machine- and human-readable versions of sentences, references and a number of tables that exist in the source literature. The classification of the tools according to certain criteria is now available to both human users and reasoning applications. Memory protection, in figure 5(a), contains e.g. subconcepts for stating that a tool is either a C library wrapper, a compiler patch or works by using non-executable memory. Again, all concepts are defined with descriptions from Wilander (2005) and all tools are referred with a link to their documentation or publication. C-source code analysis describes tools for lexical analysis and syntax or (partially) semantic analysis. The latter group is further subdivided according to certain criteria from Wilander and Kamkar (2003) as shown in figure 5(b). The tools make up the leaf nodes.

Figure 4. Threat classification

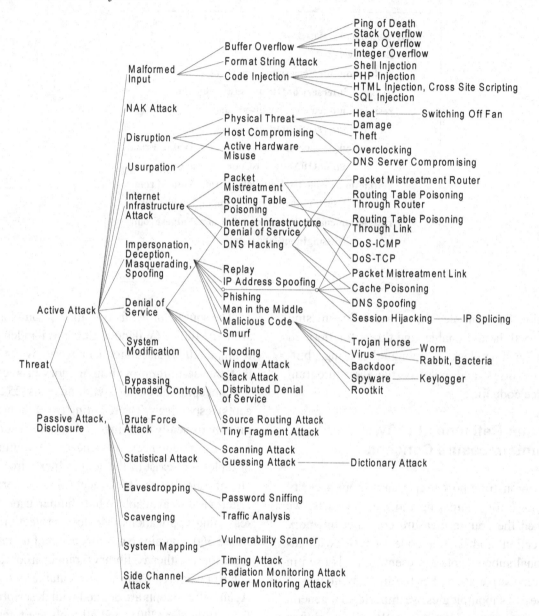

ADVANCED USES OF THE ONTOLOGY

So far we have described the hierarchy of the ontology and the information it provides for specific concepts. Now we use this hierarchy and information to categorise, for example, threats or countermeasures according to their security goal, asset or defense strategy. A query language offers additional possibilities to find and process information in an ontology.

Inference

This section describes the contents of the ontology called SecurityViews.owl, accessible at http://www.ida.liu.se/~iislab/projects/secont. This ontology imports the general security ontology

Figure 5. Subontology of tools for (a) memory protection, (b) C source code analysis. Text in italics denotes the sorting criteria.

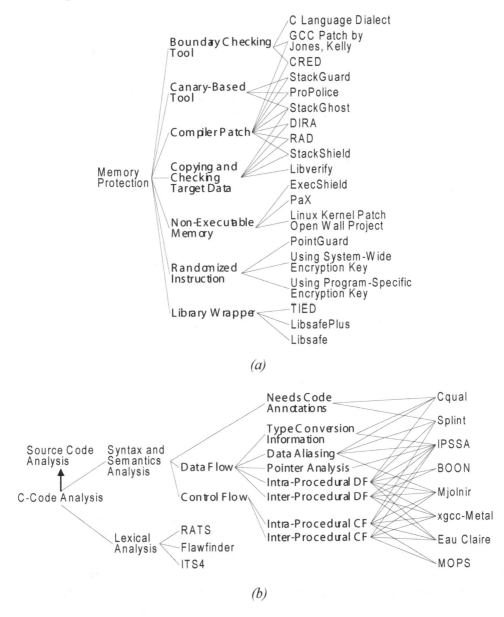

(a)

(b)

of Figure 1 and allows the grouping of counter-measure and threat concepts according to certain criteria described below. The grouping is achieved by defining view concepts and by letting a reasoner such as FaCT, Racer, Pellet etc. (see www.w3.org/2001/sw/WebOnt/impls) infer subclasses for these view concepts.

We are, for example, interested in finding all threats that threaten the confidentiality of data. To achieve this, we define a categorising view class *ThreatByConfidentialityOfData* which is defined as a threat that threatens the confidentiality of data (Box 5).

After inference, this class contains all threats that threaten the confidentiality of data. The result is seen in Figure 6(a).

Figure 6. Inference results: (a) threats that violate the confidentiality of data, (b) countermeasures that protect the confidentiality of data.

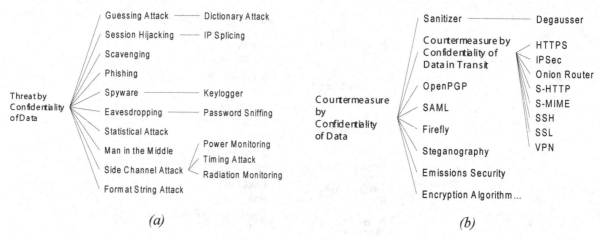

(a)   *(b)*

Box 5.

```
Class (ThreatByConfidentialityOfData complete
        intersectionOf(
                Threat
                restriction(threatens someValuesFrom(
                        intersectionOf(_Confidentiality _Data)))
        )
)
```

Countermeasures that thwart the above threats are found in a similar way. One creates a class *CountermeasureByConfidentialityOfData* which is defined as a countermeasure that protects confidentiality of data (Box 6).

The result of this inference is shown in Figure 6(b).

The inference mechanism supports even more detailed formulations. After inference, the following class contains the inferred countermeasures that detect or prevent violation of integrity of data (Box 7).

The inferred subconcepts are all block ciphers, all signature algorithms, memory protection, message digest and checksum creation systems and some of the secure network communication

concepts such as SAML (Security Assertion Markup Language), OpenPGP (Open Pretty Good Privacy), S-MIME (Secure/Multipurpose Internet Mail Extensions), SSL, IPSec, Firefly, SSH, SHTTP (Secure Hypertext Transfer Protocol), DNSSEC and HTTPS (Hypertext Transfer Protocol over SSL).

Inference is also useful for finding countermeasures against specific threats.

We assume that one wishes to find countermeasures against the specific threat of a rootkit. The rootkit threat is a subconcept of malicious code and threatens the integrity of a host (Box 8).

We propose a three-step procedure for finding countermeasures against specific threats.

Box 6.

```
Class (CountermeasureByConfidentialityOfData complete
        intersectionOf(
                Countermeasure
                restriction(protects someValuesFrom(
                        intersectionOf(_Confidentiality _Data)))
        )
)
```

Box 7.

```
ClassSS(CountermeasureByDetPrevIntData complete
        intersectionOf(
                Countermeasure
                restriction(protects
                        someValuesFrom(intersectionOf(
                                _Data _Integrity
                                unionOf(_Prevention _Detection)
        ))))
)
```

Box 8.

```
Class (Rootkit partial
        MaliciousCode
        restriction(threatens someValuesFrom(
                intersectionOf(_Integrity _Host)))
        ...
))
```

(1) One must find those countermeasures that protect what the rootkit threatens, namely integrity of host. This is done by the view class

```
Class(CountermeasureByIntegrityOfHost complete
        intersectionOf(
        Countermeasure
        restriction(protects someValuesFrom(
        intersectionOf(_Integrity _Host)))))
```

that infers all countermeasures that protect the integrity of a host or subclasses of 'host' such as 'networked host' or 'router'. The user should then browse the result and decide with the help of the countermeasure documentation which countermeasure is most suitable.

(2) There may be additional suitable countermeasures that protect against rootkits, and they can be found by inferring those countermeasures that protect the integrity of any asset.

Class(CountermeasureByIntegrity complete
   intersectionOf(
     Countermeasure
     restriction(protects **someValuesFrom**(_Integrity))))

The inference result for this view class is imprecise with regard to the goal of finding countermeasures against rootkits and retrieves a lot of goal-irrelevant countermeasures such as digital signature algorithms (which protect the integrity of data, with data being an—for this query irrelevant—sibling concept of host). This can be remedied with a ranking algorithm that matches results from step two to the asset that is used in step one. Countermeasures that protects assets that are direct superclasses of the asset of step one (for the rootkit: host) are more likely to thwart the given threat of a rootkit than countermeasures that protect assets which are sibling concepts of host (such as CPU) or sibling concepts of direct superclasses of host (such as data, network or human).

(3) There may be countermeasures that protect security goals that are related to integrity, such as correctness and policy compliance. These countermeasures could be potential countermeasures

against rootkits, too. They are found by defining a view class that makes use of the relation named *has related goal*, which denotes which security goals are similar to each other.

In this ontology, inference is primarily used for sorting and categorising threats and countermeasures according to security goals, assets and defence strategies. Inference also assists in finding countermeasures against a given threat. In future work, we will implement an algorithm that suggests and ranks countermeasures against a given threat following the three steps described above so as to relieve the user from performing these steps manually.

Querying with SPARQL

We showed before that inference with view classes can find e.g. threats that can compromise the confidentiality of data and thus provide a means of categorising concepts in the ontology. The standard query language SPARQL (SPARQL Protocol and RDF Query Language) (Prud'hommeaux and Seaborne, 2006) allows additional degrees of freedom in retrieving data from an OWL ontology. SPARQL can e.g. be used to do some post-processing of results as shown in Box 9.

This query returns all inferred countermeasures that protect the confidentiality of data using the previously described view class *Counter-*

Box 9.

```
PREFIX ns: <http://www.ida.liu.se/~iislab/projects/secont/SecurityViews.owl#>
PREFIX rdfs: <http://www.w3.org/2000/01/rdf-schema#>
PREFIX owl: <http://www.w3.org/2002/07/owl#>
PREFIX rdf: <http://www.w3.org/1999/02/22-rdf-syntax-ns#>
SELECT DISTINCT ?c
WHERE {
        ?c rdfs:subClassOf ns:CountermeasureByConfidentialityOfData
        FILTER ( ?c != owl:Nothing)
}
ORDER BY (?c)
```

measureByConfidentialityOfData and orders the result alphabetically.

SPARQL also supports yes/no-questions, sorting, filtering, string matching etc. The following advanced SPARQL code, which makes use of sorting and filtering, finds all leaf classes of the countermeasure hierarchy (Box 10).

IMPLEMENTATION

Users that are not familiar with OWL files and OWL-specific tools can still use the ontology for reference by browsing through it. Browsing is possible with the ontologies' html-representations at http://www.ida.liu.se/~iislab/projects/secont. The html representation shows an OWL ontology complete with properties, individuals, restrictions and pointers to where each concept is used, all in javadoc style. Together with the overview provided in figure 1 the ontology should be useful for human users "as is".

A convenient but less detailed overview of the tree of concepts without comments, definitions and restrictions is the dumpont service: http://www.daml.org/cgi-bin/dumpont?http://www.ida.liu.se/~iislab/projects/secont/Security.owl

Our ontologies are created using the Protege OWL tool (protege.stanford.edu) with the Pellet reasoner (www.mindswap.org/2003/pellet). The editor Swoop (www.mindswap.org/2004/SWOOP) was useful for finding the sources of inconsistencies in the knowledge base. Images from the ontology are produced using Protege with the Jambalaya plugin (www.cs.uvic.ca/~chisel/projects/jambalaya/jambalaya.html) and the OWLViz plugin (www.co-ode.org/downloads/owlviz/). Certain programming, e.g. for creating the helper classes and retrieving countermeasures for certain threats, was done using the Jena API (jena.sourceforge.net). For querying OWL files, we used the SPARQL language of the ARQ implementation (jena.sourceforge.net/ARQ/), Jena and Pellet. A convenient web interface for both the Pellet reasoner and SPARQL queries exists on www.mindswap.org/2003/pellet/demo.shtml. Our ontology imports the general Dublin Core ontology (www.dublincore.org) for making annotations such as describing a class, citing a source etc.

RELATED WORK

Schumacher (2003) describes a core security ontology for maintaining a knowledge base of security patterns. The ontology consists of the concepts asset, threat, attack, vulnerability, attacker, risk,

Box 10.

```
PREFIX ...
SELECT DISTINCT ?c
WHERE {
        ?c rdfs:subClassOf ns:Countermeasure .
        OPTIONAL {
                ?c2 rdfs:subClassOf ?c .
                FILTER (?c2 != owl:Nothing && ?c2 != ?c)
        }
        FILTER (!bound(?c2))
}
ORDER BY (?c)
```

countermeasure, stakeholder and security objective (confidentiality, integrity, availability etc.) and their relations. However, the ontology has the following problems: (1) Countermeasures are not directly related to security objectives or assets but only to threats. This makes it unclear what a countermeasure protects. (2) If an attack is described as the realisation of a threat, it is difficult to distinguish between the concepts 'threat' and 'attack'. (3) A risk, being a probability, should not be modelled as a concept but as a property of a threat. Refinements of the core ontology are not available. Thus, there is no technical domain terminology such as specific threats or security countermeasures, and the ontology can consequently not be used for queries.

Kim et al. (2005) have put up a number of small ontologies, which they use for matching security services. These ontologies are online at http://chacs.nrl.navy.mil/projects/4SEA/ontology.html and show quite a level of detail e.g. in the areas of encryption algorithms and credentials. However, a core that shows the connections between concepts is missing. Assets, threats and vulnerabilities are not modelled, and the countermeasure branch is less refined than our work.

Other ontologies in the domain of information security are used for more specific purposes e.g. reasoning about privacy settings or negotiations (Jutla and Bodorik, 2005; Squicciarini et al., 2006), policy settings (Nejdl et al., 2005), automatic intrusion classification (Undercoffer et al., 2004), risk assessment of organisations (Tsoumas et al., 2005), learning about encryption in network security (Takahashi et al., 2005) and rarely are the actual ontologies made available. Especially the work of Tsoumas et al. (2005) may be based on an interesting core ontology but only a few concepts are exposed in the publication and the actual ontology is not made available. One strength of our ontology is that it is publicly available, general and thus of use for a broad audience.

Domain knowledge is also collected in taxonomies—non-overlapping concept classifications with a single top-level concept and no relations between concepts. These can refine general concepts of the core ontology and are therefore of interest.

Threat taxonomies (Lindqvist and Jonsson, 1997; Chakrabarti and Manimaran, 2002; Álvarez and Petrovic, 2003; Welch and Lathrop, 2003; DeLooze, 2004; Simmonds et al., 2004) are rich and well-developed. There is even a rudimentary threat ontology, but it is not available online anymore (Undercoffer et al., 2004). Also text books (Amoroso, 1994; Bishop, 2003; Stallings, 2006; Ször, 2005; Whitman and Mattord, 2005) are usually good in grouping or classifying threats. Thus for the threat branch of our ontology we could harvest from many sources. The same sources also supply useful input for the vulnerability branch. However, countermeasure taxonomies are less well-developed.

The security technology taxonomy of Venter and Eloff (2003) puts high-level concepts like 'access control', 'biometrics' or 'cryptography' on the same level as technical concepts like 'VPN' (virtual private network), 'digital signature' or 'digital certificate'. The six concepts above and ten more are grouped into proactive and reactive technologies as well as by their level of interaction: network, host or application level. In contradiction with the authors' own definition, access control and passwords are classified as reactive measures.

Irvine and Levin (1999) show a countermeasure taxonomy and use it for determining the cost of network security services. The taxonomy starts out by grouping security technologies by security goals like CIA (confidentiality, integrity, availability) but does not remain consistent. Both 'data confidentiality' and 'audit and intrusion detection' figure as grouping criteria. The former is a security goal, the latter however are two security technologies.

Wang and Wang (2003) put up a countermeasure taxonomy of four concepts: 'standards and policies', 'library and tools', 'administration and system management' and 'physical tools'. However, the important concept of encryption is missing and it is unclear where it should be added. Also, the authors mix between more general concepts like 'PKI' (public-key infrastructure) and 'biometric authentication' and products such as 'Secure SQLnet' and 'Tripwire' in a list of only 19 concepts.

Better-developed taxonomies can be found in the area of intrusion detection (Axelsson, 2000; Carver and Pooch, 2000; Debar et al., 1999) but these naturally do not cover other security technologies.

DISCUSSION AND FUTURE WORK

In the introduction, we put up goals for our ontology. We set out to achieve an ontology that provides a general *overview*, contains detailed *domain vocabulary*, allows *queries*, supports *machine reasoning* and may be used *collaboratively*.

The core ontology provides the *overview* over the domain by focusing on the four pillars of risk assessment—assets, threats, vulnerabilities and countermeasures—and their relations. The core ontology is refined by a great number of subconcepts that make up the *domain vocabulary*. These refinements of the core provide details and allow *queries* for specific problems and solutions in the domain of information security.

Our work contains definitions and explanations of concepts and relations in natural language, which makes it easy for human users to understand them.

The ontology is implemented in a standard language that supports *machine reasoning*. We have made first steps towards *collaborative use* of the ontology by the choice of the ontology implementation language and by making the ontology available online. Users can download our ontologies and edit them to their liking; or they can integrate our work with any existing ontology through aligning and merging. Tools for

this are readily available, both in Protege and in the research community (Lambrix and Tan, 2005, 2007). But as we have shown with our extensions—memory protection, source code analysis, security views— it is also possible to import the general ontology from the web and extend it with new concepts. Hopefully, these possibilities for extension will make our work interesting for others and can lead to an ontology of information security that is accepted by the community.

An issue for discussion is *concept naming* and *concept classification*. We had to make choices that may not be acceptable to everyone. An example is that the concept of 'credential'—for example 'password' or 'smart card'—is sometimes used as a pars-pro-toto (part of something is used as name for the whole) to denote a system that verifies the credential. Some use the concept 'password' as a countermeasure. However, we model a password as a credential, which is a subconcept of asset, not a countermeasure. A system that verifies credentials is called 'login system' (a countermeasure) in our ontology. An object property denotes that login systems *verify credentials* such as a 'password'. At the moment, there are no subconcepts to login systems because they would duplicate the credential hierarchy and confuse more than help. When the need arises, subconcepts of 'login system' can be created that can then show that e.g. a 'password system' verifies 'passwords'. If someone insists on using 'password' as the name for a system that administrates and verifies passwords, a different name must be chosen because OWL does not allow use of the same name for two different concepts. Easier to resolve are issues of synonyms that can easily be declared in OWL, using equivalent classes.

Security technologies, threats and vulnerabilities are quickly changing. Thus, an important part in the life-cycle of an ontology like ours is *maintenance*. In the future we plan to increase the ontologies' availability to the public, for example by using a wiki to make them editable by contributors. So far we provide the raw OWL files, illustrations and html-documentation of the ontology, but we would also like to offer a *web interface* for finding threats given a countermeasure, or finding countermeasures given a threat, or finding threats and countermeasures given an asset.

Extensions and refinements on all levels can be envisioned. General concepts that may make interesting extensions are 'attacker', 'stakeholder' and 'impact' of a threat. Technical details in all branches can be found; the ontology is far from complete. We envision refinements for the concepts of vulnerability, threat, and the countermeasure subconcepts of firewall, backup, intrusion detection system and more. Also procedures and written policies—being countermeasures (and thus also assets)—may need to be integrated.

CONCLUSION

This article shows how the need for a general and specific, machine-usable and extensible ontology for the security community can be met. We have described an OWL-based ontology with its core concepts *asset, threat, vulnerability, countermeasure, security goal* and *defence strategy*. All the core concepts are subclassed or instantiated to provide the domain vocabulary of information security. Relations connect concepts. Axioms, implemented as OWL restrictions, model constraints on relations and are used to express, for example, which countermeasure protects which asset and which security goal. Inference and the query language SPARQL allow additional views on the ontology. They can show countermeasures that protect the confidentiality of data, countermeasures that detect integrity violations, threats that can compromise the availability of a host etc. Inference also assists in finding countermeasures for a given threat.

Our work can be used as online learning material for human users, as a framework for comparing security products, security attacks or security

vulnerabilities, as a publicly available knowledge base for rule-based reasoning with semantic web applications and as a starting point and framework for further extensions and refinements.

We hope that our ontology will be a trigger for discussions leading to even more detailed and acceptable ontologies in the area of information security.

ACKNOWLEDGMENT

We would like to thank Christoph Schuba and Patrick Lambrix for fruitful discussions on the content, structure and implementation of the ontology. The developers of the Jena API and Pellet reasoner—especially Chris Dollin, Dave Reynolds, Andy Seaborne, Bijan Parsia, Evren Sirin—helped clarify implementation issues.

REFERENCES

Álvarez, G., & Petrovic, S. (2003). A new taxonomy of web attacks suitable for efficient encoding. *Computers & Security, 22*(5), 435–449.

Amoroso, E. (1994). *Fundamentals of Computer Security Technology*. Prentice-Hall.

Axelsson, S. (2000). *Intrusion detection systems: A survey and taxonomy*. Technical Report 99-15, Dept. of Computer Engineering, Chalmers University of Technology.

Bechhofer, S., van Harmelen, F., Hendler, J., Horrocks, I., McGuinness, D. L., Patel-Schneider, P. F., & Stein, L. A. (2004). *OWL Web Ontology Language Reference*. http://www.w3.org/TR/owl-ref/ (visited 21-Apr-2006).

Bishop, M. (2003). *Computer Security—Art and Science*. Addison Wesley.

Carver, C. A., & Pooch, U.W. (2000). An intrusion response taxonomy and its role in automatic intrusion response. In *Proceedings of the IEEE Workshop on Information Assurance*. IEEE.

Chakrabarti, A., & Manimaran, G. (2002). Internet infrastructure security: A taxonomy. *IEEE Internet Computing, 16*(6), 13–21.

Chen, P. P.-S. (1976). The entity-relationship model—toward a unified view of data. *ACM Transactions on Database Systems (TODS), 1*(1), 9–36.

Debar, H., Dacier, M., & Wespi, A. (1999). Towards a taxonomy of intrusiondetection systems. *Computer Networks, 31*, 805–822.

DeLooze, L. L. (2004). Classification of computer attack using a selforganizing map. In *Proceedings of the IEEE Workshop on Information Assurance*, (pp. 365–369). IEEE.

Donner, M. (2003). Toward a security ontology. *IEEE Security and Privacy, 1*(3), 6–7.

Gruber, T. R. (1995). Toward principles for the design of ontologies used for knowledge sharing. *International Journal of Human-Computer Studies, 43*(5–6), 907–928.

Ince, D. (2001). *A Dictionary of the Internet*. Oxford University Press.

Irvine, C., & Levin, T. (1999). Toward a taxonomy and costing method for security services. In *Proceedings of the 15th Annual Computer Security Applications Conference (ACSAC'99)*, (pp. 183–188). IEEE.

Jutla, D. N., & Bodorik, P. (2005). Sociotechnical architecture for online privacy. *IEEE Security and Privacy, 3*(2), 29–39.

Kim, A., Luo, J., & Kang, M. (2005). Security ontology for annotating resources. In *Proceedings of the On the Move to Meaningful Internet Systems: CoopIS, DOA, and ODBASE*, LNCS 3761, (pp. 1483–1499). Springer-Verlag.

Lambrix, P. (2004). Ontologies in bioinformatics and systems biology. In W. Dubitzky, & F. Azuaje (Eds.), *Artificial Intelligence Methods and Tools for Systems Biology*, (pp. 129–146). Springer-Verlag.

Lambrix, P., & Tan, H. (2005). A framework for aligning ontologies. In *Proceedings of the 3rd Workshop on Principles and Practice of Semantic Web Reasoning, LNCS 3703*, 17–31. Springer-Verlag.

Lambrix, P., & Tan, H. (2007). Ontology alignment and merging. In Burger, A., Davidson, D., and Baldock, R., editors, *Anatomy Ontologies for Bioinformatics: Principles and Practice*. Springer-Verlag. To appear.

Lambrix, P., Tan, H., Jakoniene, V., & Strömbäck, I. (2007). Biological ontologies. In Baker, C. J. and Cheung, K.-H., editors, *Semantic Web: Revolutionizing Knowledge Discovery in the Life Sciences*, (pp. 85–99). Springer-Verlag.

Lindqvist, U., & Jonsson, E. (1997). How to systemactically classify computer security intrusions. In *Proceedings of the IEEE Symposium on Security and Privacy (S&P'97)*, (pp. 154–163). IEEE.

Neches, R., Fikes, R., Finin, T. W., Gruber, T. R., Patil, R., Senator, T. E., & Swartout, W. R. (1991). Enabling technology for knowledge sharing. *AI Magazine, 12*(3), 36–56.

Nejdl, W., Olmedilla, D., Winslett, M., & Zhang, C. C. (2005). Ontologybased policy specification and management. In *Proceedings of the 2nd European Semantic Web Conference (ESCW'05), LNCS 3532*, 290–302. Springer-Verlag.

Neumann, P. G. (1995). *Computer-related risks*. Addison Wesley.

Noy, N., & Rector, A. (2006). *Defining N-ary Relations on the Semantic Web*. http://www.w3.org/TR/swbp-n-aryRelations/ (visited 24-Apr-2006).

Oxford University Press (2004). A Dictionary of Computing. Oxford Reference Online. Oxford University press.

Patel-Schneider, P. F., Hayes, P., & Horrocks, I. (2004). *OWL Web Ontology Language Semantics and Abstract Syntax*. http://www.w3.org/TR/owl-absyn/ (visited 21-Apr-2006).

Powers, S. (2003). *Practical RDF*. O'Reilly.

Prud'hommeaux, E., & Seaborne, A. (2006). *SPARQL query language for RDF*. W3C.

Rector, A., Drummond, N., Horridge, M., Rogers, J., Knublauch, H., Stevens, R., Wang, H., & Wroe, C. (2004). OWL pizzas: Practical experience of teaching OWL-DL: Common errors & common patterns. In *Proceedings of the 14th International Conference of Engineering Knowledge in the Age of the Semantic Web (EKAW'04)*, LNCS 3257, pages 63–81. Springer-Verlag.

Schumacher, M. (2003). *Security Engineering with Patterns: Origins, Theoretical Model, and New Applications*. LNCS 2754. Springer-Verlag.

Simmonds, A., Sandilands, P., & van Ekert, L. (2004). An ontology for network security attacks. In *Proceedings of the 2nd Asian Applied Computing Conference (AACC'04), LNCS 3285*, 317–323. Springer-Verlag.

Squicciarini, A. C., Bertino, E., Ferrari, E., & Ray, I. (2006). Achieving privacy in trust negotiations with an ontology-based approach. *IEEE Transactions on Dependable and Secure Computing*, 3(1), 13–30.

Stallings, W. (2006). *Cryptography and Network Security—Principles and Practices, 4th Edition*. Prentice-Hall.

Stevens, R., Goble, C. A., & Bechhofer, S. (2000). Ontology-based knowledge representation for bioinformatics. *Briefings in Bioinformatics*, 1(4), 398–414.

Ször, P. (2005). *The Art of Computer Virus Research and Defense*. Addison Wesley.

Takahashi, Y., Abiko, T., Negishi, E., Itabashi, G., Kato, Y., Takahashi, K., & Shiratori, N. (2005). An ontology-based e-learning system for network security. In *Proceedings of the 19th International Conference on Advanced Information Networking and Applications (AINA'05)*, *1*, 197–202. IEEE.

Tsoumas, B., Dritsas, S., & Gritzalis, D. (2005). An ontology-based approach to information systems security management. In Gorodetsky, V., Kotenko, I., and Skormin, V., editors, *Computer Network Security: Third International Workshop on Mathematical Methods, Models, and Architectures for Computer Network Security (MMM-ACNS'05)*, *LNCS 3685*, 151–164. Springer-Verlag.

Undercoffer, J., Joshi, A., Finin, T., & Pinkston, J. (2004). Using DAML+OIL to classify intrusive behaviors. *The Knowledge Engineering Review*, (pp. 221–241).

Venter, H. S., & Eloff, J. H. P. (2003). A taxonomy for information security technologies. *Computers & Security*, 22(4), 299–307.

Wang, H., & Wang, C. (2003). Taxonomy of security considerations and software quality. *Communications of the ACM*, 46(6), 75–78.

Welch, D., & Lathrop, S. (2003). Wireless security threat taxonomy. In *Proceedings of the IEEE Workshop on Information Assurance*, (pp. 76–83). IEEE.

Whitman, M. E. & Mattord, H. J. (2005). *Principles of Information Security*. Thomson Course Technology, 2nd edition.

Wilander, J. (2005). Modeling and visualizing security properties of code using dependence graphs. In *Proceedings of the 5th Conference on Software Engineering Research and Practice in Sweden*, (pp. 65–74). http://www.idt.mdh.se/serps-05/SERPS05.pdf (visited 1-Jun-2006).

Wilander, J., & Kamkar, M. (2003). A comparison of publicly available tools for dynamic buffer overflow prevention. In *Proceedings of the 10th Network and Distributed System Security Symposium (NDSS'03)*, (pp. 149–162). Internet Society.

APPENDIX: INTRODUCTION TO OWL

This section introduces concepts and keywords of OWL in the context of our information security ontology.

An OWL ontology typically consists of the concepts that are to be modelled. These concepts are called *classes*, which can have *subclasses*. *Object properties* describe the relation between classes. *Datatype properties* denote attributes of a class. *Individuals* are instances of a class; and *restrictions* on properties model axioms that e.g. constrain the values of that property.

OWL is a description-logic based language and based on RDF. RDF can be used to model the world using subject-predicate-object statements called *triples*. Example: THREAT *isEnabledBy* VULNERABILITY. N-ary relations like COUNTERMEASURE *Protects* SECURITYGOAL *and* ASSET *through* DEFENCESTRATEGY cannot be expressed directly and need to be resolved with helper patterns (Noy and Rector, 2006).

The actual OWL code, being a derivative of XML, is verbose. The following example defines a class called 'Data' which is a subclass of a class called 'Technology', which is defined elsewhere in the local ontology.

```
<owl:Class rdf:ID="Data">
    <rdfs:subClassOf>
        <owl:Class rdf:about="#Technology"/>
    </rdfs:subClassOf>
</owl:Class>
```

Humans prefer the more dense, abstract OWL syntax (Patel-Schneider et al., 2004)

Class (Data **partial** Technology)

which is what we will use when we want to show OWL code. Keywords of OWL are provided in bold face.

Object properties, as shown in the code example below, describe relations between classes. The object property *existsOnAsset*, for example, is a property between *vulnerability*—the domain—and *asset*—the range. A vulnerability exists on an asset. The inverse property between asset and vulnerability is named *assetHasVulnerability*.

```
ObjectProperty(existsOnAsset
    inverseOf(assetHasVulnerability)
    domain(Vulnerability)
    range(Asset))
```

Class definitions can contain restrictions that define constraints on the use of properties. Our ontology makes heavy use of these restrictions, therefore we explain these in detail. The countermeasure class 'vulnerability scanner', with its OWL code below, is our guiding example.

```
Class (VulnerabilityScanner partial
Countermeasure
restriction(protects someValuesFrom(_Correctness))
restriction(protects someValuesFrom(_Host))
restriction(protects someValuesFrom(_Detection))
restriction(protects someValuesFrom(_Integrity))
restriction(protects allValuesFrom(intersectionOf(
    unionOf(_Correctness _Integrity)
    _Host
    unionOf(_Detection _Correction)
)))
)
```

The class 'vulnerability scanner' is a subclass of *countermeasure*. Every vulnerability scanner protects *at least* the correctness and integrity of a host through detection. This statement is implemented with the someValuesFrom-restrictions on the *protects*-property. Some vulnerability scanners also allow certain correction of found vulnerabilities. This possibility is expressed in the closure axiom, in the allValuesFrom-restriction, which expresses that a vulnerability scanner *at best* protects the correctness or integrity of a host using detection or correction. The syntax of the allValuesFrom-restriction combines intersection and union of the three components—security goal, asset, defence strategy—of the protects-property. In concise format, the restriction is

$$\forall protects.((\_Correctness \cup \_Integrity) \cap \_Host \cap (\_Correction \cup \_Detection))$$

If the closure of the allValuesFrom-restriction were not given, it would be possible for a reasoner or human to erroneously believe that a vulnerability scanner protects, for example, the privacy of a human, because nothing contradicts this. If the someValuesFrom-restrictions were not given and only the allValuesFrom-restriction existed, a reasoner would not find the vulnerability scanner as a countermeasure that protects a host because the knowledge base would only express that a vulnerability scanner *at best* could protect a host, but is not required to do so. It could actually protect nothing at all. This kind of reasoning is called the *open world assumption*, which is typical for reasoning on the semantic web.

In the example, the classes starting with an underscore (e.g. _Integrity) are helper classes that denote yet another restriction, namely a restriction on a property of the class that implements the quaternary *protects*-relation. The pattern of helper classes is described in Noy and Rector (2006) and not further explained here.

Restrictions are not only useful as descriptions of constraints. They are a natural starting point for applying inference: Given restrictions on the *protects*-property, it is straightforward for a reasoner to find all countermeasures that protect a certain asset, that protect confidentiality, that use detection or a combination of these. How this is done is shown in section 4.

Synonyms, such as 'encryption' and 'cryptography', can be handled by declaring two or more classes as equivalent. Thus, all subclasses of 'encryption' are also subclasses of 'cryptography' and vice versa.

For more about OWL we recommend the tutorial in Rector et al. (2004). The concise language definition is in Bechhofer et al. (2004). Tools for editing, viewing or reasoning about OWL files are presented in the main body of this article.

Section VI
Evaluating Information Security and Privacy:
Where are We Going from Here?

Chapter XIX
Information Security Effectiveness:
Conceptualization and Validation of a Theory

Kenneth J. Knapp
U.S. Air Force Academy, USA

Thomas E. Marshall
Auburn University, USA

R. Kelly Rainer, Jr.
Auburn University, USA

F. Nelson Ford
Auburn University, USA

ABSTRACT

Taking a sequential qualitative-quantitative methodological approach, the authors propose and test a theoretical model that includes four variables through which top management can positively influence security effectiveness: user training, security culture, policy relevance, and policy enforcement. During the qualitative phase of the study, the authors generated the model based on textual responses to a series of questions given to a sample of 220 information security practitioners. During the quantitative phase, we analyzed survey data collected from a sample of 740 information security practitioners. After data collection, we analyzed the survey responses using structural equation modeling and found evidence to support the hypothesized model. They also tested an alternative, higher-order factor version of the original model that demonstrated an improved overall fit and general applicability across the various demographics of the sampled data. They then linked the finding of this study to existing top management support literature, general deterrence theory research, and the theoretical notion of the dilemma of the supervisor.

INTRODUCTION

With modern national economies dependent upon information technology for survival, the need to protect information and mitigate risk has become paramount. One can find evidence of poor information security in the frequency of media reports about security breaches and from published survey data. As of this writing, media headlines about security incidents have become a regular occurrence with one of the more embarrassing breaches occurring when a laptop went missing that contained sensitive information of millions of U. S. veterans and military personnel (Files, 2006). Multiple national surveys confirm a high number of attacks against organizational information resources (Bagchi & Udo, 2003; Computer Emergency Response Team (CERT), 2004; Gordon, Loeb, Lucyshyn, & Richardson, 2005). Between 1998 and 2003, the number of reported incidents to the U.S. Computer Emergency Response Team (CERT) has nearly doubled each year with 137,529 reported incidents in 2003 alone.[1] An Ernst and Young analysis found that security incidents can cost companies between $17 and $28 million each occurrence (Garg, Curtis, & Halper, 2003). Because incidents are frequent and costly, management must take security seriously to protect organizational information.

Noting the disappointing state of information systems (IS) security in organizations, Dhillon & Backhouse (2001) called for more empirical research to develop key principles that will help in the management of IS security. Despite the call, few studies have developed and empirically tested theoretical models of IS security (Kotulic & Clark, 2004). In some studies, the sensitive nature of the security topic (Straub & Welke, 1998) impeded the collection of a sufficient sample willing to participate in the research (Kotulic & Clark, 2004). The few empirical studies that contained information security effectiveness as a dependent variable used general deterrence theory as a research foundation (Kankanhalli,

Hock-Hai, Bernard, & Kwok-Kee, 2003; Straub, 1990). Sensing that other variables in addition to those related to deterrence theory might significantly predict information security effectiveness, we engaged in a study to develop and empirically test a model of effectiveness that is not based on predetermined independent variables.

Using a sequential quantitative-qualitative methodological approach, we developed and tested a theoretical model that illustrates four practices through which top management can positively influence security effectiveness. The role of management support has been identified as a critical success factor in a wide area of information system implementations and IT projects (Jasperson et al., 2002; Sharma & Yetton, 2003). Management support has been called the variable most frequently hypothesized as contributing to IS success but empirical analysis has limited modeling 'success' as a simple linear function of management support (Sharma & Yetton, 2003, p. 535). Our model offers a more comprehensive view by including four critical mediator variables through which management can improve security effectiveness: user training, security culture, policy relevance, and policy enforcement. By doing so, the theoretical model proposed in this study provides practical help to professionals and researchers who seek to advance the managerial effectiveness of information security programs.

The following methodology section describes our qualitative approach used to conceptualize the theoretical model and the survey instrument to test the model. Using survey data, we then quantitatively test the model using structural equation modeling (SEM). We also proposed and analyzed an alternate structural model. To add credibility to the results of this study, the discussion section links our findings to related theory including previous IS studies based on general deterrence theory. We close our paper with limitations, implications and a conclusion.

RESEARCH METHODOLOGY

Rather than developing a theoretical model based on existing theory in the literature, we used a qualitative strategy that closely followed grounded theory to develop a theoretical model. For this reason, we are going straight into the methodology section. Later in the discussion section, we will appropriately link our findings to theory in the literature. This format is consistent with the grounded theory approach which aims to discover theory directly from a corpus of data rather than from theory generated by logical deduction based on *a priori* assumptions (Glaser & Strauss, 1967). Using a coding process consistent with developing grounded theory, question responses provided by a sample of information security practitioners are analyzed to identify key issues in IS security. A theoretical model emerges based on the categorical relationships among the key managerial issues identified in the responses. After developing and giving the survey to a sample of information security practitioners, we test the model using structural equation modeling. We then explore an alternative model where the four mediator variables are represented by a higher order factor.

Our study combines qualitative and quantitative techniques over a six step methodological process. Figure 1 illustrates the methodological steps of the study. The following subsections describe each of these steps.

Step One: Qualitative Data Collection

An announcement was placed on the International Information Systems Security Certification Consortium [(ISC)²] web site (www.isc2.org) calling for Certified Information System Security Professionals (CISSPs) to volunteer for this research project. (ISC)² is a non-profit organization that manages the CISSP program. Among the requirements to earn a CISSP designation, candidates must pass a rigorous exam, consent to an ethical code, and possess a minimum of four years of professional experience in the field or three years experience plus a college degree. To maintain certification, a CISSP must earn continuing professional education credits.

Two hundred and twenty CISSPs responded to the first question: What are the top five information security issues facing organizations today? Respondents gave a short title and rationale for

Figure 1. Methodology steps

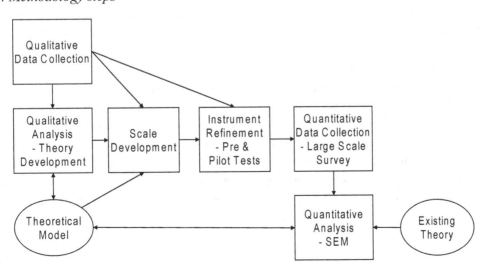

each issue. By asking respondents to identify and describe their top issues, we took as our starting point the concerns of the participants, which is a practical approach for grounded theory studies (Galal, 2001). In the process of gathering and analyzing the responses, we asked several follow-on questions both to the entire sample (N=220) and to specific individuals for the purpose of obtaining clarifications, getting additional details, or receiving feedback on researcher analysis. After this series of interactions with the participants, we accumulated a database containing over 146,000 words of question responses suitable for the purposes of our study.

Step Two: Qualitative Analysis

The grounded theory approach entails a series of highly structured steps involving the systematic comparison of units of data and the gradual construction of a system of categories describing the observed phenomena. This approach involves the discovery of emergent theory from qualitative, empirical data. The grounded theory methodology we used was introduced by Glaser and Strauss (1967) and further refined as a series of structured steps by Strauss and Corbin (1998). Using these steps, we coded respondent statements into logical categories where each category represented a critical information security issue. Through a process of continuous interplay between the researchers and the data (Strauss & Corbin, 1998, p. 13), a list of 58 logical categories emerged. A committee of two university faculty members and one (ISC)² board member reviewed the categories for clarity and accuracy resulting in minor improvements.

Next, we iteratively integrated and refined the categories to discover patterns in the data that suggested theoretical relationships among the categories (Strauss & Corbin, 1998, p.143). This process led to a model with top management support as the independent variable, security effectiveness as a dependent variable, and four

variables mediating the relationship. A mediator is defined as a variable or mechanism through which an independent or predictor variable influences an outcome (Frazier, Barron, & Tix, 2004). Our data suggested that top management can influence security effectiveness through various security programs and policies. Yet, some responses stated that management can also directly influence security effectiveness suggesting that the four mediator variables are partial mediators since they do not fully explain the relationship between the independent and dependent variables. Practically interpreted, top management can influence effectiveness directly, such as through the employee perception that management has taken ownership of an organization's security program, or indirectly, such as by supporting security training goals.

Figure 2 illustrates the hypothesized model and Table 1 contains formal statements of hypotheses. Table 2 provides ten examples of respondent statements supporting the six hypotheses. Underlined words refer to the predictor variables of the hypothesized model. These statements are representative of the larger body of responses.

Step Three: Scale Development

We developed measurement items through a process of extracting words and phrases from the participant responses to build a pool of candidate items. Extracting items directly from the responses assured that both the content and the language of the questionnaire items would be familiar to the likely sample and thus reduce possible construct bias (Karahanna, Evaristo, & Srite, 2004). Psychometricians emphasize that the validity of a measurement scale is built in from the outset. Careful construction of the initial scale items helps to ensure that they will representatively cover the specified domain of interest, and thus possess content validity (Nunnally, 1978).

We extended the technique of theoretical saturation (Strauss & Corbin, 1998) as a guide to

Figure 2. Hypothesized model

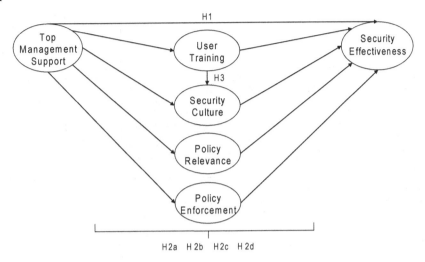

Table 1. Formal hypotheses

H1	Top management support is positively associated with security effectiveness.
H2a	Top management support and security effectiveness is partially mediated by user training.
H2b	Top management support and security effectiveness is partially mediated by security culture.
H2c	Top management support and security effectiveness is partially mediated by policy relevance.
H2d	Top management support and security effectiveness is partially mediated by policy enforcement.
H3	User training is positively associated with security culture.

help determine the number of items appropriate for the item pool (DeVellis, 2003). Theoretical saturation implies that when adding items to the pool contributes little marginal value to the scale or seems counterproductive, the item pool may be theoretically saturated. This approach links the size of the candidate item pool to the assessed content domain. Applying this method, we generated candidate items until the addition of new items contributed little to the scale, indicating that a construct is theoretically saturated. Testing for instrument construct validity began once the quality and quantity of the item pool seemed satisfactory with the concept of theoretical saturation.

Step Four: Instrument Refinement

This step had two major objectives. The first concerned the construct validity of the candidate survey items. The second concerned the perceived sensitive nature of the questions asked. An expert panel of twelve CISSPs evaluated every candidate item from the two perspectives (construct validity and intrusiveness). We invited the twelve CISSPs to be members of this panel based on their high quality and critical answers to the earlier questions while also trying to preserve the demographic diversity of the CISSP population. Combined, the twelve expert panelists earned forty professional IT certifications, fourteen bachelor degrees, five graduate degrees, while representing four countries and five industries.

Table 2. Participant responses supporting the hypothesized model

Representative responses from the qualitative data	H1	H2a	H2b	H2c	H2d	H3
"It is imperative to have <u>top management</u> support <u>all security programs</u>…If there's no <u>management</u> support, real or perceived, <u>all INFOSEC programs</u> will fail."	√					
"The importance of information security by the company's <u>leadership</u> permeates throughout the organization resulting in either successful or poor <u>information security programs</u>."	√					
"Without support and understanding of both <u>management</u> and <u>employee</u>, an effective security program is impossible."	√	√				
"Obviously, without <u>top management</u> support and involvement, the <u>creation</u>, <u>training</u> and <u>enforcement</u> of the organization's security <u>policies</u>…would not be taken seriously by the employees. <u>Top management</u> support must happen first if the <u>other issues</u> are to be handled effectively."		√			√	
"<u>Management</u> direction will set the expectations of employees and form a security-aware organization <u>culture</u>."			√			
"Without <u>top down support</u> for security, the enterprise <u>culture</u> cannot reflect a security conscious business practice and security cannot gain a significant foothold in a business."			√			
"Frequent security <u>policy</u> <u>updates</u> need to happen in a timely manner…we see policy updates as an important task."				√		
"<u>Management</u> must not only communicate the "contents" of the policy, but also the need for it. Management should reinforce the need and importance with consistent <u>enforcement</u> as well as a clearly defined process for <u>updates and reviews</u>."				√	√	
"<u>Enforcement</u> (and) <u>policy</u> violations may also be an excellent indicator for security staffs on the effectiveness of their policies, … and the general security state of the organization."					√	
"Without an established and widespread <u>awareness</u> and education effort it is difficult if not impossible to integrate security into the corporate <u>culture</u>."						√

For construct validity, expert panelists matched each item in the item pool to one of seven constructs in two separate evaluation rounds. The seven constructs in the scale included the independent and mediating variables from the study plus two decoy variables (policy development and organizational governance). Items that obtained at least a 75% agreement rate among the panelists were retained for the survey (Hinkin, 1998). If the agreement rate was less than 75%, then the item was dropped or modified and reevaluated. Although this item-to-construct matching process does not guarantee construct validity, this refinement effort produced a list of 70 questionnaire items that exhibited preliminary evidence of construct validity for the constructs of this study.

This important step helped minimize potential problems such as cross-loading of items across constructs.

The second objective concerned the issue of the perceived sensitive nature of security-related questions. Some consider information security research an extremely sensitive research topic (Straub & Welke, 1998) and recommend a cautious research approach because of a general mistrust by practitioners of attempts to gain data about the behaviors of security professionals (Kotulic & Clark, 2004). To minimize the problem of unacceptably high levels of perceived intrusiveness, the same expert panel evaluated each item using a willingness-to-answer scale specifically developed for this study and provided in Table

Table 3. Willingness-to-answer scale

Scale		Definition
1.	Unacceptably Intrusive	Many respondents may be unwilling to answer; a problem question.
2.	Moderately Intrusive	Some respondents may be unwilling to answer.
3.	Slightly Intrusive	A small number of respondents may be unwilling to answer.
4.	Not Intrusive	Respondents should be willing to answer; the question is OK

3. While a certain level of perceived intrusiveness is unavoidable, we removed items with the higher intrusive scores. This step is critical in the domain of security because items perceived to be unacceptably intrusive may discourage or influence survey completion.

In addition to scoring every item on the willingness-to-answer scale, some of the feedback from the expert panel addressed the more intrusive items in the pool. For instance, one panelist commented about an item, "(I) find it hard to believe you would get an honest or accurate answer" and subsequently rated the item as *unacceptably intrusive*. Based on this and other feedback, the item was dropped. We compared both the quantitative intrusiveness scores of each item with the qualitative feedback when evaluating problematic items. Through this analysis, we established the following guidelines to help us judge the perceived intrusiveness of each item. We judged an acceptable item to:

- be rated as either slightly (3) or not intrusive (4) by at least 70% of the panelists and
- have a mean score from all the panelists of at least a 2.75 on a 4.0 scale.

Based on the expert panel results, perceived intrusiveness problems did not surface with four of the six constructs in the theoretical model. All of the items intending to measure the top management support, security culture, user training, and policy relevance constructs met the two intrusive-ness guidelines. However, 22% of the initial policy enforcement and 33% of the security effectiveness items did not meet the two guidelines. Table 4 contains the panelists' intrusiveness scores for the dropped policy enforcement and effectiveness questions from the initial item pool.

The willingness-to-answer scale was not the only consideration for reducing perceived intrusiveness. Other factors may influence a potential respondent's participation more than simply perceived intrusiveness of the questionnaire's items. Some of these possible factors include the visible sponsorship of a research project by a reputable organization such as (ISC)^2, clearly written survey instructions, approval of a university human subjects office, implementation of secure sockets layer encryption at the survey web site, a posted privacy policy, and a general impression of professionalism. This study addressed all of these factors in an effort to minimize the perception of intrusiveness.

The expert panel process produced a survey instrument containing 63 candidate items. We then pilot tested the instrument with a convenience sample of 68 CISSPs who did not participate in previous steps of the project. Based on a confirmatory factor analysis of each construct modeled in isolation, we removed 28 of the 63 items because of high-cross loads and poor fit. The pilot test resulted in a 35-item instrument exhibiting six dimensions that was ready for a larger scale test. The Appendix lists all 35-items.

Table 4. Intrusiveness scores of dropped items

Proposed Survey Question (Item)	Slightly or Not Intrusive	Mean Score (4.0 max)
Dropped Policy Enforcement Items		
Security policies have no teeth. [Reverse Code (RC)]	50%	2.75
There is conflict between security staff and employees regarding policy enforcement. (RC)	67%	3.00
Policies are selectively enforced. (RC)	67%	3.00
Computer security abuses often go unpunished. (RC)	67%	2.75
Dropped Security Effectiveness Items		
Sensitive information is sufficiently protected.	45%	2.42
Valuable information is effectively secured.	64%	2.58
Our organization has adequate computer security.	64%	2.67

Step Five: Quantitative Data Collection

For the large-scale survey, we collected data in three phases to help control for the potential validity threat of common method variance. Common method variance is a type of method bias where variable correlations are vulnerable to artificial inflation (or deflation) due to the method used during data collection. Common method variance is one of the main sources of measurement error that can threaten the validity of empirical research conclusions (Campbell & Fiske, 1959; Podsakoff, MacKenzie, Lee, & Podsakoff, 2003). It is a particular concern with self-report surveys where predictor and criterion variables come from the same source. Fortunately, investigators can strengthen their research studies by taking steps to control and even eliminate this validity threat. The key to controlling method variance is to identify what the measures of the predictor and criterion variables have in common and to minimize this commonality through the design of the study. For example, time gaps in data collection is a remedy that helps ensure that respondents are in different cognitive mood states when providing answers to predictor and crite-

rion variables. Gaps can also reduce the chance of respondents engaging in hypothesis guessing (Straub, Limayem, & Karahanna-Evaristo, 1995) and minimize the tendency to answer in a socially desirable manner (Podsakoff et al., 2003). While it is impossible to eliminate all forms of bias in a study, our goal is to reduce the plausibility of method bias as an explanation of the relationships between the constructs.

We used two design remedies to reduce common method variance (Podsakoff et al., 2003). First, at least a 48-hour hiatus separated the collection of the independent, mediator, and dependent variables. Second, we designed a different response format and Likert scale for collection of the independent variable, top management support. Figure 3 illustrates the phased data collection approach used in this study.

Step Six: Quantitative Data Analysis

The results section presents an analysis of the data collected in step five. We used structural equation modeling (SEM) software to test our proposed model.

Figure 3. Three-phased approach to data collection

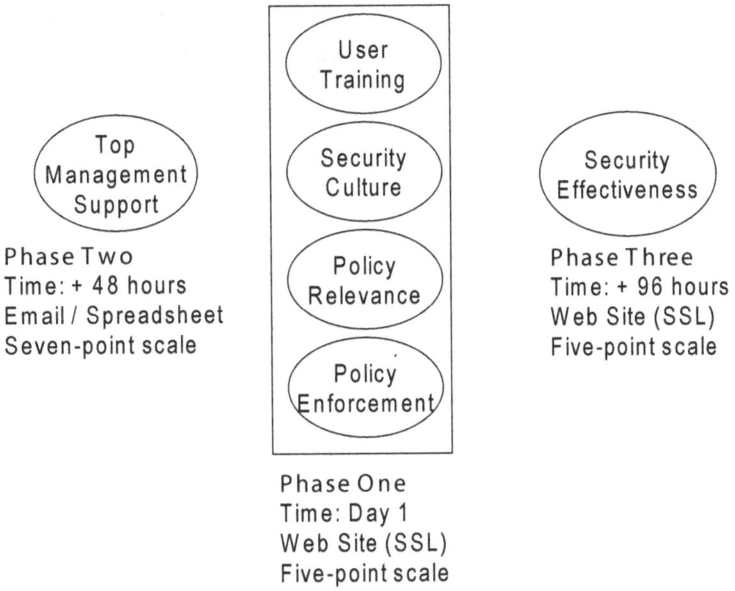

RESULTS

This section is divided into three parts. First, we describe our sample demographics. Second, we provide a statistical analysis of each construct modeled in isolation. Third, we evaluate the hypothesized model as well as an alternative, second-order factor model. We also provide a sub-sample analysis using the two models.

Demographics

A single email notification (no reminders) was sent to approximately 30,000 constituents of (ISC)^2, inviting them to participate in a three-phased research survey. The message was an official 'e-blast' containing one other unrelated item of (ISC)^2 business. Table 5 lists the survey response rates by phase and the actual average time that respondents took to complete each of the phases. Tables 6 and 7 provide sample demographics (N = 740).

Statistical Analysis of Each Construct

We used the Amos 5.0.1 program to test the theoretical model. We modeled each of the measured factors in isolation, then in pairs, and then as a collective network (Segars & Grover, 1998). To support convergent validity, all item loadings should be statistically significant and above .707

Table 5. Sample size and response rates by phase

	Phase 1	Phase 2	Phase 3	Usable
N	936	760	743	740
Response Rate	3% of 30,000	81% of Phase 1	79% of Phase 1	79% of Phase 1
Actual Mean of Temporal Separation	Day 1	84 hours after Phase 1	192 hours after Phase 1	---

Table 6. Country demographics

Country	Count	Percent	Country	Count	Percent
United States	402	54.3%	Malaysia	6	0.8%
Canada	60	8.1%	Sweden	6	0.8%
United Kingdom	36	4.9%	Italy	5	0.7%
Hong Kong	20	2.7%	New Zealand	5	0.7%
Australia	18	2.4%	Saudi Arabia	5	0.7%
India	17	2.3%	Belgium	4	0.5%
Netherlands	16	2.2%	Denmark	4	0.5%
Finland	12	1.6%	France	4	0.5%
Singapore	12	1.6%	Germany	4	0.5%
China	9	1.2%	Ireland	4	0.5%
South Africa	8	1.1%	Mexico	4	0.5%
Russian Federation	7	0.9%	Nigeria	4	0.5%
Brazil	6	0.8%	Others	53	7.2%
Korea, South	6	0.8%	Not provided	3	0.4%
			Total	740	100%

Table 7. Industry demographic

Industry	Count	Percent
Info Tech, Security, Telecommunications	201	27.2%
Finance, Banking, Insurance	187	25.3%
Government	184	24.9%
Consulting	166	22.4%
Manufacturing	69	9.3%
Healthcare	63	8.5%
Other	50	6.8%
Consumer Products, Retail, Wholesale	47	6.4%
Education, Training	47	6.4%
Professional Services (legal, marketing, etc.)	30	4.1%
Utilities	29	3.9%
Energy	24	3.2%
Transportation, Warehousing	15	2.0%
Industrial Technology	14	1.9%
Non-Profit	13	1.8%
Travel & Hospitality	11	1.5%
Entertainment	6	0.8%
Publishing	5	0.7%
Real Estate, Rental, Leasing	4	0.5%

Note: Respondents were free to indicate multiple industries indicating that over half the variance is captured by the latent construct. Supporting both convergent and discriminant validity, GFI, NFI, AGFI, CFI and RMSEA should be within acceptable ranges (Straub, Boudreau, & Gefen, 2004). Table 8 presents a list of acceptable cut-off values.

During this process, we dropped six items from 35-item instrument due to low item reliability and high cross-loads resulting in a more parsimonious 29-item instrument. The Appendix provides the 35-item instrument and identifies the six dropped items. Table 9 presents the measurement properties of the final six constructs, each modeled in isolation. The results indicate acceptable scale reliability and construct validity (convergent and discriminant). We conducted an additional test for discriminant validity between each pair of constructs by comparing the chi-square statistic of a constrained and an unconstrained two-construct model based on procedures provided in Segars & Grover (1998, p.153). The chi-square differences between each construct showed significant differences (p < .001) suggesting the six constructs are distinct conceptual entities.

Theoretical Models

Next, we tested the original hypothesized model as a collective network. Table 10 provides the measurement model: standardized factor loadings, critical value (z-statistic), and squared multiple correlations (SMC) for each of the 29 indicators of the final instrument. Figure 4 presents the path model: the standardized causal path findings, selected fit indices, and SMC values.[2] All hypothesized paths are significant with indices indicating the data is consistent with the hypothesized model. Based on this analysis, each of the hypotheses from Table 1 is supported.

In the survey, respondents provided demographic information that aided in sub-sample analysis. We used this information to detect differences among demographics based on geography, organizational size, and industry. Table 11 provides results of testing the hypothesized model using key demographic sub samples. Because of the smaller size of some of the sub samples (e.g. n < 200), interpretations should be made with caution.

Table 8. Summary of acceptable cut-off values of reliability and fit

Measure	Cut-Off Value
Cronbach's alpha	≥ .70
Item loadings	Significant and ≥ .707
Adjusted chi-square	≤ 3.0
GFI	≥ .90
AGFI	≥ .80
CFI	≥ .90
NFI	≥ .90
RMSEA	≤ .08

Table 9. Measurement properties of constructs (29-item instrument)

Construct	Phase	Items	Alpha	χ^2/df	GFI	AGFI	CFI	NFI	RMSEA
Top Mgt Support	2	6	.93	4.98	.98	.95	.99	.99	.073
User Training	1	5	.93	3.95	.99	.97	1.00	.99	.063
Security Culture	1	5	.90	2.33	.99	.98	1.00	1.00	.042
Pol. Relevance	1	4	.90	.379	1.00	1.00	1.00	1.00	.000
Pol. Enforcement	1	4	.87	1.55	.99	.99	.99	1.00	.027
Sec. Effectiveness	3	5	.91	1.32	1.00	.99	1.00	1.00	.020

Table 10. Measurement model

Constructs	Indicators	Loadings	Critical Value	SMC
Top Management Support alpha = .93	TM1	.84	31.33	0.71
	TM2	.79	27.53	0.62
	TM3	.78	27.34	0.62
	TM4	.87	33.83	0.77
	TM5	.88	---	0.78
	TM6	.83	30.13	0.68
Employee Training alpha = .93	UT1	.81	31.39	0.66
	UT2	.88	37.56	0.78
	UT4	.92	---	0.85
	UT5	.85	34.77	0.72
	UT6	.81	31.20	0.66
Security Culture alpha = .90	SC1	.75	23.54	0.57
	SC3	.77	24.52	0.59
	SC4	.83	27.12	0.69
	SC5	.85	---	0.72
	SC6	.84	28.35	0.70
Policy Relevance alpha = .90	PR1	.90	34.98	0.81
	PR2	.73	24.01	0.53
	PR4	.80	27.98	0.64
	PR5	.90	---	0.81
Policy Enforcement alpha = .87	PE1	.85	---	0.72
	PE2	.78	23.78	0.60
	PE3	.83	26.32	0.70
	PE4	.72	21.29	0.51
Security Effectiveness alpha = .91	EF1	.85	31.36	0.72
	EF2	.83	30.69	0.70
	EF3	.75	25.31	0.56
	EF4	.89	---	0.79
	EF5	.77	26.84	0.60

Note: All loadings significant at p < .001

In addition to the original model, we tested an alternative model that posits a second-order factor governing the correlations among *user training, security culture, policy relevance,* and *policy enforcement*. Illustrated in Figure 5, this model provides an additional perspective on the factor analytic structure of the original model. The motivation for proposing and testing the alternative model is the recognition that a more general latent construct may determine the first-order latent constructs. The four mediator variables may be influenced by a second-order factor that does not have direct effects on the observed variables of the study (Bollen, 1989). This alternative model is an exploratory investigation of the original. Unlike the original, it was not conceptualized from reading the qualitative responses. Yet, it is valuable because it offers a different way of think-

Figure 4. Path diagram of hypothesized model

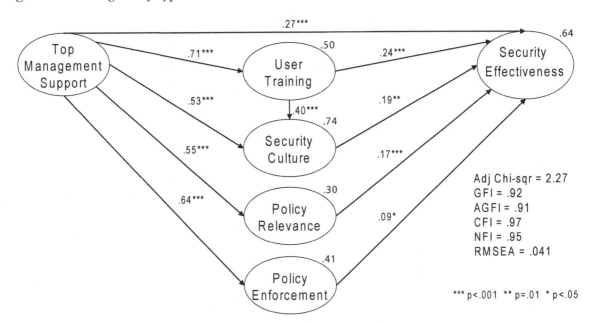

Note. Each endogenous variables' SMC estimate is to the upper-right of the construct

ing about the relationships among the constructs. Our interpretation of the second-order factor is *managerial practice* in information security. In the model, managerial practice represents the repeated actions and instructions of management to promote information security effectiveness in their organization. Table 12 illustrates the results of running the alternative model using the same demographic sub samples from Table 11.

Empirical support for both the original and alternative models are found in the magnitude and significance of the estimated parameters as well as the amount of variance explained by the structural equations (Segars & Grover, 1998). The alternative model is a more parsimonious representation of the observed covariance (six paths versus ten paths in the original model). Unlike the original model, all paths in the alternative model are significant at $p < .001$. The amount of explained variance measured by SMC is higher in each variable in the alternative model. Additionally, every model fit index improved in the alternative model including those measures that

account for degrees of freedom (e.g. AGFI). In the demographic analysis using the alternate model, every path is significant at $p < .001$ including the smaller sub samples such as from Asia-Pacific respondents (n=104). Moreover, the model-fit generally improved from the original model for each sub sample. Thus, results suggest that the alternative model has general applicability across the demographic categories of the sampled data of this study.

The improved fit in the alternative model does not necessarily mean it is the better of the two models. The original model, for instance, had the advantage of measuring the magnitude of the direct effect of each mediator variable on the dependent variable. This advantage was lost in the alternative model due to the inclusion of the more general second-order factor. This advantage of the original model was instrumental in bringing about one of the findings of the study pertaining to policy enforcement that we will discuss in the next section of this paper.

Table 11. *Demographic tests of the hypothesized model*

Sample	n	Top Mgt Support					UT	UT	SC	PR	PE	Fit
		EF	UT	SC	PR	PE	SC	Security Effectiveness				GFI CFI RMSEA
US & Canada	462	***	***	***	***	***	***	***	**	**	NS	.91 .97 .042
Europe	121	*	***	***	***	***	***	NS	*	**	NS	.79 .96 .051
Asia-Pacific	104	*	***	***	***	***	**	NS	NS	NS	NS	.76 .93 .065
Government Sector	184	NS	***	***	***	***	***	***	*	*	NS	.84 .97 .046
Finance, Banking Sector	187	**	***	***	***	***	***	NS	NS	*	**	.84 .96 .050
Info Tech (IT) Sector	201	*	***	***	***	***	***	**	NS	*	NS	.84 .96 .052
Small (< 500 employees)	193	NS	***	***	***	***	***	**	*	**	**	.84 .96 .049
Med. (500-15,000 employees)	302	***	***	***	***	***	***	NS	NS	***	NS	.88 .97 .048
Large (> 15,000 employees)	245	*	***	***	***	***	***	***	NS	NS	NS	.85 .95 .054
No top officer in organization[#]	267	***	***	***	***	***	***	NS	*	**	*	.87 .96 .044
Yes top officer in organization	460	**	***	***	***	***	***	***	*	***	NS	.91 .97 .041

Notes: ***p<.001; **p<.01; *p<.05; NS Not Significant
EF: security effectiveness; UT: user training; SC: sec. culture; PR: policy relevance; PE: policy enforcement
[#] Does the organization have a top security officer (e.g. Chief Security Officer, Director of Information Security)?

Figure 5. *Alternative, second-order factor model*

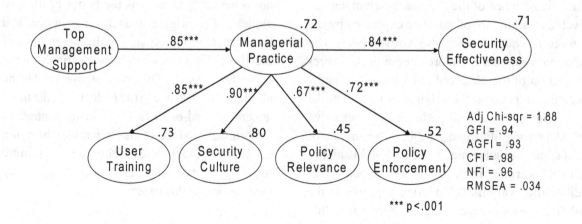

*** p<.001

Table 12. Demographic tests of second-order factor model

Sample	n	Top Mgt Support	Managerial Practice				Mgt Practice	Fit
		Mgt Practice	UT	SC	PR	PE	Sec Effect	GFI CFI RMSEA
US & Canada	462	***	***	***	***	***	***	.92 .98 .035
Europe	121	***	***	***	***	***	***	.80 .96 .045
Asia-Pacific	104	***	***	***	***	***	***	.77 .94 .062
Government sector	184	***	***	***	***	***	***	.84 .97 .045
Finance, Banking, sector	187	***	***	***	***	***	***	.84 .96 .050
Info Tech (IT) sector	201	***	***	***	***	***	***	.85 .97 .045
Small (< 500 employees)	193	***	***	***	***	***	***	.84 .97 .045
Medium (500-15,000 employees)	302	***	***	***	***	***	***	.89 .97 .041
Large (> 15,000 employees)	245	***	***	***	***	***	***	.87 .96 .049
No top officer in organization	267	***	***	***	***	***	***	.88 .97 .039
Yes top officer in organization	460	***	***	***	***	***	***	.92 .98 .035

Tests were conducted to estimate the amount of common method variance in the collected data (N=740) using confirmatory procedures provided in the literature (Facteau, Dobbins, Russell, Ladd, & Kudisch, 1995; Williams, Cote, & Buckley, 1989). Confirmatory factor analysis shows that a single latent factor representing common variance did not fit the data well (χ^2/df = 14.1). For comparison, the alternative model (Figure 5) provides a better fit (χ^2/df = 1.9). The Chi-square difference between the single latent factor and alternative models is significant at *p <.001* [$\Delta\chi^2$ (6 df) = 4598.4]. Since there was a significant improvement in model fit between the single latent factor model and the alternative model, we have evidence that common method variance is not problematic in the sampled data. This finding is not surprising since the procedural remedies used during data collection aimed to minimize the effect of undesirable method variance among the constructs of the study. Researchers considering using this instrument can take further steps to minimize common method variance by obtaining measures of the dependent variable from a different source. For example, data for security effectiveness can come from employees other than full-time security professionals.

Based on the empirical results presented, we found support for both the original and alternative theoretical models. The next section discusses the findings of the study.

LINKS TO EXISTING THEORY

In their seminal text, Glaser & Strauss (1967) stated that it is desirable to link grounded models to existing theory to enhance internal validity and generalizability (see also Orlikowski, 1993). In this section, we link aspects of this study to three existing theories and make suggestions for future research. These aspects include top management support, general deterrence theory, and the 'dilemma of the supervisor' notion.

Existing Notions of Management Support

Top management support refers to the degree that senior management understands the importance of the security function and the extent to which management is perceived supporting security goals and priorities. By virtue of their position, top management can significantly influence resource allocation and act as a champion of change in creating an organizational environment conducive to security goals. Support from top management has been recognized for at least four decades as necessary for computer security management. For example, Joseph Wasserman discussed the importance of executive support stating, "Computer security thus involves a review of every possible source of control breakdown…one factor that has made the job more difficult is lack of awareness by many executives of new control concepts required for computer systems" (1969, p. 120).

The qualitative data from this study suggests that obtaining top management support is important for an effective information security program. As one CISSP stated, "Management buy-in and increasing the security awareness of employees is key. Technology is great, but without…management's backing, all the bits in the world won't help." The quantitative results of this study also suggest that management support is especially important to information security effectiveness. Among the results from the SEM portion of this study, the positive association between *top management support* and *security effectiveness* was significantly demonstrated in a wide-range of demographic data (see Figures 4, 5 and Tables 11, 12).

A substantial IS literature stream exists about the management support construct. With few exceptions, much of the empirical analysis has limited the effect of management support on a dependent 'success' variable to a simple linear function (Jarvenpaa & Ives, 1991; Sharma & Yetton, 2003). Consequently, the current study contributes to the IS literature by offering a model that substantially mediates the relationships between management support and a dependent variable. This finding is valuable because the mediator variables of the study help show the complex relationship between management support and an appropriate dependent variable.

Both the original and alternative models of this study may be structured in a general form, which we illustrate in Figure 6. Future research can apply these forms to areas outside the realm of IS security, especially in organizational environments where top management support is critical to success. For instance, based on a meta-analysis of research published in 82 articles, Jasperson et al (2002) offered several metaconjectures about environments where top management support may be especially critical. One such environment is characterized by resource conflict of IT projects. Research that studies organizational environments with considerable resource conflict may be able to benefit from the general models by applying them in their research setting.

We do not suggest that the general models are all-comprehensive depictions of mediators between top management support and information security effectiveness. Depending on the study, researchers can add different mediator variables to the model. For example, an added mediator variable could represent financial resource support. For this study, we considered adding such a variable during the qualitative steps of the study since many respondents indicated that obtaining financial resources for security programs is a critical organizational issue. However, we felt that asking financially related survey questions could have an adverse effect on the perceived

Figure 6. General forms of the theoretical models of this study

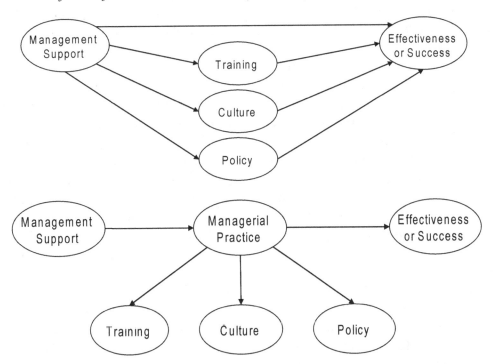

intrusiveness of the survey instrument. Other studies where perceived intrusiveness is less of a concern could consider adding a financial resource type of variable to the model.

Deterrence Theory

The criminology theory of general deterrence emphasizes policing as a means of warding off potential abusive acts primarily through the fear of sanctions and unpleasant consequences (Parker, 1981; Straub, 1990). In the IS realm, deterrents are passive, administrative controls that can include security training sessions and policy statements that specify the proper use of an information system (Straub & Nance, 1990). Administrative deterrent efforts have been empirically demonstrated to result in fewer IS abuses (Straub, 1990). In the IS literature, the application of deterrence theory has been widely applied in related security studies to include software piracy (Gopal & Sanders, 1997; Peace, Galletta, & Thong, 2002), ethics (Harrington, 1996), risk management (Straub & Welke, 1998), abuse detection (Straub & Nance, 1990), social control theory (Lee, Lee, & Yoo, 2004), and security effectiveness (Kankanhalli et al., 2003; Straub, 1990).

Our study has parallels with the Kankanhalli et al. (2003) and Straub (1990) studies that are worth discussing. First, the Kankanhalli et al study included top management support in a model of IS security effectiveness that was based on both deterrence and preventive efforts. Although their results of the hypothesized model were mixed, the top management support variable demonstrated a significant relationship on effectiveness through a mediating variable identified as *preventive efforts*. Second, while discussing the practical implications from his empirical study, Straub (1990, p. 272) suggests four actions to improve security effectiveness. First, managers who desire security improvements should establish policies as the precondition to effective deterrence efforts. Second, once polices are established, management needs to ensure users are educated and informed about proper IS use. Security officers should stress that policy violations will be accordingly punished. Third, with policy in place, managers can ensure that appropriate monitoring and surveillance programs of employee activities are utilized to enforce policy. Security officers should then follow up on all identified violations to help deter potential abusers. Finally, management should ensure the implementation of preventive mechanisms with security software that proactively helps to minimize security incidents. When comparing Straub's action plan to our study, four of the five predictor variables in our model are implied in Straub's suggested actions. The variable in our model not in Straub's suggestions is security culture. Yet, the literature supports culture as an important part of successful security programs (Leach, 2003; von Solms & von Solms, 2004). The culture construct has also been suggested for inclusion in future deterrence based security studies (Kankanhalli et al., 2003). Hence, while we did not base our study *a priori* on deterrence, the variables in our model may be interpreted through the lens of general deterrence theory.

The Dilemma of the Supervisor

The *policy enforcement* construct, while demonstrating acceptable scale reliability ($\alpha = .87$) and fit (e.g. GFI = .99; CFI = .99), had the weakest effect on the dependent variable compared to the other variables of the study. This weaker relationship is apparent in two areas. First, in the original theoretical model, the relationship between policy enforcement and the dependent variable had the lowest level of statistical significance compared to the other variables in the study. Second, as Table 11 shows, eight of the eleven sub-samples had non-significant *policy enforcement – security effectiveness* paths.

We propose that the 'dilemma of the supervisor' notion may help explain the weaker relationship between *policy enforcement* and

security effectiveness. This dilemma is described by Strickland (1958) as occurring when the excessive use of surveillance, monitoring, and authority leads to management's distrust of employees and the perception of an increased need for more surveillance and control. Because managers see employees as motivated by the controls in place, managers develop a jaundiced view of their people (Ghoshal, 2005, p. 85). Too much surveillance and monitoring of employee activities to enforce policy compliance is then perceived by employees as overly controlling which may damage employee self-perception, deteriorate trust, and decrease intrinsic motivation (Ghoshal, 2005). Applying this notion to our study, the relationship between *policy enforcement* and *security effectiveness* may be non-linear. If organizations want to encourage employees to intrinsically behave in a security-minded fashion, then an optimum level of policy enforcement may exist. Either too much or too little enforcement may have negative consequence on effectiveness.

A careful review of the qualitative data did not reveal participants identifying potential problems associated with excessive monitoring. However, this notion has been identified in the IS literature. While monitoring can help enforce important security policies, some employees may regard this as negatively affecting their work habits and privacy (Ariss, 2002). Managers have a key role to play in designing monitoring and enforcement systems that are effective, yet not viewed as too onerous or invasive. In this way, employees not only tolerate the monitoring system, but understand and approve of it (George, 1996). Based on this discussion, future research can further study the potential non-linear relationship between policy enforcement and security effectiveness.

LIMITATIONS

This study developed and empirically tested a theory of information security effectiveness in organizations. However, the findings are limited in that the sample was homogeneous to the (ISC)² constituency. Participant concerns from this population may have biased the models in favor of organizational environments that typically hire certified security professionals. Before generalizing the results to other populations, researchers should apply these theoretical models to samples from different national cultures, specific industries, organization contexts, or in case studies. Research has shown that certain management practices can be compatible and others incompatible depending on the culture of a society (Hofstede, 1993). We recommend that any application of the models in culture-specific settings (i.e. consulting or case studies) should take national culture into account (McCoy, Galletta, & King, 2005). In our study, the CISSP certification requirements and the global nature of modern Internet security threats may have acted to minimize many cultural differences (Yang, 1986). The proliferation of IT certification bodies with rigorous entrance requirements like (ISC)² and their role in minimizing cross-cultural differences is a potential question for future research.

Another limitation of this study is the use of self-report, perception-based variables versus objective measures. The literature contains arguments both for and against the use of subjective measures (Podsakoff & Organ, 1986; Spector, 1994; Straub et al., 2004). Some evidence suggests that perceived and objective measures are positively associated (Venkatraman & Ramanujam, 1987) while others suggest they are not positively associated (Srinivasan, 1985). The use of objective data can be especially problematic in the area of security. Many companies are hesitant to provide hard data regarding computer abuse or security ineffectiveness because they may not want to risk embarrassing media reports. In addition, it is difficult to know if hard data (e.g. number of incidents, financial loss) is accurate and complete considering that security incidents often are underreported or undiscovered (Gordon et al., 2005;

Straub & Nance, 1990). An alternative to hard data is to measure security effectiveness using a professional subjective judgment as accomplished in this study. One can even argue that a qualified judgment about an organization's overall security program is more sensitive than the sharing of hard, objective data since a professional judgment can take a holistic view of an organization's security program while taking into account aspects that are difficult to measure objectively. Despite the limitation of using perception-based variables, subjective measures can be an appropriate research tool for exploratory studies into a phenomenon of interest (Spector, 1994). Taken as a whole, it would be prudent for organizations attempting to measure security effectiveness to take a multifaceted approach by collecting both hard, objective data as well as soft, subjective perceptions. This type of combined approach is most likely to lead to an accurate view of the state of an organization's information security program.

IMPLICATIONS AND CONCLUSION

The models proposed in this study emerged from an analysis of qualitative data. Grounded models are especially relevant to practitioners because the practitioner community provided the data from which the models emerged. This is important considering that IS researchers continue to struggle to make research relevant to practitioners (Baskerville & Myers, 2004) despite the frequent calls for IS researchers to do so (Benbasat & Zmud, 1999). Since the constructs of this study embody relevant issues of IS security, managers can improve security effectiveness by thinking about and applying the theoretical model of this study in their organizations. While the scales and the model do not include every aspect that should be important to managers, the model does focus on some of the most critical areas that managers can influence to bring about an effective information security program. We believe a key implication of this research is the development of a theoretical model that is useful and relevant to information security practitioners.

Considering that many IT executives now consider security among their top issues, the findings of this study should be highly relevant to IT management. While no organization can have perfect security, there are specific practices that management can do to maximize the protection of their critical information resources. Results of this study suggest that sufficient levels of top management support, user training, security culture, policy relevance and appropriate policy enforcement are significant predictors of the effectiveness of an information security program. Because many computer and information security problems today require managerial solutions, the model proposed in this study can help management focus their efforts in the areas where they can make the most difference.

We summarize our findings by suggesting the following proposition: An organization's overall security health can be accurately predicted by asking a single question: Does top management visibly and actively support the organization's information security program? The answer to this question is a strong indicator and predictor into the overall health and effectiveness of the organization's information security program. If answered in the affirmative, it is likely that an organization's information security program is achieving its goals. If answered in the negative, it is less likely the program is accomplishing its goals. We argue that the findings of this study support this proposition.

NOTE

Opinions, conclusions and recommendations expressed or implied within are solely those of the authors and do not necessarily represent the views of USAF Academy, USAF, the DoD or any other government agency.

REFERENCES

Ariss, S. S. (2002). Computer monitoring: Benefits and pitfalls facing management. *Information & Management, 39*(7), 553-558.

Bagchi, K., & Udo, G. (2003). An analysis of the growth of computer and internet security breaches. *Communications of the AIS, 12*(46), 684-700.

Baskerville, R. L., & Myers, M. D. (2004). Special issue on action research in information systems: Making IS research relevant to practice. Forward. *MIS Quarterly, 28*(3), 329-335.

Benbasat, I., & Zmud, R. W. (1999). Empirical research in information systems: The practice of relevance. *MIS Quarterly, 23*(1), 3-16.

Bollen, K. A. (1989). *Structural equations with latent variables*. New York: John Wiley & Sons.

Campbell, D. T., & Fiske, D. W. (1959). Convergent and discriminant validation by the multi-trait-multimethod matrix. *Psychological Bulletin, 56*(2), 81-105.

Computer Emergency Response Team (CERT). (2004). *CERT statistics*. Retrieved May, 2004, from http://www.cert.org/stats/cert_stats.html#incidents

DeVellis, R. F. (2003). *Scale development. Theory and applications* (2nd ed. Vol. 26). Thousand Oaks, CA: Sage Publications.

Dhillon, G., & Backhouse, J. (2001). Current directions in IS security research: Towards socio-organizational perspectives. *Information Systems Journal, 11*(2), 127-153.

Facteau, J. D., Dobbins, G. H., Russell, J. E. A., Ladd, R. T., & Kudisch, J. D. (1995). The influence of general perceptions of training environment on pretraining motivation and perceived training transfer. *Journal of Management, 21*(1), 1-25.

Files, J. (2006, June 29). Missing laptop with veterans' data is found. *New York Times.*

Frazier, P. A., Barron, K. E., & Tix, A., P. (2004). Testing moderator and mediator effects in counseling psychology. *Journal of Counseling Psychology, 51*(1), 115-134.

Galal, G. H. (2001). From contexts to constructs: The use of grounded theory in operationalising contingent process models. *European Journal of Information Systems, 10,* 2-14.

Garg, A., Curtis, J., & Halper, H. (2003). The financial impact of IT security breaches: What do investors think? *Information Systems Security, 12*(1), 22-34.

Gefen, D. (2003). Assessing unidimensionality through LISREL: An explanation and example. *Communications of the AIS, 12,* 23-46.

George, J. F. (1996). Computer-based monitoring: Common perceptions and empirical results. *MIS Quarterly, 20*(4), 459-480.

Ghoshal, S. (2005). Bad management theories are destroying good management practices. *Academy of Management Learning & Education, 4*(1), 75-91.

Glaser, B. G., & Strauss, A. L. (1967). *The discovery of grounded theory: Strategies for qualitative research.* New York: Aldine Publishing Company.

Gopal, R. D., & Sanders, G. L. (1997). Preventive and deterrent controls for software piracy. *Journal of Management Information Systems, 13*(4), 29-47.

Gordon, L. A., Loeb, M. P., Lucyshyn, W., & Richardson, R. (2005). *10th annual CSI/FBI computer crime and security survey.* San Francisco, CA: Computer Security Institute.

Harrington, S. J. (1996). The effect of codes of ethics and personal denial of responsibility on computer abuse judgments and intentions. *MIS Quarterly, 20*(3), 257-278.

Hinkin, T. R. (1998). A brief tutorial on the development of measures for use in survey questionnaires. *Organizational Research Methods, 1*(1), 104-121.

Hofstede, G. (1993). Cultural constraints in management theories. *Academy of Management Journal, 7*(1), 81-94.

Jarvenpaa, S. L., & Ives, B. (1991). Executive involvement and participation in the management of information technology. *MIS Quarterly, 15*(2), 205-221.

Jasperson, J. S., Carte, T. A., Saunders, C. S., Butler, B. S., Croes, H. J. P., & Zheng, W. (2002). Power and information technology research: A metatriangulation review. *MIS Quarterly, 26*(4), 397-459.

Kankanhalli, A., Hock-Hai, T., Bernard, C. Y. T., & Kwok-Kee, W. (2003). An integrative study of information systems security effectiveness. *International Journal of Information Management, 23*(2), 139-154.

Karahanna, E., Evaristo, R., & Srite, M. (2004). Methodological issues in MIS cross-cultural research. In M. E. Whitman & A. B. Woszczynski (Eds.), *The handbook of information systems research* (pp. 166-177). Hershey, PA: Idea Group Publishing.

Kotulic, A. G., & Clark, J. G. (2004). Why there aren't more information security research studies. *Information & Management, 41*(5), 597-607.

Leach, J. (2003). Improving user security behavior. *Computers & Security, 22*(8), 685-692.

Lee, S. M., Lee, S. G., & Yoo, S. (2004). An integrative model of computer abuse based on social control and general deterrence theories. *Information & Management, 41*(6), 707-718.

MacKinnon, D. P., Krull, J. L., & Lockwood, C. (2000). Mediation, confounding, and suppression: Different names for the same effect. *Prevention Science, 2,* 15-27.

McCoy, S., Galletta, D. F., & King, W. R. (2005). Integrating national culture into IS research: The need for current individual-level measures. *Communications of the Association for Information Systems, 15*, 211-224.

Nunnally, J. (1978). *Psychometric theory*. New York: McGraw-Hill.

Orlikowski, W. (1993). CASE tools as organizational change: Investigating incremental and radical changes in systems development. *MIS Quarterly, 17*(3), 309-340.

Parker, D. B. (1981). *Computer security management*. Reston, Virginia: Reston Publishing Company.

Peace, A. G., Galletta, D. F., & Thong, J. Y. L. (2002). Software piracy in the workplace: A model and empirical test. *Journal of Management Information Systems, 20*(1), 153-177.

Podsakoff, P. M., MacKenzie, S. B., Lee, J. Y., & Podsakoff, N. P. (2003). Common method bias in behavioral research: A critical review of the literature and recommended remedies. *Journal of Applied Psychology, 88*(5), 879-903.

Podsakoff, P. M., & Organ, D. W. (1986). Self-reports in organizational research: Problems and prospects. *Journal of Management, 12*(4), 531-544.

Segars, A. H., & Grover, V. (1998). Strategic information systems planning success: An investigation of the construct and its measurement. *MIS Quarterly, 22*(2), 139-163.

Sharma, R., & Yetton, P. (2003). The contingent effects of management support and task interdependence on successful information systems implementation. *MIS Quarterly, 27*(4), 533-555.

Spector, P. E. (1994). Using self-report questionnaires in OB research: A comment on the use of a controversial method. *Journal of Organizational Behavior, 15*, 385-392.

Srinivasan, A. (1985). Alternative measures of system effectiveness: Associations and implications. *MIS Quarterly, 9*(3), 243-253.

Straub, D. W. (1990). Effective IS security: An empirical study. *Information Systems Research, 1*(3), 255-276.

Straub, D. W., Boudreau, M. C., & Gefen, D. (2004). Validating guidelines for IS positivist research. *Communications of the AIS, 13*(24), 380-427.

Straub, D. W., Limayem, M., & Karahanna-Evaristo, E. (1995). Measuring system usage: Implications for IS theory testing. *MIS Quarterly, 41*(8), 1328-1342.

Straub, D. W., & Nance, W. D. (1990). Discovering and disciplining computer abuse in organizations: A field study. *MIS Quarterly, 14*(1), 45-60.

Straub, D. W., & Welke, R. J. (1998). Coping with systems risk: Security planning models for management decision making. *MIS Quarterly, 22*(4), 441-469.

Strauss, A., & Corbin, J. (1998). *Basics of qualitative research. Techniques and procedures for developing grounded theory* (2nd ed.). Thousand Oaks, CA: Sage.

Strickland, L. H. (1958). Surveillance and trust. *Journal of Personality, 26*, 200-215.

Venkatraman, N., & Ramanujam, V. (1987). Measurement of business economic performance: An examination of method convergency. *Journal of Management, 13*(1), 109-122.

von Solms, R., & von Solms, B. (2004). From policies to culture. *Computers & Security, 23*, 275-279.

Wasserman, J. J. (1969). Plugging the leaks in computer security. *Harvard Business Review, 47*(5), 119-129.

Williams, L. J., Cote, J. A., & Buckley, M. R. (1989). Lack of method variance in self-reported affect and perceptions at work: Reality or artifact? *Journal of Applied Psychology, 74*, 462-468.

Yang, K. S. (1986). Will societal modernization eventually eliminate cross-cultural psychological differences. In M. H. Bond (Ed.), *The cross-cultural challenge to social psychology*. Newbury Park, CA: Sage.

ENDNOTES

[1] In part because attacks against Internet-connected systems have become so commonplace, the CERT no longer publishes incident numbers. See http://www.cert.org/stats

[2] We also conducted various mediation tests described in the literature (MacKinnon, Krull, & Lockwood, 2000). In our model, the total percent mediated by the four mediator variables on the dependent variable was 61%. The percent mediated of each variable: user training 25%, security culture 15%, policy relevance 13%, and policy enforcement 8%.

APPENDIX.   SURVEY INSTRUMENT.

The pilot test supported a 35-item instrument. During the large-scale survey, we dropped six items resulting in a 29-item instrument. We coded reasons for dropping each item as follows:

[X] = high cross loading with other constructs.
[R] = low reliability.
[U] = high residual covariance with other items (Gefen, 2003)

Constructs: TM = top management support; UT = user training; SC = security culture; PR = policy relevance; PE = policy enforcement; EF = security effectiveness

Code Item. Each begins with, "In the organization,"

TM1   Top management considers information security an important organizational priority.
TM2   Top executives are interested in security issues.
TM3   Top management takes security issues into account when planning corporate strategies.
TM4   Senior leadership's words and actions demonstrate that security is a priority.
TM5   Visible support for security goals by senior management is obvious.
TM6   Senior management gives strong and consistent support to the security program.
UT1   Necessary efforts are made to educate employees about *new* security polices.
UT2   Information security awareness is communicated well.
UT3 [R]   A variety of business communications (notices, posters, newsletters, etc.) are used to promote security awareness.
UT4   An effective security awareness program exists.
UT5   A continuous, ongoing security awareness program exists.

UT6	Users receive adequate security refresher training appropriate for their job function.
SC1	Employees value the importance of security.
SC2 [X]	A culture exists that promotes good security practices.
SC3	Security has traditionally been considered an important organizational value.
SC4	Practicing good security is the accepted way of doing business.
SC5	The overall environment fosters security-minded thinking.
SC6	Information security is a key norm shared by organizational members.
PR1	Information security policy is consistently updated on a periodic basis.
PR2	Information security policy is updated when technology changes require it.
PR3 [X R U]	Policy is updated when legal & regulatory changes require it.
PR4	An established information security policy review and update process exists.
PR5	Security policy is properly updated on a regular basis.
PR6 [X]	Information security policies are aligned with business goals.
PR7 [X]	Information security policies reflect the objectives of the organization.
PR8 [X]	Risk assessments are conducted prior to writing new security polices.
PE1	Employees caught violating important security policies are appropriately corrected.
PE2	Information security rules are enforced by sanctioning the employees who break them.
PE3	Repeat security offenders are appropriately disciplined.
PE4	Termination is a consideration for employees who repeatedly break security rules.
EF1	The information security program achieves most of its goals.
EF2	The information security program accomplishes its most important objectives.
EF3	Generally speaking, information is sufficiently protected.
EF4	Overall, the information security program is effective.
EF5	The information security program has kept risks to a minimum.

Chapter XX
A Simulation Model of IS Security

Norman Pendegraft
University of Idaho, USA

Mark Rounds
University of Idaho, USA

ABSTRACT

The value of IS security evaluated by simulating interactions between an information system, its users and a population of attackers. Initial results suggest that the marginal value of additional security may be positive or negative as can the time rate of change of system value. This implies that IT security policy makers should be aware of the relative sensitivity of attackers and users to security before setting IT security policy.

INTRODUCTION

This paper offers a simulation model of the interaction between an information system (IS) and populations of users and attackers. The model incorporates plausible interactions between the rate of attacks, the value of the IS, user sensitivity to security, user specific response curve to security and the level of security. These interactions are incorporated into a reservoir / flow model using the IThink simulation software.

The purpose of this research is to develop a model sufficiently robust to provide management insight into the merits of alternative responses. For example: does it make more sense to train users to be more productive with existing security or to make a system more robust while under attack. There are many variables that cannot be controlled with certainty, so answering this question precisely would be difficult. But even the capacity to perform relative assessments has potential value to an IS manager. Given the current state of the art in quantifying the value of security measures and the difficulty of accurately assessing attack costs, it is unlikely that exact quantitative comparisons between possibilities will be possible any time soon. However, a comparative model will still provide value in decision making and will also be valuable as an educational tool. Ultimately, we hope to extend the work to better determine under what circumstance each of these strategies might prove superior. The chapter should be viewed as exploratory.

This chapter is organized as follows. Section two examines previous work and the security problem; in section three, the methodology and the model are described. Section four includes the results and our discussion.

BACKGROUND

Previous Work

Much of the research on information systems security focuses on the costs and risks of various security schemes. A common practice is to analyze the level of risk for any given security outcome and perform cost/benefit analysis on the results as exemplified by Gordon and Loeb (2002).

For the purposes of this research, we model attackers as a homogeneous group of rational criminals. While there are many sorts of attackers this simplification makes the results much more understandable. We base the rational activities of our attacker upon the economics of criminal activity, first studied by Becker (1968). He assumed that criminals responded rationally to a set of incentives and studied the impact of issues like likelihood of punishment and severity of punishment on their behavior. Others extended this work, for example, Block and Heineke (1975) offered a labor theoretic model of criminal activity.

Rogers (1962, 1976) offers a model of user. In his model early adopters of technology behavior

differently from late adopters. There are several theoretical models of IS (Information System) use that have seen empirical justification. TAM, the Technology Acceptance Model (Davis 1989) offers a means of analyzing the impact of ease of use upon Usage. It has been successful in establishing such a link, but does not explicitly consider other IS quality issues such as data quality and completeness.

The IS Success Model (ISM) explicated by DeLone and McLean (1992) includes constructs of information and system quality and posits that system and information quality lead to increased user satisfaction and increased use which in turn leads to net benefits. DeLone and McLean (2003) recently revised that model to expand measure of quality to include service quality and to explicitly include a feedback loop from net benefits to intention to use.

Wixom and Todd (2005) recently integrated TAM and ISM, and their results suggest that there is a link between system and data quality on the one hand and system usage on the other. On the other hand, Zhu and Kraemer (2005) argue that firm value is increased by IS usage in E-business applications.

TAM also supports a link from security to usage. In general, security will reduce ease of use which TAM predicts will reduce usage. Recent reports in the popular press (Richmond 2004, Grow 2005) suggests that attackers are motivated by economic interests and therefore are attracted by high value targets. These reports confirm the notion that increases in system value lead to increases in attacks.

We have also assumed that the security and value functions are continuous in nature. While security decisions are at least partially discrete, Rajuput, Chen, and Hsu (2005) demonstrate that security is being broken up into ever smaller increments as the users are given more and more options and the systems are more refined and complex. The result is that security choices are reasonably continuous.

Computer Security Problem

For the four most recent years surveyed by the US Census, the revenue generated through e-commerce has increased each year. Further, the rate of increase is itself increasing. In 2000 $28.35 billion in revenue was generated by e-commerce in this country. In 2001 $34.6 Billion, in 2002 $43.5 Billion and for last year surveyed 2003 $54.9 Billion was generated. The rate of increase in 2001 was 22%, in 2002 it was 25% and in 2003 it was 26% (U.S. Census, 2004). This includes only e-commerce, this does not include all those business functions that are supported and abetted by networked systems but have not been given a monetary value.

The threat is also on the rise. A defacement attack on e-commerce sites is one of the easiest types of attacks to measure. If we use this as a proxy for the total number of attacks, we can easily see that the threat is increasing. For example, according to Articsoft (2001) the number of defacement attacks in 1999 was approximately 3,000; in 2000 the number jumped to 6,000; in 2001 the number significantly increased to 30,000; in 2002, the last year for which we have figures, the number of defacement attacks was over 65,000. See Figure 1.

While the amount of money spent on computer security has increased, it has not kept up with e-commerce revenue. According to the Fredonia Group (Security Systems News, October 2002), spending in this country security related issues for 2000 was approximately $2.64 Billion, in 2001, it was approximately $2.9 billion for a 10% increase. In 2002 the spending was approximately $3.4 Billion (18% increase), showing significant post 9/11 increases. For 2003, spending was projected to be $3.95 Billion for an increase of just 15%. Clearly, the computer security community is being asked to protect ever more valuable assets with relatively less. See Figure 2.

Clearly, the problem of computer security is not going away, and the figures above show that the threat is increasing and that the resources to protect the rapidly expanding e-commerce market are being spread ever more thinly. This being the case, it becomes apparent that allocation of these scarce resources is a significant problem.

Methodology / Simulation Background

The model is a reservoir flow model similar to that used by Senge (1990). He studied the behavior of complex systems and offered several "archetypes" for complex interactions. (Our model is similar to his "Limits to Growth" model.) In particular, he discussed the implications of delayed feedback on systems. It is often the case that delayed feedback loops result in highly complex behaviors.

Figure 1. Defacement attacks

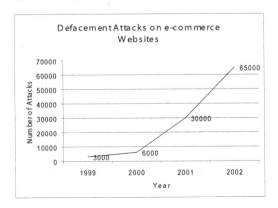

Figure 2. Revenue vs. security expense

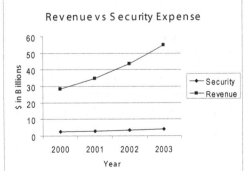

In such models, there are two types of object: reservoirs and flows. Reservoirs represent constructs whose values change over time, and the flows represent changes in the values of the reservoirs. In effect, the flows are derivatives of the reservoirs. In the current research for example, we use a reservoir to represent the value of the information system. The flows represent changes to the value of the system based on both use of the system and attacks on the system. In general in our model, usage of the system results in an inflow, increasing the value of the IS, and attacks result in an outflow decreasing the value of the system. IThink transforms the model into a set of finite difference equations which are solved iteratively (High Performance Systems).

We use a graphical model like Senge rather than the differential equation model like Becker because we believe that it is easier to understand, and it is easier to extrapolate the behavior of the system via simulation. Further, simulation makes it possible to study the behavior of systems of differential equations which cannot be solved in closed form. We adhere to Senge's caution that a model not be made too complicated. We readily concede the simplicity of our model, yet it produces interesting and informative behavior. Clearly, it makes no sense to construct a more complete (and therefore complex) model until one can fully understand the behavior of a simple model.

THE MODEL

Conceptual Background

Our model depends on four fundamental constructs: VALUE, USAGE, ATTACKS, and SECURITY. These are inherently fuzzy terms, and we deliberately do not attempt rigorous definitions in this paper. Our VALUE construct is a reservoir. USAGE and ATTACKS are flows, and SECURITY is a control parameter representing the management decision.

VALUE subsumes several distinct issues of the IS Success Model. In particular, we combine issues of system and data quality which are held distinct in that model. In addition, VALUE includes aspects of firm value per Zhu and Kraemer (2005). Separating these notions of value in our model presents an interesting opportunity for future work. The revised ISM model suggests that increases in VALUE lead to further USAGE. Zhu and Kraemer show that use leads to increases in firm value, and it seems clear that legitimate use of an information system increases the system's value. For example, adding records to a database, a common use, increases the value of that database. Hence, we assume in our model that increases in VALUE lead to increases in USAGE.

These models link these two constructs through intermediary constructs which we omit in the interest of simplicity. We justify our simplification on the grounds that the more detailed links supported in the empirical literature would add little insight at this point in our work. Further, including them would substantially increase the complexity of your model. Thus, our model assumes a macro perspective while leaving substantial room for additional work to bring it into closer alignment with the empirical literature.

VALUE includes properties such as data quality, data volume, etc. VALUE is increased by USAGE which is in turn increased by VALUE. This is a reinforcing process represented by a rolling snow ball (Senge). However, increased system value also increase attacks which in turn decrease value. This is a limiting or balancing process represented by a balance beam. See Figure 3.

To ease the development of the mathematics, we simplify the notation in the following. We let V be the system value (VALUE in the computer code). V is assumed to change additively due to usage and attacks. In the particular time interval $\Delta V = R * U(V, S) - A(V, S)$ where S, U, and A are SECURITY, USAGE, and ATTACKS respectively and are of the form noted below. R

Figure 3. Basic model

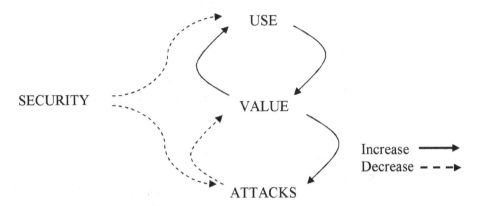

is a measure of the relative importance of usage compared to attacks.

We assume that users and attackers constitute two internally homogeneous groups. Each group is described in terms of a representative agent. The behavior of the representative agents is described by their utility functions:

U(V, S) = level of usage and
A(V, S) = level of attacks where
V = system value
S = security level.

We further assume that these functions are multiplicatively separable:

U(V, S) = UV(V) * US(S)
A(V, S) = AV(V) * AS(S)

UV and AV are assumed to be S shaped as discussed below.

Figure 4 typifies UV and AV. First we assume that Usage is positively influenced by value. Second, we assume that for low values of V, there will be little use beyond the minimum mandated by management. But, as value approaches and then exceeds some critical value, V*, usage will increase rapidly being highly sensitive to V at the margin. At some point, usage will taper off.

Figure 5 shows the shape of typical US and AS responses. We assume that low levels of security

do not impact the user and hence there is little effect, however as security climbs, it has more impact on the users so USAGE and ATTACKS decrease.

The idea that the responses are "S" shaped, while an assumption on our part, is supported by Yamada, Ouba, and Osaki (1983). We implemented this behavior with a piecewise exponential function:

$$UV = \begin{array}{ll} -1+\exp(MV_U (V-V_U^*)) & \text{for } V \le V_U^* \\ 1 - \exp (MV_U (V_U^*-V)) & V > V_U^*. \end{array}$$

So, each agent's reaction to value is determined by two values.

VU* determines the point of inflection and MV_U determines the steepness of the curve.

Figure 4. Impact of value

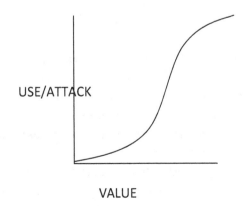

Figure 5. Response to security

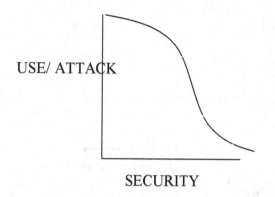

USE/ ATTACK

SECURITY

There are professional crackers who are motivated by profit and amateurs who are doing it for notoriety. In the user community, there are trusted users who rankle at all security and users who value a modicum of security. In this model we have chosen the former in both attacker and user populations, and we intend to relax this assumption in future work.

IThink Model

The simulation model was built with IThink and is illustrated in Figure 6. The equations of the model are listed in Figure 7. The reservoir (rectangle) represents system VALUE. Its value can change depending on the inflows and outflows indicated by large arrows. The flow on the left (USE) causes increases in VALUE. The flow on the right (ATTACKS) is an outflow which decreases VALUE. The drain was included to model the possibility that VALUE might naturally decrease over time as data and technology become obsolete.

After some experimentation we settled on the inflection points in the security response curves (SA*, SU*) as our primary state variables. This simplification greatly reduces the size of the parameter space and still displays a rich set of behavior. In the Model these parameters are labeled S_a_Star and S_u_Star. We treated several parameters as pairs with the attacker's value fixed and the users value expressed as a ratio with respect to the attackers value. For example, M_{AS} is fixed at .2 and M_{US} is determined by the value of the parameter RATIO MUS OVER MAS. In most cases in the current model, this ratio is set equal to 1, reflecting the two parameters being equal. This format made it possible to in effect reduce the side of the state space. The fixed values (.2) was chosen arbitrarily.

The state variables can be varied by the sliders, which in IThink are graphical controls to adjust parameters in the model, and the level of security can be controlled using the dial. The dial works in a similar manner to the slider but

In similar fashion, we assume that agents have negative utility for security. This is the case for attackers and for employee users for whom security is a burden. Hence, we exclude from current examination customers who are attracted by security. These users will be a focus of future study.

$$US = 2 - \exp [MS_U (S-S_U{}^*)] \text{ for } S <= S_U{}^*$$
$$+ \exp [MS_U (S_U{}^*-S)] \quad S > S_U{}^*.$$

The attacker is described in a similar fashion.

$$AV = -1 + \exp [MV_A (V-V_A{}^*)] \text{ for } V <= V_A{}^*$$
$$1 - \exp [MV_A (V_A{}^*-V)] \quad V > V_A{}^*.$$

and

$$AS = 2 - \exp [MS_A (S-S_A{}^*)] \text{ for } S <= S_A{}^*$$
$$+ \exp [MS_A (S_A{}^*-S)] \quad S > S_A{}^*.$$

Thus to fully characterize each agent requires four parameters: V*, MV, S*, MS for a total of 8 parameters. As will be seen we reduced the size of the state space by fixing the attackers' parameters, and defining the users' parameters as ratios with respect to the attackers' values.

We acknowledge that it is a strong assumption that both attackers and users are homogeneous.

Figure 6. IThink model

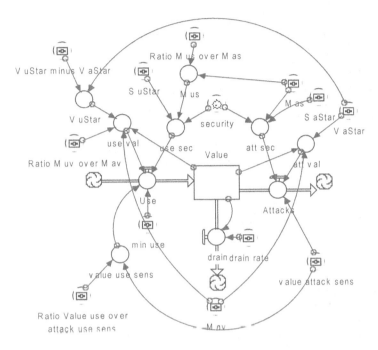

in a rotary fashion. The sliders are used to set the environmental state by identifying the sensitivity of the users and attackers to security and to system value. It is important to emphasize that the various constructs are not intended to measure in specific units any particular system property. Rather, they represent general notions related to the indicated concepts.

RESULTS AND DISCUSSION

We observed 4 basic responses (see Figures 8, 9, 10, and 11). The graphs show the VALUE of the system over time for values of security ranging from .1 to .9 in steps of 0.2. Runs are numbered consecutively; thus run #1 has security = 0.1, run #2 has security =0.3 and so on. Thus they show the change in value over time (∂V/∂T) and the change in value with respect to security (∂V/∂S). The results show that there exist conditions in which ∂V/∂T and ∂V/∂S can be either positive or negative. This suggests that there may be two classes of users (and attackers) whose behavior

is similar to that of early and late adopters (Rogers, 1976).

Note that one policy implication is immediately apparent: in those regions where ∂V/∂S<0 it makes sense to change the state, perhaps by educating users, rather than to increase security. In particular, while we have taken Security Use Sensitivity to be given, it may in fact be subject to influence. For example training might make users less sensitivity to security. Perhaps simplifying the security system by use of single sign on or biometrics we might also make users less sensitive.

These four extreme cases can be readily understood by comparing the responses to security of the users and attackers. The four graphs (Figures 8a,9a,10a, and 11a) illustrate these extreme situations. (They correspond to the similarly named graph.) In each graph the solid line represents the response to security of the attackers. The dotted line represents the response of users. In the extreme case noted, one of the players has S* of .5. That player will be affected by security changes within the range under the control of the manager. The other player has S* at such an extreme, that

Figure 7. Model equations

```
Value(t) = Value(t - dt) + (Use - Attacks - drain) * dt
INIT Value = 1000

INFLOWS:
Use = (use_sec*use_val+min_use)*value_use_sens
OUTFLOWS:
Attacks = att_sec*att_val*value_attack_sens
drain = delay(Value,1)*drain_rate
att_sec = 1+(if (security-S_aStar<0)
then 1-exp(10*M_as*(security-S_aStar))
else -1+exp(10*M_as*(-security+S_aStar))
)
att_val = 1+(if (Value-V_aStar<0)
then -1 + exp(M_av*(Value-V_aStar))
else 1-exp(M_av*(-Value+V_aStar))
)
drain_rate = 0
min_use = 0
M_as = .2
M_av = .0003
M_us = M_as*Ratio_M_us_over_M_as
Ratio_M_us_over_M_as = 1
Ratio_M_uv_over_M_av = 1
Ratio_Value_use_over_attack_use_sens = 1
security = 0.1
S_aStar = .5
S_uStar = .5
use_sec = 1+(if (security-S_uStar <0)
then 1 -exp(10*M_us*(security-S_uStar))
else -1+exp(10*M_us*(-security+S_uStar))
)
use_val = 1+(if (Value<V_uStar)
then -1 + exp(Ratio_M_uv_over_M_av*M_av*(Value-V_uStar))
else 1-exp(Ratio_M_uv_over_M_av*M_av*(-Value+V_uStar))
)
value_attack_sens = 1
value_use_sens = Ratio_Value_use_over_attack_use_sens*value_attack_sens
V_aStar = 1000
V_uStar = V_uStar_minus_V_aStar+V_aStar
V_uStar_minus_V_aStar = 0
```

she is unaffected. If S* is to the left (i.e. is <0), then that player is already highly deterred and the additional security under consideration has no impact. If S* is the right (i.e. >1), then that player is not deterred by the level of security in question. So, Figure 9 which shows increasing system value and increasing returns to security, in the extreme has Su* large. In other words, the users are largely unaffected by the security in question, while the attackers are. Figure 9a shows the general relationship of their security responses. Thus increased security is a good thing, and the system grows in value. By contrast Figure 10 and Figure 10a, show a system in which Sa* is large. Here the attacker is unaffected by the security available while the user is. This results not only

Figure 8.

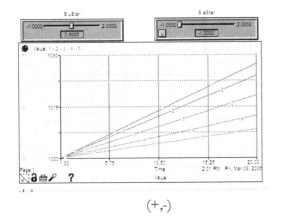

(+,-)

Figure 10.

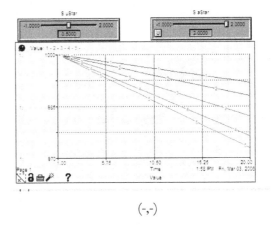

(-,-)

Figure 9.

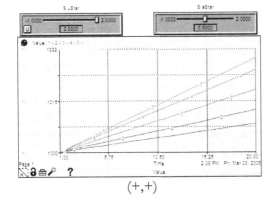

(+,+)

Figure 11.

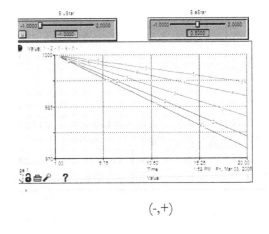

(-,+)

in negative changes in system value, but in negative returns to security as the increased security does not affect the attackers, but does drive users from the system.

The clear implication of this result is that system managers need to be aware of their situations. Further, the results may be applied to situations in which the manager does not have complete control over security. Letting SECURITY range from 0 to 1 maps into the security options available to the manager, but still allows for other security measures to be in place, or not be available at a particular level.

In order to better understand what is happening, we investigated several more extreme cases and plotted the response as a function of

S_A^* and S_U^*. The graph in Figure 12 illustrates our findings. In each of several extreme cases we characterize the behavior with a tuple whose elements are +,0, or -. The first element of the tuple indicates the sign on the slope of the Value vs. time curve, i.e. $\partial V/\partial T$. A 0 indicates that there is no change over time. Similarly the second element in the tuple gives the sign of $\partial V/\partial S$; similarly, 0 indicates no change with respect to S.

In the central region of the graph both the attackers and the users are responsive to changes in SECURITY. Here we observe more complex behavior. The response in Figure 13 shows that the value of the system increases with SECURITY for a while and then begins to decrease with increased SECURITY. The response to

Figure 8a.

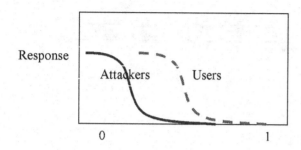

Figure 9a.

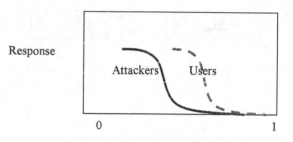

Figure 10a.

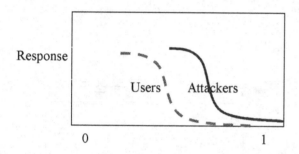

Figure 11a.

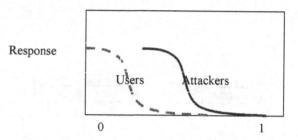

SECURITY is concave, hence the concave curve on the graph. Thus there is an optimal level of SECURITY (here around 3). Similarly in the region identified by a convex curve, at low and high levels of SECURITY, VALUE is high, but it decreases for middle levels of SECURITY. Similarly, Figure 14 shows a situation in which the response is convex. Figures 15, 16, and 17 respectively show conditions labeled (0,0), (+,0), and (-,0) in Figure 12.

We believe that the model has shown sufficient validity to be worth extending. For example, VALUE is probably more complex. In particular, it may be a function of system value and rate of use. As we note above, our notion of VALUE contains aspects of system value and firm value. In essence we assume that these values are tightly related. Our model also assumes that legitimate users and attackers will use similar metrics for VALUE. These are strong assumptions and will need to be relaxed in subsequent work. Similarly, we assume that all users will be deterred by

increased security, while it is likely that some customers will in fact be attracted by increases in security. Similarly, SECURITY is also fuzzy. Explicating these issues remains to be done.

The models may also be extended in other ways. For example we might include non-homogenous attackers, so called crackers and hackers with differing motives. The early late adopter model of user behavior should also be examined. We also believe that there are various classes of attackers with a specific response curve and inflection point. These different population can be modeled and have predictive value. The current model assumes static users and attackers; that is, their characteristics do not change over time. This is a strong assumption, which we hope to relax. We have also noted certain similarities between the two major classes of users and a body of marketing research on Early Adopters of a new product vs. Late Adopters. This is clearly a linkage that needs to be researched. We continue to develop the model. Unfortunately all of these various

Figure 12.

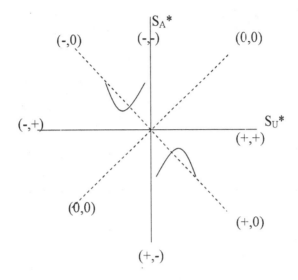

Figure 13.

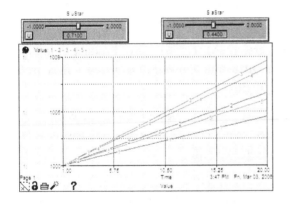

Figure 14.

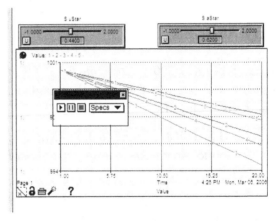

Figure 15.

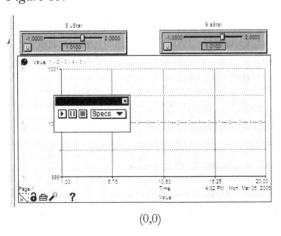

(0,0)

Figure 16.

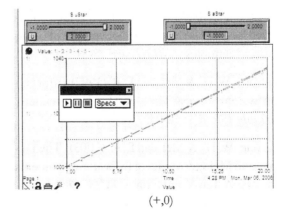

(+,0)

Figure 17.

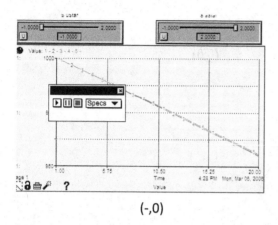

(-,0)

refinements introduce considerable complexity into the model. A path of stepwise refinement of the model with evaluation at each step appears to be the prudent approach.

REFERENCES

Articsoft Limited (2001). *Changing Face of Web Security,* www.arcticsoft.com/wp-changingface.htm, revised May 21.

Becker, G.S. (1968). Crime and Punishment: An Economic Approach. *Journal of Political Economy, 78,* 169-217.

Block, M. K., & Heineke, J. M. (1975). Labor Theoretic Analysis of Criminal Choice. *American Economic Review, 65,* 314-325.

Davis, F. D. (1989). Perceived Usefulness, Perceived Ease of Use, and User Acceptance of Information Technology. *MISQuart, 13*(3), 319-340.

DeLone, W. H., & McLean E. R. (1992). Information System Success: The Quest for the dependent. *Variable ISR, 3*(1) 60-95.

DeLone, W. H., & McLean E. R. (2003). The DeLone and McLean Model of Information Systems Success: A Ten-Year Update. *JMIS, 19*(4) 9-30.

Gordon, G. A., & Loeb, M. P. (2002). The Economics of Information Security Investment. *Transactions on Information and System Security (TISSEC), 5*(4), 438-457.

Grow, B. (2005). Hacker Hunters. *Business Week,* 30 May, (pp. 74-82).

High Performance Systems, IThink / Stella Technical Documentation, Lebanon NH.

Rajput, S. A., Chen., J., & Hsu, S. (2005). State Based Authentication. *Proceedings of the 43rd Annual Association for Computing Machinery South East Conference, Volume 2,* March 18-20 160-165.

Richmond, R. (2004). Money Increasingly Is Motive For Computer-Virus Attacks. *Wall Street Journal, 19,* Sept., B5.

Rogers, E. M. (1962). *Diffusion of Innovations.* The Free Press. New York.

Rogers, E. M. (1976). New Product Adoption and Diffusion. *Journal of Consumer Research. 2,* 290-301.

Security Systems News (2002). www.security-systemsnews.com/october2002/securitystats/09.ssn.pages.02.pdf.

Senge, P. M. (1990). The Fifth Discipline, Currency Doubleday, New York.

US Census Bureau Retail Indicators Branch (2004). Retail E-commerce Sales In First Quarter 2004 Were 15.5 Billion Up 28.1 Percent From First Quarter 2003 Census Bureau Reports (2003). www.census.gov/mrts/www/current.html, Revised May 21.

Yamada, S., Ouba, M., and Osaki, S. (1983). S-Shaped Reliability Growth Modeling for Software Error Detection. *IEEE Transactions on Reliability, R-32,* 5, December 475-478.

Wixom, B., & Todd P. A. (2005). A Theoretical Integration of User Satisfaction and Technology Acceptance. *ISR16*(1), 85-102.

Zhu, K., & Kraemer, K. L. (2005). Post-Adoption Variation in Usage and Value of E-Business by Organizations: Cross-Country Evidence from the Retail Industry, *ISR 16*(1) 61-84.

Compilation of References

Achlioptas, D. (2001). Database-Friendly Random Projections. In Proc. of the 20th ACM Symposium on Principles of Database Systems (p. 274-281). Santa Barbara, CA, USA.

Ackerman, M., Cranor, L. F., & Reagle, J. (1999). *Beyond Concern: Understanding Net Users' Attitudes About Online Privacy.* AT&T Research Technical Report. Retrieved May 20, 2005, from http://www.research.att.com/library/trs/TRs/99/99.4/

Ackerman, M., Darrell, T., & Weitzner, D. J. (2001). Privacy in context. *HCI, 16*(2), 167-179.

Ackerman, M., Darrell, T., & Weitzner, D.J. (2001). Privacy In Context. *Human-Computer Interaction, 16*(2), 167-176.

ACNielson (2001). *ACNielsen Internet Confidence Index.* Retrieved December 10, 2005 from http://acnielsen.com/news/corp/001/20010627b.htm

Adam, N. R., & Wortman, J. C. (1989). Security-control Methods for Statistical Databases. *ACM Computing Surveys, 21*(4), 515-556.

Adkinson, W., Eisenach, J., & Lenard, T. (2002). *Privacy Online: A Report on the Information Practices and Policies of Commercial Web Sites.* Retrieved November 4, 2005 from http://www.pff.org/publications/privacy-onlinefinalael.pdf

Agrawal, D., & Aggarwal, C. C. (2001, May 2001). *On the design and quantification of privacy preserving data mining algorithms.* Paper presented at the Proceedings of the twentieth ACM SIGMOD-SIGACT-SIGART symposium on Principles of database systems, Santa Barbara, California, United States.

Agrawal, R., & Srikant, R. (2000). Privacy-preserving data mining. In *ACM SIGMOD Record , Proceedings of the 2000 ACM SIGMOD international conference on Management of data SIGMOD '00* (Vol. 29, pp. 439-450): ACM Press.

Ahmet, M. E., Town, J., & Delp, E. J. (2003, April). Security of digital entertainment content from creation to consumption. *Signal Processing: Image Communication, Special Issue on Image security, 18*(4), 237-262.

Ajzen, I., & Fishbein, M. (1980). *Understanding attitudes and predicting social behavior.* Englewood Cliffs, NJ: Prentice-Hall.

Ali Eldin, A., & Wagenaar, R. (2003). *Towards a Component based Privacy Protector Architecture.* Paper presented at the 15. CAiSE 2003 Short Papers, Klagenfurt, Austria.

Ali Eldin, A., & Wagenaar, R. (2004). *Towards a users driven privacy control.* Paper presented at the the IEEE conference on Systems, Man, and Cybernetics (SMC 2004), The Hague.

Ali Eldin, A., van den Berg, J., & Wagenaar, R. (2004). *A Fuzzy reasoning scheme for context sharing decision making.* Paper presented at the the 6th International Conference on Electronic Commerce, Delft, The Netherlands.

Allen, J., Alberts, C., Behrens, S., et al. (2000). Improving the Security of Networked Systems, *CrossTalk: The Journal of Defense Software Engineering*, October 2000.

Álvarez, G., & Petrovic, S. (2003). A new taxonomy of web attacks suitable for efficient encoding. *Computers & Security, 22*(5), 435–449.

Amoroso, E. (1994). *Fundamentals of Computer Security Technology.* Prentice-Hall.

Andrew, K. (2002). *Formal theory for political science – Lecture Notes.*

Andrew, T. et al. (2003). *Business Process Execution Language for Web Service Version 1.1.* June 1, 2006, from http://www.ibm.com/developerworks/library/ws-bpel

Anonymous. (2004). *Privacy Legislation Affecting the Internet: 108th Congress.* Retrieved August, 2006, from http://www.cdt.org/legislation/108th/privacy/

Anonymous. (2006). Retrieved August, 2006, from http://www.hhs.gov/ocr/index.html

Anthony, N., Chris, K., Phillip H., & Ronald, M. (2004). *Web Services Security: SOAP Message Security 1.0 (WS-Security 2004).* June 1, 2006, from http://docs.oasis-open.org/wss/2004/01/oasis-200401-wss-soap-message-security-1.0

Antoniou, G., & Harmelen, F. V. (2004). *A Semantic Web Primer.* MIT press.

Arbuckle, J., & Wothke, W. (1999). *AMOS 4.0 user's guide.* Chicago, IL: Smallwaters Corporation.

Ariss, S. S. (2002). Computer monitoring: Benefits and pitfalls facing management. *Information & Management, 39*(7), 553-558.

Armstrong, M. P.; Rushton, G.; Zimmerman, D. L. (1999). Geographically Masking Health Data to Preserve Confidentiality. *Statistics in Medicine, 18*, 497–525, 1999.

Articsoft Limited (2001). *Changing Face of Web Security,* www.arcticsoft.com/wp-changingface.htm, revised May 21.

Atallah, M., Elmagarmid, A., Ibrahim, M., Bertino, E., & Verykios, V. (1999). *Disclosure Limitation of Sensitive Rules.* Paper presented at the Proceedings of the 1999 Workshop on Knowledge and Data Engineering Exchange.

Auer, J. W. (1991). *Linear Algebra With Applications.* Prentice-Hall Canada Inc., Scarborough, Ontario, Canada.

Avcybasb, I., Memon, N., & Sankurb, B. (2001, February). Steganalysis based on image quality metrics. *Proceedings of International Conference on Security and Watermarking of Multimedia contents.*

Awad, N. F., & Krishnan, M. S. (2006) The Personalization Privacy Paradox: An Empirical Evaluation of Information Transparency and the Willingness to be Profiled Online for Personalization. *Management Information Systems Quarterly*, March 2006, (30)1, 13-28.

Axelsson, S. (2000). *Intrusion detection systems: A survey and taxonomy.* Technical Report 99-15, Dept. of Computer Engineering, Chalmers University of Technology.

Bagchi, K., & Udo, G. (2003). An analysis of the growth of computer and internet security breaches. *Communications of the AIS, 12*(46), 684-700.

Bajaj, S. et al. (2004). *Web Services Policy Framework (WS-Policy).* June 1, 2006, from http://www-106.ibm.com/developerworks/library/specification/ws-polfram/

Bart, Y., Shankar, V., Sultan, F., & Urban, G. L., (2005). Are the Drivers and Role of Online Trust the Same for All Web Sites and Consumers? A Large-Scale Exploratory Empirical Study. *Journal of Marketing, 69*, 133-152.

Bartmann, D. jun (2000). *Benutzerauthentisierung durch Analyse des Tippverhaltens mit Hilfe einer Kombination aus statistischen und neuronalen Verfahren.* Dissertation, Technical University of Munich.

Bartmann, D., & Bartmann, D. (1997). *Method for Verifying the Identity of a User of a Data Processing Unit with a Keyboard Designed to Produce Alphanumeric Characters.* European patent number: EP 0 917 678 B1.

Bartmann, D., & Breu, C. (2004). Eignung des biometrischen Merkmals Tippverhalten zur Benutzerauthentisierung. In D. Bartmann, (Eds.), *Überbetriebliche Integration von Anwendungssystemen* (pp. 321-343). FORWIN-Tagung, Aachen.

Baskerville, R. L., & Myers, M. D. (2004). Special issue on action research in information systems: Making IS research relevant to practice. Forward. *MIS Quarterly, 28*(3), 329-335.

Bayardo, R. J., & Agrawal, R. (2005). *Data privacy through optimal k-anonymization.* Paper presented at the ICDE.

Bechhofer, S., van Harmelen, F., Hendler, J., Horrocks, I., McGuinness, D. L., Patel-Schneider, P. F., & Stein, L. A. (2004). *OWL Web Ontology Language Reference.* http://www.w3.org/TR/owl-ref/ (visited 21-Apr-2006).

Becker, G.S. (1968). Crime and Punishment: An Economic Approach. *Journal of Political Economy, 78*, 169-217.

Bellovin, S. M. (2004). Spamming, phishing, authentication, and privacy. *Communications of the ACM, 47*(12), 144.

Bellovin, S., & Merritt, M. (1992). *Encrypted key exchange: password-based protocols secure against dictionary attacks.* Paper presented at the IEEE Symposium on Security and Privacy, Oakland, California.

Bellovin, S., & Merritt, M. (1994). An attack on the Interlock Protocol when used for authentication. *IEEE Transactions on Information Theory, 40*(1), 273-275.

Bellwood, T. et al. (2003). *UDDI Version 3.0.1.* June 1, 2006, from http://uddi.org/pubs/uddi_v3.htm

Benbasat, I., & Zmud, R. W. (1999). Empirical research in information systems: The practice of relevance. *MIS Quarterly, 23*(1), 3-16.

Bennett, C. H., & Brassard, G. (1984). BB84. *Proceedings of IEEE International Conference on Computers, Systems, and Signal Processing.* Los Alamitos, CA: IEEE Press (pp. 175-184).

Bento, A., & Bento, R. (2004) Empirical Test of Hacking Framework: An Exploratory Study. *Communications of the AIS, 14*, 678-690.

Berners Lee, T., et al. (2001, May). *The Semantic Web.* Scientific American.

Berry, M., & Linoff, G. (1997). *Data Mining Techniques - for Marketing, Sales, and Customer Support.* New York, USA: John Wiley and Sons.

Bertino, E. et al. (2004). Secure Third Party Publication of XML Documents. To appear in *IEEE Transactions on Knowledge and Data Engineering.*

Bertino, E., et al. (2002). *Access Control for XML Documents, Data and Knowledge Engineering, 43*(3).

Bingham, E., & Mannila, H. (2001). Random Projection in Dimensionality Reduction: Applications to Image and Text Data. *In Proc. of the 7th ACM SIGKDD International Conference on Knowledge Discovery and Data Mining* (pp. 245-250). San Francisco, CA, USA.

Bishop, M. (2003). *Computer Security—Art and Science.* Addison Wesley.

Blake, C., & Merz, C. (1998). *UCI Repository of Machine Learning Databases*, University of California, Irvine, Dept. of Information and Computer Sciences.

Block, M. K., & Heineke, J. M. (1975). Labor Theoretic Analysis of Criminal Choice. *American Economic Review, 65*, 314-325.

Bojadziev, G., & Bojadziev, M. (1997). *Fuzzy Logic for Business, Finance, and Management*: World Scientific.

Bolle, R. M., Ratha, N. K., & Pankanti, S. (1999). Evaluating Authentication Systems Using Bootstrap Confidence

Intervals. *Proceedings of the 1999 IEEE Workshop on Automatic Identification Advanced Technologies (WAIAT-99)*, Morristown NJ, USA.

Bollen, K. A. (1989). *Structural equation modeling with latent variables*. New York: John Wiley & Sons Inc.

Bollen, K. A. (1989). *Structural equations with latent variables*. New York: John Wiley & Sons.

Bolton, R. J., & Hand, D. J. (2001). Unsupervised profiling methods for fraud detection. *Proceedings of the Conference on Credit Scoring and Credit Control*, Edinburgh, UK.

Boneh, D., & Boyen, X. (2004). Short signatures without random oracles. *Proceedings of Eurocrypt 2004, LNCS 3027*, 56-73.

Boser, B. E., Guyon, I. M., & Vapnik, V. N. (1992). *A training algorithm for optimal margin classifiers*. In D. Haussler, (Ed.), *5th Annual ACM Workshop on COLT*, (pp. 144-152). Pittsburgh, PA. ACM Press.

Brancheau, J. C., Janz, B. D., & Wetherbe, J. C. (1996). Key issues in information systems management: 1994-95 SIM Delphi Results. *MIS Quart., 20*(2), 225-242.

Brown, E. (2002, April 1). Analyze This. *Forbes, 169*, 96-98.

Bryan, W. L., & Harter, N. (1897). Studies in the Physiology and Psychology of the Telegraphic Language. *Psychological Review, 4*(1), 27-53. Cho, S., Han, C., Han, D., & Kim, H. (2001). Web based keystroke dynamics identity verification using neural networks. *Journal of Organisational Computing & Electronic Commerce, 10*(4), 295-307.

BSI. (1999). *Information Security Management – Part 1, Code of Practice for Information Security Management*, BS 7799-1, BSI Group, London, UK.

Businessweek. (2001), Privacy in an Age of Terror. *Businessweek*.

Caldelli, R., Bartiloni, F., & Cappellini, V. (2003). Standard metadata embedding in a digital image. *Proceedings of 14th International Workshop on Database and Expert Systems Applications*.

Calhoun, K. J., Teng, J. T. C., & Cheon, M. J. (2002). Impact of National Culture on Information Technology Usage Behavior: An Exploratory Study of Decision Making in Korea and the USA. *Behavior and Information Technology, (21.4)*, July/August 2002, 293-302.

Camenisch, J., & Herreweghen, E. V. (2002). *Design and Implementation of Idemix Anonymous Credential System*: IBM Zurich Research Laboratory.

Campbell, D. T., & Fiske, D. W. (1959). Convergent and discriminant validation by the multi-trait-multimethod matrix. *Psychological Bulletin, 56*(2), 81-105.

Carminati, B., et al. (2004). Security for RDF. *Proceedings of the DEXA Conference Workshop on Web Semantics*, Zaragoza, Spain.

Carver, C. A., & Pooch, U.W. (2000). An intrusion response taxonomy and its role in automatic intrusion response. In *Proceedings of the IEEE Workshop on Information Assurance*. IEEE.

Casal, C. R. (2001). *Privacy Protection For Location Based Mobile Services in Europe*. Paper presented at the the 5th World Multi-Conference on Systems, Cybernetics, and Informatics (SCI2001), Orlando, Florida USA.

Center for Democracy & Privacy (2004). *Privacy Legislation Affecting the Internet: 108th Congress*. Retrieved December 12, 2005 from http://www.cdt.org/legislation/108th/privacy/

Chakrabarti, A., & Manimaran, G. (2002). Internet infrastructure security: A taxonomy. *IEEE Internet Computing, 16*(6), 13–21.

Chan, P. K., Fan, W., Prodromidis, A. L., & Stolfo, S. J. (1999). Distributed Data Mining in Credit Card Fraud Detection. *IEEE Intelligent Systems*, (pp. 67-74).

Chen, P. P.-S. (1976). The entity-relationship model—toward a unified view of data. *ACM Transactions on Database Systems (TODS), 1*(1), 9–36.

Chinnici, R. et al. (2004). *Web Services Description Language (WSDL) Version 2.0 Part 1: Core Language*, June 1, 2006, from http://www.w3.org/TR/wsdl20/

Christandl, M., & Wehner, S. (2005). Quantum Anonymous Transmissions. *Proceedings of 11th ASIACRYPT, LNCS 3788*, 217-235.

Claessens, J., Preneel, B., & Vandewalle. J. (2003). How can mobile agents do secure electronic transactions on untrusted hosts? *ACM Trans. Internet Tech, 3*(1), 28-48.

Clarke, N., Furnell, S., Reynolds, P., & Lines, B. (2003). Using Keystroke Analysis is a Mechanism for Subscriber Authentication on Mobile Handsets. *SEC*, (pp. 97-108).

Clarke, R. (1999). *Introduction to Dataveillance and Information Privacy, and Definitions of Terms.* Retrieved November 20, 2006, from, http://www.anu.edu.au/people/Roger.Clarke/Intro.html

Clearly Business (2005). *Clearly Business – Card Fraud.* Website: http://www.clearlybusiness.com/cb/articles/

Clifton, C., Kantarcioglu, M., Vaidya, J., Lin, X., & Zhu, M. (2002). Tools for privacy preserving distributed data mining. *ACM SIGKDD Explorations Newsletter, 4*(2), 28-34.

Collberg, C., Thomborson, C., & Low, D. (1997). *A Taxonomy of Obfuscating Transformations.* Technical report, TR–148, Department of Computer Science, University of Auckland, New Zealand, July.

Common Criteria Project (2006, November 16). *The Common Criteria.* Retrieved November 16, 2006, from, http://www.commoncriteriaportal.org/

Complete Website (2005). *Complete Website and E-commerce Solutions.* Website: http://www.haveninternet.com/welcome.htm

Computer Emergency Response Team (CERT). (2004). *CERT statistics.* Retrieved May, 2004, from http://www.cert.org/stats/cert_stats.html#incidents

Conca, C., Medlin, D., & Dave, D. (2005). Technology-based security threats: taxonomy of sources, targets and a process model of alleviation. *International Journal Information Technology Management, 4*(2) 166-177.

Coppersmith, D., Stern, J., & Vaudenay, S. (1993). Attacks on the birational permutation signature schemes. *CRYPTO 1993, LNCS 773*, 435-443.

Cormen, T. H., Leiserson, C. E., & Rivest, R. L. (1999). Introduction to Algorithms. *The MIT Press and McGraw-Hill,* (pp. 489-490).

Courtois, N. (2004) *Short signatures, provable security, generic attacks and computational security of multivariate polynomial schemes such as HFE, Quartz and Sflash.* Eprint 2004/143.

Cox, I. J., Miller, M. L., & Bloom, J. A. (2002). *Digital Watermarking.* Morgan Kaufmann Publishers.

Cranor, L., Langheinrich, M., & Marchiori, M. (2002). *A P3P Preference Exchange Language 1.0 (APPEL1.0) W3C Working Draft.*

Cranor, L., Langheinrich, M., Marchiori, M., Presler-Marshall, M., & Reagle, J. (2004). *The Platform for Privacy Preferences 1.1 (P3P1.1) Specification W3C Working Draft.*

CSC (2006). *Aligning technology and corporate goals is top concern again in annual CSC survey—networks seen as key competitive tool; Outsourcing gaining support, Computer Sciences Corporation.* Available at: http://www.csc.com/newsandevents/news/1298.shtml. Retrieved: 05/03/2006.

CSI/FBI (2004). *CSI/FBI Computer Crime and Security Survey 2004*, Computer Security Institute and Federal Bureau of Investigation (CSI/FBI). Available at: http://i.cmpnet.com/gocsi/db_area/pdfs/fbi/FBI2004.pdf

Culnan, M. J. (1993). How did they my name?" An exploratory investigation of consumer attitudes toward secondary information use. *MIS Quart., 17*(3), 341-363.

D'Amico, A. (2000). What Does a Computer Security Breach Really Cost? Retrieved from http://www.avatier.com/files/docs/CostsOfBreaches-SANSInstitute.doc on June 9, 2008.

Daskapan, S., Vree, W. G., & Ali Eldin, A. (2003). *Trust metrics for survivable security systems.* Paper presented at the The IEEE International Conference on Systems, Man & Cybernetics,, Washington.

Davis, F. D. (1989). Perceived Usefulness, Perceived Ease of Use, and User Acceptance of Information Technology. *MISQuart, 13*(3), 319-340.

Davis, F. D. (1989). Perceived usefulness, perceived ease of use, and user acceptance of information technology. *MIS Quarterly, 13*(3), 319-329.

Davis, F. D., Bagozzi, R. P., & Warshaw, P. R. (1989). User acceptance of computer technology: A comparison of two theoretical models. *Management Science, 35*, 982-1002.

Davison, R. M., Clarke R., Smith, J., Langford, D., & Kuo, B. (2003). Information Privacy in a Globally Networked Society: Implications for IS Research. *Communications of the Association for Information Systems, 12*, 341-365.

Debar, H., Dacier, M., & Wespi, A. (1999). Towards a taxonomy of intrusiondetection systems. *Computer Networks, 31*, 805–822.

DeCew, J. (2002). *Privacy. The Stanford Encyclopedia of Philosophy.* E. N. Zalta online at: http://plato.stanford.edu/archives/sum2002/entries/privacy/ (accessed 8-31-2006).

DeLone, W. H., & McLean E. R. (1992). Information System Success: The Quest for the dependent. *Variable ISR, 3*(1) 60-95.

DeLone, W. H., & McLean E. R. (2003). The DeLone and McLean Model of Information Systems Success: A Ten-Year Update. *JMIS, 19*(4) 9-30.

DeLooze, L. L. (2004). Classification of computer attack using a selforganizing map. In *Proceedings of the IEEE Workshop on Information Assurance*, (pp. 365–369). IEEE.

Denker, G., et al. (2003). Security for DAML Web Services: Annotation and Matchmaking. *International Semantic Web Conference.*

Denning, D. (1980). Secure statistical databases with random sample queries. *ACM Transactions on Database Systems (TODS), 5*(3), 291-315.

Denning, D. (1982). *Cryptography and Data Security*: Addison-Wesley.

Deutsch, D., Ekert, A., Jozsa, R., Macchiavello, C., Popescu, S., & Sanpera, A. (1996). Quantum privacy amplification and the security of quantum cryptography over noisy channels. *Physics Review Letters, 77*(13), 2818-2821.

DeVellis, R. F. (2003). *Scale development. Theory and applications* (2nd ed. Vol. 26). Thousand Oaks, CA: Sage Publications.

Dhillon, G., & Backhouse, J. (2001). Current directions in IS security research: Towards socio-organizational perspectives. *Information Systems Journal, 11*(2), 127-153.

Dhillon, G., & Moores, T. (2001). Internet privacy: Interpreting key issues. *Information Resources Management Journal, 14*(4).

Dictionary.com. (2006). Retrieved July 2006, 2006, from http://dictionary.reference.com/browse/privacy

Diffie, W., & Hellman, M. E. (1976). New directions in cryptography. *IEEE Transactions on Information Theory, IT-22*, 644-654.

Digital C. (2005). *N. Korea's Hackers Rival CIA*, Expert Warns.

Digital Signature Algorithm (DSA), (ECDSA; as specified in ANSI X9.62), RSA (as specified in ANSI X9.31), and Elliptic Curve DSA FIPS 186-2.

Dillard, K. (2005). What is a rootkit? from *SearchWindowsSecurity.com*

Dittmann, J. (2001, December). Using cryptographic and watermarking algorithms. *IEEE Multimedia and Security*, (pp. 54-65).

Donner, M. (2003). Toward a security ontology. *IEEE Security and Privacy, 1*(3), 6–7.

Doorn, L. v. et al. (2006). *4758/Linux Project*. June 1, 2006, from http://www.research.ibm.com/ secure_systems_department/projects/linux4758/index.html

Dowland, P. S., & Furnell, M. S., & Steven M., & Papadaki, M. (2002). Keystroke Analysis as a Method of Advanced User Authentication and Response. *Proceedings of IFIP/SEC - 17ᵗʰ International Conference on Information Security,* Cairo, Egypt, (pp. 215-226).

Drennan, J., Mort, G. S., & Previte, J. (2006). Privacy, Risk Perception, and Expert Online Behavior: an exploratory study of household end users. *Journal of Organizational and End User Computing*: (18)1, 1-22.

Dubois, D., & Prade, H. (1995). What does fuzzy logic bring to AI? *ACM Computing Surveys (CSUR),, 27*(3).

Dyson, E. (1998). Release 2.0 : A Design for Living in the Digital Age. *Bantam Doubleday Dell Pub.*

E&Y (2005). *5th Annual Information Security Survey,* Ernest and Young.

Earp, J. B. & Baumer, D. (2003). Innovative Web Use to Learn about Consumer Behavior and Online Privacy. *Communications of the ACM,* (46)4, 81-83.

Eckerson, W., & Watson, H. (2001). Harnessing Customer Information for Strategic Advantage: Technical Challenges and Business Solutions, Industry Study 2000, Executive Summary. In *The Data Warehousing Institute.*

Economist. (2001, February 17). The slow progress of fast wires, *358.*

Edjlali, G., Acharya, A., & Chaudhary, V. (1998). *History-based access control for mobile code. ACM CCS 1998,* (pp. 38-48).

Eklund, E. (2006). *Controlling and securing personal privacy and anonymity in the information society.* http://www.niksula.cs.hut.fi/~eklund/Opinnot/netsec.html

EPIC (2003). *Privacy and Human Rights 2003. Electronic Privacy Information Centre.* Retrieved October 9, 2006, from http://www.epic.org

Erradi, A., & Maheshwari, P. (2005). wsBus: QoS-aware Middleware for Reliable Web Services Interactions. *Proc. of IEEE EEE05,* (pp. 634-639).

Ester, M., Kriegel, H-P., Sander, J., & Xu, X. (1996). A density-based algorithm for discovering clusters in large spatial databases with noise. *Proceedings of the Second International Conference on Knowledge Discovery and Data Mining.*

Estivill-Castro, V., Brankovic, L., & Dowe, D. L. (1999). *Privacy in Data Mining.* Retrieved August, 2006, from http://www.acs.org.au/nsw/articles/1999082.htm

European Directive. (2002). Directive 2002/58/EC of the European Parliament and of the Council of 12 July 2002, electronic communications sector (Directive on privacy and electronic communications). *Official Journal of the European Communities, L,* 201-237.

Evfimievski, A., Srikant, R., Agrawal, R., & Gehrke, J. (2002). Privacy preserving mining of association rules. In *Proceedings of the eighth ACM SIGKDD international conference on Knowledge discovery and data mining, July 2002, Edmonton, Alberta, Canada* (pp. 217-228).

Facteau, J. D., Dobbins, G. H., Russell, J. E. A., Ladd, R. T., & Kudisch, J. D. (1995). The influence of general perceptions of training environment on pretraining motivation and perceived training transfer. *Journal of Management, 21*(1), 1-25.

Faja, S. (2005). Privacy in E-Commerce: Understanding User Trade-Offs. *Issues in Information Systems, 6*(2).

Faloutsos, C., & Lin, K.-I. (1995). FastMap: A Fast Algorithm for Indexing, Data-Mining and Visualization of Traditional and Multimedia Datasets. *In Proc. of the 1995 ACM SIGMOD International Conference on Management of Data* (pp. 163-174). San Jose, CA, USA.

Farmer, D., & Venema, W. (1999). *Murder on the Internet Express, Computer Forensic Analysis Seminar.* IBM T.J. Watson Research Centre, Yorktown Heights, NY, USA.

Featherman, M. S., & Pavlou, P. A. (2003). Predicting e-services adoption: a perceived risk facets perspective. *International Journal of Human-Computer Studies, 59,* 451-474.

Federal Trade Commission Identity Theft Clearing House, Retrieved on January 23, 2006 from http://www.consumer.gov/idtheft/http://www.consumer.gov/idtheft/.

Ferguson, S. (2006). Study: Security Breaches Afflict Most Enterprises, Governments. *eWeek*, July 7, 2006. http://www.eweek.com/article2/0,1895,1986066,00.asp (accessed 8-31-2006).

Ferguson, T. S., & Melolidakis, C. (1998). On the inspection game. *Naval Research Logistics 45*, 327-334.

Fern, X. Z., & Brodley, C. E. (2003). Random Projection for High Dimensional Data Clustering: A Cluster Ensemble Approach. *In Proc. of the 20th International Conference on Machine Learning (ICML 2003).* Washington DC, USA.

Fernandez, A., & Miyazaki, A. (2001). Consumer perceptions of privacy and security risks for online shopping. *The Journal of Consumer Affairs, 35*(1), 27-44.

Files, J. (2006, June 29). Missing laptop with veterans' data is found. *New York Times.*

Findlaw.com. (2006). *Findlaw Homepage.* Retrieved July, 2006, from http://public.findlaw.com/

Finin, T., & Joshi, A. (2002). Agents, Trust, and Information Access on the Semantic Web, *ACM SIGMOD.*

Finkel, A. (1993). The Minimal Coverability Graph for Petri Nets. *Advances in Petri Nets 1993, Springer Verlag Lecture Notes in Computer Science, 674,* 210-243. Galileo International. (2006) June 1, 2006, from http://www.galileo.com/galileo/

Fishbein, M., & Ajzen, I. (1975). *Belief, attitude, intention, and behavior.* Reading, MA: Addison-Wesley.

Fletcher, K. (2003). Consumer power and privacy: the changing nature of CRM. *International Journal of Advertising, 22,* 249-272.

Fox, S. (2000). *Trust and Privacy Online: Why Americans want to re-write the rules.* Pew Internet & American Life Project. Retrieved December 20, 2004 from http://www.pewinternet.org/reports/pdfs/PIP_Trust_Privacy_Report.pdf

Frankwood (2000). *Introduction to Accounting.* UK: Prentice Hall.

Fraud Detection Suite (2005). *Fraud Detection Suite-White Paper.* Website: http://www.authorizenet.com/files/fdswhitpaper.pdf

Frazier, P. A., Barron, K. E., & Tix, A., P. (2004). Testing moderator and mediator effects in counseling psychology. *Journal of Counseling Psychology, 51*(1), 115-134.

Friel, A. L. (2004). Privacy Patchwork. *Marketing Management, 13*(6), 48-51.

FTC (2000). *Privacy Online: Fair Information Practices in the Electronic Marketplace a Report to Congress.* Retrieved May 23, 2005 from http://www..gov/reports/privacy2000/privacy2000.pdf

FTC (2004). Federal Trade Commission. *National and State Trends in Fraud and Identity Theft.* Retrieved May 23, 2005 from http://www.consumer.gov/sentinel/pubs/Top10Fraud2003.pdf

FTC (2000). Federal Trade Commission. *Online Profiling: A Report to Congress.* June 2000, Retrieved May 23, 2005 from http://www.ftc.gov/os/2000/06/onlineprofilingreportjune2000.pdf

Fukunaga, K. (1990). Introduction to Statistical Pattern Recognition. 2nd. Edition. Academic Press.

Furnell S. M., & Dowland P. S. (2000). Enhancing Operating System Authentication Techniques. *In Proceedings of the Second International Network Conference,* Plymouth, England (pp. 253-261).

Gable, R. K., & Wolf, M. B. (1993). *Instrument development in the affective domain* (second edition). Boston, MA: Kluwer Academic Publishing.

Galal, G. H. (2001). From contexts to constructs: The use of grounded theory in operationalising contingent process models. *European Journal of Information Systems, 10,* 2-14.

Game Theory (2005). *Game Theory.* Website: http://plato.stanford.edu/entries/game-theory/

Garbarino, E., & Strahilevitz, M. (2002). Gender differences in the perceived risk of buying online and the effects of receiving a site recommendation. *Journal of Business Research 57*(7), 768-775.

Garcia, J. D. (1986). *Personal identification apparatus.* United States patent number: 4 621 334.

Garfinkel, R., Gopal, R., & Goes, P., (2002). Privacy Protection of Binary Confidential Data Against Deterministic, Stochastic, and Insider Threat. *Management Science, 48*(6), 749 - 764.

Garg, A., Curtis, J., & Halper, H. (2003). The financial impact of IT security breaches: What do investors think? *Information Systems Security, 12*(1), 22-34.

Geer, D. (2005). Security technologies go phishing. *IEEE Computer, 38*(6), 18 - 21.

Gefen D. (2002). Customer Loyalty in E-Commerce. *Journal of the Association of Information Systems, 3,* 27-51.

Gefen, D. (2000). E-Commerce: The Role of Familiarity and Trust. *Omega 28*(6), 735-737.

Gefen, D. (2003). Assessing unidimensionality through LISREL: An explanation and example. *Communications of the AIS, 12,* 23-46.

Gellman, R. (2002). *Privacy, Consumers, and Costs: How the Lack of Privacy Costs Consumers and Why Business Studies of Privacy Costs are Biased and Incomplete.* Retrieved January 8, 2006 from http://www.epic.org/reports/dmfprivacy.html

George, J. F. (1996). Computer-based monitoring: Common perceptions and empirical results. *MIS Quarterly, 20*(4), 459-480.

Ghosh, S., & Reilly, D. L. (1994). Credit card fraud detection with a neural network. *Proceedings of the 27th Annual Hawaii International Conference on System Sciences,* (pp. 621-630).

Ghoshal, S. (2005). Bad management theories are destroying good management practices. *Academy of Management Learning & Education, 4*(1), 75-91.

Giedke, G. (2006, March 14). *What is Quantum Information Processing.* MagiQ, retrieved March 14, 2006, from http://www.magiqtech.com/index.php

Glaser, B. G., & Strauss, A. L. (1967). *The discovery of grounded theory: Strategies for qualitative research.* New York: Aldine Publishing Company.

Global Consumer Attitude (2006). Global Consumer Attitude Towards Online Shopping. Website: http://www2.acnielsen.com/reports/documents/2005_cc_onlineshopping.pdf

Golbeck, J., & Hendler, J. (2004). *Reputation network analysis for email filtering.* In CEAS.

Goldberg I. (2002). Privacy-enhancing technologies for the Internet II: Five years later. *Proceedings of the Workshop on Privacy Enhancing Technologies, LNCS 2009,* 1-12.

Goldreich, O., Micali, S., & Wigderson, A. (1987). How to Play Any Mental Game - A Completeness Theorem for Protocols with Honest Majority. In *Proc. of the 19th Annual ACM Symposium on Theory of Computing,* (pp. 218–229), New York City, USA, May.

Gopal, R. D., & Sanders, G. L. (1997). Preventive and deterrent controls for software piracy. *Journal of Management Information Systems, 13*(4), 29-47.

Gordon, A. A., & Loeb, M. P. (2002). The economics of information security investment. *ACM Transactions on Information and System Security, 5*(4), 438-457.

Gordon, L. A., Loeb, M. P, Lucyshyn, W., & Richardson, R. (2004). Ninth Annual CSI/FBI Computer Crime And Security Survey, Computer Security Institute.

Gordon, L. A., Loeb, M. P., Lucyshyn, W., & Richardson, R. (2005). *10th annual CSI/FBI computer crime and security survey.* San Francisco, CA: Computer Security Institute.

Gosh, A. K. & Swaminatha, T. M. (2001). Software Security and Privacy Risks in Mobile E-Commerce: Examining the risks in wireless computing that will likely influence the emerging m-commerce market. *Communication of the ACM,* (44)2, 51-57.

Goth, G. (2005). Phishing attacks rising, but dollar losses down. *IEEE Security and Privacy, 3*(1), 8.

Grandison, T., & Sloman, M. (2000). A Survey of Trust in Internet Applications. *IEEE Communications Surveys,* (pp. 2-16).

Gritzalis, D. A. (2004). Embedding privacy in IT applications development. *Information Management and Computer Security, 12*(1), 8-26.

Grover, L. (1997). Quantum Mechanics helps in searching for a needle in a haystack. *Physics Review Letter, 79*(22), 325-328.

Grow, B. (2005). Hacker Hunters. *Business Week*, 30 May, (pp. 74-82).

Gruber, T. R. (1995). Toward principles for the design of ontologies used for knowledge sharing. *International Journal of Human-Computer Studies, 43*(5–6), 907–928.

Gunetti, D., & Picardi, C. (2005). Keystroke Analysis of Free Text. *ACM Transactions on Information and System Security, 3*(5), 312-347.

Gutierrez-Osuna, R. (2005). *Introduction to Pattern Analysis, Cross-validation.* http://research.cs.tamu.edu/prism/lectures/pr/pr_l13.pdf, last visited on 2006-11-13.

Haller, N., Metz, C., Nesser, P., & Straw, M. (2005). A one-time password system. Retrieved May 5, 2006, from http://www.faqs.org/rfcs/rfc2289.html

Hamilton, S. N., Miller, W. L., Ott, A., & Saydjari, O. S. (2002). Challenges in applying game theory to the domain of information warfare. *Proceedings of the Fourth Information Survivability Workshop.*

Hamilton, S.N., Miller, W.L., Ott, A., & Saydjari, O.S. (2002). The role of game theory in information warfare. *Proceedings of the Fourth Information Survivability Workshop.*

Han, J., & Kamber, M. (2001). *Data Mining: Concepts and Techniques*: Morgan Kaufmann Publishers.

Han, J., & Kamber, M. (2001). *Data Mining: Concepts and Techniques.* Morgan Kaufman.

Han, J., & Kamber, M. (2006). *Data Mining: Concepts and Techniques.* Morgan Kaufmann Publishers, San Francisco, CA.

Han, S., & Chang, E. (2006). *New efficient undetachable sigantures.* Technical Report, IS-CBS2006.

Han, S., Chang, E., & Dillon, T. (2005b). Secure transactions using mobile agents with TTP. *Proceedings of the Second IEEE Conference on Service Systems and Service Management, 2,* 856-862, Jun. 13-15, Chongqing University.

Han, S., Chang, E., & Dillon, T., (2005a). Secure e-transactions using mobile agents with agent broker. *Proceedings of the Second IEEE Conference on Service Systems and Service Management, 2,* 849-855, Jun.13-15, Chongqing University, China.

Hardy, Q. (2004, May 10). Data of Reckoning. *Forbes, 173,* 151-154.

Harrington, S. J. (1996). The effect of codes of ethics and personal denial of responsibility on computer abuse judgments and intentions. *MIS Quarterly, 20*(3), 257-278.

Hastie, T., Tibshirani, R., & Friedman, J. (2001). *The Elements of Statistical Learning; Data Mining, Inference.* New York: Spring-Verlag.

Hauser, C., & Kabatnik, M. (2001). *Towards Privacy Support in a Global Location Service.* Paper presented at the the IFIP Workshop on IP and ATM Traffic Management (WATM/EUNICE 2001), Paris.

He, Y., & Dawn N., & Jutla, N. D. (2006). Contextual e-Negotiation for the Handling of Private Data in e-Commerce on a Semantic Web. HICSS. *Proceedings of the 39th Annual Hawaii International Conference on System Sciences (HICSS'06),* 62-66.

Heijden, H., Verhagen, T., & Creemers, M. (2003). Understanding online purchase intentions: contributions from technology and trust perspectives. *European Journal of Information Systems, 12,* 41-48.

Henderson, S. C. & Snyder, C. A. (1999). Personal Information Privacy: Implications for MIS Managers. *Information & Management*, (36), 213-220.

Herlocker, J. L., & Konstan, J. A. (2001). Content-Independent Task-Focused Recommendation. *IEEE Internet Computing, 5*(6), 40-47.

Herzberg, A. (2004). *Web spoofing and phishing attacks and their prevention.* Paper presented at the The Fifth Mexican International Conference in Computer Science, Colima, Mexico.

High Performance Systems, IThink / Stella Technical Documentation, Lebanon NH.

Hinkin, T. R. (1998). A brief tutorial on the development of measures for use in survey questionnaires. *Organizational Research Methods, 1*(1), 104-121.

Hodge, J. G., Gostin, L. O., & Jacobson, P. (1999). Legal Issues Concerning Electronic Health Information: Privacy, Quality, and Liability, JAMA. *The Journal of the American Medical Association, 282*(15), 1466-1471.

Hoffman, D. L., Novak, T. P., & Peralta, M. (1999). Building consumer trust online. *Communications of the ACM, 42*(4), 80-85.

Hoffman, D.L., Novak, T.P., & Peralta, M. (2004). Building consumer trust online" Association for Computing Machinery. *Communications of the ACM, (42)*4, 80-86.

Hofstede, G. (1993). Cultural constraints in management theories. *Academy of Management Journal, 7*(1), 81-94.

Honeypot (2006). http://www.honeypots.net/

http://www.sarc.com/avcenter/venc/data/w32.beagle.bg@mm.html

Huhns, M. N., & Buell, D. A. (2002). Trusted autonomy. *IEEE Internet Computing,* (pp. 92-95).

Hulme, G. V. (2002). *Rude Worm Insults.* then Wreaks Havoc. http://www.itnews.com.au/newsstory.aspx?CIaNID=10532

IBM Corporation (2003). *Web Services Level Agreements.* June 1, 2006, from http://www.research.ibm.com/wsla/WSLASpecV1-20030128.pdf

IBM Research (2003, September). *Views of Privacy: Business Drivers, Strategy, and Directions.* IBM Research Division. Retrieved November 16, 2006, from, www.zurich.ibm.com/pdf/privacy/IBM_RC_on_Views_of_Privacy.pdf

IBM Survey: Consumers Think Cybercrime Now Three Times More Likely Than Physical Crime: Changing Nature of Crime Leads to Significant Behavior-Changes. Retrieved on January 27, 2006 from http://www 03.ibm.com/press/us/en/pressrelease/19154.wss

IBM, BEA Systems, Microsoft, Layer 7 Technologies, Oblix, VeriSign, Actional, Computer Associates, Open-Network Technologies, Ping Identity, Reactivity and RSA Security, (2004). *Web Services Trust Language.* June 1, 2006, from http://www-128.ibm.com/developerworks/webservices/library /specification/ws-trust/

Ince, D. (2001). *A Dictionary of the Internet.* Oxford University Press.

Inomata, A., Rahman, M., Okamoto, T., & Okamoto, E. (2005). *A novel mail filtering method against phishing.* Paper presented at the IEEE Pacific Rim Conference on Communications, Computers and signal Processing, Victoria, B.C., Canada.

Intellidimension, the RDF Gateway. http://www.intellidimension.com/

International Journal of Psychology, 41(4) 287-292.

Internet World Stats (2005). http://www.internetworld-stats.com/stats.htm

Irvine, C., & Levin, T. (1999). Toward a taxonomy and costing method for security services. In *Proceedings of the 15th Annual Computer Security Applications Conference (ACSAC '99)*, (pp. 183–188). IEEE.

ISO/IEC, Ed. (2005). ISO/IEC 17799:2005 Information technology - Security techniques - Code of practice for information security management, International Organization forStandardization.

ITIM International (2006). http://www.geert-hofstede.com/

ITRC 2008 Breach List. (2008). Retrieved from http://www.idtheftcenter.org/artman2/publish/lib_survey/ITRC_2008 on June 11, 2008.

Iyengar, V. S. (2002). *Transforming data to satisfy privacy constraints.* Paper presented at the KDD.

Jackson, L. A., von Eye, A., Barbatsis, G., Biocca, F., Zhao, Y., & Fitzgerald, H. (2003). Internet attitudes and Internet use: some surprising findings from the HomeNetToo Project. *International Journal of Human-Computer Studies, 59,* 355–382

Jaeger, M. C. et al. (2005). QoS Aggregation in Web Service Compositions. *Proc. of IEEE EEE05*, (pp. 181-185).

Jagadish, H. V. (1991). A Retrieval Technique For Similar Shapes. *In Proc. of the 1991 ACM SIGMOD International Conference on Management of Data* (pp. 208-217). Denver, Colorado, USA.

Jahankhani, H., & Nkhoma, M. Z. (2005). Information Systems Risk Assessment. *International Conference on information and Communication Technology in Management, Challenges and Prospects,* 23-25 May 2005, Malaysia.

Jarvenpaa, S. L., & Ives, B. (1991). Executive involvement and participation in the management of information technology. *MIS Quarterly, 15*(2), 205-221.

Jarvenpaa, S. Tactinsky, N., & Vitale, M. (2000). Consumer Trust in an Internet Store. *Information Technology and Management, 1,* 45-71.

Jasperson, J. S., Carte, T. A., Saunders, C. S., Butler, B. S., Croes, H. J. P., & Zheng, W. (2002). Power and information technology research: A metatriangulation review. *MIS Quarterly, 26*(4), 397-459.

JENA. http://jena.sourceforge.net/.

John, G. H., & Langley, P. (1995). *Estimating Continuous Distributions in Bayesian Classifiers. In the Proceedings of the Eleventh Conference on Uncertainty in Artificial Intelligence* (pp. 338-345)., San Mateo: Morgan KaufMann Publishers.

Johnson, W. B., & Lindenstrauss, J. (1984). Extensions of Lipshitz Mapping Into Hilbert Space. *In Proc. of the Conference in Modern Analysis and Probability* (pp. 189-206). Volume 26 of Contemporary Mathematics.

Jones, M. C., Arnett, K. P., Tang, J. T. E., & Chen, N. S. (1993). Perceptions of computer viruses a cross-cultural assessment. *Computers and Security, 12,* 191-197.

Jutla, D. N., & Bodorik, P. (2005). Sociotechnical architecture for online privacy. *IEEE Security and Privacy, 3*(2), 29–39.

Kagal, L., Finin, T., & Joshi, A. (2003) A Policy Based Approach to Security for the Semantic Web. *International Semantic Web Conference.*

Kalakota, R. & Whinston, A. B. (1996). Frontiers of Electronic Commerce, 1st edition, Addison Wesley Publishing Co., New York, NY, USA

Kankanhalli, A., Hock-Hai, T., Bernard, C. Y. T., & Kwok-Kee, W. (2003). An integrative study of information systems security effectiveness. *International Journal of Information Management, 23*(2), 139-154.

Kantarcioglu, M., & Clifton, C. (2004). Privacy-Preserving Distributed Mining of Association Rules on Horizontally Partitioned Data. *IEEE Trans. Knowledge Data Eng., 16*(9), 1026-1037.

Kar, E. A. M. v. d. (2004). *Designing mobile information services; An Approach for Organisations in a Value Network.* Unpublished Doctoral dissertation, Delft University of Technology, Delft, The Netherlands.

Karahanna, E., Evaristo, R., & Srite, M. (2004). Methodological issues in MIS cross-cultural research. In M. E. Whitman & A. B. Woszczynski (Eds.), *The handbook of information systems research* (pp. 166-177). Hershey, PA: Idea Group Publishing.

Kaski, S. (1999). Dimensionality Reduction by Random Mapping. *In Proc. of the International Joint Conference on Neural Networks* (pp. 413-418). Anchorage, Alaska.

Kavantzas, N. et al. (2004). *Web Services Choreography Description Language Version 1.0.* June 1, 2006, from http://www.w3.org/TR/2004/WD-ws-cdl-10-20041217/

Keen, P. G. W. (1999). Competing in chapter 2 of internet business: Navigating in a new world. Eburon Publishers, Delft, The Netherlands.

Keller, A., & Ludwig, H. (2003). The WSLA Framework: Specifying and Monitoring Service Level Agreements for Web Services. *Plenum Publishing, Journal of Network and Systems Management, 11*(1), 57-81.

Kelloway, E. K. (1998). *Using LISREL for structural equation modeling: A researcher's guide.* Thousand Oaks, CA: Sage Publications.

Kifer, D., & Gehrke, J. (2006). *Injecting utility into anonymized datasets.* Paper presented at the Proceedings of the 2006 ACM SIGMOD international conference on Management of data, Chicago, IL, USA.

Kim, A., Luo, J., & Kang, M. (2005). Security ontology for annotating resources. In *Proceedings of the On the Move to Meaningful Internet Systems: CoopIS, DOA, and ODBASE,* LNCS 3761, (pp. 1483–1499). Springer-Verlag.

Kim, H.-A., & Karp, B. (2004). Autograph: Toward Automated, Distributed Worm Signature Detection. *In the Proceedings of the 13th Usenix Security Symposium (Security 2004),* San Diego, CA, August, 2004.

Kim, S. & Leem, C. S. (2005). Security of the internet-based instant messenger: Risk and safeguards. *Internet Research,* (15)1, 68-98.

Kim, S. S., & Malhotra, N. K. (2005a). A longitudinal model of continued IS use: An integrative view of four mechanisms underlying postadoption phenomena. *Management Science, 51*(5), 741-755.

Kim, U., & Park, Y. S. (2006). Indigenous psychological analysis of academic achievement in Korea: The influence of self efficacy, parents, and culture.

Kirda, E., & Kruegel, C. (2005). *Protecting users against phishing attacks with antiPhish.* Paper presented at the 29th Annual International on Computer Software and Applications Conference, Edinburgh, Scotland.

Kirk, J. (2005). Yahoo users get phished. Retrieved May 6, 2006, from http://www.pcworld.com/news/article/0,aid,122707,00.asp

Kodialam, M., & Lakshman, T.V. (2003). Detecting network intrusions via sampling: A game-theoretic approach. *Proceedings of the IEEE INFOCOM,* (pp. 1880-1889).

Kolaczek, G. (2003). *Specification and verification of constraints in role based access control for enterprise security system.* WETICE 2003, (pp. 190-195).

Kolodzinski, O. (2002). Aligning Information Security Imperatives with Business Needs, *The CPA Journal, 27*(7), 20.

Konar, A. (2000). *Artificial Intelligence and Soft Computing: Behavioral and Cognitive Modeling of the Human Brain.* New York: CRC Press.

Korean Times (2005) Technology. It's English. *The Korean Times.*http://times.hankooki.com/lpage/tech/200512/kt2005120216444111780.htm

Kotani, K., & Horii, K. (2005). Evaluation on a keystroke authentication system by keying force incorporated with temporal characteristics of keystroke dynamics. *Behaviour & Information Technology, 4*(24), 289-302.

Kotulic, A. G., & Clark, J. G. (2004). Why there aren't more information security research studies. *Information & Management, 41*(5), 597-607.

Kotzanikolaou, P., Burmester, M., & Chrissikopoulos, V. (2000). Secure transactions with mobile agents in hostile environments. *ACISP 2000, LNCS 1841,* 289-297.

Kramarenko, D. (2003, January 25) Hackers or Cyber-soldiers? *Computer Crime Research Center.* http://www.crime-research.org/interviews/hacker0904/

Kristol, D. M. (2001). HTTP Cookies: Standards, Privacy, and Politics. *ACM Transactions on Internet Technology, 1*(2) 151-198.

Kruskal, J. B., & Wish, M. (1978). *Multidimensional Scaling.* Sage Publications, Beverly Hills, CA, USA.

Kuper, P. (2005). The state of security. *IEEE Security and Privacy 3*(5), 51-53.

Kutter, M., & Petitcolas, F. A. P. (1999, January). A fair benchmark for image watermarking systems. *Proceedings of SPIE: Security and Watermarking of Multimedia Contents, 3637*, 226-239. San Jose, USA.

Kutter, M., & Petitcolas, F. A. P. (1999, January). A fair benchmark for image watermarking systems. *Proceedings of SPIE: Security and Watermarking of Multimedia Contents, 3637*, 226-239. San Jose, USA.

Labuschagne, L. & Eloff, J. H. P. (2000). Electronic Commerce: the information-security challenge. *Information Management & Computer Security,* (8)3, 54-159.

Lakshmanan, L. V. S., Ng, R. T., & Ramesh, G. (2005). *To do or not to do: the dilemma of disclosing anonymized data.* Paper presented at the Proceedings of the 2005 ACM SIGMOD international conference on Management of data, Baltimore, Maryland.

Lambrix, P. (2004). Ontologies in bioinformatics and systems biology. In W. Dubitzky, & F. Azuaje (Eds.), *Artificial Intelligence Methods and Tools for Systems Biology,* (pp. 129–146). Springer-Verlag.

Lambrix, P., & Tan, H. (2005). A framework for aligning ontologies. In *Proceedings of the 3rd Workshop on Principles and Practice of Semantic Web Reasoning, LNCS 3703,* 17–31. Springer-Verlag.

Lambrix, P., & Tan, H. (2007). Ontology alignment and merging. In Burger, A., Davidson, D., and Baldock, R., editors, *Anatomy Ontologies for Bioinformatics: Principles and Practice.* Springer-Verlag. To appear.

Lambrix, P., Tan, H., Jakonieṅe, V., & Strömbäck, L. (2007). Biological ontologies. In Baker, C. J. and Cheung, K.-H., editors, *Semantic Web: Revolutionizing Knowledge Discovery in the Life Sciences,* (pp. 85–99). Springer-Verlag.

Landwehr, C. E. (2001). Computer security. *International Journal of Information Security, 1*(1), 3-13.

Larsen, B., & Aone, C. (1999). Fast and Effective Text Mining Using Linear-Time Document Clustering. *In Proceedings of the 5th ACM SIGKDD International Conference on Knowledge Discovery and Data Mining* (pp. 16-22). San Diego, CA, USA.

Lauter, K. (2004). The advantages of elliptic curve cryptography for wireless security. *IEEE Wireless Communications Magazine.*

Leach, J. (2003). Improving user security behavior. *Computers & Security, 22*(8), 685-692.

Lee, S. M., Lee, S. G., & Yoo, S. (2004). An integrative model of computer abuse based on social control and general deterrence theories. *Information & Management, 41*(6), 707-718.

Lee, Y., Kozar, K. A., & Larsen, K. R. T. (2003). The technology acceptance model: Past, present, and future. *Communications of AIS, 12*(50), 752-780.

Lemos, R. (1999a). *Can you trust TRUSTe?* Retrieved Oct 14, 2002, from http://zdnet.com.com/2100-11-516377.html?legacy=zdnn

Lemos, R. (1999b). *RealNetworks rewrites privacy policy ZDNet News.* Retrieved 1999, October 31, from http://zdnet.com.com/2100-11-516330.html?legacy=zdnn

Lemos, R. (2001) Web Worm Targets White House. *CNet News.com*

leskerov, E., Freisleben, B., & Rao, B. (1997). CARD-WATCH: A neural network based database mining system for credit card fraud detection. *Proceedings of the Computational Intelligence for Financial Engineering Conference,* (pp. 220-226).

Li, Y., & Zhang, X. (2004). A security-enhanced one-time payment scheme for credit card. *Proceedings of the 14th International Workshop on Research Issues in Data Engineering,* (pp. 40-47).

Libsvm. (2006). *A library for Support Vector Machine.* http://www.csie.ntu.edu.tw/~cjlin/libsvm/

Liew, C. K., Choi, U. J., & Liew, C. J. (1985). A data distortion by probability distribution. *ACM Transactions on Database Systems (TODS), 10*(3), 395-411.

Lindell, Y., & Pinkas, B. (2002). Privacy Preserving Data Mining. *J. Cryptology, 15*(3), 177-206.

Lindqvist, U., & Jonsson, E. (1997). How to systematically classify computer security intrusions. In *Proceedings of the IEEE Symposium on Security and Privacy (S&P'97)*, (pp. 154–163). IEEE.

Liu, C., Marchewka, J. T., Lu, J., & Yu, C. (2005). Beyond Concern - a Privacy -Trust - Behavioral Intention Model of Eclectronic Commerce. *Information & Management,* (42), 289-304.

Liu, J. T., Marchewka, J. L., & Yu, C. S. (2004). Beyond concern: a privacy-trust-behavioral intention model of electronic commerce. *Information & Management*(42), 127-142.

Liu, P., & Li, L. (2002). A game-theoretic approach for attack prediction. Technical Report, PSU-S2-2002-01, Pennsylvania State University.

Liu, W., Huang, G., Liu, X., Deng, X., & Zhang, M. (2005). *Phishing web page detection.* Paper presented at the Eighth International Conference on Document Analysis and Recognition, Daejeon, Korea.

Lo, V. S. Y. (2002). The True Lift Model - A Novel Data Mining Approach to Response Modeling in Database Marketing. *SIGKDD Explorations, 4*(2), 78-86.

Lu, C-S., & Lia, M Y. A. (2003, June). Structural digital signature for image authentication: An incidental distortion resistant scheme. *IEEE Transactions on Multimedia, 5*(2), 161-173.

Machanavajjhala, A., Gehrke, J., Kifer, D., & Venkitasubramaniam, M. (2006). *l-Diversity: Privacy Beyond k -Anonymity.* Paper presented at the 22nd International Conference on Data Engineering (ICDE'06).

MacKinnon, D. P., Krull, J. L., & Lockwood, C. (2000). Mediation, confounding, and suppression: Different names for the same effect. *Prevention Science, 2,* 15-27.

Macqueen, J. (1967). Some Methods for Classification and Analysis of Multivariate Observations. *In Proc. of the 5th Berkeley Symposium on Mathematical Statistics*

and Probability (pp. 281-297). Berkeley: University of California Press, Vol. 1.

Malhotra, N. K., Kim, S. S., & Agarwal, J., (2004). Internet users' Information Privacy concerns (IUIPC): The Construct, the Scale and a Casual Model. *Information Systems Research,* (15)4, 336-355.

Mamdani, E. H. (1976). Advances in the Linguistic Synthesis of Fuzzy Controllers. *Journal of Man-Machine Studies, 8,* 669-678.

Manber, U., Patel, A., & Robinson, L. (2000). Experience with Personalization on Yahoo! *Communications of the ACM, 43*(8), 35-39.

Mani, A. and Nagarajan, A. (2002). *Understanding Quality of Service for Web Services.* June 1, 2006, from http://www-106.ibm.com/developerworks/webservices/library/ws-quality.html

Mansfield, A. J., & Wayman, J. L. (2002). *Best Practices in Testing and Reporting Performance of Biometric Devices - Version 2.01.* http://www.npl.co.uk/scientific_software/publications/biometrics/bestprac_v2_1.pdf, last visited on 2006-11-14.

Margulis, S. T. (1977). Conceptions of privacy: current status and next steps. *J. of Social Issues*(33), 5-10.

Margulis, S. T. (2003). On the Status and Contribution of Westin's and Altman's Theories of Privacy. *Journal of Social Issues, 59*(2), 411-429.

Martin, S., Sewani, A., Nelson, B., Chen, K., & Joseph, A. D. (2005). *A Two-Layer Approach for Novel Email Worm Detection.* Submitted to USENIX Steps on Reducing Unwanted Traffic on the Internet (SRUTI).

Martin, S., Sewani, A., Nelson, B., Chen, K., & Joseph, A.D. (2005). Analyzing Behavioral Features for Email Classification. *In the Proceedings of the IEEE Second Conference on Email and Anti-Spam (CEAS 2005),* July 21 & 22, Stanford University.

Mason, R. O. (1986). Four ethical issues of the information age. *MIS Quart., 10*(1), 4-12.

Maximilien, E. M., & Singh, M. P. (2002). Conceptual Model of Web Service Reputation. *SIGMOD Record, 31*(4), 36–41.

Maximilien, E. M., & Singh, M. P. (2004). A Framework and Ontology for Dynamic Web Services Selection. *IEEE Internet Computing, 8*(5), 84–93.

MAXMIND (2005). *MAXMIND – Geolocation and Credit Card Fraud Detection.* Website: http://www.maxmind.com/

Mayer, T. S. (2002). Privacy and Confidentiality Research and the U.S. Census Bureau Recommendations Based on a Review of the Literature. *Statistical Research Division U.S. Bureau of the Census.*

McClure, S., Scambray, J., & Kurtz, G. (2003). Hacking Exposed, *Network Security Secrets & Solutions*, 4th edition. McGraw-Hill Ryerson.

McCoy, S., Galletta, D. F., & King, W. R. (2005). Integrating national culture into IS research: The need for current individual-level measures. *Communications of the Association for Information Systems, 15*, 211-224.

Memon, N., Vora, P., Yeo, B-L., & Yeung, M. (2000, February). Distortion bounded authentication techniques. *Proceedings of International Conference on Watermarking and Multimedia Contents.*

Mendenhall, W., & Beaver, R. J. (1999). Introduction to Probability and Statistics. *Duxbury Press,* (pp. 442-446).

Merchant Account (2005). *Merchant Account Credit Card Processing.* Website: http://www.aaa-merchant-account.com/

Meregu, S., & Ghosh, J. (2003). Privacy-Preserving Distributed Clustering Using Generative Models. *In Proc. of the 3rd IEEE International Conference on Data Mining (ICDM'03)* (pp. 211-218). Melbourne, Florida, USA.

Miklau, G., & Suciu, D. (2004). A Formal Analysis of Information Disclosure in Data Exchange. In *SIGMOD 2004* (pp. 575-586).

Milberg, S. J., S. J., B., Smith, H. J., & Kallman, E. A. (1995). Values, personal information privacy, and regulatory approaches. *Comm. of the ACM, 38*, 65-74.

Miller, M. L., Cox, I. J., Linnartz, J-P. M. G., & Kalker, T. (1999). A review of watermarking principles and practices. *Digital Signal Processing in Multimedia Systems*, pp. 461-485). Marcell Dekker Inc.

Miller, R. (2006). Retrieved from http://news.netcraft.com/archives/security.htm on February 2, 2006.

Milne, G. R., & Boza, M.E. (1998). Trust and Concern in Consumers' Perceptions of Marketing Information Management Practices. *Marketing Science Institute Working Paper Report*, 98-117.

Milne, G. R., & Culnan, M. J. (2004). Strategies for reducing online privacy risks: Why consumers read (or don't read) online privacy notices. *Journal of Interactive Marketing*, (18)3, 15-29.

Mitchell, T. (1997). *Machine Learning.* McGraw Hill.

Mitra, N. (2003). *SOAP Version 1.2 Part 0: Primer.* June 1, 2006, from http://www.w3.org/TR/2003/REC-soap12-part0-20030624/.

Monrose, F., Reiter, M. K., & Wetzel, S. (2001). Password hardening based on keystroke dynamics. *International Journal of Information Security, 1*(2). New York: Springer-Verlag,

Murata, T. (1989). Petri Nets: Properties, Analysis and Applications. *Proceedings of the IEEE, 77*(4), 541-580.

Naraine, R. (2006, January 18) eWeek.com When's a Rootkit Not a Rootkit? http://www.eweek.com/article2/0,1759,1913083,00.asp

Naraine, R. (2007, May 15) Rutkowska Announces Invisible Things Lab Startup. *ZDNet,* http://blogs.zdnet.com/security/?p=199.

Narayanan, S., & McIlraith, S. A. (2002). Simulation, Verification and Automated Composition of Web Services. *Proceedings ACM WWW 2002,* (pp. 77-88).

Neches, R., Fikes, R., Finin, T. W., Gruber, T. R., Patil, R., Senator, T. E., & Swartout, W. R. (1991). Enabling technology for knowledge sharing. *AI Magazine, 12*(3), 36–56.

Nejdl, W., Olmedilla, D., Winslett, M., & Zhang, C. C. (2005). Ontology based policy specification and management. In *Proceedings of the 2nd European Semantic Web Conference (ESCW'05), LNCS 3532*, 290–302. Springer-Verlag.

Nemati, H., Barko, R., & Christopher, D. (2001). Issues in Organizational Data Mining: A Survey of Current Practices. *Journal of Data Warehousing, 6*(1), 25-36.

Neumann, P. G. (1995). *Computer-related risks*. Addison Wesley.

Newman, M. E. J., Forrest, S., & Balthrop, J. (2002). Email networks and the spread of computer viruses. *Physical Review, E 66*, 035101.

Newsome, J., Karp, B., & Song, D. (2005). Polygraph: Automatically Generating Signatures for Polymorphic Worms. *In Proceedings of the IEEE Symposium on Security and Privacy,* May 2005.

Niederman, F., Brancheau, J. C., & Wetherbe, J. C. (1991). Information systems management issues for the 1990's. *MIS Quart., 15*, 474-500.

Nilsson, M., Lindskog, H., & Fischer-Hübner, S. (2001). *Privacy Enhancements in the Mobile Internet.* Paper presented at the the IFIP WG 9.6/11.7 working conference on Security and Control of IT in Society, Bratislava.

Noy, N., & Rector, A. (2006). *Defining N-ary Relations on the Semantic Web.* http://www.w3.org/TR/swbp-n-aryRelations/ (visited 24-Apr-2006).

NSTISSC (1999). *National Information Systems security (INFOSEC) Glossary, National security Telecommunications and Information Systems security Committee (NSTISSC): 4.*

Nunnally, J. (1978). *Psychometric theory.* New York: McGraw-Hill.

Obaidat, M. S., & Sadoun, B. (1997). Verification of Computer User Using Keystroke Dynamics. *IEEE Transactions on Systems, Man, and Cybernetics - Part B, 27*(2), 261-269.

Oliveira, S. R. M. (2005). *Data Transformation For Privacy-Preserving Data Mining.* PhD thesis, Department of Computing Science, University of Alberta, Edmonton, AB, Canada, June.

Oliveira, S. R. M., & Zaïane, O. R. (2004). Achieving Privacy Preservation When Sharing Data For Clustering. In *Proc. of the Workshop on Secure Data Management in a Connected World (SDM'04) in conjunction with VLDB'2004,* (pp. 67–82), Toronto, Ontario, Canada, August.

Oliveira, S. R. M., & Zaïane, O. R. (2004). Privacy-Preserving Clustering by Object Similarity-Based Representation and Dimensionality Reduction Transformation. *In Proc. of the Workshop on Privacy and Security Aspects of Data Mining (PSADM'04) in conjunction with the Fourth IEEE International Conference on Data Mining (ICDM'04)* (pp. 21-30). Brighton, UK.

Olivero, N., & Lunt, P. (2003). Privacy versus willingness to disclose in E-commerce exchanges: the effect of risk awareness on the relative role of trust and control. *Journal of Economic Psychology, 25*, 243-262.

Online Fraud (2005). *Online Fraud is 12 Times Higher than Offline Fraud.* Website: http://sellitontheweb.com/ezine/news0434.shtml

Orlikowski, W. (1993). CASE tools as organizational change: Investigating incremental and radical changes in systems development. *MIS Quarterly, 17*(3), 309-340.

Oxford University Press (2004). A Dictionary of Computing. Oxford Reference Online. Oxford University press.

Pan, S. L., & Lee, J.-N. (2003). Using E-CRM for a Unified View of the Customer. *Communications of the ACM, 46*(4), 95-99.

Papadimitriou, C. H., Tamaki, H., Raghavan, P., & Vempala, S. (1998). Latent Semantic Indexing: A Probabilistic Analysis. *In Proc. of the 17th ACM Symposium on Principles of Database Systems* (pp. 159-168). Seattle, WA, USA.

Parker, D. B. (1981). *Computer security management.* Reston, Virginia: Reston Publishing Company.

Patarin, J., Courtois, N., & Goubin, L. (2001). QUARTZ, 128-bit long digital signatures. *CT-RSA 2001*, (pp. 282-297).

Patel-Schneider, P. F., Hayes, P., & Horrocks, I. (2004). *OWL Web Ontology Language Semantics and Abstract Syntax.* http://www.w3.org/TR/ owl-absyn/ (visited 21-Apr-2006).

Peace, A. G., Galletta, D. F., & Thong, J. Y. L. (2002). Software piracy in the workplace: A model and empirical test. *Journal of Management Information Systems, 20*(1), 153-177.

Peacock, A., Ke, X., & Wilkerson, M. (2004). Typing Patterns: A Key to User Identification. *IEEE Security and Privacy, 5*(2), 40-47.

Personalization Consortium. (2000). *Survey Finds Few Consumers Unwilling to Provide Personal Information to Web Marketers in Exchange for Better Services.* Retrieved March 15, 2005 from http://www.personalization.org/surveypress.html

Personalization Consortium. (2001). *New Survey Shows Consumers are More Likely to Purchase at Web Sites That Offer Personalization* Retrieved March 15, 2005 from http://www.personalization.org/pr050901.html

Peters, M.E. (2002). Emerging eCommerce credit and debit card protocols. *Proceedings of the 3rd International Symposium on Electronic Commerce*, (pp. 39-46).

Peterson, D. K., & Kim, C. (2003). Perceptions on IS Risks and Failure Types: A Comparison of Designers from the United States, Japan and Korea. *Journal of Global Information Management, 11*(3), 19-20, Jul-Sep.

Peterson, Robert A. (1994). A meta analysis of Cronbach's coefficient alpha. *Journal of Consumer Research*, 21(2), 381-391.

Pezzini, M. (2003). Composite Applications Head Toward the Mainstream. *Gartner Group*, ID Number AV-21-1772.

Piller, K., & Wolfgarten, S. (2004). Honeypot Forensics – No stone unturned or logs, what logs? *Risk Advisory Services.* Berlin: Ernst & Young.

Pinkas, B. (2002). Cryptographic Techniques For Privacy-Preserving Data Mining. *SIGKDD Explorations, 4*(2), 12–19, December 2002.

Pinkas, B. (2002). Crytographic techniques for privacy-preserving data mining. *SIGKDD Exploreations, 4*(2), 12-19.

Pitofsky, R. (2006). *Privacy Online: Fair Information Practices in the Electronic Marketplace, a Report to Congress.* Retrieved August, 2006, from http://www.ftc.gov/reports/privacy2000/privacy2000.pdfFTC

Podsakoff, P. M., & Organ, D. W. (1986). Self-reports in organizational research: Problems and prospects. *Journal of Management, 12*(4), 531-544.

Podsakoff, P. M., MacKenzie, S. B., Lee, J. Y., & Podsakoff, N. P. (2003). Common method bias in behavioral research: A critical review of the literature and recommended remedies. *Journal of Applied Psychology, 88*(5), 879-903.

Ponemon, L. (2005). *Lost Customer Information: What Does a Data Breach Cost Companies?* Ponemon Institue, Tucson, Arizona, USA. (online at: http://www.securitymanagement.com/library/Ponemon_DataStudy0106.pdf) (accessed 8-31-2006)

Ponemon, L. (2005). *The National Survey on Data Security Breach Notification*, Ponemon Institute, Tucson, Arizona, USA. (online at: http://www.whitecase.com/files/Publication/bdf5cd75-ecd2-41f2-a54d-a087ea9c0029/Presentation/PublicationAttachment/2f92d91b-a565-4a07-bf68-aa21118006bb/Security_Breach_Survey%5B1%5D.pdf) (accessed 8-31-2006)

Potter, G. (2001). *Business in a Virtual World: Exploiting Information for Competitive Advantage.* Houndmills, England: Macmillan.

Power, R. (2002). CSI/FBI computer crime and security survey. *Computer Security Issues & Trends VIH,* (1), 1-22.

Powers, S. (2003). *Practical RDF*. O'Reilly.

Preimesberger, C. (2006). Hackers Hit AT&T System, Get Credit Card Info. *eWeek,* August 29, 2006, http://www.eweek.com/article2/0,1895,2010001,00.asp?kc=EWNAVEMNL083006EOA (accessed 8-31-2006).

Protechnix (2006, October 9). Cryptology and Data Secrecy: The Vernam Cipher. Retrieved 9 October, 2006, from, http://www.pro-technix.com/information/crypto/pages/vernam_base.html

Prud'hommeaux, E., & Seaborne, A. (2006). *SPARQL query language for RDF*. W3C.

PWC/DTI (2004). *Information Security Breaches Survey 2004: Executive Summary,* Pricewaterhouse Coopers UK, Department of Trade and Industry UK, April 2004. Available at: http://www.pwc.com/images/gx/eng/about/svcs/grms/2004Exec_Summ.pdf.

PWC/DTI (2004). *Information Security Breaches Survey 2004: Technical Report*, Pricewaterhouse Coopers UK, Department of Trade and Industry UK, April 2004. Available at: http://www.pwc.com/images/gx/eng/about/svcs/grms/2004Technical_Report.pdf

Quinlan, J. R. (1993). *C4.5: Programs for Machine Learning*. Morgan Kaufmann Publishers.

Raab, C. D., & Bennett, C. J., (1998), The Distribution of Privacy Risks: Who Needs Protection? *The Information Society*, 14, 263-274.

Ragnathan, C., & Grandon E. (2002). An Exploratory Examination of Factors Affecting Online Sales. *Journal of Computer Information Systems, 42*(3) 87-93.

Rajput, S. A., Chen., J., & Hsu, S. (2005). State Based Authentication. *Proceedings of the 43rd Annual Association for Computing Machinery South East Conference, Volume 2*, March 18-20 160-165.

RDF Primer. http://www.w3.org/TR/rdf-primer/

Rector, A., Drummond, N., Horridge, M., Rogers, J., Knublauch, H., Stevens, R., Wang, H., & Wroe, C. (2004). OWL pizzas: Practical experience of teaching OWL-DL: Common errors & common patterns. In *Proceedings of the 14th International Conference of Engineering Knowledge in the Age of the SemanticWeb (EKAW'04)*, LNCS 3257, pages 63–81. Springer-Verlag.

Reddick, C. G. (2004). A two-stage model of e-government growth: Theories and empirical evidence for U.S. cities. *Government Information Quarterly, 21*(1), 51-64.

Richardson, R. (2003). Eighth Annual CSI/FBI Computer Crime And Security Survey, Computer Security Institute: Online at. http://www.reddshell.com/docs/csi_fbi_2003.pdf#search=%22Eighth%20Annual%20CSI%2FFBI%20COMPUTER%20CRIME%20AND%20SECURITY%20SURVEY%22 (accessed 8-31-2006)

Richmond, R. (2004). Money Increasingly Is Motive For Computer-Virus Attacks. *Wall Street Journal, 19*, Sept., B5.

Rivest, R., & Shamir, A. (1984). How to expose an eavesdropper. *Communications of the ACM, 27*(4), 393 - 394.

Rivest, R.L., Shamir, A., & Adleman, L.M. (1978). A method for obtaining digital signatures and public-key cryptosystems. *Commun. ACM 21*(2), 120-126.

Rizvi, S. J., & Haritsa, J. R. (2002). *Maintaing data privacy in association rule mining*. Paper presented at the Proceedings of the 28th International Conference on Very Large Databases.

Roberts, P. F. (2005). *Microsoft on 'Rootkits': Be Afraid, Be very Afraid*.

Robinson, S. (2000, March 7). Gauging the Limits of Quantum Computing. *The New York Times On The Web*, Retrieved November 22, 2006, from, http://www.nytimes.com/library/national/science/030700sci-quantum-computing.html.

Rockart, J. F., & DeLong, D. W. (1988). *Executive Support Systems: The Emergence of Top Management Computer Use*. Paper presented at the Dow Jones-Irwin, Homewood, IL.

Roddick, J., & Wahlstrom, K. (2001). On the Impact of Knowledge Discovery and Data Mining. *Australian Computer Society, Inc.*

Rogers, E. M. (1962). *Diffusion of Innovations.* The Free Press. New York.

Rogers, E. M. (1976). New Product Adoption and Diffusion. *Journal of Consumer Research. 2,* 290-301.

Romano, N. C., Jr., & Fjermestad, J. (2001-2002). Customer Relationship Management Research: An Assessment of Research. *International Journal of Electronic Commerce, 6*(3 Winter)), 61-114.

Romano, N.C., Jr. & Fjermestad, J. (2003). Electronic Commerce Customer Relationship Management: A Research Agenda. *Information Technology and Management, 4,* 233-258.

Roy, J. (1999). Polis and oikos in classical Athens. *Greece & Rome 46*(1), 1-18.

Rykwert, J. (2001). Privacy in Antiquity. *Social Research, 68*(1), 29-40.

Samarati, P. (2001). Protecting respondents' identities in microdata release. *IEEE Transactions on Knowledge and Data Engineering,* 1010-1027.

Samarati, P. (2001). Protecting Respondents' Identities in Microdata Release. IEEE Transactions on Knowledge and Data Engineering, 13 (6), 1010-1027.

Sander, T., & Tschudin, C.F. (1998). Protecting mobile agents against malicious hosts. *Mobile Agents and Security 1998, LNCS 1419,* 44-60.

Schmidt, M. B., & Arnett, K. P. (2005). Spyware: A Little Knowledge is a Wonderful Thing. *Communications of the ACM, 48*(8), 67-70.

Schneier, B. (2005). The failure of two-factor authentication. Retrieved May 6, 2006, from http://www.schneier.com/blob/archives/2005/03/the_failure_of.html

Schneier, B., (2005). Risks of Third-Party Data. *Communication of the ACM,* 48(5),136.

Schoder, D. & Madeja, N. (2004). Is customer relationship management a success factor in electronic commerce? *Journal of Electronic Commerce Research, 5*(1), 38-53.

Schultz, M., Eskin, E., & Zadok, E. (2001). MEF: Malicious email filter, a UNIX mail filter that detects malicious windows executables. *In USENIX Annual Technical Conference - FREENIX* Track, June 2001.

Schumacher, M. (2003). *Security Engineering with Patterns: Origins, Theoretical Model, and New Applications.* LNCS 2754. Springer-Verlag.

Schwartau, W. (2005). Securing the Enterprise. Technology alone won't make you safe. Tackle it as a management problem. *Network World,* January 27, 42.

Security Systems News (2002). www.securitysystemsnews.com/october2002/securitystats/09.ssn.pages.02.pdf.

Segars, A. H., & Grover, V. (1998). Strategic information systems planning success: An investigation of the construct and its measurement. *MIS Quarterly, 22*(2), 139 163.

Seitz, K. (2006). Taking Steps To Ensure CRM Data Security. *Customer Inter@ction Solutions 24*(11), 62-64,66.

Seltzer, L. (2005). Rootkits: The Ultimate Stealth Attack. *PC Magazine, 24,* 76.

Senge, P. M. (1990). The Fifth Discipline, Currency Doubleday, New York.

Shadbolt, N. (2002). A Matter of Trust. *IEEE Intelligent Systems,* (pp. 2-3).

Shamir, A. (1984). Efficient signature schemes based on birational permutations. *Advances in Cryptology - CRYPTO 93, LNCS 773,* 1-12.

Sharma, R., & Yetton, P. (2003). The contingent effects of management support and task interdependence on successful information systems implementation. *MIS Quarterly, 27*(4), 533-555.

Sheng, Y., Phoha, V. V., & Rovnyak, S.M. (2005). A Parallel Decision Tree-Based Method for User Authentication Based on Keystroke Patterns. *IEEE Transactions on Systems, Man, and Cybernetics - Part B, 35*(4), 826-833.

Sheth, A., & Larson, J. (1990). Federated Database Systems. *ACM Computing Surveys, 22*(3).

Sheth, J. N., Sisodia, R. S., & Sharma, S. (2000). The antecedents and consequences of customer-centric marketing. *Journal of the Academy of Marketing Science, 28*(1 Winter), 55-66.

Shim, J. P. (2005) Korea's Lead in Mobile Cellular and DMB Phone Services., *Communications of the Association for Information Systems,15*.

Shor, P. W. (1994). Polynomial-Time Algorithms for Prime Factorization and Discrete Logarithms on a Quantum Computer. *Proceedings of the 35th Annual Symposium on Foundations of Computer Science*, USA.

Sidiroglou, S., Ioannidis, J., Keromytis, A. D., & Stolfo, S. J. (2005). An Email Worm Vaccine Architecture. *Proceedings of the First International Conference on Information Security Practice and Experience (ISPEC 2005)*, Singapore, April 11-14, pp. 97-108.

Simmonds, A., Sandilands, P., & van Ekert, L. (2004). An ontology for network security attacks. In *Proceedings of the 2nd Asian Applied Computing Conference (AACC'04), LNCS 3285*, 317–323. Springer-Verlag.

Singh, M. P. (2002). Trustworthy Service Composition: Challenges and Research Questions. *Proceedings of the Autonomous Agents and Multi-Agent Systems Workshop on Deception, Fraud and Trust in Agent Societies,* (pp. 39-52).

Singh, S., Estan, C., Varghese, G., & Savage, S. (2003) *The EarlyBird System for Real-time Detection of Unknown Worms*. Technical report - cs2003-0761, UCSD.

Skinner G., Han, S., & Chang, E. (2006). The Computational View of Information Privacy for Privacy Enhancing Technologies. *The First International Conference on Legal, Security and Privacy Issues in IT (LSPI)*, Germany.

Skinner, G., & Chang, E. (2006). A Conceptual Framework for Information Privacy and Security in Collaborative Environments. *International Journal of Computer Science and Network Security, 6*(2)B, 45-51.

Skinner, G., & Chang, E. (2006). Fair Privacy Principles and Preferences (F3P) – Evaluating Context Based Privacy Preferences. *The 10th WSEAS International Conference on Computers, ICCOMP-06*, Vouliagmeni, Athens, Greece.

Skinner, G., & Chang, E. (2007). An Environmentally Adaptive Conceptual Framework for Addressing Information Privacy Issues in Digital Ecosystems. Presented at DEST2007, Cairns, Australia.

Skinner, G., & E. Chang E. (2005). PP-SDLC: The Privacy Protecting Systems Development Life Cycle. *IPSI-2005*, Carcassonne, FRANCE.

Smith, H. J. (1993). Privacy policies and practices: Inside the organizational maze. *Comm. of the ACM, 36*, 105-122.

Smith, H. J., Milberg, S. & Burke, S. (1996). Information Privacy: Measuring Individuals Concerns About Organizational Practices. *MIS Quarterly, 20*(6), 167-196.

Smith, S. & R. Jamieson (2006). Determining Key Factors In E-Government Information System Security. *Information Systems Management, 23*(2), 23-33.

Smith, S. W., & Spafford, E.H. (2004). Grand challenges in information security: process and output. *IEEE Security and Privacy, 2*(1), 69-71.

Spector, P. E. (1994). Using self-report questionnaires in OB research: A comment on the use of a controversial method. *Journal of Organizational Behavior, 15*, 385-392.

Spillane, R. J. (1975). Keyboard apparatus for personal identification. *IBM Technical Disclosure Bulletin, 17*(11), 3346.

Spinellis, D., Kokolakis, D., & Gritzalis, S. (1999). Security requirements, risks and recommendations for small enterprise and home-office environments. *Information Management & Computer security, 7*(3), 121-128.

Squicciarini, A. C., Bertino, E., Ferrari, E., & Ray, I. (2006). Achieving privacy in trust negotiations with an ontology-based approach. *IEEE Transactions on Dependable and Secure Computing, 3*(1), 13–30.

Srinivasan, A. (1985). Alternative measures of system effectiveness: Associations and implications. *MIS Quarterly, 9*(3), 243-253.

Stafford, T. F. (2005). Spyware. *Communications of the ACM, 48*(8), 34-35.

Stallings, W. (2006). *Cryptography and Network Security—Principles and Practices, 4th Edition.* Prentice-Hall.

Stars and Stripes (2001, July 27), S. Korea Indicts U.S. Service Member for Allegedly Hacking more than 50 Web Sites. http://ww2.pstripes.osd.mil/01/jul01/ed072701g.html

Stevens, R., Goble, C. A., & Bechhofer, S. (2000). Ontology-based knowledge representation for bioinformatics. *Briefings in Bioinformatics, 1*(4), 398–414.

Stinson, D. R. (1995). Cryptography: practice and theory. CRC Press, Boca Raton.

Stoica, A., & Farkas, C. (2004). Ontology Guided XML Security Engine. *Journal of Intelligent Information Systems, 3*(23).

Stolfo, S. J., Hershkop, S., Hu, C. W., Li, W. Nimeskern, O., & Wang, K. (2006). *Behavior-based Modeling and its Application to Email Analysis.* ACM Transactions on Internet Technology (TOIT), Feb 2006.

Straub, D. W. (1990). Effective IS security: An empirical study. *Information Systems Research, 1*(3), 255-276.

Straub, D. W., & Nance, W. D. (1990). Discovering and disciplining computer abuse in organizations: A field study. *MIS Quarterly, 14*(1), 45-60.

Straub, D. W., & Welke, R. J. (1998). Coping with systems risk: Security planning models for management decision making. *MIS Quarterly, 22*(4), 441-469.

Straub, D. W., & Welke, R. J. (1998). Coping with systems risk: Security planning models for management decision making. *MIS Quarterly*, (22)4, 441-469.

Straub, D. W., Boudreau, M. C., & Gefen, D. (2004). Validating guidelines for IS positivist research. *Communications of the AIS, 13*(24), 380-427.

Straub, D. W., Limayem, M., & Karahanna-Evaristo, E. (1995). Measuring system usage: Implications for IS theory testing. *MIS Quarterly, 41*(8), 1328-1342.

Strauss, A., & Corbin, J. (1998). *Basics of qualitative research. Techniques and procedures for developing grounded theory* (2nd ed.). Thousand Oaks, CA: Sage.

Strickland, L. H. (1958). Surveillance and trust. *Journal of Personality, 26*, 200-215.

Sullivan, B. (2002). *Privacy groups debate DoubleClick settlement.* Retrieved August, 2006, from http://www.cnn.com/2002/TECH/internet/05/24/doubleclick.settlement.idg/index.html

Sweeney, L. (2002). k-Anonymity: a model for protecting privacy. *International Journal on Uncertainty, Fuziness and Knowledge-based Systems, 10*(5), 557-570.

Sweeney, L. (2002). k-Anonymity: A Model for Protecting Privacy. *International Journal on Uncertainty, Fuzziness and Knowledge-Based Systems, 10*(5), 557-570.

SWRL: Semantic Web Rules Language. (2004). http://www.w3.org/Submission/SWRL/

Syeda, M., Zhang, Y. Q., & Pan, Y. (2002). Parallel granular neural networks for fast credit card fraud detection. *Proceedings of IEEE International Conference on Fuzzy Systems*, (pp. 572-577).

Symantec Co. (2005). *W32.Beagle.BG.* Online.

Ször, P. (2005). *The Art of Computer Virus Research and Defense.* Addison Wesley.

Takahashi, Y., Abiko, T., Negishi, E., Itabashi, G., Kato, Y., Takahashi, K., & Shiratori, N. (2005). An ontology-based e-learning system for network security. In *Proceedings of the 19th International Conference on Advanced Information Networking and Applications (AINA'05), 1*, 197– 202. IEEE.

Tang, Y-L., & Chen, C-T. (2004). Image authentication using relation measures of wavelet coefficients. *Proceedings of IEEE International Conference on e-Technology, e-Commerce and e-Service.*

The OWL Services Coalition. (2006). *OWL-S: Semantic Markup for Web Service Version 1.0.* June 1, 2006, from http://www.daml.org/services/owl-s/1.0/owl-s.html.

Thuraisingham, B. (1994). Security Issues for Federated Database Systems, *Computers and Security, 13*(6).

Thuraisingham, B. (2002). *XML, Databases and the Semantic Web.* CRC Press, FL.

Thuraisingham, B. (2003). *Data Mining, National Security and Privacy.* ACM SIGKDD.

Thuraisingham, B. (2005). *Standards for the Semantic Web, Computer Standards and Interface Journal.*

Thuraisingham, B. (2005). Privacy Constraint Processing in a Privacy Enhanced Database System. *Data and Knowledge Engineering Journal.*

Thuraisingham, B. (2006). *Building Trustworthy Semantic Webs.* CRC Press, To appear.

Thuraisingham, B., et al. (1993). Design and Implementation of a Database Inference Controller. *Data and Knowledge Engineering Journal, 11*(3).

Tit For Tat (2005). *TIT FOR TAT.* Website: http://www.abc.net.au/science/slab/tittat/story.htm

Tosic, V. et al. (2003). Management Applications of the Web Service Offerings Language (WSOL). *Springer-Verlag, Proc. of CAiSE03*, (pp. 468-484).

Tosic, V., & Pagurek, B. (2005). On Comprehensive Contractual Descriptions of Web Services. *Proc. of IEEE EEE05*, (pp. 444-449).

Triple A. (2006) June 1, 2006, from http://www.infoworld.com/articles/hn/xml/02/08/12/ 020812hntriplea.html?0814wewebservices

TRUST. (2005). *Team for Research in Ubiquitous Secure Technology (TRUST).* June 1, 2006, from http://trust.eecs.berkeley.edu/.

Trusted Computing Group. (2005). *Trusted Computing Group.* June 1, 2006, from https://www.trustedcomputinggroup.org/.

Tsoumas, B., Dritsas, S., & Gritzalis, D. (2005). An ontology-based approach to information systems security management. In Gorodetsky, V., Kotenko, I., and Skormin, V., editors, *Computer Network Security: Third International Workshop on Mathematical Methods, Models, and Architectures for Computer Network Security (MMM-ACNS'05), LNCS 3685*, 151–164. Springer-Verlag.

Turner, E. C. (2003). Privacy on the web: an examination of user concerns, technology, and implications for Business organizations and individuals. *Information Systems Management, 20*(1), 8-18.

Turow, J., & Lilach N. (2000). *The Internet and the family 2000: The view from parents, the view from kids.* Annenberg Public Policy Center of the University of Pennsylvania.

Undercoffer, J., Joshi, A., Finin, T., & Pinkston, J. (2004). Using DAML+OIL to classify intrusive behaviors. *The Knowledge Engineering Review*, (pp. 221–241).

US Census Bureau Retail Indicators Branch (2004). Retail E-commerce Sales In First Quarter 2004 Were 15.5 Billion Up 28.1 Percent From First Quarter 2003 Census Bureau Reports (2003). www.census.gov/mrts/www/current.html, Revised May 21.

Vaidya, J., & Clifton, C. (2003). Privacy-Preserving K-Means Clustering Over Vertically Partitioned Data. *In Proc. of the 9th ACM SIGKDD Intl. Conf. on Knowledge Discovery and Data Mining* (pp. 206-215). Washington, DC, USA.

Vaidya, J., & Clifton, C. (2004). Privacy-Preserving Data Mining: Why, How, and When. *IEEE Security and Privacy, 2*(6), 19-27.

Vaidya, J., & Clifton, C. (2005). Secure Set Intersection Cardinality with Application to Association Rule Mining. *J. Computer Security.*

van Blarkom G. W., Borking, J. J., & Olk, J. G. E. (2003). Handbook of Privacy and Privacy-Enhancing Technologies. *Privacy Incorporated Software Agent (PISA) Consortium*, The Hague, Amsterdam.

Venkatesh, V. (2000). Determinants of Perceived Ease of Use: Integrating Perceived Behavioral Control, Computer Anxiety and Enjoyment into the Technology Acceptance Model. *Information Systems Research* (11) 342-365.

Venkatesh, V., & Davis, F.D. (2000). A theoretical extension of the technology acceptance model: Four longitudinal field studies. *Management Science, 46,* 186-204

Venkatesh, V., Morris, M. G., Davis, F. D., & Davis, G. B. (2003). User acceptance of information technology: Toward a unified view. *MIS Quarterly, 27,* 425-478.

Venkatraman, N., & Ramanujam, V. (1987). Measurement of business economic performance: An examination of method convergency. *Journal of Management, 13*(1), 109-122.

Venter, H. S., & Eloff, J. H. P. (2003). A taxonomy for information security technologies. *Computers & Security, 22*(4), 299–307.

Verykios, V. S., Bertino, E., Fovino, I. N., Provenza, L. P., Saygin, Y., & Theodoridis, Y. (2004). State-of-the-art in privacy preserving data mining. In *SIGMOD Record* (Vol. 33, pp. 50-57).

Verykios, V. S., Elmagarmid, A. K., Bertino, E., Saygin, Y., & Dasseni, E. (2004). Association Rule Hiding. *IEEE Transactions on Knowledge and Data Engineering, 16*(4), 434-447.

VirusList.com (2008) Email-Worm.Win32.NetSky.q. (2008). Retrieved from http://www.viruslist.com/en/viruses/encyclopedia?virusid=22760 on June 8, 2008.

Volonino, L., & Robinson, S.R. (2004). *Principles and Practice of Information Security*. Upper Saddle River, NJ, USA, Pearson Prentice Hall.

von Solms, R., & von Solms, B. (2004). From policies to culture. *Computers & Security, 23,* 275-279.

Wahlstrom, K., & Roddick, J.F. (2001). On the Impact of Knowledge Discovery and Data Mining. In J. Weckert (Ed.), *Selected Papers from the Second Australian Institute of Computer Ethics Conference*. Australian Computer Society, Inc., Canberra, 22-27.

Wang, G. et al. (2004). Integrated Quality of Service (QoS) Management in Service-Oriented Enterprise Architectures. *Proc. of IEEE EDOC04*, (pp. 21-32).

Wang, H., & Wang, C. (2003). Taxonomy of security considerations and software quality. *Communications of the ACM, 46*(6), 75–78.

Wang, K., Fung, B. C. M., & Yu, P. S. (2005). *Template-based privacy preservation in classification problems*. Paper presented at the ICDM.

Wareham, J., Zheng, J.G., & Straub, D. (2005). Critical themes in electronic commerce research: a meta-analysis. *Journal of Information Technology, 20*(1), 1-19.

Warren, S., & Brandeis, L. (1890). The Right to Privacy. *Harvard Law Review, 4*(5 December), 193-220.

Wasserman, J. J. (1969). Plugging the leaks in computer security. *Harvard Business Review, 47*(5), 119-129.

Watson, H. J., Rainer Jr, R. K., & Koh, C. E. (1991). Executive information systems: a framework for development and a survey of current practices. *MIS Quart.*, 13-30.

WebSideStory (2001). *Cookie rejection less than 1% on the Web*. Retrieved June 13, 2004 from http://www.websidestory.com/cgi-bin/wss.cgi?corporate&news&press_2_124

Wehner, S. (2004). *Quantum Computation and Privacy*. Unpublished masters thesis, University of Amsterdam, Amsterdam.

WEKA (2006): *Data Mining Software in Java*. Online, http://www.cs.waikato.ac.nz/~ml/weka/

Welch, D., & Lathrop, S. (2003). Wireless security threat taxonomy. In *Proceedings of the IEEE Workshop on Information Assurance*, (pp. 76–83). IEEE.

Westin, A. (1967). *Privacy and Freedom*. New York, NY, USA, Atheneum.

Weston, A. F. (2005). American Attitudes on Health Care and Privacy. *I-Ways, Digest of Electronic commerce Policy and Regulation,* IOS Press, (28), 79-84.

Whitman, M. E. & Mattord, H. J. (2005). *Principles of Information Security*. Thomson Course Technology, 2nd edition.

Widmeyer, G. R. (2004). The Trichotomy Of Processes: A Philosophical Basis For Information Systems. *The Australian Journal of Information Systems, 11*(1), 3-11.

Wilander, J. (2005). Modeling and visualizing security properties of code using dependence graphs. In *Proceedings of the 5th Conference on Software Engineering Research and Practice in Sweden*, (pp. 65–74). http://www.idt.mdh.se/serps-05/SERPS05.pdf (visited 1-Jun-2006).

Wilander, J., & Kamkar, M. (2003). A comparison of publicly available tools for dynamic buffer overflow prevention. In *Proceedings of the 10th Network and Distributed System Security Symposium (NDSS'03)*, (pp. 149–162). Internet Society.

Williams, L. J., Cote, J. A., & Buckley, M. R. (1989). Lack of method variance in self-reported affect and perceptions at work: Reality or artifact? *Journal of Applied Psychology, 74*, 462-468.

Williamson, M. (1997). *Weighing the NO's and CON's CIO*, April 15, 49.

Williamson, M. (2007). A Conversation with Jamie Butler. *ACM Queue,* February 2007. 16-23.

Wilson, E. V., Mao, E., & Lankton, N. K. (2005). Predicting continuing acceptance of IT in conditions of sporadic use. In *Proceedings of the 2005 Americas Conference on Information Systems* (AMCIS), Omaha, NE.

Winer, R. S. (2001). A framework for Customer Relationship Management. *California Management Review, 43*(4), 89-106.

Wishart R., Henricksen K., & Indulska J. (2005). An access control scheme for ubiquitous computing environments based on context-dependent privacy preferences. *10ᵗʰ Australasian Conference on Information Security and Privacy*, Brisbane Australia.

Wixom, B., & Todd P. A. (2005). A Theoretical Integration of User Satisfaction and Technology Acceptance. *ISR16*(1), 85-102.

World Wide Web Consortium(W3C): www.w3c.org

Wu, C. W. (2002, September). On the design of content-based multimedia authentication systems. *IEEE Transactions on Multimedia, 4*(3), 385-393.

Wu, D-C., & Tsai, W-H. (2003). A Steganographic method for images by pixel differencing. *Pattern Recognition Letters* (pp. 1613-1626). Elsevier.

XML Encryption. http://www.w3.org/Encryption/2001/

XML Security. http://xml.apache.org/security/

XML Signature. http://www.w3.org/Signature/

Yamada, S., Ouba, M., and Osaki, S. (1983). S-Shaped Reliability Growth Modeling for Software Error Detection. *IEEE Transactions on Reliability, R-32,* 5, December 475-478.

Yang, H., & Kot, A. C. (2006, December). Binary image authentication with tampering localization by embedding cryptographic signature and block identifier. *IEEE Signal Processing Letters, 13*(12), 741-744.

Yang, K. S. (1986). Will societal modernization eventually eliminate cross-cultural psychological differences. In M. H. Bond (Ed.), *The cross-cultural challenge to social psychology*. Newbury Park, CA: Sage.

Yolum, P., & Singh, M. P. (2002). An Agent-Based Approach for Trustworthy Service Location. *Proceedings of 1st International Workshop on Agents and Peer-to-Peer Computing (AP2PC)*, (pp. 45-56).

Young, F. W. (1987). *Multidimensional Scaling.* Lawrence Erlbaum Associates, Hillsdale, New Jersey.

Young, J. R., & Hammon, R. W. (1989). *Method and apparatus for verifying an individual's identity*. United States patent number: 4 805 222.

Yu, T., & Winslett, M. (2003). A Unified Scheme for Resource Protection in Automated Trust Negotiation. *IEEE Symposium on Security and Privacy*, Oakland, CA.

Zadeh, L. A. (1973). Outline of a new approach to the analysis of complex systems and decision processes. *IEEE Trans. on Systems, Man and Cybernetics, 3*(1), 28-44.

Zaslow, J. (2002). *If TiVo Thinks You are Gay, Here's How to Set It Straight: What You Buy Affects Recommendations On Amazon.com, Too The Wallstreet Journal*, November 26, 2002. Retrieved July 6, 2004 from Http://online.wsj.com/article_email/0,,SB1038261936872356908,00.thml

Zhang, J. et al. (2004). An Approach to Help Select Trustworthy Web Services. *Proc. of IEEE CEC-East*, (pp. 84–91).

Zhu, K., & Kraemer, K. L. (2005). Post-Adoption Variation in Usage and Value of E-Business by Organizations: Cross-Country Evidence from the Retail Industry, *ISR 16*(1) 61-84.

About the Contributors

Hamid Nemati is an associate professor of information systems at the Information Systems and Operations Management Department of The University of North Carolina at Greensboro. He holds a doctorate from the University of Georgia and a Master of Business Administration from The University of Massachusetts. Before coming to UNCG, he was on the faculty of J. Mack Robinson College of Business Administration at Georgia State University. He has extensive professional experience in various consulting, business intelligence, and analyst positions and has consulted for a number of major organizations. His research specialization is in the areas of decision support systems, data warehousing, data mining, knowledge management and information privacy and security. He has presented numerous research and scholarly papers nationally and internationally. His articles have appeared in a number of premier professional and scholarly journals.

* * *

K. Anbumani obtained his bachelor's degree in engineering (Hons) from the College of Engineering, Guindy, Chennai (Presently Anna University) (1962), a master's degree in engineering with distinction and University First rank from the College of Engineering, Pune (1967), and a PhD with GPA of 4/4 from the Indian Institute of Sciences, Bangalore (1982), all in India. Dr. K. Anbumani has a total of 42 years of teaching in premier engineering institutions and also has ample industrial experience. Currently, he is the director, School of Computer Science and Technology, Karunya University, Coimbatore - 641114, India. Current research interests of Dr. K. Anbumani include information security, image processing, business intelligence and realtime systems.

Michael Achatz has successfully graduated the faculty of economics at the University of Regensburg in 2005 on the evaluation of biometrical authentication systems. Since then he has been working as an IT security specialist at the ibi research at the University of Regensburg Ltd. His main interests are in software development and biometrics.

Ashraful Alam is a PhD candidate in the Computer Science Department at the University of Texas at Dallas. He received his BS in computer science from University of Texas at Austin with an honors thesis on "Secure Internet Network Protocols." He is currently working at the Data and Application Security Lab, under the supervision of Dr. Bhavani Thuraisingham. His research interests include Semantic Web, intelligent systems, geospatial data integration, Web services and cryptography.

Kirk P. Arnett is a professor of management information systems at Mississippi State University. He was previously the College of Business and Industry Outstanding faculty member. His research focus is in information assurance. Dr. Arnett is a certified computing professional (CCP) and holds a Global Information Assurance Certificate from SANS Institute.

Idir Bakdi studied computer science at the University of Erlangen, Germany and at the University of Rennes, France. He worked within the IT security research team at Thomson Multimédia in Rennes and graduated on a subject in cryptography. Currently, he is working on his PhD thesis at the University of Regensburg on the subject of keystroke dynamics. His research interests include cryptography, smart card security, biometrics and machine learning.

Dieter Bartmann is the head of chair for banking informatics at the University of Regensburg and CEO of the ibi research at the University of Regensburg Ltd. He is the founding president of the European Research Institutes for Finance and IT (FIT), the leader of the section IF—information systems in financial management "in the "Gesellschaft für Informatik e. V. (GI)" and the founder of the Information Security Society Switzerland". He is member of numerous scientific boards and the editor of the journal BIT—Banking and Information Technology. His research areas are information systems and their impact on the finance sector.

Joseph A. Cazier is an assistant professor in the department of computer information systems in the John A. Walker College of Business at Appalachian State University. He received his PhD from Arizona State University in Boone North Carolina. He actively does research in information security, trust and ethics. Dr. Cazier has also published in Information & Management, the *Journal of Information System Security, Information Systems Security: the (ISC)2 Journal* and the *Journal of Information Privacy and Security,* among others. He has also published a book relating to business ethics and privacy, *Value Congruence and Trust Online: Their Impact on Privacy and Price Premiums.*

Elizabeth Chang is the professor of software engineering in the School of Information Systems, Curtin Business School (CBS), Curtin University of Technology, Perth, W.A., Australia, director of Curtin Tier 1 research centre - Digital Ecosystems and Business Intelligence at CBS, and founder of the Center for IT Applications and logistics Informatics at Newcastle University, Callaghan, N.S.W., Australia. She has published over 200 papers in international and national refereed journals and conferences, and has authored one book. Her research interests include user-interface analysis and design, usability evaluation, plug-and-play component-based system, Internet computing, including XML systems, trust and reputation, and ontologies. She is a member of the ACM, IEEE and the Australian Computer Society.

Tharam S. Dillon is the dean of the Faculty of Information Technology at University of Technology Sydney (UTS), Sydney, N.S.W., Australia. He has also worked with industry and commerce in developing systems in telecommunications, health care systems, e-commerce, logistics, power systems, and banking and finance. He is editor-in-chief of the International Journal of Computer Systems Science and Engineering and the International Journal of Engineering Intelligent Systems, as well as coeditor of the Journal of Electric Power and Energy Systems. He is on the advisory editorial board of *Applied Intelligence,* published by Kluwer in the U.S., and Computer Communications, published by Elsevier in the UK He has published more than 400 papers in international and national refereed journals and conferences, and has written four books and edited five other books. His research interests include data mining, Internet computing, e-commerce, hybrid neurosymbolic systems, neural nets, software engineering, database systems, and computer networks. He is a Fellow of IEEE, the Institution of Engineers (Australia) and of the Australian Computer Society.

Claudiu Duma received his MSc in computer science from the Polytechnic University of Timisoara (1998), and his PhD in computer science from Linköping University (2005). Dr. Duma has performed research in the area of secure group communication, with focus on the security-efficiency tradeoff in key management, and trust and reputation management, with focus on resilient reputation systems and integrated frameworks for trust management. His latest research interests are identity management and software security. Dr. Duma acts as a reviewer, and is part of the program committee, for several conferences and workshops on security and peer-to-peer computing.

Amr Ali Eldin graduated in 1997 with Bachelor's of Science degree in electronics engineering from Mansoura University. He was ranked the first out of his classmates with general grade Excellent. He is the receiver of the following scientific honor degree awards: El-Dakahleya state (1992, 1998), Mansoura University (1997), and Bahrain Kingdom (1990). He was appointed as a teaching assistant for the Department of Computer and Systems at Mansoura University. Parallel to that, he worked as a software engineer and an IT instructor at Mansoura university center of information and computer systems. He started his post-graduate studies in automatic-control/computer engineering as a major and his minor study was on distributed database management systems. He was awarded the Master's of Science degree in automatic control engineering in April 2001. After that, he was promoted as an assistant lecturer for the same department. He was awarded the doctoral of philosophy degree in information systems engineering from Delft University of Technology. His PhD research focused on developing consent decision-making mechanisms for privacy control architectures. He participated in various research and industrial projects. Among which he worked on the BETADE, MIES, FRUX and Multimedian projects. Furthermore, he supervised master and bachelor students and participated in the teaching programme of the information and communications department. He has more than 15 publications in international conferences, workshops and book chapters. Furthermore, he has a number of forthcoming scientific papers to appear in scientific journals in the fields of computer science and information systems.

Shantha Fernando obtained his first degree in computer science and engineering in 1993, from the University of Moratuwa, Sri Lanka. He started his career as a software engineer and worked with Linux systems in Internet environments since 1994. He extended his expertise of secure computer network designing for intranets and extranets to many internet service providers, banks and commercial organizations, governmental and non-governmental organizations in Sri Lanka. He has engaged in designing and implementing firewalls and servers, systems auditing, vulnerability assessment, ethical hacking, and business process re-engineering. He obtained his master's in philosophy in 2000, and joined the University of Moratuwa as a senior lecturer. His new research area of interest is e-learning and university education, on which he now reads for a PhD at the Delft University of Technology. He was a pioneer in developing online e-learning systems at University of Moratuwa, and currently he heads the development team. He was instrumental in setting up the first Computer Emergency Response Team in Sri Lanka, TechCERT, which is a project of the Department of Computer Science and Engineering and LK Domain Registry. Currently he works as a senior lecturer at the department of computer science and engineering and the CEO of TechCERT. He is also a chartered engineer at the Institute of Engineers, Sri Lanka.

Jerry Fjermestad is an associate professor in the School of Management at NJIT. He received his BA in chemistry from Pacific Lutheran University, an MS in operations research from Polytechnic University, an MBA in operations management from Iona College and an MBA and PhD from Rutgers University in management information systems. Dr. Fjermestad has taught courses on management information systems, decision support systems, systems analysis and design, electronic commerce, data warehousing, and graduate seminars in information systems. His current research interests are in collaborative technology, decision support systems, data warehousing, electronic commerce, global information systems, customer relationship management, and enterprise information systems. Dr. Fjermestad has published in the *Journal of Management Information Systems, Communications of the ACM, Group Decision and Negotiation*, the *Journal of Organizational Computing and Electronic Commerce, Information and Management, Decision Support Systems, Logistics Information Management, International Journal of Electronic Commerce*, and several other journals and conference proceedings. He also serves as an associate editor for J*ournal of Information Science and Technology*, the *International Journal of Electronic Collaboration*, and the *International Journal of Information Security and Privacy*.

F. Nelson Ford is associate professor and coordinator of MIS programs in the Department of Management at Auburn University. Dr. Ford has published in a wide range of journals including *MIS Quarterly, The Journal of Management Information Systems, Decision Support Systems, Interfaces, Database, Information Management and Computer Security*, and *Information & Management*.

Lixin Fu is currently an assistant professor at the Department of Computer Science in The University of North Carolina at Greensboro (UNCG). He obtained his master's in electrical engineering at Georgia Institute of Technology in 1997 and his PhD in computer and information science at University of Florida in 2001. He joined UNCG in 2001. His main research areas focus on data warehousing/data mining, databases, and algorithms. He has published more than 15 papers in referred journals and conferences in the past five year. Dr. Fu has been also awarded a NSF ITR grant.

Teik Guan is the chief security officer at Data Security Systems Solutions Pte Ltd in Singapore. He has many years of hands-on experience in designing and implementing data security solutions for many highly-sensitive projects including the Interbank RTGS Systems, Cheque Clearing Systems and several Internet banking and trading systems. Teik Guan is well-versed in the niche area of cryptographic security programming and integration, having developed numerous successful products such as CAs, smartcards (Javacard), HSMs, authentication servers, etc. Teik Guan holds an MSc from the National University of Singapore.

Song Han is research fellow at the School of Information Systems, Curtin Business School, Curtin University of Technology. He is an early career researcher within the Curtin Tier 1 Research centre - Digital Ecosystems and Business Intelligence. He holds a PhD in mathematics. His current research area includes information security, cryptography, information privacy and management, wireless network security, security in healthcare, and information hiding. He has published more than thirty refereed publications in international conferences and journals.

Almut Herzog received her MSc in medical informatics from Heidelberg University, Germany (1994). Between 1994 and 1999 she worked as a software developer in the area of medical information systems. She is currently finishing her PhD studies at the Department of Computer and Information Science, Linköpings universitet, Sweden. Her research interest is in information security, and specifically Java security and usable security.

Ha Jin Hwang received his MBA in 1986 and PhD in 1990 from Mississippi State University. He is a professor of MIS and vice-president of external relations and cooperation at Catholic University of Daegu, Korea. He has served as a steering committee member of Daegu Metropolitan City, Kyungbuk Province, and Kyungbuk Development Agency, Korea. He served as president of the Korean Association of Information Systems for 2005-2006. Prior to joining Catholic University, he taught at Minnesota State University from 1989 to 1991. His research interests include knowledge management, data mining, and component based software development.

Hamid Jahankhani is field leader and principal lecturer in secure systems and software development at the School of Computing and Technology. Hamid's expertise contributes directly to the latest in industry innovation as well as to unique degree programmes, offered exclusively at the University of East London. With his own master's and professional doctorate in information security and computer forensics, Jahankhani stresses the importance of education in order to arm and deliver the next generation of future experts to tackle our global security issues. He is research champion in the innovative informatics research group at the School of Computing and Technology and currently directs the research of six PhD students particularly in the areas of security management, cryptography, computer security and Trust. Dr. Jahankhani is the editor-in-chief of the *International Journal of Electronic Security and Digital Forensics* published by Inderscience and general chair of the annual International Conference on Global e-Security (ICGeS), www.icges.org. Also, member of the programme committee of the ECIW-06, The 5th European Conference on Information Warfare, SECRYPT 2006 International Conference on Security and Cryptography, WDFIA 2006 Workshop on Digital Forensics and Incident Analysis, International Conference on Information Science and Security. He has edited and contributed to several books and has over 70 conference and journal publications.

Allen Johnston an assistant professor in the School of Business at the University of Alabama Birmingham. He holds a BS from Louisiana State University in electrical engineering as well as an MSIS and PhD in information systems from Mississippi State University. His works can be found in such outlets as *Communications of the ACM, Journal of Global Information Management, Journal of Information Privacy and Security*, and the *Journal of Internet Commerce*. His research focus has been in the area of information assurance and security, with a specific concentration on the behavioral aspects of information security and privacy.

Latifur R. Khan is currently an associate professor in the computer science department at the University of Texas at Dallas (UTD), where he has taught and conducted research since September 2000. He received his PhD and MS degrees in computer science from the University of Southern California, in August of 2000, and December of 1996 respectively. He obtained his BSc degree in computer science and engineering from Bangladesh University of Engineering and Technology, Dhaka, Bangladesh in November of 1993.

Jongki Kim is an associate professor of MIS at the Division of Management, Pusan National University, South Korea. His research interests include information systems security management, project management methodology and research methodology in MIS. He received his PhD in MIS from Mississippi State University.

Kenneth J. Knapp is an assistant professor of management information systems at the U.S. Air Force Academy, Colorado. He has published in the *Communications of the Association for Information Systems, Information Systems Management, Information Management & Computer Security*, and *Information Systems Security*.

Xin Luo is an assistant professor of computer information systems in the Department of Computer Information Systems of School of Business at Virginia State University, USA. He received his PhD in information systems from Mississippi State University in 2007. He has an undergraduate degree in international business from Sichuan Normal University, China, an MBA from The University of Louisiana, and an MSIS in information systems from Mississippi State University. His research interests center around information security, e-commerce/m-commerce, and global IT adoption and management. He is the assistant editor of *Journal of Internet Banking and Commerce*. He has published numerous research papers and attended international & national conferences including Communications of the ACM, Information Systems Security, JIBC, AMCIS, DSI, IRMA, and etc.

Arun K. Majumdar is a professor of the Dept of Computer Science and Engineering of the Indian Institute of Technology, Kharagpur, India. Professor Majumdar received an MTech and PhD from the University of Calcutta, in applied physics (1968 and 1973, respectively). He also earned a PhD in electrical engineering from the University of Florida, Gainesville, USA (1976). He has more than 140 research publications in international journals and conferences. Professor Majumdar is a fellow of the Institute of Engineers (India), fellow of the Indian National Academy of Engineering and a senior member of the IEEE. His research interests include data and knowledge based systems, medical information systems, design automation and image processing.

Thomas E. Marshall is an associate professor of management information systems at Auburn University, Auburn, Alabama. He has published in journals such as *Omega, Information & Management, Information Systems Security, Information Management & Computer Security, Journal of Computer Information Systems, Journal of End User Computing, Information Resource Management* and *Journal of Database Management*.

B. Dawn Medlin is currently serving as an associate professor in the department of computer information systems in the John A. Walker College of Business at Appalachian State University in Boone North Carolina. She earned her doctorate at Virginia Polytechnic Institute and State University. Her teaching and research activities have been in the area of information technology, specifically in security, outsourcing, and e-commerce. Dr. Medlin's research articles have appeared in journals such as *International Journal Information Technology Management, Journal of Computer Information Systems, International Journal of Management*, among other refereed journals.

Mohammad Mehedy Masud is a PhD student at the Department of Computer Science at the University of Texas at Dallas (UTD) since August, 2005. He received his undergraduate degree in computer science and engineering (CSE) from Bangladesh University of Engineering and Technology (BUET) in 2001. Before joining UTD, he was a lecturer at the department of CSE, BUET, from 2001-2004. He is currently an assistant professor (on leave) at the same department. He is a member of the IEEE Computer Society, and the Association for Computing Machinery (ACM). His current areas of research are data mining, intrusion detection, and network security. He has already published 15 conference papers and journal articles and 3 more papers are currently under review. He is also an award-winning programmer at the ACM-International Collegiate Programming Contests (ICPC) World Finals-1999, held in Eindhoven, The Netherlands.

Haralambos Mouratidis received his BEng (Hons) in electronics with computing science from the University of Wales, Swansea; his MSc in data communications and PhD in computer science from the University of Sheffield, England. He has also received a postgraduate certificate on teaching and learning from the University of East London. He is currently a lecturer at the School of Computing and Technology at the University of East London, England.He is member of the software design and development field of the School of Computing and Technology, teaching and leading modules associated mainly with software engineering and security.

Mathews Z. Nkhoma is a postgraduate research student at the School of Computing and Technology and currently writing up his PhD thesis. Nkhoma research is on aligning network security to corporate goals: Investing on network security.

Stanley R. M. Oliveira is a researcher in computer science at the Brazilian Agricultural Research Corporation (Embrapa) in Brazil, since February 1995. He obtained his master's degree in computer science from the Federal University of Campina Grande, Brazil, in 1995, and his PhD in computer science from the University of Alberta, Canada, in 2005. His PhD thesis work focused on privacy-preserving data mining. Dr. Oliveira is also a visiting faculty member at the UNICAMP/FEAGRI (State University of Campinas/Agricultural Engineering Faculty) in Brazil. He has published several papers, most of them in international conferences. His main research interests include privacy-preserving data mining, database security, bioinformatics, text mining and feature selection.

Latha Parameswaran is currently pursuing a PhD with Bharathiar University. She has a bachelor's degree in mathematics and a master's degree in computer applications from Bharathiar University. She has 10 years experience in IT industry and 7 years experience in teaching and research. She is currently an assistant professor at the Department of Computer Science and Engineering, AMRITA University, Coimbatore – 641 105. Her research interests are information security, image processing and theoretical computer science.

Norman Pendegraft is associate professor of management information systems in the College of Business and Economics at the University of Idaho. He has taught a variety of IS courses including Database Design, Telecommunications, and IS Security. IS security is also his major research interest.

Vidyasagar Potdar is a researcher at DEBI (Digital Ecosystems and Business Intelligence Institute) at Curtin University of Technology. He has a Masters in Information Technology from the University of Newcastle, Australia and a PhD from Curtin University of Technology, Perth, Western Australia. His main areas of research include information forensics & security. His research focuses' on copyright protection, ownership verification applications, information retrieval and security in supply chain & logistics. He has undertaken several projects in robust watermarking, digital steganography, digital fingerprinting and secret sharing applications. His current research is focussing on devising tamper detection solutions for RFID tags, detecting secret communication on Internet and developing a web services search engine.

R. Kelly Rainer, Jr. is George Phillips Privett professor of management information systems at Auburn University, Alabama. Dr. Rainer has published in leading academic and practitioner outlets and is associate editor of communications of the Association of Information Systems. He is co-author, with Efraim Turban and Richard Potter, of *Introduction to Information Systems* (Wiley).

Nicholas C. Romano, Jr. is an assistant professor in the Management Science and Information Systems Department at Oklahoma State University. Romano received a PhD in MIS from the University of Arizona in 1998 and worked for IBM. His research interests involve collaborative systems including: technology-supported learning; knowledge management; collaborative project/process management; e-customer relationship management; IS accessibility; and collaborative interface evaluation. He was ranked 3rd in world in electronic commerce research journal articles from 1998-2004 in the 2006 Business Research Yearbook. He has published papers in several journals and proceedings including: *Journal of Management Information Systems, International Journal of Electronic Commerce, Small Group Research, Journal of the American Society for Information Science, Information Technology and Management, Business Process Management Journal, Information Systems Frontiers*. He serves as associate editor for *Journal of Information Systems Technology* and reviews for ISR, JMIS, IJEC, Management Science, DSS and others. He is active in the HICSS and AMCIS conferences.

Mark Rounds is an instructor of MIS in the College of Business and Economics at the University of Idaho. He worked for a time in industry as a security software developer. Security remains his primary research interest as a PhD student in computer science.

Fereidoon Sadri is a professor of computer science at The University of North Carolina at Greensboro. He studied at Tehran University (Tehran, Iran), University of Washington (Seattle, WA), and Princeton University (Princeton, NJ). Prior to joining UNCG, he worked at Isfahan University of Technology (Isfahan, Iran) and Concordia University (Montreal, Canada). He has published more than 50 papers in journals, conferences and workshops. His research has been supported by grants from NSERC (Natural Sciences and Engineering Research Council of Canada) in Canada, and by NSF (National Science Foundation) in the U.S.

Mark B. Schmidt is an assistant professor of at St. Cloud State University. He holds a BS from Southwest State University in Business and Agri-Business, an MBA from St. Cloud State University, and MSIS and PhD, degrees from Mississippi State University. He has works published in the *Communica-*

tions of the ACM, Journal of Computer Information Systems, Journal of End User Computing, Journal of Global Information Management Journal of Internet Commerce, Mountain Plains Journal of Business and Economics, and in the *International Journal of Information Security and Privacy*. His research focuses on information security, end-user computing, and innovative information technologies.

Nahid Shahmehri received her PhD in 1991, in the area of programming environments, and has been a full professor in computer science at Linköping University since 1998. Since 1994 her research activities have been concerned with various aspects of engineering advanced information systems, her main research interests being software security, security and usability, and trust/policy management. Professor Shahmehri chairs the Swedish Section of the IEEE Chapter for Computer/Software and the steering committee for the IEEE International Conference on Peer-to-Peer Computing. She is one of the founders of the iTRUST Center for Information Security.

Geoff Skinner is currently an academic with the Department of Design, Communication and Information Technology, within the Faculty of Science and IT at the University of Newcastle. He lectures in the areas of e-business, databases, and software development. His research interests include information privacy and data security, collaborative environments, intelligence analysis, and quantum computation. He is a member of three research centers across two university institutions, which include the Dampney Centre for Information Technology Applications (DCITA) at the University of Newcastle, the Centre for Extended Enterprises and Business Intelligence (CEEBI) at Curtin University of Technology, and Digital Ecosystems and Business Intelligence Institute (DEBII). He currently has twenty four international publications in the areas of privacy, collaborative environments and quantum computation.

Bhavani Thuraisingham is a professor of computer science and the director of the Cyber Security Research Center at the University of Texas at Dallas (UTD). Prior to joining UTD, she was a program director for three years at the National Science Foundation (NSF) in Arlington, VA. She has also worked for the computer industry in Minneapolis, MN for over five years and has served as an adjunct professor of computer science and member of the graduate faculty at the University of Minnesota and later taught at Boston University. Dr. Thuraisingham's research interests are in the area of Information Security and data management. She has published over 300 research papers including over 60 journals articles and is the inventor of three patents. She serves on the editorial board of numerous journals including *ACM Transactions on Information and Systems Security* and *IEEE Transactions on Dependable and Secure Computing*.

Natasha Tsybulnik is a PhD student in computer science at The University of Texas at Dallas, where she also received her BS and MS degrees. She began her college education at an early age and desires to receive multiple degrees in various fields. Currently, her research is in securing efficient data federation in a P2P environment with concern for confidentiality, privacy, and trust management under the direction of Dr. Bhavani Thuraisingham. Her other research interests include developing secure privacy policies for the Semantic Web, data security, expert systems, machine learning algorithms, and distributed systems.

Shamik Sural received the PhD from Jadavpur University in 2000. He has worked in a number of companies both in India as well as the USA in various capacities. Since 2002, he is an assistant professor at the School of information Technology, Indian Institute of Technology, Kharagpur, India. Dr. Sural has served on the program committee of a number of international conferences. He is a senior member of the IEEE. He has published more than sixty papers in reputed journals and conferences. His research interests include database security, data mining and multimedia database systems.

Thomas P. Van Dyke is an assistant professor of information systems and operations management at the University of North Carolina, Greensboro. He received his PhD in business computer information systems at the University of North Texas. His current research interests include privacy and security, IT leadership and human factors. His previous publications appear in journals such as *MIS Quarterly*, *Decision Sciences*, and *Electronic Markets*.

Vishal Vatsa is an alumnus of the Naval Engineering College and completed his graduation in mechanical engineering from Jawaharlal Nehru University, New Delhi (India) in 1997. The author completed his MTech in computer science and information technology from the Indian Institute of Technology, Kharagpur, India in 2005. He has a couple of papers to his credit. His areas of interest include data mining, cyber crime and intrusion detection systems, e-commerce and game theory. The author is serving in the Navy and presently posted at IN Ship Maintenance Authority (Mumbai), India.

E. Vance Wilson is an assistant professor in the Lubar School of Business at the University of Wisconsin-Milwaukee. He received a PhD in information systems from the University of Colorado at Boulder. Wilson's research focuses generally on organizational aspects of human-computer interaction with specific interests in patient-centered e-health, computer-mediated communication, team-based software development, and decisional guidance. His publications are strongly interdisciplinary, appearing in such journals as *Communications of the ACM, Journal of the American Medical Informatics Association, Database, Computers in Human Behavior, Journal of Organizational Computing and E-Commerce, Information & Management, Simulation & Gaming*, and *Computers & Education*.

Osmar R. Zaïane is an associate professor in computing science at the University of Alberta, Canada. Dr. Zaïane joined the University of Alberta in July of 1999. He obtained an master's degree in electronics at the University of Paris, France(1989), and an master's degree in computer science at Laval University, Canada(1992). He obtained his PhD from Simon Fraser University, Canada(1999) under the supervision of Dr. Jiawei Han. His PhD thesis work focused on Web mining and multimedia data mining. He has research interests in novel data mining algorithms, Web mining, text mining, image mining, and information retrieval. He has published more than 80 papers in refereed international conferences and journals, and taught on all six continents. Osmar Zaïane was the co-chair of the ACM SIGKDD International Workshop on Multimedia Data Mining in 2000, 2001 and 2002 as well as co-chair of the ACM SIGKDD WebKDD workshop in 2002, 2003 and 2005. He is the program co-chair for the IEEE International Conference on Data Mining 2007 and general co-chair for the conference on Advanced Data Mining Applications 2007. Osmar Zaïane is the ACM SIGKDD Explorations.

376

Index